America's Priorities

How the U.S. Government Raises and Spends
$3,000,000,000,000 (Trillion) Per Year

Charles S. Konigsberg

authorHOUSE®

America's Priorities
How the U.S. Government Raises and Spends
$3,000,000,000,000 (Trillion) Per Year

AuthorHouse books may be ordered through local and on-line booksellers or by contacting:

AuthorHouse
1663 Liberty Drive, Suite 200
Bloomington, IN 47403
888.519.5121

First published by AuthorHouse 01/09/2008

ISBN: 978-1-4343-6013-7 (soft cover)
ISBN: 978-1-4343-6012-0 (dust jacket)

Printed in the United States of America

*For my son Eddie
and all of his generation
who deserve to inherit
a strong and prosperous America
that remains the democratic ideal
for all of humanity*

Summary of Contents

Table of Contents

ABOUT THE AUTHOR

Charles S. Konigsberg is one of the few people in Washington who has served in senior-level positions in the U.S. Senate and the Administration for both Democrats and Republicans, earning bipartisan respect for his knowledge of the Federal Budget.

He served as a senior staff member in the Senate for thirteen years, becoming a recognized expert on the Federal Budget and the legislative process. Most recently, he served four years as General Counsel to the late Senator Daniel Patrick Moynihan (D-NY) at the Senate Finance Committee, where he advised the Senator on fiscal policy, health policy, and constitutional issues. As General Counsel, he managed the Finance Committee's half-trillion-dollar deficit reduction legislation in 1993.

In the Executive Branch, Mr. Konigsberg spent over four years in the Clinton White House serving as an Assistant Director at the Office of Management and Budget.

Mr. Konigsberg began his Senate career as Staff Attorney at the Senate Budget Committee, where he wrote the first two editions of the Committee's explanation of the congressional budget, authorization, and appropriations processes. He moved on to the Senate Rules and Administration Committee for six years, ultimately serving as Chief Counsel on the Committee's minority staff.

After the Clinton Administration, Mr. Konigsberg served in the Bush Administration as Director of Congressional and Intergovernmental Affairs at the Corporation for National and Community Service, the Agency that administers AmeriCorps.

His previous publications on the Federal Budget include "Amending the Congressional Budget Act of 1974," *Notre Dame Journal of Legislation*, Winter 1984; "The Congressional Budget Process: How It Works," *U.S. Senate Budget Committee*, August 1985; "Gramm-Rudman-Hollings and the Congressional Budget Process," *U.S. Senate Budget Committee*, December 1985; and "Overview of the Congressional Budget Process," *U.S. Senate Finance Committee*, May 1994.

Mr. Konigsberg is founder and editor of the *Washington Budget Report*, an e-newsletter and website (**www.washingtonbudgetreport.com**) that provides nonpartisan analysis of Federal budget, appropriations, and tax developments. He also created **www.GovBudget.com**, a unique user-friendly tool for exploring the Federal Budget. Mr. Konigsberg frequently discusses ongoing budget developments with journalists, has been profiled in Capitol Hill's *Roll Call* newspaper, has appeared on C-SPAN's *Washington Journal*, the *NewsHour with Jim Lehrer*, and addresses public, private, and nonprofit sector audiences on the Federal Budget.

Mr. Konigsberg graduated magna cum laude and Phi Beta Kappa from Kenyon College in Gambier, Ohio, in 1980 and from the Case Western Reserve School of Law in Cleveland, Ohio, in 1983, where he was executive editor of the *Law Review*.

ACKNOWLEDGMENTS

I have been privileged to serve on three Senate Committee staffs—Finance, Budget, and Rules and Administration. At the Senate Finance Committee, I had the rare opportunity of twice working for the committee's chairman and ranking member, the late Senator Daniel Patrick Moynihan, who taught me that true public service is always saying what you believe, no matter how much it might shake up the conventional wisdom—and that you better have the facts to back up your opinion. Senator Moynihan did this throughout his remarkable bipartisan career in four Administrations and the U.S. Senate and earned national respect, across the political spectrum, for his candor and insightful thinking.

On the Budget Committee staff, I had the rare good fortune to find a mentor and long-time friend, the late Sid Brown, the committee's Chief of Budget Review. I was fresh out of law school, and Sid generously and always with good humor and infinite patience taught me more about the Federal Government, Congress, and the budget process than anyone else I have known. Sid was a man of great intelligence, wit, and humanity who is deeply missed by all of his many friends and colleagues on the Hill and at National Public Radio, where he spent his later years.

I also wish to thank Alice Rivlin, Frank Raines, Jack Lew, and Chuck Kieffer who I had the great privilege to work for and learn from during my tenure at the Office of Management and Budget; Senator Ted Stevens, for the opportunity to serve on the staff of the Senate Rules Committee; Senator Pete Domenici, Steve Bell, and Gail Millar for the opportunity to serve on the staff of the Senate Budget Committee; Laura Larson, my copy editor, and Andrea Reider my typesetter, for their professionalism and infinite patience; Michael Crowley, Laura de la Torre, Lorraine Evans, Trevor Johnston, John Laird, and Eric Warren for their assistance; and all my family and friends who have provided support and encouragement during this enormous project.

FREQUENTLY USED ABREVIATIONS AND TERMS

CBO   The Congressional Budget Office supports the congressional budget process by providing Congress with nonpartisan economic and program analyses and cost information on existing and proposed Federal programs. The Budget and Appropriations Committees of the House and Senate are the major users of CBO reports.

CRS   The Congressional Research Service is the public policy research arm of the United States Congress, producing reports on a broad range of Federal programs and issues of national interest. As a legislative branch agency within the Library of Congress, CRS works exclusively and directly for Members of Congress, their Committees, and staff on a confidential, nonpartisan basis. While CRS reports are not made directly available to the public, many can be found on a variety of websites by searching "CRS" and "key words." In addition, any CRS report cited in this book can be purchased from www.pennyhill.com.

GAO   The Government Accountability Office (until recently the General Accounting Office) is a legislative branch agency established to report to Congress on the effectiveness of programs and expenditures of the Federal government. GAO, commonly called the investigative arm of Congress or the "congressional watchdog," is independent and nonpartisan. GAO also frequently advises Congress and the heads of executive agencies about ways to make government more effective and responsive.

IRS   Internal Revenue Service, Department of the Treasury

JCT   The Joint Committee on Taxation is a joint House-Senate Committee of the Congress. Unlike other committees of the Congress that develop legislation for congressional consideration, the JCT exists solely to employ a nonpartisan staff of tax professionals and economists to provide the House Ways and Means

Committee and the Senate Finance Committee with nonpartisan revenue estimates and analyses of tax proposals. The CBO uses JCT's revenue estimates in CBO budget documents.

OMB The Office of Management and Budget is an agency within the Executive Office of the President that formulates the President's Budget requests for transmittal to Congress, manages the "apportionment" (i.e., availability) of appropriated funds, and is the President's instrument for managing the overall operations of the Federal Government.

SUPER-MAJORITY A vote of the House of Representatives or Senate requiring more than 50%-plus-one for passage—typically setting the threshold for passage at three-fifths or two-thirds.

TAX CODE Refers to the *Internal Revenue Code* of 1986, the most recent comprehensive rewrite of the tax laws.

TRILLION DOLLARS A "trillion dollars" is such an enormous amount of money, even Merriam-Webster's Collegiate Dictionary can't seem to comprehend how large it really is. It defines a *trillion* as "a very large number." Consider looking at it this way: if you think about a million dollars, a "trillion dollars" is a million millions. Or if you prefer to think in billions, a "trillion dollars" is a thousand billions.

INTRODUCTION: AMERICA'S PRIORITIES

The Budget of the United States—now approaching $3 trillion—is about people and priorities. The allocation of our public resources in each year's budget process is a singular reflection of how we view our nation, our people, our collective future, and our place in the world.

Yet, the critical issues of our day are increasingly lost in a morass of growing partisanship and ideology. It is essential that we move beyond the "red" and "blue" labels and focus pragmatically on the vital national issues that profoundly impact all of us.

The Federal Budget touches all of us in many ways—some apparent, others less so. Consider, for a moment, a "snapshot" of the Federal Budget:

- Our **nation's security** is defended by 1.4 million Americans in uniform at bases throughout the world.
- 34 million seniors collect monthly **Social Security** checks—for many of them, the largest share of their monthly income—making the difference between living with dignity and living in poverty.
- Hundreds of thousands of our nation's **veterans** who fought in World War II, Korea, Vietnam, the Gulf War, Afghanistan, and Iraq receive medical care at veterans hospitals for injuries suffered during military service, and millions more receive compensation payments for combat-related injuries that impair their ability to work.
- Tens of millions of Americans live in their own **homes** due to the deductibility of monthly mortgage interest from taxable income (a priority on the "tax side" of the budget).
- More than 5 million college students receive **Pell Grants** to help pay for higher education.
- Every American enjoys the use of **160,000 miles of national highways**, vital to the nation's economy, defense, and mobility.
- 34 million seniors visit doctors of their choice, or have in-patient medical procedures, paid for by **Medicare**.
- Millions of **disabled Americans**—of all ages—receive Social Security disability insurance payments, or Supplemental Security Income, and receive medical coverage through Medicare or Medicaid.

- Millions of Americans take **prescription drugs** with confidence, knowing that their medications have undergone rigorous scrutiny by the Food and Drug Administration.
- Half of all **long-term care** in our nation is paid for by Medicaid—providing vital nursing home and other services to low-income seniors and disabled children in need of care.
- Medical researchers and scientists across the nation, and around the world, conduct groundbreaking scientific and medical research funded by the **National Institutes of Health.**
- Millions of **low-income working families** are assisted in climbing out of poverty through the Earned Income Tax Credit and Temporary Assistance for Needy Families.
- Fifteen thousand **air traffic controllers** enable millions of air travelers to visit family or conduct business throughout the country and across the globe.
- The **Centers for Disease Control and Prevention** protects the public health by monitoring disease outbreaks across the nation, and around the world, to prevent catastrophic pandemics.
- Thousands of inspectors from the Agriculture Department spot-check meat and poultry facilities to protect **America's food supply.**
- Millions of poor children receive vital **preschool services, school breakfasts,** and **school lunches** to give them a fair chance and an equal opportunity at a decent life.

The process of how we prioritize $3 trillion of national resources among these and other Federal programs, and how we raise the revenues to pay for them, is the subject of this book.

Author's Note

This book is designed so that you can begin reading at various points in the book, depending on which areas are of greatest interest to you.

- If you want to begin with a plain English overview of the **budget process**—how the President and Congress construct the massive Federal budget—continue reading, with Part II.

- Or, if you are interested in how the Federal government went from deficits in the 1980s, to surpluses in the 1990s, and back to **rapidly rising debt** in the 2000s, begin with Part VI.

- Finally, if you are interested in an **overview of America's priorities,** or how a particular program operates, skip ahead to Parts III, IV, and V.

THE BUDGET PROCESS

State of the Union Address. Courtesy: Associated Press

We're all familiar with the photograph above—the President delivering the State of the Union address.[1] What most people don't realize is the close linkage between the State of the Union and the President's Budget.

The State of the Union fulfills the President's constitutional obligation to "from time to time give to the Congress information of the State of the Union."[2] As a practical matter, it also serves as the President's platform to launch his policy proposals for the upcoming year—the details of which are set forth in the President's formal Budget document. By law, the President submits his Budget to the Congress by the first Monday in February, typically the week following the State of the Union.

The President's Budget is actually a request—albeit a very long (and heavy) request (10 pounds, 4 volumes, 2,000+ pages). In these enormous documents, the President lays out for Congress (1) the programs he believes should be funded, (2) at what levels, and (3) how he proposes to raise (or borrow) the funds to pay for those programs.

However, on matters relating to the Federal Budget, the real power is at the other end of Pennsylvania Avenue—on Capitol Hill. *The Constitution gives to Congress the exclusive power to appropriate funds, to collect taxes, and to borrow money.*[3] Sometimes Congress accepts the President's proposals; often Congress modifies the proposals; and sometimes Congress rejects the proposals outright.

Notes

1. President Clinton delivers State of the Union Address, January 25, 1994, at the U.S. Capitol.

2. U.S. Constitution, Article II, Section 3.

3. Article I, Section 9, of the Constitution provides that "No Money shall be drawn from the Treasury, but in Consequence of Appropriations made by Law." Article I, Section 8, of the Constitution provides that "the Congress shall have Power to lay and collect Taxes, Duties, Imposts and Excises, to pay the Debts and provide for the common Defence and general Welfare of the United States . . . (and) to borrow Money on the Credit of the United States."

Preparation of the President's Budget

*A nation's budget is full of moral implications: it tells what a society cares about and what
it does not care about; it tells what its values are.—Senator J. William Fulbright, 1988*[1]

Preparation of the President's Budget begins about nine months prior to transmittal of the
President's Budget to Congress. For example, formulation of the President's FY 2009 Budget began in the spring of 2007, culminating in transmittal of the Budget to Congress on February 4, 2008.

The first step in budget preparation is the President's White House Office of Management
and Budget (OMB) issuing "planning guidance" to the various departments and agencies of
government to develop budget proposals for FY 2009 based on the President's priorities and
policy objectives.

For example, the guidance might ask each agency to submit a budget proposal that continues spending at current levels, or cuts spending by 5 percent, or allows spending for current programs and government services to grow with inflation. Such guidance might apply
consistently across all government departments and agencies, or the White House might permit some agencies to increase spending to accommodate new initiatives, while instructing
other agencies to cut spending by a specific percentage. This first decision point in formulation of the President's Budget is for all practical purposes invisible to the public. But it is a
critical decision point where the President and his Administration decide the general outlines
and priorities of the forthcoming Budget transmittal to Congress.

Following OMB's planning guidance, each department and agency spends several
months preparing detailed budgets for their programs. This budget preparation work is
meticulously guided by a two-inch-thick set of instructions issued annually by OMB called
"Circular A-11." [2]

After several months of examining budget needs and priorities within the parameters of
the spring planning guidance, each department and agency in early fall submits to OMB its
initial budget request. OMB then conducts its "Fall Review," analyzing agency budget requests
in light of the planning guidance, program performance, and overall budget objectives and
constraints. During the Fall Review, OMB career program analysts raise issues and present

options to the OMB Director and senior political staff for their policy decisions. These policy decisions are incorporated into a complete set of budget proposals.

In late November, the OMB Director briefs the President and senior advisors on the draft budget and receives the President's guidance on key policy issues. After incorporating any changes that emerge from the OMB Director's meeting with the President, OMB informs departments and agencies about the decisions on their budget requests in what is commonly called the "OMB passback."

Based on the OMB passback, departments and agencies then submit all computer data and related materials to OMB for preparation of the budget documents. Simultaneously, in December, department and agency heads may appeal to the OMB Director, and ultimately the President, to reverse or modify certain decisions in the agency's passback. (The degree of presidential involvement depends, of course, on the nature of the issues being "appealed" as well as the management style of the President.)

With final decisions in hand, OMB then makes final adjustments to the budget and "locks down" the numbers around mid-January, in time to print and deliver the massive documents to Congress on the first Monday of February, as required by law.[3] At the same time, departments and agencies prepare "budget justification" materials which are released immediately after the President's Budget and provide greater detail on each of their respective budgets.

In January we often see the Washington ritual of "planned leaks." Administrations pass to reporters details of new initiatives in the President's Budget in order to build up anticipation of the President's State of the Union address—where the outlines of key proposals are typically unveiled.

Recommended Sources for More Information on Preparation of the President's Budget

- OMB Circular A-11: www.whitehouse.gov/omb/circulars/a11/current_year/a11_toc.html
- GAO: "Principles of Federal Appropriations Law," 3rd ed., vol. 1: 1-14–1-16.

Notes

1. Lewis D. Eigen and Jonathan P. Siegel, *The Macmillan Dictionary of Political Quotations* (New York: Macmillan, 1993), 25.

2. Circular A-11 is available at www.whitehouse.gov/omb/circulars/a11/current_year/a11_toc.html.

3. The President's Budget is required by law to be submitted by the first Monday in February for the fiscal year beginning October 1 (31 U.S.C. 1105(a)). The timing of the President's Budget transmittal changes in a year with a transition between outgoing and incoming Administrations. For example, President George W. Bush transmitted his first budget, the FY 2002 Budget, in April 2001. OMB Circular No. A-11 (2005), p. 3 of section 10.

The Congressional Budget Process

The House of Representatives cannot only refuse, but they alone can propose the supplies requisite for the support of the government. They, in a word, hold the purse: that powerful instrument by which we behold in the history of the British constitution an infant and humble representation of the people, gradually enlarging the sphere of its activity and importance, and finally reducing . . . all the overgrown prerogatives of the other branches of the government. —James Madison, Federalist No. 58[1]

Although Congress has held the "power of the purse" since ratification of the Constitution in 1789,[2] prior to 1974 Congress generally deferred to the President on overall budget policies and priorities. The Congress had no process of its own for formulating an overall fiscal policy. It generally acted on, and made changes to, the specific spending and tax proposals submitted by the President. It was primarily the President, and officials and staff at the Office of Management and Budget, who focused on the larger picture of total spending, total revenues, and public debt.[3]

Then came the Nixon "impoundment" controversy. In the early 1970s President Nixon attempted to "impound"—that is, he refused to spend—funds Congress had appropriated for specific purposes. Nixon's assertion of presidential impoundment authority, as well as Congress' long-standing dependence on the Administration's Office of Management and Budget, led Congress to enact the landmark Congressional Budget and Impoundment Control Act of 1974 ("Budget Act"). The Budget Act—although amended in substantial ways since 1974—continues to govern the process by which Congress assembles the $3 trillion Federal Budget.

The Three-Tier Legislative Process

Before we walk through the budget process timetable, it is worth a short detour to place the congressional budget process in context, that is, how it fits generally into Congress' multilayered legislative process.

The congressional budget process is part of a three-tier legislative process: (1) authorizations, (2) appropriations and revenue raising, and (3) the congressional budget process.

IN A NUTSHELL

In General:

Authorizing Committees (17 in each chamber) establish Federal programs and determine how they will operate.

The Appropriations Committees (1 in each chamber) *allocate available funds* to authorized programs.

The Congressional Budget Resolution determines how much *total funding* is available for appropriation in a particular year.

Example: The Homeland Security authorizing committees in the House and Senate write legislation *authorizing* a State homeland security grants program. However, the State grants program will not operate *unless* the House and Senate Appropriations Committees act on legislation that *appropriates funding* for the grants program. The Appropriations Committees cannot allocate funding for the program until Congress adopts a Budget Resolution that determines how much *total funding* is available for the upcoming fiscal year.

Entitlement programs are the big exception to this process; authorizing committees *circumvent the annual appropriations process* when they establish legal entitlements to specified benefits.

Authorizations Process. First, Congress has an *authorizations process* that creates Federal programs in response to national needs. The Senate and House each have seventeen authorizing committees, although the number of committees has varied over the years. Generally, most of the congressional hearings that you see reported in the media involve fact finding on the wide range of issues facing the nation. The task of the authorizing committees is to determine if a Federal response is needed—in the form of creating or reconfiguring Federal programs, providing assistance to state and local governments, or providing incentives to—or regulating—the private sector.

Appropriations and Revenue Raising. The second tier of the legislative process is appropriations and revenue raising. The Senate Finance and House Ways and Means committees raise revenues (through taxes, customs duties, fees, and borrowing) to finance authorized programs. The two Appropriations Committees—one in the Senate and one in the House—allocate available funds among the authorized programs.

Congressional Budget Process. The congressional budget process is the third, and newest, tier of the legislative process. Under the congressional budget process, the Congress annually establishes overall fiscal policy on how much *total* spending and revenues will be for the entire government, how much discretionary funding will be available to the Appropriations Committees, and whether the tax or authorizing committees of Congress will be directed to make budgetary changes to spending or revenue programs under their jurisdiction.

However, nothing in Congress is simple, and the three-tier process is often misunderstood. *A frequent misconception is that the Budget Resolution contains program-by-program*

THE BLURRING OF AUTHORIZATIONS AND APPROPRIATIONS

The distinction between Congress' *authorizing* and *appropriations* committees has been significantly blurred in recent decades. While the appropriators traditionally made all of the funding decisions, authorizing committees in recent decades have been spending money directly (hence the term *direct spending*), in effect bypassing the appropriators and enacting into law programs that *legally entitle* particular categories of individuals to receive specified benefits. These are the so-called *entitlement programs* (also called *mandatory spending* programs because the government is legally required to pay specified benefits to eligible individuals). These spending programs are effectively on auto-pilot. Because of a few large mandatory spending programs (Social Security, Medicare, and Medicaid), as well as interest on the debt, more total spending now results each year from entitlements under the jurisdiction of authorizing committees than from the annual discretionary decisions of the Appropriations Committees. For additional background, see Appendix D.

detail. It does not. As explained below, the Budget Resolution establishes a general framework of budgetary totals, committee allocations and enforcement mechanisms, but does not set funding levels for individual programs.

A second misconception is that the Budget Resolution is the product of negotiations with the President. The Budget Resolution is actually a "concurrent resolution" that Congress uses as an internal mechanism to guide subsequent action on spending and revenue bills. It is not a law and is not presented to the President for signature.

A third misconception is that legislation "authorizing appropriations" for a project provides funding. Authorizing bills quite often include dollar amounts. For example, an authorizing bill might establish a program and include language stating: "There are authorized to be appropriated $100 million to carry out this Act in fiscal year 2008." Even if that language is eventually passed by Congress and signed into law by the President, no money has actually been appropriated. *The "authorization" of $100 million is, in effect, simply a recommendation* by the authorizing committees, to the Appropriations Committees, that funds in that amount ought to be appropriated in order for the program to fulfill its intended purposes.

Unfortunately, this ambiguity is sometimes used to create the perception that funds have actually been provided to address a vital need, when the truth is that only an authorization has been enacted.

New Institutions Created in 1974

To implement the new congressional budget process created in 1974, the Budget Act created the House Budget Committee, the Senate Budget Committee, and the Congressional Budget Office (CBO).

The Budget Committees of the House and Senate are responsible for drafting Congress' annual budget plan for the Federal government for consideration by the full House and Senate. Unlike the authorizing and Appropriations committees described earlier, the Budget Committees focus on the Federal Budget as a whole and how it affects the national economy. In this way, the Budget Act created congressional institutions whose unique concern is Federal fiscal policy.

FIGURE 2-2.1. The Three-Tier Legislative Process

Congressional Budget Process: Setting Overall Fiscal Policy	
Total Spending, Total Revenues, and Broad Priorities	
Senate Budget Committee	House Budget Committee

Appropriations and Revenue Raising	
Senate Appropriations Committee	House Appropriations Committee
Senate Finance Committee*	House Ways and Means Committee*

Authorizing Committees: Addressing National Needs	
Senate Authorizing Committees:	**House Authorizing Committees:**
Agriculture, Nutrition and Forestry	Agriculture
Armed Services	Armed Services
Banking, Housing and Urban Affairs	Education and Labor
Commerce, Science and Transportation	Energy and Commerce
Energy and Natural Resources	Financial Services
Environment and Public Works	Foreign Affairs
Finance*	Homeland Security
Foreign Relations	House Administration
Health, Education, Labor and Pensions	Judiciary
Homeland Security and Governmental Affairs	Natural Resources
Judiciary	Oversight and Government Reform
Rules and Administration	Science and Technology
Small Business and Entrepreneurship	Small Business
Veterans' Affairs	Transportation and Infrastructure
Select Committee on Indian Affairs	Veterans' Affairs
Select Committee on Intelligence	Ways and Means*
Special Committee on Aging	Permanent Select Committee on Intelligence

*The Senate Finance and House Ways and Means Committees have responsibility for raising revenues and authorizing health and social services entitlement programs.

CBO supports the congressional budget process by providing cost projections on existing and proposed Federal programs, as well as fiscal and economic projections. The framers of the Budget Act saw a need to provide Congress with its own independent, nonpartisan budget professionals so that Congress would no longer have to rely on the President's Office of Management and Budget. The creation of CBO placed the Congress on an equal footing with the President in terms of capacity to develop a comprehensive fiscal policy.

The Congressional Budget Process: A Step-by-Step Explanation

Prior to 1974, the Federal government's fiscal year had been July 1 through June 30. However, in 1974 the Budget Act shifted the fiscal year forward to October 1 through September 30 in order to allow sufficient time for the new congressional budget process. As we walk through the various steps of the congressional budget process, keep October 1 in mind as the target date for completion of each year's budget process.

January–February: CBO Report, Hearings on the President's Budget, Committee Views

The congressional budget process begins in late January when CBO publishes its annual *Budget and Economic Outlook*. CBO's annual report lays out for Congress a *budget baseline*, or starting point, which projects Federal spending and revenues for each of the next ten years if current Federal programs and services remain in place. The baseline is constructed according to specific rules that generally adjust discretionary programs for inflation; assume the continuation of most entitlement programs; and assume that tax laws expire as scheduled in current law. (For more background on budget baselines, see chapter 2-9.)

Shortly thereafter, the President transmits his 2,000-plus page Budget to Congress on the first Monday of February. As explained in chapter 2-1, the President's Budget is the culmination of nine months of work by the departments, agencies, and OMB, and it shows in substantial detail the President's spending and tax proposals for the upcoming fiscal year.

After transmittal of the President's Budget, the Senate and House Budget Committees hold public hearings in February at which they receive testimony on the President's Budget proposals from Administration officials, experts from various disciplines, representatives from national trade associations and organizations, Members of Congress, and the general public.

At the same time, the other committees of Congress carefully review the President's Budget and transmit to the Budget Committees their own "views and estimates" on appropriate spending or revenue levels for programs within their jurisdictions. Since budget and tax priorities are among the most contentious and partisan issues on Capitol Hill, it is not uncommon for a particular committee's views and estimates to include both the views of the majority party and separate minority party views.

Toward the end of February or early March, CBO produces its own nonpartisan review of the President's Budget and reestimates the President's proposed policies using the CBO's own economic projections. The objective of this "reestimate" is to "take the politics out of the President's Budget" since Members of Congress often argue that the President's Budget uses overly optimistic economic projections in order to paint a more favorable picture of the nation's fiscal situation.

March–April: Budget Resolution

In March, the Senate and House Budget Committees—using the President's Budget request, information from their own hearings, views and estimates from other committees of Congress, and CBO's reports—each draft a congressional budget plan in meetings known as committee "mark-ups." The draft House and Senate budget plans are known as the Concurrent Resolution on the Budget, or "Budget Resolution" for short.

Budget Resolutions are required by current law to cover the upcoming budget year plus the following four fiscal years—although this requirement has varied over the years, sometimes covering as many as ten years or as few as one year. A Budget Resolution includes four standard components and two optional components. Standard in all budget resolutions are the following:

1. Budget totals (spending, revenues, deficit or surplus, debt);
2. Total spending allocated among budget functions;
3. Allocation of spending among the congressional committees (by jurisdiction); and
4. Budget enforcement provisions.

Optional Budget Resolution components are:

5. Reserve Funds; and
6. Budget Reconciliation instructions (a key procedure when invoked).

Budget totals, examples of which are shown in appendix G, set forth what the Congress considers to be the appropriate amounts for total spending, total revenues, and the resulting deficit or surplus, and Federal debt. In setting these budget totals, the Congress considers the impact of the Federal Budget on the national economy and establishes Federal fiscal policy for the coming year. (See Part VI, "Do Deficits Matter?")

Federal spending broken down by function gives Congress a way to consider broad Federal spending priorities. The Budget Resolution accomplishes this by dividing up Federal spending among twenty-one "budget functions," such as national defense, agriculture, and health. (See chapter 2-9 for a list of budget functions.) The allocation among budget functions, however, does *not* control how money is actually appropriated.[4] That responsibility belongs to the Appropriations Committees, as explained later.

Committee allocations. The House-Senate Conference Report on the Budget Resolution is accompanied by a document called the "Joint Explanatory Statement of the Committee of Conference." This Joint Statement—in addition to explaining how the Senate and House arrived at their final compromise on each provision—contains *spending allocations* to the various committees of Congress. These allocations—called "302(a) allocations" in budget-speak—divide total Federal spending among the Appropriations Committees and the authorizing committees of each House, based on jurisdiction. The Senate and House Appropriations Committees—with jurisdiction over all discretionary (i.e., nonentitlement) spending—receive large lump sum 302(a) allocations.

For example, the FY 2008 Budget Resolution allocated $953 billion to the House Appropriations Committee and the Senate Appropriations Committee.[5] The amount of the 302(a) allocations to the Appropriations Committee is one of the key decision points in each year's budget process, because they determine the size of the total pot of discretionary funds the House and Senate Appropriations Committees will divide among their respective subcommittees. (See appendix J for an example of 302(a) allocations.)

The *authorizing* committees likewise receive spending allocations for the upcoming budget year, as well as for the five-year period covered by the Budget Resolution. These allocations determine how much new direct spending a committee is permitted to bring to the Senate or House Floor, respectively. For example, if an authorizing committee's spending allocation is set at "baseline" levels (i.e., levels that reflect current law), any net new spending reported by the committee would be subject to a procedural objection for violating the committee's allocation. Alternatively, if the Budget Resolution contemplates a new direct spending program within an authorizing committee's jurisdiction, the additional spending authority would be reflected in the Budget Resolution totals, the appropriate budget function, and in the committee's 302(a) allocation.

Budget Enforcement Provisions. The Budget Resolution also typically includes various *budget enforcement provisions*, intended to add teeth to the spending and revenue totals and committee allocations set forth by the Budget Resolution. Over the years, these enforcement provisions have included new parliamentary points of order, specific caps on overall discretionary spending, pay-as-you-go requirements for new entitlement spending or tax cuts, limitations on advance appropriations, and limitations on the use of emergency designations.

Reserve Funds. An optional component of a Budget Resolution, which was used heavily in the Fiscal Year 2008 Budget Resolution, is called a "reserve fund." These are provisions that allow total spending and committee allocations to be adjusted upward to accommodate additional spending for a specifically defined purpose. The adjustment of spending levels is dependent on one or more contingencies, typically that (1) the additional spending will be "deficit neutral" and (2) that the covered legislation is dedicated to specific objectives. Because most reserve funds require that the new legislation be "deficit neutral" (paid for by new spending cuts or tax increases), the use of the term *reserve fund* is actually a misnomer, since *a Budget Resolution "reserve fund" does not provide any funds.*

In fact, the only scenarios in which a "reserve fund" has any purpose at all (other than to make a political statement) is where a mechanism is needed to allow the Budget Committees to adjust spending totals and/or committee allocations to accommodate a new program *that is to be paid for by tax increases, or by spending cuts in another committee's jurisdiction.* If a new program is paid for by spending cuts within a committee's own jurisdiction, there is no net increase in the committee's spending or in total Federal spending, so no adjustments to the Budget Resolution are required and "reserve fund" authority is unnecessary. (See Appendix I for more background on reserve funds.)

Reconciliation Instructions. The Budget Resolution may also initiate an optional—and powerful—procedure known as *Budget Reconciliation.* This procedure is used when the Congress wants to make substantial changes in tax laws or entitlement programs. Under the Reconciliation process, the Congress inserts "Reconciliation Instructions" in the Budget Resolution that direct specific authorizing committees to report legislation changing entitlement programs or tax laws within their jurisdiction by a specified amount.

As displayed in appendix H, Reconciliation Instructions in the Budget Resolution include only dollar amounts to be achieved. The authorizing committees have complete discretion to fulfill the instructions as they see fit, though the Budget Committees normally have specific, *non*binding policy assumptions in mind when drafting the instructions. What makes Reconciliation Instructions extraordinarily significant is that legislation produced under these instructions are completely protected from Senate filibuster and largely protected from Floor amendments—something discussed below in greater detail.

Completing Work on the Budget Resolution. When the House and Senate Budget Committees finish drafting a Budget Resolution, they report their respective resolutions to the full House and Senate. Members of the House and Senate then have an opportunity to alter the work of their respective Budget Committees by offering amendments to the Budget Resolutions.

When the Senate and House have both passed their respective versions of the Budget Resolution, they appoint several of their Members to a Senate-House conference committee to resolve the differences between the Senate- and House-passed resolutions. When differences have been resolved in conference, each chamber must then vote on the compromise version of the Budget Resolution called a "Conference Report." The Budget Act sets April 15 as the date for completion of this work, although this deadline is seldom met. (See appendix F for a historical table on Budget Resolutions.)

THE INFAMOUS BUDGET RESOLUTION "VOTE-A-RAMA"

The Senate has been called the world's greatest deliberative body. There are many examples throughout U.S. history where the Senate has lived up to this accolade. The Budget Resolution "vote-a-rama" is not one of them.

During the 1980s, Senators began offering scores of Floor amendments to the Budget Resolution to ostensibly increase discretionary spending for particular programs. However, as explained earlier, the Budget Resolution does not include program detail. (That responsibility belongs to the Appropriations Committee.) For example, if a Senator offers an amendment intended to move money from a natural resources program into a discretionary health program, the amendment itself would simply reduce the function 300 (natural resources) spending levels and increase the function 550 (health) spending levels. But there would be *no practical impact* because total spending levels would not change and the lump-sum 302(a) committee allocation to the Appropriations Committee would not change.

The Senate Budget Committee also permits Senators to offer amendments that increase spending in one area and "offset" the cost with a negative number in an artificial "Budget Function 970," innocuously called "Allowances," to ensure that total spending and committee allocations do not change.

Despite the fact that these amendments actually do nothing, they have proliferated to the point where dozens of such amendments are offered every year. When the fifty hours of Senate debate time on the Budget Resolution expires, the Senate must still vote on all amendments that are offered, albeit without debate. The result is the now infamous Budget Resolution "vote-a-rama"—a series of votes, sometimes taking an entire day, on amendments that for the most part have no impact.

(A new twist on the annual vote-a-rama came to pass during debate on the FY 2008 Budget Resolution when Senators offered numerous amendments to create Reserve Funds that, as explained earlier, do not actually provide any funds.)

The Budget Resolution vote-a-rama has caused the unfortunate misperception that all amendments to the Budget Resolution are just "message" amendments that have no real impact. *The reality is that some amendments to the Budget Resolution have a tremendous impact on our nation's fiscal policy.*

For example amendments that change Reconciliation instructions can have a profound impact on entitlement programs or tax laws. In 2004, I met with a Senator to ask for his support for an amendment to delete Reconciliation instructions from the Budget Resolution. The Instructions would have required the Finance Committee to report legislation cutting $10 billion (out of the Medicaid program). At first, the Senator dismissed my request, saying that he would not support Budget Resolution amendments that don't have any practical impact. Once I explained that the amendment would actually change the Reconciliation Instructions and have a profound impact on the Medicaid program, he agreed to support the amendment, and his vote became one of the pivotal votes in eliminating billions of dollars in Medicaid cuts from that year's budget process.

As noted above, the Budget Resolution is a concurrent resolution of Congress and, therefore, action is completed when both houses of Congress have adopted the Conference Report. The Budget Resolution is not a law and is not presented to the President for signature. It functions as an internal procedural mechanism of the Congress to guide its subsequent deliberations on appropriations, entitlement programs, and changes in tax laws.

May–September: Appropriations Action and Budget Reconciliation

The Appropriations Process. Following adoption of a Budget Resolution Conference Report and the issuance of committee allocations, the Appropriations Committees in the Senate and House subdivide their allocations among their twelve respective subcommittees and proceed with mark-up of the annual appropriations bills. These suballocations are known as "302(b) allocations."

Adoption of the 302(b) subcommittee allocations is a critical point in the budget process—one of the most closely-watched—because it prioritizes the total funds available for annually appropriated programs. For FY 2008, the Appropriations Committees of the House and Senate have $953 billion in budget authority to subdivide among their various subcommittees. (Appendix K displays an example of 302(b) subcommittee allocations.)

Once the Appropriations Committees vote on 302(b) allocations for their respective subcommittees, the appropriations process starts in earnest—although prior to receiving their allocations, the appropriations subcommittees have an active hearing schedule during February, March, and April as they review the President's requests and begin to formulate their own spending priorities. Figure 3 displays the appropriations process that begins with 302(b) allocations.

After hearings have concluded, each subcommittee chairman drafts an appropriations bill for the upcoming fiscal year and holds a business meeting to "mark up" the appropriations bill. This is where the immense influence of appropriations subcommittee chairmen is displayed, because it is the subcommittee chairmen who place a draft bill—known as a "chairman's

FIGURE 2-2.2: The Appropriations Process

**MAY-SEPTEMBER: THE APPROPRIATIONS PROCESS
FOR THE 12 ANNUAL APPROPRIATIONS BILLS**

Budget Resolution Generates "302(a)" Lump-Sum Allocations to:

House Appropriations Committee	**Senate Appropriations Committee**
▼	▼
"302(b)" Allocations to 12 Subcommittees	"302(b)" Allocations to 12 Subcommittees
▼	▼
Subcommittees "Mark Up" Appropriations Bills	Subcommittees "Mark Up" Appropriations Bills
▼	▼
Full Committee Mark-up of Each Appropriations Bill	Full Committee Mark-up of Each Appropriations Bill
▼	▼
House Floor Action on Each Appropriations Bill	Senate Floor Action on Each Appropriations Bill
▼	▼

House-Senate Conference Committee
on each of the 12 Appropriations Bills

▼

House: Final Action on Each Conference Report

▼

Senate: Final Action on Each Conference Report

▼

President for Signature

---

mark"—in front of their respective subcommittees for consideration. The chairman's mark distributes the subcommittee's 302(b) allocation among all of the programs, projects, and activities within their subcommittee's jurisdiction. The influence of the subcommittee chairs—in distributing billions of dollars among Federal programs—is so widely recognized that they are generally referred to as the "Appropriations Cardinals."

The most important thing to understand about the appropriations subcommittee mark-ups—and the full committee mark-ups and Floor action that follow—is that the 302(b) allocations to the appropriations subcommittees are *binding*. A procedural objection can be raised on the Senate or House Floor against any appropriations bill that exceeds its subcommittee's allocation. Waiving this budgetary constraint in the Senate requires sixty votes (a very difficult threshold to reach). *Consequently, amending an appropriations bill is a zero-sum game.* If a Senator or Representative wants to add funds to an appropriations bill at the subcommittee mark-up, or later on at the full-committee level or on the Senate or House Floor, he or she *must* propose a reduction in funding elsewhere in the bill.

For example, assume that a Member of the Senate Labor-HHS-Education subcommittee has attempted—unsuccessfully—to persuade his subcommittee chair to provide $10 million for a new initiative within the Department of Health and Human Services. If the Senator wants to offer an amendment to add the proposed $10 million to the chairman's mark at the subcommittee's mark-up, he or she must *at the same time* propose an offset—that is, a reduction of $10 million elsewhere in the bill. Needless to say, this is not easy to do; any spending reduction elsewhere in the bill will gore someone's ox, as the saying goes.

Once an appropriations subcommittee has completed marking up its appropriations bill for the upcoming Fiscal Year, the bill then goes to the full Appropriations Committee for consideration. The Senate Appropriation Committee has twenty-nine members, and the House Appropriations Committee has sixty-six members. At the full committee mark-up of an appropriations bill, any Member can offer an amendment, but—as in the case of the subcommittee mark-up—it is a zero-sum game; all proposed amendments must be offset.

Following full committee action, the appropriations bill travels to the House or Senate Floor, respectively, for consideration by the full chamber. Typically, appropriations bills reach the House Floor before the Senate Floor, because the House asserts the right to originate appropriations bills.[7] During Floor action—as in subcommittee and full committee mark-ups—Representatives and Senators may offer amendments to add spending to the bills but must include offsets in their amendments to prevent the relevant subcommittee's 302(b) allocation from being exceeded. (See appendix O for additional rules that apply to Floor consideration of Appropriations measures.)

After the House and Senate have both acted on a particular appropriations bill, the bill then goes to a House-Senate Conference Committee, generally composed of senior members of the relevant House and Senate appropriations subcommittees. The task of the conferees is to resolve all differences between the two versions of the bill, producing a compromise version known as a conference report. The major constraint under which the conferees operate is to produce a conference report that complies with the 302(b) subcommittee allocations in both the House and Senate. When they arrive at such a compromise, the House and Senate vote on the appropriations conference report and the bill is sent to the President for signature.

Budget Reconciliation. In years when the Congress has chosen to include Budget Reconciliation Instructions in the Budget Resolution, the authorizing committees of the Senate and House proceed to mark up Budget Reconciliation legislation about the same time the appropriators are working on the twelve appropriations bills (i.e., May and June).[8] *The*

Reconciliation process is used when the Congress wants to fast-track substantial changes in tax or entitlement laws. Under this *filibuster-proof* procedure, the Congress—by including Reconciliation Instructions in the Budget Resolution—*directs* specific authorizing committees to report legislation that cuts spending or increases tax revenues by changing programs within their jurisdiction.

All committees, so instructed, have *unfettered discretion* to fulfill the instructions as they see fit as long as the legislation they report is within their jurisdiction, meets the deadline set forth in the Budget Resolution, and fulfills the Budget Resolution directive to cut spending or raise revenues.

(Although Reconciliation, during the 1980s and 1990s was used to achieve *deficit reduction* in an expedited manner, in recent years it was used to fast-track legislation that cut taxes and *increased deficits.* However, this use of Reconciliation may be over, with the Senate's adoption in 2007 of a procedural prohibition on Reconciliation legislation that increases deficits.[9])

The Budget Act gives the Senate Finance Committee special flexibility in meeting Reconciliation instructions. If the Committee is instructed to cut spending by a specified amount and to raise revenues by a specified amount, the committee can choose to cut more spending and raise less revenues, or vice versa, as long as it achieves the same net amount of required deficit reduction. (We used this procedure—known as the "fungibility rule"[10]— at the Finance Committee in 1993 in order to facilitate enactment of a half-trillion-dollar deficit reduction bill.)

Surprisingly, the Budget Committee's role in the Budget Reconciliation process is largely ministerial. The Senate and House Budget Committees, respectively, simply take the legislation reported by the respective Senate and House authorizing committees and package the legislation—*without change*—into a single Senate bill and a single House bill for consideration by the respective chambers.

The most important aspect of the Reconciliation process—and the budget process itself—is that Reconciliation legislation is protected by extraordinary rules that radically limit Floor debate and amendments—short-circuiting the regular rules of the Senate.

The Standing Rules of the Senate, many of which have been in place since the founding of the Republic, generally protect the right of all Senators to engage in (1) unlimited debate and (2) the unlimited right to offer amendments. This is the heart and soul of the Senate—designed to ensure that all points of view can be fully debated.

Unlimited debate in the Senate. Votes do not occur in the Senate until all debate on a matter is completed. Consequently, *opponents of a particular measure can block it simply by engaging in extended debate.* This is the Senate *filibuster*—made famous by Jimmy Stewart's portrayal in *Mr. Smith goes to Washington.* A filibuster is nothing more than the continuation of debate in order to prevent a vote. The only way to stop a filibuster is by shutting down debate with a procedure known as "cloture." Here's the key point: invoking cloture requires a *three-fifths vote—sixty out of one hundred Senators.*[11]

In recent years, filibusters have been threatened more and more frequently. When I began working in the Senate in 1983, filibusters were a relatively rare occurrence. But opponents of legislation now routinely threaten to filibuster. It has therefore become almost an accepted fact in the Senate that major legislation requires the support of sixty, not fifty-one Senators, because sixty is the number needed to invoke cloture and bring matters to a final vote.[12]

THE REAL STORY BEHIND "COBRA"

Most Budget Reconciliation bills have very bureaucratic sounding names, such as the Omnibus Budget Reconciliation Act of 1993. But there is one Reconciliation bill that much of the American public has actually heard of: COBRA—the Consolidated Omnibus Budget Reconciliation Act of 1985. COBRA has become well known because it contains a provision requiring employers to offer extensions of health insurance to former employees—which has been a lifesaver for many American families. But why the name COBRA? In 1985, I and the rest of the Senate Budget Committee staff were sitting in Staff Director Steve Bell's office getting ready to package all of the Reconciliation submissions from the various authorizing committees into a single bill to send to the Senate Floor. Steve happened to muse about whether we should give the bill a name other than Omnibus Budget Reconciliation Act—after all, this would be the fifth in a row. Paul Heilig, the defense budget analyst on the staff jokingly suggested that instead of another "OBRA," why not "COBRA"? That got almost instant approval from the rest of the assembled staff; we just needed to figure out what the C would stand for. It wasn't long before one of the staff suggested "consolidated," since we were in the midst of packaging or "consolidating" the Reconciliation submissions from the Senate's authorizing committees. And thus was born COBRA. What we didn't know at the time was that the health insurance provisions in the bill would make it virtually a household name.

Unlimited right of Senators to offer amendments. The other major privilege of Senators is the power of unlimited amendment. *In general, Senators can offer any amendment on any subject to any bill.* This right of amendment includes "nongermane" amendments—in other words, amendments that have nothing to do with the underlying bill being debated. (This may seem like a wildly inefficient way to legislate, but it actually has the undeniable virtue of ensuring that minority points of view get public attention in the Senate—unlike the House where the majority party has the procedural means to severely limit debate and amendment.[13])

Budget Reconciliation: Short-circuiting Senate Rules. The Budget Reconciliation process effectively short-circuits Senate rules because the Budget Act protects Reconciliation bills with (1) a very strict (twenty-hour) time limit on debate *and* (2) a very strict germaneness restriction on amendments. (These same significant protections apply to Congressional Budget Resolutions: Budget Resolutions cannot be filibustered and amendments are subject to strict limitations.)

The limit on debate means that Reconciliation bills (and Budget Resolutions) cannot be filibustered. Consequently, no matter how controversial a Reconciliation bill or Budget Resolution may be, passage in the Senate requires fifty-one votes, rather than the sixty votes that would ordinarily be necessary to invoke cloture (end debate and get to a final vote) on a controversial bill.

By looking at recent political history one can easily see how significant this no-filibuster rule for Reconciliation bills has been. Most of President George W. Bush's major legislation has passed under the protection of Reconciliation rules.

In 2001, President Bush secured his massive trillion-dollar-plus tax cut legislation through the Budget Reconciliation process. When the Senate in April 2001 considered a Budget Resolution that included Reconciliation instructions for the Finance Committee to report legislation cutting taxes by $1.25 trillion over a ten-year period, Senate Republicans were able to muster only fifty-three votes—well short of the sixty votes normally needed for controversial legislation.

Similarly, in 2003, the President's second major round of tax cuts—the Jobs Growth Tax Relief Reconciliation Act of 2003—passed the Senate by a final vote of 51–50 (with the Vice President voting for the bill). As in the case of the 2001 tax legislation, Senate Republican leaders in 2003 had well short of the sixty votes normally needed to pass major, controversial legislation. Reconciliation's no-filibuster rule, once again, enabled passage of the President's legislation.

And again, in 2006, the no-filibuster rule on Reconciliation legislation worked to the President's advantage. The Congress passed cuts in Medicaid, student loans, and other entitlement programs—which Democrats strongly opposed. The bill ultimately passed the Senate 52–47, again well short of the sixty votes that would have been needed to pass the legislation absent the no-filibuster protections unique to Reconciliation Bills and Budget Resolutions.

The "germaneness" restriction on amendments to Reconciliation bills, a fact often overlooked, is equally significant. "Germaneness" is much stricter than mere relevance. An amendment is "germane" only if it strikes a provision, changes a number, limits some new authority provided in the legislation, or expresses the "sense of the Senate." Effectively, this means that *any substantive amendment offered to a Reconciliation bill on the Senate Floor is nongermane and can only be considered if the restriction is waived by a vote of sixty Senators.*

For example, assume that Reconciliation legislation reported by the Senate Finance Committee proposes to enact certain changes in Medicare in order to generate budget savings. If a Senator feels that the proposed cuts are bad policy and wants to offer alternative budget savings in the Medicare program or a different entitlement program, the amendment would be nongermane. The only way to gain consideration of the amendment would be to waive the Budget Act's germaneness rule, which requires sixty votes.

The same scenario holds for tax legislation. If the Finance Committee has proposed to increase revenues by closing a particular tax loophole, or to cut specific taxes, a Senator would have to obtain sixty votes for a Budget Act waiver in order to gain consideration of an alternative proposal.

Germaneness restrictions therefore give the committees of the Senate virtually unfettered authority over the substance of Reconciliation legislation. Once the legislation reaches the Senate Floor and is protected by the germaneness restriction on Floor amendments, it is extremely difficult to amend the legislation without garnering sixty votes to waive the germaneness restriction.

Reconciliation and the Byrd Rule. Because Budget Reconciliation is such a radical departure from the way the Senate normally does its business, Senator Robert C. Byrd (D-WV) created in 1985 what has become known as the "Byrd Rule," which limits what can be included in a Reconciliation bill. Under the Byrd Rule, all legislation reported in response to Reconciliation instructions must be "budgetary" in nature. Anything not budgetary in nature is considered "extraneous" to the purpose of Budget Reconciliation and in violation of the Byrd Rule. The concept is simple, although the rule itself is mind-numbing in its complexity.

Senator Byrd, a brilliant defender of the Senate's tradition of unlimited debate and amendment, did not want to see the Reconciliation mechanism become a way for Senate committees to fast-track *non*budgetary legislation through the Senate, immune from filibuster and amendment. In 1985, he was the driving force behind an amendment to the Budget Act[14] that permits any Senator to raise an objection on the Senate Floor to any provisions in a Reconciliation bill that are "extraneous" to the budgetary purposes of the Reconciliation bill. If the Presiding Officer in the Senate—in actuality the Parliamentarian—agrees that the provision falls into the Byrd Rule's definition of "extraneous," the provision is automatically stricken from the Reconciliation bill.

Generally, the rule defines as extraneous, provisions that (1) have no cost or (2) are significant policy changes with "merely incidental" budgetary effects. Senators may challenge a lengthy provision or very small provisions down to the subsection level. The Byrd Rule is explained in greater detail in appendix L.

Why the Tax Cuts Expire in 2010. One of the more noteworthy effects of the Byrd Rule is that the tax cuts enacted in the 2001 Reconciliation tax legislation *expire after ten years* because the Byrd Rule specifically defines as "extraneous" any provisions that have the effect of increasing spending or decreasing revenues beyond the "budget window." In this case, the Budget Resolution that generated the 2001 Reconciliation Bill covered a ten-year budget period, so if the tax cuts had extended into the eleventh year they would have violated the Byrd Rule and exposed the tax cuts to parliamentary oblivion. This is why we have the unusual situation of the estate tax phasing down to nothing by the end of this decade and springing back up in 2011 at its pre-2001 level.

There is a logical purpose behind this seemingly strange rule. Senator Byrd and his colleagues wanted to be sure that the Reconciliation process would not be misused by enacting legislation that brings deficits down during the five- or ten-year budget window and then reverses course and increases deficits in the "out-years" (i.e., the years beyond the budget window).[15]

Clearly Senator Byrd and his colleagues who joined him in framing the Byrd Rule in 1985 intended that Reconciliation, as an extraordinary departure from normal Senate procedures, be used *only to reduce deficits*. I was on the staff of the Senate Budget Committee in 1985 when the Byrd Rule was being drafted, and there is no question that the general bipartisan consensus in the Senate at that time—and until the late 1990s—was that Reconciliation was to be used for deficit reduction.

Reconciliation and the House of Representatives. Little has been said thus far about Reconciliation procedures in the House of Representatives. Unlike the Senate, where Reconciliation represents a radical departure from normal procedures, the Reconciliation limitations on debate and amendments are *not* a radical departure for the House. In the House of Representatives, the powerful Committee on Rules *routinely* imposes time limitations on debate and strict limitations on the right to offer amendments. Consequently, Budget Reconciliation procedures do not significantly change the normal order of business in the House.

October 1: Fiscal New Year, Continuing Resolutions, Omnibus Bills, and Government Shutdowns

You will not be surprised to learn that the budget process often does not work as intended. In recent years, appropriations bills have seldom been completed by the start of the new fiscal year. In fact, in the last 32 years Congress has, only four times, completed all of its annual appropriations bills by the start of the new fiscal year.[16] (See appendix N.)

However, the Constitution is very clear that "no money shall be drawn from the Treasury, but in Consequence of Appropriations made by Law."[17] In addition, in 1870 Congress enacted the Anti-Deficiency Act strictly prohibiting Federal programs from operating without specific budget authority appropriated by Congress. Put simply, without appropriations, Federal managers have no legal authority to obligate the U.S. government's resources. Federal managers who attempt to do so are subject to disciplinary action and criminal prosecution. (See appendix C.) Therefore, if appropriations are not enacted by October 1, the beginning of the new fiscal year, Federal departments and agencies must shut down (although special provisions permit certain "essential government employees" to continue working).

Continuing Resolutions. To avoid a shutdown of government programs not funded by the start of the fiscal year, the Congress typically passes stop-gap measures called "continuing resolutions" or "CRs." These joint resolutions of Congress (requiring presidential signature) authorize agencies to continue current programs for a period of time according to a formula, usually the previous year's levels, or the lower of the funding levels in either the House-passed or Senate-passed bill.[18] The number of continuing resolutions needed until all programs are funded for the new fiscal year can vary dramatically depending on how contentious the funding issues are. For fiscal year 1993, one CR was adopted, while in fiscal year 1996, when President Clinton and Congress had a major political showdown over budget cuts, thirteen CRs were adopted.

Omnibus Appropriations Bills. In addition to temporarily continuing funding to avoid government shutdowns, continuing resolutions are also frequently used as the legislative vehicle for "omnibus appropriations bills." These are bills that package together all of the unfinished appropriations bills. Many will remember the image of President Ronald Reagan at a State of the Union Address, putting an eighteen-inch stack of paper on the dais—the previous year's omnibus appropriations bill—and declaring that he would never again sign an omnibus bill.

There is much opposition to the use of omnibus appropriations bills both within and outside the Congress, because the sheer length of the bills makes it impossible for any Member of Congress to exercise anything close to due diligence in understanding the totality of what they are voting on. Yet, getting to closure on the new year's funding levels at the end of a congressional session very often leads to the legislative vehicle everyone loves to hate—the omnibus appropriations bill. (In recent years, when eight, ten, or all eleven of the regular appropriations bills are packaged together, they are referred to as an omnibus appropriations bill. When four

Ronald Reagan declares that he will never again sign an omnibus appropriations bill. Vice President George Bush and House Speaker Jim Wright preside over the Joint Session. By Permission, Ronald Reagan Library.

or five bills are packaged together, it has become common—in budget-speak—to call them a "minibus.")

As an example of how an appropriations season might proceed, consider funding for FY 2004. By the beginning of the fiscal year (October 1, 2003), only three of the thirteen appropriations bills had been enacted.[19] A government shutdown was averted by adopting a series of five CRs. Between October and December, three more appropriations bills became law. Funding for FY 2004 was finally completed January 23, 2004, when President George W. Bush signed into law an omnibus appropriations act including the remaining seven appropriations bills.[20]

Government Shutdowns. When fiscal politics become extremely intense, Congress and the President have on occasion failed to enact continuing resolutions to avert a shutdown of Federal departments and agencies at the start of the fiscal year. The longest such shutdown, causing the furloughing of 284,000 employees,[21] lasted for three weeks, from December 16, 1995, through January 6, 1996. President Clinton and Republican congressional leaders were in a tense stand-off over tax cuts and proposed cuts to Medicare, Medicaid, education and environment programs, and AmeriCorps. (As the political stand-off continued, I had the dubious honor during the government shutdown of generating OMB's daily report to Congress on the worsening impact of the shutdown.)

Following the shutdown of FY 1996, there have been numerous proposals to prevent future shutdowns by providing for "automatic continuing resolutions" when funding deadlines are missed. However, because of the intense political fallout from the standoff of 1996 (primarily blaming Congress for the shutdown), recent Congresses have studiously avoided shutting down the government, eliminating any political momentum for enacting an "automatic CR."

Supplemental Appropriations

In the eyes of its supporters, supplemental spending gives the Congress flexibility to respond to problems or priorities that may not have been anticipated during the regular cycle of annual appropriations. In the view of its detractors, supplemental spending allows lawmakers to circumvent budgetary enforcement mechanisms.[22] —CBO

During the course of a fiscal year, it is routine for the President to request, and Congress to enact, "supplemental appropriations" to provide funding for:

- Mandatory or discretionary programs that turn out to have greater spending needs than earlier anticipated;
- Disaster response (natural disasters such as Hurricanes Katrina and Rita, and "nonnatural" disasters such as the Oklahoma City bombing in 1995 and the 9/11 attacks in 2001);
- Ongoing military needs, particularly during a war; and
- New programs authorized after enactment of the regular appropriations bill.

Supplemental appropriations bills are typically enacted in the spring, midway through a fiscal year—anywhere from March to June. Items of spending included in supplemental appropriations are generally classified as "emergency requirements"—exempted from spending limits—in order to avoid breaching the Budget Resolution 302(a) allocation to Appropriations Committees and the aggregate spending limits in the Budget Resolution.[23] According to CBO, 92% of the discretionary supplemental appropriations enacted during the 1990s were designated as emergency spending in order to be exempted from spending limits.

In addition to the use of "emergency designations," the Congress often rescinds budget authority from other programs to "pay for" the cost of the supplemental bill. For example, according to CBO, Congress provided almost $138 billion in supplemental appropriations in the 1990s, which were accompanied by $52 billion in rescissions.[24] Critics argue, however, that some of the rescinded budget authority would never have been used anyway, and other BA would have spent out more slowly than the supplemental funds they're intended to "offset."[25] More recently, the practice of rescinding BA to pay for supplemental appropriations has waned. Between 2003 and 2006, CRS calculates, less than 8% of supplemental appropriations were offset, compared with 36% in the 1990s.[26]

CRS conducted an extensive study of supplemental appropriations since 1981 and concluded that "the major purposes of supplemental appropriations have changed over the past 25 years." Their study notes that "in the 1980s, almost half of supplemental appropriations were for mandatory[27] programs such as unemployment compensation, and the rest were for discretionary spending." After 1990, the analysis continues, "over 90% of supplemental appropriations have been for discretionary spending, as the major purpose has shifted toward funding natural disaster relief."[28]

A recent example of major disaster relief is the supplemental funding provided following Hurricanes Katrina and Rita in 2005—which caused widespread loss of life, displacement, food and medical shortages, flooding, and unemployment. As reflected in table 2-2.1, within two weeks after the Hurricanes struck, Congress passed two supplemental appropriations bills

TABLE 2-2.1: Supplemental Appropriations, Fiscal Years 2000–2007

Fiscal Year	Budget Authority (in billions of dollars)	Date Enacted
Military Construction, 2000	$15.2	07/13/00
Defense, 2000	$1.8	08/09/00
Emergency Supplemental and Rescission, 2001	$7.5	07/24/01
Recovery and Response to Terrorism Acts, 2001	$20.0	09/18/01
Defense, 2002	$20.0	01/10/02
Emergency Supplemental & Rescission, 2002	$25.3	08/02/02
Emergency Wartime Supplemental Appropriations Act, 2003	$79.2	04/16/03
Emergency Supplemental Appropriations for Disaster Relief, 2003	$1.0	08/08/03
Legislative Branch, 2003	$0.9	09/03/07
Supp for Defense/Iraq/Afghanistan, 2004	$87.5	11/06/03
FY 05 Defense Appropriations (titles 8, 9, 10 provided '04 supp. funds)	$28.2	08/05/04
Emergency Disaster Relief Supp, 2004	$2.0	09/08/04
Emergency Supp for Hurricane Disasters Assistance Act, 2005	$14.5	10/13/04
Emergency Supp Approps for Defense, GWOT, Tsunami Relief, 2005	$82.1	05/11/05
Interior Appropriations, 2005	$1.5	08/02/05
Emergency Supp, Hurricane Katrina, 2005	$10.5	09/02/05
Second Emergency Supp, Katrina, 2005	$51.8	09/08/05
Defense Appropriations, 2006	$50.0	12/30/05
Emergency Supp for Defense, Hurricane Recovery, 2006	$94.5	06/15/06
Supplemental for defense and Katrina relief, 2007	$120.0	05/25/07

Source: Congressional Budget Office

providing a combined $62 billion for relief and recovery needs.[29] In addition, Congress has provided additional Katrina relief in FY 2006 and FY 2007 supplementals.

The other heavy use of supplemental funding in recent years has been for the wars in Iraq and Afghanistan. From the beginning of the Afghanistan war in FY 2002, through funding of both Iraq and Afghanistan in FY 2007, nearly all of the funding for both military operations has been provided through emergency supplemental appropriations.[30] According to CRS, this contrasted with the funding of prior military conflicts where supplemental bills generally funded the "initial stages of military operations," but Administrations transitioned to funding through *regular appropriations* bills "as soon as even a limited and partial projection of costs could be made."[31]

The continuing practice of funding operations in Iraq and Afghanistan through supplemental bills led to increasing discontent among Members of Congress who wanted the war funding requests included in the President's regular February Budget. The principal reason is that *regular annual budget requests, unlike supplemental requests, are accompanied by highly detailed "budget justifications."* For example, in an early 2007 article investigating war costs, *Congressional Quarterly* reported the following:

> Though the armed services send congressional committees thousands of pages of copiously detailed justifications for their regular budget requests each year, the supplemental requests that go to Congress are almost terse. The request from the Department of Defense for about $68 billion in supplemental spending for fiscal 2006, for example, was 73 pages long. . . . One line item, $5.9 billion for "Iraqi and Afghan Security Forces," was justified in about three and one-third pages, mostly composed of brief descriptions of various expenditures. . . The request also included $296 million, with no further explanation, for "police assets maintenance—to develop Ministry of Interior's capability to maintain equipment and buildings, to include the maintenance of a large volume of American-made vehicles; stocks must be established and maintained."[32]

In response to the growing frustration over inadequate detail on war funding requests, Congress mandated in the FY 2007 Department of Defense Authorizations Act that beginning with FY 2008 the *President's Annual Budget* must include "(1) a request for the appropriation of funds. . .for ongoing military operations in Afghanistan and Iraq; (2) an estimate of all funds expected to be required in that fiscal year for such operations; and (3) a detailed justification of the funds requested."[33] The Administration responded by including in its FY 2008 Budget a $145 billion request for Iraq, Afghanistan and other Global War on Terror operations for FY 2008. However, eight months later the Administration increased their FY 2008 request to $196 billion.

Notes

1. Lewis D. Eigen and Jonathan P. Siegel, *The Macmillan Dictionary of Political Quotations* (New York: Macmillan, 1993), 26.

2. U.S. Constitution, Article I, Section 9, Clause 7: "No money shall be drawn from the treasury, but in consequence of appropriations made by law."

3. For a good overview of the budget process prior to 1974, see U.S. General Accounting Office, Office of the General Counsel, "Principles of Federal Appropriations Law," 3rd ed., vol. 1, GAO-04-261SP, pp. 1-14–1-24.

4. However, the split between mandatory spending and discretionary spending within a particular budget function impacts the size of the total discretionary allocation to the House and Senate Appropriations Committees and the amount of direct spending allocated (or "crosswalked") to the authorizing committees.

5. H.Rpt. 110–153, Conference Report to accompany S.Con.Res. 21, Concurrent Resolution on the Budget for Fiscal Year 2008.

6. The Budget Resolution is therefore in the form of a "concurrent resolution" (S.Con.Res. __ or H.Con.Res. __), which is a legislative vehicle requiring approval by both houses of Congress, but is not presented to the President.

7. Article I, Section 7, of the Constitution provides that "All Bills for raising Revenue shall originate in the House of Representatives." Over the generations, the House has chosen to interpret "Revenue" broadly to include all tax *and* spending bills (which is consistent with the Framers' intent as set forth in the Federalist Papers).

8. Reconciliation instructions were first used in the FY 1980 Budget Resolution and since then have been included in 18 of the 26 Budget Resolutions. Source: review of each Budget Resolution since FY 1980.

9. Section 202 of the FY 2008 Budget Resolution, S.Con.Res. 21 (110th Cong., 1st Sess.).

10. Section 310(c) of the Congressional Budget Act.

11. The process of bringing debate to a close, and ending a filibuster is known as "invoking cloture" and is established by Senate Rule XXII. Although invoking cloture now requires sixty votes, at the time *Mr. Smith Goes to Washington* was made, Senate Rules still required a two-thirds vote to end a filibuster.

12. The reference to fifty-one votes refers to a "simple majority" of 50 percent plus one, assuming all one hundred Senators are voting.

13. In the House, the Rules Committee—which is heavily weighted toward the majority party—writes the rules of debate and amendment for all major legislation.

14. Section 313 of the Congressional Budget and Impoundment Control Act, as amended.

15. Section 313(b)(1)(E) of the Congressional Budget and Impoundment Control Act, as amended, states, "A provision of a Reconciliation bill . . . shall be considered extraneous (i.e. in violation) if it increases, or would increase, net outlays, or if it decreases, or would decrease, revenues during a fiscal year after the fiscal years covered by such Reconciliation bill . . . and such increases or decreases are greater than outlay reductions or revenue increases resulting from other provisions in such title in such year."

16. David Baumann, "Congress: How We Got Here—Again," *National Journal*, November 13, 2004.

17. U.S. Constitution, Article I, Section 9, Clause 7.

18. For example, under the initial FY 2007 CR: (1) where both houses had passed their regular versions of an appropriations bill, funding was continued at the *lower of* the amounts provided in the House-passed version, the Senate-passed version, or the '06 level; (2) an account funded by only House or Senate was protected until final '07 funding decisions were made; (3) accounts funded in '06, but not by either house, were not funded; and (4) entitlements that were not permanently appropriated received stopgap funding sufficient to fulfill the legally required payments. Sandy Streeter, "Continuing Appropriations Acts: Brief Overview of Recent Practices," CRS Report No. RL30343, (Washington, D.C.: Congressional Research Service, Library of Congress, November 15, 2006), 3–4.

19. At that time there were thirteen regular appropriations bills. Under reorganization of the appropriations subcommittees, beginning in 2007, there are twelve bills.

20. Kevin Kosar, "Shutdown of the Federal Government: Causes, Effects, and Process," CRS Report No. 98-844, (Washington, D.C.: Congressional Research Service, Library of Congress, September 20, 2004), 2.

21. Another 475,000 federal employees, deemed to be "essential," continued to work in a nonpay status. "Essential employees . . . are those performing duties vital to national defense, public health and safety, or other crucial operations." Essential employees, although not paid during the shutdown, were paid retroactively. Kosar, "Shutdown of the Federal Government," 3.

22. "Supplemental Appropriations in the 1990s" (Washington, D.C.: Congressional Budget Office, March 2001), ix.

23. Regular appropriations bills generally "consume" the entire Budget Resolution allocation of Budget Authority to the Appropriations Committees. Supplemental Appropriations must therefore be exempted from the Budget Resolution spending limits.

24. "Supplemental Appropriations in the 1990s," ix.

25. "Supplemental Appropriations in the 1990s," xiii.

26. Thomas Hungerford, "Supplemental Appropriations: Trends and Budgetary Impacts Since 1981," RL33134 (Washington, D.C.: Congressional Research Service, November 8, 2006), 1, 6.

27. "Mandatory spending" refers generally to entitlement programs, which are explained in chapter 2-9 on "Budget Concepts."

28. Thomas Hungerford, "Supplemental Appropriations," summary page.

29. Hungerford, "Supplemental Appropriations," 1.

30. In a June 13, 2006 report, the Congressional Research Service calculated that "since the terrorist attacks of September 11, 2001, Congress has appropriated $331 billion for military operations in Afghanistan, Iraq, and elsewhere. Of that amount, $301 billion, or 91%, has been provided either in supplemental appropriations bills or as additional 'emergency' funding in separate titles of annual defense appropriations acts." Stephen Daggett, "Military Operations: Precedents for Funding Contingency Operations in Regular or in Supplemental Appropriations Bills," RS22455 (Washington, D.C.: Congressional Research Service), 1.

31. Daggett, "Military Operations," 2.

32. John Cochran, "Penetrating the Fog of War Costs," *CQ Weekly,* January 1, 2007, 14.

33. Section 1008 of H.R. 5122, the John Warner National Defense Authorization Act of Fiscal Year 2007, P.L. 109-364.

Implementation of Spending Laws

After the fiscal year begins and appropriations bills are enacted, the next phase of the budget process is implementation of spending laws.

Budget Execution and Control: The Apportionment Process

Appropriations (in the form of budget authority[1]) are not immediately available to Federal agencies. A key step in making these funds available is for OMB to release the funds to agencies in a process known as *apportionment.*

The purpose of the centralized apportionment process is to ensure that agencies spend their funds effectively, reduce the need to request supplemental appropriations, and avoid exceeding their appropriated budget authority.[2] Exceeding congressional appropriations is a serious matter. The Antideficiency Act makes it a criminal offense for any government official to obligate the government in excess of congressional appropriations.[3]

OMB apportions budget authority to departments and agencies in one of two ways: (1) by time periods (usually quarterly) or (2) by projects or activities.

After OMB apportions budget authority to an agency, the agency then makes "allotments" to officials within the agency allowing them to incur obligations on behalf of the Federal government.[4]

Impoundment Control

As discussed above, one impetus for enactment of the Budget Act was an executive-legislative power struggle that erupted during the Nixon Administration over presidential authority to impound budget authority appropriated by Congress.[5] Title X of the Budget Act established legal procedures to prevent a recurrence of this dispute and is separately referred to as the "Impoundment Control Act" (ICA).

Under the procedures put in place by the Impoundment Control Act, the President may (1) "defer" (delay) using an amount of budget authority *until later in the fiscal year* or (2) propose to "rescind" (cancel) an amount of budget authority.

The authority of the President to defer budget authority and propose rescissions of budget authority does *not* apply to the nearly two-thirds of the budget that is consists of mandatory spending and interest payments. The portion of the budget that is susceptible to rescissions or deferrals is the 38% portion of the budget that is "discretionary" and subject to annual funding decisions.

Deferrals. The purpose of the deferral mechanism is to permit the Executive Branch to set money aside until later in the year in order to provide for a contingency or to save money due to changes in operations. The President may *not* propose a deferral simply because he disagrees with the Congress' appropriations decision. A further restriction is that funds may not be deferred for a period of time that is too long to allow the agency to obligate the funds prudently by the end of the fiscal year. *A deferral proposed by the President takes effect unless Congress passes, and the President signs, a law disapproving the deferral in which case the funds must be released.*

Rescissions. Conversely, a rescission (cancellation) of budget authority, proposed by the President, does *not* occur unless Congress affirmatively passes a law approving the cancellation within 45 days (of continuous session).[6] Consequently, if either the House or Senate fails to enact the President's proposed rescission of budget authority in a timely manner, the President has no choice but to release the budget authority to the agency after expiration of the 45-day period.[7] This gives Congress the upper hand in the rescission process.

As reflected in a 1999 GAO study, during the Impoundment Control Act's first quarter century, Congress agreed to rescind only about one-third of the proposed $76 billion in presidential rescissions.[8] Congress, however, has unfettered authority to initiate its own rescission legislation in order to revise earlier appropriations decisions and has increasingly made use of this authority.[9]

Both the President and the Congress have used rescissions primarily as a mechanism to shift priorities, rather than to reduce overall spending.[10]

In drafting the 1974 Impoundment Control Act, Congress put teeth in its limitations on presidential impoundment by empowering the Comptroller General (who heads the Congress' investigative arm, the GAO) to file suit in Federal Court to require the release of appropriated funds that have been illegally deferred or rescinded.

Notes

1. Budget authority, as explained in chapter 2-1, is legal authority provided by Congress to Federal departments and agencies to enter into obligations that will result in outlays.

2. Executive Office of the President, Office of Management and Budget, *OMB Circular No. A-11: Preparation, Submission, and Execution of the Budget*, June 2005, §120, 3.

3. Anti-Deficiency Act (enacted in 1870 as part of the legislative appropriations bill). 31 U.S.C. 1341-42; 1511–1519.

4. GAO: "Principles of Federal Appropriations Law," 3rd ed., GAO/04-261SP, January 2004, I-31.

5. For historical background on presidential assertions of impoundment authority, see Virgina A. McMurty, "Item Veto and Expanded Impoundment Proposals," IB89148 (Washington D.C.: Congressional Research Service, September 26, 2005), 1–2.

6. In counting the 45 days, continuity of session is broken by final (or *sine die*) adjournment at the end of a session or a mid-session adjournment of more than 3 days. If a Congress ends before the 45

days has run, then the President's proposed rescission is deemed to be resubmitted at the opening of the new Congress and the 45 days permitted for enactment of the rescission starts over. Congressional Budget and Impoundment Control Act, §1011.

7. The Budget Act, in Section 1017, provides procedures for expedited consideration of legislation to enact a proposed rescission.

8. Statement of Gary L. Kepplinger, U.S. General Accounting Office, "Impoundment Control Act: Use and Impact of Rescission Procedures," Testimony before the Subcommittee on Legislative and Budget Process, Committee on Rules, House of Representatives, Report No. GAO/T-OGC-99-56, July 30, 1999.

9. See Kepplinger, "Impoundment Control Act," Attachment I, where the GAO estimates that between 1974 and 1998, Congress initiated $105 billion in rescissions. Compare this with the same time period when Congress accepted $25 billion of the $76 billion in the Presidents' proposed rescissions.

10. Kepplinger, "Impoundment Control Act," 5.

Budget Enforcement

"We might hope to see the finances of the Union as clear and intelligible as a merchant's books," President Thomas Jefferson wrote to his Secretary of the Treasury, *"so that every member of Congress and every man of any mind in the Union should be able to comprehend them, to investigate abuses, and consequently to control them."* [1]

MYTH: The Congressional Budget Resolution does not become law, and the budget process produces little more than a nonbinding budget blueprint with trivial practical impact.

FACT: Key parts of the Budget Resolution are enforceable through parliamentary points of order, and in many fiscal years since enactment of the 1974 Budget Act, the Budget Resolution has impacted the overall amount of appropriations, as well as the enactment of key entitlement reforms and tax legislation. Moreover, the enactment of "PAYGO procedures" and "spending limits" strengthened the congressional budget process throughout the 1990s—a key factor in achieving budget surpluses.

The misperceptions of the Congressional Budget Resolution as ineffective or irrelevant are quite understandable. Congress failed to pass a Budget Resolution 4 times in the last 10 years (see Appendix F)—and the government continued to function. Moreover, the proliferation of nonbinding provisions in the Budget Resolution—

- nonbinding "sense of the Congress" provisions,
- nonbinding "policy statements,"
- the Senate's "vote-a-rama,"[2] and
- the recent proliferation of "reserve funds" that don't actually fund anything[3]—

has led many observers to conclude that the Budget Resolution is ineffectual and not worth much attention.

However, there are three ways in which the congressional budget process *is* enforceable and has significantly impacted Federal spending and tax policies: (1) parliamentary points of order; (2) Budget Reconciliation; and (3) in the 1990s, the addition of PAYGO and discretionary spending limits to the budget process.

Parliamentary Points of Order: Giving Individual Members of Congress Power to Enforce the Budget Resolution

In general, a parliamentary point of order allows a Senator or Representative to "rise" or "be recognized" by the Presiding Officer[4] to make a *procedural objection* to a bill, a provision of a bill, an amendment to a bill, or a conference report under consideration by the Senate or House. The Presiding Officer of the chamber (based on advice from the Parliamentarian) will then rule on the point of order. If the point of order is "sustained" (i.e., if the Parliamentarian agrees with the objection), the bill or amendment "falls"—meaning it is no longer under consideration by the Senate or House (or in the case of the Byrd Rule in the Senate, the offending provision is stricken from the bill).

The Budget Act includes numerous points of order to enforce the spending and revenue aggregates and committee spending allocations, as well as to impose limits on creation of new entitlements, extension of Federal credit, and creation of unfunded mandates. In addition, Budget Resolutions often establish additional points of order to enforce the budget policies reflected in the Resolution. Current Budget Act and Budget Resolution points of order are summarized below.

Budget Act points of order are more significant in the Senate than in the House of Representatives for two reasons. First, the House majority (i.e., the party in power) strictly controls the procedures for consideration of all major legislation by adopting "Rules" that determine whether points of order may be raised (as well as what amendments may be offered and how much time a measure will be debated). In the Senate, by contrast, any Senator can raise a point of order at any time.

Second, most Budget Act points of order in the Senate can be waived only by a three-fifths vote of the Senate (i.e., 60 votes). The importance of this "supermajority" requirement cannot be overemphasized. Particularly in today's political circumstances where the Senate is nearly evenly split, *it is exceedingly difficult to muster 60 votes to overcome a budget point of order—making the points of order strong enforcement mechanisms.*

Following are points of order that enable the Budget Resolution to be "enforced." For a comprehensive list of all points of order, see Appendix B.

- **Exceeding aggregate spending limit**: The Budget Act prohibits consideration of *any* spending legislation—discretionary spending *or* entitlement spending—that would cause the Budget Resolution's *aggregate* spending levels for budget authority *or* outlays to be exceeded. (Sixty votes are required to waive this point of order in the Senate.)
- **Controlling discretionary spending**: The Budget Act prohibits consideration of any appropriations bill that would cause the relevant subcommittee's 302(b) suballocation to be exceeded. This is one of the most potent budget enforcement mechanisms. By ensuring that each subcommittee remains within its suballocation, this point of order keeps discretionary spending within the total levels established by the Budget Resolution. (Sixty votes are required to waive this point of order in the Senate.)

- **Controlling mandatory spending**: Similarly, the Budget Act prohibits consideration of direct spending legislation—usually a change to an entitlement program—that would cause the relevant authorizing committee's direct spending allocation (their 302(a) allocation) under the Budget Resolution to be exceeded. In effect, this means that if the Budget Resolution did not incorporate increased spending in the relevant authorizing committee's 302(a) allocation, any Senator can object to legislation proposing a new or expanded program (with 60 votes required to waive the point of order).
- **Breaching the revenue floor**: As explained earlier, the Budget Resolution sets forth total levels for both spending *and* revenues. The Budget Act prohibits consideration of tax cut legislation that would cause Federal revenues to drop below the Budget Resolution's revenue floor in the upcoming budget year, or over the period of years covered by the Budget Resolution.

It is important to note that these "points of order" only provide budget enforcement when the Congress has adopted a Budget Resolution. In the last 10 years, the Congress has failed to complete work on a Budget Resolution four times. (See Appendix F.) However, in such years, the House and Senate typically adopt one-house resolutions "deeming" specified numbers to be Budget Resolution totals or committee allocations for the purposes of Budget Act points of order.

Budget Reconciliation: A Powerful Enforcement Mechanism

As explained in detail in chapter 2-2, Budget Reconciliation—when utilized—is a potent mechanism for implementing a fiscal plan set forth in a Budget Resolution. There are four reasons for this. Reconciliation:

- *Requires* congressional committees to report legislation to the Senate and House achieving specified budgetary results;
- *Packages* the legislation into a single bill;
- *Protects* the legislation from Senate filibuster; and
- *Immunizes legislation from most amendments* on the Senate Floor.

The proof of Budget Reconciliation's importance is readily apparent if one examines the history of Reconciliation legislation. (See the historical table on Budget Reconciliation in Appendix M.) In reviewing the Senate votes on Reconciliation bills enacted since 1980, it turns out that seven of those bills might never have become law without the filibuster-proof protections of Reconciliation, because they lacked the 60 votes necessary to shut down a filibuster. These include the following:

- TEFRA, the Tax Equity and Fiscal Responsibility Act of 1982, which passed the Senate by a slim margin of 52-47.
- The Omnibus Budget Reconciliation Act of 1990, the first of the major deficit reduction agreements of the 1990s, which was quite controversial and passed the Senate by a vote of only 54-45.

- The Omnibus Budget Reconciliation Act of 1993, the second major deficit reduction bill of the 1990s, that barely passed the Senate 51–50 but resulted in more than a half trillion dollars of deficit reduction.
- The 2001 tax cuts, which remain an ongoing source of controversy and which were enabled by Budget Reconciliation instructions in a Budget Resolution that passed the Senate with a narrow 53–47 margin.
- The controversial 2003 tax cuts that reduced dividend and capital gains taxes passed the Senate by a razor-thin margin of 51–50.
- The Deficit Reduction Act of 2005 that included controversial entitlement reforms, particularly in the Medicaid program, passed by a narrow margin of 52–47.
- The tax cuts of 2006, which extended the 2003 capital gains and dividend tax cuts and which passed the Senate by 54–44, well short of a filibuster-proof margin.

When examining the vast impact these Reconciliation bills have had on tax policy and entitlement programs, it is clear that Budget Reconciliation has become an important and effective mechanism for enforcing a Budget Resolution—far more important, in fact, than originally intended. (The Reconciliation process was originally conceived as a procedure at the end of a fiscal year to make minor changes to spending bills in order to "reconcile" them to a second budget resolution.)[5]

SHOULD RECONCILIATION BE RESERVED FOR DEFICIT REDUCTION?

To fully understand the evolving role of Reconciliation, it is also important to be aware of an ongoing debate, with significant repercussions, over the "appropriate use" of Reconciliation. Reconciliation bills were used from 1980 through 1993 exclusively to achieve *net deficit reduction* through entitlement and tax reforms. Then in 1999, the Republican majority in Congress passed a Reconciliation bill that would have cut taxes by $792 billion over 10 years. This was the first time Budget Reconciliation was used to pass deficit-increasing legislation.

That bill, HR 2488, was ultimately vetoed. But since the door was opened in 1999 to using the filibuster-proof Reconciliation procedures to pass major tax cuts, the Congress followed suit in 2000, 2001, 2003, and 2006. In each of those years, Reconciliation's filibuster-proof, expedited procedures were used to pass major tax cuts. (The bill in 2000 was vetoed by President Clinton, but President Bush supported and signed the other three bills.)

The impact on fiscal policy has been enormous. The 2001 Reconciliation Act cut taxes by $1.349 trillion over 10 years, the 2003 Act cut taxes by $320 billion over 10 years, and the 2006 Reconciliation Act cut taxes by $69 billion.[6]

In 2007, Senate Budget Committee Chairman Kent Conrad (D-ND), believing that the use of Budget Reconciliation to increase deficits is an inappropriate use of Reconciliation's fast-track procedures, included in the FY 2008 Congressional Budget Resolution a new point of order effectively prohibiting the use of Reconciliation procedures to increase deficits.[7]

Using the Budget Process to Achieve Deficit Reduction

Although Congress continues to debate the "appropriate use" of Reconciliation, it is fairly well settled that the congressional budget process was originally designed more than three decades ago to be result-neutral; that is, it was not designed to achieve any particular fiscal objective.[8] Rather, it was designed to give Congress the *institutional means*—through the Budget Committees and CBO—to review the broad range of fiscal policy options and to establish the *Budget Resolution as a means to implement* desired policies.

However, Congress has twice superimposed an additional layer of procedures on the Budget Act in order to reorient the budget process toward the specific goal of a balanced budget.

The first attempt to enforce a balanced budget, the so-called Gramm-Rudman-Hollings law, failed. The second attempt, the Budget Enforcement Act, was generally regarded as a success until it was effectively repealed in 2001.

Gramm-Rudman-Hollings

When deficits began to grow rapidly in the early 1980s (from $74 billion in 1980 to $212 billion in 1985[9]), a group of Senators drafted new budget procedures designed specifically to *force* a reduction in Federal deficits. The result was the Balanced Budget and Deficit Control Act of 1985, also known as Gramm-Rudman-Hollings (GRH),[10] a procedural overlay on top of the congressional budget process that sought to balance the budget by 1991 through a series of *declining deficit targets* ("maximum deficit amounts") and *automatic cuts* ("sequesters"). Senator Warren Rudman, one of the authors of GRH, called it "a bad idea whose time has come."[11]

To enforce the declining deficit targets, GRH enacted into law procedures to make automatic uniform percentage reductions in all (nonexempt) budget accounts to eliminate any excess deficit amount in any of the covered years. Half of the excess deficit was to be eliminated by cutting defense programs and the other half from nondefense programs.

GRH was designed to be a budgetary Sword of Damocles[12] hanging over the Congress. There was a substantial consensus at the time that this across-the-board "meat axe" approach was an irresponsible way to budget. The idea, however, was that facing the prospect of automatic cuts the Congress would be goaded into making policy decisions to comply with the statutory deficit targets, leading to a balanced budget by 1991.

Not surprisingly, in 1987 Congress revised the maximum deficit amounts (in a law often referred to as "son of Gramm-Rudman") extending the balanced budget target year to FY 1993—having realized that the cuts required to achieve budgetary balance in 1991 were unacceptable.

The GRH sequester mechanism triggered across-the-board cuts three times—in 1985 when the law was first enacted, and automatic cuts in 1987and 1989, although in the latter two cases Congress limited the amount of the cuts since the amounts required to bring deficits down to the statutory targets were politically unacceptable.[13]

The Budget Enforcement Act of 1990

By 1990, it had become clear that GRH had failed. Despite the statutory requirement to balance the budget by FY 1993, CBO's July 1990 *Update* report projected deficits in excess of $230 billion in 1991 and 1992.[14]

Consequently, in the fall of 1990, senior officials from the Bush Administration and Congress held a "budget summit" at Andrews Air Force Base outside Washington, D.C. They hammered out a deficit reduction agreement that proved to be the first of three major deficit reduction laws of that decade—the other two in 1993 and 1997—that ultimately led to a balanced budget in FY 1998.

Central to the budget summit agreement—and the subsequent path toward a balanced budget—was enactment of the Budget Enforcement Act of 1990 (BEA).[15] The Budget Enforcement Act of 1990 replaced GRH with two types of budget restraints: (1) discretionary spending limits; and (2) a pay-as-you-go ("PAYGO") requirement for changes in entitlement programs or tax laws.

Discretionary Spending Limits. The concept of the *discretionary spending limits* was to set statutory ceilings for discretionary spending (i.e., spending controlled through annual appropriations bills) in each fiscal year. Limits were established on both budget authority and outlays, and they were set at levels consistent with the desired fiscal objective of bringing projected deficits under control.

In order to achieve the desired deficit reduction, the 1990 budget law set discretionary spending limits for FY 1991–FY 1993. Separate limits were set for three spending categories: defense, domestic, and international programs. Total discretionary spending limits, without categories, were also set for fiscal years 1994 and 1995.

In 1993, President Clinton and the Democratic Congress passed the second major, multiyear deficit reduction legislation of the 1990s—the Omnibus Budget Reconciliation Act of 1993—extending discretionary spending limits through FY 2008.[16]

In 1997, the third major deficit reduction legislation of the 1990s, negotiated by President Clinton and the Republican Congress, extended discretionary spending limits through FY 2002 and, for the first time, established separate limits for defense and nondefense discretionary spending.[17]

The key to the statutory spending limits was the enforcement mechanism. If OMB determined that appropriations legislation exceeded the statutory limits, the President was required by law to execute an automatic across-the-board cut ("sequester") to eliminate the overage.[18]

Across-the-board cuts were triggered by spending overages in only one fiscal year, 1991.[19] However, as deficits turned into surpluses at the end of the 1990s and the beginning of the new millennium, Congress enacted measures to allow spending to substantially exceed the limits that had been set in the 1997 Budget Act. Congress allowed spending for FY 2001 to exceed the statutory limits for that year by $97 billion, and for FY 2002—the last year of the statutory limits—Congress and the Administration agreed to increase the statutory limit on budget authority by $137 billion.[20]

The triggering of only one discretionary sequester during the 1990s was also due in part to the existence of an escape valve in the enforcement mechanism: *an exemption for emergency spending.* Under the BEA, any appropriations declared by *both the President and Congress* to be an "emergency requirement" were effectively exempted from the discretionary spending limits.[21] As reflected in the text box, this allowed for substantial amounts of additional spending.

EMERGENCY SPENDING: THE LOOPHOLE IN DISCRETIONARY SPENDING LIMITS

The discretionary spending limits enacted in the 1990 Budget Enforcement Act, and extended in 1993 and 1997, played a significant role in restraining spending in the 1990s, contributing to the elimination of deficits and the emergence of surpluses. However, the effectiveness of the spending limits was diminished to some extent by use of the "emergency spending" designation.

Under the Budget Enforcement Act, spending designated jointly by the President and Congress as "emergency spending" was effectively exempted from the discretionary spending limits (by triggering an automatic upward adjustment in the spending limits to accommodate the emergency spending).[22]

In theory, the "emergency" designation was to be seldom used. Federal law requires that the President's Budget should each year request "an allowance for unanticipated uncontrollable expenditures."[23] In other words, the President should ask Congress to set aside money for unexpected emergencies, as many States do.

However, as a practical matter, neither the Administration nor Congress attempted to anticipate disaster relief and other emergency requirements when preparing their annual budgets and instead responded, on an ad hoc basis, by utilizing the emergency designation. This led to the "routine" enactment of "emergency supplemental appropriations bills" as well as the designation of provisions in regular appropriations bills as "emergencies" as reflected in the following chart:

Emergency Spending per Fiscal Year: Budget Authority (in Billions of Dollars)

Emergency Spending in:	*1991*	*1992*	*1993*	*1994*	*1995*	*1996*	*1997*	*1998*	*1999*
Supplemental Appropriations	$44.9	$15.9	$5.2	$12.0	$6.2	$4.6	$7.4	$5.6	$12.9
Number of emergency designations*	42	91	54	51	39	54	38	57	111
Regular Appropriations	$1.0	$0.3	$0.9	$1.9	$1.7	$0.5	$2.1	$0.3	$21.4
Number of emergency designations*	1	2	5	11	9	7	72	3	103

Source: CBO Memorandum, December 1998; updated June 8, 1999.

Note: The large amount of emergency supplemental spending in FY'91 was due to the Gulf War, and in FY'99 to military action in Kosovo.

*Refers to the number of budget accounts that contain emergency designations.

(Continued)

As observed in CBO testimony in 1998, policymakers have "acknowledged the need for a budgetary safety valve for true emergency needs as part of recent budget enforcement disciplines. They are concerned, however, that the safety valve has served as an excuse to avoid planning for those needs and has provided a budgetary loophole for excessive spending."[24]

In response to concerns on the part of Members who objected to what they perceived as the overuse of the emergency designation, in 1995 the House adopted a rule to prevent nonemergency spending from being added to emergency supplemental bills.[25]

The Senate took a different approach, in 1999 adopting a point of order that, in effect, required 60 votes to include any emergency designation in an appropriations bill.[26] Ironically, the largest number of emergency designations occurred in that year.

PAYGO: Controlling Entitlement Spending and Tax Cuts. The concept of *PAYGO*—the other budget enforcement mechanism established by the 1990 budget law—was, literally, to "pay as you go." The concept was simple: if sponsors of new legislation wanted to enact new entitlement programs, expand existing entitlements, or enact new tax cuts, they had to find *offsets* to "pay for" the cost of the new benefits or tax cuts. Offsets could be reductions in entitlement (mandatory) spending or tax increases.

Put simply, under the PAYGO regime, new tax cuts would have to be paid for by raising other taxes or cutting entitlement spending, or a combination of the two. Similarly, new entitlement spending would have to be paid for by cutting other entitlement spending or raising taxes, or a combination of the two.

Similar to the discretionary spending limits, the teeth in the PAYGO requirement was a sequester mechanism. OMB would be required to execute automatic cuts in nonexempt[27] mandatory spending programs if the cumulative effect of tax and entitlement legislation was to increase the deficit. Under this new system of budget discipline, a negative balance on OMB's cumulative "PAYGO scorecard" was something to be carefully avoided since Medicare would take the brunt of a PAYGO sequester.[28] Other nonexempt programs that would be hit by a PAYGO sequester included farm price supports, child support enforcement, and social services block grants.

In other words, PAYGO borrowed from Gramm-Rudman-Hollings the Sword of Damocles approach to budget discipline: the automatic across-the-board cuts in Medicare and other programs that would result from violating the PAYGO requirement would be so politically unpalatable that Congress would avoid enacting new entitlement spending or new tax cuts without the required offsets. And, in fact, no PAYGO sequesters were ever triggered.

The PAYGO discipline was further augmented beginning in FY 1994 with a new *10-year pay-as-you-go point of order in the Senate.* The new point of order, first created in the FY 1994 Budget Resolution, created a parliamentary point of order against any legislation that would result in revenue losses or entitlement spending increases in the upcoming fiscal year, as well as cumulatively for the upcoming 5 years, and the subsequent 5 years, *unless* fully paid for by offsetting revenue increases or entitlement spending cuts.

Expiration of the Budget Enforcement Act. Beginning with the new Administration in 2001, PAYGO was effectively terminated. In order to enact the massive tax cut legislation of 2001 without triggering a PAYGO sequester, provisions were enacted to circumvent (and effectively repeal) the PAYGO process.[29] Congress and the Administration subsequently allowed the Budget Enforcement Act, including PAYGO and the statutory discretionary spending limits, to expire on October 1, 2002.

In addition, the Senate's PAYGO point of order, which during the 1990s had strengthened the budget enforcement regime by requiring 60 votes to waive PAYGO, was seriously weakened by the FY 2000 Budget Resolution and effectively gutted by the FY 2004 Budget Resolution.[30]

Part VI of this book will discuss in some detail the return of deficits in the 2000s, but for purposes of this discussion of budget enforcement, it is important to underscore that between 2001 (when PAYGO was effectively repealed) and 2006, there was a surge in deficit spending to pay for $2 trillion in tax cuts and the largest entitlement expansion in four decades.[31]

2007: The Return of PAYGO. Following the midterm elections of 2006, when Democrats became the majority party in Congress, one of their early priorities was to reestablish the traditional PAYGO regime with automatic cuts as an enforcement mechanism.

The Bush Administration, however, was adamantly opposed to reenactment of the Budget Enforcement Act as it existed in the 1990s, believing it would hinder extension of tax cuts due to expire in 2010. Instead, the Administration proposed restoring PAYGO for mandatory spending only. Under the Administration's proposal, entitlement expansions or other new direct spending would have to be paid for with offsetting spending cuts, but new tax cuts would not have to be offset.[32]

Believing that fiscal discipline needed to be restored on the spending and revenue sides of the budget, congressional Democrats reestablished a PAYGO requirement for new spending and new tax cuts, but as *internal rules of the House and Senate* because disagreement with the Administration ruled out reenacting statutory PAYGO.

In January 2007, the House adopted a new PAYGO rule that created a parliamentary point of order against consideration of direct spending or tax legislation that would increase deficits in either the upcoming 5-year budget period or the upcoming 10-year budget period.[33]

In May 2007, the Senate followed suit with adoption of the FY 2008 Congressional Budget Resolution including a PAYGO point of order against all new spending or tax legislation that would increase deficits in either of the two budget periods. Waiver of the new Senate point of order requires 60 votes.[34]

The House PAYGO rule, as part of the Standing Rules of the House, must be readopted at the beginning of the 111th Congress to remain in effect. The Senate rule is in effect through FY 2017.

What remains to be seen is how effective these internal rules of the House and Senate will be as compared with the Budget Enforcement Act of the 1990s, which included automatic cuts to enforce its PAYGO requirement.

The Debt Limit: No Restraint on Debt

As explained in chapter 2-9 on "Budget Concepts," Federal law contains a statutory limit on the Federal debt commonly called the "debt ceiling."[35] One might assume that a mechanism called the "statutory limit on the Federal debt" serves as a form of budgetary restraint or enforcement. However, the debt ceiling does not restrain the growth of Federal debt. *Rather than being an instrument of fiscal policy, the debt ceiling is a consequence of fiscal policy.*

Gross (total) Federal Debt—which is the sum of **Debt Held by the Public** and **Debt Held by Government Accounts**—grows *automatically* for two reasons. *First, Gross Debt grows as a consequence of deficits* that occur when Congress approves Federal spending in excess of revenues. When the Federal government's *total* spending in a fiscal year exceeds *total* revenues, the Treasury[36] covers the annual deficit by borrowing from (issuing securities to) the public. In this circumstance, Debt Held by the Public increases.

**Gross Federal Debt
(End of FY 2007)**
$9.0 Trillion

$3.9 Trillion
**Debt Held by
Govt. Accounts**
(Social Security & Other
Trust Funds)

$5.1 Trillion
**Debt Held
by the Public**

Source: OMB, FY 2008 Budget.

Second, Gross Federal debt grows automatically because government trust funds are required to invest their surpluses in Treasury securities in order to protect their funds. These include the Social Security, Medicare, Highway, and Civil Service Trust Funds. In most years, these trust fund surpluses are used entirely to finance budget deficits together with additional funds borrowed from the public—causing both Gross Federal Debt and Debt Held by the Public to increase.[37]

Issuance of securities to government trust funds to protect their surpluses, and to the public to cover annual deficits, is *not a discretionary action*. In the case of annual deficits, once Congress has authorized agencies to enter into spending obligations that exceed Federal revenues, the Treasury has no choice but to raise the necessary cash by issuing securities and adding to the accumulated debt.

Nevertheless, a statutory limit on outstanding Federal debt has been in effect since 1940, when "debt subject to limit" stood at $43 billion. The debt ceiling reached $269 billion by the end of World War II and then declined to $250 billion during the postwar boom. It surpassed $500 billion in 1975 and $1 trillion in 1982. Since the early 1980s, the debt ceiling has increased rapidly to $2 trillion in 1986, $3 trillion in 1990, $4 trillion in 1993, $5 trillion in 1996, $6 trillion in 2002, $7 trillion in 2004, $8 trillion in 2006, and nearly $10 trillion in FY 2008.[38]

Congress has taken up debt ceiling legislation 85 times since it was first imposed in 1940.[39] Since the increases in the debt must occur in order to fulfill the obligations of the U.S. government and preserve the U.S. government's creditworthiness, why do we have a statutory ceiling on the public debt?

The short answer is that *the debt ceiling is a political instrument, not a fiscal instrument.* As a political instrument, the debt ceiling serves two purposes.

First, Members of Congress concerned about annual deficits and increases in the accumulated debt have historically only been willing to increase the debt in relatively small increments to be certain that *every time the debt ceiling is reached a fiscal policy debate will take place in Congress to reexamine the nation's fiscal policy.* (Unfortunately, it also allows the more cynical Members of Congress to feign "fiscal responsibility" by voting against authorizing more debt, without making the difficult spending and tax decisions required to balance the budget.)

Second, since increasing the debt ceiling is *"must-pass" legislation* (since the Treasury must have the ability to raise cash to fulfill U.S. government obligations), the debt ceiling has often served as an attractive legislative vehicle to which Members of Congress can attach legislation. A prime example is Gramm-Rudman-Hollings, discussed earlier, which was enacted in 1985 as an amendment to that year's debt ceiling legislation and was revised in the 1987 debt ceiling legislation.[40] (However, at times, congressional leaders have used procedural maneuvers to preclude amendments to a debt limit increase.[41])

Notes

1. Excerpt from a letter President Thomas Jefferson wrote to his Secretary of the Treasury in 1802, quoted by Comptroller General David Walker, op-ed, New York Times, February 4, 2004.

2. See chapter 2-2.

3. See chapter 2-2.

4. In the Senate, the Presiding Officer is the Vice President. However, the Vice President is seldom present, except to break ties, and the gavel belongs to the President Pro Tempore, who by tradition is the senior member of the majority party—currently Senator Robert C. Byrd (D-WV). The President Pro Tempore, in turn, delegates his duties to other members of the majority party, usually for one hour at a time. As a practical matter, whoever is presiding relies on the Senate Parliamentarian to guide him or her in the performance of their duties. In the House of Representatives, the Presiding Officer is the Speaker or, in her absence, the Speaker Pro Tempore. Often, the House conducts legislative business as a "committee of the whole," in which case the presiding officer is "Chairman of the Committee of the Whole House."

5. As originally enacted the Budget Act required Congress to adopt a first and second budget resolution each year. The first Budget Resolution spending and revenue totals served only as targets for congressional action on spending and revenue bills. Spending and revenue totals were not binding (i.e., not enforced by parliamentary points of order) until adoption of a second Budget Resolution. Beginning with FY 1983, the Congress discontinued the formulation of second Budget Resolutions and made first Budget Resolution totals binding with the start of the fiscal year on October 1. Beginning with FY 1987, GRH made the Budget Resolution totals immediately binding upon adoption of the one Budget Resolution each spring. U.S. Senate Committee on the Budget, "Gramm-Rudman-Hollings and the Congressional Budget Process," 99th Cong., 1st sess., 1985, S.Prt. 99-119, Appendix I (uncredited author: Charles S. Konigsberg, Staff Attorney).

6. See table 6.1.

7. Section 202 of S.Con.Res. 21 (110th Congress, First Session), adopted May 17, 2007.

8. Conversations over 1983-86 with the Senate Budget Committee's first Chief of Budget Review Sid Brown.

9. CBO, *The Budget and Economic Outlook: FYs 2007 to 2016*, table F-1, 140.

10. So named for the legislation's authors Senators Phil Gramm (R-TX), Warren Rudman (R-NH), and Ernest "Fritz" Hollings (D-SC).

11. Senator Warren B. Rudman of New Hampshire quoted in the *Washington Post*, October 8, 1989.

12. According to the legend, when Damocles spoke in extravagant terms of his sovereign's happiness, Dionysius invited him to a sumptuous banquet and seated him beneath a naked sword that was suspended from the ceiling by a single thread. In this way, the tyrant demonstrated that the fortunes of men who hold power are as precarious as the predicament in which he had placed his guest. "Damocles," *Encyclopaedia Britannica*, from Encyclopaedia Britannica 2006 Reference Suite DVD (accessed May 25, 2007).

13. The first sequester was actually integrated into the GRH law itself in 1985, since a political backlash to growing deficits was the impetus for enactment of GRH. This first sequester cut $11.7 billion in outlays from the fiscal year 1986 budget by cutting defense accounts across the board by 4.9%, and nonexempt nondefense programs across the board by 4.3%. In 1987, an automatic sequester of 10.5% in defense and 8.5% in nondefense was triggered at the beginning of FY 1988, but the $20 billion in cuts were political unsustainable and were superseded by the Budget Summit Agreement of November 20, 1987. The third, and last, GRH sequester was triggered in 1989 and would have resulted in outlay cuts of $16.1 billion for FY 1990, but it was superseded by the Omnibus Budget Reconciliation Act of 1989 which reduced the sequester to $4.6 billion. Robert Keith, "Budget Sequesters: A Brief Review," RS20398 (Washington, D.C.: Congressional Research Service, March 8, 2004), 4–5.

14. CBO, *The Economic and Budget Outlook: An Update*, July 1990, ix.

15. The BEA of 1990 is Title XIII of P.L. 101-508, the Omnibus Budget Reconciliation Act of 1990, 104 Stat. 1388. The BEA amended the Balanced Budget and Emergency Deficit Control Act of 1985, P.L. 100-119, otherwise known as Gramm-Rudman-Hollings.

16. Subsequently, the 1994 Violent Crime Control and Law Enforcement Act, P.L. 103-322, established separate spending limits for violent crime reduction through FY 2000 (designed to ensure a desired multiyear level of spending for crime reduction). Bill Heniff, "Discretionary Spending Limits," RS20008 (Washington, D.C.: Congressional Research Service, March 19, 2001), 1.

17. Title X of the 1997 law, P.L. 105-33, was enacted as the "1997 Budget Enforcement Act." It established separate limits for defense and nondefense spending for fiscal years 1998–1999, violent crime reduction spending for fiscal years 1998–2000, and all other discretionary spending for fiscal years 2000–2002. Subsequently, the 1998 highway bill, known as the Transportation Equity Act for the 21st Century, P.L. 105-178, created two additional spending limits on outlays for highway and mass transit spending for fiscal years 1999–2002. And in 2000, the Interior Appropriations Act for FY 2001, P.L. 106-291, established limits for conservation spending, including six subcategories. Heniff, "Discretionary Spending," 1. The separate categories for highway spending and conservation spending, as with crime reduction spending, were designed more as a guarantee of spending than a budget control mechanism.

18. A sequester of nonexempt discretionary programs would have been triggered by a report issued by the OMB Director within 15 days after the end of a congressional session. If the Director's report indicated that spending cuts must be made to eliminate a breach of the spending limits, then the President was required to issue a sequestration order directing that the necessary across-the-board cuts be made. A further sequester for a fiscal year was required during the following session of Congress (through June 30) if the enactment of a supplemental appropriations act caused a breach of the limits (known as a "within-session sequester"). Enactment of a supplemental after June 30, causing an overage, would not have caused a sequester; instead, the spending limits for the following fiscal year were to be reduced. Keith, "Budget Sequesters," 2. See also Robert Keith, "Sequestration Procedures under the 1985 Balanced Budget Act," RL31137 (Washington, D.C.: Congressional Research Service, September 27, 2001).

19. There were two sequesters in FY 1991. On November 9, 1990, $395 million in budget authority was sequestered (canceled) in the international spending category, leading to estimated outlay savings of $191 million; however, that sequester was ultimately rescinded the following spring. On April 25, 1991, $2.4 million in budget authority was sequestered in the domestic category, leading to estimated outlay savings of $1.4 million. Keith, "Budget Sequesters," 5.

20. The Military Construction Appropriations Act for FY 2001 prevented a sequester to eliminate overages of $2.3 billion in BA and $6.8 billion in outlays that would have been required because of the inclusion of FY 2000 supplemental appropriations in the bill. Keith, "Sequestration Procedures," 10–11.

In November 2000, President Clinton and the Republican leadership in Congress increased the FY 2001 discretionary budget authority limit from $541 billion (as set forth in the 1997 law) to $637 billion in H.R. 4811, the Foreign Operations Appropriations Act, P.L. 106-429. Robert Keith, "Discretionary

Spending Limits for FY 2001: A Procedural Assessment," RL30696 (Washington, D.C.: Congressional Research Service, August 31, 2001), 4–7.

In December 2001, Congress and the Bush Administration substantially increased the statutory Budget Authority limit for FY 2002 to $686 billion, $137 billion above the $549 billion statutory limit set for that year in the 1997 Budget Enforcement Act. The legislative vehicle for the increase was the FY 2002 Defense Appropriations Act, H.R. 3338, P.L. 107-117. Robert Keith, "Budget Enforcement for FY 2002: An Overview of Procedural Developments," RS21084 (Washington, D.C.: Congressional Research Service, May 23, 2002), 3–5.

21. Section 251(b)(2)(A) of the Deficit Control Act of 1985, as amended by the Budget Enforcement Act of 1990. The way emergency exemptions actually operated is that the discretionary spending limits, as well as the Budget Resolution spending totals and committee allocations were adjusted upward to accommodate emergency spending. James V. Saturno, "Emergency Spending: Statutory and Congressional Rules," RS21035 (Washington, D.C.: Congressional Research Service, May 11, 2005), footnote 9. In addition, section 314 of the Congressional Budget Act provides for an adjustment of Budget Resolution aggregates as well as committee allocations to reflect spending designated as an emergency under the BEA.

22. Section 251(b)(2)(A) of the Balanced Budget and Emergency Deficit Control Act of 1985, P.L. 100-119 (Gramm-Rudman-Hollings), provided for the automatic adjustment of the statutory discretionary spending limits. Section 314(a) of the Congressional Budget Act provides for adjustment of Budget Resolution aggregates and committee allocations to reflect spending designated as an "emergency."

23. 31 U.S.C. §1105(a)(14).

24. James Blum, Deputy Director, CBO, Testimony on "Budgeting for Emergency Spending" before the Task Force on the Budget Process, House Budget Committee, June 23, 1998, 24.

25. House Rule XXI, clause 2(e).

26. Sec. 206(b), H.Con.Res. 68 (106th Cong.).

27. About 80% of outlays associated with direct spending programs were statutorily exempt from automatic sequestration cuts. Exempt programs included Social Security, Federal retirement and disability programs, net interest, certain low-income programs, veterans' compensation and pensions, regular State unemployment insurance benefits, and certain types of resources such as unobligated balances of budget authority for nondefense programs.

28. Under the automatic sequestration of nonexempt programs, the sequester calculations were made so that two programs with automatic spending increases (COLAs)—the special milk program, and vocational rehabilitation—were cut first, followed by two special-rule programs (Stafford loans, formerly called guaranteed student loans, and foster care and adoption assistance), and then Medicare and the remaining nonexempt direct spending programs. The automatic cuts in Medicare under PAYGO were limited to 4%.

29. Section102 of P.L. 107-117 "zeroed out" the PAYGO scorecard for the effects of the 2001 tax cuts and other direct spending and receipts legislation in 2001 and 2002, thereby precluding a PAYGO sequester. P.L. 107-312 zeroed out the PAYGO scorecard for additional legislation in FY 2002, as well as FY 2003, and prospectively eliminated the possibility of a sequester for fiscal years 2004 through 2006 by setting those PAYGO balances at zero. Robert Keith, "Termination of the 'Pay-As-You-Go' (PAYGO) Requirement for FY 2003 and Later Years," Library of Congress, RS21378 (Washington, D.C.: Congressional Research Service, December 31, 2002).

30. The Conference Report on the FY 2000 Budget Resolution (H.Con.Res. 68, 106th Congress) stated that the Senate's PAYGO point of order was being modified to "permit on-budget (non–Social Security) surpluses to be used for . . . tax reductions or spending increases." H.Rept. 106-91, 72.This modification remained in effect through FY 2002 and paved the way for the conferees on the FY 2002 Budget Resolution (H.Con.Res. 83, 107th Congress) to state that the $1.25 trillion in tax cuts called for

in the resolution "would not result in a violation of the Senate pay-as-you-go point or order." H.Rept. 107-60, 91. Then in the FY 2004 Budget Resolution (H.Con.Res. 95, 108th Congress), the Senate reinstated a PAYGO point of order, but in name only. The conference report noted that the PAYGO requirement would "apply on a post-budget resolution policy basis," meaning that any tax cuts or entitlement increases brought to the Floor would only violate the point of order if they had not been contemplated in the Budget Resolution. H.Rept. 108-71, 122. This effectively threw the "pay-as-you-go" concept out the window, since Budget Resolutions could henceforth call for any amount of new tax cuts or entitlement increases without requiring any offsets.

31. The entitlement expansion was the enactment of Medicare Part D. This is not meant to suggest that the enactment of a Medicare prescription drug benefit was a bad idea. The point here is that with the expiration of PAYGO discipline, no effort was made to offset the enormous costs of the entitlement expansion. In fact, at the same time that entitlement spending was being dramatically increased, taxes were being cut and hundreds of billions dedicated to emergency war spending.

32. Office of Management and Budget, "Budget of the U.S. Government, FY 2008: Analytical Perspectives" (Washington, D.C.: Government Printing Office, February 2007), 211.

33. Section 405 of H.Res. 6 added the PAYGO language to Clause 10 of House Rule XXI (110th Congress):

"10. It shall not be in order to consider any bill, joint resolution, amendment, or conference report if the provisions of such measure affecting direct spending and revenues have the net effect of increasing the deficit or reducing the surplus for either the period comprising the current fiscal year and the five fiscal years beginning with the fiscal year that ends in the following calendar year or the period comprising the current fiscal year and the ten fiscal years beginning with the fiscal year that ends in the following calendar year. The effect of such measure on the deficit or surplus shall be determined on the basis of estimates made by the Committee on the Budget relative to—(a) the most recent baseline estimates supplied by the Congressional Budget Office consistent with section 257 of the Balanced Budget and Emergency Deficit Control Act of 1985 used in considering a concurrent resolution on the budget; or (b) after the beginning of a new calendar year and before consideration of a concurrent resolution on the budget, the most recent baseline estimates supplied by the Congressional Budget Office consistent with section 257 of the Balanced Budget and Emergency Deficit Control Act of 1985."

34. Section 201 of S.Con.Res. 21 (110th Congress).

35. 31 USC 3101.

36. The Treasury Department handles almost all borrowing by the Federal government. In a few instances, agencies such as the Tennessee Valley Authority operate within their own borrowing limits. Bill Heniff Jr., "Legislative Procedures for Adjusting the Public Debt Limit: A Brief Overview," RS21519 (Washington, D.C.: December 29, 2006), 1-2.

37. But in those rare fiscal years, 1998–2001, when the government ran a unified budget surplus, Debt Held by the Public declined (as surpluses were used to retire outstanding debt), while Gross Federal Debt continued to increase to accommodate investment of the trust fund surpluses. The government's surpluses during those four years *reduced Debt Held by the Public by $448 billion.* At the same time, Social Security and the other government trust funds increased their holdings by $853 billion. The combination ($853 billion minus $448 billion) *raised Gross Federal Debt by $405 billion.* Philip D. Winters, "The Debt Limit: The Ongoing Need for Increases," RL31967 (Washington, D.C.: Congressional Research Service, March 21, 2006), summary page.

38. "Federal Debt," Historical Tables, Section 7, Budget of the U.S. Government, FY 2008. See also "Federal Borrowing and Debt," Analytical Perspectives, Budget of the U.S. Government, Fiscal Year 2008 (Washington, D.C.: Office of Management and Budget), 232.

39. "Federal Debt," Historical Tables, 7.3.

40. For additional examples, see Philip Winters, "Debt Limit Increases: Fact Sheet on Uses of the Debt Limit for Other Legislation," 97-297E (Washington, D.C.: Congressional Research Service, February 29, 1997).

41. In the House, the so-called Gephardt Rule (House Rule XXVII) automatically generates a debt limit increase bill to have been passed by the House upon adoption of a Budget Resolution that calls for a debt limit increase. (Budget Resolutions include the "appropriate levels of debt subject to limit" in order to accommodate policies in the Budget Resolution.) While this avoids amendments to the debt ceiling bill in the House, it does not avoid amendments in the Senate. Another device that has been used to avoid considering a free-standing debt ceiling bill is inclusion of the debt ceiling increase in a Budget Reconciliation bill that, as previously explained, cannot be filibustered and is virtually immune to Floor amendments in the Senate. Of the total 85 debt limit measures enacted since 1940, 68 were enacted under regular legislative procedures, 13 pursuant to the Gephardt rule, and 4 as part of Reconciliation legislation. Heniff, "Legislative Procedures," 3.

The Government as Banker: Federal Credit Reform

Along with the Budget Enforcement Act, the 1990 "Budget Summit Agreement" gave birth to another milestone in budget enforcement—the Federal Credit Reform Act of 1990 (FCRA)[1]—which dramatically changed the budget process for enacting new Federal credit programs. These budget reforms are significant, because direct loans and loan guarantees have, for many years, been critical components of Federal education, housing, agriculture, small business, disaster assistance, and trade programs.

Prior to credit reform, all credit transactions were recorded in the fiscal year in which they occurred on a strictly cash basis. Direct loans were recorded as outlays in the year the loan was made, direct loan repayments were recorded as receipts in the year paid, loan guarantee claim payments were recorded as outlays in the year disbursed, and any fees charged for direct loans or loan guarantees were recorded as receipts in the year received. However, this approach *distorted the budgetary impact of creating or modifying credit programs.*

For example, because the Federal Government did not have to show any outlays for loan guarantees until lenders filed claims on defaulted loans, the granting of new loan guarantees appeared to have no cost when enacted, while direct loans—which were treated like grants in the year they were issued—appeared to be very expensive. This created a misleading bias in favor of loan guarantees over direct loans.

Congress enacted FCRA to address these flaws. FCRA changed the budget rules for credit programs by *requiring Congress to appropriate budget authority up front* to cover projected delinquencies, defaults and interest rate subsidies over the life of credit programs. By requiring the up-front appropriation of budget authority to cover the projected future costs of credit programs, FCRA allows Congress to compare in an apples-to-apples way the budgetary costs of direct loans, loan guarantees, and more traditional grant programs.

For example, in the President's FY 2008 Budget, he requested that Congress authorize $34 billion in new direct loans. If Congress agrees with the President's requests, FCRA will require that Congress appropriate for FY 2008, $1.4 billion to cover interest subsidies and estimated uncollectible principal and interest. In considering the President's request, the Congress can compare the up-front costs of the proposed direct loans with other program options.

On the loan guarantee side, the President's Budget requests $290 billion in new loan guarantees for FY 2008. If Congress agrees with the President's requests, FCRA will require that Congress appropriate for FY 2008, $2.4 billion to cover projected liability for loan defaults.[2] Prior to the enactment of FCRA, the authorization of these new loan guarantees in FY 2008 would have shown up as costing nothing, and in fact it might actually have been scored as bringing in revenue due to loan guarantee fees.

The magnitude of the Federal government's credit programs underscores the importance of FCRA's budgetary controls. In FY 2006, the most recent year for which actual numbers are available, the Federal Government had $251 billion in *total outstanding direct loans*, with an estimated total future cost of $47 billion due to subsidy costs and uncollectible principal and interest. The largest direct loan programs are student loans and rural development, housing and utility loans.

On the loan guarantee side, the Federal Government had $1.1 trillion in outstanding loan guarantees in FY 2006, with an estimated future cost of $66 billion attributable to projected liability for loan defaults. The largest loan guarantee programs are for Federal Housing Administration mortgage guarantees, veterans' mortgage guarantees, and guaranteed student loans.[3] The various program areas are reviewed in Part III of this book.

Nearly two decades after enactment of FCRA, considerable debate remains among Administration and congressional budget estimators about the best methodologies for estimating the future costs of direct loans, loan guarantees and other credit programs.[4] But importantly, that debate is now taking place, and policymakers are now comparing the efficacy and actual costs of direct loans, loan guarantees, and other program options in addressing national needs.

Recommended Sources for Further Reading on Federal Credit Reform

- CRS: "Federal Credit Reform: Implementation of the Changed Budgetary Treatment of Direct Loans and Loan Guarantees," RL30346, April 25, 2006; "Federal Credit Reform Act of 1990," 96-792 E, September 11, 1997.
- CBO: *Estimating the Value of Subsidies for Federal Loans and Loan Guarantees*, August 2004.
- GAO: *Credit Reform*, GAO/AIMD-94-57, July 1994; see Appendix I for useful background material on credit reform.

Notes

1. FCRA became the new Title V of the Congressional Budget Act.

2. Office of Management and Budget, *The Budget for Fiscal Year 2008*, "Analytical Perspectives," Table 7-5.

3. Office of Management and Budget, *The Budget for Fiscal Year 2008*, "Analytical Perspectives," Table 7-1.

4. See, for example, Congressional Budget Office, *A CBO Study: Estimating the Value of Subsidies for Federal Loans and Loan Guarantees*, August 2004; and Congressional Budget Office, *Assessing the Government's Costs for Mortgage Insurance Provided by the Federal Housing Administration*, July 19, 2006 (http://www.cbo.gov/ftpdocs/74xx/doc7412/07-17-FHA.pdf

The Federal Unfunded Mandates Reform Act

Many federal . . . initiatives, in areas ranging from homeland security to health care and environmental protection, involve shared responsibilities. . . . To aid in the implementation of these programs and initiatives, and to share their costs, federal statutes and regulations often require nonfederal parties to expend their resources in support of . . . national goals. Determining the appropriate balance of fiscal responsibility between the federal government, state, local and tribal governments, and the private sector . . . is a constant challenge. —Government Accountability Office, 2005[1]

The Unfunded Mandates Reform Act[2] (UMRA) was enacted in 1995 in response to concerns that the Federal Government was frequently enacting legislation that imposed new and costly duties or responsibilities on States and localities *without providing funding to fulfill those responsibilities.* Similar concerns were raised about new mandates imposed on the private sector.

The legislation was enacted as part of the House Republicans' Contract with America and was supported by the Clinton Administration. At the time of its enactment, supporters of the legislation viewed it as part of a "new federalism" agenda designed to free up the resources of state and local governments for locally determined priorities. Opponents viewed it as a potential obstacle to national mandates on health, safety, and environmental concerns. In retrospect, UMRA has had less impact than supporters hoped or opponents feared.

UMRA contains requirements that new unfunded mandates be *identified* in congressional committee reports accompanying new authorizing legislation.[3] UMRA also establishes procedures to *curb enactment* of new unfunded mandates, although it does *not* preclude their enactment or implementation as discussed below.

UMRA addresses two types of mandates. A **Federal Intergovernmental Mandate** refers to provisions in Federal authorizing legislation that impose enforceable duties on State or local governments, make existing duties more stringent, reduce funds available to cover the costs of existing duties, or preempt state or local revenue-raising authority.[4] UMRA requires congressional committees and CBO to prepare detailed analyses of intergovernmental mandates in legislation that total up to more than $50 million per year, adjusted for inflation ($66 million for FY 2007).

According to CBO, since UMRA's enactment in 1995, seven intergovernmental mandates, with costs above the threshold, have become law including: an increase in the minimum wage, a reduction in Federal funding for the food stamp program, a preemption of state taxes on premiums for prescription drugs, a temporary preemption of states' authority to tax Internet services and transactions, a requirement that state and local governments meet certain standards for drivers' licenses, and the elimination of Federal matching payments for child support enforcement.[5]

Private Sector Mandates refer to similar types of provisions applied to private sector entities. UMRA requires congressional committees and CBO to prepare detailed analyses of private sector mandates in legislation that total up to more than $100 million per year, adjusted for inflation ($131 million for FY 2007).

According to CBO, Congress has enacted 40 private sector mandates exceeding the statutory threshold since 1995 including an increase in the minimum wage, 12 revenue-raising provisions, 6 mandates that impact health insurance, and 9 that affect specific industries including mining, telecommunications, food processing, and chemical facilities.[6]

UMRA *excludes* a number of key areas from the informational and procedural requirements of the Act. In particular, Federal requirements designed to protect constitutional rights and prohibit discrimination are not subject to review under the Act. Legislation pertaining to national security and treaty implementation are also excluded. In addition, duties that are imposed as a condition of Federal assistance or that arise from participation in a voluntary Federal program are not "mandates" under UMRA.

Identifying New Mandates. The central function of UMRA is to make certain that policymakers and affected parties have adequate information about requirements in proposed legislation that would establish new Federal mandates. UMRA seeks to make new mandates more transparent by requiring that congressional authorizing committees include in their reports accompanying legislation a statement identifying all intergovernmental or private sector mandates and a CBO estimate of the mandates' costs to state and local governments and/or

---

**Excerpt from CBO Cost Estimate on H.R. 5815,
Department of Homeland Security Authorization Act for FY 2007
October 17, 2006**

ESTIMATED IMPACT ON STATE, LOCAL, AND TRIBAL GOVERNMENTS

H.R. 5814 contains intergovernmental mandates as defined in UMRA because it would require certain public transportation agencies to conduct vulnerability assessments and to create and implement security plans. While CBO cannot estimate the aggregate costs of those mandates, based on information from industry and government sources, we estimate that the costs to state, local, and

tribal governments would exceed the threshold ($64 million in 2006, adjusted annually for infla-
tion) in at least one of the first five years after enactment. The bill would authorize appropriations
of funds to cover those costs.

Mandates on Public Transit Entities
H.R. 5814 would require certain public transportation agencies to conduct vulnerability

Assessments....
...CBO estimates that the aggregate costs to transit and ferry systems likely would exceed the
threshold established in UMRA ($64 million in 2006, adjusted annually for inflation) in at least
one of the first five years after enactment. The bill would authorize the appropriation of $400
million in fiscal year 2007 to cover these costs.

Other Impacts
Other provisions of the bill would make several changes to existing grant programs for state,
local, and tribal governments.... On balance, state, local, and tribal governments would benefit
from provisions that require DHS to create, with input from local first responders and trade representatives, essential capabilities and voluntary standards for equipment and training.

ESTIMATED IMPACT ON THE PRIVATE SECTOR
H.R. 5814 would impose several private-sector mandates, as defined in UMRA, on rail carriers,
transportation systems, and certain individuals. CBO estimates that the direct cost of comply-
ing with most of those mandates would be small and fall well below the annual threshold for private-sector mandates established by UMRA ($128 million in 2006, adjusted annually for
inflation). However, because the cost of one of the mandates would depend on regulations that
have not yet been issued, CBO cannot determine whether the aggregate cost of all the private-
sector mandates in the bill would exceed the annual threshold.

Vulnerability Assessments and Security Plans
Section 901 would require the Secretary of the Department of Homeland Security to establish
by regulation standards, protocols, and procedures for vulnerability assessments and security
plans for rail or public transportation systems....

Security Screening Inspection Claims
Section 914 would impose a new private-sector mandate on certain individuals filing claims for
civil damages as a result of a security screening inspection....

Recurrent Aircraft Training
Section 916 would impose a new mandate on individuals applying for recurrent training to operate aircraft having maximum take-off weight of more than 12,500 pounds by requiring them to
pay a fee for threat assessment as determined by DHS....

Prohibited Items on Passenger Aircraft...

For a complete text of this CBO report, see http://www.cbo.gov/ftpdocs/76xx/doc7674/hr5814b.pdf.

the private sector. The CBO estimate must be a detailed, year-by-year analysis for any mandates exceeding the statutory threshold amounts.

UMRA enforces this informational requirement by allowing any Member of Congress to raise a procedural objection against legislation that fails to include the required unfunded mandates statement in its committee report. However, the point of order can be waived by a simple majority (50% plus one). The text box above is an example of an UMRA report provided to Congress as part of a CBO cost estimate.

"Curbing" New Intergovernmental Mandates. UMRA seeks "to curb the practice of imposing Federal mandates"[7] by allowing any Representative or Senator to raise a procedural objection (point of order) against any legislation that includes intergovernmental mandates costing more than the threshold amount ($66 million per year for FY 2007)—*unless* the legislation either "authorizes appropriations" or provides funding to cover the costs. Typically, authorizing committees insert provisions authorizing appropriations, since it has become increasingly rare for authorizing committees to create new mandatory spending programs that circumvent the appropriations process.

However, an "authorization of appropriations" does not actually provide funding. An authorization is simply a "request" or "recommendation" by the authorizing committee that the appropriations committee provide funding for a particular program.[8] Therefore, UMRA attempts to put teeth in the funding "requirement" by providing that an authorization is adequate *only if* the legislation requires the administering agency to monitor whether the mandate in the legislation is *actually* funded in each year. The authorizing legislation must also require that, in the event funds are not actually appropriated, the administering agency must submit legislation to Congress to reduce the cost of, or eliminate the mandate. This is the Achilles' heel of the enforcement mechanism, because a requirement that the Administration request funding in no way assures that Federal funding will be provided. (In addition, this requirement can be waived by a simple majority in the Congress.)

In a nutshell, while UMRA successfully focuses attention on whether proposed legislation includes new Federal mandates, it does not actually preclude unfunded mandates.

Regulations. UMRA also requires Federal agencies to assess the financial impact of proposed rules, assess costs and benefits where the proposed regulations exceed a threshold,[9] determine whether federal resources are available to cover the costs, consider the input of those affected, and select the least costly or burdensome regulatory option. An example of a regulatory mandate imposing costs is the Environmental Protection Agency's regulations in 2001 setting new standards for the maximum level of arsenic in drinking water that affected both publicly-owned and privately-owned water systems.[10] In a review of UMRA's impact on Federal rulemaking, the GAO found that "UMRA appeared to have had little effect on agencies' rulemaking and most significant rules promulgated were not subject to (UMRA) requirements."[11] The reason for this is likely due to the weak judicial review provision, under which a court can order agencies to do the required analysis, but cannot invalidate a rule.[12]

Assessment of UMRA. Overall, UMRA has undeniably made progress in focusing congressional and public attention on proposed legislation that would establish new mandates.[13] Less conclusive is whether UMRA has had a significant deterrent effect on enactment of new unfunded mandates. One measure of the law's impact may be that, in its annual review of unfunded mandates, the Congressional Budget Office noted that "few bills or proposals with mandates exceeding the (statutory) thresholds ultimately became law" in 2006.[14]

Whether CBO's findings reflect an actual deterrent effect, or UMRA's narrow definition of unfunded mandate, is open to debate. In its 2005 report on UMRA, GAO found that parties from many sectors shared concerns that UMRA's coverage is "too narrow"[15] due to the amount of legislation excluded from the statute's reach. GAO noted, however, that public interest advocates would strongly oppose expanding the reach of UMRA, because it could have a weakening effect on the ability of the Federal government to mandate measures to protect public health, safety, and welfare.[16]

Recommended Sources for More Information on Unfunded Mandates

- GAO: "Unfunded Mandates: Views Vary about Reform Act's Strengths, Weaknesses, and Options for Improvement," March 2005, http://www.gao.gov/new.items/d05454.pdf.
- CBO: A Review of CBO's Activities in 2006 under the Unfunded Mandates Reform Act, April 2007, http://www.cbo.gov/ftpdocs/79xx/doc7982/04-03-UMRA.pdf.
- CRS: "Unfunded Mandates Reform Act Summarized," RS20058, January 25, 2005.
- National Conference of State Legislatures Mandate Monitor: http://www.ncls.org/standcommscbudg/manmon.htm.
- U.S. Advisory Commission on Intergovernmental Relations draft report on mandates: http://www.library.unt.edu/gpo/acir/mandates.html. (A final report was never completed.)

Notes

1. U.S. Government Accountability Office, "Unfunded Mandates: Views Vary about Reform Act's Strengths, Weaknesses, and Options for Improvement" (Washington, D.C.: March 2006), 1.

2. P.L. 104-4, 109 Stat. 48 *et seq.*

3. For a full explanation of the respective roles of authorizing and appropriations legislation, see chapter 2-2.

4. Duties that are imposed as a condition of federal assistance or that are associated with participation in voluntary federal programs are generally not regarded as mandates.

5. Congressional Budget Office, "A Review of CBO's Activities in 2006 under the Unfunded Mandates Reform Act," 8–9.

6. Congressional Budget Office, "A Review of CBO's Activities in 2006," 9.

7. Preamble to the Unfunded Mandates Reform Act of 1995, P.L. 104-4, March 22, 1995.

8. For a complete discussion of authorizations versus appropriations, see chapter 2-2.

9. $131 million for FY 2007, adjusted annually for inflation.

10. U.S. Government Accountability Office, "Unfunded Mandates," 1.

11. See U.S. General Accounting Office, "Unfunded Mandates: Reform Act Has Had Little Effect on Agencies' Rulemaking Actions," GAO/GGD-98-30 (Washington, D.C.: , February 4, 1998).

12. A 2005 GAO-sponsored conference on UMRA found no interested parties that viewed the judicial review provision to be meaningful or effective. U.S. Government Accountability Office, "Unfunded Mandates," 5. The same GAO report, on page 16, noted that "if a court finds that an agency has not prepared a written statement or developed a plan for one of its rules, the court can order the agency to do the analysis and include it in the regulatory docket for that rule but the court may not block or invalidate the rule."

13. See U.S. Government Accountability Office, "Unfunded Mandates," 6, which found that "all the sectors provided . . . generally positive, comments about the . . . usefulness of UMRA information in policy debates."

14. Congressional Budget Office, "A Review of CBO's Activities in 2006," 2. According to CBO, "The Congress and the President enacted 321 public laws in 2006, 30 of which contained one or more inter-governmental mandates as defined by UMRA, and 39 of which contained one or more private-sector mandates. Of the public laws that included intergovernmental mandates, two contained mandates with costs exceeding the statutory threshold. By comparison, over the 10-year period leading up to 2006, five intergovernmental mandates with costs that exceeded the threshold were enacted. Of the public laws with private-sector mandates, eight contained mandates with costs exceeding the statutory threshold. By comparison, of the 79 public laws with private-sector mandates enacted from 2002 through 2005, 12 laws contained mandates with costs above the threshold."

15. U.S. Government Accountability Office, "Unfunded Mandates," 10.

16. U.S. Government Accountability Office, "Unfunded Mandates," 13.

Performance-Based Budgeting

High-performing organizations consistently strive to ensure that their organizational missions and goals drive day-to-day activities. —U.S. General Accounting Office, July 1999

Since World War II, various initiatives have been undertaken to implement "performance-based budgeting" (sometimes called results-oriented budgeting). The concept of performance budgeting is to "promote greater efficiency, effectiveness, and accountability in federal spending" by linking budget levels to results.[1] The most recent iterations of performance-based budgeting are the Government Performance and Results Act (GPRA)[2] and the Program Assessment Rating Tool (PART).

Various attempts to establish performance-based budgeting occurred in the decades prior to GPRA and PART:

1949: The Commission on the Organization of the Executive Branch. The Commission made a number of recommendations relating to the Executive branch, including the first formal recommendation that performance budgeting be incorporated into the Federal Budget process.

1960s: Planning-Programming-Budgeting-System (PPBS). PPBS was an attempt at performance budgeting originated in the Department of Defense under Secretary Robert McNamara, who brought his skills in modern systems analysis and cost-benefit analysis from the Ford Motor Company to the Federal Government. President Lyndon Johnson eventually mandated the use of PPBS across all government departments. However, PPBS was short-lived. The Nixon Administration terminated PPBS in 1971.

1973: Management by Objectives. The Nixon Administration's replacement for PPBS was Management by Objectives, which was primarily focused on holding agency managers accountable for achieving outcomes set forth in the respective agencies' budget requests.

1977: Zero-Based Budgeting. President Carter's Zero-Based Budgeting, initiated by Office of Management and Budget (OMB) Director Bert Lance, required that a series of packages for different funding levels be prepared, with the overall intent being to directly link expected program results with a level of spending.[3]

According to the GAO, there is consensus that these early efforts "failed to significantly shift the focus of the Federal Budget process from its long-standing concentration on the items of government spending to the results of its programs."[4]

Government Performance and Results Act (GPRA)

Contrary to popular belief, GPRA was not invented to Get People Really Angry! — Anonymous federal manager in a memorandum to staff

GPRA was enacted into law by Congress in 1993. (By contrast, the previous performance-based initiatives were initiated by Executive Order, rather than having the force of law.) The essential concept of GPRA was to "shift the focus of government decision making and accountability away from a preoccupation with the activities that are undertaken—such as grants dispensed or inspections made —to a focus on the results of those activities, such as real gains in employability, safety, responsiveness, or program quality."[5]

GPRA's approach to achieving this shift in decision making was to require that agencies set goals, devise performance measures, and assess their results on a regular basis. More specifically, GPRA established three types of ongoing requirements for most Federal agencies:[6]

- **strategic plans** (covering five years and to be revised at least every three years),[7]
- **annual performance plans**,[8] and
- **annual program performance reports** (covering the previous three fiscal years).[9]

Strategic plans, submitted by Federal agencies to the OMB and the Congress beginning in the fall of 1997, were to contain a comprehensive mission statement, general goals and objectives, and a description of how they are to be achieved.[10] The agency strategic plans were to be the starting point for agencies to set annual goals for programs and to measure the performance of programs.[11] A key element of the new process was to require mandatory consultations between agencies and Congress on program performance.

Annual performance plans, beginning with plans for FY 1999,[12] were to provide the direct linkage between the strategic goals and what managers and employees do day-to-day.[13] More specifically, the plans were to provide a quantifiable basis for comparing actual program results with the established performance goals.[14]

Annual program performance reports, at the end of each fiscal year, were to complete the picture by comparing "actual program performance" with the goals set forth in the performance plan.[15] Where a performance goal has not been met, the performance reports were to explain why not and set forth a plan for achieving the stated goal or explain why the goal is unrealistic.

While the concept of GPRA is sound, overcoming bureaucratic inertia can be difficult. In 1998, congressional leadership asked the GAO to evaluate the first round of performance plans. The GAO found that while "all of the plans showed how agencies' missions . . . related to their performance goals, ...most of the plans . . . contained major weaknesses that undermined their usefulness. . . . [T]hey did not consistently provide clear pictures of agencies' intended performance" and lacked credible criteria for providing accurate performance data."[16]

In a follow-up report prepared in 1999, the GAO found "moderate improvements" over the prior year's performance plans but noted continuing weaknesses in attention to management challenges, presentation of how personnel and other resources are used to achieve results, and credibility of data.[17]

By the end of the Clinton Administration in 2000, CRS noted growing congressional involvement with GPRA. CRS noted that 74 laws enacted in the 106th Congress (1999–2000) included GPRA-related provisions.[18]

The beginning of the Bush Administration saw an increasing emphasis on performance-based budgeting but a *shift away from GPRA*. In August 2001, the President's Management Agenda was announced, emphasizing "budget and performance integration" as one of five government-wide initiatives.[19] This was followed up in February 2002 with inclusion in the President's Budget of a new effort to measure performance of over 100 programs, separate and apart from the GPRA process.

Building on that effort, in the summer of 2002 OMB announced a new "Program Assessment Rating Tool" (PART) to be used by OMB and agencies to evaluate over 200 programs during the course of preparing the President's FY 2004 budget. OMB explained that PART was intended to "inform and improve agency GPRA plans and reports, and establish a meaningful, systematic link between GPRA and the budget process."[20]

Program Assessment Rating Tool (PART)

The Bush Administration's PART is a set of questionnaires to be completed annually by Federal managers to assess the effectiveness of Federal programs. The questionnaires include 25 questions divided into four categories (see table 2-7.1).

TABLE 2-7.1: Overview of PART Questions

SECTION	DESCRIPTION	WEIGHT
I. Program Purpose and Design	To assess whether the purpose of is clear and the program design makes sense.	20%
II. Strategic Planning	To assess whether the agency sets valid programmatic annual goals and long-term goals.	10%
III. Program Management	To rate agency management of the program, including financial oversight and program improvement efforts.	20%
IV. Program Results and Accountability	To rate program performance on goals reviewed in the strategic planning section and through other evaluations.	50%

A complete list of PART questions is set forth in appendix P. Based on responses to these questions, and the prescribed weighting of the various categories of questions, OMB gives each program one of five overall ratings: 1, effective; 2, moderately effective; 3, adequate; 4, ineffective; or 5, results not demonstrated.[21]

While PART has been the subject of considerable criticism, the GAO has found that "PART has helped to structure and discipline OMB's use of performance information for its internal program analysis and budget review, made the use of this information more transparent, and stimulated agency interest in budget and performance integration. . . . Several agency officials also told us that the PART was a catalyst of bringing agency budget, planning, and program staff together since none could fully respond to the PART questionnaire alone."[22]

One of the ironies of the PART process is that it appears to be biased against block grants—despite the fact that block granting is often favored by conservative public policy analysts. One analysis notes that under PART, "programs that operate through grants, whether competitive grants or block grants, are rated lower on average than all other programs. When OMB rated block/formula grant programs . . . in FY 2005, . . . it found no block/formula grant programs were 'effective' . . . [and] found 43 percent of block/formula grant programs to be ineffective while determining only 5 percent of programs overall were 'ineffective.'"[23]

GPRA versus PART

The Bush Administration made explicit its preference for PART as the primary mechanism for performance-based budgeting: "[W]hile well-intentioned, . . . [GPRA] did not meet its objectives. Through the President's Budget and Performance Integration initiative, augmented by the PART, the Administration will strive to implement the objectives of GPRA."[24] In 2004, OMB issued guidance formally instructing agencies to submit a "performance budget" for FY 2005 that would *replace* the annual GPRA performance plan.[25]

There has been considerable debate, however, about the wisdom of replacing GPRA with PART. For example, GPRA requires an agency, in developing its strategic plan, to "solicit and consider the views and suggestions of those entities potentially affected by or interested in such a plan."[26] PART does not require the involvement of impacted stakeholders. In addition, GPRA requires mandatory consultations with Congress; PART does not.

Others have questioned the objectivity, openness, and accuracy of PART's assessment methodology, suggesting that the PART process ignores congressional intent, conflicts with GPRA and inappropriately preoccupies agency planners and resources.[27] The GAO has concluded that "by using the PART process to review and sometimes replace GPRA goals and measures, OMB is substituting its judgment for a wide range of stakeholder interests. . . . Although PART can stimulate discussion on program-specific measurement issues, it cannot substitute for GPRA's focus on thematic goals and department-and-governmentwide . . . comparisons."[28]

Moreover, the GAO continues to favor GPRA as an effective framework for improving information sharing and cooperation among Federal agencies. The GAO report also reiterated previous recommendations that (1) OMB develop a *governmentwide performance plan* (as required by GPRA but never implemented); and (2) Congress consider amending GPRA to require a *governmentwide strategic plan*.[29]

Cautionary Notes about Performance-Based Budgeting

The GAO correctly points out that "pursuing a closer alignment between performance planning, budgeting, and financial reporting is essential in supporting the transition to a more results-oriented and accountable federal government."[30] GPRA was a useful management tool before taking a back seat to PART, and its full potential has yet to be tapped. At the same time, it is also important to understand the limitations of GPRA and other performance-based budgeting tools such as PART.

Budgeting, ultimately, is about the allocation of limited national resources among competing priorities.[31] GPRA, PART, and other performance measures can tell us—within limits—whether an existing program is fulfilling its objectives and how programs can be restructured to do a better job of achieving objectives, but they cannot tell us what our budgetary priorities should be.

For example, negative performance assessments of FEMA's handling of Hurricane Katrina can tell us that the management systems at FEMA and DHS require substantial restructuring and that resources can be more effectively used and better outcomes achieved. However, those performance assessments do not necessarily lead to budgetary conclusions. The appropriate response to FEMA's poor performance in the Katrina catastrophe could lead policymakers to seek a restructuring at the same budgetary level, a restructuring with a smaller budget, or a restructuring with a larger budget. The poor outcomes alone do not tell us the appropriate level of funding for emergency management, nor do they set the relative priority of such funding compared to other high priorities, such as homeland security.

Moreover, even the best performance measures have limits, for a variety of reasons: (1) some outcomes are inherently difficult to measure, like foreign aid programs and research and development programs; (2) there is frequently a time lag between programmatic actions and outcomes; and (3) it may be difficult to distinguish or separate out the outcomes of a particular federal effort from various nonfederal influences, such as state, county, local, and nonprofit activities.[32]

In short, performance-based assessments should be used to maintain an ongoing commitment to achieve the best possible results or "outcomes" from the programs Congress has chosen to fund, but they should never be used as a principal basis for setting budgetary levels. The allocation of resources among competing priorities are decisions that belong to elected policymakers in the Congress.

Notes

1. Virginia McMurtry, "Performance Management and Budgeting in the Federal Government: Brief History and Recent Developments," RL32164 (Washington, D.C.: Congressional Research Service, March 16, 2005), summary page.

2. *Government Performance and Results Act of 1993*, P.L. 103-62, August 3, 1993.

3. McMurtry, "Performance Management," 1–2.

4. U.S. General Accounting Office, "Performance Budgeting: Observations on the Use of OMB's Program Assessment Rating Tool for the FY 2004 Budget," GAO-04-174 (Washington, D.C.: January 2004), 1.

5. U.S. Government Accountability Office, "Reports on the Government Performance and Results Act," http://www.gao.gov/new.items/gpra/gpra.htm.

6. Some agencies were explicitly exempted in the Act: the CIA, GAO, Panama Canal Commission, and Postal Rate Commission (the USPS itself was exempted from the standard requirements of the

GPRA and given separate, but similar, requirements through its own section in the Act). Also, any agency with annual outlays less than $20 million and the OMB itself were exempted.

7. GPRA, P.L. 103-62, §3 (new sec. 306).

8. GPRA, P.L. 103-62, §4 (new sec. 1115).

9. GPRA, P.L. 103-62, §4 (new sec. 1116).

10. GPRA, P.L. 103-62, §3 (new sec. 306)

11. U.S. General Accounting Office, "Executive Guide: Effectively Implementing the Government Performance and Results Act" (Washington, D.C.: GAO, June 1996), appendix 1.

12. Note that this is timing is aligned with the schedule for preparation of the President's Budget. As noted in chapter 2-1, the Executive Branch prepared the President's Budget request for FY 1999 in the fall of 1997; the Budget was then rolled out in February 1998; the congressional budget process operated during the spring, summer and early fall of 1998, and FY 1999 began on October 1, 1998.

13. GAO, "Executive Guide," appendix 1.

14. GPRA, P.L. 103-62, §4 (new sec. 1115).

15. GPRA, P.L. 103-62, §4 (new sec. 1116).

16. U.S. General Accounting Office, "Managing for Results: An Agenda to Improve the Usefulness of Agencies' Annual Performance Plans," GAO/GGD/AIMD-98-228 (Washington, D.C.: Author, September 1998).

17. U.S. General Accounting Office, "Managing for Results: Opportunities for Continued Improvements in Agencies' Performance Plans," GAO/GGD/AIMD-99-215 (Washington, D.C.: Author, July 1999).

18. Virginia McMurtry, "Government Performance and Results Act: Overview of Associated Provisions in the 106th Congress," RL31678 (Washington, D.C.: Congressional Research Service, December 20, 2002).

19. Genevieve Knezo, "Government Performance and Results Act: Brief History and Implementation Activities," RS20257 (Washington, D.C.: Congressional Research Service, June 7, 2004), 5.

20. See OMB Memorandum M-02-10, July 16, 2002, as cited in CRS, "Government Performance and Results Act: Brief History and Implementation Activities," 6.

21. U.S. General Accounting Office, "Performance Budgeting: Observations on the Use of OMB's Program Assessment Rating Tool for the FY 2004 Budget," GAO-04-174 (Washington, D.C.: Author, January 2004), 10–11.

22. U.S. General Accounting Office, "Performance Budgeting," 4.

23. See Testimony of Adam Hughes, Director of Federal Fiscal Policy at OMB Watch, before the Senate Homeland Security and Governmental Affairs Subcommittee on Federal Financial Management, Government Information and International Security, June 13, 2006, http://hsgac.senate.gov/_files/061306Hughes.pdf, 6.

24. U.S. Office of Management and Budget, *Budget of the United States Government, FY 2004, Performance and Management Assessments* (Washington, D.C.: February 2003), 9.

25. U.S. General Accounting Office, "Performance Budgeting," 7.

26. 5 U.S.C. § 306

27. See Testimony of Adam Hughes.

28. U.S. General Accounting Office, "Performance Budgeting," summary page.

29. U.S. Government Accountability Office, "Results-Oriented Government: Practices That Can Help Enhance and Sustain Collaboration among Federal Agencies," GAO-06-15 (Washington, D.C.: October 2005), 28-29.

30. U.S. General Accounting Office, "Managing for Results: Agency Progress in Linking Performance Plans with Budgets and Financial Statements," GAO-02-236 (Washington, D.C.: January 2002), 1.

31. McMurtry, "Performance Management," summary page.

32. See Clinton Brass, "The Bush Administration's Program Assessment Rating Tool (PART)," RL32663 (Washington, D.C.: Congressional Research Service, November 5, 2004).

Budget Process Reform Proposals

It has become an axiom of political life in Washington that whenever budget deficits get seriously out of control, "budget process reform" proposals proliferate. Administration officials and Members of Congress look to procedural mechanisms to get deficits under control. But as my friend Sid Brown, the first Chief of Budget Review at the Senate Budget Committee, used to say, no procedural reform can substitute for the political will to make hard choices.

To be fair, certain budget process reforms have made a difference—the case in point being the Budget Enforcement Act of 1990 (BEA). As explained earlier, the BEA's spending caps and pay-as-you-go (PAYGO) requirements were an important factor in reaching a surplus in the late 1990s. Nevertheless, budget process reform proposals are often political diversions from the real work of setting national priorities, assessing program results, and crafting responsible budgets. Ultimately, the policy decisions reflected in the deficit reduction agreements of 1990, 1993, and 1997 were principally responsible for driving deficits down.

Balanced Budget Constitutional Amendment

The clearest example of a budget process reform that is more political theater than substance is the Balanced Budget Constitutional Amendment (usually referred to as "Balanced Budget Amendment," or BBA). Congressional interest in a constitutional amendment to require a balanced Federal Budget emerged in the early 1980s, when deficits began to soar. In the ensuing years, one or both houses of Congress voted on various forms of the BBA five times: 1982, 1986, 1992, 1995, and 1997.[1] The BBA nearly passed Congress in 1995, achieving the required two-thirds support in the House, but it fell two votes short of the required two-thirds support in the Senate.[2] (Article V of the U.S. Constitution requires a two-thirds[3] vote of the House and Senate, *and* ratification by three-fourths of the States to amend the Constitution.)

In the 1980s, the country also came perilously close to a Constitutional Convention (the first since 1787), when nearly two-thirds (32 of the required 34) State legislatures passed resolutions calling for a Constitutional Convention to consider a Balanced Budget Amendment.[4] (One of my first duties as Staff Attorney at the Senate Budget Committee, fresh out of law school, was to track the actions of State legislatures as they considered resolutions calling for a Constitutional Convention. Fortunately, we never reached the two-thirds threshold that would have compelled the convening of a Convention, since this could have opened up a Pandora's box of additional constitutional amendments.

The Balanced Budget Amendments considered by Congress varied in their respective details, but generally all included the following common elements:

- Directing the President to submit a balanced budget to Congress;
- Prohibiting total outlays from exceeding total revenues for a fiscal year *unless* three-fifths of the House and Senate vote to waive the requirement; and
- Waiving the balanced budget requirement in the event of a declaration of war

Various other provisions of BBA proposals would have required a three-fifths vote to increase the debt ceiling, roll call votes on tax increases, or would have extended the declaration of war waiver to "imminent and serious" military threats.

Proponents have, for years, argued that Congress and the President need the authority of a constitutional balanced budget requirement to force Congress and the President to be fiscally responsible. However, the four budget surpluses achieved between FY 1998 and FY 2001 proved that a constitutional amendment is unnecessary. The surpluses were achieved because Congress and the President passed major deficit reduction legislation in 1990, 1993, and 1997 (see Part VI) and enacted the ongoing fiscal restraints of the Budget Enforcement Act of 1990.

In addition to being unnecessary, the BBA could do serious harm for several reasons:

1. **The BBA is bad economic policy**. It makes no allowance for the reality that government spending goes up and tax revenues go down during a recession. The difficulty of getting a three-fifths vote in both chambers to secure a balanced budget waiver could *force spending cuts and tax increases during a recession* which, most economists agree, would deepen the recession.
2. **The BBA constrains public policy**. The budgetary straitjacket would limit the Federal government's ability to respond to natural disasters, international crises, and long-term defense needs.[5] In addition, it would prohibit the Federal government from borrowing to finance investments with a long-term pay-off—a practice available to every State and local government.[6]
3. **The BBA would damage the Federal Government's separation of powers**. It would involve unelected Federal judges in spending and tax policy, and it could be construed as giving the President constitutional authority to impound appropriations—a dangerous erosion of Congress' constitutional authority over Federal spending and tax policy.
4. **The BBA would force midyear draconian cuts in essential Federal services**. For example, if early projections of a balanced budget are replaced by midyear estimates of a $100 billion deficit, the consequences could be serious. Since entitlement benefits must, by law, be paid, the burden of cutting $60 billion in spending—halfway through the year—would fall disproportionately on discretionary spending, most likely nondefense discretionary spending. The result could be drastic cuts, or even shutdowns, of vital programs.
5. Versions of the BBA that require a three-fifths vote to increase the debt ceiling would **allow a minority of either chamber to hold the Federal Treasury—and America's cred-**

itworthiness—**hostage** whenever the nation's finances require the issuance of additional debt.

6. Allowing Congress to waive the balanced budget requirement (by a three-fifths vote), the BBA would **diminish the public's respect for the U.S. Constitution**. Consider the scenario of press reports that Congress is yet again "waiving" the Constitution's balanced budget requirement. There are no other examples where Congress votes to waive a constitutional requirement.

Unfortunately, the soaring deficits of the current decade have yielded renewed calls for a Balanced Budget Constitutional Amendment. Already, as of October 2007, six measures have been introduced calling for a Balanced Budget Amendment.[7] Hopefully, the Congress will not turn to this phony and dangerous meddling with the U.S. Constitution to create the illusion of having "taken action" to restore fiscal responsibility. Real fiscal responsibility requires serious, bipartisan reforms to our nation's spending programs and tax laws.

Tax Limitation Constitutional Amendment

Another budget reform proposal involving an amendment to the Constitution is commonly called the "Tax Limitation Amendment" (TLA), which would impose a supermajority requirement for passage of tax increases. The House of Representatives considered Tax Limitation Amendments each year from 1996 to 2002.

Tax limitations have been proposed in a variety of forms. Many would have required a two-thirds supermajority in the House and Senate for passage of any tax legislation increasing revenues by more than a "de minimus" (very small) amount. Some would have required a supermajority to increase revenues above a set percentage of the economy (usually measured as Gross Domestic Product, or GDP). Others would limit tax increases to growth in "national income."[8]

The tax limitation proposals are premised on the view that the Federal government's size as a percentage of the economy is too large (although current revenue levels remain close to the 40-year average of 18.2% of GDP[9]) or that deficit reduction should be achieved exclusively through spending cuts.

In each instance that Congress has voted on a version of the TLA, the proposal failed to achieve the two-thirds majority required for passage of a constitutional amendment. The closest the Amendment came to passage was in 1996 when it received 243 votes, 47 short of the two-thirds required for passage of a constitutional amendment.

The various versions of the Tax Limitation Amendment raise a considerable number of concerns:

- The TLA would place future Congresses in a constitutional straitjacket when considering fiscal policy options.
- Under the TLA, "tax loopholes" creating special interest tax cuts could be enacted by a simple majority, but a two-thirds supermajority would be required to close the loopholes.
- A minority of legislators in either chamber could block revenue-raising measures needed to prepare for potential military conflicts or to respond to other national emergencies.

- Courts could be drawn into policy and political disputes better resolved by the elected branches of government—for example, determining whether a tax increase is "de minimus," or distinguishing between a "fee" and a "tax." Alternatively, if judicial enforcement is precluded under the terms of the TLA, those who would seek to enforce the TLA would be left without a remedy, and the public's confidence in the Constitution would be diminished.[10]

Earmark Reform

Well, we cuss the lawmakers. But I notice we're always perfectly willin' to share in any of the sums of money that they might distribute.—Will Rogers, 1935[11]

In general, a provision in an appropriations bill may be described as an earmark when Congress directs a portion of a lump-sum appropriation to a particular project, location, or institution—rather than deferring to Executive branch agencies on how and where the money will be spent.[12] (To be fair, some executive branch funding decisions can also be described as political earmarks.[13])

Earmarks are not well understood because they usually do not appear in the legislative text of appropriations bills. Rather, most earmarks appear in "report language" accompanying an appropriations bill.

There are two types of report language:
- *Committee Reports* explain the reasons for and costs of legislation voted out of committee; and
- *Joint Explanatory Statements of Managers* accompany compromise legislation emerging from House-Senate conference committees.

A recent Congressional Research Service review of the FY 2006 appropriations process calculated that more than 95% of all earmarks that year appeared in report language.

A classic example of legislation with numerous earmarks is the multibillion-dollar Energy and Water Appropriations Act which, among other purposes, appropriates budget authority for water projects—dams, levees, and so forth. An earmark is a line in the bill, or a line in the committee report accompanying the bill indicating the committee's intention that a specified amount of budget authority is to be obligated for a particular water project.

What is often confusing to people is that report language *does not become law* and is technically *not binding* on Executive branch agencies. Nevertheless, it has been the common practice of Executive departments and agencies to follow closely the wishes of Congress as set forth in report language because they know that failure to do so will—to put it mildly—"displease" the appropriations subcommittees that control their respective budgets. (In 1987, then OMB Director Jim Miller, attempted to ignore report language earmarks, causing a political firestorm.[14])

Earmarks can appear in the Senate or House version of the appropriations bill or report, or they sometimes appear for the first time in the Senate-House conference agreement (i.e., the final version) of the appropriations bill (or the joint statement of managers accompanying the conference report). The appearance of 11th-hour earmarks in conference agreements—dubbed "air-dropped language"—is what often attracts a great deal of criticism from media and watchdog groups.

The earmark process typically begins in March or April when Members of Congress submit their "earmark requests" to the relevant appropriations subcommittees. Not surprisingly, members of the House and Senate Appropriations Committees typically have greater success in landing earmarks than nonmembers. The heaviest incidence of earmarks generally occurs in highway projects, military construction projects, energy and water development projects, defense procurements, and research and development funding (although the Congress thus far has wisely protected the National Institutes of Health and the National Science Foundation from earmarks.)[15]

Critics of earmarks pointed out that the number of earmarks more than tripled since 1994[16] and reports of inappropriate or wasteful earmarks were surfacing with greater frequency.[17] According to CRS, the number of earmarks in FY 2006 exceeded 13,000, not including more than 5,600 earmarks contained in the multiyear highway authorization bill.[18]

Supporters of earmarking authority argue that it is appropriate for a Senator or Representative to seek appropriations for urgent projects in their States and Districts, rather than leaving constituents' needs to an impersonal government agency grants process. But opponents of earmarks assert a growing number of low-priority or wasteful earmarks that presumably could be avoided through an impartial review of funding needs by an Executive Branch agency. Earmark opponents also express concern that time spent pursuing earmarks has diverted Congress' attention from broader policy issues confronting the nation.

In FY 2007, the trend of escalating earmarks came to an abrupt halt. Prior to the 2006 midterm elections, Congress had enacted only 2 of the 11 regular appropriations bills (defense and homeland security). The rest of the government's annually funded programs were placed on auto-pilot under "continuing resolutions" (see chapter 2-2 for an explanation of CRs). After Democrats won majorities in the House and Senate, the outgoing Republican leadership decided to extend the continuing resolutions until February 15, leaving the nine unfinished appropriations bills for the incoming Democratic majorities to complete in the new Congress.

The incoming Democratic Appropriations Chairmen—Senator Robert C. Byrd (D-WV) and Representative David R. Obey (D-WI)—announced on December 11, 2006, their intention to enact a "year-long joint resolution" to dispose of the nine unfinished appropriations bills, which would continue most programs at FY 2006 levels (with some increases or decreases for specific programs).[19] To the surprise of many, they also announced "there would be no Congressional earmarks in the joint funding resolution . . . [and] we will place a moratorium on all earmarks *until a reformed process is put in place…subject to new standards for transparency and accountability*"[20] (emphasis added).

True to their word, the appropriators included in the $463.5 billion FY 2007 funding resolution (H.J.Res. 20, 110th Congress), a provision making explicit Congress' intent that earmarks included in committee reports for FY 2007 were not binding.[21] After the funding measure was signed into law by the President on February 15, the Office of Management and Budget underscored the no earmarks policy by sending a memorandum to all agency heads instructing them to ignore earmarks included in FY 2007 committee reports.[22]

The Byrd-Obey decision to place a moratorium on all earmarks until earmark reform measures were adopted was the equivalent of an earthquake in Washington, D.C., where interest groups and lobbyists had been working for a year with Members of Congress to secure thousands of earmarks—from water projects to agricultural and health research. (The earmark moratorium did not affect military earmarks in the already-enacted defense appropriations bill.)

Earmark reform measures were adopted by the House soon after the convening of the new Congress in January 2007. The House adopted a new rule (H.Res. 6, 110th Congress) requiring disclosure of earmark sponsors, as well as justifications for earmarks, and written certification that earmarks will not benefit their House sponsor. The House Rule became effective immediately.

The Senate's earmark reform became effective in September 2007 as part of S. 1, the lobbying and ethics reform bill. The new Senate Rule defines an earmark as "a congressionally directed spending item, limited tax benefit, and limited tariff benefit," and prohibits consideration of legislation unless the committee chair or majority leader certifies that all earmarks in legislative or report language have been identified by sponsor, and have been publicly available on the Internet for 48 hours. Senators must also provide to the committee, the name and location of the earmark beneficiary, and Senators must certify that they have no financial interest in the earmark. The Rule also prohibits placing *new* earmarks into conference reports.

As the new House and Senate Rules on earmark transparency and accountability take effect for the 110th Congress, it is possible that we will see fewer examples of quid pro quo lobbying scandals and fewer examples of expenditures that annoy taxpayers and defy common sense.

However, these reforms will not lead to a reduction in Federal deficits or accumulated debt. Earmark reform is more about *how funds are spent* on a project-by-project basis than about reducing overall spending.

Those who suggest that earmark reform is the answer to rapidly rising Federal debt are unfortunately diverting the public's attention away from the enormous fiscal issues that face our nation, particularly, exploding entitlements due to the "perfect storm" of rapidly rising health care inflation and the baby boomer retirement.

Recommended Sources for More Information on Earmarks

- Senate Appropriations Committee Press Releases on Earmark Reform, "Byrd-Obey Announce FY 2007 Plan," December 11, 2006, and April 17, 2007, http://appropriations.senate.gov/news.cfm.
- CRS: "Earmark Reform Proposals," RL33397, December 8, 2006; "Earmarks in FY 2006 Appropriations Acts," March 6, 2006; "Earmarks in Appropriation Acts: FY 1994, FY 1996, FY 1998, FY 2000, FY 2002, FY 2004, FY 2005," January 26, 2006.
- OMB: Database on more than 13,000 earmarks in FY 2005 appropriations bills: http://earmarks.omb.gov.
- GAO: "Principles of Federal Appropriations Law," 3d ed., Vol. II, chap. 6 (B): Line-Item Appropriations and Earmarks, February 2006, 40–47. Available online at http://www.gao.gov/special.pubs/d06382sp.pdf.
- National Journal Group, "Earmark Heartburn," March 31, 2007.
- Congressional Quarterly Weekly: "C-17s: A Primer in Directed Spending," January 8, 2007; "Budget Villain, Local Hero," June 12, 2006.
- Testimony of Steve Ellis, Taxpayers for Common Sense Action, on "Earmark Reform" before the Senate Subcommittee on Federal Financial Management, Committee on Homeland Security and Governmental Affairs, March 16, 2006.

The Line-Item Veto and Expedited Rescission

"From the nature of the Constitution" George Washington said, "I must approve all the parts of a bill, or reject it in toto."[23]

The line-item veto (LIV) is a budget process reform proposal that repeatedly emerges when budget deficits get out of control or wasteful earmarks make the headlines. A legislative grant of line-item veto authority was enacted into law in 1996—and subsequently struck down by the Supreme Court as unconstitutional in 1998. However, memories in Washington are short, because the LIV has once again emerged as an "answer" to burgeoning deficits. Before looking at more recent proposals, it is useful to recall how the LIV Act of the 1990s operated and why it was struck down by the Court.

The U.S. Constitution (Article I, §7, cl. 2) sets forth a very clear process for enacting a law:

> Every bill which shall have a passed the House of Representatives and the Senate, shall, before it become a Law, be presented to the President of the United States; if he approve he shall sign it, but if not he shall return it, with his Objections to that House in which it shall have originated.

This provision of the Constitution unambiguously gives the President the option of signing a bill or returning (vetoing) the bill. The Constitution clearly does not allow the President to sign or return a "part" or a "provision" of a bill.

Nevertheless, in 1994, Republicans swept the midterm elections promising to enact into law a "Contract with America" that called for enactment of a line-item veto. President Clinton, who had, himself, called for LIV authority during his campaign for President, instructed his staff to negotiate LIV legislation with the Republican Congress. The result of these negotiations was the Line Item Veto Act of 1996.

The LIV Act attempted to finesse the absence of constitutional authority to veto an individual provision of a bill, by empowering the President to "cancel" a dollar amount of discretionary budget authority, an item of direct spending, or a limited tax benefit (i.e., a tax earmark).

The concept of the LIV Act drafters was that "canceling" an item of discretionary budget authority would amount to a congressionally authorized rescission and was therefore a constitutional delegation of congressional authority to the President.

The cancellation of items of direct spending (entitlement provisions) and tax earmarks by the President was more complicated. The concept developed by Administration and congressional negotiators was that such cancellations would result in the direct spending and tax items having no "legal force or effect."

Not surprisingly, the Justices didn't accept the distinction between an item veto and a "cancellation." The Court in 1998 struck down the LIV Act, holding that the "cancellation" scheme did in fact amount to an unconstitutional grant of item veto authority to the President. The Court reaffirmed what George Washington had clearly and unambiguously written more than two centuries ago—that the President has authority to sign or veto an *entire* bill, not a portion of a bill.[24]

The Supreme Court's clear decision has not dissuaded backers of the item veto from once again advocating passage of an LIV. In his first budget transmittal to Congress, President

Be Careful What You Ask For . . .

I was an Assistant Director at the Office of Management Budget during negotiation of the LIV Act, its implementation, and its review by the Supreme Court. Needless to say, this gave me an interesting perspective on the item veto. I offer the following observations to this and future Administrations who may seek to amend the Constitution to create an item veto, or to expand the President's rescission authority in ways that might simulate an item veto. Be careful what you ask for, Mr. President.

The item veto immediately changes the political dynamic between the President and the Congress. From the congressional perspective, it is quite obviously a negative change because the President suddenly has powerful leverage over programs and projects of immense importance to individual members of Congress.

But the item veto is also a negative change for the President. After the enactment of each appropriations bill, the item veto presents the President with the unenviable task of deciding which of the hundreds (or thousands) of items of spending in each bill is so bad that it's worth singling out a particular Member of Congress for vetoing a spending item they sponsored.

With the item veto power in hand the President can't very well let major appropriations bills go by without vetoing *any* item. That would be an endorsement of each and every item in the bill—and in a representative democracy where legislation is developed through compromise and give-and-take, there are no bills completely free of low-priority items or items of questionable national importance. Yet, singling out particular projects, and the project's congressional sponsor(s), places the President in a very tough political dilemma following enactment of each and every appropriations bill. And the same dilemma applies to items in tax bills and entitlement bills.

To put it bluntly, the item veto requires the President to decide, after each budget bill, how many political enemies to make—all in the interests of retargeting a relatively small amount of money.

Moreover, the item veto also adds great complexity to development of the President's Budget. I found that with the item veto power available, our legislative affairs office at OMB was deluged in the fall with letters from Members of Congress asking the President to include their high-priority projects in the President's budget—as a way of inoculating them from later use of the item veto. Suddenly, the task of putting together the President's Budget became far more complicated.

In sum, the item veto makes the political dynamics between the President and Congress far more complicated, with comparatively little budgetary savings. Do we really want the President mired in petty political fights, when he or she should be focused on the broad issues facing the nation?

Be careful what you ask for, Mr. President. The fiscal crises facing the nation cannot possibly be fixed by an item veto, but the item veto can imperil the delicate balance of powers that has served our nation so well for more than two centuries.

George W. Bush included a call to "restore the President's line item veto authority" and has frequently renewed the request. The House obliged the President's request and on June 22, 2006, passed the "Legislative Line Item Veto Act of 2006" by a vote of 247–172.[25] However, the Senate did not take up the measure.

In reality, the House-passed measure was not a line-item veto. It was an enhancement of the "rescission" authority the President already has, masquerading as an LIV.

As explained in chapter 2-6, under the 1974 Budget and Impoundment Control Act, the President is permitted to *propose* to Congress "rescissions" of appropriated funds. The President can withhold the funds for 45 days, but if Congress does not enact the rescissions into law, the President must release the funds. (This requirement was placed in law as a result of President Nixon's "impoundment" of funds.)

The House-passed bill would have augmented the existing rescission authority by *requiring that Congress vote* on the President's proposed rescissions (often referred to as "expedited rescission authority"). In addition, the proposal would expand the reach of proposed rescissions, beyond appropriations, to include tax benefits and new entitlement spending. The bill would also prohibit rescinded funds from being used as "offsets" for other new spending (as they often have been by the Appropriations Committees).

The House-passed measure died at the end of the 109th Congress without any Senate action on the bill. However, the Senate did take up a variation of the House "item veto" bill in January 2007.[26] The measure was rejected when Senate supporters failed to get the 60 votes needed to overcome a filibuster by opponents of the measure.

Despite all of the recent political rhetoric about granting the President a "constitutional" LIV, these and similar proposals are not "constitutionally valid" line-item veto mechanisms. LIV is not constitutional; the Court made clear that Presidents do not have constitutional authority to veto pieces of bills. These are simply proposals to expand the President's current rescission authority by requiring Congress to vote on his proposals.[27]

The important issue here is whether expanding the President's current rescission authority would upset the balance of powers between the Executive and Legislative Branches. In a nutshell, after the Congress sends the President a bill, should the President have the authority to *require* Congress to vote again on selected provisions of that bill?

Proponents of expedited rescission say yes—it would allow the President to bring wasteful spending or tax loopholes to light, providing an opportunity to eliminate such provisions as well as serving as a deterrent for their enactment in the first place.

Opponents of expedited rescission say no—it would allow a President to put undue pressure on individual Members of Congress by requiring special votes on provisions important to their States or Districts.

Opponents also point out that major legislative packages are often the result of extensive compromises among competing interests. Giving the President's authority to force separate votes, after the fact, on individual provisions of such legislation *could undermine Congress' ability to assemble important legislation without advance presidential assurances.* These are not minor or arcane issues of procedure, especially at a time when many have argued that the pendulum of authority has swung too far in the direction of the Executive Branch.

Moreover, say opponents:

- The President's existing authority to propose rescissions has been used sparingly casting doubt on the need to augment that authority;[28] and
- Even if such authority were heavily used, it would not make a dent in the fiscal crises we face, particularly, exploding entitlements due to rapidly rising health care inflation.

Biennial Budgeting

The Budget Act calls for Congress to adopt a new Budget Resolution and all of the regular appropriations bills (currently numbering 12) each year. Some have argued that the annual budget process—in all of its complexity—is duplicative and inefficient, leaving little time for thoughtful oversight and long-range planning both in Congress and the Executive Branch.

Members of Congress, Administration officials, and outside observers have offered a variety of proposals since the late 1970s to switch the Federal budget process from an annual timetable to a two-year, or "biennial," timetable. Most of these proposals call for lawmakers to use the first year of each Congress to adopt a biennial (two-year) budget resolution and biennial appropriations. The second year of each Congress would be devoted to multiyear authorization bills and oversight. Biennial budget proposals also typically require the President to submit two-year budgets to the Congress and conduct performance reviews on a two-year cycle as well.

One of the oddities of biennial budgeting is that it has received widespread support of all Democratic and Republican Administrations since the 1980s, various bipartisan commissions, key congressional committees, and majorities in surveys of the House and Senate, but it has never passed the Senate or House.[29]

Proponents of biennial budgeting argue that it would reduce the enormous amount of time consumed by the annual budget process, giving Congress more time to review the effectiveness of existing programs in meeting the nation's needs. In addition, they suggest that biennial budgeting would afford agency program managers and recipients of federal funds more financial stability and, consequently, the potential for better planning and greater efficiencies.

Opponents of biennial budgeting argue (convincingly, in my view) that *the most effective oversight actually occurs through the process of annual appropriations*—from budget hearings, to drafting the annual appropriations bills, to negotiating with the Administration. Opponents also suggest that realistically, if regular appropriations were biennial, Congress would have to enact significant midcourse corrections through supplemental appropriations in the "off-years" and possibly revised budget resolutions, eliminating the supposed advantages of "increased time for oversight." Such midcourse corrections would be essential due to the difficulties of budgeting too far in advance.

Notes

1. See "Statement by the President" on defeat of the Balanced Budget Amendment, The White House, March 4, 1997.
2. H.J.Res. 1, 104th Congress.

3. Two-thirds of the Members present and voting, not two-thirds of the entire membership.

4. See David C. Huckabee and Meredith McCoy, "Constitutional Conventions: Political and Legal Questions," IB80062 (Washington, D.C.: Congressional Research Service, July 8, 1985). See also James V. Saturno, "A Balanced Budget Constitutional Amendment: Background and Congressional Options," 97-379 GOV (Washington, D.C.: Congressional Research Service, March 20, 1997), Part IV.

5. While some versions of the BBA waive the requirement when war has been declared or a military threat is "imminent," none provide a waiver for vital homeland security investments or preparation for longer-term threats such as the Global War on Terror.

6. States impose balanced budget requirements only on their "operating budgets" but allow substantial borrowing and investment through their "capital budgets." The Federal government, by contrast, lumps together all operating and investment expenditures in one "unified budget."

7. Balanced Budget Amendments introduced in the 110th Congress: S.J.Res. 1, H.J.Res. 1, H.J.Res. 7, H.J.Res. 10, H.J.Res. 21, and H.J.Res. 45 (as of October 28, 2007).

8. "National Income" is the total income earned in generating the U.S. Gross Domestic Product (the total value of goods and services produced by the U.S. economy).

9. Congressional Budget Office, "The Budget and Economic Outlook: Fiscal Years 2008 to 2017" (Washington, D.C.: January 2007), 77.

10. See Statement of Administration Policy, April 15, 1999, Office of Management and Budget.

11. *Will Rogers Says,* ed. Reba Collins (n.p.: Neighbors and Quaid, 1993), 76.

12. CRS notes, correctly, that "there is not a single specific definition of the term *earmark* accepted by all practitioners and observers of the appropriations process, nor is there a standard earmark practice across all . . . regular appropriations bills. . . . For one bill, an earmark may refer to a certain level of specificity within an account. For other bills, an earmark may refer to funds set aside within an account for individual projects, locations, or institutions." Sandy Streeter, "Earmarks and Limitations in Appropriations Bills," 98-518 GOV (Washington, D.C.: Congressional Research Service, December 7, 2004), 1.

13. See Jackie Calmes, "In Search of Presidential Earmarks," *Wall Street Journal,* February 21, 2006.

14. James C. Miller III, "Earmarks Infection," *Washington Times,* May 24, 2006.

15. For a discussion of defense earmarks, see Center for Defense Information, www.cdi.org, "Congress' Earmark Reform Fiasco," by Winslow Wheeler, March 20, 2006. For background on all earmarks, see Congressional Research Service Memorandum, "Earmarks in Appropriations Acts: FY 1994, FY 1996, FY 1998, FY 2000, FY 2002, FY 2004, FY 2005" (Washington, D.C.: January 26, 2006).

16. Congressional Research Service Memorandum, January 26, 2006.

17. See, for example, Ken Silverstein, "Inappropriate Appropriations," *Harper's Magazine,* April 26, 2006; Danielle Knight, "Loading the Pork Train," *U.S. News & World Report,* May 29, 2006; and Peter Whoriskey, "Priorities of Earmarks are Disputed," *Washington Post,* May 24, 2006, A-03.

18. CRS notes in its report, "because of the varying ways that earmarks are defined and applied in appropriations bills, we have *not* attempted to combine and summarize earmarks across the 11 appropriations bills covered. . . . To the greatest extent possible, we have maintained a consistent definition of earmarks *within each entry,* so that even in the absence of universally accepted terminology, the data for a particular bill were collected using common methodology." Therefore, the author's aggregation of the earmark data in the line marked "total" should be reviewed with the CRS caveat in mind. Congressional Research Service, "Earmarks in FY 2006 Appropriations Acts" (Washington, D.C.: March 6, 2006), 3.

19. H.J.Res. 20 (110th Congress).

20. Statement of U.S. Senator Robert C. Byrd (D-WV) and U.S. Representative Dave Obey (D-WI), December 11, 2006.

21. Title I, section 112 of the bill stated that "any language specifying an earmark in a committee report or statement of managers accompanying an appropriations Act for fiscal year 2006 shall have no legal effect with respect to funds appropriated" under the joint resolution.

22. Office of Management and Budget, Memorandum M-07-10 for the Heads of Departments and Agencies, February 15, 2007.

23. *Writings of George Washington,* ed. J. Fitzpatrick 1940), 96.

24. *Clinton v. City of New York,* 524 U.S. 417 (1998), http://supct.law.cornell.edu/supct/html/97-1374.ZS.html.

25. HR 4890 (109th Congress). Roll Call No. 317.

26. Senator Gregg (R-NH) offered the measure as an amendment to legislation increasing the minimum wage (HR 2, 110th Congress). On a 49–48 vote on January 24, 2007, the Senate fell 11 votes short of the 60 required to end a filibuster of the amendment.

27. "Expedited" rescission refers to proposals to expedite or require congressional voting on proposed presidential rescissions. "Enhanced" rescission, by contrast, refers to proposals to flip the burden of action so that presidential rescission proposals would take effect unless overturned by Congress, as opposed to current law, where rescission proposals do not take effect unless approved by Congress. "Enhanced rescission" was effectively ruled unconstitutional when the Supreme Court struck down the Line Item Veto Act of 1996.

28. According to the Congressional Budget Office, "Presidents have made very little use of the authority to recommend rescissions. From 1976 through 2005, Presidents proposed about $73 billion in rescissions, about one-half of 1 percent of the more than $15 trillion in total discretionary budget authority legislated in those years. Moreover, in dollar terms, the Congress enacted only about one-third of the proposed rescissions." Congressional Budget Office, "CBO's Comments on H.R. 4890, the Legislative Line Item Veto Act of 2006" (Washington, D.C.: March 15, 2006), 2.

29. See James Saturno, "Biennial Budgeting: Issues and Options," RL30550 (Washington, D.C.: Congressional Research Service, August 10, 2006).

Key Budget Concepts

The Federal Budget

There are two separate and distinct Federal Budgets: (1) the President's Budget and (2) the Congressional Budget Resolution.

Not later than the first Monday in February of each year, the President submits to the Congress the Administration's budget plan for the fiscal year that will start on October 1 of that year. The President's Budget sets forth the overall levels of recommended spending and revenues as well as a detailed listing of the dollar amounts the President proposes for each individual program, project, and activity of government.[1]

The Congressional Budget Resolution is a "concurrent resolution of Congress"[2] reported from the House and Senate Budget Committees and adopted by the Congress. Unlike the very detailed President's Budget, the Congressional Budget Resolution does *not* include detailed programmatic budget levels. Instead, it establishes overall budget aggregates (*total spending, total revenues, annual deficits, public debt*) and spending authority allocated among the committees of Congress. The Budget Resolution also includes a breakdown of total spending among broad "functional" categories such as "Energy," "Agriculture," and "Health," but this breakdown is not binding on annual funding decisions made by the Appropriations Committees.

Both the President's Budget and the Congressional Budget Resolution are essentially planning documents designed to guide the Congress as it works on the separate pieces of legislation (appropriations, entitlement, and tax bills) that actually determine the amount of Federal spending, revenues, and resulting deficits or surpluses.[3]

The Fiscal Year

To keep track of its revenues and expenditures in an orderly way, the Federal government has established a 12-month period known as the "fiscal year" (FY). Since fiscal years are determined by the calendar year in which the fiscal period ends, the October 1, 2007 to September 30, 2008 fiscal period is FY 2008.

Understanding Federal Spending: Budget Authority versus Outlays

Spending levels in the Federal Budget process consist of two types of numbers: (1) budget authority and (2) outlays.

Outlays are simply disbursements by the Treasury. When the Treasury issues a check in FY 2007, that disbursement is an FY 2007 outlay.

Budget authority (usually referred to as "BA") is more important, but less understood. BA is *legal authority* Congress gives to a Federal department or agency to enter into obligations that will result in outlays. *It is important to understand that when Congress appropriates funds for a particular program, it is enacting BA—not outlays.* In short, *appropriations are a form of budget authority.*

To illustrate the relationship of budget authority to outlays, consider the following example. The Department of Defense Appropriations Act for FY 2006 provided $2.4 billion in new budget authority to the Department of the Navy to build a nuclear submarine. This means that the Congress gave the Department of the Navy legal authority to sign contracts to build the submarine. However, this budget authority will only result in outlays when the contractors are issued checks by the Treasury. Since contractors on a lengthy construction contract are typically paid only upon completion of each stage of the construction, the $2.4 billion of budget authority could result in outlays over several years, as reflected in the following table.[4]

FUNDING OF A NEW NUCLEAR SUBMARINE
(in billions of dollars)

	FY '06	FY '07	FY '08	FY '09
Budget authority (BA)	2.4	0.0	0.0	0.0
Outlays (OT)	0.2	0.2	1.0	1.0

In other cases, new budget authority appropriated for a Fiscal Year will "spend out" immediately, which means the budget authority will result in outlays during the same Fiscal Year. Examples of appropriations with a quick spend-out rate are salaries of Federal workers and benefit programs such as veterans' benefits.

Even though outlays often flow from budget authority over a number of years, the BA itself must be used in the year, or years, for which it is appropriated by Congress. Typically, budget authority is provided for one year only and is available beyond the end of a fiscal year only if Congress specifically states in the appropriations law that the budget authority is to remain available for an extended period of time.

Forms of Budget Authority

Budget Authority is the legal authority provided by Congress for Federal agencies to enter into obligations that will result in immediate or future outlays of Federal funds. Budget authority can take several forms, but the three most important are as follows:

1. *Appropriations*—An Act of Congress that permits Federal agencies to incur obligations for specified purposes and to make payments out of the Treasury for those purposes. An appropriation is the most common form of Budget Authority.
2. *Borrowing authority*—An Act of Congress that permits a Federal agency to incur obligations and to make payments for specified purposes out of money borrowed from the Treasury, the Federal Financing Bank, or the public. (The Budget Act generally requires that new borrowing authority must be approved in advance in an appropriations act.)
3. *Contract authority*—An Act of Congress that permits a Federal agency to enter into contracts for specified purposes that obligate the Federal government, for example, highway projects (see chapter 3-9). Such contracts must then be followed by appropriations that permit payments out of the Treasury to liquidate those obligations. (The Budget Act generally requires that new contract authority must be approved in advance in an appropriations act.)

Permanent versus Annual Appropriations

Although most budget authority is appropriated for one year, and less frequently for two or more years, some budget authority has been made *permanent* by statute. This consists mainly of budget authority for trust funds (such as Social Security), interest on the public debt (for which budget authority is automatically provided under a permanent appropriation enacted in 1847), and the authority to spend certain government receipts called offsetting collections.

Major Categories of Federal Spending

In recent years, the President and Members of Congress often formulate budget plans in terms of four major categories of spending: (1) defense spending, (2) nondefense discretionary spending, (3) entitlement or mandatory spending, and (4) interest payments. Each of the four major categories is described below.

Defense Spending

Defense spending refers primarily to spending by the Department of Defense, but also by the Department of Energy which is responsible for nuclear weapons. Nearly all defense spending is discretionary in nature. It is often broken out as a separate budgetary category because of the size of the defense budget, $631 billion for FY 2007. Currently, defense spending constitutes more than one-fifth of the Federal Budget (excluding spending on military retirement and healthcare, and veterans, which are generally included in the entitlements category).[5]

Nondefense Discretionary Spending

Nondefense discretionary spending, often referred to by the shorthand "NDD," refers to nondefense programs that are subject to annual funding decisions in the appropriations process. Examples include funding for law enforcement, education, homeland security, environmental protection, transportation, national parks, disaster relief, food inspection, medical research, and foreign aid. Currently, NDD constitutes about 18 percent of the Federal Budget.[6]

Entitlements, Mandatory Spending, and Direct Spending

Entitlements are benefit programs established by law, such as Social Security, Medicare, and Medicaid that *require the Federal government to pay specified benefits to eligible individuals.* From a budgetary perspective, *the fundamental characteristic of an entitlement is the absence of annual, discretionary decisions on funding levels.* Instead, *formulas* included in laws establishing the entitlement programs determine how much money the Federal government is *obligated* to pay. For this reason, entitlements constitute the bulk of a larger budget category called "mandatory spending"—reflecting the absence of annual discretionary funding decisions. A synonymous term for *mandatory spending* often used in budget deliberations is *direct spending* because the entitlement or other mandatory spending flows *directly* from entitlement or other statutes—without any intervening discretionary appropriations decisions.

An example of how an entitlement operates is Social Security, the nation's largest entitlement program (at $612 billion in FY 2008). The Social Security laws prescribe formulas under which retired workers receive benefits based on the length of time they have worked and their earnings (up to certain limits). The total cost of Social Security for a particular fiscal year is determined by the number of qualifying retirees and the benefits formula established in law—not by annual appropriations decisions. In this way, entitlement programs like Social Security, Medicare, and Medicaid are regarded as nondiscretionary, or "mandatory," since their funding requirements are determined by legal formulas rather than annual funding decisions.[7]

"Entitlements" constitute more than half of all Federal spending. Nearly one-quarter of this spending is means tested—that is, paid to beneficiaries who must prove their need based on limited income or assets. Medicaid, a joint Federal-state health program, accounts for half of all means-tested spending.[8]

The remaining three-quarters of mandatory spending dollars go to beneficiaries who do not have to satisfy a means test. Social Security is the largest non-means-tested program.

Entitlements may also be differentiated based on their various objectives. Social Security and unemployment compensation are based on principles of *social insurance.* Other programs are categorized as *public assistance programs* because they provide income support for specific categories of needy individuals (e.g., needy families; or aged, blind, or disabled individuals). *Health entitlements* pay medical expenses of the elderly on a social insurance basis and medical expenses of the poor on a means-tested basis. Other entitlements provide benefits to a variety of disparate groups: veterans, Federal retirees, coal miners suffering from black lung disease, college students, and children.

The term *entitlement* had become widely used in public policy discussions by the time Congress turned to enactment of the Congressional Budget and Impoundment Control Act of

---

ORIGIN OF THE TERM ENTITLEMENT

One of the great privileges of my career as a Senate staffer was to serve twice as Finance Committee General Counsel for the late Senator Daniel Patrick Moynihan of New York. In addition to being a brilliant thinker, the Senator had an insatiable curiosity for history. With entitlements being the fastest-growing part of the Federal Budget, in 1993 he asked me to research the origin of the term *entitlement*. In a memorandum dated May 5, 1993, I reported to "DPM," as we called him, that the term *entitlement* appears to have originated in a June 1965 *Yale Law Journal* article by Yale Law Professor Charles A. Reich (volume 74, number 7, p. 1245). In the article, entitled "Individual Rights and Social Welfare: The Emerging Legal Issues," Reich forcefully introduced the concept of entitlement:

> Society today is built around entitlement. . . . Many of the most important of these entitlements now flow from government. . . . Such sources of security, whether private or public, are no longer regarded as luxuries or gratuities; to the recipients they are essentials, fully deserved, and in no sense a form of charity. It is only the poor whose entitlements, although recognized by public policy, have not been effectively enforced. . . . Since the enactment of the Social Security Act, we have recognized that (the poor) have a right—not a mere privilege—to a minimal share of the commonwealth. Even were this not so, the experience of thirty years has shown how much danger there is to society as a whole when any group in the population lacks entitlements and hence chronically suffers from insecurity and dependence. . . . The idea of entitlement is simply that when individuals have insufficient resources to live under conditions of health and decency, society has obligations to provide support, and the individual is entitled to that support as of right.

Reich's article was then quoted by Mr. Justice Brennan in the Supreme Court case *Goldberg v. Kelly*, 397 U.S. 254 (1970), a case that introduced *entitlement* into the legal arena. The entitlement concept was a basis for the opinion of the majority, written by Brennan, in which the Court affirmed a lower court decision that a pretermination evidentiary hearing is necessary to provide welfare recipients with procedural due process. In so doing, the Court held that "welfare benefits are a matter of *statutory entitlement* for persons qualified to receive them" (emphasis added) and quoted the Reich article.

FIGURE 2-9.1. FY 2007 Outlays by Major Budget Category (in billions of dollars)

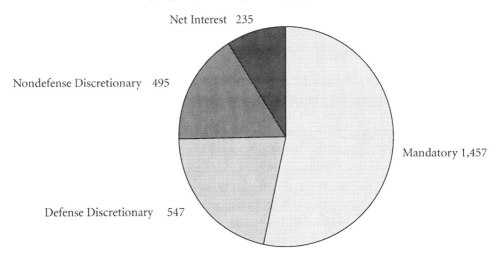

Source: Congressional Budget Office, August 2007

1974 (Budget Act). During debate on the Budget Act, the Committee on Rules and Administration made the following statement in its report:

> This Section (§401 of the Budget Act) deals with advance spending authority of the type generally known as mandatory entitlement legislation. Simply stated, this is legislation which, when enacted entitles persons or governments who meet the requirements established in the legislation to receive payments from the Federal Government, the budget authority for which has not been provided in advance through appropriations Acts. The basic legislation determines the level of budget authority needed to implement the program; once enacted, it mandates an appropriation Act containing such budget authority.[9]

Net Interest

Net interest, a fourth major budget category, refers to payments to individuals, corporations, foreign governments, or other nongovernmental entities that hold bonds and notes that finance the Federal debt.[10] In FY 2007, net interest was approximately $235 billion—approaching 9 percent of the Federal Budget.[11]

Budget Functions

Federal spending (i.e., budget authority and outlays) is sometimes divided into 19 conceptual categories known as "budget functions." This is a system of classifying spending according to

050: National Defense

150: International Affairs

250: General Science, Space, and Technology

270: Energy

300: Natural Resources and Environment

350: Agriculture

370: Commerce and Housing Credit

400: Transportation

450: Community and Regional Development

500: Education, Training, Employment, and Social Services

550: Health

570: Medicare

600: Income Security

650: Social Security

700: Veterans Benefits and Services

750: Administration of Justice

800: General Government

900: Net Interest

950: Undistributed Offsetting Receipts

the national needs being addressed. Congress's annual Budget Resolution allocates budget authority and outlays among the various functions in the Federal Budget. However, while the functions are a useful display of Federal spending priorities, they have little practical impact on the annual process of allocating discretionary Federal funds.

Federal Revenues

Our Constitution is in actual operation; everything appears to promise that it will last; but nothing in this world is certain but death and taxes.—Benjamin Franklin, 1789[12]

The Federal Budget is customarily viewed as having two "sides"— a spending side and a revenue side. Another term often used in the congressional budget process for revenues or taxes is *governmental receipts*. Governmental receipts are collections from the public based on the government's exercise of its sovereign powers. They include individual and corporate income taxes, social insurance taxes (e.g., Social Security payroll taxes), excise taxes, estate and gift taxes, and customs duties.

Congress's authority to raise revenues is set forth in Article I, Section 8, Clause 1, of the Constitution: "The Congress shall have Power to lay and collect Taxes, Duties, Imposts and Excises." The Constitution also requires that revenue bills originate in the House of Representatives.[13]

Offsetting Receipts

A practice that frequently causes confusion is that revenues do *not* include receipts received by the Federal government for sale of products or services rendered (e.g., sale of timber from Federal lands or entrance fees for national parks). Such receipts are *netted against Federal spending* and thus called "offsetting collections" or "offsetting receipts."

It is not uncommon for issues to arise concerning whether particular government user charges are more appropriately regarded as governmental receipts (on the revenue side of the budget) or as offsetting collections/receipts (on the spending side).[14]

Deficits, Debt, and Debt Ceiling

A budget deficit or surplus is simply *the difference between outlays and revenues* for a given fiscal year. (Note that outlays are used in this calculation, rather than budget authority, because outlays reflect dollars actually disbursed.) For example in FY 2007, revenues and outlays were $2.568 trillion and $2.731 trillion, respectively, yielding a budget deficit of $163 billion.[15]

In contrast to an annual deficit, the *Federal debt* is the *accumulated* debt of the Federal government. Whenever the Federal government runs a budget deficit, the additional borrowing to finance that deficit adds to the Federal debt. By contrast, whenever the Federal government runs a budget surplus, as it did during Fiscal Years 1998 through 2001, the Federal debt *decreased* because the Treasury used the surplus to redeem some of the outstanding debt, rather than borrowing additional funds to redeem the debt (known as "rolling over the debt").

Federal law also contains a statutory limit on the Federal debt, commonly called the "debt ceiling." If the activities of the Federal government require a higher limit, Congress must enact a law to raise the debt ceiling. President Bush on September 29, 2007, signed into law an increase in the debt ceiling to $9.815 trillion.[16] Note that the debt ceiling approximates *Gross Federal debt*—which includes: (1) *Debt Held by the Public* (money borrowed by selling Treasury securities in the capital markets to various buyers including foreign investors, mutual funds, state and local governments, commercial banks, insurance companies and individuals); and (2) *debt held by Federal government accounts*, such as the Social Security Trust Funds and various federal retirement trust funds. (The Social Security and other trust funds, by law, invest all of their surpluses in nonmarketable Treasury securities.)

While a lot of political attention is paid to the debt ceiling, many economists view Debt Held by the Public as more significant economically than Gross Federal Debt, because Debt

---

Taxes, Fees, and the Duck Test

Not surprisingly, there's no shortage of political banter about what a "tax" is and what a "fee" is. This issue became part of a *Time* magazine cover story shortly after George H. W. Bush's presidential inauguration. During his 1988 campaign, Bush had famously pledged, "No new taxes." But the following week, at a Senate hearing, Bush's Budget Director cast a haze over what the pledge actually meant. As reported by *Time* on January 30, 1989:

> Last week's signals from Budget Director-designate Richard Darman were intriguing. At the outset, Darman seemed willing to raise new revenues if euphemisms like "definitional changes" and "user fees" could be substituted for the word tax. Then, in a yin-yang reminiscent of the early 1980s, when he helped craft Reagan's acceptance of revenue enhancements, Darman backed off, invoking the "duck test." No matter what a revenue raiser is called, he told Congress, if it looks like a tax and sounds like a tax, and people perceive it to be a tax, it is a tax—and thus violates the President's pledge. Unless, he concluded cryptically, there are special circumstances.[17]

Held by the Public reflects the total amount the Federal government is borrowing from the private credit markets—with the implications that has for available credit.

The Dance between the Unified Budget and Social Security

A fact that causes immense confusion both inside and outside Washington is that Social Security is—technically—excluded from budget totals and considered to be "off-budget."[18]

In 1967, President Johnson's Commission on Budget Concepts[19] decided that the most meaningful way to develop fiscal policy is with a "unified budget" that looks at the impact of *total* Federal spending and revenues on the economy. The principal objective of the unified budget, in their view, was to present a comprehensive picture of the full range of Federal activities. This permits policymakers to gauge the full fiscal effect of Federal activities on the economy. For example, many economists believe large Federal deficits, and the accompanying Federal borrowing needs, drive up interest rates and ultimately slow down economic growth. (For a discussion of whether Federal deficits matter, see Part VI.)

However, during the early 1980s, the Congress enacted Social Security legislation that, in part, set the Social Security program on a path designed to bring in significant annual Social Security surpluses for about 30 years, the purpose of which is to build up a huge "Social Security Trust Fund" to pay for the benefits of baby-boomers who will begin retiring around 2010.[20] This means that for the past 25 years, Social Security payroll tax receipts have far exceeded Social Security payments, yielding significant Social Security surpluses.

Because the *unified budget* consists of *total* Federal spending and revenues, *including* Social Security spending and revenues, Federal policymakers—budget "hawks" in particular—began to argue that these large and *temporary* annual surpluses in the Social Security program would have the effect of "masking" non–Social Security deficits—sometimes called "structural" (or ongoing) deficits. So, in 1985, the Balanced Budget and Emergency Deficit Control Act provided for the removal of the Social Security Trust Funds from the Federal Budget—and the previously unified budget was split into "on-budget" (non–Social Security) totals and "off-budget" (Social Security) totals. Social Security was now to be "off-budget," and everything else would be referred to as "on-budget" spending and revenues.[21]

Nevertheless, despite the legal requirement that Social Security surpluses *not* be included in the Budget, policymakers in both the Administration and Congress have continued to use unified budget numbers—alongside the legally required on-budget and off-budget numbers. The reason is simple: as reflected in Table 2-9.1, as long as Social Security is running surpluses, *unified* budget deficits are a lot smaller than *on-budget (non–Social Security)* deficits.

For example, in FY 2007, the on-budget deficit was $344 billion, whereas the unified budget deficit (including the $181 billion of Social Security surpluses for that year) was 163 billion.[22] Table 2 gives additional examples of how the inclusion or exclusion of Social Security—due to its ongoing surpluses—has a major impact on deficit numbers.

There was, however, a short period of time when policymakers focused on non–Social Security, rather than unified budget totals. This was during the brief period of time—FY 1999 and 2000—when the Federal government was running a non–Social Security (i.e., "on-budget") surplus. With the existence of *non*–Social Security surpluses, both political parties began vigorously debating how to safeguard Social Security surpluses in so-called "lock boxes" that would ensure that Social Security surpluses would "never again be spent on anything other than Social Security."

The truth is, however, that *the proposed Social Security "lock-box" mechanisms would have had no practical effect.* The reason is that by law, all Social Security surpluses are required to be invested in Federal bonds (because they are a safe investment). Therefore:

- When there is a non-Social Security *deficit*, Social Security Trust Fund surpluses, because they are invested in Federal bonds, lend funds to the Treasury to cover costs of non-Social Security programs; and
- When there is a *surplus*, as we had in Fiscal Years 1998 through 2001, the Social Security Trust Fund surpluses, pay down accumulated Debt Held by the Public.

These financial transactions would have been completely unaffected by any of the so-called "lock-boxes." In short, Social Security surpluses are already "locked away" in the safest investments possible—U.S. Treasury securities.

In recent years, the lock box debate has receded into the background because the Federal government is again running high deficits. Once again, policymakers are routinely using

TABLE 2-9.1: Revenues, Outlays, Deficits, Surpluses, and Debt Held by the Public
(billions of dollars rounded to the nearest billion)

Fiscal Year	Revenues	Outlays	Unified Deficit or Surplus*	On-Budget Deficit or Surplus	Social Security Surplus	End-of-Year Debt Held by the Public
1985	734	946	−212	−222	9	1,507
1987	854	1,004	−150	−168	20	1,890
1989	991	1,144	−153	−205	52	2,191
1991	1,055	1,324	−269	−321	54	2,689
1993	1,155	1,410	−255	−300	47	3,248
1995	1,352	1,516	−164	−226	60	3,604
1997	1,579	1,601	−−22	−103	81	3,772
1998	1,722	1,653	69 surplus	−30	99	3,721 decline
1999	1,828	1,702	126 surplus	2 surplus	125	3,632 decline
2000	2,026	1,789	236 surplus	86 surplus	152	3,410 decline
2001	1,991	1,863	128 surplus	− 32	163	3,320 decline
2002	1,853	2,011	−158	−317	159	3,540
2003	1,783	2,160	−378	−538	156	3,913
2004	1,880	2,293	−413	−568	151	4,296
2005	2,154	2,472	−318	−494	174	4,592
2006	2,407	2,654	−248	−434	185	4,829
2007[23]	2,568	2,731	−163	−344	181	4,993

Source: CBO, Budget and Economic Outlook
*Total numbers also include Postal Service. The U.S. Postal Service, like Social Security is also "off-budget"; however, its impact on the total deficit or surplus numbers is relatively minimal.

unified budget totals—*including Social Security surpluses*—in order to make deficits appear lower. However, this masking of the structural non–Social Security deficits will not go on for long, because with the impending retirement of the baby boomers and the consequent increase in Social Security outlays, annual surpluses in the Social Security program will soon disappear (by the middle of the next decade). Ironically, in the postboomer world, politicians will be anxious to use *non*–Social Security (nonunified) budget totals, because *annual Social Security deficits* (due to arrive in 2017) will make unified budget numbers look progressively worse.[24]

And so continues the dance between the unified budget and Social Security.

Budget Baselines: The Starting Point for Budgeting

To formulate a Federal Budget, the President and the Congress must have a starting point. The starting point is known as a "baseline." The rules used to establish budget baselines are the source of tremendous confusion, as well as endless partisan finger pointing about "truth-in-budgeting."

The concept of the baseline is simple: what would the budget look like next year without any policy changes. This is generally called the "current services" baseline. Sounds simple enough—until you take a closer look.

What about anticipated inflation? If you want current programs to continue providing services without change, you need to build in an inflation adjustment, right?

What about entitlement programs or other mandatory spending that is scheduled to expire at the end of this year? Does current policy mean that we assume the program expires or that it continues?

And what about expiring tax provisions? Should the baseline assume that the expiring tax provisions continue unchanged or actually expire? (This, in fact, was one of the most hotly contested issues in the budget debate in the spring of 2007.)

In 1985, Congress wrote into the law[25] the answers to each of these questions:

Revenues—Tax laws are assumed to expire as set forth in current law; however, excise taxes dedicated to a trust fund are assumed to be extended.

Entitlement programs—Entitlement and other direct spending programs, with estimated current year outlays greater than $50 million, are assumed to continue.[26]

Discretionary spending—The Congressional Budget Office's baseline *assumes that discretionary spending programs continue with annual adjustments for projected inflation.* The January and March CBO baselines and the summer update (August or September) baseline also incorporate, and project into the future, any supplemental appropriations *already enacted* for that Fiscal Year.[27] However, this latter rule causes some anomalies in budgetary projections, as explained in the box.

The baseline rules have generated considerable political demagoguery. You've heard, "Only in Washington would an increase in spending be called a cut." What this comment usually refers to is one of the following two scenarios:

First scenario: Assume that CBO, in its baseline, has said that a particular discretionary spending program that costs $100 million this year will, due to inflation, cost $103 million next year to perform the same functions and deliver the same services. If the President or a congressional committee proposes to spend $101 million on the program, that is regarded as a $2 million "cut" below the baseline level of $103 million since the program will be constrained to deliver fewer services (taking inflation into account). One could say that the program is actually being increased (from $100 million to $101 million), but that would not be accurate from the perspective of the current services baseline, which looks at services provided—not dollars.

Second scenario (and this one actually happened): The President's Office of Management Budget projected in January 2006 that Medicare would cost the Federal government $343 billion in FY 2006 and that *without any changes in the law*, the program would cost $395 billion in FY 2007. The expenditures were projected to increase without any changes in the program

Timing and Discretionary Spending Baselines

Timing plays an important role in calculating baselines for discretionary spending. A case in point is funding for the Iraq and Afghanistan wars, which (until FY 2008) were largely funded through emergency supplemental appropriations—not through funding requested in the President's February budget transmittals. For example, consider FY 2007 war funding. In the President's transmittal of his FY 2007 budget in *January 2006*, he included only $50 billion for ongoing operations in Iraq and Afghanistan— a number widely viewed as far below actual needs. Congress added $20 billion to the President's request, appropriating $70 billion in war funding in the FY 2007 regular defense appropriations bill in *September 2006*. Even though it was apparent to everyone that the President would be requesting substantial supplemental war funding for FY 2007, CBO's *January 2007 baseline* based its defense projections and deficit projections on the enacted FY 2007 war funding level of $70 billion. This had the practical effect of "masking" actual defense needs and deficit projections for FY 2007 and later years. As expected, a few weeks after CBO released its January 2007 baseline, the President requested an additional $100 billion in war funding for FY 2007 which Congress approved in May 2007. This example illustrates that the *timing* of the President's war funding requests—that is, requesting a fraction of anticipated war needs for the regular appropriations process, followed by large supplemental requests—has had the effect, in recent years, of distorting both defense numbers and deficit projections in CBO's January report.

due to an increasing number of people who are eligible for Medicare benefits, as well as general health care inflation (i.e., paying more for the same services).

The President's Budget proposal for FY 2007 proposed to "cut" Medicare spending over a period of five years by $36 billion, allowing the program to grow at a rate of 7.7 percent instead of the 8.1 percent projected in the current services baseline. President Bush, in a speech on February 7, 2006, pitched his Medicare reform proposals by saying, "It is the difference between slowing your car down to the speed limit or putting your car into reverse."

The President was correct that even with enactment of his proposed Medicare changes, the actual dollars spent on Medicare would still be higher in FY 2007 than in FY 2006. However, his budget proposal called for a *reduction in Medicare services* below the current services baseline levels for FY 2007 and beyond. Using the President's metaphor, his budget proposal would in fact "put the car in reverse" for the people who would lose the services resulting from the proposed Medicare changes. The key point here is that *significant cuts in government services can occur even when actual dollars spent are still going up.*

There have been proposals, from time to time, to switch government budgeting from a current services baseline to a nominal, or actual, dollars baseline. However, in all likelihood, the Congress would return to a current services baseline because, inevitably, policymakers would ask the fundamental question: if the government continues providing the same level of services next year as we are providing this year, how much is it going to cost?

Budgeting and the Economy: The Debate over Dynamic Scoring

In considering economic behavior, humor is especially important for, needless to say, much of that behavior is infinitely ridiculous." –John Kenneth Galbraith[28]

As explained earlier, the budget baseline is a *starting point* for policymakers. The next step in budgeting is to estimate the impact of proposed policy changes. How would increasing or decreasing budget authority for a particular program impact budget outlays? How would tax cuts or tax increases impact projected revenues? This process of estimating proposed changes in revenue and spending policies is known as "budget scorekeeping" or "scoring."

CBO scores proposed changes in *spending* programs for congressional consideration, and OMB scores spending proposals for the President.

Proposed changes in *tax* policy are scored for the President by the Treasury Department's Office of Tax Analysis (OTA) and for the Congress by the Joint Committee on Taxation (JCT)—a joint House-Senate "Committee" that exists to employ a nonpartisan staff of tax experts to analyze and score revenue proposals for the Congress. CBO combines its own spending estimates with JCT's revenue estimates when reporting to the Congress on the overall budget and economic outlook, and OMB uses OTA's revenue estimates when preparing the President's Budget.

A controversial issue in budget scoring is whether—and how—to incorporate the economic effects of spending and revenue proposals. For example, suppose the Congress is considering imposing a luxury tax on boats. The revenue estimators would assess the number of boats sold in the United States in a given year, multiply the number of sales by the proposed tax rate, and come up with an estimate of additional revenues to be raised by the tax. But consider this: should the estimators also figure into their analysis a possible drop-off in the number of boat sales as a consequence of the new tax and the more generalized impact that might have on employment or GDP? This would be known as a "dynamic" approach to scoring because it takes into account changes in the economy, rather than the simple mathematics of calculating the tax receipts (which is known as a "static" approach to scoring).

Consider another more complex and controversial example. In 2003, the Congress was considering the President's proposal to cut the tax rate on capital gains. What is normally portrayed as a static approach to scoring the rate cut would look at the anticipated capital gains "realizations" (i.e., the sale of capital gains) and the aggregate dollar amount of the gains, and determine the revenue loss associated with lowering the tax rate on those gains. A dynamic approach, by contrast, would integrate into the scoring an analysis of whether the lower tax rate would increase economic activity (often called the "feedback effect") and whether the increased activity would increase gross domestic product (GDP), employment, taxable income, and federal tax receipts (thereby partially offsetting some of the revenue loss attributable to the tax rate cut). Not surprisingly, supporters of the capital gains cut favored a dynamic approach to scoring the proposed rate reduction, and opponents of the cut favored a static approach.

Unfortunately, the ongoing debate over dynamic versus static revenue scoring has oversimplified and mischaracterized current scoring practices. The current misimpression is that revenue estimators at OTA and JCT generally use a purely static approach. In actuality, the current practice of revenue estimators lies somewhere *between* static and dynamic. For example, in the 1990s, when scoring the effect of the proposed luxury tax on boats, estimators did take into account a projected reduction in boat sales as a consequence of the tax.[29] (This type of analysis, focusing on the impact of the proposed tax change on *individual economic activities*, is known as *micro*economics.) However, the revenue estimators did not analyze how a contraction in this particular industry might impact the economy more generally (an area of study called *macro*economics). The current practice is therefore not static (because microeconomic factors are considered) but also not fully dynamic—which would require highly complex and controversial macroeconomic analysis.

In recent years, there has been an ongoing, vigorous debate in Washington about whether revenue estimators should move to a more dynamic scoring approach in estimating tax cuts. Proponents argue that proposed policy changes such as the capital gains rate reduction cannot be accurately assessed unless dynamic macroeconomic effects are incorporated into revenue estimates. However, opponents argue that (1) incorporating macroeconomic effects of major tax proposals would be extremely complex and achieving consensus among estimators would be elusive; and (2) dynamic scoring, with its numerous assumptions about macroeconomic activity, could result in underestimating revenue losses, risking higher deficits.

In addition, opponents of dynamic scoring point out that consistency would require using dynamic scoring on the *spending* side of the budget. This could result in underestimating the cost of proposed changes in spending programs. For example, a significant increase in defense spending could be projected to cause a quantifiable increase in general economic activity, accompanied by increases in taxable income and higher Federal tax revenues. The higher Federal tax revenues would then be applied as an offset, causing the estimated *net budgetary costs* of the projected spending to decrease.

Efforts to incorporate dynamic scoring into the budget process have been increasing. In February 2006, the President's FY 2007 Budget proposed creation of a Division of Dynamic Analysis within the Department of Treasury. In July 2006, the Treasury Department released "A Dynamic Analysis of Permanent Extension of the President's Tax Relief."[30] A dynamic analysis of the recent tax cuts was also included in OMB's 2006 Mid-Session Review of the Budget.[31] And in February 2007, the President's FY '08 Budget included a dynamic analysis of how the tax proposals would affect the economy. It remains to be seen whether the proliferation of dynamic "analyses" will translate into the actual use of fully dynamic scoring in the budget process.

The only certainty is that this arcane and complex debate will continue because the stakes are very high. The revenue estimates associated with tax cuts or increases, and the spending estimates associated with Federal program changes, frame the debates on a wide range of critically important public policy issues.

Recommended Sources for More Information on Dynamic Scoring

- Debate in the *Ripon Forum*, April/May 2006: "Dynamic Scoring: The Time Is Now," by William Beach (Heritage Foundation); and "Dynamic Scoring: Not So Fast!" by Rudolph Penner (Urban Institute and former CBO Director).
- Testimony from a House Budget Committee Hearing on "Dynamic Estimating," September 13, 2006, which can be accessed at www.budget.house.gov/hearings.htm.
- CRS: Issues in Dynamic Revenue Estimating," by Jane Gravelle, April 26, 2007; "Comments on the Treasury Dynamic Analysis of Extending the Tax Cuts," by Jane Gravelle, July 27, 2006.
- Alan J. Auerbach, University of California, Berkeley, "Dynamic Scoring: An Introduction to the Issues," *Journal of Economic Perspectives*, January 2005.

• Joint Committee on Taxation, U.S. Congress, "Exploring Issues in the Development of Macroeconomic Models for Use in Tax Policy Analysis," June 16, 2006.

Notes

1. U.S. Senate, Committee on Finance, *Program Descriptions and General Budget Information for FY 1995*, S. Prt. 103-80, 103d Congress, 2d Session, p. 128, uncredited author: Charles S. Konigsberg, General Counsel.

2. Concurrent resolutions of Congress are not laws and are not presented to the President for signature. Rather, they are internal guidelines the Congress sets for its own legislative operations—in this case, legislative action on appropriations and tax laws that follow adoption of the concurrent resolution on the budget.

3. U.S. Senate, Committee on Finance, *Program Descriptions and General Budget Information for FY 1995*, S. Prt. 103-80, 103d Congress, 2d Session, p. 128, uncredited author: Charles S. Konigsberg, General Counsel.

4. Sandy Streeter, "The Congressional Appropriations Process: An Introduction," 97-684 (Washington, D.C. Congressional Research Service, September 8, 2006), 4.

5. Office of Management and Budget, *FY 2008 Historical Tables* (Washington, D.C.: Government Printing Office, 2006), 135.

6. Office of Management and Budget, 135.

7. U.S. Senate Budget Committee, "The Congressional Budget Process: How It Works," S. Prt. 99-74 (Washington, D.C.: August 1985), 10, uncredited author: Charles Konigsberg, Staff Attorney.

8. Office of Management and Budget, FY 2008 Historical Tables (Washington, D.C.: Government Printing Office, 2007), 133.

9. U.S. Senator Report 93-688, p. 56.

10. *The Congressional Budget Process: How It Works*, 10.

11. Office of Management and Budget, *FY 2007 Historical Tables* (Washington, D.C.: Government Printing Office, 2006), 135.

12. Daniel B. Baker, ed., *Political Quotations* (Detroit: Gale Research Inc., 1990), 219.

13. U.S. Constitution, Article I, Section 7.

14. U.S. Senate, Committee on Finance, Program Descriptions and General Budget Information for FY 1995, S. Prt. 103-80, 103d Congress, 2d Session, p. 128, uncredited author: Charles S. Konigsberg, General Counsel.

15. Department of the Treasury and Office of Management and Budget, Joint Statement on Fiscal Year 2007, October 11, 2007.

16. H.J.Res.43, "Increasing the Statutory Limit on the Public Debt," Public Law No. 110-184.

17. "A New Breeze is Blowing," *Time*, January 30, 1989.

18. The U.S. Postal Service is also excluded from budget totals on the rationale that it is intended to be operated as an independent business-like entity.

19. U.S. Government Printing Office, *Report of the President's Commission on Budget Concepts* (Washington, D.C.: Author, October 1967).

20. All of the surplus funds are, by law, invested in U.S. Treasury securities—deemed to be the safest repository for the funds. However, the practical result of the Social Security Trust Funds buying so many Treasury bonds is that the Treasury has much lower requirements to borrow money by issuing bonds to the public—so that debt held by the public has been artificially held down by the availability of Social Security surpluses to finance non–Social Security government programs. In addition, when the Social Security program begins running a deficit, around the year 2017, the Social Security Trust Funds will need to begin redeeming the Treasury bonds they hold—which will require substantial tax increases or increases in borrowing from the public.

21. The history of moving Social Security "off-budget" is actually a bit more complicated, as follows:

1983: P.L. 98-121, the Social Security Amendments of 1983, including a provision providing for the removal of the Social Security (and the Medicare Hospital Insurance) trust funds from the budget totals beginning in 1993.

1985: P.L. 98-177, the Balanced Budget and Emergency Deficit Control Act of 1985 (Gramm-Rudman-Hollings), made the removal effective immediately for Federal Budget totals, but Social Security receipts and outlays continued to be counted for purposes of enforcing deficit targets.

1990: P.L. 101-508, the Budget Enforcement act of 1990, took Social Security out of all calculations of the budget totals. See Budget Enforcement Act §13301, 104 Stat. 1388-573, 1388-673 (1990). Consequently, Social Security was excluded from the PAYGO sequestration process. However, Social Security's administrative expenses are subject to the discretionary spending caps.

U.S. Senate, Committee on Finance, *Program Descriptions and General Budget Information for FY 1995*, S. Prt. 103-80, 103d Congress, 2d Session, p. 128, uncredited author: Charles S. Konigsberg, General Counsel. The U.S. Postal Service is also off-budget.

22. Department of the Treasury and Office of Management and Budget, Joint Statement on Fiscal Year 2007, October 11, 2007.

23. Treasury and OMB Joint Statement on Fiscal Year 2007; and CBO Budget and Economic Outlook Update, August 2007.

24. U.S. Government Printing Office, *The 2005 Annual Report of the Board of Trustees of the Federal Old-Age and Survivors Insurance and Disability Insurance Trust Funds*, 109th Congress, 1st Session, House Document 109-18, 2.

25. The baseline rules are set forth in Section 257 of the Balanced Budget and Emergency Deficit Control Act of 1985. Although these rules technically expired at the end of September 2006, the CBO opted to continue following the law's specifications in preparing baseline projections. CBO, "Economic and Budget Outlook," January 2007, 5.

26. This baseline rule applies to programs established on or before the enactment of the Balanced Budget Act of 1997. Programs established after that are not automatically assumed to continue. CBO, "Economic and Budget Outlook," January 2006, 6, fn. 7.

27. More specifically, CBO projects growth in discretionary spending as specified in the Balanced Budget an Emergency Deficit Control Act of 1985, using the "GDP deflator and the employment cost index for wages and salaries." CBO, "The Economic and Budget Outlook," January 2005, p. xiv.

28. Lewis D. Eigen and Jonathan P. Siegel, *The Macmillan Dictionary of Political Quotations* (New York: Macmillan Publishing Company, 1993), 138.

29. Memorandum from the author to Senate Finance Committee Chairman Moynihan, dated November 22, 1994.

30. U.S. Department of the Treasury, "A Dynamic Analysis of Permanent Extension of the President's Tax Relief," July 25, 2006.

31. Office of Management and Budget, Fiscal Year 2007 Mid-Session Review, 3-4. See also Jane Gravelle, Congressional Research Service, "Comments on the Treasury Dynamic Analysis of Extending the Tax Cuts," July 27, 2006.

PART

III

SPENDING: HOW AMERICA SPENDS $3 TRILLION PER YEAR

Three trillion dollars . . . $3,000,000,000,000—that's how much the Federal government will be spending in a single year by FY 2009. It is a number so large it is difficult to truly grasp.

And it is a number clouded by political rhetoric and popular myths. For example, surveys show that a majority of Americans believe foreign aid spending is over 20% of the budget.[1] It is actually less than 1% as reflect in Figure 3.1.

This part of the book is designed to give you an overview of how we, as a nation, are spending this gargantuan amount of money each year.

The Federal Budget is about far more than numbers. It is about our nation's priorities—how we defend our nation, enforce our laws, care for our seniors, respond to disasters, build our transportation infrastructure, protect our health and environment, educate our children, and care for the poor and disabled.

The following program summaries are not designed to be exhaustive. Rather, the nation's largest programs are summarized along with prominent small programs, in order to provide a useful overview of how the Federal government is prioritizing our tax dollars.

Note

1. *Americans on Foreign Aid and World Hunger: A Study of U.S. Public Attitudes* from Program on International Policy Attitudes, February 2, 2001, [http://www.pipa.org/].

FIGURE 3.1 Overview of FY 2007 Federal Spending

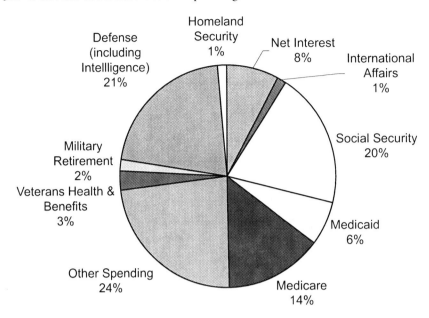

Source: OMB, CBO, CRS

Note: This pie chart is intended to convey an overview of how Federal spending is distributed among major items. "Other Spending" includes a broad range of mandatory *and* discretionary spending programs. For a complete breakdown of "other spending," as well as updated numbers, see www.GovBudget.com.

Note: As this book goes to print, Congress and the President have not reached agreement on appropriations levels for FY 2008 (the new fiscal year that began on October 1, 2007). Therefore, Part III of this book provides **FY 2007 appropriations levels for discretionary spending programs**; FY 2008 numbers will be posted on www.GovBudget.com when available. **FY 2008 spending levels are provided for entitlements** and other mandatory spending programs, because they operate on "automatic pilot" unless changed by new legislation. (See chapter 2-9 for an explanation of discretionary and entitlement spending.)

Defense (and Intelligence) Spending: From "Peace Dividend" in the 1990s to Rapid Growth Since 2000

A certain degree of preparation for war . . . affords also the best security for the continuance of peace.—James Madison[1]

> **FY 2007 Defense Spending: $631 billion[2]**
> **21% of Federal Spending**

See www.GovBudget.com for updated numbers

The major political changes that swept across Eastern Europe and the former Soviet Union in the late 1980s, along with domestic pressure to bring down record deficits, led to a significant downsizing of the U.S. armed forces in the 1990s. Military personnel levels dropped from 2.1 million in 1988 to 1.4 million in 1998. During the 1990s, defense discretionary spending declined by 27% after adjusting for inflation (see figure 3-1.1).[3] This reduction in spending was described at the time as a "peace dividend."

However, the peace dividend was short-lived. Since FY 2000, the defense budget has doubled in dollar terms.[4] Even after adjusting for inflation, defense outlays have increased by more than 50%.[5]

This chapter explores the factors that have driven the rapid growth in defense spending since 2000.

In a Nutshell

The national defense budget[6] includes the military activities of the Department of Defense (DoD) and the nuclear weapons activities of the Department of Energy (DoE). Programs include operations and maintenance, military pay and benefits, procurement of ships, planes, tanks, satellites, missiles and other weapons, research and development, construction of military housing and other facilities, and all nuclear weapons activities including

FIGURE 3-1.1. Defense Spending, FY 1990–2008

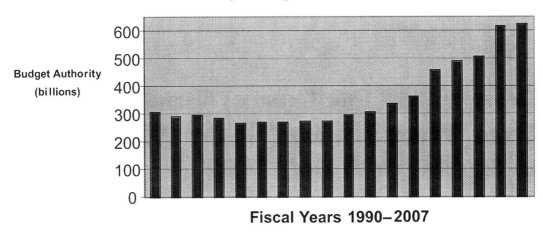

Defense spending *declined* in 1990s due to end of Cold War and deficit reduction agreements; defense spending *doubled* over FY 2000–2007

Budget Authority (billions)

Fiscal Years 1990–2007

research, development, maintenance, clean-up, and nonproliferation.[7] The breakdown of these expenditures is reflected in table 3-1.1.

Two terms that recur frequently in defense policy are the "**QDR**," the congressionally mandated *Quadrennial Defense Review*, which is a long-term planning document, most recently published in February 2006; and ***defense transformation,*** a term initiated by Defense Secretary Donald Rumsfeld at the beginning of the Bush Administration referring to the belief that our national defense would be best served by transforming U.S. forces into smaller, more agile units that can be more easily deployed.[8]

TABLE 3-1.1: How Defense Dollars Are Spent (FY 2007 Budget Authority Including Supplemental)

Category of Spending	Description	$ in billions	% of total
Operations and Maintenance*	Equipment operating costs; recruiting and training; base operations; facilities maintenance; utilities; civilian labor; travel; logistics services; Defense Health Program (the TRICARE System for active duty, dependents, and retirees under 65); drug interdiction; Nunn-Lugar Cooperative Threat Reduction Program	243*	39*
Military Personnel*	Basic and Special Pay; allowances for food, clothing, and off-base housing; recruitment and retention bonuses; DoD contributions to: military retirement[9], Social Security, and the Medicare-Eligible Retiree Health Care Fund	133*	21*

Category of Spending	Description	$ in billions	% of total
Procurement	Acquisition of aircraft, tanks, ships, combat vehicles, satellites/launch vehicles, weapons, ammunition, and missiles	131	21
Research, Development, Testing and Evaluation	Basic research for all branches of the military, as well as the development of prototype weapons and equipment	77	12
Atomic Energy (Nuclear) Defense Activities	DoE's National Nuclear Security Administration oversees nuclear weapons maintenance and development, naval reactors, and nuclear nonproliferation through detection, preventing the spread of technologies and securing inventories; Also includes environmental clean-up, waste disposal, and compensation for radiation exposure	17	3
Military Construction	Training facilities, office buildings, barracks, facilities for new weapons systems, upgrading existing facilities, Base Realignment and Closure (BRAC), U.S. share of NATO facilities	13	2
Family Housing	All costs associated with construction, improvements, operations, maintenance and leasing of military family housing	4	0.6
Other	Includes the National Defense Stockpile, Pentagon maintenance and protection, national defense sealift, defense logistics agency, and defense commissary.	13	2
TOTAL DEFENSE	**Total for "Budget Function 050." In the budget world, this is generally regarded as "total" defense spending. This amount includes funding for Iraq and Afghanistan and other Global War on Terror operations.**	631	100

*Note: Most of the $44 billion in national intelligence spending is hidden within the accounts of the defense budget, most likely concentrated in O&M and Personnel. Consequently we do not know the true level of expenditures on those categories of national defense.

In addition to the $631 billion spent on national defense (and intelligence) in FY 2007, other defense-related expenditures include: **$44 billion** for Federal payments to military retirees and survivors[10]; **$8 billion** for the TRICARE for Life program which provides supplemental medical coverage for military retirees; and **$80 billion** for veterans benefits (reviewed in detail in chapter 3-3). Including these defense-related expenditures, **total defense-related spending was $763 billion in FY 2007.**

Background

Sorting through the Gaggle of Numbers. One of the challenges inherent in explaining the Federal Budget is that budget statistics can be framed in different ways to make seemingly contradictory arguments. For instance, all of the following statements are true:

- Defense discretionary outlays have nearly *doubled* since FY 2000.[11]
- *After adjusting for inflation,* defense discretionary outlays have increased about 50% since FY 2000.[12]
- As reflected in table 3-1.2, defense discretionary outlays have increased more than 10-fold since 1962.
- After adjusting for inflation, the increase since 1962 has been 40%.
- Defense discretionary outlays *as a percentage of the Federal Budget* declined from 49% in 1962 to 17% in 2000, but increased to about 20% in 2007.
- As a percentage of GDP, defense has declined from 9.3% in 1962 to 3% in 2000 and 4.1% in 2007.

U.S. Defense Spending Compared with Other Nations. What about defense spending compared with other nations? Is it myth or fact that the United States spends more on defense than any other nation?

Once again, it depends how you look at it. According to the most recently available CIA data, the U.S. ranks 27th in terms of defense spending as a percentage of GDP. Twenty-six other countries, including China and Russia, spend a greater percentage of their economy on defense (see table 3-1.3).

However, in terms of actual expenditures on defense, the United States far outstrips all other countries—spending nearly half of the world's entire defense expenditures.

What do all these numbers tell us? The United States is not spending an inordinate amount on defense when looking at expenditures as *percentages* of GDP or the Federal Budget. However, percentage figures are not the most revealing measures of defense spending for

TABLE 3-1.2: Defense Spending Is 40% Higher Than at the Height of the Cold War[13]

Defense Outlays in Billions of Dollars		
FY Defense Outlays	*Outlays*	*Outlays Adjusted for Inflation (Constant FY 2000 Dollars)*
1962 defense outlays	53	317
2000 defense outlays	295	295
2007 defense outlays (projected)	569	444

Source: Office of Management and Budget, Executive Office of the President

TABLE 3-1.3: U.S. Accounts for Close to One-Half of the World's Total Military Expenditures

Rank among All Countries	Country	FY 2005 Military Expenditures (in US $ at constant 2003 prices and exchange rates)*	Rank among All Countries	Country	Military Expenditures (% of GDP)†
1	**United States**	478	5	Saudi Arabia	10.0
2	United Kingdom	48	7	Israel	9.0
3	France	46	21	Russia	4.8 ('02)‡
4	Japan	42	23	China	4.3
5	China	41	**27**	**United States**	**4.1** (OMB)
6	Germany	33	50	Australia	2.5
7	Italy	27	53	South Korea	3.0
8	Saudi Arabia	25	55	France	2.6
9	Russia	21	58	India	2.7
10	India	20	62	United Kingdom	2.4
11	South Korea	16	**77**	**World Average**	**2.00**
12	Canada	11	89	Italy	1.8
13	Australia	11	107	Germany	1.5
14	Spain	10	127	Spain	1.2
15	Israel	10	129	Canada	1.1
WORLD 1,001.00			135	Japan	0.9

*Source: SIPRI (Stockholm International Peace Research Institute), http://www.sipri.org/contents/milap/milex/mex_major_spenders.pdf.

†Source: https://www.cia.gov/cia/publications/factbook/geos/sa.html (accessed 05/12/07).

‡Source: International Institute for Strategic Studies.

two reasons. First, the United States has a larger economy than any other nation.[14] Second, the overall size of the Federal Budget has increased dramatically over the last four decades, due principally to entitlement spending. Given this explosion of nondefense spending, historical trends on defense as a percent of the total budget are misleading.

A better measure of defense spending is actual dollars appropriated. Using this metric, as noted earlier, defense appropriations have more than doubled since 2000. The major factors driving the rapid increase in the defense budget are examined next.

Major Issues

Issue 1: The Escalating Cost of the War in Iraq. The potential budgetary costs of the Iraq war were grossly underestimated in the lead-up to the invasion, as reflected in the following statements.

UNDERESTIMATING THE COSTS OF THE IRAQ WAR

- On September 15, 2002, White House economic advisor Lawrence Lindsey estimated the upper limit on the cost to be **$100 to $200 billion**. (*Wall Street Journal*, "Cost of Iraq War," September 15, 2002)
- In January 2003, White House Budget Director Mitch Daniels, in a prewar interview with the *New York Times*, significantly downgraded the estimated total war cost to **$50 to $60 billion**, saying that Lindsay's earlier estimates were too high. According to the *Times*, "Mr. Lindsey was criticized inside and outside the administration for putting forth such a large number, which helped pave the way for his ouster earlier this month." (*New York Times* interview by E. Bumiller, reported January 2, 2003)
- ABC's *This Week* interview of Defense Secretary Donald Rumsfeld on January 29, 2003:
  Rumsfeld: The Office of Management and Budget estimated it would be something under $50 billion.
  George Stephanopoulos: Outside estimates say up to $300 billion.
  Rumsfeld: Baloney.
- March 27, 2003: One week after the invasion, Deputy Defense Secretary Paul Wolfowitz suggested Iraqi oil revenues would largely cover post invasion costs: "There's a lot of money to pay for this that doesn't have to be U.S. taxpayer money, and it starts with the assets of the Iraqi people. . . . The oil revenues of that country could bring between $50 and $100 billion over the course of the next two or three years. . . . **We're dealing with a country that can really finance its own reconstruction**, and relatively soon." (Testimony before the House Committee on Appropriations, emphasis added)

As displayed in table 3-1.4, the nonpartisan Congressional Budget Office estimates the budgetary costs of U.S. operations in Iraq and the war on terrorism exceeded $600 billion by the end of FY 2007, and will reach nearly $800 billion in FY 2008 if the President's request is fully funded.[15] The costs are significantly higher if one includes debt service due to additional Treasury borrowing.

A recent analysis suggests that enactment of the Administration's FY 2008 request for Iraq war funding would make the Iraq war the second-most costly in U.S. history, exceeding the costs of the Vietnam and Korean wars (adjusted for inflation).[16]

Long-Term Budgetary and Economic Costs Could Top $2 trillion. The current military costs of the war are only the tip of the proverbial iceberg. A study by Nobel laureate economist Joseph Stiglitz at Columbia University and Harvard economist Linda Bilmes, released in January 2006[17] and updated in November 2006,[18] estimates long-term budgetary costs for the Iraq war exceeding $1 trillion and *total budgetary and economic* costs exceeding $2 trillion.[19] According to Stiglitz and Bilmes :

> The full costs of the war are still largely hidden below the surface. Our calculations include not just the money for combat operations but also the costs the government will have to pay

TABLE 3-1.4: Estimated War-Related Funding, Iraq and Afghanistan

(CBO estimates in billions of dollars of budget authority)

	FY 2001– FY 2007 enacted	President's FY 2008 Budget Request	President's FY 2008 Supplemental Request*	FY 2001–2008 Enacted and Requested
Military Operations				
—Iraq	368			
—Afghanistan and other	165			
—**Subtotal**	**533**	**137**	**51**	
Indigenous Security Forces				
—Iraq	19			
—Afghanistan	11			
—**Subtotal**	**30**	5		
Diplomatic Operations & Foreign Aid				
—Iraq	25			
—Other	14			
—**Subtotal**	**39**	3		
Veterans Benefits and Services				
—Iraq				
—Other				
—**Subtotal**	**3**			
TOTAL	**$604 billion**	145	51	**$798 billion**

*Supplemental requests in July and October 2007 *Source*: Congressional Budget Office, 10/24/07

for years to come. These include lifetime health care and disability benefits for returning veterans and special round-the-clock medical attention for many of the (thousands of) Americans who have already been seriously wounded. We also count the increased cost of replacing military hardware because the war is using up equipment at three to five times the peacetime rate. In addition, the military must pay large reenlistment bonuses and offer higher benefits to reenlist reluctant soldiers.[20] On top of this, because we finance the war by borrowing more money (mostly from abroad), there is a rising interest cost on the extra debt.[21]

Other prominent economists have projected total budgetary and economic costs at $1 trillion or less, arguing, for example, that the military costs of containing Saddam Hussein prior to 2003 should be deducted from the war costs.[22]

Whether one is persuaded by estimates of $1 trillion or the Stiglitz-Bilmes projections of more than $2 trillion, there is general agreement that the initial projections of war costs were grossly underestimated, and by FY 2008 the *direct* costs of the Iraq war will make it the second costliest war in U.S. history.

A "Deficit-Financed" War. The budgetary costs of the war are "hidden" in another way. The United States is financing the war through borrowing, shifting the costs to future generations. A recent CRS report observed that the Iraq war "is not financed through higher tax revenues or lower non-military outlays. Therefore, the war can be thought to be *entirely* deficit financed. As opposed to past conflicts where taxes were raised, taxes were cut in 2003."[23] (emphasis added)

Myth: The amount of U.S. reconstruction and security assistance to Iraq is still far less than the massive aid provided to Germany and Japan following World War II.

Fact: According to a January 2007 report by CRS: "Total U.S. assistance to Iraq thus far is about a fifth more than total assistance (adjusted for inflation) provided to Germany—and somewhat more than double that provided to Japan—from 1946–1952."[24]

Issue 2: Iraq War Generates Troop Increases, Following Post–Cold War Troop Reductions. Throughout the Cold War, U.S. active duty forces never dropped below 2.0 million (peaking at more than 3.5 million during the Korean and Vietnam Wars). However, after the Cold War, from 1989 to 1999, troop strength *dropped from 2.1 million to 1.4 million*, where it has remained (see table 3-1.5).

TABLE 3-1.5: Department of Defense Active Duty Personnel Level, FY 1950–2003

1950	1,459	1964	2,688	1978	2,061	1992	1,808
1951	3,249	1965	2,656	1979	2,024	1993	1,705
1952	3,636	1966	3,094	1980	2,050	1994	1,610
1953	3,555	1967	3,377	1981	2,082	1995	1,518
1954	3,302	1968	3,548	1982	2,108	1996	1,472
1955	2,935	1969	3,460	1983	2,123	1997	1,440
1956	2,806	1970	3,065	1984	2,138	1998	1,406
1957	2,795	1971	2,714	1985	2,151	1999	1,386
1958	2,600	1972	2,322	1986	2,169	2000	1,384
1959	2,504	1973	2,252	1987	2,174	2001	1,385
1960	2,475	1974	2,161	1988	2,138	2002	1,387
1961	2,483	1975	2,127	1989	2,130	2003	1,390
1962	2,808	1976	2,081	1990	2,069		
1963	2,700	1977	2,073	1991	2,002		

Sources: FY2001-FY2003 from Office of Management and Budget, *Budget of the United States government for FY2003; Appendix,* February 2002; FY1950-2000 from Under Secretary of Defense Comptroller, *National Defense Budget Estimates for FY2002,* June 2001.

In a 2007 report to Congress, CRS observed, "Expectations that military requirements would diminish, however, were not realized; U.S. forces deployed to new missions in . . . the Persian Gulf, Somalia, Haiti, the Balkans and . . . Afghanistan. . . . . The most recent experience of *Operation Iraqi Freedom* suggests that U.S. ground forces are stretched thin." [25]

While there is little consensus on the wisdom of the Iraq invasion, and even less on how and when to disengage and redeploy, the conflict has generated considerable support in the Congress and the Administration on increasing the size of the Army and Marine Corps. The Administration temporarily added 30,000 troops in January 2004 and proposed in January 2007 to *permanently* increase the size of the active-duty Army by 65,000 personnel (to 547,400) and the Marine Corps by 27,000 personnel (to 202,000).[26] According to CRS, this proposal to increase permanent "end strength" of the two services by 92,000 has been "justified largely by the need to reduce the frequency of deployment for any one unit"[27] – an issue of increasing concern as the Iraq engagement continues.[28]

The growth in personnel to the recommended permanent levels would occur over a five-year period. The Administration plan would also increase the Army Reserve and National Guard by a combined 9,200 personnel and would reallocate additional military personnel from overhead functions to the operational force.

CBO has estimated the costs of implementing the plan at $108 billion over fiscal years 2007–2013, relative to levels projected in the *Quadrennial Defense Review*.[29] Annual costs for the permanent increase in personnel would be about $14 billion per year including $6.9 billion for pay and benefits, $5.2 billion for operation and maintenance, and the remainder for health care, retiree health care, family housing, and procurement.[30]

HAVE THE GUARD AND RESERVES BEEN STRETCHED TOO THIN?

There are five military reserve components that are *purely Federal* entities—the Army Reserve, Navy Reserve, Marine Corps Reserve, Air Force Reserve, and Coast Guard Reserve—and are generally referred to as the "Reserves." By contrast, the Army and Air National Guard components—descended from colonial era militias—are both *Federal and state entities* that can be called to duty by the governors or by the President for state active duty or Federal active duty, respectively. State duty typically includes responding to disasters and civil disorders; Federal duty has, recently, included service in Iraq.

From the end of World War II until 1990, the reserves were activated by the Federal government only four times. Since 1990, however, reservists have been activated six times.[31] As of the end of FY 2006, there were 1.1 million men and women serving in the "Ready Reserve," the primary manpower pool of the seven reserve components.[32] Between 2001 and 2006, about half of the ready reserve had been involuntarily activated for operations in Iraq, Afghanistan, and protecting military installations from terrorism. "The continuing mobilization of reservists to participate in these operations," observes CRS analyst Lawrence Kapp, "lends further support to the idea that the Reserve Component has been transformed from a 'force of last resort' in the Cold War era into an integrated part of the military services in the post–Cold War era."[33]

In light of these substantial costs, it is significant that the director of the GAO's Defense Capabilities and Management unit testified to Congress shortly after the Administration proposed the personnel increase that the "DoD has not clearly demonstrated the basis for military personnel requests."[34]

Issue 3: Overseas Basing and U.S. Commitments to NATO and South Korea. A significant factor in the defense budget is the more than 350,000 U.S. troops deployed around the world on a variety of missions. As reflected in table 3-1.6, these missions include active military operations, stabilization and reconstruction, strategic deployment, and peacekeeping.

Burden sharing and the U.S. commitment to NATO. Since 1949, the United States has committed itself to defending its European allies in the North Atlantic Treaty Organization (NATO), declaring that it would consider any attack on its NATO allies to be an attack on the United States. But some have asked over the years whether the United States has borne an unfair share of NATO's costs—often referred to as the "burden sharing" issue.

According to a 2001 report by CBO, "over the past 50 years, the United States has maintained as many as 300,000 military personnel in Europe and has consistently devoted more of its gross domestic product (GDP) to defense than have most of its allies. With the end of the Cold War and the demise of the Soviet threat, the U.S. cut its force presence in Europe to about 100,000…but the European allies have also cut their defense spending . . . leaving the U.S. still bearing the largest financial burden among the NATO allies."[35] Proposals are currently under consideration for additional reductions and redeployments in Europe.

At the same time, efforts are being made to enhance NATO's joint capabilities. In 2004, NATO announced that a Chemical/Biological, Radiological, and nuclear defense battalion had become fully operational. In 2006, the allies launched a NATO Response Force (NRF) with 20,000 troops, on rotation from Member nations for rapid response to a variety of military and humanitarian crises.

TABLE 3-1.6: Major Overseas U.S. Troop Deployments

Location	Number of Troops Deployed	Mission
Iraq	**162,000** troops plus 20,000 support personnel[36]	Original mission: remove Saddam Hussein who was believed to have weapons of mass destruction. With the removal of Saddam, the U.S. presence became a "stabilization and reconstruction operation."[37]
Europe	**98,000*** (when not deployed elsewhere)[38]	Forces in the U.S. European Command maintain readiness to support NATO security missions as discussed below.
Japan	**53,000**[39]	The deployment in Japan is the anchor of U.S. security strategy in East Asia. Current security concerns in the region: N. Korea. Potential concerns: China.

Location	Number of Troops Deployed	Mission
Afghanistan	28,000[40]	2 missions: U.S. Operation Enduring Freedom and NATO-led peacekeeping, both intended to prevent the Taliban[41] from returning to power and to support the current democratically elected government.
South Korea	Less than 30,000; will be reduced to less than 20,000 by 2008.	Mutual Defense Treaty, although strategic interests have been diverging as discussed below.
Kosovo	1,700 U.S. troops serving in KFOR, down from a peak of 5,500.	The NATO-led Kosovo Force, or KFOR, deployed in the wake of a 78-day air campaign launched by NATO in March 1999 to halt the massacre of ethnic Albanians by Yugoslav/Serb forces under Slobodan Milosevič.[42]
Djibouti[43] (northeast coast of the Horn of Africa)	1,500 (military and civilian personnel at Camp Lemonier)	Operations against Al Qaeda and other terrorists operating in the region. A new U.S. Africa Command will also address Africa's growing strategic importance having surpassed the Middle East as the largest supplier of oil to the United States, the ongoing presence of terrorist training camps, and ongoing concern about military and humanitarian crises in Africa.[44]
Egypt (Sinai)	700 serving as the U.S. contingent of the Multi-National Force and Observers in the Sinai Peninsula.[45]	Monitoring the Egypt-Israeli border as provided for in the 1979 Camp David peace treaty.
Bosnia & Herzegovina	100 (assigned to NATO Headquarters-Sarajevo)	Assist in defense reform and operational tasks such as counterterrorism and supporting the International Criminal Court for the Former Yugoslavia. (In 1995, the United States–facilitated Dayton peace agreement ended an ethnic and territorial conflict that erupted with the dissolution of Yugoslavia.)[46]

Total U.S. troop levels dropped to about 1.4 million in the 1990s, from a Cold War average of 2.1 million. Troop levels are currently scheduled to increase to 1.5 million by 2012, as noted in the previous section.

*Kosovo and Bosnia deployments not included in the Europe total.

**NATO Membership
(as of 2007)**
Belgium, Bulgaria, Canada, Czech Republic, Denmark, Estonia, France, Germany, Greece, Hungary, Iceland, Italy, Latvia, Lithuania, Luxembourg, Netherlands, Norway, Poland, Portugal, Romania, Slovakia, Slovenia, Spain, Turkey, United Kingdom, United States

There are also ongoing concerns at the Pentagon that European contributions to NATO missions are often subject to deployment limitations imposed by member nations, and the capabilities of the NRF could be limited by the European Union's development of its own rapid reaction forces.[47]

The U.S. deployment in South Korea. The United States has dedicated—and continues to invest—resources in the defense of South Korea. In a February 2007 report, CRS estimated the total cost of stationing U.S. troops in South Korea at nearly $3 billion per year, with South Korea contributing about $800 million of the cost (although the Pentagon has been pushing for South Korea to increase its contribution to 50%).[48] In addition, DoD has put in place a multiyear $11 billion plan to modernize U.S. forces in South Korea.

From the U.S. perspective, South Korea is vital to contain the militaristic—and now nuclear-capable—North Korea. South Korea is also the seventh-largest U.S. trading partner and is strategically located off the east coast of China.

The United States suffered over 33,000 killed and over 101,000 wounded in the Korean War (1950–1953). In the 1954 Mutual Defense Treaty, it agreed to defend South Korea from external aggression and until recently maintained about 34,000 troops there to supplement the 650,000 South Korean armed forces.

In August 2004, the United States withdrew a 3,600-person brigade from South Korea and sent the troops to Iraq. In addition, in October 2004, the United States and South Korea agreed to a plan for the withdrawal of an additional 12,500 troops by September 2008, reducing overall U.S. troop strength in South Korea to less than 20,000, with the possibility of additional reductions after 2008.

The reasons for the troop reductions include: the need for personnel in Iraq; South Korean intentions to end the Combined Forces Command, under which South Korean forces have been under the authority of the U.S. Commander; South Korea's demand for a right to veto the use of U.S. forces based in Korea in any operations in East Asia; a growing divergence of views between South Korean leaders and the Bush Administration over policies towards North Korea and China; and uneasiness among South Koreans over U.S. encouragement of Japan's strategic role in Northeast Asia.[49]

Issue 4: Domestic Base Closures (BRAC)—Short-Term Increases for Long-Term Savings. The major political changes that swept across Eastern Europe and the former Soviet Union in the late 1980s led to the downsizing of the U.S. Armed Forces (see table 3-1.5). Congress initiated in 1988 a reduction in the number of domestic military bases to accompany the force reductions, with the objective of generating long-range annual savings by cutting back on personnel, and operations and maintenance expenditures.

However, as one might expect, individual Members of Congress were likely to vigorously oppose closure of bases in their States and Districts due to jobs that would be lost and the economic ripple effects. Congress therefore established a process designed to insulate base closure decisions from political considerations. Congress created a bipartisan Base Realignment and Closure (BRAC) Commission to move the base closure process forward. The Commission was tasked with reviewing Pentagon recommendations and selecting facilities to be closed or downsized. Under the procedure, if the President approves the Commission's recommended list of bases to be closed and downsized, the Commission recommendations take effect *unless* Congress enacts a law disapproving *the entire list*.[50] The law establishes special fast-track procedures to ensure that disapproval legislation receives expedited consideration by Congress.

The initial Commission in 1988 was appointed by the Secretary of Defense, but subsequent commissions in 1991, 1993, 1995, and 2005 were appointed by the President with Senate confirmation. The presidentially appointed Commissions made recommendations to the President, who, in turn, sent the recommendations and his approval to Congress. Congress voted four times on resolutions to disapprove Commission recommendations, but all of the disapproval resolutions were overwhelmingly defeated.[51]

Under the first four BRAC rounds, DoD closed 97 major bases and downsized 55 bases, with a *20% reduction in domestic infrastructure* and projected long-range budget savings of $6.6 billion per year.[52] Under the 2005 round, DoD is slated to close 25 major bases and downsize 32 by 2011, yielding an additional $4 billion in projected long-range annual savings.

However, *in the short-term the domestic base closure process substantially increases defense spending*, particularly for military construction. For example, the FY 2007 emergency supplemental appropriations bill[53] included $3 billion in additional funds to implement the 2005 round of BRAC closures and downsizing.

Issue 5: Rapidly Accelerating Military Personnel Costs. The costs associated with military personnel have been rapidly increasing in recent years, in particular defense health care and military retirement.

Military health system. The Defense Department is facing rapidly rising health care costs, similar to the explosion in Medicare and Medicaid outlays (discussed in chapter 3-6). According to Senate testimony by the Undersecretary of Defense for Personnel and Readiness, military health spending in FY 2007 is expected to total $39 billion—*7.5 % of the defense budget*—and is estimated to continue growing rapidly due to (1) health care inflation, (2) the reduction in cost sharing, and (3) a sharp increase in usage by retirees under 65. DoD is estimating military health care costs of $64 billion by 2015—*12 % of the defense budget*.[54]

This rapid growth in military health costs is causing growing concern among military leaders that health dollars are soaking up funds needed for operations and maintenance.[55]

The Military Health System (MHS) encompasses the Defense Department's 75 hospitals, 461 clinics, and 131,000 medical personnel. Their *primary* duty is to maintain the health of military personnel so they can carry out their military missions. The system also provides, *where space is available*, health care services to dependents of active duty service members and to military retirees and their dependents.

Since space in military facilities was not always available to serve dependents and retirees, in 1966 DoD created the Civilian Health and Medical Program of the Uniformed Services (CHAMPUS). CHAMPUS was designed as the military equivalent of a health insurance plan for active duty dependents, military retirees and their dependents, and survivors. CHAMPUS operated as a fee-for-service insurance plan to reimburse civilian providers.

CHAMPUS has now been replaced by TRICARE, which brings together the health care resources of the Army, Navy, and Air Force and supplements them with civilian health care professionals. The comprehensive TRICARE system—which provides health care to over 9 million people[56]—offers active duty military (including activated Guard and Reserves[57]), military retirees, and their families[58] three options: (1) a DoD-managed health maintenance organization, TRICARE Prime, where *military treatment facilities* are the principal source of Health Care; (2) a preferred provider network, TRICARE EXTRA, where private providers agree to provide care at a reduced cost; or (3) a fee-for-service system, where private providers are reimbursed a percentage of their charges, called TRICARE Standard (based on the CHAMPUS model).

Active duty military are automatically enrolled in TRICARE Prime. Their families and retirees may select any of the three options.[59] Families of active duty personnel have a higher priority at military medical facilities (under TRICARE Prime) than military retirees. This priority is designed to help them obtain care easily so that active duty members performing military service do not have to be concerned about health care for their dependents.

TRICARE and Medicare. Military retirees become ineligible to receive TRICARE benefits when they reach 65 and become eligible for Medicare, although TRICARE pays out-of-pocket costs for Medicare Part B—a significant benefit—through a program called TRICARE for Life. The $7.7 billion FY 2007 cost of TRICARE for Life is not included in the "defense" portion of the Federal Budget, but because it is a cost of defending the nation, it is included in the aggregation of "defense-related costs" following table 3-1.1.[60]

TRICARE Reserve Select (TRS). TRICARE was expanded in 2005 to allow Guard and Reserve Members called up for full-time service after 9/11 to "buy into" the TRICARE program 90 days before reporting for duty and for extended periods after returning.[61] TRS members pay monthly premiums to cover themselves and can also obtain coverage for their families.

Military retirement. Military retirees are people who have completed a full active duty military career (usually at least 20 years of service) *or* were disabled in the line of duty

---

Myth: Military personnel and their families are entitled to free medical care for life.

Fact: Many current and former military say they were promised "free medical care for life" when they signed up. This is not true and appears to be based on the fact that non–active duty military and their families have continuing *access to* military medical facilities, *although on a space-available basis*. Nevertheless, TRICARE does provide exceptional coverage—having "expanded its benefits in recent years, eliminating almost all cost sharing (deductibles and copayments) for active-duty personnel and their family members . . . and adding TRICARE for Life to supplement Medicare coverage for beneficiaries over age 65." In fact, TRICARE benefits compare so favorably with private sector benefits that the Rand Corporation warned in 2005 that "if current trends continue, DoD risks becoming the primary insurer for all of its beneficiaries,"[62] notwithstanding other private sector coverage they or their spouses may be entitled to.

and meet certain length of service and extent of disability criteria. (By contrast, a *veteran* is any person who has served in the armed forces. *Military retirees* are therefore a subset of veterans.)

The military retirement system includes benefits for retirement after an active or reserve military career, disability benefits, and benefits for survivors of deceased retirees. There are currently about 2.1 million military retirees and survivor benefit recipients (plus 6 to 8 million family members who rely on their benefits).[63]

Expenditures for military retirement are enormous—$44 billion in FY 2007, growing to $50 billion by 2011. Technically military retirement expenditures are included in the "Income Security" portion of the Federal budget—not the "Defense" budget, but because military retirement is a cost of defending the nation, it is included in the aggregation of defense-related costs following table 3-1.1.

The expenditures for military retirement are high for several reasons. The first reason is the large number of military retirees. Second, a member of a military service becomes immediately entitled to retirement pay upon completion of 20 years of military service, regardless of age—and most retire young. (According to the DoD Office of the Actuary, in 2004 the average nondisabled service member retired from an active duty career at age 41 with nearly 22 years of service.)[64] Third, military personnel do *not* contribute a percentage of salary toward retirement—the reason being that they are already subject to Social Security payroll taxes. Fourth, military retirement benefits are fully protected against inflation through cost–of–living adjustments. Fifth, military retirement benefits are no longer offset by veterans' disability compensation; retirees receive both, concurrently. (The issue of concurrent benefits is addressed in chapter 3-2 on veterans' benefits.)[65]

Issue 6: Increasing Commitment to Missile Defense Systems. Since the Reagan Administration's Strategic Defense Initiative (SDI) was announced in the mid-1980s, the Congress has appropriated between $110 and $150 billion for ballistic missile defense programs, making it the largest acquisition program in the defense budget.[66] Annual expenditures on missile defense have significantly increased during the second Bush Administration, with appropriations increasing from $3.6 billion in FY 2000 to $7.8 billion in FY 2002—with $9.3 billion appropriated for FY 2007.[67]

Along with increased expenditures, the Administration announced in 2002 U.S. withdrawal from the 1972 Anti-ballistic Missile (ABM) Treaty[68] and in 2004 began deployment of 44 ground-based interceptors in Alaska and Hawaii, with plans to deploy up to 132 sea-based interceptors on Navy ships and 10 long-range interceptors in Poland (although as of the G-8 meeting in June 2007, this is a subject of negotiation with Russia).[69]

Supporters of missile defense systems argue that these steps are necessary because nuclear deterrence can not be relied on in an age when rogue states, such as North Korea and Iran, already have missile delivery systems and are working to build nuclear arsenals.[70] Furthermore, they believe the collapse of the Soviet Union has increased the possibility of an accidental or unauthorized launch.[71]

Critics argue that missile defense has not been proven,[72] withdrawal from the ABM treaty was provocative, plans to place interceptors in Poland may spark a new arms race with Russia,[73] and the greatest nuclear threat facing the United States is terrorists who are likely to deliver warheads in cargo containers or vehicles.[74]

Issue 7: Developing a New Generation of Nuclear Weapons. Contrary to popular assumptions, the Department of Energy (DoE), not the DoD, directs nuclear weapons research, development, and production. DoE's National Nuclear Security Administration spends more than $6 billion per year on research and development of nuclear weapons and close to $800 million related to naval reactors. In addition, DoE spends more than $6 billion year on defense nuclear cleanup and disposal.[75]

Despite the end of the Cold War, the United States is several years into a long-term, multi-billion-dollar effort to design and build a new generation of nuclear weapons known as the Reliable Replacement Warhead (RRW) program. Most warheads in the current stockpile were built in the 1970s and 1980s. The program is currently in the design phase, with plans to start engineering development by 2010 and produce the first deployable RRW between 2012 and 2016.

However, policymakers and defense analysts continue to debate the wisdom of producing a new generation of nuclear weapons, with critics of RRW arguing that the useful life of existing nuclear warhead stockpiles can be extended for at least several more decades. A key issue underlying the ongoing debate is whether, in light of the nuclear test moratorium the United States has observed since 1992, our nuclear deterrent is more reliable by extending the life of proven warhead technologies or moving forward with deployment of a new generation of warheads.[76] (This topic has generated a renewed debate on nuclear testing with the President's FY 2008 Budget stating that the Department of Energy "supports the capability to return to underground testing, if so directed by the President.")

An additional issue is cost, with advocates of RRW arguing that a simplified and uniform design could, over the long term, be less expensive to maintain than the current stockpile (although any savings would have to offset the billions spent on design, development and deployment of new warheads).

Issue 8: Procurement of Weapons Systems, Defense Transformation, and the "Budget Wedge."

> *Although DoD has doubled its planned investment in major weapon systems from $750 billion to $1.5 trillion since 2001, unanticipated cost growth has reduced the return on this investment. . . . Given the federal fiscal outlook, what was once a desire to deliver high-quality products on time and within budget has become an imperative. —GAO Comptroller General David M. Walker, March 20, 2007* [77]

There is a broad-based consensus that our national security, and the lives of our troops, depend on cutting-edge technology. However, there is little agreement on what that means in practical terms—that is, which weapons systems to continue procuring, which systems to upgrade, which systems to scrap and replace, which systems are no longer needed, and when strategic or tactical requirements warrant a new approach. These decisions have enormous consequences for our national defense, the lives of our troops, and the allocation of national defense resources. (They are also inextricably interwoven with congressional politics as decisions on major weapons systems can profoundly impact the economies of local communities.)

The 2006 *Quadrennial Defense Review* stated that in addition to traditional threats involving large-scale mechanized forces (as faced during the Cold War), the United States should increasingly prepare for three new types of national security threats: (1) *unconventional threats* relying on terrorism and guerilla operations; (2) *catastrophic threats* using weapons of mass destruction (WMDs); and (3) *disruptive threats* such as cyber-attacks, bio-attacks, or other types of novel, high-tech attacks.[78] Consistent with these new threats, DoD's defense transformation initiative calls for transforming U.S. forces into smaller, more agile units that can be more easily deployed.[79]

The cost of this transformation falls disproportionately in the area of procurement. The fundamental policy challenges will be to determine whether the tremendous investments that are currently planned are necessary and appropriate to meet actual threats to our nation, and how to shut down existing weapons programs that no longer address evolving defense priorities.

For example, some analysts have suggested that the following weapons systems are immensely expensive procurements that are more relevant to the strategic needs of the Cold War, than the new threats highlighted by the QDR:

- The Navy's DDG 1000 Zumwalt Class Destroyer program ($33 billion);
- The F/A 22 Raptor, the most expensive fighter plane ever designed ($339 million per plane—100 already purchased, with plans to acquire another 82), which was originally planned to counter a Soviet fighter that was never built;
- The V-22 Tilt-Rotor Osprey aircraft, which has been plagued with safety issues and fatalities since its development began in the 1980s ($110 million per helicopter, $50 billion total);
- The tri-service Joint Strike Fighter program (at a total program cost of $224 billion), which, according to GAO, is being fast-tracked into production in 2007 "with little demonstrated knowledge about performance" and only 2 of the plane's 8 critical technologies fully developed; and
- The Army's "Future Combat Systems" program, a high-tech ground combat system consisting of new armored vehicles, unmanned ground and air vehicles, and sensors that will be integrated into a highly complex system (with $3.7 billion requested for FY 2008 even though only 1 of 48 critical technologies is fully mature, and with a total estimated cost of $132 to $160 billion).[80]

TABLE 3-1.7: Examples of Cost Overruns and Reduced Purchasing Power on Key Weapons Systems

(billions of dollars adjusted for inflation)					
Program	Initial Estimate	Initial Quantity	Latest Estimate	Latest Quantity	Percentage Unit Cost Increase
Joint Strike Fighter	$197 b	2,866	$224 b	2,458	**33 %**
Future Combat Systems	$86 b	15	$132 b	15	**54 %**
V-22 Advanced Vertical Lift Aircraft	$37 b	913	50 b	458	**170 %**
Evolved Expenditure Launch Vehicle	$16 b	181	$29	138	**135 %**
Space Based Infrared System High	$4 b	5	$10 b	3	**312 %**
Expeditionary Fighting Vehicle	$8 b	1,025	$11 b	1,025	**34 %**

Source: Government Accountability Office, March 2007.[81]

In addition to realigning procurements with actual and evolving threats to our national security, DoD faces a significant challenge in overcoming enormous cost overruns in procurement. The GAO concluded in a March 2007 report to Congress that "while DoD is pursuing plans to transform military operations and committing more investment dollars to realize these new weapon systems, it regularly realizes a reduced return on their investment. DoD programs typically take longer to develop and cost more to buy than planned, placing additional demands on available funding."[82] Consider the examples presented in table 3-1.7, in particular the percentage unit cost increase to date.

Issue 9: The Intelligence Budget.

> *Secrecy now beclouds everything about the CIA—its cost, its efficiency, its successes, and its failures. —Mike Mansfield, widely respected and longest-serving Majority Leader of the U.S. Senate*[83]

The total intelligence budget, including the National Security Agency (NSA), Central Intelligence Agency (CIA), and 14 other intelligence agencies, was $44 billion in FY 2007.[84]

The intelligence budget, sometimes referred to as the "black budget," is being addressed in the defense chapter of this book because most intelligence budget authority is hidden within the accounts of the Defense budget, with the details spelled out in classified annexes to defense appropriations, defense authorization, and intelligence authorization bills. (There is not a separate intelligence appropriations bill, as had been recommended by the 9/11 Commission.[85]) Other departmental budgets that include smaller amounts of intelligence spending are budgets for the Departments of Justice, State, Treasury, Energy, and Homeland Security.[86]

The two major components of the intelligence budget are (1) the **National Intelligence Program** (NIP)—formerly the National Foreign Intelligence Program or NFIP—which funds foreign intelligence and counterintelligence activities; and (2) the **Military Intelligence Program** (MIP) which funds the DIA and military intelligence services (see table 3-1.6).[87]

Director of National Intelligence. Responsibility for preparing and implementing the NIP budget belongs to the Director of National Intelligence (DNI), a new position established on the recommendation of the 9/11 Commission by the Intelligence Reform and Terrorism Prevention Act of 2004.[88] Under the 2004 Act, the DNI also assumed two of the three responsibilities formerly performed by the Director of Central Intelligence (DCI): (1) providing intelligence to the President and Congress and (2) serving as head of the Intelligence Community. (The former Director of Central Intelligence is now focused exclusively on the operations of the CIA as the Director of the Central Intelligence Agency, or DCIA.)

In theory, the budgetary authority of the DNI is significantly stronger than authority previously available to the DCI. In addition to developing the NIP Budget, the 2004 Act gives the DNI authority to apportion the flow of appropriated funds to each of the agencies,[89] allot funds for intelligence activities within those agencies, ensure the effective execution of the NIP Budget, reprogram funds, transfer intelligence personnel from individual agencies to joint centers or other agencies, decide on major acquisitions, and provide guidance on DoD intelligence activities not included in the NIP.[90]

TABLE 3-1.8: The U.S. Intelligence Community's 16 Agencies
Agencies within the Department of Defense are shaded

Agency and Year Established	Functions	2007 Budget Estimate*
NIP (National Intelligence Program) Budget		
National Security Agency/ Central Security Service (NSA/CSS), 1952[91]	"Signals Intelligence": intercepts radio, phone, and other communications; and breaks codes	$6–$8 b
National Reconnaissance Office (NRO), 1960	Develops and operates reconnaissance satellites	$6–$8 b
National Geospatial– Intelligence Agency (NGA),1996	Precision maps and geospatial data necessary for targeting precision guided weapons	$2–$3 b
Defense Intelligence Agency (DIA), 1961	Performs liaison functions between defense and intel.	$1–$3 b
Central Intelligence Agency (CIA), 1947	Intelligence collection, analysis and covert action	$5 b
Federal Bureau of Investigation (FBI)	Counterterrorism and counterintelligence	$1 b
Energy Department	Intelligence on foreign nuclear programs and counterintelligence to protect U.S. nuclear secrets	$75 m
Treasury Department	Terrorist financing, international money laundering	$50 m
State: Bureau of Intel. & Research (INR)	Most of State's intelligence assets were moved to form the CIA in 1947, but State retains a small, highly regarded analytical agency	$51 m
Department of Homeland Security (DHS/IAIP), 2003	Directorate of Information Analysis and Infrastructure Protection assesses vulnerabilities	$10 m
Coast Guard (part of DHS)	Maritime security and homeland defense	
Drug Enforcement Agency	Drug enforcement intelligence	
MIP (Military Intelligence Program) BUDGET		
Estimated DoD spending on defense-wide airborne reconnaissance programs[92]		$3 b
Air Force Intelligence (USAF)	Focused on specific tactical needs of the Air Force	$6.5–$7 b
Army Intelligence	Focused on specific tactical needs of the Army	$4.5–$5 b
Navy Intelligence	Focused on specific tactical needs of the Navy and Marine Corps	$3 b
	Total intelligence spending, FY 2007	**$44 b**

*Because the intelligence budget is classified, the reliability of the estimated break-down cannot be verified. See end note for sources.[93]

Despite the objective of the 2004 Act to better clarify and rationalize roles and responsibilities in the Intelligence Community, Congress failed to resolve ongoing turf battles. Since a substantial portion of NIP funds include the activities of DoD agencies—specifically the NSA, NRO, and NGA as reflected in table 3-1.8—section 2018 of the 2004 Act requires the President to issue guidelines to ensure that the DNI exercises this authority "in a manner that respects and does not abrogate the statutory responsibilities of the heads of" the Office of Management and Budget and Cabinet departments. This proviso was primarily in response to concerns of some Members of Congress that the Defense Secretary not lose authority over agencies within DoD.[94] It remains to be seen how this will operate as a practical matter, but initial indications suggest that the turf wars may have actually intensified.[95]

The need for results-oriented budgeting for intelligence. Is the $44 billion appropriated for intelligence activities being well spent? It is difficult to say, since neither the media nor nongovernmental analysts have access to the budgetary details. But the record on major intelligence matters should cause serious skepticism, particularly the intelligence community's colossal failure to uncover the 9/11 plot[96] and the failure of intelligence on WMDs in Iraq that paved the road to war.[97] Common sense suggests that the vast expenditures on intelligence should have produced far better results.

A decade before these failures, Senator Daniel Patrick Moynihan raised similar questions about the value derived from our immense national investment in the intelligence community: "For twenty five years," said Moynihan, "the CIA told the President everything there was to know about the Russians except that they were about to collapse."[98]

To be fair, we don't know whether, or how many, attacks on Americans have been thwarted by the direct efforts of the U.S. intelligence community. But the facts that we do know should motivate Congress, the media, and the American public to ask some serious questions about the massive intelligence expenditures and demand public disclosure of at least the top-line total for the various intelligence agencies.

Issue 10: Thinking Outside the Budget Box—Integrating Defense and Homeland Security

The greatest danger of another catastrophic attack in the United States will materialize if the world's most dangerous terrorists acquire the world's most dangerous weapons. —9/11 Commission[99]

The Federal Budget continues to treat "defense" and "homeland security" as entirely distinct areas of concern. Each year Congress passes separate defense and homeland security appropriations bills, and the congressional budget rules do not permit Senators or Representatives to offer amendments on the Senate or House Floors to move money from one category to the other.[100]

Moreover, our governmental structure in the Executive Branch, as well as the committee structure in Congress, establishes a financial and strategic barrier between defense and homeland security. This artificial distinction is generating some seriously wrongheaded decisions in the allocation of Federal resources for national security. It is urgent that we reshape our thinking and combine defense and homeland security resources into one unified national security budget.

As reflected in the lead-in to this section, the 9/11 Commission determined that the greatest threat facing U.S. national security, in terms of magnitude, is the acquisition of a nuclear weapon by Al Qaeda or other terrorists. According to the Commission, "al Qaeda has tried to acquire or make nuclear weapons for at least ten years. . . . Bin Ladin's associates thought their leader was intent on carrying out a 'Hiroshima.' These ambitions continue. . . . A nuclear bomb can be built with a relatively small amount of nuclear material. A trained nuclear engineer . . . could fashion a nuclear device that would . . . level Lower Manhattan."[101]

The grave threat of nuclear terrorism to our nation's defense has been underscored repeatedly by leading policymakers and the specter of a "mushroom cloud" was explicitly used as one of the key rationales for invading Iraq. Yet the old strategy of nuclear deterrence, dubbed "mutually assured destruction" during the Cold War, is irrelevant in the face of nuclear terror. In the days of the Cold War, we could feel reasonably certain that our massive sea, land, and air-based "nuclear triad" would effectively deter leaders of the Soviet Union from attacking the U.S. or our allies.

The irrelevance of Cold War strategies. Today we face an entirely different threat. Al Qaeda and other fanatical terrorists, are not deterred by threats of nuclear retaliation. Threats of retaliation can deter rogue nations from assisting terrorists, and it might even be used as leverage to cajole reluctant nations into curbing illegal terrorist activities within their borders, but retaliation is not an effective deterrent against the terrorists themselves—since they are stateless. Moreover, many terrorist leaders and their followers are fanatically committed to suicide in order to advance their extremist world view.

Given this new reality, there is a dangerous disconnect between the seriousness of the terrorist nuclear threat (and other WMDs) and the allocation of resources in the Federal Budget. Out of the $631 billion defense budget summarized in table 3-1.1, *less than $2 billion—one-third of one percent—is dedicated to securing loose nukes or nuclear material that could fall into the hands of terrorists.*

Compare that funding with the $224 billion price tag for the Joint Strike Fighter, the $132 billion cost of the Army's Future Combat Systems, or the $3.3 billion cost for each of the Navy's new DDG high-tech destroyers.

It is vital for U.S. national security that the Administration and Congress think outside the traditional "budget box" and realign Federal resources to address the gravity of the threats we currently face. An effective strategy would include the following elements:

1. Ramp up resources for securing loose nukes and materials that can be used in developing improvised nuclear devices (INDs). The one-third of one percent of the defense budget[102] currently allocated to the National Nuclear Security Administration at the Department of Energy and the Nunn-Lugar Cooperative Threat Reduction Program at the Department of Defense is disproportionately low given the gravity of the nuclear terror threat.
2. Train and deploy numerous rapid response teams dedicated to the task of intercepting loose nuclear materials anywhere in the world, in cooperation with U.S. allies.
3. Dedicate a significant portion of the $44 billion intelligence budget to tracking WMD materials throughout the world.
4. Initiate a high-priority program, on a par with the Manhattan Project, jointly administered by DoD, DoE, and DHS, to speed the development and deployment of nuclear detection technologies. GAO has been highly critical of the progress thus far.[103]

5. In addition to preventing nuclear and other WMD attacks, a responsible national security strategy requires that the Federal government implement comprehensive emergency planning for urban areas, including the stockpiling of effective medical countermeasures.

The same type of analysis can apply to other threats, such as a catastrophic release from chemical plants. In December 2006, the Congressional Research Service reported to Congress that (1) according to the Department of Homeland Security, release of a large volume of chlorine could cause thousands of fatalities and injure tens of thousands; (2) in 2000 the Department of Justice concluded that "the risk of terrorists attempting in the foreseeable future to cause an industrial chemical release is both real and credible"; and (3) in 2005, the Environmental Protection Agency had approximately 110 industrial facilities registered, which projected potential off-site consequences to a million or more people in the event of a worst-case chemical release.[104] As in the case of the nuclear terror threat, it is reasonable to conclude that national security would be better enhanced by purchasing 7 Navy DDG Destroyers instead of 10 and using the $10 billion saved to harden and secure our nation's chemical plants.

Similar trade-offs would make sense to secure a broad range of U.S. critical infrastructure sites including water and power plants, nuclear plants, ports, bridges and tunnels, trains, and subways.

Accomplishing this will require exceptional leadership. Realigning Federal budgets and agencies, and congressional committees, is an enormous challenge in the nation's capital where budgets, bureaucratic turf, and jurisdictions are jealously guarded.

Even more difficult is overcoming the bureaucratic inertia generated by the military-industrial complex that President Dwight D. Eisenhower presciently warned about a half century ago.[105] Canceling or paring back multibillion-dollar weapons systems and redirecting the money to more urgent homeland security priorities will be no small feat, but one of the most urgent matters awaiting the next President.

In the councils of government, we must guard against the acquisition of unwarranted influence, whether sought or unsought, by the military-industrial complex. The potential for the disastrous rise of misplaced power exists and will persist. —President Dwight D. Eisenhower

---

Notes

1. Lewis D. Eigen and Jonathan P. Sigel, *The Macmillan Dictionary of Political Quotations* (New York: Macmillan, 1993), 104.

2. In Part III of this book, all dollar amounts refer to "budget authority" unless otherwise noted. Budget authority is the amount appropriated by Congress in a given year. For a discussion of budget authority and outlays, see chapter 2-9. The defense budget authority number leading off this chapter includes 2007 supplemental funds enacted on May 25, 2007 (H.R. 2206, 110th Congress).

3. Discretionary defense outlays, in constant FY 2000 dollars, declined from $390 billion in FY 1991 to $284 billion in FY 1999. Office of Management and Budget, *FY 2008 Historical Tables* (Washington, D.C.: GPO, 2007), 134.

4. The defense budget has more than doubled in budget authority from $304 billion in FY 2000 to $625 billion in FY 1007 (adjusted for recent action) (table 5.1) and nearly doubled in outlays from $294

billion to $572 billion.(table 3.2). Office of Management and Budget, *FY 2008 Historical Tables* (Washington, D.C.: GPO, 2007), 59–60 and 88–89.

5. Defense discretionary outlays, in constant FY 2000 dollars, have increased from $295 billion in FY 2000 to a projected $444 billion in FY 2008. Office of Management and Budget, *FY 2008 Historical Tables* (Washington, D.C.: GPO, 2007), 134.

6. Reflected in Budget Function 050. For an explanation of budget functions, see chapter 2-9.

7. House of Representatives, Joint Explanatory Statement of the Committee of Conference on S.Con.Res. 21, Concurrent Resolution on the Budget for Fiscal Year 2008, 110th Cong., 1st sess., 2007, H.Rept. 110-153, 26.

8. Transformation as described by Pat Towell in "Foreign Affairs, Defense, and Trade: Key Issues of the 110th Congress," RL33760 (Washington, D.C.: Congressional Research Service, December 20, 2006), 52. For more information on "Defense Transformation," see Ronald O'Rouke, "Defense Transformation: Background and Oversight Issues for Congress, RL3228 (Washington, D.C.: Congressional Research Service, April 16, 2007).

9. Public Law 98–94 provided for accrual funding of the military retirement system and for the establishment of a Department of Defense Military Retirement Fund in 1985. The fund has three sources of income: payments from the Military Personnel accounts (reflected here), which *cover the accruing costs of the future retirement benefits being earned by today's service members*; interest on investments of the fund in Treasury securities; and payments from the Treasury to cover a portion of the accrued unfunded liability for all the retirees and current members who had earned benefits *before* the accrual funding system was set up and to cover the liability for concurrent receipt of military retired pay and disability compensation paid by the Department of Veterans' Affairs (see chapter 3-2). This benefit was added in the 2004 National Defense Authorization Act (P.L. 108–136). Approximately 35% to 40% of military basic pay costs must be added to the DOD personnel budget each fiscal year to cover the future retirement costs of those personnel who ultimately retire from the military. Office of Management and Budget, FY 2008 Budget of the United States, Appendix (Washington, D.C.: GPO), 939.

10. Military retirement payments are disbursed from the Military Retirement Fund, located in the Income Security Function of the Budget, to current retirees. Since FY1985, an "accrual accounting" system has been used to budget for the costs of military retired pay. Under this system, the DOD personnel budget for each fiscal year includes the estimated amount of money that must be set aside (invested in interest-bearing Treasury securities) to cover future retirement payments for current military personnel; these funds are transferred to the Military Retirement Fund. (See previous note.) The Military Retirement Fund also receives transfers from the Treasury to cover the initial unfunded liability of the military retirement system (i.e., the total future cost of military retired pay that will result from military service performed *prior to* the implementation of accrual accounting in FY1985). Technically, because retirement benefits are paid to individuals from the Military Retirement Fund, and not from the DoD Budget, the Federal Budget shows military retirement outlays as part of the Income Security function of the Federal Budget and not as part of the Defense Budget. However, because payments to military retirees are clearly a cost of national defense, this book includes those payments as "defense-related expenditures." See also Charles Henning, "Military Retirement: Major Legislative Issues," IB85159 (Washington, D.C.: Congressional Research Service, March 14, 2006), 5–6.

11. As noted earlier, defense budget authority has more than doubled since FY2000.

12. The President's Budget (historical table 8.2) shows outlays adjusted for inflation, but not budget authority. See chapter 2-9 for an explanation of budget authority vs. outlays.

13. Office of Management and Budget, *FY 2008 Historical Tables* (Washington, D.C.: GPO, 2007), 133–34. This table shows defense outlays in "constant FY 2000" dollars; that is, it takes actual outlays in FY 2000 and adjusts prior years and subsequent years for inflation, enabling an apples-to-apples comparison of defense spending in the covered years, 1962 through 2007.

14. The U.S. economy, as measured by GDP, far outstrips any other nation. The top 10 economies, in terms of 2006 GDP (purchasing power parity) are United States, $12.98 trillion; China, $10 trillion; Japan, $4.22 trillion; India, $4.04 trillion; Germany, $2.58 trillion; UK, $1.9 trillion; France, $1.87 trillion; Italy, $1.73 trillion; Russia, $1.72 trillion; and Brazil, $1.61 trillion. Central Intelligence Agency, *The World Factbook*, https://www.cia.gov/library/publications/the-world-factbook/index.html (accessed June 4, 2007).

15. Testimony of CBO Director Peter Orszag before the Committee on the Budget, U.S. House of Representatives, October 24, 2007. See also Amy Belasco, "The Cost of Iraq, Afghanistan, and Other Global War on Terror Operations since 9/11," RL33110 (Washington, D.C.: Congressional Research Service, July 16, 2007).

16. Analysis by Steven Kosiak, budget analyst at the Center for Strategic and Budgetary Assessments, as reported by CQ.com, February 5, 2007 (Washington, D.C.: Congressional Quarterly, 2007). See also a comparison of U.S. war costs at http://www.csmonitor.com/2005/0829/p15s01-cogn.html#chart.

17. Linda Bilmes (Kennedy School, Harvard University) and Joseph Stiglitz (Columbia University), "The Economic Costs of the Iraq War: An Appraisal Three Years after the Beginning of the Conflict," January 2006, http://ksgnotes1.harvard.edu/research/wpaper.NSF/RWP/RWP06-002.

18. The Stiglitz-Bilmes study was updated in the Milken Institute Review, 4th quarter 2006, http://www.milkeninstitute.org/publications/review/2006_12/76_83mr32.pdf.

19. Milken Institute Review, 79. PBS: "Experts Calculate Billions in Long-term Costs of War," http://www.pbs.org/newshour/bb/middle_east/jan-june07/warcost_05-22.html (accessed May 30, 2007).

20. In 2005, the Army, Army National Guard, and Army Reserve fell short of recruiting goals. Congress responded by increasing the maximum enlistment bonus from $20,000 to $40,000, and DoD increased the number of recruiters. As a result, the active Army met its 2006 recruiting target, however only two of the six reserve components met their targets. Charles Henning, "Military Pay and Benefits: Key Questions and Answers," RL33446 (Washington, D.C.: Congressional Research Service, January 24, 2007).

21. Linda Bilmes and Joseph Stiglitz, "War's Stunning Price Tag," *Los Angeles Times*, January 17, 2006.

22. Scott Wallsten, AEI-Brookings Joint Center, "The Economic Cost of the Iraq War," *The Economists Voice* (2006) http://www.bepress.com/ev/vol3/iss2/art1. Steven Davis, Kevin Murphy, Robert Topel, University of Chicago, "War in Iraq versus Containment," February 15, 2006, http://faculty.chicagogsb.edu/steven.davis/research/War_in_Iraq_versus_Containment_(15February2006).pdf.

23. Marc Labonte, "Financing Issues and Economic Effects of American Wars," RL31176 (Washington, D.C.: Congressional Research Service, October 6, 2006), 15–16. See also: Brian Faler, "Bush Breaks 150-Year History of Higher U.S. Taxes in Wartime," *Bloomberg.com*, http://www.bloomberg.com/apps/news?pid=washingtonstory&sid=aCg_jCpWuAXU.

24. N. Serafino, C. Tarnoff, D. Nanto, "U.S. Occupation Assistance: Iraq, Germany and Japan Compared," RL33331 (Washington, D.C.: Congressional Research Service, January 4, 2007), summary page.

25. Edward Bruner, "Military Forces: What Is the Appropriate Size for the United States?" RS21754 (Washington, D.C.: Congressional Research Service, January 4, 2007), 1.

26. Congressional Budget Office, "Estimated Cost of the Administration's Proposal to Increase the Army's and the Marine Corps's Personnel Levels" (Washington, D.C.: Author, April 16, 2007). As explained by CBO, "military personnel levels are often expressed in terms of 'end strength,' which is the maximum number of personnel each of the military services is authorized to have on the last day of the fiscal year" (footnote 1). This growth is compared to the levels proposed in the 2006 QDR, a 4-year planning document. Actual growth is less since the Congress had already authorized and funded on a temporary emergency basis personnel levels above the 2006 QDR recommended levels.

27. S. Daggett et al., "FY 2007 Supplemental Appropriations for Defense, Foreign Affairs, and Other Purposes," RL33900 (Washington, D.C.: May 2, 2007), footnote 20.

28. Daggett, "Supplemental Appropriations," 44.

29. QDR can be accessed at http://www.defenselink.mil/qdr/.

30. CBO, "Proposal to Increase the Army's and the Marine Corps's Personnel Levels," 1.

31.As members of the Reserves, National Guardsmen (Army and Air National Guard) can be called to Federal active duty in the same way as other reservists. In such an instance, control passes from the Governor to the President. For further information on the Guard and Reserves, see Lawrence Kapp, "Reserve Component Personnel Issues: Questions and Answer," RL3082 (Washington, D.C.: Congressional Research Service, January 26, 2007), 6.

32. Ready Reserve excludes the Retired Reserve and the Standby Reserve (those individuals who have a temporary disability or hardship and those who hold key defense related positions in their civilian lives). Kapp, "Reserve Component Personnel Issues," 3–4.

33. Kapp, "Reserve Component Personnel Issues," 10.

34. Statement of Janet A. St. Laurent, Director Defense Capabilities and Management, Government Accountability Office, "DoD Needs to Provide a Better Link between Its Defense Strategy and Military Personnel Requirements," Hearing before the Subcommittee on Military Personnel, House Committee on Armed Services, January 30, 2007. See also Carl Conetta, "No Good Reason to Boost Army, Marine Corps End Strength," Briefing Report #20 (Cambridge, MA: Project on Defense Alternatives, Commonwealth Institute, January 31, 2007).

35. CBO, "NATO Burdensharing after Enlargement," August 2001, summary page.

36. Steve Bowman, "Iraq: U.S. Military Operations," RL31701 (Washington, D.C.: Congressional Research Service, May 15, 2007), summary page.

37. Nina Serafino, "Peacekeeping and Related Stability Operations: Issues of U.S. Military Involvement," RL33557 (Washington, D.C.: Congressional Research Service, January 24, 2007), 11.

38. Source: http://www.heritage.org/Research/NationalSecurity/troopMarch2005.xls.

39. Emma Chanlett-Avery, "Japan-U.S. Relations: Issues for Congress," RL33436 (Washington, D.C.: Congressional Research Service, March 28, 2007), summary page.

40. JoAnne O'Bryant and Michael Waterhouse, "U.S. Forces in Afghanistan," RS22633 (Washington, D.C.: Congressional Research Service, March 30, 2007), 1.

41. The Taliban allowed Afghanistan to be a haven for Islamic militants including Osama bin Laden, leader of al-Qaeda. The Taliban refused to extradite bin Laden to the U.S. following the attacks of 9/11.

42. Julie Kim and Steven Woehrel, "Kosovo and U.S. Policy: Background and Current Issues," RL31053 (Washington, D.C.: Congressional Research Service, April 26, 2007), 20.

43. Located on the northeast coast of the horn of Africa.

44. Lauren Plock, "Africa Command: U.S. Strategic Interests and the Role of the U.S. Military in Africa," RL34003 (Washington, D.C.: Congressional Research Service, May 16, 2007), summary page.

45. Source: http://www.mfo.org/1/9/46/base.asp.

46.Richard Grimmett, "Instances of Use of United States Armed Forces Abroad, 1798-2006," RL32170 (Washington, D.C.: Congressional Research Service, January 8, 2007), 39. See also Julie Kim, "Bosnia: Overview of Current Issues," RS22324 (Washington, D.C., Congressional Research Service, March 7, 2007).

47. Kristin Archick and Paul Gallis, "NATO and the European Union," RL32342 (Washington, D.C.: Congressional Research Service, January 23, 2007), 5–8.

48. Larry Niksch, "Korea-U.S. Relations: Issues for Congress," RL33567 (Washington, D.C.: Congressional Research Service, February 23, 2007), 27–28.

49. Niksch, "Korea-U.S. Relations," 23–27.

50. George Siehl and Edward Knight, "Military Base Closures since 1988," 96-562F (Washington, D.C.: Congressional Research Service, February 26, 2997), 2.

51. Christopher Davis, "Fast Track Congressional Consideration of Recommendations of the Base Realignment and Closure (BRAC) Commission," RS22144 (Washington, D.C.: Congressional Research Service, May 12, 2005), 6.

52. The downsizing is called a "major base realignment," which is defined as one with a net loss of 400 or more military and civilian personnel. "Military Base Closures," GAO-07-166 (Washington, D.C.: Government Accountability Office, January 2007), 7.

53. H.R. 2206 (110th Congress, 1st sess.).

54. See http://www.tricare.osd.mil/planning/congress/downloads/2006/04-04-06SASCChuWinken werderOMBFinal.pdf.

55. See Tom Philpott, "Struggle to Enact Fee Hikes Continues," *HeraldNet.com*, April 15, 2006.

56. GAO, "Defense Health Care," July 2005, letter to Chairmen Warner and Hunter.

57. Members of the Guard and Reserve get early access to TRICARE upon notification of call-up and have continued access to TRICARE for six months following active duty service for themselves and their families. Testimony before the Senate Armed Services Committee, Subcommittee on Personnel, April 4, 2006, p. 13.

58. Includes unmarried children under 21, full-time college students under 23, and most severely disabled unmarried children regardless of age.

59. In addition to covering the Army, Navy, Marine Corps, Air Force, and Coast Guard, TRICARE also covers two other uniformed services, the Public Health Service and the National Oceanic and Atmospheric Administration.

60. In addition, military retirees continue to be eligible for health care at military facilities on a space available basis.

61. See http://www.tricare.osd.mil/reserve/reserveselect/index.cfm.

62. The Rand Corporation Center for Military Health Policy Research, Statement of Susan Hosek before the Senate Armed Services Committee, Subcommittee on Personnel, April 21, 2005.

63. Charles A. Henning, "Military Retirement: Major Legislative Issues," RL33449 (Washington, D.C.: Congressional Research Service, March 14, 2006), 1.

64. Henning, "Military Retirement," 3–6.

65. *FY 2004 DOD Statistical Report on the Military Retirement System* (Washington, D.C.: DoD Office of the Actuary, September 30, 2004), 90, 105, http://www.defenselink.mil/actuary/statbook04.pdf.

66. Research and development of missile defense systems actually began in the 1950s concurrent with the beginning of the missile age. Steven Hildreth, "Ballistic Missile Defense: Historical Overview," RS22120 (Washington, D.C.: Congressional Research Service, January 5, 2007), 2–3. The $150 billion number is in Miriam Pemberton and Lawrence Korb, "A Unified Security Budget for the United States, FY 2008" (Foreign Policy in Focus, April 2007), 22.

67. Steven Hildreth, "Foreign Affairs, Defense, and Trade: Key Issues for the 110th Congress," RL33760 (Washington, D.C.: Congressional Research Service, December 20, 2006), 60.

68. The ABM Treaty negotiated by the U.S. and the Soviet Union Treaty prohibited the deployment of ABM systems for the defense of either nation's entire territory, the concept being that such a deployment could undermine the nuclear deterrent of the other nation's arsenal. However, the Treaty, as amended in 1974, permitted both countries to deploy one ABM site located either at the nation's capital or around an ICBM deployment area. The Treaty banned sea-based, air-based, space-based, or mobile systems, but it placed no restrictions on defenses against shorter range missiles. Hildreth, "Ballistic Missile Defense," 2.

69. Testimony of Lt. General Henry Obering III, Director, Missile Defense Agency, before the Strategic Forces Subcommittee of the House Armed Services Committee, March 27, 2007.

70. White House, "National Policy on Ballistic Missile Defense Fact Sheet," May 20, 2003, www.white-house.gov/news/releases/2003/05/print/20030520-15.html.

71. Hildreth, "Ballistic Missile Defense," 1.

72. One report states that "the system has failed in five out of 11 tests since 2004, and none of these tests have been conducted under anything approaching realistic conditions." Miriam Pemberton and

Lawrence Korb, "A Unified Security Budget for the United States, FY 2008" (Foreign Policy in Focus, April 2007), 23.

73. "Russia Tests New Ballistic Missile," *New York Times*, May 30, 2007, A12, reports, Russia successfully launched a new intercontinental ballistic missile as President Vladimir Putin "again chided the West for American-led plans to install an antimissile shield in Europe." Russian officials also "pointedly said that the new missile, known as the RS-24, had been fired from a mobile launcher and that it could carry as many as six warheads that could not be defeated by current or future missile-defense systems."

74. Steven Hildreth, "Missile Defense: The Current Debate" and Government Accountability Office, "Missile Defense Acquisition Strategy Generates Results but Delivers Less at a Higher Cost," GAO-07-387, March 2007.

75. Department of Energy, FY 2008 Budget Request to Congress, http://www.mbe.doe.gov/budget/08budget/Start.htm.

76. Janathan Medalia, "Nuclear Warheads: The Reliable Replacement Warhead Program and the Life Extension Program," RL33748 (Washington, D.C.: Congressional Research Service, May 7, 2007). See also National Nuclear Security Administration, Department of Energy, Testimony of Thomas P.D'Agostino, Administrator, before the House Committee on Armed Services, March 20, 2007; and "Weaponeers of Waste: A Critical Look at the Bush Administration Energy Department's Nuclear Weapons Complex and the First Decade of Science-Based Stockpile Stewardship" (Washington, D.C.: Natural Resources Defense Council, April 2004).

77. Letter accompanying U.S. Government Accountability Office, "Defense Acquisitions: assessments of Selected Weapon Programs," GAO-07-406SP (Washington, D.C.: March 2007), 1.

78. Pat Towell, "Foreign Affairs, Defense, and Trade: Key Issues of the 110th Congress," RL33760 (Washington, D.C.: Congressional Research Service, December 20, 2006), 52.

79. Transformation as described by Pat Towell in "Foreign Affairs, Defense, and Trade: Key Issues of the 110th Congress," RL33760 (Washington, D.C.: Congressional Research Service, December 20, 2006), 52. For more information on "Defense Transformation," see Ronald O'Rouke, "Defense Transformation: Background and Oversight Issues for Congress, RL3228 (Washington, D.C.: Congressional Research Service, April 16, 2007).

80. Towell, "Foreign Affairs, Defense, and Trade," 53; Miriam Pemberton and Lawrence Korb, "A Unified Security Budget for the United States, FY 2008" (Foreign Policy in Focus, April 2007), 22-24; GAO, "Defense Acquisitions."

81. GAO, "Defense Acquisitions," 11.

82.GAO, "Defense Acquisitions," 9.

83. Eigen and Sigel, *The Macmillan Dictionary of Political Quotation*, 179.

84. The Director of National Intelligence released the total amount appropriated for national intelligence for FY 2007, as required by the 9/11 Commission implementing legislation (P.L. 110-53). However, no details below the top line will be released, and the requirement to release total funding is applicable to fiscal years 2007 and 2008 only. See www.dni.gov/press_releases/20071030_release.pdf.

85. However, on January 9, 2007, the House established (H.Res. 35, 110th Congress) a select panel within the House Appropriations Committee that includes three members of the Permanent Select Committee on Intelligence to review intelligence funding issues, although the panel does not have any legislative authority. Richard Best, "Intelligence Issues for Congress," RL33539 (Washington, D.C.: Congressional Research Service, May 16, 2007), 7.

86. According to CRS, "funding for most intelligence activities included in the defense appropriations bills is not identified as such either in legislation itself or in the accompanying reports, but does appear in classified annexes to the reports which Senators and Representatives can read under guidelines designed to protect secrecy." Thomas Nicola, "9/11 Commission Recommendations: Intelligence Budget," RL32609 (Washington, D.C.: Congressional Research Service, September 27, 2004), 4.

87. The MIP is comprised of the former Joint Military Intelligence Program, or JMIP, that funded programs related to defense-wide intelligence requirements; and the Tactical Intelligence and Related Activities, or TIARA budget, which funded tactical military intelligence programs managed by the military services. JMIP and TIARA were combined by the Defense Department into the MIP in September 2005. Richard Best and Elizabeth Bazan, "Intelligence Spending: Public Disclosure Issues," 94-261 (Washington, D.C.: Congressional Research Service, February 15, 2007), 3.

88. P.L. 108-458 (108th Congress, 2d sess.). See also *The 9/11 Commission Report: Final Report of the National Commission on Terrorist Attacks upon the United States* (New York: Norton, 2004), 412; and Richard Best, Alfred Cumming, and Todd Masse, "Director of National Intelligence: Statutory Authorities," RS22112 (Washington, D.C.: Congressional Research Service, January 30, 2007).

89. See chapter 2-3 on apportionment. The 2004 Act provides that the Director of OMB, at the exclusive direction of the DNI, will apportion funds to intelligence agencies.

90. Best et al., "Director of National Intelligence," 3-5.

91. The National Security Agency has an estimated 40,000 military and civilian personnel." Hayden's Code," *GovExec.Com*, October 15, 2004.

92. See http://ftp.fas.org/irp/agency/daro/daroorg.htm.

93. Based on estimates from "The Intelligence Community," *National Journal* (March 19, 2005); Doyle McManus and Peter Spiegel, "Spy Czar, Rumsfeld in a Turf War," *Los Angeles Times*, May 6, 2006; www.globalsecurity.org/intell/library/budget/index.html (accessed June 2, 2007); and http://www.thespywhobilledme.com/the_spy_who_billed_me/2007/06/exclusive_offic.html (accessed June 4, 2007). However, because the intelligence budget is classified, the reliability of these estimates cannot be verified.

94. Best, "Intelligence Issues for Congress," 8.

95. Doyle McManus and Peter Spiegel, "Spy Czar, Rumsfeld in a Turf War," *Los Angeles Times*, May 6, 2006.

96. In 2002, Eleanor Hill, Staff Director of a joint Senate-House Intelligence investigation of the September 11 attacks summarized the inquiry's findings: "the Intelligence Community did have general indications of a possible terrorist attack against the United States or U.S. interests overseas in the spring and summer of 2001 and promulgated strategic warnings. However, it does not appear that the Intelligence Community had information prior to September 11 that identified precisely where, when and how the attacks were to be carried out Best, "Intelligence Issues for Congress," 8.

97. See CRS, "U.S. Intelligence and Policymaking: The Iraq Experience," December 2, 2005, 2, which states in part, "the prewar intelligence estimate that Iraq was reconstituting an extensive nuclear programs [sic] was in large measure discredited." See also Best, "Intelligence Issues for Congress," 13, which cites the report of the Commission on the Intelligence Capabilities of the United States Regarding WMDs (www.wmd.gov/report/index.html). According to CRS "the report described in detail a number of analytical errors that resulted in faulty pre-war judgments on Iraq's WMDs."

98. Interview, PBS, *MacNeil-Lehrer News Hour*, September 12, 1991, as quoted in Eigen and Sigel, *The Macmillan Dictionary of Political Quotations*, 100. See also "An Interview with former CIA analyst Melvin Goodman," www.cnn.com/SPECIALS/cold.war/episodes/21/interviews/goodman/, 5.

99. *The 9/11 Commission Report*, 380.

100. Section 302(f) of the Congressional Budget Act, as explained in chapter 2-4.

101. *The 9/11 Commission Report*, 380.

102. Budget function 050.

103. Letter Appropriations Subcommittees on Homeland Security, *Subject: Combating Nuclear Smuggling* (Washington, D.C.: Government Accountability Office, October 17, 2006).

104. Linda-Jo Schierow, "Chemical Facility Security," RL31530 (Washington, D.C.: Congressional Research Service, December 15, 2006), 11–15.

105. Farewell address, January 17, 1961. Daniel B. Baker, *Political Quotations* (Detroit, MI: Gale Research, 1990), 237.

Department of Homeland Security

FY 2007 DHS Spending: $43 billion[1]
Less than 1.5% of Federal Spending

See www.GovBudget.com for updated numbers

In a Nutshell

The primary mission of the Department of Homeland Security (DHS) is to prevent terrorist attacks in the United States in the aftermath of 9/11. In establishing DHS, the Homeland Security Act of 2002 brought together 22 agencies with responsibility for emergency planning, as well as securing the borders and coastal waters, transportation systems, ports, critical infrastructure, and the nation's leadership.[2] For FY 2007, the Department's budget (including supplemental appropriations) is $43 billion, including appropriations for the Federal Emergency Management Agency (FEMA), homeland security grants to State and local governments, the Coast Guard, U.S. Customs and Border Protection (CBP), Immigration and Customs Enforcement (ICE), U.S. Citizenship and Immigration Services (USCIS), the Transportation Security Administration (TSA) and Air Marshals, the Domestic Nuclear Detection Office (DNDO), and the Secret Service. Because of the wide range of activities conducted by the various agencies, *more than one-third of DHS expenditures are unrelated to homeland security.*

Background

The most difficult part of explaining what our country is spending on homeland security is defining what "homeland security" spending actually includes. There are two reasons why DHS spending cannot be equated with actual expenditures on "homeland security."

First, as reflected in figure 3-2.1, in FY 2007 less than two-thirds of the funding appropriated to the Department of Homeland Security was used for homeland security activities. This reflects the broad responsibilities of the various agencies.

FIGURE 3-2.1 Department of Homeland Security Spending in FY 2007

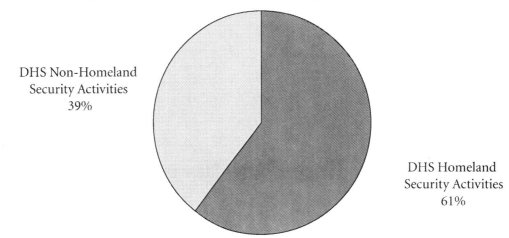

DHS Non-Homeland
Security Activities
39%

DHS Homeland
Security Activities
61%

Second, a number of homeland security programs or activities are located in other departments such as the BioShield program at the Department of Health and Human Services and nuclear nonproliferation and counterterrorism operations at the Departments of Defense and Justice.

FY 2007 DHS Budget Authority in billions of dollars
(including supplemental appropriations)

Program/Activity	FY 2007*	Description
Programs/activities related to homeland security		
Customs and Border Protection (CBP)	$9.6 b	CBP is responsible for inspecting travelers at land, sea, air ports of entry for immigration and customs compliance.
Transportation Security Administration (TSA)	$6.6 b	Screening of passengers and cargo at airports. ($2.3 b in security fees offset the TSA budget.) Also includes $719 m for air marshals.
Immigration and Customs Enforcement (ICE)	$4.2 b	Investigation/enforcement of immigration and customs laws
State and local grant programs	$3.7 b	State and local homeland security (details in table 3-1.1)
Coast Guard	$2.6 b	Coastal and other defense operations (30% of CG budget)
Secret Service	$1.5 b	Protection of officials, buildings (and lead agency on counterfeiting and other financial fraud crimes)

Program/Activity	FY 2007*	Description
National Protection and Programs Directorate	$973 million	US-VISIT (monitors entry & exit of aliens), infrastructure protection, cybersecurity. emergency communications
Science and Technology	$853 million	Detection, destruction of chemical/biological agents and conventional explosives; research on interoperability
Domestic Nuclear Detection Office	$581 million	Detect and identify the origins of nuclear and radiological materials
Rail, transit, trucking, bus security (administered by TSA)	$ 37 million	Entire TSA budget for surface transportation is $37 million. ($399 million included in "state and local grants" is also aimed at improving surface transportation security.)
Other	$1.4 b	DHS operations, Inspector General, Law Enforcement Training Center
Non–Homeland Security Programs/Activities		
FEMA Disaster Relief	$10 b	Preparing for disasters, coordinating response efforts, providing recovery assistance, and working to mitigate risks of future disasters
Coast Guard (non-HS)	$5.9 b	Search & rescue, marine safety, navigation support, ice operations, environmental protection, marine resources, law enforcement, drug interdiction
Citizenship and Immigration Services (USCIS)	$2 b	Processes all applications for citizenship, work authorization, residency, asylum, and refugee status.
National Flood Insurance Program	$2.8 b	Covers flood losses, which are rarely covered by private insurers. (This reflects gross spending, which is offset in the budget by insurance premiums.)

*Adjusted to reflect '07 Supplemental Appropriations. See www.GovBudget.com for updated numbers.

Some have suggested that the Homeland Security Act of 2002 merely reshuffled the bureaucracy but didn't add any real money to homeland security. This is a misperception: *total funding for homeland security activities—at DHS and other agencies—has substantially increased since 9/11.* According to CBO's most recent analysis, total funding for homeland security more than doubled between FY 2001 and FY 2006, from $21 billion to nearly $49 billion.[3] *New resources* include funding for TSA to screen all airline passengers and baggage, homeland security grants to state and local governments, and research and development of new preparedness and detection technologies. *Additional resources* have been appropriated to

CBP and ICE for border and customs security, as well as for operations at other departments including DoD funding for security at military bases and domestic counterterrorism activities of the FBI.

The question of whether the establishment of DHS has actually improved the nation's homeland security is a separate issue that will be addressed at the end of this chapter.

State and Local Homeland Security Grants

In a Nutshell

State and local homeland security grants are aimed at improving preparedness of state and local governments, particularly first responders, to respond to terrorist incidents. The numerous grant programs include general state grants and grants focused on law enforcement terrorism prevention; high-threat urban areas; ports, rail, and transit; intercity buses; trucking; buffer zone areas near nuclear plants; national exercises to promote readiness; state and local training; first-responder equipment; technical assistance; medical response; community involvement; rural preparedness; emergency management; and assistance to firefighters. Grants in FY 2007 amounted to $3.7 billion.

Background

A core function of the Department of Homeland Security has been the allocation of State and local homeland security grants. For FY 2007, Congress appropriated funds for numerous types of grants, as reflected in table 3-2.1. The Office of Grant Programs, now part of FEMA, administers the grants, which collectively are aimed at improving the readiness of State and local governments for terrorism incidents and catastrophic events. Much of this assistance is aimed at strengthening "first responders"—that is, police, fire, rescue, and emergency personnel who are first on the scene of a terrorist attack or major disaster.

Two ongoing issues with regard to state and local homeland security preparedness grants have been whether the grant funds are adequate, and whether the allocation process makes sense.

Amount of Funding. With regard to the amount of funding, many have argued that considering the extent to which the nation depends on state and local governments to protect critical infrastructure, identify potential terrorist activity, and respond to emergencies, the total amount of funding is seriously inadequate. Debate on this issue is intensifying given the Administration's reduced requests for FY 2008 funding for state and local grants.

Allocation of Funding. Regarding the allocation of appropriated funds, some have argued that all States and cities should have access to Federal homeland security grants. Others have argued that Congress should allocate the funds based purely on an assessment of risk (i.e., which States and cities are most vulnerable to terrorist attack). The results of this debate have been a gradual evolution from population- to risk-based allocation.

In FY 2004, Congress gave DHS discretion on how to allocate grant funds, and it chose to allocate based on population *rather than* assessments of the highest-risk targets. In FY 2005, Congress *required* that grants be allocated based on population rather than risk. In FY 2006 and FY 2007, Congress gave DHS discretion on how to allocate grant funds, knowing that

TABLE 3-2.1: FY 2007 State and Local Preparedness Grants

(Budget Authority in Millions of Dollars)

Grant	FY 2007 Funding	Purpose/Description
Grants based on risk assessment, but including a minimum state allocation		
State Homeland Security Grants	$533 m*	Grants to States to support the implementation of State homeland security strategies. Grants are allocated by the Secretary on the basis of risk and effectiveness and then adjusted to ensure that each State receives at least 0.25% of the program total.
Law Enforcement Terrorism Prevention Program	$375 m	Grants to law enforcement for terrorism prevention including coordination with other government agencies and the private sector. Allocated on the same basis as state grants (risk with a minimum state allocation).
Discretionary grants based on risk assessment and effectiveness		
Urban Area Security Initiative (High-threat, high-density urban areas)	$805 m*	Grants to address the security needs of high-threat, high-density urban areas and to assist in building a capacity to prevent, respond to, and recover from acts of terrorism
Port Security	$320 m*	Grants to the owners and operators of ports, terminals, passenger vessels and ferries, as well as port authorities and State and local agencies for enhancements to security at the Nation's seaports[5]
Rail and Transit Security	$275 m	Grants to transit systems in high-risk urban areas for the protection of critical infrastructure and preparedness
Intercity Bus Security	$12 m	Grants to owners/operators of fixed route, intercity bus services serving high risk urban areas
Trucking Security	$12 m	Grants to the American Trucking Association to continue the Highway Watch Program
Buffer Zone Protection	$50 m	Grants to increase the preparedness capabilities of jurisdictions responsible for security of communities located around select, high-risk critical infrastructure
National Exercise Program	$49 m	Funds Federal, State, and local exercises for WMD events and other major incidents
State and Local Training Program (National Domestic Preparedness Consortium)	$ 145 m	Supports the unique training facilities managed by the Center for Domestic Preparedness and other members of the National Domestic Preparedness Consortium

(Continued)

TABLE 3-2.1: FY 2007 State and Local Preparedness Grants (Continued)

(Budget Authority in Millions of Dollars)

Grant	FY 2007 Funding	Purpose/Description
CEDAP: Commercial Equipment Direct Assistance Program	$50 m	Equipment for first responders
Technical Assistance, Evaluation	$39 m*	Technical assistance for grantees and program evaluation
Metropolitan Medical Response System	$33 m	MMRS funds local preparedness efforts to respond to all-hazards mass casualty incidents
Citizen Corps	$15 m	Coordinate community involvement in emergency preparedness, response, and recovery
Training Grants	$61 m	Demonstration training grants; continuing training grants
Rural Domestic Preparedness Consortium	$12 m	Earmark for five colleges to develop rural emergency preparedness training
Emergency Management Performance Grants	$250 m*	Assistance for states and local governments in planning and implementing emergency management activities
Assistance to Firefighters	$662 m	Direct assistance for local fire departments: training, equipment, protective gear needed for terrorism response
TOTAL	**$3.698 billion**	State and local homeland security assistance programs

*Includes funding from FY 2007 Supplemental Appropriations.

DHS had decided to move to risk-based grant allocations, resulting in over 80% of the grants being based on risk (with a small state minimum applied to the basic State grant program).[6]

FEMA and Related Programs

In a Nutshell

FEMA has four basic areas of responsibility: preparing for disasters, coordinating emergency response efforts, providing recovery assistance, and working to mitigate risks of future disasters.[7] Much of FEMA's activity is concentrated in response and recovery as reflected in the $10 billion appropriated for the Disaster Relief Fund for FY 2007. The Fund is tapped for presidentially declared "major disasters" and "emergencies." (The amounts appropriated for the Fund vary dramatically from year to year based on the occurrence of disasters and emergencies.)

Background

The Federal Emergency Management Agency was established by President Carter in 1979[8] to centralize disaster prevention, preparedness, and response in a single agency. In its early years, the agency received a great deal of criticism. In response to this criticism, in 1993 President Clinton appointed James Lee Witt, the first professional emergency manager to direct the agency, and elevated the agency to Cabinet-level status. Under Witt, FEMA received considerable praise for improving responsiveness to natural disasters.[9]

Most disaster relief funds are provided by Congress as "emergency spending" (see chapter 2-4) and are therefore outside the constraints of the annual Congressional Budget Resolution. For example, for FY 2007, Congress had (as of June 2007) appropriated $10 billion to FEMA for disaster relief, most of it as emergency spending. The President's request for FY 2008 for FEMA was $2.7 billion, with the expectation that disaster relief would be appropriated on an as-needed emergency basis as the 2008 hurricane season unfolds and other emergency situations arise.

Under a law known as the Stafford Act, "major disasters" (e.g., hurricanes, tornadoes, earthquakes, fires, floods, or explosions) or "emergencies" (situations that threaten lives, public safety, or property) may be declared by the President *when a State requests Federal assistance and certifies that the disaster or emergency is beyond the State's capacity to respond.*[10]

Upon presidential declaration of a "major disaster" or "emergency," a broad range of Federal resources automatically become available depending on the type of assistance needed— for example, cash grants for the immediate needs of individuals and families; disaster unemployment assistance; assistance to individuals with special needs; crisis counseling; temporary shelter and housing; and repairs to (and rebuilding of) State, local, and nonprofit infrastructure.[11] Table 3-2.2 summarizes FEMA's functions:

Issue: Moving FEMA to DHS and the Hurricane Katrina debacle

When the Department of Homeland Security was established in 2003, FEMA (along with its 2,600 full-time and 4,000 standby employees) was moved to DHS, the rationale being that disaster response, whether for a natural disaster or a terrorist attack, involves similar activities.

However, given the catastrophically poor performance of FEMA in responding to Hurricanes Katrina and Rita in August 2005,[12] many have questioned the wisdom of the 2002 decision to relocate the previously independent agency to DHS. Irwin Redlener, Director of the National Center for Disaster Preparedness at Columbia University, observed that while Katrina could have overwhelmed any bureaucracy, the problems were made worse because FEMA had been weakened and underfunded when it was moved into DHS.[13]

After a major post-Katrina debate about whether to keep FEMA under the DHS umbrella or reestablish it as an independent agency, Congress decided in 2006 to keep FEMA within DHS but made a number of significant reforms in the Post-Katrina Emergency Management Reform Act of 2006 (Post-Katrina Act).[14] Key among these reforms (effective March 1, 2007):

- Provides FEMA more autonomy within DHS to function as a distinct entity and gives the Administrator (who still reports to the DHS Secretary) a statutory advisory relationship

TABLE 3-2.2. Summary of FEMA's Comprehensive Emergency Management (CEM) Functions[15]

Preparedness	Financial assistance for State and local disaster planning • Coordinates Federal interagency planning for disaster response and continuity of government • Coordinates business and government leaders willing to volunteer for government service in emergency situations • Awards grants to state and local governments for exercises and simulations • Trains first-responder units (firefighters, emergency rescue, hazardous materials teams).
Response	Coordinates delivery of Federal and nonfederal resources to communities stricken by major disasters • Administers funds to nonprofit organizations that aid the homeless[16] • Monitors the response of Federal interagency teams to hazardous material incidents • Awards funds for response associated with storage of chemical agents • Awards assistance to State and local officials responding to major disasters and catastrophic situations.
Recovery	Provides funds to individuals and families in need of temporary shelter or cash grants due to losses incurred in major disasters • Awards grants to state and local governments and nonprofit organizations for the reconstruction or repair of structures • Reimburses National Flood Insurance policy holders for losses from floods • Provides Community Disaster Loans (CDLs) to assist local governments that experience revenue losses as the result of a disaster.[17]
Mitigation	Assists property owners seeking to reduce future losses by elevating, relocating, or reinforcing buildings in disaster-prone areas such as flood plains or earthquake zones • Awards grants to help non-federal fire agencies fight wildfires before they result in more catastrophic losses • Publishes flood zone maps and funds efforts to update the maps • Provides technical assistance and funding for updating land use plans and building codes • Funds efforts to prevent terrorist attacks.

to the President and the Homeland Security Council during emergencies, as well as authority to make recommendations directly to Congress;

- Reintegrates into FEMA the "preparedness" function for disasters (which had been moved from FEMA to a Preparedness Directorate when DHS was created) and requires the FEMA Administrator to establish a comprehensive National Preparedness System and a national exercise program to evaluate the nation's preparedness;
- Includes in FEMA's preparedness responsibilities, the administration of the State and local first-responder grants;
- Establishes a Disability Coordinator and a Small State and Rural Advocate inside FEMA;
- Establishes regional offices and working groups to improve Federal, State, and local coordination; and
- Tasks FEMA with establishing a National Emergency Family Registry and Locator System, planning for continuity of government, and responsibility for distribution of homeland security grants to State and local governments.[18]

FEMA's Response to Hurricane Katrina

Senate Report (2006): "Hurricane Katrina was . . . the most destructive disaster in American history, laying waste to 90,000 square miles of land, an area the size of the United Kingdom. . . . [M]ore than 1,500 people died. . . . [T]he suffering that continued in the days and weeks after the storm passed . . . continued longer than it should have because of . . . the failure of government at all levels to plan, prepare for and respond aggressively to the storm. These failures . . . were pervasive."[19]

House Report (2006): "The Select Committee identified failures at all levels of government that significantly undermined and detracted from the heroic efforts of first responders, private individuals and organizations, faith-based groups, and others. . . . The preparation for and response to Hurricane Katrina show . . . that we are woefully incapable of storing, moving, and accessing information—especially in times of crisis. . . . The Select Committee believes Katrina was primarily a failure of initiative."[20]

Courtesy: The Times-Picayune

GAO (2006): "Hurricane Katrina raised major questions about our nation's readiness and ability to respond to catastrophic disasters."[21] "Over 50,000 National Guard and 20,000 active (military) personnel participated in the response. . . . [N]one of the exercises that were conducted prior to Katrina had called for a major deployment of DOD capabilities to respond to a catastrophic hurricane."[22]

In addition, responding to widespread criticism of former FEMA Administrator Michael Brown's lack of emergency management experience, the legislation also instructed the President to nominate an administrator who has "a demonstrated ability in and knowledge of emergency management and homeland security" and has "not less than 5 years of executive leadership and management experience in the public or private sector." However, the President's "signing statement," a document often issued by the White House when a bill is signed into law, asserts the provision could rule out good candidates and the provision will be interpreted "in a manner consistent with the Appointments Clause of the Constitution."[23] Translation: White House attorneys believe the bill's qualifications requirement abridges the President's constitutional appointment authority, and the Administration does not consider itself to be bound by the new requirement.[24]

Issue: The Escalating Costs of the Gulf Coast Hurricanes.

As of June 2007, the combined costs of Federal assistance (spending and tax relief) in response to Hurricanes Katrina and Rita reached $128.8 billion, far more than any other domestic emergency, as reflected in table 3-2.3.[25]

Moreover, Federal spending and tax relief dispensed thus far may only be the tip of the iceberg. In June 2007, GAO reported that "while the federal government has provided billions of dollars in assistance to the Gulf Coast, a substantial portion of this aid was directed to short-term needs, leaving a smaller portion for long-term rebuilding. . . . [T]he Congressional Budget Office put capital losses resulting from Hurricanes Katrina and Rita in the range of $70 billion to $130 billion. . . . [T]he State of Louisiana estimates that the economic impact on its state alone would reach $200 billion."[26]

Emergency Food and Shelter Program

Tucked away inside FEMA, and now under the huge umbrella of DHS, is a small $151 million program (small, that is, by Federal standards) called the Emergency Food and Shelter Program (EFSP). EFSP is one of the best examples of a highly effectively public-nonprofit

TABLE 3-2.3 Comparison of Federal Response to Domestic Emergencies
(in inflation-adjusted constant 2006 dollars)

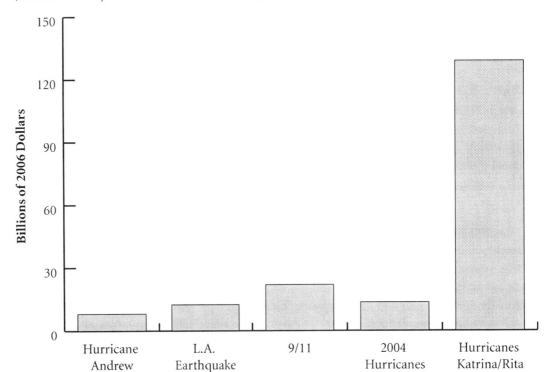

Source: Senate Budget Committee, June 4, 2007.

partnership. EFSP was established in 1983 to help meet the needs of hungry and homeless people throughout the United States by allocating Federal funds for the provision of emergency food and shelter. The program is governed by a national board composed of representatives of the American Red Cross; Catholic Charities, USA; United Jewish Communities; The National Council of the Churches of Christ in the U.S.A.; The Salvation Army; and United Way of America. The Board is chaired by a representative from FEMA. During its 20 years of operation, the program has disbursed over $2 billion to over 11,000 local providers in more than 2,500 counties and cities. The program has very little overhead and no government bureaucracy. It gets money out the door to soup kitchens, food banks, shelters, and homeless prevention services quickly and efficiently.

National Flood Insurance Program

The National Flood Insurance Program (NFIP) was established to reduce flood losses through flood hazard identification, flood plain management (by encouraging land use controls and building codes), and insurance protection in a market rarely covered by private insurers.

If you have a homeowner's policy, you know that flooding is excluded from your coverage. Because of the catastrophic nature of flooding and the likelihood of flooding along many bodies of water, private insurance companies have largely been unwilling to underwrite and bear the risk of flood insurance.[28] Nevertheless, "flooding has been the most common natural disaster in the U.S., costing more in property damages than any other natural disaster."[29]

In response to the increasing cost of damages caused by flooding, in 1968 Congress established the NFIP (1) to make flood insurance widely available; and (2) to reduce flood damage by encouraging states and cities—through various incentives—to establish land use controls and building codes.[30] NFIP, administered by FEMA, offers flood insurance to all homeowners, renters, and business owners—regardless of risk—provided their communities use the NFIP's strategies for reducing flood risk.[31] In order to spread the costs of flood insurance claims, Federal law requires that *all* property owners in high-risk areas purchase NFIP policies—although compliance has been a problem.

In an October 2005 report, GAO found that "the NFIP . . . is not actuarially sound" because it does not collect sufficient premiums to meet future expected flood losses.[32] The GAO points out, though, that this imbalance is "by design" reflecting a policy decision by Congress to subsidize premiums for high-risk properties.[33] The imbalance is covered by authorizing the program to borrow from the Treasury. Due to Hurricanes Katrina and Rita in 2005, the program's borrowing authority had to be increased in late 2005 from $3.5 billion to $18.5 billion to pay claims from the two hurricanes.[34]

An ongoing problem in the NFIP is the high cost of paying for repetitively flooded properties (RLPs), which were "grandfathered" into the NFIP when the program was created.[35]

Hurricanes Katrina and Rita raised other policy questions as well. According to CRS, "the disasters have renewed public concerns about reliability of the nation's aging flood control levees and dams . . . what is an acceptable level of risk—especially for low-probability, high-consequence events—and who should bear that risk."[36] The response to these questions could have enormous budgetary consequences.

Transportation Security Administration (TSA)

Targeting travel is at least as powerful a weapon against terrorists as targeting their money. The United States should combine terrorist travel intelligence, operations, and law enforcement in a strategy to intercept terrorists, find terrorist travel facilitators, and constrain terrorist mobility. —The 9/11 Commission[37]

In a Nutshell

The Transportation Security Administration (TSA), with an FY '07 budget of $6.6 billion and 49,000 employees, is responsible for securing the nation's air and surface transportation from all forms of attack. ($2.3 billion in passenger and airline security fees offset TSA spending yielding a net budget of $4.3 billion). The vast majority of TSA's resources are allocated to employing a Federal workforce at the nation's airports to screen passengers and check baggage for weapons and explosives. The Secure Flight program prescreens passengers against terrorist watch lists. Other functions include deploying Federal Air Marshals to deter and defeat attacks on board U.S. airlines, with a budget of $719 million; and security for surface transportation (rail, transit, trucking, and intercity buses) with a minimal budget of $37 million.

Background

Two months after the attacks of 9/11, the President signed into law the Aviation and Transportation Security Act[38] (ATSA) establishing the Transportation Security Administration. The new agency was established to restore confidence in air travel and prevent another 9/11. Although originally part of the Department of Transportation, TSA was integrated into the new Department of Homeland Security in March 2003.

TSA's air security functions include prescreening prospective passengers against terrorism watch lists (the Secure Flight program), screening passengers at the airport with metal detectors and random searches, X-raying carry-on luggage, and screening all checked baggage with explosive detection systems (EDS) equipment. Other air security functions include the security of air cargo, limiting access to restricted areas at airports, securing airport perimeters, and conducting background checks for baggage handlers and other airport personnel.

In 2003, the Federal Air Marshall program was moved from TSA to ICE, but it was transferred back to TSA in 2006.

TSA got high marks for meeting its original benchmarks. In less than 6 months, TSA trained more than 25,000 individuals to be federal screeners[39] and installed 1,000 explosive detection system machines and 6,000 tabletop explosive trace detection (ETD) machines at commercial airports.[40] However, TSA's management practices and effectiveness, as well as Congress's funding decisions, have been subject to criticism in a number of important areas.

Issues

- Significant concerns have been raised about the lack of security for surface transportation, particularly passenger rail systems and commuter trains, given the attacks in Mumbai, London, Madrid, and Moscow. In addition, security experts are concerned about attacks on hazardous materials carriers, as well as the vulnerability of imported cargo containers to tampering during transportation to their destinations. Over 11 million marine cargo containers enter the U.S. annually, as well as 11 million truckloads of cargo and over 2 million railcars.[41] Despite these vulnerabilities, the total TSA appropriations for truck, rail and other surface transportation is *only $37 million*, with an additional $399 million appropriated in FY 2007 through the State and local grants programs. This raises, once again, the issue of the imbalance between defense and homeland security spending and the need to view both as part of a single national security budget. (See chapter 3-1.) For example, reducing the defense research and development, and procurement budgets by only 1% would free up enough funds to increase surface transportation security funding to over $2 billion annually.[42]
- TSA has had major problems implementing a system to prescreen air passengers. A controversy over detecting potential terrorists by "mining personal data" led to TSA scrapping its proposed Computer Assisted Passenger Prescreening (CAPPS II) program in 2004. CAPPS II is being replaced by a new system called "Secure Flight," although similar concerns about data protection, falsely identifying passengers as terror risks, and mismanagement of costs have delayed implementation of the new system.[43]
- TSA has also faltered in implementing the 9/11 Commission's recommendation that it give priority attention to implementing technology and procedures for screening passengers for explosives. TSA has been testing so-called puffer machines, which would be a secondary walk-through device following the current metal detectors, but the technology is still not deployed.[44]
- While current policies are aimed at ensuring that all passenger baggage is screened prior to a flight, only a small amount of air cargo is screened. According to the Senate Appropriations Committee, more than 50,000 tons of air cargo are transported each day, of which 7,500 tons is on domestic passenger aircraft; a majority of that cargo "is not inspected and virtually none is screened for radiation."[45] In FY 2007, Congress appropriated only $55 million for the task of screening air cargo.[46]
- TSA has not developed a strategy for reducing the risks associated with U.S.-bound air cargo.[47]
- Currently a majority of the 800,000 airport employees are not screened before entering secure areas of their respective airports.[48]

Customs, Border Protection, and Immigration

The border and immigration system of the United States must remain a visible manifestation of our belief in freedom, democracy, global economic growth, and the rule of law, yet serve equally well as a vital element of counterterrorism. —The 9/11 Commission[49]

In a Nutshell

U.S. Customs and Border Protection (CBP), with a budget of $9.6 billion and more than 44,000 employees, is responsible for preventing illegal immigrants, terrorists, and weapons of mass destruction from entering the U.S., conducting immigration, customs, and agricultural inspections at air, land, and sea ports of entry, and patrolling 7,500 miles of U.S. borders between ports of entry. **SBI*net*** is the program within CBP responsible for deploying a "virtual-fence" along the southwest border combining high-tech sensors, cameras, and fencing. **U.S. Immigration and Customs Enforcement (ICE),** with a budget of $4.2 billion and nearly 17,000 employees, investigates immigration and customs violations in the interior of the country, including work site enforcement, detention and removal of illegal aliens, and drug interdiction. **U.S. Citizenship and Immigration Services (USCIS),** with a budget of $2 billion, facilitates entry, residence, employment, and naturalization of legal immigrants; and adjudicates (i.e., approves or denies) applications for citizenship, work authorization, residency, asylum, and refugee status.[50] More than 90% of the USCIS budget is offset by immigration fees.[51]

Background

When the attacks of 9/11 occurred, the Congress and Administration were deeply involved in ongoing negotiations over restructuring the U.S. Immigration and Naturalization Service (INS), which had operated as a single agency within the Department of Justice since 1940. Independent commissions, many in Congress, and the last two INS Commissioners, Doris Meisner (1993–2000) and James Ziglar (2001–2003), were in agreement that a single agency could not effectively administer the competing priorities of *providing immigration services* and *enforcing immigration laws.*[52]

The Homeland Security Act of 2002 (HSA)[53] separated those competing functions and placed them in separate agencies within the new Department of Homeland Security. On March 1, 2003, the responsibilities of providing *immigration services* were moved from INS at the Department of Justice to USCIS at the Department of Homeland Security. USCIS func-

FIGURE 3-2.2: Reorganization of INS into DHS

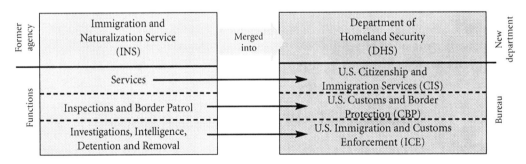

Source: GAO

tions include facilitating entry, residence, employment, and naturalization of legal immigrants; and adjudicating (i.e., approving or denying) millions of applications each year for citizenship,[54] legal permanent resident status,[55] and refugee or asylum status.

The Homeland Security Act of 2002 placed INS's immigration inspections, investigations, detention, removal, and border patrol functions into a Bureau of Border Security and kept the U.S. Customs Service intact. However, in 2003, the President exercised authority provided in the HSA to direct further organizational changes and split up the U.S. Customs Service and the Bureau of Border Security, reconfiguring them into two new agencies: one focused on *security at the border* (CBP) and the other focused on *interior investigations* (ICE). Specifically, **CBP is responsible for:**

- Immigration and customs inspections at all ports of entry (land, sea, and air) in order to detect and prevent the entry of terrorists, weapons of mass destruction (WMDs), unauthorized aliens, and drug smugglers;
- Inspecting all imports and exports for compliance with U.S. law and regulations, collect customs duties, and guard against smuggling of contraband;
- Operating the Container Security Initiative, a program in which CBP inspectors prescreen U.S.-bound marine containers at foreign ports of loading;
- Achieving effective control over U.S. land borders beginning with the southwest border— a program called SBI*net* (part of the Secure Border Initiative);
- Patrolling U.S. borders, in coordination with the Coast Guard to prevent illegal aliens from entering the country and to secure the United States from terrorists (functions implemented by the United States Border patrol (USBP), which is on a projected growth trajectory from about 9,000 agents in 2001 to 18,000 by the end of 2008);[56]
- Conducting passenger and cargo *pre-inspections* at foreign airports and other selected sites abroad;
- Inspecting animals, plants, and agricultural goods; and
- Overseeing issuance of visas by the State Department in a manner consistent with homeland security.

Immigration and Customs Enforcement (ICE), and its more than 11,000 agents,[57] is responsible for (*in order of priority*):[58]

- Detention and removal of criminal aliens;
- Dismantling alien smuggling and trafficking operations;
- Responding to community complaints about illegal immigration;
- Immigrant benefits and document fraud; and
- Employers' use of unauthorized aliens.[59]

In addition, ICE tracks nonimmigrant aliens who pose an "elevated security risk," tracks foreign students studying in the U.S., collects, analyzes and disseminates immigration-related intelligence, and performs the functions of the former Federal Protective Service, securing more than 8,800 federal facilities nationwide.

US-VISIT. CBP and ICE together administer the US-VISIT entry-exit data system that was established to use biometrics (finger scans and digital photography) to track entries *and* exits from the country—a key function for stopping potential terrorists at the borders and curbing illegal immigration by making sure that temporary visitors leave the country when their visas expire.[60] US-VISIT is funded by DHS's National Protection and Programs Directorate.[61]

Issues Relating to Customs, Borders, and Immigration

Issue 1: The Southwest Border Fence

> *Some months before I declared (for the presidency), I asked for a meeting and crossed the border to meet with the president of Mexico. I did not go with a plan. I went, as I said in my announcement address, to ask him his ideas—how we could make the border something other than a locale for a nine-foot fence.*—President Ronald Reagan[62]
>
> Fact: The U.S. border with Mexico, including Texas, New Mexico, Arizona, and California, is 1,933 miles long.[63]

The "Border Fence." In 1990, the U.S. Border Patrol (USBP), an agency now part of CBP, first began erecting near San Diego a 10-foot-high welded steel barrier known as the "primary fence" to deter illegal entries and drug smuggling.[64] In addition to the 14-mile barrier near San Diego, the Border Patrol erected stretches of primary fencing near other population centers: Yuma, Tucson, El Centro, and El Paso. In 1996 Congress authorized construction of a secondary layer of fencing in the San Diego sector, and authority to expedite completion of the San Diego fence was provided in the REAL ID Act of 2005.[65] In 2006, Congress passed the Secure Fence Act,[66] which directs DHS to construct five separate stretches of fencing, lights, cameras and electronic sensors (SBI*net*) along the southwest border totaling 850 miles.[67]

Implementing the Secure Fence Act comes with a high price tag. For FY 2007, Congress appropriated $1.5 billion for "border security fencing, infrastructure, and technology."[68] The FY 2008 Homeland Security Appropriations bills working their way through Congress call for another $1 billion. The Administration's projected total cost for completing work at the southwest border is $7.6 billion from fiscal years 2007 through 2011, although DHS's inspector general warned in November 2006 that the cost could rise to *$30 billion.*[69]

According to GAO, "of this total, approximately $5.1 billion is for the design, development, integration, and deployment of fencing, roads, vehicle barriers, sensors, radar units, and command, control, and communications and other equipment, and $2.5 billion is for. . .logistics and operations. . . . [W]ork on the northern border is not projected to begin before fiscal year 2009."[70]

There is cause to be skeptical about the billions that will be spent on border fencing. According to a 2007 report to Congress:

> In the limited urban areas where border fencing has been constructed, it has typically reduced apprehensions. However, there is also strong indication that the fencing, combined with added enforcement, has re-routed illegal immigrants to other less fortified areas of the border. Additionally, in the limited areas where fencing has been erected, there have been numerous breaches of the border fencing and a number of tunnels discovered crossing underneath the fencing. It stands to reason that even if border fencing is constructed over a significant portion of the land border, the incidences of fence breaches and underground tunnels would increase. . . . In San Diego, where (double layer) fencing has been constructed, smugglers have dug numerous tunnels underneath the border fence. One such tunnel was almost a kilometer long and was built from reinforced concrete—evidence of a rather sophisticated smuggling operation.[71]

Another reason to be skeptical about the effectiveness of border fencing is that *roughly 40% to 50% of the people who are now in the United States illegally entered the country by legal means.* In other words they came here on short-term visas of various types and remained.[72] (As noted above, the "exit" portion of US-VISIT is not in place so there is currently no effective way to track aliens who overstay their visas.)

Is the Border Fence a Homeland Security Issue? Advocates of border fencing have recently argued that sealing the borders is necessary for purposes of homeland security to stop terrorists with WMDs from entering the country. However, advocacy for the southern border fence began in the 1980s in reaction to illegal immigration, long before terrorism became a national concern.

Moreover, from a homeland security perspective, a sound strategy to keep terrorists and weapons of mass destruction out of the country requires deployment of new technologies at the 326 U.S. ports of entry, as well as up-to-date terrorist databases and no-fly lists. The billions of dollars the U.S. is poised to spend on border fencing could be far better spent developing and deploying nuclear, biological, and chemical detection technologies as quickly as possible.

Issue 2: Do U.S. Social Services Attract Illegal Immigrants?

Illegal aliens have always been ineligible for U.S. benefits, except for emergency medical services (see Table 3-2.4). Legal permanent residents (i.e., immigrants) are, in general, not eligible for benefits until they have been in the United States for five years, with significant exceptions for refugees and asylees, and those with a military connection.

These limitations on legal immigrants were imposed by the 1996 welfare overhaul with the intent of discouraging immigration primarily for the purpose of obtaining U.S. public assistance. Prior to 1996, legal permanent residents were generally eligible for Federal benefits on the same basis as citizens.

TABLE 3-2.4 Eligibility of Foreign-born Persons for Federal Benefits[74]

Program/Benefits	Legal Permanent Residents (LPRs)	Illegal Aliens	Naturalized Aliens (foreign-born who have become citizens)
Medicaid (health care for low-income Americans) *(see chapter 3-5 for explanation of Medicaid)*	Not eligible (except for emergency medical care) until 5 years after becoming LPR and then at State's option. Exceptions: military,* residents with 10-year work history, and refugees/asylees are immediately eligible.	Not eligible (except for emergency medical care—i.e., arriving at the hospital in a medically unstable condition)	Eligible
SCHIP: State Children's Health Insurance Program *(see chapter 3-6 for explanation of SCHIP)*	Not eligible until 5 years after becoming LPR and then at State's option. Exceptions: military* and refugees/asylees are immediately eligible.	Not eligible (unless a victim of trafficking)	Eligible
Food Stamps *(see chapter 3-10 for explanation of Food Stamps)*	Not eligible until 5 years after becoming LPR. Exceptions: refugees, asylees, children, military,* and disabled are immediately eligible.	Not eligible	Eligible
SSI: Supplemental Security Income for Aged, Blind, Disabled *(see chapter 3-10 for explanation of SSI)*	Noncitizens are ineligible. (Exceptions: • refugees/asylees are immediately eligible for 7 years; • military residents as of August 22, 1996, and residents with 10-year work history are eligible)	Not eligible	Eligible

Program/Benefits	Legal Permanent Residents (LPRs)	Illegal Aliens	Naturalized Aliens (foreign-born who have become citizens)
TANF: Temporary Assistance for Needy Families *(see chapter 3-10 for explanation of TANF)*	States may opt to cover after 5 years. Exceptions: military,* residents with 10-year work history, and refugees/asylees are immediately eligible.	Not eligible	Eligible
EITC: Earned Income Tax Credit *(see chapter 3-10 for explanation of EITC)*	Eligible	Not eligible	Eligible
Social Security *(See chapter 3-4 for Soc. Sec. explanation)*	Eligible	Not eligible	Eligible
Medicare *(see chapter 3-6 for Medicare explanation)*	No restrictions on Part A (hospitalization coverage); not eligible for Part B until 5 years after becoming LPR	Not eligible	Eligible

*Active duty military personnel, veterans, and their families.

Issue 3: Insufficient Funds Provided for Workplace Enforcement

Out of the estimated 12 million illegal aliens currently in the United States, an estimated 7.2 million have been absorbed into the U.S. workforce.[76] Given the intensity of the current debate over illegal immigrants residing in the United States, a surprisingly small amount of funding is provided for workplace enforcement (i.e., investigating employment of illegal aliens by U.S. employers). According to a 2006 report to Congress:

> While the amount of U.S. Border Patrol (USBP) resources almost doubled between FY1997 and FY2003, time spent on other enforcement activities increased only slightly, while the number of inspection hours decreased. . . . . [I]n FY2003, the largest amount of staff time was devoted to locating and arresting criminal aliens (39%), followed by administrative and non-investigative duties (23%) and alien smuggling investigations (15%). *Only 4% was devoted to worksite enforcement (i.e., locating and arresting aliens working without authorization, and punishing employers who hire such workers)* (emphasis added).[77]

BACKGROUND: THE IMMIGRATION DEBATE

- The number of foreign-born people residing in the U.S. is 37 million, or 12% of the population, *a percentage similar to the early 20th century.*[78]
- Of the foreign-born residents in the U.S., approximately one-third have become citizens, one-third are legal permanent residents, and one-third, an estimated 12 million, are illegal aliens resulting from aliens who fail to depart when their temporary visas expire as well as illegal entries.[79]
- There are two paths for the legal admission of noncitizens ("aliens"): Permanent (immigrant) admission under which aliens are accorded the status of Legal Permanent Residents (LPRs). They are more commonly known as "green card" holders and can apply (usually within 3–5 years) to become citizens. The second path is temporary (nonimmigrant) admission (tourism, study, temporary work).[80]
- U.S. immigration law reflects four objectives: (1) reuniting families; (2) addressing labor shortages; (3) providing refuge for people experiencing political, racial, or religious persecution; and (4) promoting diversity by admitting people from countries with historically low rates of immigration to the United States.[81]
- Under current law, the annual immigration ceiling is 675,000 per year,[82] which includes 480,000 family-sponsored immigrants, 140,000 employment-based immigrants, and 55,000 diversity immigrants (with no more than 7% of the ceiling from any individual country).[83] However, this is a flexible ceiling that permits an *unlimited number* of immediate relatives, and an *unlimited number* of refugees and asylees.[84]
- For example, in 2006, 1.27 million aliens were admitted as legal permanent residents. Of this total, 581,000 were immediate relatives of U.S. citizens (spouses, parents, children), 222,000 were non-immediate relatives, 159,000 were employment sponsored (the cap can be exceeded with unused slots from other categories), 216,000 were refugees and asylum seekers, 44,000 were diversity admissions, and 43,000 were admitted on other grounds.[85]
- Each year, an estimated 400,000–700,000 *unauthorized* aliens successfully enter the United States. Each year approximately 1 million aliens are apprehended trying to enter the United States illegally.[86]
- As of 2005, about 56% (6.2 million) of the illegal immigrants residing in the United States were from Mexico, and 22% were from other Latin American countries.[87]
- Most Mexicans who enter the United States, legally or otherwise, come for jobs. According to the CIA's latest analysis of the Mexican economy, "per capita income in Mexico is one-fourth that of the US [and] income distribution remains highly unequal."[88] Some have argued that NAFTA has been a catalyst for increased illegal immigration, although this is a subject of debate.[89]
- A majority of illegal immigrants have found a broad variety of work opportunities in the United States, cited by some as evidence of a labor shortage and the need for increasing the supply of temporary foreign workers, commonly referred to as guest workers.[90] A recent analysis estimated unauthorized employment by sector (in

2005) as follows: private households, 21%; food manufacturing, 14%; agriculture, 13%; furniture manufacturing, 13%, construction, 12%, textile, apparel and leather manufacturing, 12%, food services; 12%, administrative and support services, 11%; and accommodations, 10%.[91]

- The immigration reform debate is focused on the appropriate number of guest worker visas,[92] how to tighten border security, and whether to offer an "earned legalization" opportunity to illegal aliens. Congress has debated various proposals for "earned legalization" that would require illegal aliens to document some combination of: physical presence in the United States over a period of time, employment for a certain period, payment of income taxes, family ties, or education and training.

- Opponents of earned legalization view it as unjustified amnesty for lawbreakers and encouragement for others to immigrate illegally. As evidence, they point to the 1986 Immigration Reform and Control Act, signed into law by President Reagan, which legalized nearly 2.7 million illegal aliens who had entered the United States before 1982, and was followed by an even larger wave of illegal immigrants.[93]

- Supporters of earned legalization argue that it is the absence of a sufficient guest worker program, together with the economic needs of employers and workers that have resulted in 12 million illegal aliens living in the shadows. In addition, they point to the national security benefits of knowing the identities of currently unknown individuals in the country and of legalizing the inflow of temporary workers—thereby freeing border personnel to concentrate on terrorist threats.[94]

Issue 4: Has US-VISIT Been Effective in Stopping Suspect Individuals at the Borders and Tracking Their Departure from the Country?

According to a recent GAO report to Congress:

> After investing about $1.3 billion over 4 years, DHS has delivered essentially one-half of US-VISIT.... [O]perational entry capabilities have reportedly produced results.... However, DHS still does not have the other half of US-VISIT (an operational exit capability) despite the fact that its funding plans have allocated about one-quarter of a billion dollars since 2003 to exit-related efforts.... The prospects for successfully delivering an operational exit solution are as uncertain today as they were 4 years ago.... [T]he longer the department goes without exit capabilities, the more its ability to effectively and efficiently perform its border security and immigration enforcement missions will suffer.... DHS immigration and customs enforcement entities will continue to spend limited resources on investigating potential visa violators who have already left the country.[95]

Issue 5: Has CBP Been Effective at Stopping Radioactive Materials at the Border?

According to GAO undercover investigators, as reported in July 2006, they were able to cross the northern and southern borders "with enough radioactive sources in the trunks of their vehicles to make two dirty bombs."[96] (Dirty bombs, rather than causing a nuclear explosion, use a mix of explosives and radioactive material to irradiate people in proximity to the explosion sight; also known as radiation dispersal devices, or RDDs.)

Issue 6: The USCIS Backlog

USCIS is responsible for adjudicating (i.e., approving or denying) millions of applications each year for citizenship, legal permanent resident status, employment authorization and refugee or asylum status. In FY 2000, USCIS's beleaguered predecessor agency, the INS, had an application backlog of about 3.8 million.[97] Backlogs and long waiting periods for adjudications can cause major disruptions for immigrants, their families, and prospective employers.

By June 2005, USCIS estimated it had reduced the backlog to about 1.2 million applications. However, it is unclear how accurate that estimate is because, according to GAO, USCIS's data systems cannot provide reliable data on how long an application has been pending.[98]

On May 30, 2007, USCIS published a new fee schedule for immigration and naturalization adjudications that would increase fees by an average of 88%—the amount necessary, according to USCIS, to avoid further backlogs. The new fees follow from a policy established two decades ago for the INS to become a fee-based operation. Announcement of the near doubling of fees is generating renewed debate about whether USCIS operations should be covered by appropriations, fees, or a combination of the two.[99]

The U.S. Coast Guard

A few armed vessels, judiciously stationed at the entrances of our ports, might at small expense be made useful sentinels of the laws.—Alexander Hamilton, Federalist Paper No. 12

In a Nutshell

The U.S. Coast Guard, with an FY 2007 budget of $8.5 billion and nearly 40,000 military and 6,000 civilian employees, is the lead agency for the maritime component of homeland security and is also responsible for the non–homeland security functions of search and rescue, marine safety, navigation support, ice operations, environmental protection, marine resources, law enforcement and drug interdiction.[100]

Background

The United States Coast Guard (the "Service"), one of the uniformed military services of the United States, was moved from the Department of Transportation (DoT) into the new Department of Homeland Security (DHS) in 2003. Despite its incorporation into DHS, the Coast Guard still operates as part of the Navy during times of war, the most recent example being the Iraq War.

The Coast Guard's homeland security duties include securing 95,000 miles of U.S. coastline, 360 ports and waterways, and safeguarding maritime transportation. The transfer of the Coast Guard to DHS, unlike the transfer of FEMA discussed earlier, was met with little controversy. There was broad agreement that the increased homeland security role was well suited

FIGURE 3-2.3 Major Coast Guard FY 2007 Expenditures by Mission

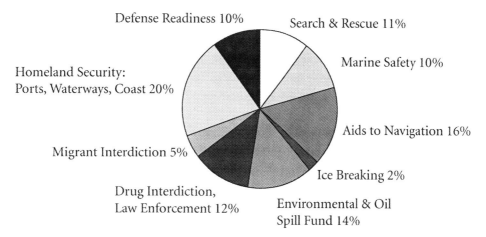

Data source: Office of Management and Budget.

to the Coast Guard's military and national defense duties. Due to those increased responsibilities, the Coast Guard's personnel increased by 5,000 between 2001 and 2006, along with a 65% increase in its operating budget and a tripling of its capital acquisition budget.[101]

In addition to its homeland security responsibilities, the Coast Guard's broad mission includes law enforcement, aids to navigation, search and rescue, marine inspection and safety, migrant interdiction, licensing of U.S. merchant marine personnel, marine environmental protection, regulating deepwater ports, and ice breaking.

The broad responsibilities of the Coast Guard evolved considerably during its lengthy history. The earliest predecessor of the Coast Guard was the Revenue Marine, established in 1790 at the urging of Alexander Hamilton as a Federal maritime law enforcement agency. The fleet of "cutters," being the only armed vessels at the time, also performed military duties.[102] After the sinking of the *Titanic* in 1912, the Revenue Cutter Service (the successor to the Revenue Marine) took over the polar ice breaking duties of the Navy, which did not have the resources to perform both national defense and nondefense duties.

In 1915, the Revenue Cutter Service was combined with the U.S. Lifesaving Service to create the Coast Guard (which was placed in the Department of Treasury, due to the origins of the Cutter Service as the Revenue Marine). Later on, the U.S. Lighthouse Service, the Steamboat Inspection Service, and the Bureau of Navigation were also brought into the Coast Guard.[103]

In 1967, the Coast Guard became part of the Department of Transportation where it was located until the recent move to DHS.[104] Today's Coast Guard has nearly 40,000 active duty personnel, nearly 8000 reservists, more than 6,000 civilian workers, and more than 30,000 auxiliarists.[105]

Coast Guard servicemen, as a branch of the military, are eligible for military health and veterans benefits (see chapters 3-1 and 3-3).

During Hurricane Katrina, the Coast Guard was credited as one of the few successful federal responses—not only in rescuing more than 33,000 people but also in responding to more than a hundred oil spills.[106]

Issue: The Deepwater Project

The Service is in the midst of a 25-year, $24 billion major acquisition program called "Deepwater" to modernize the Coast Guard with 91 new ships, 124 small boats, 195 new or rebuilt helicopters, and 40 unmanned aerial vehicles (UAVs).[107] The aim is to acquire a fully integrated fleet equipped with modern surveillance, intelligence, reconnaissance, and communications capabilities. To date, it is the largest and most complex acquisition in Coast Guard history.[108]

The Deepwater project is unusual in that the Coast Guard contracted with a consortium of private companies led by Lockheed Martin Corp. and Northrop Gruman Corp. to handle everything from designing and building ships, planes, and information systems, to *management* of the entire multiyear project. According to the DHS Inspector General, "the Coast Guard's technical role was limited to that of an expert 'advisor.'"[109] The Deepwater project, and particularly the outsourcing of management to the contractors, has been the subject of considerable criticism on Capitol Hill. In a June 2007 report to Congress, the GAO reported that "five years into the Deepwater contract, some assets have been delivered . . . but several other assets have encountered significant problems. . . . For example, the Vertical and Landing Unmanned Aerial Vehicle has experienced delays as the Coast Guard assesses alternatives; the Fast Response Cutter . . . experienced design problems and the Coast Guard suspended all work, and the first two hulls of the National Security Cutter have structural design issues."[110]

As of summer 2007, legislation was moving through Congress to overhaul Deepwater including a prohibition on a private company managing the program.[111]

Domestic Nuclear Detection Office (DNDO) and Defending against Weapons of Mass Destruction

In a Nutshell

DNDO, with an FY 2007 budget of $581 million, is dedicated to research, development, and acquisition of nuclear detection technologies to prevent smuggling of nuclear bomb making or other radiological materials at U.S. ports of entry. In general, six departments of the Federal Government have FY 2007 funding for protecting the homeland from terrorists acquiring and using nuclear and other weapons of mass destruction (WMDs), amounting to $3.3 billion. Activities include assisting Russia and other States of the former Soviet Union with improving security at various sites, nuclear weapons storage and disposal, chemical weapons destruction, biosecurity, employing nuclear scientists, various nonproliferation initiatives, and detecting nuclear bomb making and other WMD materials at U.S. ports of entry.

Background

Preventing nuclear and other radioactive material from being smuggled into the United States is a key national security objective because of the catastrophic implications of terrorists detonating an atomic bomb or, to a lesser extent, a dirty bomb (a conventional bomb that spreads radioactive material). When DHS was established, CBP managed an effort to develop and deploy radiation detection technology. In April 2005, the President established DNDO, with a mission to support development and acquisition of a full range of radiation technology devices including fixed, mobile, backpack, and handheld devices to be deployed at the nation's ports of entry, as well as in high-risk urban areas.

Current nuclear portal monitors are rudimentary and cannot distinguish between harmless radiological materials, such as naturally occurring material in ceramic tile, and dangerous nuclear materials such as highly enriched uranium (HEU), which is used to build nuclear bombs.

In July 2006, DHS announced that it had awarded contracts to three vendors to continue development and purchase $1.2 billion worth of new portal monitors over 5 years.

Issue: GAO Concerns about DNDO Effectiveness

In a highly critical letter to congressional appropriators in October 2006 evaluating the DHS contracts, the GAO reported that DNDO's decision to purchase the new equipment could not be justified, given the agency's *own test results*. According to the GAO, the Nuclear Detection Office "instead relied on potential future performance to justify the purchase." Performance tests showed that the ability of the new radiation detection monitors to correctly identify HEU was "limited." GAO also reported that DNDO "did not consider how well [the] new portal monitor technology can correctly detect or identify other dangerous radiological or nuclear materials." The report concluded that DNDO did not focus on the technology's effectiveness at identifying nuclear material but instead "focused its analysis on reducing the time necessary to screen traffic at border check points and reduce the impact of any delays on commerce."[112] GAO reiterated these alarming findings in reports to Congress in March 2007.

In short, in the rush to deploy "new technology," DNDO is replacing currently ineffective nuclear detection technology with higher-priced ineffective technology.

Since 1993, the Departments of Defense and Energy have worked to improve security at sites housing weapons-grade nuclear material and warheads in Russia and other countries. Following is an overview of FY 2007 spending on nuclear security and nonproliferation by DoD, DoE, DHS, and the State and Justice Departments. (Figure 3-2.7 compares this spending with other defense spending and the estimated cost of securing all fissile material worldwide.)

FY 2007 Spending to Defend the U.S. from Terrorists
Acquiring and Using Nuclear and Other Weapons of Mass Destruction

1	(DoD) Nunn-Lugar Cooperative Threat Reduction (CTR) program	$371 million[113]
2.	(DoE) Nuclear Nonproliferation Programs	$1.621 billion[114]
3.	(DHS) Science and Technology, DNDO, Port Security	$1.255 billion[115]
4.	(State) Global Threat Reduction Program	$182 million[116]
5.	(DOJ) Defending against Catastrophic Threats	$40 million[117]
	TOTAL	**$3.469 billion**

DoD/CTR Program: The Nunn-Lugar CTR program is focused on securing and dismantling WMDs in Russia and other countries of the former Soviet Union (FSU). Recent projects include construction of a chemical weapons destruction facility at Shchuch'ye, Russia, and security upgrades at Russian warhead storage sites; and there are plans to upgrade security at vulnerable borders and expand the Biological Threat Reduction program for FSU States (except Russia).

DOE/Nuclear Nonproliferation: Addresses the danger that hostile nations or terrorist groups may acquire WMD or weapons-usable material or production technology or WMD expertise. Major elements of the program include: R&D on detection systems; international security efforts to control export of technology useful for WMDs; reducing the potential for diversion of nuclear warheads and nuclear materials from Russia and other countries of proliferation concern; screening of containerized cargo at strategic international seaports; assisting Russia in ceasing its production of weapons-grade plutonium production by providing replacement power production capacity; and a variety of global threat reduction initiatives.

Recommended Sources for More Information on Nuclear Detection at Ports of Entry and Protecting the U.S. from Terrorist WMDs

- **GAO:** "DHS' Decision to Procure and Deploy the Next Generation of Radiation Detection Equipment Is Not Supported by Its Cost-Benefit Analysis," GAO-07-581T, March 14, 2007; "Combating Nuclear Smuggling: DNDO Has Not Yet Collected Most of the National Laboratories' Test Results on Radiation Portal Monitors in Support of DNDO's Testing and Development Program," GAO-07-347R, March 9, 2007; "Nuclear Nonproliferation: Progress Made in Improving Security at Russian Nuclear Sites, but the Long-term Sustainability of U.S.-Funded Security Upgrades Is Uncertain," GAO-07-404, February 2007;
- **Partnership for Global Security:** Publications on Federal appropriations for nonproliferation and other WMD-related programs, www.partnershipforglobalsecurity.org.
- **Nuclear Threat Initiative:** www.nti.org.

Science and Technology Directorate: R&D on Chemical, Biological, and Other Threats, and Interoperability

In a Nutshell

DHS's Science and Technology Directorate (S&T), with an FY 2007 budget of $853 million, directs R&D on chemical and biological agents and other threats, and R&D to achieve communications interoperability (addressing the incompatibility of most police, fire, and emergency response radios). (R&D on nuclear detection technologies are handled by the Domestic Nuclear Detection Office [DNDO],discussed earlier.) S&T and DNDO together spend more than a *billion dollars per year* on homeland security research. S&T also *coordinates* homeland security–related research at other Federal departments and agencies.

Background

R&D priorities. S&T's largest appropriations for R&D in FY 2007 include $350 million for biological countermeasures, $87 million for explosives countermeasures, $60 million for chemical countermeasures, $40 million to counter shoulder-fired missiles, and $27 million for communications interoperability.

Interoperability and SAFECOM. The 9/11 Commission observed that "the inability to communicate was a critical element at the World Trade Center, Pentagon, and Somerset County, Pennsylvania, crash sites, where multiple agencies and multiple jurisdictions responded. The occurrence of this problem at three very different sites is strong evidence that compatible and adequate communications among public safety organizations at the local, state, and federal levels remains an important problem."[118] Ensuring communications among various first responders using different types of wireless radio communications is called "interoperability."

The continuing urgency to achieve interoperability as quickly as possible was underscored during the response to Hurricanes Katrina and Rita when—similar to the 9/11 tragedy four years earlier—police, fire, and other rescue workers were once again unable to communicate. It was not until the Army was deployed to assist with rescue operations that the communications situation improved.

SAFECOM, a communications program located in the S&T Directorate,[119] funds R&D on interoperability, as well as providing "guidance, tools, and templates" on communications-related issues to State, local, and Federal emergency response agencies.[120] While SAFECOM is located in the S&T Directorate, most of its functions are now under the overall direction of a reinvigorated FEMA, as called for in the post-Katrina legislation.[121]

The Federal Communications Commission and Commerce Department also play important roles in addressing the urgent need for interoperable communications. In early 2009, the FCC is required to allocate 24 MHz of spectrum to public safety. According to CRS, "the channels designated for public safety are among those currently held for TV broadcasters; they are to be cleared as part of the move from analog to digital television." When the vacated channels are auctioned by the FCC, up to a billion dollars of the proceeds are to be made available for grants by the NTIA[122] at the Commerce Department for public safety agencies to take advantage of the new public safety channels at 700 MHz.[123]

Coordinating Homeland Security R&D at Other Agencies. S&T's roles in coordinating homeland security–related R&D at other Federal departments and agencies includes NIH's work on medical countermeasures for exposure to weapons of mass destruction, DoD's work on countering chemical and biological threats, the Agriculture Department's work on the security of the U.S. food supply, the National Science Foundation's work on protection of critical infrastructure and cybersecurity, EPA's work on toxic materials research, DoE's work on DNA-based diagnostics, NASA's work on aviation safety and remote sensing, and the National Institute of Standards' work on protecting information systems. Total Federal government R&D related to homeland security is estimated at about $5 billion for FY 2007.[124]

Issue: Interoperability

In an April 2007 report to Congress, GAO noted that $2.15 billion in grant funding had been awarded to states and localities for communications interoperability. However, GAO found that the States they reviewed (New York, Kentucky, Oregon, and Florida) "had generally not used strategic plans to guide investments toward broadly improving interoperability (and that) no national plan was in place to coordinate investments across states." GAO concluded that "until DHS takes a more strategic approach to improving interoperable communications . . . progress by states and localities in improving interoperability is likely to be impeded."[125]

National Protection and Programs Directorate: Infrastructure Protection, Information Security, and Emergency Communications

In a Nutshell

DHS's National Protection and Programs Directorate, with a $941 million budget in FY '07, funds the US-VISIT program, which monitors entry and exit of aliens, and programs in support of infrastructure protection, cybersecurity, protecting national telecommunications infrastructure, and emergency communications.

Background

The **US-VISIT entry-exit data system,** as discussed in more detail earlier under "Customs, Border Protection, and Immigration," was established to use biometrics (finger scans and digital photography) to track entries and exits from the country.

Critical Infrastructure Protection. The specific goals of infrastructure protection activities are to *identify* critical infrastructure, *assess risk*, and provide leadership on *preparedness* for attacks on critical infrastructure.

Cybersecurity. DHS seeks to identify critical points in our nation's information infrastructure that could be exploited by terrorists, and facilitate cooperation between government and private sector cybersecurity experts to address potential threats.

Emergency Communications. Originally within the Department of Defense, the National Communications System (NCS) in DHS's Protection and Programs Directorate "supports and promotes the ability of emergency response providers and federal officials to continue to communicate in the event of natural disasters, acts of terrorism, or other man-made disasters."[126] For example, NCS coordinates public and private sector efforts to restore communications in the aftermath of a disaster.[127] (As already discussed, research and development activities on interoperability are funded by the Science and Technology Directorate, with significant direction from FEMA.)

United States Secret Service

In a Nutshell

The United States Secret Service, with an annual budget of $1.5 billion and 5,000 employees, protects the President, Vice President, their families, former Presidents, presidential candidates, and foreign heads of state. The Service also investigates financial crimes including counterfeiting of currency or government bonds, money laundering, bank fraud, credit card fraud, identity theft, and computer-based attacks on our nation's financial system.

Background

In 1865, the Civil War ended and half the money supply in the United States was counterfeit. To restore faith in American currency, the Department of the Treasury established the United States Secret Service (USSS) to stop the spread of counterfeit dollars.[128] A few years later, the USSS was tasked with stopping fraud against the U.S. government, and following the assassination of President William McKinley in 1901, the USSS formally became responsible for the protection of the President.

The Service is responsible for protecting, and investigating threats against the President, Vice President, their families, former Presidents, and foreign heads of state.[129] In 1968, following the assassination of Senator Robert F. Kennedy, the Service began protecting presidential candidates. For the 2008 presidential election, Congress appropriated $18.4 million for candidate nominee protection.

In 1997, Congress passed legislation that restricted protection of former Presidents and their families to 10 years after leaving office. President Clinton was the last president to receive lifetime protection, making Hillary Clinton the only Senator with Secret Service protection. Protection costs for former presidents and their families are not disclosed.[130]

In addition to its protection services, the USSS has substantial federal law enforcement responsibilities, working in cooperation with FBI and the US Marshals. The service is active in uncovering counterfeiting and other financial crimes; countering identity theft; investigating computer fraud; and protecting the nation's financial, banking and telecommunications infrastructure against computer-based attacks.

In 2002, the Secret Service was transferred from the Treasury to the Department of Homeland Security.[131] The Service was given the authority to be "maintained as a distinct entity,"[132] which allows the Service to carry on with duties and jurisdiction it had prior to the move. While the two primary responsibilities of the service have remained the same, the service now plays a greater role in counterterrorism and antiterrorist financing.[133]

Has DHS Improved Our Nation's Security?

Considered collectively, the 9/11 hijackers: included known al Qaeda operatives who could have been watchlisted; presented passports manipulated in a fraudulent manner; presented passports with suspicious indicators of extremism; made detectable false statements on visa applications; made false statements to border officials to gain entry into the United States; and violated immigration laws while in the United States.—9/11 Commission[134]

The Department of Homeland Security was established in response to 9/11. Since that time, the Department has been reorganized nine times.[135] The core issue with respect to the Department of Homeland Security is whether its establishment and subsequent reorganizations, along with the infusion of billions of dollars in new and increased resources, has effectively addressed the breakdown in the system highlighted by the 9/11 Commission. Thus far, assessments of DHS performance have been highly critical:

- **October 2002**: "[A] year after 9/11, America remains dangerously unprepared to prevent and respond to a catastrophic attack on U.S. soil."[136]—Rudman-Hart Commission

FIGURE 3-2.4 Organizational Overview of DHS

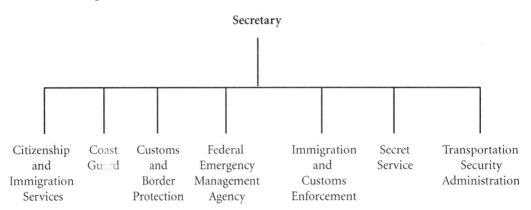

- **September 2005:** "Despite testimony from the Director of Central Intelligence that the chemical industrial infrastructure is vulnerable to a terrorist attack, no Federal security measures have been established for the chemical sector."[137]—House-Senate conference report for FY 2006
- **December 2005:** "The Federal government received failing and mediocre grades yesterday from the former Sept. 11 commission, whose members said in a final report that the Bush Administration and Congress have balked at enacting numerous reforms that could save American lives and prevent another terrorist attack on U.S. soil."[138]—*Washington Post.*
- **January 2006:** "The administration made pursuit of weapons of mass destruction in Iraq the front line of its counter-proliferation strategy. Since failing to find any such weapons, officials now are focused on interdicting suspected weapons shipments at sea, breaking up black markets, and stopping North Korea and Iran from developing big stores of nuclear weapons. But those initiatives will hardly make a dent in what most nonproliferation experts see as the greatest potential source of deadly weapons for terrorists: the thousands of so-called 'loose nukes' scattered around the states of the former Soviet Union; many of these weapons aren't secured, and experts fear that terrorists could steal them or buy them on the black market."—*National Journal*[139]
- **May 2006:** DHS has still not set priorities for critical infrastructure needing protection and "the private sector has not been effectively integrated into response and recovery planning for major disasters."[140]—Council on Foreign Relations
- **May 2006:** Most critical infrastructure, about 80%, is privately held, including civilian nuclear power plants, chemical plants, electric and other utilities, and facilities for production, storage and distribution of food.[141] According to a senior congressional aide, DHS has a "consistent pattern for relying on the private sector to meet security needs and then providing no funds, no regulations, no standards, no analytical framework to actually invest in security. So, no chemical security grants or regulations, no grants to secure our water systems, almost no funds even to assess the vulnerability of water systems and other utilities. They have a list of critical infrastructure . . . but they have not provided any funds, or security standards to actually build fences, put up cameras or train guards."[142]

- **May 2006:** "[T]he Katrina catastrophe revealed . . . confusion delay, misdirection, inactivity, poor coordination, and lack of leadership. . . . All of this unfolded nearly four years after the terror attacks of September 11, 2001; after a massive reorganization . . . and billions of dollars of expenditures."—Senate Committee on Homeland Security and Governmental Affairs[143]

- **August 2006:** "Five years after September 11, 2001, the United States remains dangerously unprepared to deal with the aftermath of a terrorist attack involving nuclear weapons, dirty bombs or explosions at nuclear power plants. . . . We found that the U.S. government lacks a workable plan to respond to the likely medical needs. Thousands of American civilians injured by a nuclear terrorist attack could survive with better preparedness." Physicians for Social Responsibility[144]

- **September 2006:** DHS "has fallen woefully short in efforts to equip emergency responders with interoperable radios and met only half of its goals of building a compute network to track foreign visitors.[145] Last year's bungled federal response to Hurricane Katrina, moreover, cast lingering doubts on the government's ability to respond to future crises."—*CQ Weekly*[146]

- **December 2006:** "A multibillion-dollar effort to modernize the Coast Guard's fleet has suffered delays, cost increases, design flaws and, most recently, the idling of eight 123-foot patrol boats that were found to be not seaworthy after an $88 million refurbishment. . . . Congressional critics warn that early mistakes in the 25-year modernization program, called Deepwater. . .are hobbling the service's transformation into a front-line homeland security force."—*Washington Post*[147]

- **January 2007:** "The Department of Defense must be prepared to respond to and mitigate the effects of weapons of mass destruction (WMD) attacks at home and abroad. . . . Most Army units tasked with providing chemical and biological defense support are not adequately staffed, equipped, or trained to perform their mission. . . . Most of the Army's chemical and biological units, particularly in the National Guard and Reserve, are reporting the lowest readiness rating."—GAO[148]

- **March 2007:** "Experts and government documents suggest that, absent a major preparedness push, the U.S. response to a mushroom cloud could be worse than the debacle after Hurricane Katrina . . . costing thousands of lives. 'The U.S. is unprepared to mitigate the consequences of a nuclear attack,' Pentagon analyst John Brinkerhoff concluded in a July 31, 2005 draft of a confidential memo to the Joint Chiefs of Staff. '*We are unable to find any group or office with a coherent approach to this very important aspect of homeland security.*' "—McClatchy Newspapers,[149] emphasis added

- **April 2007:** "Until DHS takes a more strategic approach to improving interoperable communications, such as including in its decision making an assessment of how grant requests align with statewide communications plans, and conducts a thorough assessment to identify strategies to mitigate obstacles between federal agencies and state and local agencies, states and localities are likely to make limited progress in improving interoperability." —GAO[150]

- **April 2007:** "TSA and CBP . . . do not have a systematic process in place to share information that could be used to strengthen the department's efforts in securing inbound air cargo."—GAO[151]

- **May 2007:** "GAO designated implementing and transforming DHS as high risk in 2003 because DHS had to transform and integrate 22 agencies—several with existing program and management challenges—into one department, and failure to effectively address its challenges could have serious consequences for our homeland security. Despite some progress, this transformation remains high risk. . . . DHS must overcome continued challenges related to such issues as cargo, transportation, and border security; systematic visitor tracking; efforts to combat the employment of illegal aliens; and outdated Coast Guard asset capabilities."—Comptroller General of the United States David M. Walker[152]

- **June 2007:** "Roughly 75 percent of all cargo entering the country is not screened for nuclear material."—Senate Appropriations Committee[153]
- **July 2007:** "The Bush Administration has failed to fill roughly a quarter of the top leadership posts at the Department of Homeland Security, creating a 'gaping hole' in the nation's preparedness for a terrorist attack or other threat, according to a congressional report."[154]—*Washington Post*

Finally, consider the sobering chart presented in figure 3.2-5, comparing:

- Resources appropriated in FY 2007 for weapons systems (many of which were conceived to maintain technological superiority over the Former Soviet Union);[155]
- FY 2007 appropriations for Operation Iraqi Freedom;[156]
- FY 2007 funds appropriated to defend against catastrophic terrorist threats;[157] and
- The estimated amount of funds required to secure the world's entire supply of fissile material (the essential ingredient required to build a nuclear bomb).[158]

If the 9/11 Commission is correct that "the greatest danger of another catastrophic attack in the United States will materialize if the world's most dangerous terrorists acquire the world's most dangerous weapons," we have a serious imbalance to correct in the allocation of national security resources.[159]

> *Since the advent of the Nuclear Age, everything has changed save our modes of thinking and we thus drift toward unparalleled catastrophe.—Albert Einstein*[160]

Notes

1. In Part III of this book, all dollar amounts refer to "budget authority" unless otherwise noted. Budget authority is the amount appropriated by Congress in a given year. For a discussion of "budget authority" and "outlays" see chapter 2-9. The homeland security budget authority number leading off this chapter includes '07 supplemental funds enacted on May 25, 2007 (H.R. 2206, 110th Congress). The sum of program activity described later exceeds this total, because the DHS total is offset in the budget by various fees (e.g., TSA airport fees, flood insurance premiums, and immigration application fees). In budget-speak the fees are called "offsetting receipts."

2. Government Accountability Office, "Homeland Security: Management Challenges Remain in Transforming Immigration Reforms," GAO-05-81 (Washington, D.C.: Author, October 2004), 7.

3. Congressional Budget Office, "Federal Funding for Homeland Security: An Update" (Washington, D.C.: Author, July 20, 2005), 5.

4. This CBO report, as of June 2007, had not been updated.

5. See also the provisions of the Security and Accountability for Every (SAFE) Port Act of 2006, P.L. 109-347. The SAFE Port Act called for interagency operational centers at high-risk ports, port security

FIGURE 3-2.5: Comparing the 2007 Budget for Defending against Catastrophic Terrorist Threats and the Potential Costs of Securing All Fissile Material Worldwide *versus* 2007 Funding for Weapons Systems and the War in Iraq

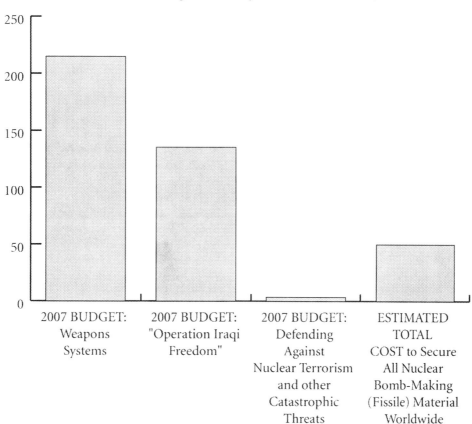

(FY 2007 Budget Authority in billions of dollars)

exercise programs, an expansion of foreign port security assessment, and enhanced technologies for scanning containers.

6. Shawn Reese, "FY 2006 Homeland Security Grant Guidance Distribution Formulas" (Washington, D.C.: Congressional Research Service, December 9, 2005); and interview with senior congressional staffer.

7. Keith Bea, "Transfer of FEMA to the Department of Homeland Security: Issue for Congressional Oversight," RL31670 (Washington, D.C.: Congressional Research Service, December 17, 2002), 12.

8. Pursuant to general reorganization authority granted the President in the Reorganization Act of 1949, as amended (P.L. 95-17, 91 Stat. 29-35, 5 U.S.C. 901), reorganization plans submitted to the Congress for consideration were implemented if Congress did not pass resolutions of disapproval within 60 days. This reorganization authority expired in 1984.

9. Eric Holdeman, "Destroying FEMA," *Washington Post*, August 30, 2005, A17.

10. Specifically, the Robert T. Stafford Disaster Relief and Emergency Act, 42 U.S.C. §5121 *et seq.* (Stafford Act) provides in section 5170 that "all requests for a declaration by the President that a *major disaster* exists shall be made by the Governor of the affected State. Such a request shall be based on a finding that the disaster is of such severity and magnitude that effective response is beyond the capabilities of the State and the affected local governments and that Federal assistance is necessary" (emphasis added). Similar language is included in section 5191 of the Stafford Act for the declaration of an

"emergency." See Elizabeth Bazan, "Robert T. Stafford Disaster Relief and Emergency Assistance Act: Legal Requirements for Federal and State Roles in Declarations of an Emergency or a Major Disaster," RL33090 (Washington, D.C.: Congressional Research Service, October 19, 2005); and Keith Bea, "Federal Stafford Act Disaster Assistance: Presidential Declarations, Eligible Activities, and Funding," RL33053 (Washington, D.C.: Congressional Research Service, March 6, 2007).

11. Congress generally appropriates budget authority to the Disaster Relief Fund on an as-needed basis, and usually with an emergency designation that exempts the funds from annual limitations on discretionary spending. In other words, the Federal government does not put money aside for emergencies because to do so would either increase projected deficits or deplete funds available for other purposes.

12. See U.S. Senate Committee on Homeland Security and Governmental Affairs, "Hurricane Katrina: A Nation Still Unprepared" (Washington, D.C.: Author, May 2006).

13. *Orlando Sentinel*, "Can FEMA handle the hurricanes of 2006," May 2, 2006.

14. HR 5441, the Post-Katrina Management Reform Act of 2006, Title VI of the FY 2007 Homeland Security Appropriations bill, P.L. 109-295 (October 4, 2006).

15. Source: Keith Bea, "Transfer of FEMA to the Department of Homeland Security: Issues for Congressional Oversight," RL31670 (Washington, D.C.: Congressional Research Service, December 17, 2002), 12.

16. Emergency Food and Shelter program. See http://efsp.unitedway.org/.

17. See Nonna Noto, Steven Maquire, "FEMA's Community Disaster Loan Program," RL33174 (Washington, D.C.: Congressional Research Service, June 28, 2007).

18. Keith Bea, "Federal Emergency Management Policy Changes after Hurricane Katrina: A Summary of Statutory Provisions," RL33729 (Washington, D.C.: Congressional Research Service, March 6, 2007), 9-13.

19. U.S. Senate Committee on Homeland Security and Governmental Affairs, "Hurricane Katrina: A Nation Still Unprepared," May 2006, 2.

20. House Select Bipartisan Committee to Investigate the Preparation for and Response to Hurricane Katrina, "A Failure of Initiative" (Washington, D.C.: U.S. House of Representatives, February 15, 2006), 1.

21. Statement of David M. Walker, Comptroller General of the United States, "Hurricane Katrina: GAO's Preliminary Observations Regarding Preparedness, Response, and Recover," GAO-06-442T (Washington, D.C.: Government Accountability Office, March 8, 2006), highlights.

22. Statement of Sharon Pickup, Director, Defense Capabilities and Management, "Hurricane Katrina: Better Plans and Exercises Need to Guide the Military's Response to Catastrophic Natural Disasters," GAO-06-808T (Washington, D.C.: Government Accountability Office, May 25, 2006), highlights.

23. Bea, "Federal Emergency Management Policy Changes after Hurricane Katrina," Keith Bea, "Federal Emergency Management Policy Changes after Hurricane Katrina: A Summary of Statutory Provision," RL33729 (Washington, D.C.: Congressional Research Service, March 6, 2007), 9–13.23.

24. This is part of a larger trend by the Bush Administration to declare, upon signing bills, that they object to specific provisions on constitutional grounds and do not feel obliged to comply with the provisions. See T. J. Halstead, "Presidential Signing Statements: Constitutional and Institutional Implications," RL33667 (Washington, D.C.: Congressional Research Service, April 13, 2007).

25. The costs, broken down, are as follows: Emergency Supplemental Appropriation (September 2, 2005) P.L. 109-61: $10.5 billion; Emergency Supplemental Appropriation (September 8, 2005) P.L. 109-62: $51.8 billion; Emergency Supplemental Appropriations (December 30, 2005) P.L. 109-148: $5.2 billion; Emergency Supplemental Appropriation (June 15, 2006) P.L. 109-234: $19.3 billion; Emergency Supplemental Appropriation (May 25, 2007) P.L. 110-28: $6.3 billion; Mandatory (Entitlement) Spending and Tax Relief: $35.7 billion. Source: Senate Budget Committee Minority Staff, "Senate Budget Committee Releases Updated Tally of Hurricane-Related Spending," June 5, 2007. See also Richard Skinner, Inspector General of DHS, Statement before the House Committee on Homeland Security, February 7, 2007; Matt Fellowes and Amy Liu, "Federal Allocations in Response to Katrina, Rita and Wilma," (Washington, D.C.: Brookings Institution, March 21, 2006); and Keith Bea, "Emergency Supplemental Appro-

priations for Hurricane Katrina Relief," RS22239 (Washington, D.C.: Congressional Research Service, August 22, 2006), 1–2.

26. Stanley Czerwinski, "Preliminary Information on Rebuilding Efforts in the Gulf Coast," GAO-07-809R (Washington, D.C.: Government Accountability Office, June 29, 2007), 3–4.

27. CRS reports pertaining to Hurricane Katrina include the following report numbers: RS22269, RS22233, RL33082, RL33084, RL33104, RL33236, RS22280, RS22344, RS22282, RS22358, and RS22264. To access the reports, go to http://opencrs.com or http://www.pennyhill.com.

28. "Testimony: Challenges Facing the National Flood Insurance Program," October 18, 2005.

29. Rawle O. King, "Federal Flood Insurance: The Repetitive Loss Problem" (Washington, D.C.: Congressional Research Service, June 30, 2005).

30. Typically referred to as "flood risk management." See Nicole T. Carter, "Flood Risk Management," RL33129 (Washington, D.C.: Congressional Research Service, October 26, 2005).

31. www.floodsmart.gov.

32. GAO, "Testimony: Challenges Facing the National Flood Insurance Program," October 18, 2005.

33. "Properties that suffer repeated flooding but generally pay subsidized flood insurance rates—so-called repetitive-loss properties—constitute a significant drain on NFIP resources. These properties account for roughly 1 % of properties insured under the NFIP, but account for 25 % to 30 % of all claim losses." GAO, "Testimony: Challenges Facing the National Flood Insurance Program," October 18, 2005.

34. Congress Daily, "Shelby Sees FEMA's Red Ink and Suggest and Overhaul," *National Journal*, January 25, 2006.

35. See Rawle O. King, "Federal Flood Insurance: The Repetitive Loss Problem," RL32975 (Washington, D.C.: Congressional Research Service, June 30, 2005).

36. Nicole T. Carter, "Flood Risk Management: Federal Role in Infrastructure," RL33129 (Washington, D.C.: Congressional Research Service, October 26, 2005), 8.

37. National Commission on Terrorist Attacks upon the United States, *The 9/11 Commission Report* (New York: Norton, 2004), 385.

38. P.L. 107-71.

39. However a few airports are enrolled in a partnership allowing them to hire private screeners who work under Federal supervision. "Federal Response to Sept. 11 in Retrospect," *CQ Weekly*, September 11, 2006, 2382.

40. "Federal Response," 2382.

41. David Peterman, Bart Elias, John Frittelli, "Transportation Security: Issues for the 110th Congress," RL33512 (Washington, D.C.: Congressional Research Service, March 26, 2007), 12.

42. Peterman et al.,, "Transportation Security," 11–15.

43. GAO, "Significant Management Challenges May Adversely Affect Implementation of the TSA's Secure Flight Program," GAO-06-374T, February 9, 2007.

44. Peterman et al., "Transportation Security," 6.

45. U.S. Senate Committee on Appropriations, Press Release: "Senate Appropriations Homeland Security Subcommittee Clears Fiscal 2008 Funding Legislation," June 13, 2007, 4. http://www.washingtonbudgetreport.com/Senate_Homeland_Sub.pdf.

46. Peterman et al., "Transportation Security," 6.

47. See GAO, "Federal Efforts to Secure U.S.-Bound Air Cargo Are in the Early Stages and Could Be Strengthened," GAO-07-660 (Washington, D.C.: Government Accountability Office, April 2007).

48. U.S. Senate Committee on Appropriations, Press Release: "Senate Appropriations Homeland Security Subcommittee Clears Fiscal 2008 Funding Legislation," June 13, 2007, 4.

49. *The 9/11 Commission Report*, 387.

50. GAO, "Homeland Security: Management Challenges," 7.

51. Ruth Wasem, "U.S. Immigration Policy on Permanent Admissions," RL32235 (Washington, D.C.: Congressional Research Service, May 11, 2007), 16.

52. Ruth Ellen Wasem, "Toward More Effective Immigration Policies: Selected Organizational Issues," RL33319 (Washington, D.C.: Congressional Research Service, RL33319), 2–9.

53. P.L. 107-296.

54. In adjudicating citizenship applications, USCIS adjudicators must determine whether applicants have continuously resided in the United States for a specified period of time, have good moral character, have the ability to read, write, speak, and understand English, and have passed an exam on U.S. government and history. Wasem, "Toward More Effective Immigration Policies," 14.

55. USCIS adjudicators determine eligibility for immigration of immediate relatives of U.S. citizens, spouses and children of legal permanent residents, employees that U.S. businesses have demonstrated they need, and other foreign nationals meeting certain criteria. Wasem, "Toward More Effective Immigration Policies," 14.

56. The projected growth is based on President Bush's request. See GAO, "Border Patrol: Costs and Challenges Related to Training New Agents," GAO-07-997T (Washington, D.C.: Government Accountability Office, June 19, 2007), highlights.

57. The number of agents has grown from about 8,000 in 2002 to more than 11,000. Source: Speech by President George W. Bush to the Associated Builders and Contractors, June 14, 2007, http://www.whitehouse.gov/news/releases/2007/06/20070614-1.html.

58. Alison Siskin, "Immigration Enforcement Within the United States," RL33351 (Washington, D.C.: Congressional Research Service, April 6, 2006), 7.

59. It is unlawful for an employer to knowingly hire, recruit for a fee, or continue to employ an illegal alien. See Andora Bruno, "Unauthorized Employment in the U.S.: Issues and Options," RL 33973 (Washington, D.C.: Congressional Research Service, April 20, 2007).

60. United States Visitor and Immigrant Status Indicator Technology Program. See Lisa Seghetti and Stephen Vina, "U.S. Visitor and Immigrant Status Indicator Technology Program," RL32234 (Washington, D.C.: Congressional Research Service, January 26, 2006).

61. The National Protection and Programs Directorate has an FY 2007 budget of nearly a billion dollars and, in addition to US-VISIT, also funds programs for infrastructure protection, cybersecurity, emergency preparedness communications, and communications interoperability (enabling police, fire and other first responders to communicate with each in coordinating emergency response.

62. *Wall Street Journal* editorial, May 21, 2006, quoting *Reagan: His Life in Letters*, http://www.opinionjournal.com/editorial/feature.html?id=110008406.

63. Janice Cheryl Beaver, "U.S. International Borders: Brief Facts," RS21729 (Washington, D.C.: Congressional Research Service, February 1, 2007), 2.

64. For more background on the San Diego fence, see Blas Nunez-Neto and Michael Garcia, "Border Security: The San Diego Fence," RS22026 (Washington, D.C.: Congressional Research Service, May 23, 2007).

65. The San Diego fence was authorized by the Illegal Immigration Reform and Immigrant Responsibility Act (IIRIRA), P.L. 104-208. The REAL ID Act of 2005 (P.L. 109-13), provided authority to waive environmental regulations to expedite completion of the San Diego fence. See Michael Garcia and Margaret Lee, "Immigration: Analysis of the Major Provisions of the REAL ID Act," RL32754 (Washington, D.C.: Congressional Research Service, May 25, 2005).

66. P.L. 109-367.

67. Blas Nunez-Neto and Michael John Garcia, "Border Security: Barriers along the U.S. International Border," RL33659 (Washington, D.C.: Congressional Research Service, June 5, 2007), 24.

68. Nunez-Neto and Garcia, "Border Security: Barriers along the U.S. International Border," 18–19. According to the CRS report, "The exact appropriation for border fencing in FY2007 is not discernible. In FY2007, the appropriations committee created a new Border Security Fencing, Infrastructure, and Technology (BSFIT) account within the CBP appropriation and allocated $1.2 billion (see H.Rept. 109-699). Combined with the $300 million already appropriated in the emergency supplemental, the overall BSFIT appropriation for FY2007 was $1.5 billion. This account funds the construction of fencing, other infrastructure such as roads and vehicle barriers, and border technologies such as cameras and sensors. The appropriators did not offer guidance on how this funding was to be allocated between these different purposes, and CBP has not responded to several requests concerning how much funding was allocated to fencing in FY2007 from the BSFIT account.

69. Spencer Hsu, "DHS Plan for 'Virtual' Border Fence Still Has Gaps," *Washington Post,* December 5, 2006, A27.

70. Richard Stana and Randolph Hite, GAO, Testimony before the House Appropriations Subcommittee on Homeland Security, February 27, 2007, GAO-07-504T, 1.

71. Nunez-Neto and Garcia, "Border Security: Barriers along the U.S. International Border," 26–27, 35.

72. Paul Cullinan, Statement before the Senate Budget Committee, 8.

73. http://www.newsregister.com/photos/upload/20050428154454_medium.jpg

74. Ruth Wasem, "Noncitizen Eligibility for Federal Public Assistance: Policy Overview and Trends," RL33809 (Washington, D.C.: Congressional Research Service, January 19, 2007), 18-21; National Immigration Law Center, *Guide to Immigrant Eligibility for Federal Programs,* revised March 2005 (accessed June 29, 2007, at http://www.nilc.org/pubs/guideupdates/tbl1_ovrvw_fed_pgms_032505.pdf). See also, Committee on Ways & Means, U.S. House of Representatives, *2004 Green Book* (Washington, D.C.: Committee Print 108-6, 108th Congress, 2d Session), appendix J: "Welfare Benefits for Noncitizens": http://frwebgate.access.gpo.gov/cgi-bin/getdoc.cgi?dbname=108_green_book&docid=f:wm006_25 .pdf.

75. National Center for Children in Poverty, Columbia University

76. Andorra Bruno, "Unauthorized Employment in the United States: Issues and Options," RL33973 (Washington, D.C.: Congressional Research Service, April 20, 2007), summary.

77. Alison Siskin, "Immigration Enforcement within the United States," RL33351 (Washington, D.C.: Congressional Research Service, April 6, 2006), summary page.

78. Ruth Ellen Wasem, "Immigration Reform: Brief Synthesis of Issue," RS22574 (Washington, D.C.: Congressional Research Service, May 10, 2007), 1.

79. Wasem, "Immigration Reform," 1. Source for the 12 million estimate: Interview of Senator Ted Kennedy (D-MA), *This Week with George Stepanopoulos,* ABC News, June 24, 2007. For more information on nonimmigrant overstays, see Ruth Wasem, "Nonimmigrant Overstays: Brief Synthesis of the Issue," RS22446 (Washington, D.C.: Congressional Research Service, May 22, 2006).

80. Congressional Budget Office, "Immigration Policy in the United States" (Washington, D.C.: Author, February 2006), vii.

81. Congressional Budget Office, "Immigration Policy," vii.

82. This is a "flexible cap"—that is, unused slots from one year may carry forward to the next year.

83. However, there are exceptions for family-sponsored and employment-based immigrants. Ruth Wasem, "U.S. Immigration Policy on Permanent Admissions," RL32235 (Washington, D.C.: Congressional Research Service, May 11, 2007), 5.

84. Ruth Wasem, Congressional Research Service, Hearing before the Judiciary Subcommittee on Immigration, Citizenship, Refugees, Border Security and International Law, House of Representatives, June 6, 2007, 5.

85. March 2007 Annual Flow Report, (Washington, D.C.: Department of Homeland Security, Office of Immigration Statistics), table 2; http://www.dhs.gov/xlibrary/assets/statistics/publications/IS-4496_LPRFlowReport_04vaccessible.pdf.

86. Estimates of unauthorized resident alien population vary from 400,000 to 500,000 to 700,000. See Jeffrey Passel, "Unauthorized Migrants: Numbers and Characteristics" (Washington, D.C.: Pew Hispanic Center, June 14, 2005), 5, http://pewhispanic.org/files/reports/46.pdf; Allison Siskin, "Immigration Enforcement within the United States," RL33351 (Washington, D.C.: Congressional Research Service, April 6, 2006), 1; Andorra Bruno, "Immigration: Policy Considerations Related to Guest Worker Programs," RL32044 (Washington, D.C.: Congressional Research Service, May 10, 2007), 6-7.

87. Ruth Wasem, "Unauthorized Aliens Residing in the U.S.: Estimates since 1986," RL33874 (Washington, D.C.: Congressional Research Service, February 28, 2007), 5.

88. CIA website accessed July 9, 2007: https://www.cia.gov/library/publications/the-world-factbook/geos/mx.html#Econ.

89. Erica Dahl-Bredine, "U.S. helped create migrant flow," National Catholic Reporter, September 22, 2006, NCRonline.org; See also Colleen W. Cook, "Mexico-U.S. Relations: Issues for the 110th Congress, RL32724 (Washington, D.C.: Congressional Research Service, May 30, 2007); Sandra Polaski, "Mexican Employment, Productivity and Income, A Decade after NAFTA, February 25, 2004; Jeff Fugate, "A Recipe for Success," *Yale Economic Review,* Spring 2005, http://www.yaleeconomicreview .com/issues/spring2005/nafta.php.

90. Under current law, there are a number of categories of visas for temporary workers: H-1B visas for professional specialty workers, H-2A visas for agricultural visas, and H-2B visas for nonagricultural workers. Wasem, "Immigration Reform," 3–5. See also Bruno, "Guest Worker Programs."

91. Jeffrey Passel, "Size and Characteristics of the Unauthorized Migrant Population in the U.S." (Washington, D.C.: Pew Hispanic Center, March 7, 2006).

92. For a review of this issue, see Andorra Bruno, "Immigration: Policy Considerations Related to Guest Worker Programs," RL32044 (Washington, D.C.: Congressional Research Service, May 10, 2007).

93. P.L. 99-603, signed November 6, 1986.

94. Bruno, "Guest Worker Programs," 38.

95. GAO, "Prospect for US-VISIT Biometric Exit Capability Remain Unclear," GAO-07-1044T (Washington, D.C.: Author, June 28, 2007), highlights.

96. GAO, "Border Security: Investigators Transported Radioactive Sources Across Our Nation's Borders at Two Locations," GAO-06-939T (Washington, D.C.: Author, July 5, 2006).

97. GAO, "Immigration Benefits: Several Factors Impede Timeliness of Application Processing," GAO-01-488 (Washington, D.C.: Author, May 2001).

98. GAO, "Immigration benefits: Improvements Needed to Address Backlogs and Ensure Quality of Adjudications," GAO-06-02 (Washington, D.C.: Author, November 2005), highlights.

99. Chad Haddal, "U.S. Citizenship and Immigration Services' Immigration Fees and Adjudication Costs: The FY 2008 Adjustments and Historical Context," RL34040 (Washington, D.C.: Congressional Research Service, June 12, 2007). See also "The Endless Wait: Will Resources Match the Resolve to Reduce the Immigration Case Backlog?" (Washington, D.C.: The American Immigration Law Foundation, July 2004), www.ailf.org/ipc/endlesswaitprint.asp; USCIS, Backlog Elimination Plan, http://149.101.23.2/graphics/aboutus/repsstudies/backlog.htm.

100. Blas Nunez-Neto, "Border Security: Key Agencies and Their Missions," RS21899 (Washington, D.C.: Congressional Research Service, April 19, 2007), 5.

101. Testimony before the House Coast Guard and Maritime Transportation Subcommittee, March 1, 2006.

102. United States Coast Guard, "U.S. Coast Guard: America's Maritime Guardian," *U.S.C.G Publication 1*, http://www.uscg.mil/overview/Pub%201/contents.html.

103. *U.S. Coast Guard: A Historical Overview*, 1–2, www.uscg.mil/history/h_USCGhistory.html.

104. *U.S. Government Manual* (Washington, D.C.: Government Printing Office, 2005–2006); "U.S. Coast Guard – A Historical Overview," www.uscg.mil/history/h_USCGhistory.html.

105. See *Coast Guard 101 Executive PPT Brief* at www.uscg.mil/overview/index.shtm.

106. Katrina statistics derived from testimony before the House Coast Guard and Maritime Transportation Subcommittee, March 1, 2006. Note also that Coast Guard expenditures related to oil spills are covered by the Oil Spill Liability Trust Fund.

107. Eric Lipton, "Failure to Navigate: Billions Later, Plan to Remake the Coast Guard Fleet Stumbles," *New York Times*, December 9, 2006.

108. CRS, "Coast Guard Deepwater Program: Background and Issues for Congress," July 22, 2005.

109. Statement of Richard Skinner before the Senate Commerce Subcommittee on Oceans, Atmosphere, Fisheries and Coast Guard, February 14, 2007, 3.

110. GAO, "Coast Guard: Challenges Affecting Deepwater Asset Deployment and Management and Efforts to Address Them," GAO-07-874 (Washington, D.C.: Author, June 2007), highlights.

111. The Deepwater reform bill is HR 2722. Kathleen Hunter, "Two Coast Guard Bills Advance; Panel Seeks Deepwater Overhaul," *CQ Weekly*, July 9, 2007, 2047.

112. GAO, Letter to the Homeland Security Appropriations Subcommittees on "Combating Nuclear Smuggling," GAO-07-133R, October 17, 2006, 2–4, 9.

113. OMB, FY 2008 Budget of the United States, *Analytical Perspectives*, table 28-1, 34, http://www.whitehouse.gov/omb/budget/fy2008/pdf/ap_cd_rom/28_1.pdf. For background on the CTR program, see Isabelle Williams, "Analysis of the U.S. Department of Defense's Fiscal Year 2008 Cooperative Threat Reduction Budget Request (Washington, D.C.: Partnership for Global Security, March 19, 2007), 7, http://www.partnershipforglobalsecurity.org/. See also www.NTI.org.

114. OMB, FY 2008 Budget of the United States, appendix, 354. See also Isabelle Williams and Kenneth Luongo, "Analysis of the U.S. Department of Energy's Fiscal Year 2008 International Nonproliferation Budget Request" (Washington, D.C.: Partnership for Global Security, February 26, 2007), 6, http://www.partnershipforglobalsecurity.org/. See also www.NTI.org.

115. Includes the following DHS programs: Science & Technology, Domestic Nuclear Detection Office, and Port Security. OMB, FY 2008 Budget of the United States, appendix.

116. Isabelle Williams, "Preliminary Analysis of the U.S. State Department's Fiscal Year 2008 Budget Request for Global WMD Threat Reduction Programs" (Washington, D.C.: Partnership for Global Security, April 2007), 5, http://www.partnershipforglobalsecurity.org/.

117. OMB, FY 2008 Budget of the United States, *Analytical Perspectives*, Table 3-7.

118. *The 9/11 Commission Report*, 397.

119. Located in the Office for Interoperability and Compatibility.

120. http://www.safecomprogram.gov/SAFECOM/about/faq.

121. When FEMA was first absorbed into DHS, it was stripped of responsibilities for emergency communications.

122. National Telecommunications and Information Administration (NTIA). See chapter 3-19.

123. Linda Moore, "Public Safety Communications Policy," RL32594 (Washington, D.C.: Congressional Research Service, January 31, 2007), 5–6.

124. Genevieve Knezo, "Homeland Security Research and Development Funding, Organization, and Oversight," RS21270 (Washington, D.C.: Congressional Research Service, December 29, 2006), 2.

125. GAO, "First Responders: Much Work Remains to Improve Communications Interoperability," GAO-07-301 (Washington, D.C.: Author, April 2007), highlights.

126. OMB, FY 2008 Budget of the United States, appendix, 479.

127. Moore, "Public Safety Communications Policy," 30–31.

128. Stefan Lovgren, "U.S. Secret Service's Other Job: Fighting Fake Money," *National Geographic News*, October 22, 2004.

129. In 1998, President Clinton issued Presidential Decision Directive 62, which first identifies events of national interest, known as National Special Security Events, and then organizes federal antiterrorism and counterterrorism assets. The Secret Service is the lead agency for the design and implementation of security operations.

130. Stephanie Smith, "Former Presidents: Federal Pension and Retirement Benefits," 98-249 (Washington, D.C.: Congressional Research Service, February 26, 2007).

131. Public Law 107-296.

132. Pursuant to Public Law 109-177, section 607, the United States Secret Service shall be maintained as a distinct entity within the Department of Homeland Security. The Director of the United States Secret Service shall report directly to the Secretary of Homeland Security.

133. CRS, "Terrorist Financing: U.S. Agency Efforts and Inter-Agency Coordination," August 3, 2005.

134. The 9/11 Commission, "Executive Summary: Final Report of the National Commission on Terrorist Attacks upon the United States," 13, http://www.9-11commission.gov/report/911Report_Exec.pdf.

135. Senate Committee on Appropriations, Press Release, "Senate Appropriations Homeland Security Subcommittee Clears Fiscal 2008 Funding Legislation," 7, http://www.washingtonbudgetreport.com/Senate_Homeland_Sub.pdf.

136. Council on Foreign Relations, "America Still Unprepared, Still in Danger," Press Release on Hart-Rudman Report, October 24, 2002.

137. Joint Explanatory Statement of the Committee of Conference, H.R. 2360, H.Rpt. 109-241, 34.

138. Dan Eggen, "U.S. is Given Failing Grades by 9/11 Panel," *Washington Post*, December 6, 2005, A01.

139. Shane Harris and Greta Wodele, "Cover Story: Miles to Go," *National Journal*, January 14, 2006.

140. Council on Foreign Relations, "News Release: U.S. Government Failing to Mobilize Private Sector in Homeland Security Efforts, Warns Council Special Report," May 3, 2006.

141. "Homeland Security and the Private Sector" (Washington, D.C.: Congressional Budget Office, December 2004), ix and interview with senior congressional staff member on May 16, 2006.

142. Background interview with senior congressional staff member, May 15, 2006.

143. U.S. Senate Committee on Homeland Security and Governmental Affairs, "Hurricane Katrina: A Nation Still Unprepared," May 2006, introductory "Note to Readers" from Senators Collins and Lieberman.

144. Ira Helfand, "The U.S. and Nuclear Terrorism: Still Dangerously Unprepared," press conference, Physicians for Social Responsibility, August 31, 2006, Washington, D.C., http://www.psr.org/site/Doc-Server/Good_PSR_Nuclear_Terrorism_News_Release_Printing.doc?docID=801.

145. See earlier section on U.S.-VISIT.

146. "Cover-Story: Federal Response to Sept. 11 in Retrospect," *CQ Weekly*, September 11, 2006.

147 Renae Merle and Spencer Hsu, "Costly Fleet Update Falters," *Washington Post*, December 8, 2006, A01.

148. GAO, "Management Actions Are Needed to Close the Gap between Army Chemical Unit Preparedness and Stated National Priorities," GAO-07-143 (Washington, D.C.: Author, January 2007), highlights.

149. Greg Gordon, "U.S. Unprepared for Nuclear Terror Attack, Experts Say," McClatchy Newspapers,[[NOT AN ACTUAL PAPER NAME, but a company name (like Reuters or AP), correct? Thus no italics.]] March 1, 2007.

150. GAO, "First Responders: Much Work Remains to Improve Communications Interoperability," 41.

151. GAO, "Aviation Security—Federal Efforts to Secure U.S.-Bound Air Cargo Are in the Early Stages and Could Be Strengthened," GAO-07-660 (Washington, D.C.: Author, April 2007), highlights.

152. David M. Walker, Comptroller General of the United States, "Management and Programmatic Challenges Facing the Department of Homeland Security," GAO-07-833T, Testimony before the Subcommittee on Oversight of Government Management, Senate Committee on Homeland Security and Governmental Affairs, May 10, 2007.

153. Senate Committee on Appropriations, Press Release, "Senate Appropriations Homeland Security Subcommittee Clears Fiscal 2008 Funding Legislation," 7, http://www.washingtonbudgetreport.com/Senate_Homeland_Sub.pdf.

154. Spencer S. Hsu, "Job Vacancies at DHS Said to Hurt U.S. Preparedness," *WashingtonPost.com*, July 9, 2007, A01. See also Robert O'Harrow Jr., "Costs Skyrocket as DHS Runs up No-Bid Contracts," *WashingtonPost.com*, June 28, 2007, A01, reporting on the use of costly no-bid contracts to compensate for the unfilled positions at DHS.

155. Includes FY 2007 budget authority for Research, Development, Testing and Evaluation; Procurement; and the Reliable Replacement Warhead program.

156. Amy Belasco, "The Cost of Iraq, Afghanistan, and Other Global War on Terror Operations since 9/11," RL33110 (Washington, D.C.: Congressional Research Service, June 28, 2007), 3.

157. See the earlier text box, "FY 2007 Resources Invested in Protecting the Homeland from Terrorists Acquiring and Using Nuclear and Other Weapons of Mass Destruction."

158. Graham Allison, *Nuclear Terrorism* (London: Constable & Robinson, 2006), 223.

159. *The 9/11 Commission Report*, 380.

160. Quoted in Allison, *Nuclear Terrorism*, 1.

Veterans Benefits

FY 2007 Veterans Spending: $79 billion

See www.GovBudget.com for updated numbers

*With malice toward none, with charity for all, with firmness in the right as God gives us to see the right, let us strive on to finish the work we are in, to bind up the nation's wounds, **to care for him who shall have borne the battle and for his widow and his orphan**, to do all which may achieve and cherish a just and lasting peace among ourselves and with all nations.*[1]

—President Abraham Lincoln

In a Nutshell

Veterans, and in some cases their spouses, dependents, and survivors, may be eligible for a broad range of benefits including health care services, compensation for service-connected injuries or disabilities, disability pensions for low-income veterans, educational (Montgomery GI Bill) assistance, vocational training, career assistance, low-interest housing loans, life insurance, and burial benefits. At the end of FY 2006, there were an estimated 24 million veterans, with 5 million receiving health care services, 3 million veterans (and survivors/dependents) receiving disability compensation, and a half million low-income veterans (and survivors) receiving pension benefits (see figure 3-3.1).

Background

The Department of Veterans Affairs (VA) traces its origins to 1789 when the first U.S. Congress appropriated funds to pay benefits to veterans of the Revolutionary War. The broader mission of the VA was eloquently defined by President Lincoln who, in his second inaugural address, called on the Nation to "care for him who shall have borne the battle and for his widow and his orphan."[2] (The Civil War is not as distant as it may seem. As of May 2006, the VA reported that "five children of Civil War veterans still draw VA benefits."[3])

It is important to understand the distinction between military retirees and veterans. *Military retirees* are people who have completed a full active duty military career, usually at least 20 years of service. A *veteran* is any person who has served in the armed forces.

Veterans' Health Care

VA health care appropriations in FY 2007 were more than $34 billion. The VA provides a full range of medical services to veterans including outpatient, in-patient, nursing home, psychiatric, rehabilitative, and home health.

Because there is an enormous demand for VA health care, services are provided on a priority basis. There are eight priority levels or "groups." Assignment to a particular priority group depends on whether a veteran has a service-connected injury or disability, the veteran's disability rating, and income level.

The *highest priority* (group 1) is reserved for veterans with service-connected disabilities rated at 50% or higher. The *lowest priority* (group 8) is for veterans without service-connected disabilities and income that exceeds the low-income threshold.

The VA delivers health care through the Veterans Health Administration (VHA), the nation's largest health care system, with over 200,000 employees at 154 hospitals, 135 nursing homes, 850 outpatient clinics, and 200 readjustment counseling centers. In 2005, about 5 million veterans received health care in VA facilities across the nation—a 20% increase since 2001.[4]

A **service-connected** injury or disability is one that was incurred or aggravated during military service. Veterans' **disability ratings range from zero to 100% (the most severe)** and are designed to reflect the veteran's reduction in earnings capacity. A 100% rating therefore indicates a severe disability resulting in no earnings capacity.

Myth: Veterans health care is an entitlement program.

Fact: Veterans health care is *not* an entitlement; it is a discretionary program. Each year Congress determines how much to appropriate to the program and the VA allocates available resources based on its priority system, giving priority to service-connected conditions and low-income veterans.

Veterans' Disability Programs: Compensation and Pensions

Unlike VA Health Care, which is a discretionary program, the VA's two disability programs are entitlements. The Veterans Disability Compensation program, costing $35 billion in FY

2007, entitles veterans to *compensation for a loss of earning capacity as a result of disabilities sustained or worsened during military service.*[5] The amount of compensation is tied to the veteran's "disability rating" as reflected in the chart.

The Veterans Disability Pensions program, costing approximately $3 billion in FY 2007, is aimed at assisting *low-income veterans* who served during wartime and are permanently disabled, or age 65 or older.[7]

2007 VA Disability Compensation Rates

Disability Rating[6]	*Monthly Disability Compensation*
10%	$ 115
20%	$ 225
30%	$ 348
40%	$ 501
50%	$ 712
60%	$ 901
70%	$ 1,135
80%	$ 1,319
90%	$ 1,438
100%	$ 2,471

Other VA Benefits

Additional VA benefits include:

- The Montgomery GI Bill, which assists vets in paying costs for higher education and various types of training.;
- Vocational rehabilitation and employment programs aimed at helping disabled vets obtain employment and live as independently as possible;
- "Vet Centers" across the country that provide trauma, substance abuse, readjustment, and bereavement counseling for veterans and their families;
- Home loan guarantees that enable vets to buy a home without a down payment;
- Grants for specially adapted housing and automobiles for disabled vets;
- Life insurance including automatic $400,000 coverage of all active duty personnel, as well as optional low-cost term life insurance and coverage for traumatic injuries; and
- Burial benefits.

Reservists and National Guard

Reservists called to active duty may, depending on the length of active duty service, qualify for the full range of VA benefits. Reservists not called to active duty qualify for more limited benefits. National Guard members may establish eligibility by being called to Federal service.[8]

Issues

- **Increasing demands on the veterans health care system.** An issue of continuing concern is the rapidly escalating costs of the veterans health care system. The Congress appropriated $31.2 billion for VA health care in FY 2006; $34.2 billion in FY 2007; and pending appropriations for FY 2008 would provide more than $37 billion.[9] The rapid growth is a consequence of three factors: (1) the easing of eligibility rules in the mid-1990s; (2) general health care inflation impacting all U.S. health care providers; and (3) the growing number of Iraq and Afghanistan veterans in need of extensive and continuing medical care upon their return to the U.S. According to the House Appropriations Committee, the Veterans Health Administration is anticipating treating "more than 5.8 million

WHATEVER HAPPENED TO THE GI BILL?

After World War II, the famous "GI Bill"[10] sent nearly 8 million veterans to college, covering their tuition and fees, and providing a monthly allowance for living expenses. In addition to the higher education boom, the GI Bill's low-interest home mortgages to 11 million families spurred an enormous housing boom, and the GI Bill's low-interest business loans assisted thousands of small businesses in getting off the ground.[11] This generous entitlement not only reflected the thanks of a grateful nation; it also built up the

Courtesy: National Archives

middle class, literally transforming America; the GI bill was dubbed the "Magic Carpet to the Middle Class."[12] However, current veterans' education benefits (under the Montgomery GI bill[13]) are somewhat limited by comparison. Returning vets from Iraq and Afghanistan receive a maximum of $1,075 per month for 36 months, which the recipients may use to cover tuition, fees, and living expenses. The College Board estimates that the current undergraduate budget for a public university is over $16,000 per year for residents and $26,000 out of State, and $33,000 per year for a private university.[14] Today's lawmakers might want to take a page out of history and reinvigorate one of the most successful government programs. Iraq and Afghanistan vets deserve it, recruitment would improve (at a time when the armed forces are stretched thin), cash-strapped universities and the ailing housing market would benefit from the infusion of resources, thousands of new businesses would open up, and the American middle class would be strengthened. The original GI Bill made "the American dream" of equal opportunity a tangible reality for millions.

patients in 2008 including more than (263,000) veterans of Iraq and Afghanistan, 54,000 more than fiscal 2007" (emphasis added).[15]

- **When is a medical condition service connected?** A key issue with regard to qualifying for veterans' compensation is establishing the "service connection." After considerable debate, certain disabilities are now *presumed* to have a service connection—for example, where the veteran was exposed to Agent Orange in Vietnam, exposed to radiation during nuclear weapons tests, or served in the Gulf War and suffers from Gulf War Syndrome.
- **The growing backlog of benefits claims.** In a recent report, GAO reported to Congress that the "VA continues to face challenges in improving service delivery to veterans, specifically speeding up the process of adjudication and appeal, and reducing the existing backlog of claims." Total pending disability claims, as well as claims pending for more than 6 months, have increased in each year since 2003.[16]
- **Homeless veterans.** The VA estimates that 196,000 veterans are homeless on any given night, comprising one-fifth to one-quarter of the U.S. homeless population. Suggested causes are post-traumatic stress disorder (PTSD) and drug or alcohol addictions. In FY 2006, $238 million was appropriated to a variety of programs designed to assist homeless veterans.

- **Concurrent receipt.** An issue that has received much attention in recent years is whether military retirees should be allowed to receive *both* military retired pay *and* VA disability compensation to which they would otherwise be entitled. Until 2004, military retired pay had to be reduced by the amount of VA disability compensation received by the retiree. However, beginning in 2004, military retirees began receiving "Combat Related Special Compensation" as a substitute for the VA disability compensation they were losing, and the concurrent receipt offset began phasing out for all veterans with a disability rating of 50% or more. As of 2005, the concurrent receipt offset was completely eliminated for veterans with a 100% service-connected disability. There still remain some limited categories of military retirees subject to the concurrent receipt offset.[17]

Notes

1. The bolded words from Lincoln's second inaugural address became the VA's motto in 1959, adorning the main entrance to VA headquarters in Washington, D.C.

2. This became the official motto of the VA in May 1959. This phrase is excerpted from President Lincoln's second inaugural address, when he uttered one of the most eloquent statements of any leader in human history: "With malice toward none, with charity for all, with firmness in the right as God gives us to see the right, let us strive on to finish the work we are in, to bind up the nation's wounds, to care for him who shall have borne the battle and for his widow and his orphan, to do all which may achieve and cherish a just and lasting peace among ourselves and with all nations." See http://www .75anniversary.va.gov/history/lincoln_motto.htm.

3. Department of Veterans Affairs Fact Sheet, May 2006, http://www1.va.gov/opa/fact/docs/ vafacts.pdf.

4. "Facts about the Department of Veterans Affairs," May 2006, 3, http://www1.va.gov/opa/fact/ docs/vafacts.pdf.

5. The amount of disability compensation ranges from $112 to $2,393 per month, depending on the extent of disability. The extent of disability is set in percentages of impairment, from 0% to 100%. Additional amounts may be paid in cases of: severe disabilities; loss of limb(s); have a spouse, child(ren), or dependent parent(s); or have a seriously disabled spouse.

6. Veterans with at least a 30% disability rating are eligible for additional payments for spouse and dependents. "Federal Benefits for Veterans and Dependents" (Washington, D.C.: Department of Veterans Affairs, 2007), 16.

7. The VA pension program pays the difference between countable family income and the yearly income limit which ranges from $10,579 for veterans without dependents to $20,924 for a veteran who needs aid and attendance and has one dependent.

8. Carol Davis, "Veterans' Benefits: Issues in the 110th Congress," RL33985 (Washington, D.C.: Congressional Research Service, April 26, 2007), 5.

9. Press Release, Senate Committee on Appropriations, "Senate Military Construction and Veterans Affairs Appropriations Subcommittee Clears Fiscal 2008 Funding Legislation," June 13, 2007; Press Release, House Committee on Appropriations, "Summary: 2008 Military Construction and Veterans Affairs Appropriations," June 6, 2007.

10. The official name of the bill was "The Servicemen's Readjustment Act of 1944."

11. Stephen Ambrose, historian, interviewed on PBS's *NewsHour*, July 4, 200, www.pbs.org/newshour/ bb/military/july-dec00/gibill_7-4.html.

12. See Christine Davenport, "The Middle Class Rose, as Did Expectations," *Washington Post*, May 27, 2004, B01.

13. Established in 1985, http://www1.va.gov/opa/fact/docs/vafacts.pdf.

14. *Trends in College Pricing 2006* (New York: College Board, 2006), table 2, http://www.collegeboard.com/prod_downloads/press/cost06/trends_college_pricing_06.pdf.

15. Press Release, House Committee on Appropriations, "Summary: 2008 Military Construction and Veterans Affairs Appropriations," June 6, 2007, 1.

16. GAO, "Veterans' Disability Benefits: Processing of Claims Continues to Present Challenges," GAO-07-562T (Washington, D.C.: Government Accountability Office, March 13, 2007).

17. Charles Henning, "Military Retirement, Concurrent Receipt, and Related Major Legislative Issues," RL33449 (Washington, D.C.: Congressional Research Service, January 24, 2007).

Social Security: Is It Stable or Facing Collapse?

> **Projected FY 2008 Social Security Spending: $612 billion**
> **20% of Federal Spending**

See www.GovBudget.com for updated numbers

[I]t took a depression to dramatize for us the appalling insecurity of the great mass of the population, and to stimulate interest in social insurance in the United States. We have come to learn that the large majority of our citizens must have protection against the loss of income due to . . . old age, death of the breadwinners and disabling accident and illness, not only on humanitarian grounds, but in the interest of our National welfare. If we are to maintain a healthy economy and thriving production, we need to maintain the standard of living of the lower income groups in our population who constitute 90 per cent of our purchasing power.— National Radio Address by Frances Perkins, President Roosevelt's Secretary of Labor, February 25, 1935

In a Nutshell

Social Security consists of two separate parts: **Old Age and Survivors Insurance** (OASI) and **Disability Insurance** (DI). Under OASI, monthly benefits are paid to **retired workers**, their spouses and dependent children, and **survivors of deceased workers** (spouses, dependent children and dependent parents). Under DI, monthly benefits are paid to **disabled workers**

Author's note: This chapter is dedicated to the late Senator Daniel Patrick Moynihan, who I had the privilege to work for as General Counsel at the Senate Finance Committee. Senator Moynihan was well known for his eloquent leadership on all matters relating to Social Security and his deep understanding of the foundational principles on which this monumental program was built.

(who have not yet reached retirement age) and their families. The Social Security system is sustained by payroll taxes of 12.4%—half paid by employers and half by employees (with self-employed individuals paying roughly the full amount). Social Security payroll taxes are assessed on income up to a maximum amount ($97,500 for 2007).[1] At the beginning of FY 2007, more than 150 million workers were paying Social Security taxes to fund current benefits for nearly 50 million beneficiaries.[2]

President Roosevelt signs the landmark Social Security Act of 1935. Standing behind the President is Secretary of Labor Frances Perkins, architect of the plan and the first woman cabinet member in U.S. history. Courtesy: SSA

Background

Social Security is the nation's largest Federal program with an FY 2008 budget of $612 billion, amounting to one-fifth of the Federal Budget. (Total defense spending for FY 2008 is higher than Social Security, but the "base" defense budget—excluding Iraq war spending—is less than Social Security.)

Looking at objective measures of poverty, Social Security has been the most effective antipoverty program in U.S. history. One recent study estimated that without Social Security, nearly half of elderly Americans would have incomes below the poverty line; but taking Social Security benefits into account, the percentage living in poverty is under 10%.[3] As a "social insurance" program, Social Security spreads the cost of providing basic retirement and disability guarantees among all working Americans, as well as providing greater stability to the economy by insulating beneficiaries from economic downturns, which would otherwise depress consumer spending.

Social Security is actually **two distinct programs**: the Old Age and Survivors Insurance Program and the Disability Insurance Program.

Old Age and Survivors Insurance program (OASI)

OASI provides monthly cash benefits to retired workers, their spouses[4] and dependent children, and survivors of deceased workers (spouses, dependent children, and dependent parents). Average monthly benefits for the more than 31 million retired workers is $1,050 per month. Generally, a worker must have 10 years (40 quarters) of covered employment to be eligible for retirement benefits.[5]

Initial benefits are based on a worker's past average monthly earnings, indexed to reflect *changes in national wage levels* (and adjusted upward for low earners). Each subsequent year, benefits are adjusted upward to compensate for consumer price *inflation*. These annual adjustments are called "cost of living adjustments," or COLAs. The COLA for 2007 was 3.3%.[6]

The Survivors Insurance component of Social Security is similar to life insurance. When a worker dies, his or her spouse, dependent children, disabled children over 16, dependent parents, and former spouse caring for children may qualify for Social Security survivors benefits.[7]

The Social Security amendments of 1983 established a gradual schedule for increasing the full retirement eligibility age from 65 to 67. Workers born before 1938 were eligible to retire at age 65, and workers born 1960 or later will be eligible for full retirement at age 67. Between those two groups, the retirement eligibility age slowly increases from 65 to 67. For example, for workers born in 1948, the full retirement age is 66, and for people born in 1958 the full retirement age is 66 and 8 months.[8]

The Social Security benefit formula is progressive, returning a higher percentage of a lower-wage worker's average monthly earnings. For example, in 2007, the benefit formula for most workers returns 90% of a worker's first $680 in monthly earnings, 32% between $680 and $4,100, and 15% over $4100.[9]

Until 1984, Social Security benefits were exempt from the income tax. In 1983, Congress made up to 50% of Social Security benefits taxable for higher income beneficiaries; and in 1993, up to 85% was made taxable. The taxes collected are credited to the OASDI Trust Funds and the Medicare Hospital Insurance (Part A) Trust Fund, respectively. According to CBO, about 40% of beneficiaries are impacted by the tax.[10]

Social Security Disability Insurance (SSDI)

Disability Insurance replaces a portion of a worker's income when illness or disability prevents him or her from working. Social Security's Disability Insurance program, established in

TABLE 3-4.1 Average Monthly Social Security Benefits (2007)

Beneficiaries (where the worker's benefits are vested due to 40 quarters of contributions)	Average Monthly
Benefit	
Old-Age Insurance	
Retired workers	$ 1,050
Retired worker and spouse	$ 1,569
Retired couple, both receiving benefits	$ 1,713
Dependent children of retired workers	$ 523
Survivors Insurance	
Aged widow(er) alone	$ 1,008
Widow(er) with two dependent children (under age 16)	$ 2,167
Dependent child (under age 16) of deceased worker	$ 687
Disability Insurance	
Disabled workers	$ 979
Disabled worker and spouse	$ 1,236
Disabled worker, spouse, and one or more children	$ 1,646

Source: Social Security Administration.[11]

1956, provides monthly cash benefits for disabled workers (and their dependents[12]) who have paid into the system, met minimum work requirements, and qualify as unable to engage in "substantial gainful activity" due to a physical or mental impairment.[13]

SSDI requires that a person wait five months from the onset of a disability before receiving SSDI benefits,[14] the purpose being to discourage fraudulent claims. Twenty-four months after SSDI coverage begins, the disabled worker is also entitled to Medicare coverage.[15]

SSDI benefits, once approved, continue as long as the individual remains disabled or until he or she reaches the normal retirement age, at which time the benefits automatically convert to retirement benefits. Periodically, SSA conducts "continuing disability reviews" (CDRs) to determine whether the individual is still disabled.

Similar to retirement benefits, *initial benefits* are based on a worker's past average monthly earnings, indexed to reflect *changes in national wage levels* and adjusted upward for low earners. *Each subsequent year*, benefits are adjusted upward to compensate for consumer price inflation.

At the end of 2006, SSDI was paying out an average of $937 per month to disabled workers, $249 for spouses of disabled workers, and $281 for children.[16] There were a total of 8.6 million beneficiaries and dependents.[17]

COMMON MYTHS ABOUT SOCIAL SECURITY

Myth: There are no Social Security Trust Funds.

Fact: Payroll taxes withheld from workers' paychecks are deposited in the U.S. Treasury and credited to the Old Age, Survivors, and Disability Insurance Trust Funds in the form of U.S. Treasury securities. When benefit checks are issued by the U.S. Treasury, equivalent amounts of U.S. securities are debited from the Trust Funds. When payroll taxes exceed benefits in a particular year, the surpluses are reflected as increasing amounts of U.S. securities held by the Trust Funds.[18]

Myth: Congress has been "raiding" the Social Security Trust Funds to pay for other government programs.

Fact: As noted above, Social Security surpluses are, by law, invested in U.S. Treasury securities. *As with any public or private funds invested in Treasury securities*, the Social Security surpluses become available for expenditure on other Federal programs. Beginning in 2017, when Social Security payroll taxes are projected to be insufficient to cover benefit payments, the Treasury will begin to draw down the accumulated Treasury securities held by the Trust Funds to cover the shortfall in payroll taxes.

Myth: Each worker has his or her own Social Security retirement "account" at the Social Security Administration.

Fact: No—Social Security is not a personal investment program. It is a "pay-as-you-go" Federal entitlement program where *current workers* fund benefits for *current retirees and disabled Americans.*

Myth: *Congress doesn't pay into Social Security.*

Fact: Prior to 1984, Members of Congress, like all Federal employees, were not covered by Social Security and did not pay into the system; they had a separate Civil Service Retirement System. In 1984, Congress established a new Federal retirement system requiring all Federal employees, including Members of Congress, to participate in Social Security.

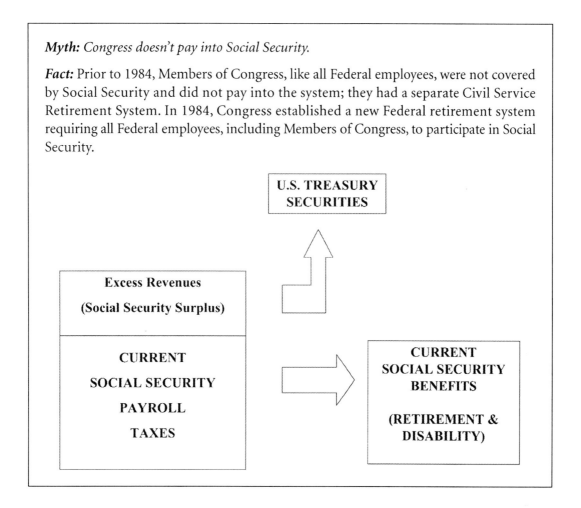

Issue: Does the Social Security program face collapse due to the "perfect storm" of (1) the baby boom retirement, (2) longer life spans, and (3) low birthrates?

It is true that these three factors will, if unaddressed, place a significant burden on the U.S. Treasury and private credit markets. However, the Social Security system does not face imminent collapse and, more importantly, can be fixed with fairly simple adjustments if the two political parties can muster the political will to make the necessary changes.

(By contrast, as discussed in chapter 3-6, the explosive growth of Medicare and Medicaid pose far more serious—and complex—challenges to the nation.)

The basic facts on the long-term outlook for Social Security are (1) annual Social Security benefits are projected to exceed payroll tax revenues between 2017 and 2019;[19] (2) at that time, the Social Security system will begin to draw down the significant surpluses it has been accumulating ($2.2 trillion at the end of FY 2007); (3) the surpluses, by law, are invested in U.S. Treasury bonds (the safest securities available); (4) between 2041 and 2046,[20] the surpluses will be depleted and will no longer be able to cover the gap between revenues and expenditures; (5) at that time, payroll taxes will only cover 74%–79% of program costs[21] (assuming current law remains unchanged); and (6) SSA would no longer have legal authority to pay full benefits.

TABLE 3-4.2 The Declining Ratio of Covered Workers to Beneficiaries[22]

Note: Between 2010 and 2030, the number of people age 65 and older is projected to grow by 76%. In contrast, the number of workers supporting the system is projected to grow by 6%.[23]

	Covered Workers	Beneficiaries	Ratio of Covered Workers per Beneficiary
1950	48,280,000	2,930,000	16.5 to 1
1960	72,530,000	14,262,000	5.1 to 1
1970	93,090,000	25,186,000	3.7 to 1
1980	113,649,000	35,118,000	3.2 to 1
1990	133,672,000	39,470,000	3.4 to 1
2000	154,732,000	45,166,000	3.4 to 1
2005	158,718,000	47,993,000	3.3 to 1
2010 (projected)	166,717,000	52,604,000	3.2 to 1
2020 (projected)	176,049,000	67,977,000*	2.6 to 1*
2030 (projected)	181,110,000	83,524,000*	2.2 to 1*
2040 (projected)	186,581,000	91,077,000	2.0 to 1
2050 (projected)	191,869,000	95,340,000	2.0 to 1
2060 (projected)	196,467,000	100,389,000	2.0 to 1
2070 (projected)	200,744,000	105,828,000	1.9 to 1

*Note the massive increase in beneficiaries as the baby boom generation retires and the concurrent decline in covered workers per beneficiary, from 3.2 in 2010 to 2.2 by 2030.

We can be certain the Treasury will redeem the bonds held by the Social Security Trust Funds as the surpluses are needed to cover annual shortfalls. However, the Treasury's obligation to do so in 2017 and beyond will place substantial fiscal pressures on credit markets and the economy. To redeem the securities, the Treasury will have to borrow funds, raise taxes, or cut spending, or some combination of the three. The most likely scenario is borrowing; that is, the debt currently held by the Social Security Trust funds will be "rolled over" (converted) into debt held by the public.

If America's current non–Social Security budget deficits[24] continue, *the combined pressures of borrowing to cover budget deficits and to redeem bonds held by the Social Security Trust Funds risk higher interest rates, inflation, and greater indebtedness to foreign nations.* Clearly, to avoid this dismal economic scenario, Social Security needs to be "adjusted" so that benefits do not outpace income.

Issue: Are Individual Accounts the Solution?

Shortly after the 2004 presidential election, President George W. Bush proposed creating "individual accounts" (IAs) to address the long-term solvency issues facing Social Security. President Bush was correct that Social Security solvency needs to be addressed—and the sooner the better. Regrettably, his proposal for individual accounts would have worsened the solvency of Social Security and increased the nation's debt.[25]

Under the IA proposal, existing beneficiaries would keep the current system, as would workers above a specified cutoff age. Younger workers who choose to participate would be able to divert a portion of their payroll taxes (between 2% and 4% of payroll) into an individual account up to a maximum contribution. In exchange, they would accept a future reduction in guaranteed Social Security benefits, wagering that their IA would earn a return larger than the reduction in benefits.[26] It is this reduction in future benefits that allows the IA approach to claim that it fixes long-term solvency. Unfortunately, the IA proposal is seriously flawed for the following reasons:

1 Social Security is a "pay-as-you-go" program, with current workers' payroll taxes paying for current retirees' benefits. Consequently, allowing younger workers to divert a significant chunk of their payroll taxes from the Social Security Trust Funds into IAs would leave the Trust Funds without sufficient funds to deliver benefits to current retirees, necessitating government borrowing in excess of *$2.5 trillion.*[27]

2 The plan would achieve long-term "solvency" for Social Security exclusively through large benefit cuts.

3 If market returns on the IAs are lower than anticipated, millions of retirees could end up with insufficient retirement funds to cover basic necessities.

4 Linking IA proceeds to stock prices would undermine Social Security's fundamental strength as *social insurance* that *guarantees* benefits to retirees, their dependents and survivors to prevent poverty.

Ultimately, the various IA proposals are driven by ideological assertions that may appear compelling at first glance: giving those who are less well-off a chance to accumulate financial assets; limiting the government's role in retirement planning; encouraging individuals to assume greater responsibility for their own well-being; and improving the overall economy by pumping IA contributions into financial markets (which seems to ignore the $2 trillion the government would have to borrow from the markets during the transition to the new system).[28] Unfortunately, the ideology is not supported by fiscal realities.

Issue: Fixing Social Security

An effective Social Security "fix" is not technically complicated but is politically complicated in today's highly partisan environment. Fixing the system requires a commitment by both parties to work together, as they did on the Greenspan Commission appointed by President Reagan in the early 1980s and on which Senator Moynihan (D-NY) and Senator Bob Dole (R-KA) served. What is needed is a *carefully balanced package* of:

- small and gradual increases in the retirement age[29] (reflecting longer life spans, improving the worker-to-retiree ratio, and increasing the payroll tax base);
- correcting the calculation of annual COLAs or placing modest limits on COLAs;[30]
- using "progressive indexing" to slow the growth in initial benefits for higher income retirees;[31]
- a modest increase in the taxation of Social Security benefits for high-income individuals;[32] and

- increasing or lifting the cap on income subject to Social Security taxes[33] coupled with a reduction in the FICA tax rate, which would yield more total revenue, while reducing the payroll tax burden on lower- and middle-income Americans, generating a more progressive payroll tax. (The current payroll tax is highly regressive, with the wealthiest 1% of American families paying a smaller proportion of their income in payroll taxes than the poorest 20% of families.)[34]

The sooner these adjustments are made the better, considering the fiscal crunch the Treasury will face when the Social Security Trust Funds begin redeeming bonds in 2017.

Individual accounts are worthy of careful consideration, but as an *optional add-on to the current system* to stimulate further national savings—not as a substitute for the current system of guaranteed retirement and disability benefits, which has successfully prevented tens of millions of Americans from slipping into poverty when they are no longer able to work.

RR workers and the Railroad Retirement Board (FY 2007: $5.9 billion)

Many of the nation's railroad workers receive Railroad Retirement Board (RRB) benefits *instead of* Social Security benefits.[35]

This practice dates back to 1936 when Congress sought to shore up the stability of the nation's railroads by assuming responsibility for administration of the railroad industry's employee benefits. The Railroad Retirement Board (RRB)—an independent Federal agency established by Congress to fulfill this responsibility—administers retirement, survivor, disability, and other benefits for railroad workers and their families.

Railroad retirees receive the equivalent of Social Security benefits (known as Tier I benefits) funded by the Social Security Trust Funds. They may also receive a rail industry pension collectively bargained like other private pension plans "but embedded in Federal law" and funded by the rail sector (known as Tier II benefits).[36]

Tier I benefits are financed with a payroll tax identical to the Social Security payroll tax. The Tier II tax is 12.1% for employers and 3.9% for employees on earnings up to $72,600 in 2007.[37] In addition to Tier I and Tier II payroll taxes, RRB payments to beneficiaries are also funded by the financial interchange with the Social Security trust funds, interest earned on surpluses, and income taxes levied on RRB benefits. In FY 2007, net budget authority for RRB was $5.9 billion and beneficiaries numbered 573,000.[38]

Notes

1. Social Security payroll taxes are often called FICA taxes, after the legislation that created them: the Federal Insurance Contribution Act. The *self-employed* pay the SECA tax, named for the Self-Employed Contribution Act, which roughly equals the total of the employer and employee contributions. Total FICA taxes amount to 15.3%, with most of the FICA tax (12.4% of payroll) going into the Social Security Trust Funds. The remaining 2.9% of payroll goes into the Medicare Part A (Hospital Insurance) Trust Fund and is often called the "Medicare Tax." (See chapter 3-6 for an explanation of Medicare.) For tax year 2007, the Social Security portion of FICA is imposed on the first $97,500 of income (adjusted annually for inflation), while the Medicare portion is imposed on *all* income. Important note on the SECA tax: While it may appear that the self-employed pay exactly double a worker's

tax, it is actually somewhat less than double because 7.65% of taxable income is excluded from SECA tax, and one-half of the SECA tax is deductible from income (as it is when employers pay their share of payroll taxes).

2. Social Security Administration, Monthly Statistical Snapshot, June 2007, http://www.ssa.gov/ policy/docs/quickfacts/stat_snapshot/.

3. Arloc Sherman and Isaac Shapiro, "Social Security Lifts 13 Million Seniors above the Poverty Line: A State-by-State Analysis" (Washington, D.C.: Center on Budget and Policy Priorities, February 24, 2005).

4. "Spousal benefits are intended for individuals who are financially dependent on spouses who work in Social Security-covered positions. Individuals who qualify for both a Social Security worker benefit . . . based on their own work history and a Social Security spousal benefit based on their spouse's work history are 'dually-entitled' and are subject to the dual entitlement rule [which] requires that 100% of a Social Security . . . benefit earned as a worker (based on one's own Social Security-covered earnings) be subtracted from any Social Security spousal benefit one is eligible to receive." Laura Haltzel, "Social Security: The Government Pension Offset," RL32453 (Washington, D.C.: Congressional Research Service, March 8, 2007), summary.

5. Dawn Nuschler and Alison Siskin, "Social Security Benefits for Noncitizens: Current Policy and Legislation," R32004 (Washington, D.C.: Congressional Research Service, June 25, 2007).

6. The inflation adjustment is tied to the Consumer Price Index for Urban Wage Earners and Clerical Works or

CPI-W. Gary Sidor, "Social Security: The Cost-of-Living Adjustment in January 2007," 94-803 EPW (Washington, D.C.: Congressional Research Service, January 2007), 1.

7. Kathleen Romig and Scott Szymendera, "Social Security Survivors Benefits," RS22294 (Washington, D.C., Congressional Research Service, January 18, 2007, 1.

8. See Social Security's "Full Retirement Age Schedule," at http://www.ssa.gov/retire2/retirechart .htm#chart.

9. Laura Haltzel, "Social Security: The Windfall Elimination Provision (WEP)," 98-35 (Washington, D.C.: Congressional Research Service, March 8, 2007), 1.

10. Christine Scott, "Social Security: Calculation and History of Taxing Benefits," RL32552 (Washington, D.C.: Congressional Research Service, May 10, 2007."

11. "Monthly Statistical Snapshot," June 2007, www.socialsecurity.gov/policy/docs/quickfacts/stat _snapshot/; and "Fact Sheet: 2007 Social Security changes," www.ssa.gov/pressoffice/factsheets/ colafacts2007.pdf.

12. Spouses, surviving disabled spouses, and children. Scott Szymendera, "Primer on Disability Benefits," RL32279 (Washington, D.C.: Congressional Research Service, December 26, 2006), 1.

13. SSA uses a five-part test to determine whether an individual qualifies as disabled: work test, severity test, medical listings test, previous work test, and any work test. Scott Szymendera, "Primer on Disability Benefits," RL32279 (Washington, D.C.: Congressional Research Service, December 26, 2006), 4, 8–9.

14. Scott Szymendera, "Social Security Disability Insurance: The Five-Month Waiting Period for SSDI Benefits," RS22220 (Washington, D.C.: Congressional Research Service, December 26, 2006), 1.

15. Scott Szymendera, "Primer on Disability Benefits," RL32279 (Washington, D.C.: Congressional Research Service, December 26, 2006), 5. For a discussion of the purpose of the 24-month waiting period, see Julie M. Whittaker, "Social Security Disability Insurance (SSDI) and Medicare: The 24-month Waiting Period for SSDI Beneficiaries under Age 65," RS22195 (Washington, D.C.: Congressional Research Service, July 14, 2005).

16. Scott Szymendera, "Primer on Disability Benefits," RL32279 (Washington, D.C.: Congressional Research Service, December 26, 2006), 3.

17. Current law requires that a person wait five months from the onset of a qualifying disability before receiving Social Security disability benefits. CRS, "Social Security Disability Insurance: The Five-Month Waiting Period for SSDI Benefits," Library of Congress: August 15, 2005.

18. For more information on the Trust Funds, see Christine Scott, "Social Security: The Trust Fund," RL33028 (Washington, D.C.: Congressional Research Service, April 24, 2007); Geoffrey Kollman, "Social Security: Where Do Surplus Taxes Go and How Are They Used?" 94-593 EPW (Washington, D.C.: Congressional Research Service, September 8, 2003), 1.

19. The Social Security Trustees' report projects 2017 and the Congressional Budget Office projects 2019. "The 2007 Annual Report of the Board of Trustees of the Federal Old-Age and Survivors Insurance and Federal Disability Insurance Trust Funds" (Washington, D.C.: April 23, 2007), 16; and CBO, "Updated Long-Term Projections for Social Security" (Washington, D.C.: Congressional Budget Office, June 2006), 1.

20. The Social Security Trustees' report projects 2041 and the Congressional Budget Office projects 2046. "The 2007 Annual Report of the Board of Trustees of the Federal Old-Age and Survivors Insurance and Federal Disability Insurance Trust Funds" (Washington, D.C.: April 23, 2007), 16; and CBO, "Updated Long-Term Projections for Social Security" (Washington, D.C.: Congressional Budget Office, June 2006), 1.

21. The Social Security Trustees' report projects 75% and CBO projects 79%. "The 2007 Annual Report of the Board of Trustees of the Federal Old-Age and Survivors Insurance and Federal Disability Insurance Trust Funds" (Washington, D.C.: April 23, 2007), 16; and CBO, "Updated Long-Term Projections for Social Security" (Washington, D.C.: Congressional Budget Office, June 2006), 1.

22. Gary Sidor, "Social Security: Brief Facts and Statistics," 94-27 (Washington, D.C.: Congressional Research Service, January 26, 2006), 10.

23. Dawn Nuschler, "Social Security Reform," IB98048 (Washington, D.C.: Congressional Research Service, May 1, 2006).

24. When Congress and the President asserted during 2007 their adoption of a "balance budget" by 2012, they were using ongoing Social Security surpluses to "mask" underlying structural deficits in the budget. See "The Dance between the Unified Budget and Social Security Spending" in chapter 2-9.

25. See Laura Haltzel, "Social Security Reform: President Bush's 2005 Individual Account Proposal," RL32879 (Washington, D.C.: Congressional Research Service, March 9, 2006), 9.

26. This reflects the plan proposed by President George W. Bush shortly after reelection in 2004, as explained in a *CRS Memorandum*, by Laura Haltzel, to the Honorable Charles Rangel dated March 31, 2005. The proposal is based on "Model 2" of the President's Commission to Strengthen Social Security which released its final report on December 21, 2001. See: http://www.csss.gov/.

27. Dawn Nuschler and Geoffrey Kollmann, "Social Security Reform: Effect on Benefits and the Federal Budget of Plans Proposed by the President's Commission to Strengthen Social Security," RL32006 (Washington, D.C.: Congressional Research Service, July 15, 2003).

28. Lawrence H. Thompson, "Administering Individual Accounts in Social Security" (Washington, D.C.: Urban Institute, February 1, 1999).

29. The retirement age, under current law, is gradually increasing to age 67.

30. Social Security benefits are adjusted upward annually to reflect inflation as measured by the Bureau of Labor Statistics' (BLS) Consumer Price Index (CPI). However, some argue that the methodology for calculating the CPI overstates annual inflation. In 1994, CBO estimated that the overstatement ranges from 0.2 to 0.6 percentage points, and a 1996 report to the Senate Finance Committee estimated it could be as high as 1.1 percentage points. The BLS has made adjustments to its calculations, but some observers suggest that CPI continues to be somewhat overstated. Slowing Social Security benefit growth by "fixing" the CPI, or slowing the annual increases by using CPI-minus-1% each year rather than the full CPI, could dramatically improve Social Security's fiscal outlook. SSA estimates that CPI-minus-1 "would

improve the long-range actuarial balance by an estimated 80%." Dawn Nuschler, "Social Security Reform," IB98048 (Washington, D.C.: Congressional Research Service, May 1, 2006).

31. "Progressive indexing" would constrain the growth of initial benefits for future retirees by tying lower wage earner benefits to wage growth (as under current law) and higher wage earner benefits to price growth (inflation). Price growth is lower than wage growth, so that higher wage earners' initial benefits would grow more slowly than lower wage earners' initial benefits. See Dawn Nuschler, "Social Security Reform: Current Issues and Legislation," RL33544 (Washington, D.C.: Congressional Research Service, May 18, 2007), 17.

32. A portion of Social Security benefits are currently taxable for higher-income beneficiaries. See Gary Sidor, "Social Security: Brief Facts and Statistics," 94-27 (Washington, D.C.: Congressional Research Service, January 26, 2006, 20–21.

33. $97,500 in 2007.

34. Thomas Hungerford, "Increasing the Social Security Payroll Tax Base: Options and Effects on Tax Burdens," RL33943 (Washington, D.C.: Congressional Research Service, April 6, 2007).

35. Lifelong railroad workers receive their benefits from the RRB. Others with experience inside and outside the railroad industry receive benefits from either RRB or Social Security, depending on length of service. Kathleen Romig, "Railroad Retirement Board: Retirement, Survivor, Disability, Unemployment, and Sickness Benefits," RS22350 (Washington, D.C.: Congressional Research Service, January 16, 2007).

36. Office of Management and Budget, Budget of the United States, FY 2008, Appendix, 1119–24.

37. Tier II taxes are used to finance Tier II benefits, supplemental annuities, and a portion of Tier I benefits. Romig, "Railroad Retirement Board," 5.

38. Romig, "Railroad Retirement Board," 6.

Interest Payments—The Fourth-Largest Federal "Program"

Estimated FY 2008 *Net* Interest Payments: $253 billion[1]
8% of Federal Spending

See www.GovBudget.com for updated numbers

In a Nutshell

Net interest is the amount of interest the Federal government pays over the course of a year to domestic and foreign investors holding U.S. Treasury securities. Net interest does *not* include interest paid to Federal Trust Funds (such as the Social Security Trust Funds) because those are intragovernmental transactions that do not result in Federal outlays. However, net interest *does* include interest paid to the Federal Reserve System because the Federal Reserve's operations are independent of the Federal Budget.

KEEPING THE TERMINOLOGY STRAIGHT:
NET INTEREST VERSUS GROSS INTEREST,
"PUBLIC DEBT" VERSUS "DEBT HELD BY THE PUBLIC"

To fully understand what *net interest* refers to, it is necessary to be acquainted with some of the terminology used in the world of federal borrowing and debt:

- A budget *deficit* is the amount by which spending exceeds revenues in a single fiscal year. The Federal Government covers the revenue shortfall by borrowing funds. Funds are borrowed by issuing U.S. Treasury securities (bills, notes, and bonds) to individual and institutional investors.
- In general, *Federal Debt* is the accumulation of annual deficits (which continue to pile up until the government runs a surplus to pay down some of the Debt). As illustrated in Figure 3-5.1, there are two types of Federal Debt:

1. **Debt Held by Government Accounts** are Treasury securities issued to Federal trust funds (such as Social Security), which must by law invest all operating surpluses in Federal securities.
2. **Debt Held by the Public** is the accumulated debt issued to all *non-Federal* sources including individual investors, businesses, financial institutions, state and local governments, and foreign governments. In addition, Debt Held by the Public includes securities purchased by the Federal Reserve System (because its operations are independent of the Federal Budget).

- **Gross Federal Debt** (often referred to as *Public Debt*) is the *total* of "Debt Held by the Public" plus "Debt Held by Government Accounts."
- Many economists believe that **Debt Held by the Public** is significant as the **best measure** of how much available credit is being consumed by the Federal Government.
- **Gross Interest** is total interest paid on Gross Federal Debt (i.e., interest paid to government trust funds *plus* interest paid to all individual and institutional investors).
- **Net Interest is interest paid on Debt Held by the Public** (i.e., interest paid to all non-Federal holders of Treasury securities, as well as to the Federal Reserve System).

Background

As illustrated in figure 3-5.1, the Federal Government's net interest costs are determined by two factors: (1) the amount of Debt Held by the Public and (2) prevailing interest rates. Consequently, net interest is the only category of Federal spending that cannot be directly reduced by legislative action.

Treasury securities may be purchased from the U.S. Treasury or in the secondary market by individual investors, businesses, financial institutions in the U.S. or overseas, the Federal Reserve System (to increase the money supply[2]), State and local governments, and foreign individuals or governments.

Federal debt is held in a variety of forms with varying interest rates tied to maturity dates. The Treasury Department uses a variety of instruments—Bills, Notes, Bonds, and Treasury Inflation-Protected Securities (TIPS) to finance the Federal debt. Bills mature in less than one year, Notes and TIPS between two and twenty years, and Bonds in ten years or longer. As with certificates of deposit, short-term securities typically have lower interest rates than longer-term securities, giving the Treasury some small degree of maneuvering room in holding down interest payments through "debt management."

As reflected in table 3-5.1, interest payments dipped in the early part of this decade due to falling interest rates as the Federal Reserve responded to the 2001 recession[3] by reducing the Federal Funds Rate (the rate charged by Federal Reserve Banks to member banks). More recently, interest rates have moved higher with the increasing Federal debt and the efforts of the Federal Reserve to combat inflationary pressures with a higher Federal Funds Rate.

Issue: Foreign Holdings of U.S. Debt

Foreign investment in Federal debt has grown in recent years, prompting some observers and policymakers to express concerns about foreign ownership of U.S. securities. As reflected in

FIGURE 3-5.1 Relationship of Net Interest Payments to Debt Held by the Public (at the end of FY 2007[4])

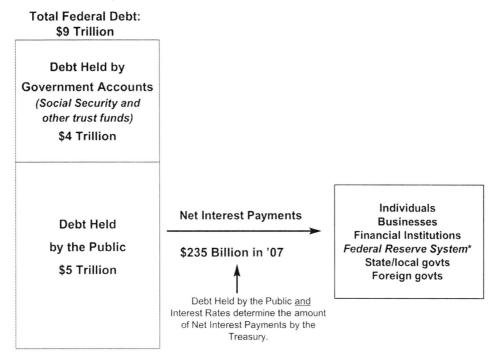

Note on Federal Reserve System: Securities purchased by the Federal Reserve System are included in "Debt Held by the Public" (rather than Debt Held by Government Accounts) because *the Federal Reserve System and its operations are independent of the Federal Budget.* The "Fed" operates without appropriations from Congress and derives income from fees for banking services and interest on Treasury securities. In FY 2006, nearly 16% of "Debt Held by the Public" consisted of securities held by the Federal Reserve System. The Fed "purchases" Treasury securities in the secondary market to ease credit conditions by increasing the money supply. This is a more direct means of impacting the money supply and general credit conditions than the much publicized adjustment of the interest rate charged by Federal Reserve Banks to member financial institutions (Federal Funds Rate).[5]

table 3-5.2, foreign holdings as a percentage of debt held by private investors[6] increased from 37.5% in March 2002 (about $1.1 trillion) to 51.5% in March 2007 ($2.2 trillion). Of that amount, approximately 60% is held by foreign governments and the remainder by private foreign investors.[7]

As illustrated in figure 3-5.2 Japan continues to be the largest foreign holder of U.S. Treasury Securities, holding almost one-third of all foreign investment in both 2001 and 2006. China, with its rapidly expanding economy and large trade surpluses, has nearly tripled its share of foreign holdings in U.S. securities, from 6.6% in 2000 to 19.1% in 2007 ($414 billion).

Some believe that this trend represents a risk to U.S. economic security. Specifically, the concern is that a foreign government holding a large amount of U.S. securities, such as China, or a group of nations collectively holding a large amount of securities, could engage in a "rapid diversification out of dollar assets" as a form of economic pressure on the United States. Such a move could cause a collapse of the dollar's value, increase interest rates, and trigger a major downturn in U.S. stock markets, putting the U.S. economy at risk of recession.[8]

TABLE 3-5.1 Net Interest Payments Determined by Debt Held by the Public and Interest Rates

(Debt and Net Interest Payments in Billions of Dollars)								
Fiscal Year	*2000*	*2001*	*2002*	*2003*	*2004*	*2005*	*2006*	*2007*
Gross Federal Debt *(end of year)*	5,629	5,770	6,198	6,760	7,355	7,905	8,451	8,964
Debt Held by Govt. Accounts	2,219	2,450	2,658	2,847	3,059	3,313	3,622	3,907
Debt Held By the Public	3,410	3,320	3,540	3,913	4,296	4,529	4,829	5,057
Interest Rates								
Federal Funds Rate	6.24	3.88	1.67	1.13	1.35	3.22	4.97	5.25[9]
6-month Treasury Bills	5.92	3.39	1.69	1.06	1.58	3.40	4.81	4.865[10]
10-year Treasury Notes	6.03	5.02	4.61	4.01	4.27	4.29	4.80	5.10[11]
Net Interest Payments	223	206	171	153	160	184	227	235

Note: This table illustrates that net interest payments are determined by two factors: the amount of "debt held by the public" and interest rates. For example, note that net interest payments declined from 2000 to 2001 for two reasons: debt held by the public declined at the end of the Clinton Administration when the Federal Government was running a budget surplus *and* interest rates declined during 2001 as the Federal Reserve responded to a recession. Net interest payments continued to decline in 2002 and 2003, despite increases in debt held by the public, because of the dramatic decline in interest rates as the Federal Reserve maintained its efforts to stimulate the economy with dramatic reductions in the Federal Funds Rate. Thereafter, the increases in net interest payments reflect the growing debt held by the public and increasing interest rates.

TABLE 3-5.2: Foreign Ownership of U.S. Treasury Securities[12]

($ in billions)			
End of Month	*Debt Held by Private Investors**	*Debt Held by Foreign Investors*	*Foreign Holdings as a Percentage of Debt Held by Private Investors*
March 2007	$4,273	$2,199	51.5%
March 2006	$4,114	$2,085	50.7%
March 2005	$3,855	$1,956	50.7%
March 2004	$3,503	$1,677	47.9%
March 2003	$3,070	$1,286	41.9%
March 2002	$2,849	$1,067	37.5%

*Reflects Debt Held by the Public *excluding* debt held by the Federal Reserve System.

Others, however, regard this scenario as highly unlikely. In a recent report to Congress, CRS concluded that "the special role that the dollar plays in international finance and the strength and stability of the U.S. financial markets (including Treasury securities) make them attractive sources for foreign investment. These factors generally encourage the retention of dollar assets by foreigners. As a result, the levels of foreign holdings of federal debt are currently neither a threat nor a problem for the nation."[13]

Regardless of one's attitude regarding the distribution of U.S. debt, most would agree that the vast foreign holdings of U.S. securities is a symptom of the rapid and unsustainable growth in U.S. debt.

FIGURE 3-5.2 Major Foreign Holders of U.S. Securities: 2001 (top) versus 2007 (bottom)[14] in billions of dollars

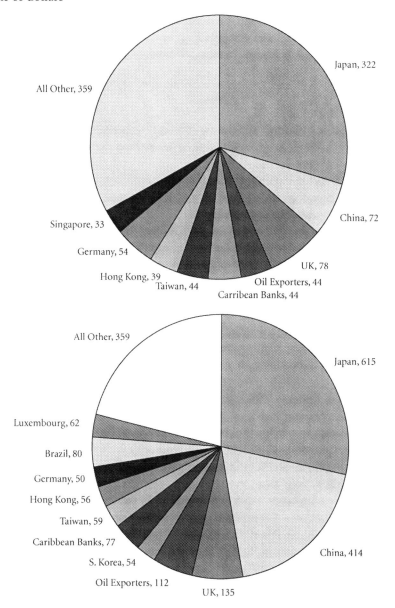

Recommended Sources for More Information on Net Interest and Foreign Holdings of Federal Debt

- **Treasury Department:** "The Debt to the Penny and Who Holds It": http://www.treasurydirect.gov/NP/BPDLogin?application=np.

- **OMB:** "Federal Borrowing and Debt," Analytical Perspectives, chapter 16, Budget of the U.S. Government, FY 2008; Mid-Session Review, FY 2008, Table S-13.
- **Council of Economic Advisors, Executive Office of the President:** *Economic Report of the President*, February 2007.
- **GAO:** "Federal Debt: Answers to Frequently Asked Questions," August 2004, http://www.gao.gov/new.items/d04485sp.pdf.
- **CBO:** "Budget and Economic Outlook," January 2007, pp. 19–22.
- **CRS:** "Interest Payments on the Federal Debt: A Primer," RS22354, May 4, 2007; "Structure and Functions of the Federal Reserve System," RS20826, April 17, 2007; "Foreign Holdings of Federal Debt," RS22331, March 14, 2007; "Growth in Foreign Holdings of Federal Debt," RL33723, November 13, 2006.

Notes

1. Office of Management and Budget, "Mid-Session Review: Budget of the U.S. Government, Fiscal Year 2008" (Washington, D.C.: OMB, July 2007), 32, http://www.whitehouse.gov/omb/budget/fy2008/pdf/08msr.pdf.

2. See Pauline Smale, "Structure and Functions of the Federal Reserve System," RS20826 (Washington, D.C.: Congressional Research Service, April 17, 2007), for an explanation of how the Fed's purchase of Treasury securities increases the money supply.

3. For more information on the 2001 recession, see Business Cycle Dating Committee, National Bureau of Economic Research, http://www.nber.org/cycles/recessions.html (accessed July 22, 2007).

4. Numbers are rounded. OMB's July 2007 midsession review projected debt outstanding at the end of FY 2007 as follows: Debt held by Govt Accounts: 3,907 billion; Debt held by the public: 5,057 billion, Gross Federal Debt: $8,964 billion. For current numbers, visit http://www.treasurydirect.gov/NP/BPDLogin?application=np.

5. Pauline Smale, "Structure and Functions of the Federal Reserve System," RS20826 (Washington, D.C.: Congressional Research Service, April 17, 2007), 1–2.

6. Debt held by private investors is "Debt Held by the Public" minus debt held by the Federal Reserve System.

7. Justin Murray and Marc Labonte, "Foreign Holdings of Federal Debt," RS22331 (Washington, D.C.: Congressional Research Service, March 14, 2007), 4.

8. Phillip Winters, "Growth in Foreign Holdings of Federal Debt," RL33723 (Washington, D.C.: Congressional Research Service, November 13, 2006), summary.

9. Federal funds rate, as of June 28, 2007, Federal Reserve Release: http://www.federalreserve.gov/boarddocs/press/monetary/2007/20070628/.

10. As of July 18, 2007, www.bankrate.com/brm/ratewatch/treasury.asp.

11. As of July 18, 2007, www.bankrate.com/brm/ratewatch/treasury.asp.

12. Table OFS-2, Estimated Ownership of U.S. Treasury Securities, from the March 2007 *Treasury Bulletin*, Financial Management Service of the U.S. Treasury, http://www.fms.treas.gov/bulletin/ (click on link for "ownership of Federal securities").

13. Winters, , "Growth in Foreign Holdings of Federal Debt," summary.

14. The U.S. Treasury Department International Capital System provides *historical* data on Major Foreign Holders of Treasury Securities http://www.treas.gov/tic/mfhhis01.txt; and *current estimates* at http://www.treas.gov/tic/mfh.txt. Oil exporters include Ecuador, Venezuela, Indonesia, Bahrain, Iran, Iraq, Kuwait, Oman, Qatar, Saudi Arabia, the United Arab Emirates, Algeria, Gabon, Libya, and Nigeria. Caribbean Banking Centers include the Bahamas, Bermuda, the Cayman Islands, Netherlands Antilles, and Panama. Beginning with a new series for June 2006, they also include the British Virgin Islands.

Health Care: The Nation's Greatest Fiscal Challenge

*Rising health care costs and their consequences for federal health insurance programs constitute the nation's central fiscal challenge. . . . If health care costs continue growing at the same rate over the next four decades as they did over the past four decades, federal spending on **Medicare and Medicaid alone** would rise to about 20 percent of GDP by 2050—roughly the share of the economy now accounted for by the **entire federal budget**.—Peter Orszag, director of the Nonpartisan Congressional Budget Office, June 21, 2007[1] (emphasis added)*

As highlighted in the opening excerpt from CBO Director Orszag's recent congressional testimony, exploding health care costs—particularly Medicare and Medicaid—pose a staggering challenge to America's fiscal and economic future.

Paradoxically, while our nation spends more and more of our public resources on health care, the number of uninsured Americans—now estimated at 47 million—continues to grow.[2]

This chapter surveys the broad array of Federal and Federal-State programs that are threatening to consume all of our public resources but paradoxically have left tens of millions of Americans without access to basic health care.

TABLE 3-6.1 The Patchwork Quilt of America's Health Care "System"

In America, you have access to affordable health care if:
- You are *65 or older* (Medicare).
- You work for an *employer* who provides group health insurance.
- You recently worked for an employer who provided group health coverage, and you can afford to pay for *COBRA continuation coverage* (which allows you to continue the coverage for 18 months by paying the employee's share *and* the employer's share of the monthly health premium—often costing over $1,000 per month for a family).

(Continued)

TABLE 3-6.1 The Patchwork Quilt of America's Health Care "System" (Continued)

- Your COBRA coverage recently ended, and you can afford to buy a *HIPAA health insurance policy*, often costing over $2000 per month for a family (HIPAA refers to a Federal law that prevents health insurers from refusing coverage based on a preexisting condition, provided you have had group coverage for at least 18 months without a break in coverage).[3]
- You are a *child or pregnant woman* in a family at or below the Federal Poverty Level (Medicaid).
- You are *aged, blind, or disabled*, and your income is less than 75% of the Federal Poverty Level (Medicaid).
- You live in a State that provides coverage to *parents of children at the Federal Poverty Level* (Medicaid).
- You are a *child in a low-income family* that earns too much for Medicaid but is poor enough to qualify for the State's SCHIP-funded program (State Children's Health Insurance Program).
- You are *active duty military, a military retiree, or an immediate family member of a military person* (TRICARE coverage).[4]
- You are a *veteran in a "high-priority" group* (i.e., service-connected disability and/or low-income) (Veterans Health Administration).[5]
- You are a *dependent or survivor of a veteran permanently and totally disabled* from a service-connected condition (CHAMPVA).[6]
- You *cannot work due to a disability* (after two years[7] on Social Security disability, you are entitled to Medicare coverage).
- You are an *American Indian or an Alaskan Native* and live near an Indian Health Service facility.
- You live in one of the States that has enacted health reform legislation aimed at helping the uninsured gain access to affordable health insurance. Examples are the plans adopted by Massachusetts[8] and Vermont.[9] Other States, including California, are actively considering universal health coverage plans.[10]
- You live in one of the 34 states (e.g., Maryland) that have established a *"high-risk health insurance pool,"* and you qualify because you or a member of your family has a *preexisting health condition* that precludes you from obtaining or affording health insurance in the private market.[11]

In America, you do not have access to affordable health care if:
- You are a full-time worker but your *employer does not offer group health insurance or has recently dropped health coverage.* (According to CRS, more than half of the nonelderly uninsured are full-time, full-year workers or their family members.[12])
- You are a *low-income, childless adult*; States cannot use Federal funds to extend Medicaid to adults without children, unless they are pregnant or disabled (this gap in Medicaid coverage accounts for one-third of America's uninsured).
- You are a *Medicaid parent* (i.e., your children qualify for Medicaid because your family is at or below the poverty level, but you—the parents—do not qualify for Medicaid under your State's program).
- You work for a *small business* that cannot afford a group health insurance plan.
- You are *self-employed, and someone in your family has a preexisting medical condition* (and you do not live in one of the 34 states that have a high risk insurance pool).

TABLE 3-6.1 The Patchwork Quilt of America's Health Care "System" (Continued)

- You are *disabled, under 65, not poor enough to be on Medicaid, and do not qualify for Social Security disability* (or qualify but are in the two-year waiting period).
- You were *injured in the Iraq war* but are nonmilitary (private contractors provide a wide range of services to the military).
- You are *unemployed*.
- The temporary *COBRA continuation coverage*[13] for which you are eligible following the loss of a job *is unaffordable or has expired*, and the *HIPAA portability coverage*[14] that follows COBRA (often costing a family $2,000 per month or more) **is unaffordable**.
- You are a *part-time* worker ineligible for your employer's health plan.
- You are a *legal immigrant and have been in the United States for less than five years* (and qualify only for emergency Medicaid, under which coverage is limited to treatment required after the sudden onset of a medical emergency).

Medicare: National Health Insurance for Seniors and (Some) People with Disabilities

> Estimated FY 2008 Total Medicare Spending: $456 billion[15]
> 15% of Federal Spending[16]

See www.GovBudget.com for updated numbers

I am proposing that every person over sixty-five years of age be spared the darkness of sickness without hope.—President Lyndon B. Johnson, in a message to Congress proposing Medicare[17]

In a Nutshell

Medicare is a national health insurance entitlement program for nearly all Americans 65 and older. The program also covers workers who have become disabled[18] and people diagnosed with end-stage renal disease or amyotrophic lateral sclerosis (ALS, or Lou Gehrig's disease).[19] Medicare has four parts:

- **Part A Hospital Insurance,** financed by current workers' *payroll* taxes and covers hospital services, posthospital services, and hospice care;
- **Part B Supplementary Medical Insurance**, financed by *general* tax revenues and premiums, and provides *optional* coverage for physician services, outpatient hospital care, home health care and medical equipment;
- **Part C "Medicare Advantage"** provides managed care options for beneficiaries enrolled in Parts A and B; and
- **Part D Prescription Drug Coverage,** financed by general tax revenues and premiums, and provides *optional* prescription drug coverage for the elderly and disabled.

Medicare pays doctors, hospitals, and most other providers using a "prospective payment system" under which predetermined payment amounts are established for specific services, with

Myth: "National health insurance" is inconsistent with America's free market culture.

Fact: The United States has had national health insurance for more than 40 years. *America's national health insurance is the Medicare program,* which has broad public support. Almost all persons age 65 and older, and many disabled Americans under 65, are entitled to Medicare coverage. Under Medicare, beneficiaries select their own doctors and hospitals, and Medicare pays the health care providers directly. In 2006, Medicare's national health insurance covered over 36 million Americans 65 and older, and 7 million disabled Americans.[20] Unfortunately, political rhetoric has obscured the difference between "national health insurance" (Medicare being a good example) and "socialized medicine" which generally refers to national health systems in other countries where doctors and other medical providers are government employees and health care is rationed by the government. As we address the growing health care crisis in America, it is important for all Americans to understand that national health insurance protects patients' right to choose doctors and hospitals, and it is not "socialized medicine."

The two most dangerous words in the English language are not "nuclear war." They are "socialized medicine."—President Lyndon B. Johnson[21]

annual "updates" and limitations on patient cost sharing (deductibles, coinsurance, and copayments). Rapidly rising Medicare expenditures are a source of widespread concern, with outlays projected to double (in dollar terms) over the next decade and triple (as a percent of the economy) by 2050.

Background

According to a recent report, Medicare's beneficiaries are "highly satisfied with their coverage and feel confident in their ability to obtain care."[22] Together with Social Security, Medicare has contributed dramatically to the economic security of older Americans "resulting in the lowest rates of elderly impoverishment experienced by any generation."[23]

Part A: Hospital Insurance

Medicare Part A covers in-patient hospital services, posthospital services (including skilled nursing facility, or SNF, services and home health care), and hospice care. Medicare Part A is financed primarily by payroll taxes of 1.45%—paid by *current* employers and employees (with self-employed paying 2.9%). Together with the 6.2% Social Security payroll tax, this adds up to the familiar 7.65 % payroll tax that most American workers and employers pay. However, unlike Social Security payroll taxes that are applied to the first $97,500[24] of income, the Medicare payroll tax is now applied to *all* income.[25] Part A requires some beneficiary "cost sharing" including deductibles for hospital care and daily charges for long hospital stays.

Part B: Doctor Visits, Lab Fees, Medical Equipment

Medicare Part B[26] is an optional part of Medicare that covers visits to the doctor, laboratory services, outpatient hospital services, physical and other therapy, medical equipment, home health care not covered under Part A, ambulance services, and some preventive medicine. Participation rates in Part B are high: 95%.[27] Medicare Part B is financed by general revenues (Federal tax dollars) and monthly premiums paid by seniors who opt to participate. In 1997, Congress permanently set the Part B premium at 25% of program costs. Based on this requirement, the 2007 monthly premium was $93.50 (low-income beneficiaries pay less).[28] Part B requires some beneficiary "cost sharing," including an annual deductible and 20% coinsurance[29] of Medicare's approved charges (although mental health coinsurance is 50%). *Net* FY 2007 Federal spending for Part B, after offsetting premiums are included, is $131 billion.

Part C: Medicare Advantage (Managed Care Alternative)

People who are eligible for Medicare Part A and are enrolled in Part B have the option to receive all of their Medicare benefits through managed care plans such as health maintenance organizations (HMOs), preferred provider organizations (PPOs), and special needs plans (SNPs). The managed care alternatives are part of the "Medicare Advantage" (MA) program.[30] Unlike traditional fee-for-service Medicare, in which medical providers are paid for each service, managed care providers in Medicare Advantage are paid a monthly per enrollee amount (known as a "capitation" payment) to provide benefits to enrollees. The total cost of MA in calendar year 2006 was $64 billion—funded about equally by Parts A and B. *Although the objective of MA is to lower total Medicare costs through competition, payments to MA plans have been higher than costs per beneficiary in traditional fee-for-service Medicare—12% higher according to one study.*[31] As of January 2007, nearly 20% of all Medicare beneficiaries were enrolled in a Medicare Advantage plan.[32]

Part D: Prescription Drug Coverage

Beginning in 2006, Medicare beneficiaries became eligible for optional prescription drug coverage—subsidized by Medicare—under which they are able to purchase drug coverage through PDPs (prescription drug plans) *or* Medicare Advantage prescription drug plans. Each plan, to qualify for Federal subsidies, must offer a minimum set of benefits. As reflected in table 3-6.2, by the end of 2006, 28 million—about two-thirds—of Medicare's 43 million eligible beneficiaries had enrolled in Part D. The new program is financed primarily by general revenues (tax dollars), as well as transfers from states[33] and modest monthly premiums paid by enrollees.[34] Enrollees with incomes below 150% of the Federal poverty level[35] receive assistance with their premiums and cost-sharing charges.[36] However, the Centers for Medicare and Medicaid Services (CMS) estimated that as of January 2007, 3.3 million persons eligible for low-income subsidies had not enrolled.[37]

Issue: Rapidly Rising Costs Threaten Medicare Sustainability

In general, most policymakers and interest groups involved in the Medicare debate agree on the following:

TABLE 3-6.2 A Snapshot of Medicare Income and Expenditures (Calendar Year 2006) (billions of dollars)

	Hospital Insurance (HI)	Supplementary Medical Insurance (SMI)		
	Part A	Part B	Part D	Total
Total Income	**212**	**177**	**48**	**437**
Payroll Taxes	181	—	—	181
Interest on Treasury Bonds	16	2	—	18
Taxation of Benefits	10	—	—	10
Premiums	2.6	43	4	49
General Revenue	0.5	133	39	172
Transfers from States	—	—	6	6
Other	1	—	—	1
Total Expenditures	**192**	**169**	**47**	**408**
Hospitals	121	27	—	148
Skilled Nursing Facilities	20	—	—	20
Home Health Care	6	7	—	13
Physician Services	—	58	—	58
Managed Care (Part C)	33	31.5	—	64
Prescription Drugs	—	—	47	47
Other	9	42	—	51
Administrative	3	3	0.3	6.3
Enrollment (millions)				
Aged	36	34		
Disabled	7	6		
Total	43	40	28	43

Source: 2007 Medicare Trustees Report, table II.B1.

1. Medicare's projected growth rates are unsustainable.
2. The causes of Medicare's projected fiscal crisis include:
   - rapidly rising health care costs,
   - the approaching baby boom retirement,
   - increasing longevity of Medicare beneficiaries, and
   - enactment of the new prescription drug benefit.

However, that's where the agreement ends. There is no consensus on how to bring Medicare costs under control while sustaining quality coverage.

Nevertheless, building a bipartisan consensus on Medicare cost control and sustainability is urgent and essential. The *total Medicare population* is projected to grow to 46 million in 2010, 61 million in 2020, and 77 million in 2030;[38] and according to the 2007 Medicare Trustees report, *total Medicare expenditures* as a percentage of GDP are expected to increase dramatically from 3.2% in 2007, to 11.3% by 2081.[39] In dollar terms, Medicare outlays are

---

THE INFAMOUS "DOUGHNUT HOLE"

The new Medicare drug benefit has a *gap in coverage* (fashioned by the authors of the legislation to hold down the overall costs of the program). The gap is commonly called the "doughnut hole." Here's how it works: the *standard Medicare drug plan*[40] will pay 75% of drug costs up to $2,400 (in 2007), after a $265 deductible for most seniors. But after enrollees reach $2,400 in total drug expenses, *the standard drug benefit pays nothing until the beneficiary's total drug expenses reach $5,450 (in 2007)*. Above that amount, the standard Medicare drug plan essentially provides catastrophic drug coverage, paying all costs except for 5% coinsurance. The important point here is that under the *standard drug plan*, by the time a participant in the plan reaches $5,450 in total drug expenses, they will have paid *out-of-pocket costs of $3,850*—while the Medicare-approved drug plan will have covered only $1,600 in costs.

Medicare-approved drug plans can, however, vary widely and some plans do in fact offer coverage of some prescriptions in the doughnut hole, although a recent Kaiser Foundation report found that *most Part D plans have a coverage gap*.[41] In addition, in 2007, 13 states reportedly have no plans offering relief from the doughnut hole gap in coverage—an increase from 4 states in 2006.[42] Moreover, plans that do offer doughnut hole coverage have substantially increased their premiums. When seniors with high drug costs find themselves in the doughnut hole coverage gap, they must still continue to pay monthly premiums to remain in the prescription drug program.

The irony is that people normally expect insurance to protect them from high costs, but the standard Medicare drug plan actually phases out when costs get high (i.e., between $2,400 and $5,450 of total drug costs), which some might view as an upside-down "insurance policy." Put another way: Under the standard plan, sicker patients with higher drug costs end up paying a higher share of their drug costs than those with fewer prescriptions.[43]

---

projected to nearly double over the next decade alone from $432 billion in FY 2007 to $853 billion by FY 2017 (see table 3-6.3).[44]

To put this in perspective, according to the Trustees, "the level of Medicare expenditures is expected to exceed that for Social Security in 2028 and, by 2081, to be 80 percent more than the cost of Social Security."[45]

Issue: HI Trust Fund—2007 Spending Exceeds Revenues; Trust Fund Depleted by 2019

Medicare Part A, Hospital Insurance, is operated as a separate "trust fund," financed primarily by payroll taxes. Beginning in 2007, the Medicare HI Trust Fund spent more than it took in from payroll taxes and other smaller sources of revenue. Treasury securities and interest earnings held by the HI Trust Fund will keep Medicare Part A afloat for a few years, but by 2019, the HI Trust Fund will be exhausted.[46] In reality, *the financial pressures have already begun*, because the Treasury is borrowing funds to pay off the bonds and interest earnings held by the Trust Fund.

TABLE 3-6.3 Medicare as a Percentage of Gross Domestic Product

1970	0.7	2030	6.5
1980	1.3	2040	8.0
1990	1.9	2050	9.0
2000	2.3	2060	9.9
2005	2.7	2070	10.7
2010	3.4	2080	11.3
2020	4.6		

Source: 2007 Medicare Trustees Report: Intermediate Estimates.[47]

WHEN IS A "TRUST FUND" NOT A REAL TRUST FUND?

Medicare Part B and Part D are often referred to as components of the Supplementary Medical Insurance (SMI) Trust Fund. However, since general revenues are automatically pumped into this "trust fund" to cover expenditures not paid for by premiums and copayments, it is *not* a trust fund in any meaningful sense. This stands in contrast to the III Trust Fund, which is a bona fide trust fund, financed by a dedicated revenue source (payroll taxes and interest on Treasury securities).

Issue: The 45% "Medicare Funding Warning"

The percentage of total Medicare outlays covered by payroll taxes, premiums and other dedicated funding sources is shrinking, and the *amount of general revenues required to keep the program afloat is rapidly increasing.* As a consequence of this trend, the 2003 Medicare prescription drug legislation[48] (known as the Medicare Modernization Act, or MMA) required the Trustees of the Medicare Trust Funds to report each year on the amount of general revenues required to finance Medicare; and if the percentage of general revenues was to exceed 45% of total Medicare outlays for two consecutive years, the Trustees are directed by the MMA to issue a "Medicare funding warning." The Trustees made such a finding in 2006 and 2007 and issued the finding in their April 2007 Annual Report. Under the MMA, the President is now required to submit to Congress, within 15 days after release of his FY 2009 Budget, proposed legislation to respond to the warning (with reforms that would eliminate the need to expend general revenues in excess of 45% of Medicare outlays). The House is then required to consider the legislation on an expedited basis, although there is no requirement that the Senate take up the legislation.[49]

Medicaid: Health Care for People at (or Near) Poverty

**Estimated FY 2008 Federal Medicaid Spending: $209 billion[50]
7% of Federal Spending**

See www.GovBudget.com for updated numbers.

In a Nutshell

Medicaid is the nation's health and long-term care program for over 55 million low-income Americans.[52] Unlike Medicare, which is available *without regard to income*, Medicaid is designed primarily for people who have incomes at or below the Federal Poverty Level (FPL). To qualify, beneficiaries must also fall within one of the several dozen specific eligibility categories that divide into three general groups: families with children, elderly people, and people with mental or physical disabilities.[53] Medicaid is jointly financed by the Federal and State governments, with the Federal government helping States pay for Medicaid services by means of a matching formula. The Federal payment is based on a State's per capita income, with the poorest States receiving Federal payments up to 76%. While the Federal government usually pays more than half the cost of Medicaid services, the program itself is *administered by the States*—subject to minimum Federal requirements on basic benefits that must be provided.

Background

Medicare and Medicaid are often confused. Although they were both created in the same 1965 legislation,[54] they are very different programs, as reflected in table 3-6.4.

TABLE 3-6.4 Medicare versus Medicaid

	MEDICARE	*MEDICAID*
Type of Entitlement	Medicare is an **entitlement** based on age (65 or older) or disability **without regard to income.**	Medicaid is a **means-tested entitlement** where eligibility is based on being at or near the Federal poverty level, as well as satisfying other eligibility criteria such as age, family structure, and health status.
Type of Program	**Medicare is a health insurance program,** similar to private sector health insurance plans, with specified coverage and beneficiary cost sharing (premiums, deductibles, coinsurance).	**Medicaid is a health coverage program;** it is *not* a typical health insurance plan or a health care delivery system.
	Medicare is *not* a health care delivery system. Medicare reimburses providers in the health care sector (according to complicated provider	**States pay health care providers** for services on behalf of Medicaid beneficiaries. For *children and families*, **services are often delivered through managed care, while the** *elderly and disabled* **typically receive care on a fee-for-service basis.**

(Continued)

TABLE 3-6.4 Medicare versus Medicaid (Continued)

	MEDICARE	*MEDICAID*
	payment rules) for providing services to Medicare enrollees.	Until recently, Federal law strictly limited the ability of States to impose premiums, cost-sharing and other insurance-like mechanisms. But the 2005 Deficit Reduction Act allows cost-sharing options.[55]
What Services are Covered?	**Part A** covers hospital services, posthospital services, and hospice care; **Part B** provides *optional* coverage for physician services, outpatient hospital care, home health care, and medical equipment; **Part C** provides managed care options for beneficiaries enrolled in Parts A and B; and **Part D Prescription Drug Coverage,** provides *optional* prescription drug coverage for the elderly and disabled.	Medicaid pays for a broad range of services with an emphasis on: —comprehensive care for children, — mental health services, and —long-term care for the elderly and disabled (Medicaid covers 60% of nursing home residents in the U.S.[56]). Medicaid also assists over 7 million low-income *Medicare* enrollees (called "dual eligibles") by paying Medicare's premiums, deductibles, and coinsurance.
Flexibility	Medicare has a **highly structured payment system** to reimburse hospitals, physicians, skilled nursing facilities, home health care agencies, and other providers.	Medicaid sets forth basic Federal requirements, but **States have significant flexibility** in program design, optional benefits, and provider payments. In addition, many States receive Federal waivers that permit additional flexibility in how Medicaid funds are used.
How Many People Are Covered?	44 million people (37 million seniors and 7 million disabled)	55 million low-income Americans
Financing	Funded by Federal payroll taxes, general tax revenues, and premiums	Jointly funded by the Federal and State governments out of general tax revenues, with the Federal government matching Medicaid spending *at least* dollar for dollar.

TABLE 3-6.4 Medicare versus Medicaid (Continued)

	MEDICARE	*MEDICAID*
Administration	Administered by CMS (Centers for Medicare and Medicaid Services, located within HHS)	However, in most States, the Federal government covers more than 50% of Medicaid percentages, reaching 76% in the poorest states. The percentage Federal contribution is known as FMAP (the Federal Medical Assistance Percentage). Administered by *the States*, subject to Federal minimum requirements.
Cost Growth[57]	Medicare annual cost growth is projected to average 7.4% from 2008 to 2017	Federal Medicaid payments to States are projected to grow, on average, 7.8% per year from 2008 to 2017.

The "Swiss Cheese" of Medicaid Eligibility

While Medicaid is intended to assist low-income Americans, *not all of the poor are eligible*, as reflected in figure 3-6.1. Less than half (43%) of the poorest nonelderly Americans are covered by Medicaid.[58]

Since Medicaid's establishment in 1965, eligibility rules have reached a level of mind-numbing complexity in which there are now more *than 50 distinct population groups* poten-

FIGURE 3-6.1 Health Insurance Coverage of the Nonelderly by Federal Poverty Level (FPL) 2005

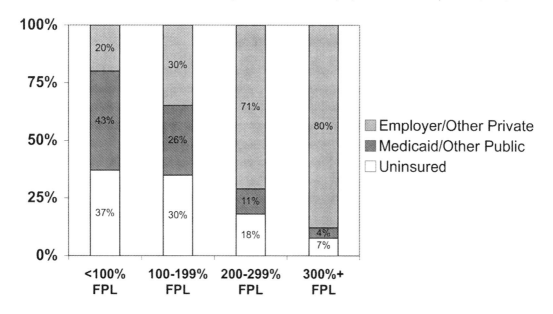

tially eligible for Medicaid.[59] As summarized in table 3-6.5, States are *required* to cover certain "mandatory" eligibility groups and have *discretion* to cover certain "optional" eligibility groups.

Why so much complexity? Medicaid began as a limited health care program for people receiving cash assistance under the Aid to Families with Dependent Children (AFDC) program—the old "welfare" program. In the 1980s, Congress expanded Medicaid six times—transforming it into a program that provides broad health services for three groups of low-income Americans: children and parents (including pregnant women), the elderly, and people with mental or physical disabilities. In general, the populations eligible for AFDC were entitled to mandatory coverage, and States were given discretion to provide coverage (and receive Federal reimbursements) for optional population categories.

But, like Swiss cheese, Medicaid has significant holes in coverage—the most notable being that *childless adults without a qualifying disability are not eligible for Medicaid no matter how poor they are.*

Mandatory and Optional Medicaid Benefits[60]

The medical services covered by Medicaid are as complex as the eligibility rules. Certain benefits are mandatory and others are optional, resulting in *different types of coverage in different states.*

Benefits that are *mandatory* for most Medicaid eligibility categories include inpatient and outpatient hospital services, physician services, pregnancy-related services, nursing facility services, and home health care. *Optional benefits offered by many states* include inpatient psychiatric care for the elderly and individuals under 21; psychological, dental, optometry, and podiatry services; and transportation.

In addition, certain special benefits are mandatory for specific populations. For example, Medicaid eligible children are entitled to special services known as *Early and Periodic Screening, Diagnostic and Treatment (EPSDT)—which is one of the key Medicaid benefits for children.*[61] Also, Medicaid pays *Medicare* premiums, deductibles, and coinsurance for individuals whose income is at or below 100% of the FPL.[62]

FMAP: The Federal Medical Assistance Percentages

Medicaid is jointly financed by the Federal and State governments, with the Federal government helping States pay for Medicaid services by means of a matching formula. The reimbursement rate for each State depends on the states' respective per capita personal income levels, with the poorer states receiving higher reimbursements. Federal Medicaid reimbursements range from a low of 50% for New York State to 76% in Mississippi (as of FY 2006). States receiving the minimum dollar-for-dollar match are said to have a "50% FMAP," or Federal Medical Assistance Percentage.[63]

State Flexibility: Medicaid Section 1115 Waivers

Federal law gives the Secretary of Health and Human Services broad authority to grant "waivers" of standard Medicaid requirements to enable states to use their Federal Medicaid

TABLE 3-6.5 Medicaid Eligibility Categories[64]

MANDATORY COVERAGE FOR:	*OPTIONAL COVERAGE FOR:*

Note: "FPL" is the acronym for "Federal Poverty Level." See Appendix Q.

FAMILIES WITH CHILDREN	**FAMILIES WITH CHILDREN**
• Pregnant women and young children at or below 133% of the FPL • Children ages (6 through 18) in poor families up to 100% of FPL • Recipients of adoption assistance and foster care (under age 18)	• Pregnant women and infants at 133%-185% of FPL • Children who are in State-sponsored foster care, institutionalized, or inpatients in psychiatric facilities
ELDERLY	**ELDERLY**
• Supplemental Security Income (SSI) recipients (i.e., people who are aged, below 75% of FPL)	• Aged with incomes 75%–100% FPL • Recipients of State supplemental payments to Federal SSI • Nursing home residents above SSI levels, but below 300% of SSI
PEOPLE WITH DISABILITIES	**PEOPLE WITH DISABILITIES**
• Supplemental Security Income (SSI) recipients (i.e., people who are blind or disabled below 75% of FPL) • Certain working disabled	• Disabled individuals with incomes above SSI but below 100% FPL • Recipients of State supplemental payments to Federal SSI • Working individuals with disabilities between ages 16 and 64 who were previously eligible for SSI or would be severely impaired without Medicaid coverage
OTHERS	**OTHERS**
• Legal immigrants *only if* they are refugees, asylees, or military veterans. Otherwise, legal immigrants can receive only emergency services during their first five years.	• "Medically needy" individuals up to 133 1/3% of FPL • Uninsured women under 65 with breast or cervical cancer • Uninsured persons with tuberculosis • States may opt to cover legal immigrants after their first five years in the U.S.

dollars in a manner that controls costs and/or expands coverage—so long as the waiver projects are "budget neutral."[65] This "1115 waiver authority" (so-called because the authority is provided in section 1115 of the Social Security Act) can be used, for example, to impose new cost sharing to reduce government outlays, provide services to individuals not otherwise eligible for services, or temporarily expand Medicaid coverage as was done in New York City after 9/11 and in the Gulf Coast states after Hurricanes Katrina and Rita.[66] Nearly half the states have sought waivers to try various approaches to controlling costs and boosting coverage.[67] However, significant concerns have been mounting about the impact of waivers on access to Medicaid services.

Medicaid Is the Largest Source of Long-Term Care Coverage in the United States

Medicaid pays an enormous share of the nation's nursing home and other long-term care expenses, covering nearly half of all long-term care expenditures and paying for 60% of the nation's nursing home residents. Increasingly, Medicaid is also covering intermediate care facilities (e.g., services for individuals with mental retardation) as well as home- and community-based long-term care services, such as adult day care.[68] In addition to covering elderly persons in need of long-term care, Medicaid pays for long-term services for people with disabilities and chronic illnesses.[69]

Medicaid and Children

Medicaid is the largest source of health coverage for children in the United States, covering 28 million as of 2005, equal to one in every four. By contrast, the State Children's Health Insurance Program (SCHIP), discussed later, covers about six million low-income children.[70] Medicaid therefore covers nearly five times more children than SCHIP.

Medicaid Is Not Universal Coverage for Low-Income Americans

All poor children (at or below the Federal poverty level) are eligible for Medicaid, but many of their parents are not. In 14 states, working parents with incomes as low as to half the FPL do not qualify for Medicaid. Moreover, childless adults do not qualify for Medicaid.[71]

Issue: Escalating Medicaid Costs Reflect Growing Poverty and Rising Health Care Costs

Medicaid Expenditures.—The costs of Medicaid, both at the Federal level and the State level, are exploding. Medicaid spending has grown by more than 49% since 2000, *exceeding growth in general inflation and medical inflation, and exceeding the rates of growth in spending for both Medicare and Social Security.*[72] Looking ahead, Federal outlays for Medicaid are projected to more than double over the next decade—growing from $193 billion in FY 2007 to $410 billion by 2017.[73]

These rapidly rising costs reflect (1) significant growth in program enrollment due to increasing poverty and a reduction in employer-sponsored health coverage and (2) rising

Myth: Hospitals that accept large caseloads of low-income and uninsured patients bear the entire cost of providing these services.

Fact: Hospitals with large caseloads of low-income and uninsured patients get special Federal and State assistance through Medicaid called Disproportionate Share Hospital (DSH) payments. Under this provision, hospitals treating large numbers of low-income and Medicaid patients receive upward adjustments to their Medicaid payments (known as "DSH adjustments"). In FY 2004, Federal Medicaid DSH allotments ranged from $100,000 in Wyoming to $1.5 billion in New York State.[74] The *Medicare* program also makes DSH payments to hospitals serving large caseloads of low-income patients, but based on a different formula.

health care costs.[75] In addition, escalating costs will be increasingly exacerbated by demographics, as baby boomers become eligible for Medicaid long-term care services.[76]

Importantly, program inefficiency is *not* regarded as a cause of escalating costs. According to CRS, Medicaid is viewed as a cost-efficient program. "The percentages of the program's spending on administrative costs (3 to 4%) are small compared to the administrative costs of private health insurance plans (often in excess of 20%)."[78]

Enrollment Growth.—For the five-year period from 1998 to 2003, total enrollment in Medicaid increased by 30% and Medicaid enrollment is projected to increase from 54 million enrollees in 2003 to 65 million in 2015—a 21% increase.[79]

Poverty.—Thirty-seven million Americans lived below the poverty line in 2004. According to sociologist Mark Rank of Washington University in St. Louis, "There's strong evidence that over the past five years, record numbers of lower-income Americans find themselves in a more precarious economic position than at any time in recent memory."[80] This is reflected in the startling fact that Medicaid is now the primary insurer for almost 40% of all births.[81]

Rising Health Care Costs.—The Agency for Health Care Research and Quality at the Department of HHS recently reported that "Medicaid spending on outpatient drugs more than doubled in recent years," reflecting "a rise in both the number of prescriptions written for Medicaid enrollees . . . and the rapid uptake of newer classes of drugs."[82]

Public Support of Teaching Hospitals

Estimated FY 2007 Spending on Graduate Medical Education: $11.7 billion
(Funded through Medicare, Medicaid, and HRSA)

In a Nutshell

Academic medical centers, often called "teaching hospitals," are hospitals associated with nearby medical schools. Teaching hospitals play a vital role in training doctors, providing highly specialized medical care, and care for the uninsured. The United States has more than

1,100 teaching hospitals that train nearly 100,000 physicians annually.[83] The Federal government provides substantial public support of teaching hospitals through Medicare and, in lesser amounts, through Medicaid and grants from the Health Resources and Services Administration (HRSA).

Background

The U.S. health care system relies heavily on "teaching hospitals" for three vital functions.

First, teaching hospitals are the focal points for clinical training of medical students and hospital residents. During the last year of medical school, students apply for postgraduate "residencies." Residency programs range from three years for primary care training (such as internal medicine or pediatrics) to five or more years for subspecialties (such as surgery, cardiology, or gastroenterology). Training of postgraduate residents is known as graduate medical education, or "GME."

Second, teaching hospitals are centers for *highly specialized medical care.* Many of the medical advances initiated in the research laboratories of medical schools are incorporated into around-the-clock patient care at teaching hospitals. Teaching hospitals care for some of the nation's sickest patients and, together with NIH, are the engines of medical innovation.

Third, many teaching hospitals provide *vital medical services to uninsured and underserved populations* in our nation.[84]

The Federal government is the largest single financing source for graduate medical education, primarily through Medicare. The rationale for these special Medicare payments is that teaching hospitals incur higher costs—relative to other hospitals—for the treatment of Medicare patients.[85]

One type of support adjusts Medicare payments to teaching hospitals to cover the *direct costs of graduate medical education* (DGME), such as resident and faculty salaries (estimated at $2.4 billion in FY 2007).[86] A second type of support—known as *Indirect Medical Education* (IME) payments—adjusts individual Medicare payments upward to compensate hospitals for the added demands placed on staff as a result of teaching activities, the greater number of tests and procedures ordered by residents, the presence of on-site clinical research and advanced technology, and treating patients with more complex conditions[87] (estimated at $5.8 billion in FY 2007).[88]

A third type of Federal support for teaching hospitals relates to Medicare's capital payments to hospitals.[89] Teaching hospitals receive a larger capital payment per patient than non-teaching hospitals.

In short, "if two otherwise identical hospitals each admit a Medicare beneficiary for the same diagnosis, the teaching hospital will receive a higher payment than the nonteaching hospital. And the percentage add-on increases as the teaching hospital's ratio of residents to beds grows."[90]

In addition to support by the Medicare program, teaching hospitals also receive GME support through Medicaid and a pediatric GME program.

Many States currently boost Medicaid inpatient reimbursement rates for teaching hospitals in order to cover DGME costs; triggering a higher Medicaid reimbursement (estimated at $3.2 billion in FY 2007).[91] However, the Administration—in a cost-cutting effort—is seeking to eliminate Medicaid funding for DGME, asserting that "GME is outside of Medicaid's primary purpose, which is to provide medical care to low-income individuals."[92] As of summer 2007, the Congress had blocked Administration efforts to end Medicaid GME payments.

Pediatric GME—funded by HRSA[93]—is the Children's Hospitals Graduate Medical Education Payment Program. The program provides both DGME and IME payments to children's hospitals and was funded at nearly $300 million in FY 2006.[94]

The late Senator Daniel Patrick Moynihan—renowned for many years as the Senate's leading supporter of teaching hospitals—advocated improving the system of public support for teaching hospitals by creating a trust fund that would be financed by existing DGME and IME payments, plus a new assessment on all health insurance premiums. Senator Moynihan felt that teaching hospitals are a "public good" and deserve solid and dependable public funding.[95] This "all-payer" proposal passed the Senate Finance Committee in 1994 as part of its comprehensive health care reform bill, but the overall legislation stalled on the Senate Floor. The all-payer concept has been reintroduced in subsequent Congresses, but without successful action.[96]

The general issue of public support for teaching hospitals will come to the fore as the baby-boom generation begins to retire. The Association of American Medical Colleges estimates that enrollment in medical schools should be increased by 30% by 2015 in order to handle the rapidly growing number of aging boomers.[97]

SCHIP: Health Coverage for Low-Income Children

> **FY 2007 Federal SCHIP Spending: $5.4 billion**[98]
> **0.2% of Federal Spending**

See www.GovBudget.com for updated numbers.

In a Nutshell

The State Children's Health Insurance Program is a Federal grant program, operated by CMS,[99] that allots about $5 billion per year among the States, based on their number of low-income, uninsured children. The objective of the program, established in 1997, is to expand health coverage for children in families *whose incomes are low but somewhat higher than Medicaid's tight income eligibility limits.*[100] Medicaid covers about 28 million children; SCHIP covers about 6 million children during the course of a year.[101] with another 9 million remaining uninsured. Similar to Medicaid, SCHIP programs are administered by the States.

Background

At the time of its enactment in 1997, the Congress appropriated $40 billion for a 10-year period. Generally, SCHIP covers children in families up to 200% of the FPL, though some states select upper eligibility limits above or below 200%.[102] The program operates like Medicaid, with joint Federal-State funding and State administration of the program. However, the Federal reimbursement rate for SCHIP is somewhat higher than in the Medicaid program, ranging from 65% to 83% (compared with Medicaid's 50%–76%).[103]

SCHIP is *not* an individual entitlement like Medicaid.[104] Rather, it is a capped entitlement to States, under which States each year receive a certain percentage (allotment) of available SCHIP funds. The amount of funds available for fiscal years 1998 through 2007 was established by authorizing legislation when SCHIP was enacted into law in 1997 (with some additional funds appropriated for FY 2007 to cover shortfalls).[105]

According to the Kaiser Commission on Medicaid and the Uninsured, "over the last decade the percentage of low-income children without health insurance has fallen by over one-third" due to the establishment of SCHIP, *as well as expansions in Medicaid coverage.*[106] (The creation of SCHIP has had the spillover effect of causing many low-income families to inquire about health coverage for their children, with the result that many children have been located who were already eligible for Medicaid.)

States are permitted to use SCHIP funds in one of three ways: (1) they can enroll SCHIP children in Medicaid, (2) they can create a separate children's health program within Federal guidelines, or (3) they can devise a combination of the two approaches. If a State chooses the Medicaid option, the State may not turn away applicants who qualify for eligibility—even after the SCHIP funds run out. The Medicaid option, therefore, effectively expands the Medicaid entitlement.

As of February 2007, 10 States and D.C. used the Medicaid option, 18 established separate State programs, and the remaining 22 used a combination of the two.[107] States selecting the Medicaid option must provide all mandatory *and* optional services covered under the State plan. States may also obtain additional flexibility in how they use SCHIP funds by seeking a section 1115 waiver, similar to the Medicaid waiver process. Some States have obtained waivers to use SCHIP funds to also provide coverage to parents or caretaker relatives of eligible children.[108]

Issue: Expand SCHIP?

The legislation authorizing the SCHIP program expired at the end of FY 2007. Although there is general agreement that SCHIP should be continued beyond its expiration date of September 30, 2007, as this book goes to print Congress and the President are locked in a debate over whether to *expand* the SCHIP program. Many in Congress want to add funds over the next five years to expand the program to cover *more eligible children who have not yet enrolled* (as well as to cover *increased health care costs* for children already covered).

Recommended Sources for More Information on SCHIP

- **CBO**: "The State Children's Health Insurance Program," May 2007.
- **GAO**: Testimony before the House Subcommittee on Health, GAO-07-558T, March 1, 2007.
- **National Conference of State Legislatures**: www.ncsl.org/programs/health/sncslweb.htm.
- **National Academy for State Health Policy**, "Perspectives on Reauthorization—SCHIP Directors Weigh In": http://www.nashp.org/Files/CHIP25_final.pdf.
- **Kaiser Commission on Medicaid and the Uninsured**: "Outreach Strategies for Medicaid and SCHIP," April 2006; "Opening Doorways to Health Care for Children," April 2006.
- **Alliance for Health Reform**: "SCHIP and Medicaid Enrollment: What's Next?" http://www.allhealth .org/issue_briefs_SCHIP.asp.
- **American Public Health Association:** "SCHIP and Its Meaning for Public Health" http://www.apha .org/ppp/schip/SCHIP.pdf.

- **CRS:** "SCHIP: A Brief Overview," RL30473, January 30, 2007; "SCHIP Financing," RL32807, January 30, 2007; "SCHIP Original Allotments: Description and Analysis," RL33366, March 12, 2007.

U.S. Public Health Service (PHS) Agencies: Preventing and Treating Disease and Injury

Despite leading the world in health expenditures, the U.S. is not fully meeting its potential in health status and lags behind many of its peers.—Institute of Medicine, National Academy of Sciences[109]

In a Nutshell

The mission of "public health" is to promote health and prevent disease, injury, and disability. Within the Department of Health and Human Services, agencies authorized by the Public Health Service Act are collectively referred to as the *U.S. Public Health Service (PHS)*. As illustrated in figure 3-6.2, PHS agencies include (alphabetically) the Agency for Healthcare Research and Quality (AHRQ), the Agency for Toxic Substances and Disease Registry (ATSDR), the Centers for Disease Control and Prevention (CDC), the Food and Drug Administration (FDA), the Health Resources and Services Administration (HRSA), the Indian Health Service (IHS), the National Institutes of Health (NIH), and the Substance Abuse and Mental Health Services Administration (SAMHSA).

The Surgeon General and the Public Health Service Commissioned Corps (USPHSCC)

FY 2007 Spending for USPHSCC: $370 million

In a Nutshell

The U.S. Public Health Service Commissioned Corps consists of more than 6,000 public health professionals assigned to a variety of public health and disease prevention programs. USPHSCC is one of the seven uniformed services in the United States—the other six being the Army, Navy, Marines, Air Force, Coast Guard, and the National Oceanic and Atmospheric Administration (NOAA). The $370 million figure cited here reflects military retirement and medical benefits for USPHSCC commissioned officers. Generally, the agencies to which the officers are assigned pay the officers' salaries.

Background

In addition to the more than 50,000 civil servants working for PHS agencies, the PHS also has a military-style Commissioned Corps consisting of more than 6,000 officers.

The idea of initiating a mobile, military-style component of the PHS (originally the Marine Hospital Service) was conceived by the first "Supervising Surgeon" John Maynard Woodworth in 1871, and it was formalized by legislation enacted in 1889. The Supervising

FIGURE 3-6.2 Organization of Health Programs at the Department of Health and Human Services

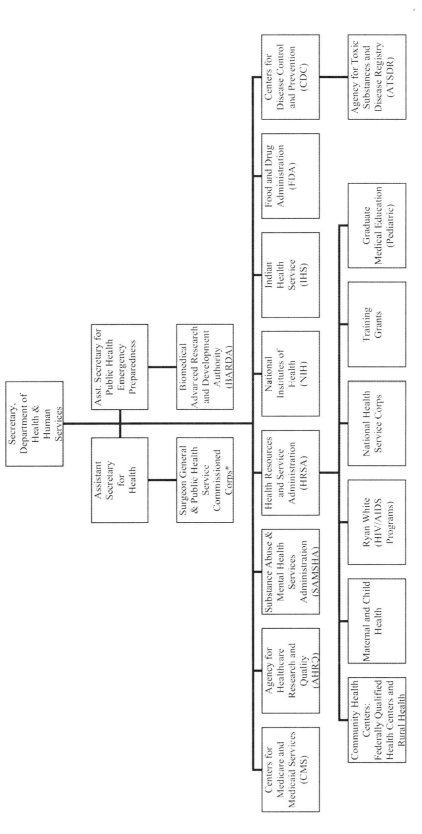

Note: All of the above agencies (except for CMS) are authorized by the Public Health Service Act and are collectively referred to as the U.S. Public Health Service.

Surgeon ultimately became today's Surgeon General—often a visible public figure, as in the case of C. Everett Koop in the 1980s.

At first, the USPHSCC was open only to physicians but expanded to include dentists, pharmacists, nurses, and other health professionals.[110]

The duties of the USPHSCC mirror those of the Public Health Service: (1) providing health care and related services to medically underserved populations; (2) preventing and controlling disease; (3) improving the nation's mental health; (4) working to ensure that food, drugs, and medical devices are safe; (5) conducting and supporting biomedical, behavioral, and health services research and communicating research results to health professionals and the public; and (6) working with other nations and international agencies on global health problems and their solutions. In addition, the USPHSCC provides physicians to the U.S. Coast Guard.

Issue: Are the Added Costs of Maintaining the USPHSCC Justified?

In a 1996 report, the GAO found that the functions performed by the USPHSCC "are essentially civilian in nature [and] some PHS employees carry out the same functions as Corps members." The report also noted that "the PHS Corps does not meet the criteria and principles cited in a DOD report as a justification for the military compensation system." The report concluded that personnel costs at that time could be reduced by 22% per year if civilian employees were used for the functions carried out by Corps members.[111]

One could conclude from these findings either that the extra expenses of maintaining the Corps are not justified *or* that the Corps is not being well utilized. The latter is a more compelling conclusion, particularly given the threats of terrorism and weapons of mass destruction facing our nation and the incompetent response to Hurricanes Katrina and Rita (discussed in the homeland security chapter). A military-style medical corps makes great sense, but it needs to operate in a military manner with rapid deployment capabilities, continuous training, and a high state of readiness.

Agency for Healthcare Research and Quality (AHRQ)

FY 2007 AHRQ Spending: $319 million[112]

In a Nutshell

The Agency for Healthcare Research and Quality (AHRQ), one of the eight Public Health Service agencies, is the lead Federal agency supporting *research* aimed at improving the quality of health care and the efficiency of its delivery. Specifically, the agency funds and conducts research on patient safety, health information technology, and comparative effectiveness of medical treatments.

Centers for Disease Control and Prevention (CDC) and ATSDR

FY 2007 CDC Spending: $6 billion
FY 2007 ATSDR Spending: $75 *million*

See www.GovBudget.com for updated numbers.

In a Nutshell

The Atlanta-based CDC is the nation's lead public health agency, responsible for coordinating *infectious disease prevention and response* efforts with State, local, and international public health agencies. In addition to emergency response, CDC supports public health activities including preparedness for bioterrorism and pandemics, immunization programs, HIV prevention, chronic disease prevention and health promotion, reducing the occurrence of birth defects and developmental disabilities, and occupational safety and health. About three-quarters of the agency's budget is disbursed as grants. CDC's sister agency, the Agency for Toxic Substances and Disease Registry (ATSDR), examines the specific health effects of hazardous waste sites and unplanned releases of toxins.[113]

Background

The CDC was originally created in 1946 to focus on communicable diseases, such as malaria and typhus. (The acronym CDC at that time stood for Communicable Disease Center.) Since then, the CDC has grown into a major agency with a broad portfolio of public health responsibilities.

CDC's workforce includes personnel in the U.S. Public Health Service Commissioned Corps (discussed earlier), although most of CDC's staff are permanent civil service employees. Examples of specific CDC programs include the following:

- CDC administers the Vaccines for Children (VCF) program that provides vaccines free of charge to children who are Medicaid recipients, uninsured, underinsured, or Native Americans. More than $2 billion of CDC's budget is allocated for VCF.
- The National Breast and Cervical Cancer Early Detection Program has provided more than six million screening tests since 1991.
- CDC collected data which defined the problem of inadequate folic acid as a cause of spina bifida, resulting in policies that have reduced the rates of that birth defect.
- CDC research led to a regimen that has virtually eliminated perinatal AIDS transmission.[114]
- The CDC's website on developmental delays—which impact nearly *one-fifth of U.S. children*—was accessed by more than 120,000 visitors in 2005, of particular importance because early recognition and treatment of developmental delays can significantly improve the chances of healthy development.
- CDC's efforts helped eliminate the rubella virus in the United States.
- CDC's National Institute for Occupational Health and Safety (NIOSH) in 2005 certified the first respirators with chemical and biological protection for first responders.

- In the wake of Hurricane Katrina, CDC developed species-specific antibodies to a fungus linked to serious health problems.
- Epidemic Intelligence Service officers respond to health outbreaks across the country and globally.
- In the area of preparedness, the CDC has set up labs in all 50 states to test for anthrax, smallpox, and other possible bioterrorism agents.
- The CDC is the lead agency in preparing for the avian flu.[115]

Food, Drug, and Consumer Product Safety: FDA, FSIS, and CPSC

> **FY 2007 Total FDA Spending: $1.6 billion**
> **USDA Food Safety and Inspection Service: $887 million**
> **Consumer Product Safety Commission: $62 million**

See www.GovBudget.com for updated numbers.

In a Nutshell

The **Food and Drug Administration (FDA),** located within the Public Health Service at HHS, oversees the safety of the food supply (except for meat and poultry) and all human drugs, biologics (blood, tissue, etc.), medical devices, and equipment that emits radiation (such as MRI machines and microwave ovens). The **Food Safety and Inspection Service (FSIS),** located in the Department of Agriculture, regulates and inspects meat, poultry, and processed egg products. The **Consumer Product Safety Commission (CPSC)** is a small independent Federal agency charged with protecting the public against risks of injury or death from more than 15,000 types of consumer products.

Background

The FDA, the oldest U.S. consumer protection office, dates back to 1906, when President Teddy Roosevelt signed the Food and Drug Act and assigned implementation to the Bureau of Chemistry at the U.S. Department of Agriculture. The Bureau eventually became the FDA, an agency located in the Department of Health and Human Services. Today, the FDA has responsibility for the safety of the national food supply—except for meat, poultry, and egg products, which are regulated by the Agriculture Department—as well as all human drugs, biologics, medical devices, equipment that emits radiation (such as MRI machines, lasers and microwave ovens), and animal drugs and food.[117] It is estimated that the FDA regulates about 25 cents of every consumer dollar spent.[118]

Food Inspection by the FDA.—Food-borne diseases are estimated to cause approximately 76 million illnesses, 325,000 hospitalizations, and 5,000 deaths every year in the United States.[119] The FDA's mission is to minimize illnesses and death from food-borne illnesses by ensuring that food is free of contaminants, approving new additives before they can be used, ensuring that drugs given to animals raised to be used for human food do not cause health problems, monitoring the safety of dietary supplements and the contents of infant formulas, and regulating food and nutrition labeling.

The FDA's food inspection resources are very limited considering their responsibilities. The FDA has about 2,800 personnel devoted to food inspection. This translates into unannounced FDA compliance inspections "roughly once every five years." State agencies handle the bulk of food safety inspections.[120]

U.S. Department of Agriculture (USDA) and Food Safety.—The Food Safety and Inspection Service at USDA regulates meat, poultry, and processed egg products. FSIS resources are substantially greater than FDA's. FSIS has about 8,000 inspectors and Federal law requires that an inspector be present for at least part of every shift while a firm is processing meat products for human consumption.[121] Former Agriculture Secretary Dan Glickman has observed that while meat and poultry are generally well regulated due to the USDA's commitment of resources, other food products are not well regulated due to insufficient inspection resources at the FDA.[122]

Other Federal Agencies with Food Safety Responsibilities.—The National Marine Fisheries Service at the Department of Commerce is responsible for assuring the safety of commercial fisheries products. CDC tracks food-borne illness incidents and outbreaks. NIH is responsible for research on the health effects of food-borne illness and efficacy of possible treatments. The Environmental Protection Agency (EPA) is responsible for regulating the amount of residues from pesticides and other chemicals that can be found in or on food.[123]

State and Local Agencies.—Eighty-five State and 3,000 local regulatory and licensing agencies play a major role in licensing and inspecting retail food establishments. Forty-four States have adopted State laws and regulations based on an FDA guidance manual called the *Food Code*—designed to ensure that food is not a vehicle for communicable disease.[124]

Medicines, Biologics, and Medical Devices.—The FDA must *pre*approve all new medicines, biologics (vaccines, blood products, tissues for transplantation, biotechnology products and gene therapy), and medical devices for safety *and* effectiveness before they can be marketed. In the early 1990s, the FDA levied fees on pharmaceutical manufacturers to beef up its resources and speed up the approval process.[125]

There is continuing controversy, however, about the backlog of applications for approval of low-cost generics. As of 2006, the FDA had a backlog of more than 800 applications to bring new generic products to the market.[126] From a budget perspective, adding millions to speed up the approval of generics could save hundreds of millions, or more, in Medicare and Medicaid prescription drug costs.

The FDA also has responsibility for the safety of drugs already on the market, although in March 2006, in a highly critical report, GAO concluded "FDA lacks clear and effective processes for making decisions about . . . postmarket safety issues." The GAO recommended that "Congress consider expanding FDA's authority to require drug sponsors to conduct postmarket studies [and] that FDA systematically track postmarket drug safety issues."[127] Experts explain that preapproval "clinical trials are not designed to detect events that occur in as few as one in 1000 patients. Many risks and adverse effects cannot be observed until after a treatment has been approved and used by a large and diverse population. That is why post-approval monitoring is key to protecting patient health."[128]

*"We've come a long way from the time when the safety of food additives
was determined by feeding them to a 'Poison Squad' of Federal employees."*[129]
Photograph: The Dining Room of the "Poison Squad." Courtesy: FDA History Office

FDA also regulates labeling of drugs and medical devices. The FDA recently announced
changes in prescription drug labeling that aim to reduce the appalling level of medical errors
in the United States—errors that kill an estimated 100,000 people and injure 300,000 in hospitals every year. The dispensing of inappropriate medications is viewed as a major cause of
the staggering error rate.[130]

FDA has also recently moved forward with an initiative requiring drug companies to elec-
tronically tag all pharmaceuticals in order to track them from the manufacturing plant to the
pharmacy in order to counter the growing problem of counterfeit prescription drugs slipping
into the United States from abroad.[131]

Consumer Product Safety Commission.—One of the first items we learn in law school
about personal injury (tort) law is that until modern times, the old British common law principle of *caveat emptor,* "let the buyer beware," prevailed in U.S. courts. Fortunately, this is no
longer the case. States have adopted commercial codes that imply warranties that merchan-
dise is of "merchantable" quality and fit for its intended purpose, and various levels government have established consumer protection agencies.

The Consumer Product Safety Commission (CPSC), an independent Federal agency led
by three commissioners appointed by the President, was established in 1972 to protect the
public against unreasonable risks of injury or death from more than 15,000 types of consumer
products (not including cars, boats, motorcycles, alcohol, tobacco, firearms, food, drugs, cosmetics, pesticides, and medical devices).[132]

According to the Commission, over *25,000 deaths and 33 million injuries* each year are associated with consumer products under CPSC's jurisdiction. In order to protect the public from
hazardous products, the CPSC has authority to (1) encourage manufacturers to adopt voluntary standards and impose mandatory standards where voluntary standards are inadequate

(although mandatory standards are rarely imposed), (2) ban products that can not be made safe, (3) recall hazardous products already on the market, (4) impose fines on company's failing to report product defects having the potential to injure or kill consumers, (5) maintain a clearinghouse of information on product-related injuries, and (6) conduct research on product hazards.

CPSC, in national budgetary terms, has a very small budget that—in inflation-adjusted terms—has decreased significantly. According to the CPSC's website, "we may or may not investigate your product complaint. We receive about 10,000 reports of product-related injuries and deaths a year from consumers and others. Due to our small staff size, we can investigate only a few of them." CPSC's staff level declined from 518 in 1994 to 446 in 2006.[133]

Issues—Beefing up Food Inspections and Consumer Product Safety

The GAO has recommended consolidating food safety under a single agency. According to GAO, more than 30 laws administered by 12 agencies operating under 50 interagency agreements govern food safety. In January 2007, GAO designated food safety as a "high risk" area, noting that "the current fragmented federal system has caused inconsistent oversight, ineffective coordination, and inefficient use of resources."[134]

However, the GAO recommendation should be considered very carefully before moving ahead with a consolidation, given the poor results of the DHS consolidation. Better and faster results might be achieved by beefing up the budgets and workforces of existing agencies, as well as creating a Food Safety and Security Council to improve coordination among agencies before charging ahead with yet another reshuffling of agencies.

In addition to adding food inspectors at the FDA, the CPSC clearly needs more personnel given the increasing number of recalls of imported consumer products, for example, children's toys imported from China.

Health Resources and Services Administration (HRSA): Access to Health Care

The Health Resources and Services Administration (HRSA) in the Department of Health and Human Services is the primary Federal agency dedicated to improving access to health care services for people who are uninsured, isolated geographically, or medically vulnerable. The major components of HRSA are community health centers, health care for people with HIV/AIDS, maternal and child health, training and recruitment grants, and the National Health Service Corps. (See www.hrsa.gov.)

Community Health Centers: Assistance to Medically Underserved Areas (Federally Qualified Health Centers and Rural Health Clinics)

FY 2007 Spending for Community Health Centers: $1.9 billion

See www.GovBudget.com for updated numbers,

In a Nutshell

Enactment of the landmark Economic Opportunity Act of 1964 is often viewed as the birth of America's community health centers. The concept was to combine the resources of local communities with State and Federal funds to establish *community-owned* neighborhood clinics in both urban and rural areas across America. There are two types of community centers: **Federally Qualified Health Centers (FQHCs)** and **Rural Health Clinics (RHCs)**. Supporters of community health centers believe the centers have successfully "reduced health disparities, lowered infant mortality rates, and reduced chronic disease" as well as reduced "the need for acute care at hospital emergency rooms."[135]

Background

Federally Qualified Health Centers.—All FQHCs have several characteristics in common; most importantly, they are required to provide a comprehensive set of *primary care services to any individual, regardless of ability to pay*. In addition, they are governed by a community board on which patients are a majority, and they generally provide services that help patients gain access, such as outreach, translation, and transportation. While a separate program is dedicated to rural clinics (discussed later), FQHCs are located in *both* urban and rural areas. According to the GAO, "FQHCs vary considerably. . . . For example, an FQHC may be located in an urban area with a large uninsured or Medicaid population . . . or in a rural area, where it serves as the only source of primary care for several communities." There are more than *1,000 FQHCs* across the country serving nearly 15 million people—about half living in economically depressed inner-city neighborhoods and the other half in rural areas.[136] Nearly 70% of health center patients have family incomes at or below poverty.

The two largest revenue sources for FQHCs are Medicaid (more than a third of total revenue) and Federal grant funds administered by HRSA.[137] Total Federal funding for health centers is approximately $2 billion.[138] Other significant sources of revenue are State and local sources and private grants.

FQHCs have been credited with improving access to primary and preventive care, effectively managing chronic illness, and reducing health disparities for racial and ethnic minorities in key areas such as infant mortality, prenatal care, tuberculosis case rates, and death rates.[139] The great success of community heath centers led to increased Federal funding since 2001, with 600 new and expanded health centers. The President in 2005 called for "expanding community health centers to every poor county in America . . . [so that] the poor and the indigent (are) able to get good primary care at . . . community health centers and not [end up] in . . . emergency rooms."[140] Yet, a March 2005 report by George Washington University and the National Association of Community Health Centers found that due to insufficient resources, half of all poor counties still lacked community health centers.[141] In addition, a 2006 study published by the *Journal of the American Medical Association* found that expansion of health centers is limited by a shortage of primary care physicians.[142]

Rural Health Clinics.—While community health centers (now called FQHCs) historically covered both urban and rural areas, rural Americans experienced a unique problem— a shortage of primary care physicians and emergency services. To address these shortages, the Rural Health Clinics (RHCs) program was established in 1977 to facilitate the establishment of health clinics staffed by physician assistants (PAs) and nurse practitioners (NPs).[143] RHCs are funded by Medicaid and Medicare, as well as private insurance and patients (self-pay). Due to incentives from State governments and Congress, the RHC program grew from fewer than 600 in 1990 to 3,600 in 2004. RHCs can operate either independently or as part of a hospital, skilled nursing facility, or home health agency.[144] In addition to primary care and emergency services, RHCs have also been authorized to provide immunization services for rural children.[145] RHCs have been credited with stabilizing local rural economies, in addition to providing much needed health care services.

Recommended Sources for More Information on FQHCs and RHCs

- **History of the Community Health Center Movement:** National Association of Community Health Centers, http://www.nachc.com/about/aboutcenters.asp; Alice Sardell, *The U.S. Experiment in Social Medicine: The Community Health Center Program, 1965–86* (Pittsburgh: Pittsburgh Press: 1988).
- **GAO:** "State and Federal Implementation Issues for Medicaid's New Payment System (for FQHCs and RHCs)," GAO-05-452, June 2005; "Community Health Centers: Adapting to Changing Health Care Environment Key to Success," GAO/HEHS-00-39, March 2000.
- **Rural Health Centers:** www.narhc.org; www.kff.org/uninsured/upload/The-Uninsured-in-Rural-America-Update-PDF.pdf; www.oig.hhs.gov/oei/reports/oei-05-03-00170.pdf; www.aapa.org/gandp/rhc.html.
- **Kaiser Foundation:** "Health Centers Reauthorization: An Overview of Achievements and Challenges," March 2006, http://www.gwumc.edu/sphhs/healthpolicy/chsrp/downloads/7471.pdf.
- **National Association of Community Health Centers:** "A Nation's Health at Risk: Growing Uninsured, Budget Cutbacks Challenge President's Initiative to Put a Health Center in Every Poor County," March 2005, http://www.nachc.com/research/Files/poorcountiesSTIB9.pdf.
- **National Health Policy Forum/George Washington University:** "The Fundamentals of Community Health Centers," August 31, 2004.

Ryan White CARE Act: Health Care for People with HIV/AIDS

> *FY 2007 Spending for the Ryan White CARE Act (HIV/AIDS): $2.1 billion*

See www.GovBudget.com for updated numbers.

In a Nutshell

The Ryan White Comprehensive AIDS Resources Emergency (CARE) Act, administered by HRSA, provides grants to states and cities for treatment and medications for a half million low-income and uninsured persons with HIV/AIDS. CARE Act funds are used for medical care, drug treatments (known as the ADAP[146] program), dental care, home health and hospice care, and outpatient mental health and substance abuse treatment.[147]

Background

Acquired immune deficiency syndrome (AIDS) impairs the immune system and leaves people infected with the virus susceptible to a variety of infections and cancer. Since 1981, nearly a million AIDS cases in the United States have been reported to the CDC. Out of the total number of reported AIDS cases, over 400,000 persons were reported to be living with AIDS as of the end of December 2003, and more than 350,000 persons were known to be infected with the human immunodeficiency virus (HIV).[148]

CARE Act expenditures are part of the estimated $23.3 billion spent annually by the Federal government on HIV/AIDS, domestically and internationally, with about two-thirds spent on treatment programs, 13% on research, 11% on prevention, and 9% on income support (cash and housing assistance).[149] The funding flows through a number of government programs (see table 3-6.6).

Global Efforts.—Internationally, AIDS has reached pandemic levels. As of FY 2007, the United States was spending nearly $4.5 billion annually on global AIDS relief programs. The funds flow through the President's Emergency Plan for AIDS Relief (PEPFAR), contributions to the Global AIDS Trust Fund, and international activities of NIH and CDC.[150]

According to the Joint UN Program on HIV/AIDS, nearly 40 million people are currently living with HIV/AIDS, including nearly 2.2 million children under age 15. The pandemic is heavily concentrated in Sub-Saharan Africa, which has 11% of the world's population but nearly 65% of the world's HIV cases. By the end of 2005, an estimated 27.5 million Africans had died of AIDS.[151] Another catastrophic AIDS issue is the exploding number of orphaned children. By 2010, it is expected that more than 25 million children will be orphaned due to AIDS.[152]

From FY 1981 through FY 2004, the Federal government invested a total of $150 billion in HIV/AIDS programs.[153]

Maternal and Child Health (MCH)

> ### FY 2007 Spending for MCH: $835 million[154]

See www.GovBudget.com for updated numbers.

In a Nutshell

HRSA's Maternal and Child Health Bureau administers several programs aimed at improving access to maternal and child health services. The largest of these programs is the Maternal and

TABLE 3-6.6 FY 2007 AIDS Funding Breakdown (billions of dollars)

Medicaid	$6.8	Supplemental Security Income	$0.4
International Aid (State/AID/HHS)	$4.5	Other HHS Discretionary	$0.3
Medicare	$3.5	HUD	$0.3
NIH Research	$2.5	SAMHSA	$0.2
Ryan White CARE	$2.1	Federal Employee Health Benefits	$0.1
Social Security Disability	$1.4	Defense Health Care	$0.1
CDC	$0.7	Prisons	$0.02
Veterans	$0.5	**Total 2007 HIV/AIDS Spending**	**$23.3 B**

Source: CRS, Report # RL30731, March 8, 2007.

Child Health Block Grant that provides funds ($700 million in FY 2007) to States for services that address infant mortality, women's health, primary care and diagnostic services for children, and coordinated care for special needs. Annually, the MCH Block Grant serves 27 million women and children in the United States.[155]

Background: Title V Block Grant

The MCH Block Grant was created by the Omnibus Budget Reconciliation Act of 2001 (OBRA-2001). A State's share of the MCH Block Grant is based on the respective State's share of the seven programs that were consolidated to create the block grant; those programs dealt with adolescent pregnancy, lead poisoning, sudden infant death syndrome (SIDS), hemophilia, and other genetic conditions.

Enacted in Title V of the Social Security Act, the MCH Block Grant requires that States use at least 30% of their allocation for preventive and primary care services for children and another 30% for services for children with special health care needs. States have discretion over how they use the remaining 40% within broad guidelines.

Typical uses for the grant funds include prenatal care, immunizations, vision and hearing screening, services to screen for lead poisoning and counseling for parents in the aftermath of SIDS.

MCH is a matching grant program; in order to receive MCH Block Grant funds, States must provide $3 for every $4 they receive in Federal funds.

National Health Service Corps (NHSC)

FY 2007 Spending for NHSC: $125 million

See www.GovBudget.com for updated numbers.

In a Nutshell

The NHSC places primary care health professionals at facilities in medically underserved areas in exchange for scholarships or loan repayments. The current field strength of NHSC is 4,000 health care professionals.[156]

Background

Unlike the PHS Commissioned Corps, which is a Federal uniformed service, NHSC[157] is a program that places private citizens—primary care health professionals including medical and dental students, residents, and practitioners—at facilities in "medically underserved areas." The primary care health professionals who sign up for the NHSC agree to serve in a *medically underserved area* upon completion of training or residency for a minimum of two years in exchange for scholarships or loan repayments.

NHSC also provides matching grants to states that operate similar grant and loan programs and operates as a placement service for health care professionals desiring to work in medically underserved areas. Underserved areas are locations where there is a shortage of medical, dental or mental health professionals. The areas tend to be located in inner cities, farm towns, remote areas and migrant communities.

Since 1972, more than 24,500 health professionals have participated in the NHSC program. One of the great successes of the program is that two-thirds of NHSC participants remain in underserved communities after fulfilling their two-year service commitments.[158]

Recommended Sources for More Information on NHSC

- **National Health Service Corps**: http://nhsc.bhpr.hrsa.gov/.
- **Eric Redman**, *The Dance of Legislation* (New York: Simon & Shuster, 1973; Seattle: University of Washington Press, 2001).

Indian Health Service and Other Programs for Native Americans

> **FY 2007 Federal Spending for Indian Health: $3.2 billion**
> **Total Spending for Indian Programs: $6.1 billion**

See www.GovBudget.com for updated numbers.

In a Nutshell

A variety of Federal government programs provide assistance to Indian Tribes and Alaska Native Corporations, among them the Indian Health Service (IHS), with an FY 2007 budget of $3.2 billion. IHS is a *direct provider* of health services. About 1.8 million Indians and Alaska Natives are eligible for services, and 1.6 million are active users of the system.[159]

Background on IHS

American Indian Tribes ("Tribes") and Alaska Native Corporations (ANCs) have a unique "government-to-government" relationship with the United States. The 560 Tribes and ANCs are recognized as sovereign entities. The U.S. government has a "Federal trust responsibility" for the health and well-being of American Indians and Alaska Natives rooted in a long history of court decisions, treaties, Acts of Congress, and executive orders.[160]

IHS is not a health insurance program; rather, it is a *direct* provider of health services with a health system consisting of more than 600 health care facilities—located primarily in Western, remote regions of the United States—and employing 900 physicians and 2,700 nurses. Tribes and ANCs also have the option of assuming responsibility for administration and operation of their own health services. Many have chosen this option; Tribes and ANCs administer 15 hospitals, 221 health centers, 9 residential treatment centers, and 176 Alaska village clinics.

Medicaid reimburses IHS for services to Medicaid enrollees. One recent analysis notes that while the Indian Health Service budget has remained inadequate, health care services are "thriving among the Northwest tribes" because they have worked closely with State Medicaid officials and have been increasingly able to access Medicaid funding.[161]

Myth: American Indians and Alaska Natives no longer experience major health disparities compared with the general population.

Fact: Death rates from a variety of factors are significantly higher for Native Americans compared with the general population, including tuberculosis (600% higher), alcoholism (510% higher), motor vehicle crashes (229% higher), diabetes (189% higher), homicide (61% higher), and suicide (62% higher).[162] According to a recent analysis, "the geographic isolation of many tribes and the grossly inadequate behavioral health staff and service levels across Indian country are spurring problems to epidemic proportions—for instance, youth suicide and violent death in some Alaska Native villages."[163]

Other Programs for American Indians and Alaska Natives

Other Federal programs for American Indians and Alaska Natives are administered by the Bureau of Indian Affairs (BIA) and the Bureau of Indian Education (BIE)—both in the Department of the Interior. Because Tribes and ANCs are sovereign entities, BIA and BIE spend more than $2 billion per year providing many of the same services as State and local governments:

- education for over 48,000 elementary and secondary students;
- 26 tribal colleges, universities, and postsecondary schools;
- social services and housing;
- law enforcement;
- fire protection;
- natural resources management on Trust lands;
- economic development programs;
- guaranteed loans for small business development;
- administration of tribal courts;
- repair and maintenance of roads and bridges; and
- operation and maintenance of irrigation infrastructures and dams.

Issue: Unemployment and Poverty among Native Americans

Notwithstanding this wide-ranging network of Federal programs, a recent Federal report issued the startling finding that *two-thirds* of the Indian workforce was unemployed or living in poverty in 2003.[164]

Recommended Sources for More Information on Native American Programs

- **Indian Health Service:** www.ihs.gov.
- **Bureau of Indian Affairs:** http://www.doi.gov/budget/2007/07Hilites/BH79.pdf.
- **Urban Institute:** A National Roundtable on the Indian Health System and Medicaid Reform, August 31, 2005, http://www.urban.org/UploadedPDF/411236_indian_health_system.pdf.
- **National Indian Health Board:** http://www.nihb.org/.

National Institutes of Health (NIH)

> *FY 2007 Federal Spending for NIH: $28.8 billion*

See www.GovBudget.com for updated numbers.

In a Nutshell

The National Institutes of Health consists of 27 institutes and centers dedicated to biomedical, behavioral, and basic scientific research. In addition to research, NIH is a lead agency in health information dissemination. Most of the NIH budget—over 80%—is disbursed through grants to scientists working in universities, teaching hospitals, and independent research institutions in the United States and abroad.[165] The NIH budget doubled between 1998 and 2003 but has been virtually flat in recent years.

Background

NIH is a collection of 20 semi-independent "Institutes" and 7 "Centers" dedicated to biomedical and behavioral research. Each of the Institutes and Centers receives a separate appropriation from Congress. Congress therefore sets broad spending priorities among the various components of NIH, but it does *not* earmark funds for specific research projects or funding recipients.

Nineteen of the Institutes are dedicated to specific areas of biomedical research: (1) Cancer; (2) Eye Disease; (3) Heart, Lung, and Blood; (4) Human Genome; (5) Aging; (6) Alcohol Abuse; (7) Allergy and Infectious Diseases; (8) Arthritis, Musculoskeletal, and Skin Diseases; (9) Biomedical Imaging and Bioengineering; (10) Child Health and Human Development; (11) Deafness and Other Communication Disorders; (12) Dental and Craniofacial Research; (13) Diabetes, Digestive, and Kidney Diseases; (14) Drug Abuse; (15) Environmental Health Sciences; (16) General Medical Sciences; (17) Mental Health; (18) Neurological Disorders and Stroke; and (19) Nursing Research. The 20th Institute is the National Library of Medicine, which collects and organizes biomedical science information on a grand scale.

The seven Centers conduct a variety of functions: incorporating advanced computer technology into biomedical research, peer review of research proposals, promotion of scientific research internationally, the study of alternative medicine, promotion of minority health and eliminating health disparities, improving research resources and infrastructure, and clinical research.

From FY 1998 through 2003, Congress—responding to a massive advocacy campaign by health care and research organizations[166]—agreed to *double* NIH funding from $13.6 billion to $27.1 billion.[167] However, the five-year doubling period has been followed by flat funding in dollar terms and a *decrease* in inflation-adjusted terms.

The current trend of flat NIH funding has generated a great deal of concern in both the medical and scientific research communities. According to a recent analysis in the *New England Journal of Medicine*, "This downturn is more severe than any we have faced previously, since it comes on the heels of the doubling of the budget and threatens to erode the benefits of that investment. It takes many years for institutions to develop investigators skilled in

Myth: As in other Federal research programs, Congress "earmarks" NIH funds for particular research projects at specific institutions in their States and congressional districts.

Fact: NIH is the most prominent *exception* to Congress' earmarking practices. Members of the Appropriations Committees long ago decided not to earmark NIH funds for specific disease research projects. If earmarks were permitted, every disease advocacy group and research institution would engage in ongoing, massive lobbying Campaigns to secure earmarks; and saying yes to one disease group and no to another would be a political no-win situation. The Congress has instead adopted the practice of appropriating large chunks of funding to each of the Institutes and Centers, and it very deliberately refrains from going a step further and earmarking any of those funds for specific research projects. To be sure, the Appropriations Committees *do* frequently include report language "urging" NIH to focus research dollars on particular diseases; but unlike most appropriations report language, which is viewed by Federal agencies as "binding" from a practical political perspective, NIH report language on research priorities is generally viewed as *non*binding. In reality, research grants are awarded based on a scientific "peer review"[168] process—without regard to language in committee reports. Table 3-6.7 and figure 3-6.3 display how the FY 2007 Appropriations Act divided funds among the various Institutes; the pie chart illustrates the relative size of research budgets.

Myth: Most NIH research is conducted by NIH doctors and scientists.

Fact: Only 10% of NIH research funds are allocated for "intramural" research—that is, research conducted by NIH scientists and doctors.[169] The bulk of NIH's $27 billion is allocated to what is known as "extramural" research—research conducted off-campus by scientists working in universities, academic health centers, and hospitals.[170]

Myth: Almost one-third of biomedical research grant proposals to NIH are able to receive funding.

Fact: That was true during the "doubling years," when the success rate was more than 30%. However, NIH estimated the percentage of research grant proposals that could be funded at less than 20% for FY 2007. In general, this trend reflects "more and more applicants chasing fewer and fewer awards. . . . The increase in applications stems from both the expanded research capacity at many academic medical centers [teaching hospitals] and the increase in the number of applications submitted per applicant, as researchers try more than one route to obtain funding."[171]

Table 3-6.7: FY 2007 NIH APPROPRIATIONS BY INSTITUTES AND CENTERS ($ in billions)*

National Cancer Institute	4.798
National Institute of Allergy and Infectious Diseases	4.417
National Heart, Lung, and Blood Institute	2.923
National Institute of General Medical Sciences	1.936
Institute of Diabetes & Digestive & Kidney Diseases	1.706
National Institute of Neurological Disorders & Stroke	1.536
National Institute of Mental Health	1.405
Institute of Child Health and Human Development	1.255
National Center for Research Resources	1.133
National Institute on Aging	1.047
National Institute on Drug Abuse	1.001
National Eye Institute	0.667
National Institute of Environmental Health Sciences	0.642
Arthritis & Musculoskeletal & Skin Diseases	0.508
National Human Genome Research Institute	0.487
National Institute on Alcohol Abuse and Alcoholism	0.436
Nat'l Inst. on Deafness & Other Communication Disorders	0.394
National Institute of Dental & Craniofacial Research	0.390
National Library of Medicine	0.321
Institute of Biomedical Imaging & Bioengineering	0.297
Center on Minority Health & Health Disparities	0.199
National Institute of Nursing Research	0.137
Center for Complementary & Alternative Medicine	0.122
Fogarty International Center	0.066

Note: Explanation: 1.0 = $1 billion; 0.667 = $667 million.
Source: Congressional Research Service.[172]
*The NIH Director has nearly a half billion dollars in discretionary funds to allocate for various priorities.

For estimates of funding for various diseases/conditions: www.nih.gov/news/fundingresearchareas.htm

FIGURE 3-6.3 Relative Size of NIH Research Budgets

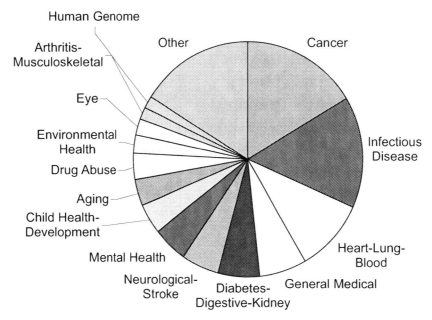

modern research techniques and to build the costly, complicated infrastructure necessary for biomedical research. Rebuilding the investigator pool and the infrastructure after a downturn is expensive and time-consuming and weakens the benefits of prior funding."[173]

Substance Abuse and Mental Health Services Administration

> *FY 2007 Federal Spending for SAMHSA: $3.2 billion*
> *0.1% of Federal Spending*

See www.GovBudget.com for updated numbers.

In a Nutshell

SAMHSA provides block grants and program grants to State and local governments and community-based organizations aimed at preventing and treating substance abuse and mental health disorders. Grantees use the funds for education and training, translating new research findings into prevention and treatment services, and early intervention. (However, Medicaid provides the bulk of public funds invested in mental health services, and the National Institute of Mental Health at NIH conducts and supports mental health research).

Background

Estimates are that 20 million adults and 6 million children and teenagers in the United States suffer from mental disorders. Half the people with disorders do not receive treatment due, in part, to lack of access to effective mental health services. In July 2003, the President's New Freedom Commission on Mental Health found the U.S. mental health system "fragmented and in disarray, lead[ing] to unnecessary and costly disability, homelessness, school failure and incarceration."[174] The Commission called for a "fundamental transformation."

However, advocacy groups highlight that in the two years immediately following release of the Commission's report:

- 63,000 Americans died by suicide—more than by homicide,
- more than 300,000 Americans with mental illnesses were incarcerated instead of treated, and
- the American economy lost $150 billion in productivity due to unaddressed mental health needs.[175]

SAMHSA's mission is to support State and local efforts to treat substance abuse and mental health disorders. Despite the broad scope of this mission, in FY 2007 SAMHSA had a national budget of less than $900 million to address mental health issues and about $2.3 billion for substance abuse prevention and treatment grants.

Issue: No Funding to Follow-up on Commission Findings

Despite the grave assessment of the President's Commission—that is, the pervasiveness of untreated mental health disorders; the implications for American society in the areas of crime, homelessness, and worker productivity; and the ineffectiveness of the current U.S. "mental health system"[176]—the Administration has requested *reduced* levels of funding for SAMHSA's mental health activities for the last three years.[177]

One bright spot was Congress' recent enactment of the Garrett Lee Smith Memorial Act, which provides grants to support youth suicide prevention activities in States and on college campuses.[178]

Recommended Sources for More Information on SAMHSA and Mental Health

- **President's New Freedom Commission on Mental Health**: "Interim Report" and "Final Report," http://www.mentalhealthcommission.gov/.
- **Kaiser HealthCast**: March 29 reconvening of the President's New Freedom Commission. http://www.kaisernetwork.org/health_cast/hcast_index.cfm?display=detail&hc=1687 (including discussion of returning war veterans and mental health).
- **SAMHSA**: www.samhsa.gov; www.samhsa.gov/Budget/FY2008/index.aspx.
- *Mental Health: A Report of the Surgeon General* (1999): http://www.surgeongeneral.gov/library/mentalhealth/home.html.
- *Out of the Shadow:* a widely acclaimed documentary that puts a human face on mental illness; http://www.outoftheshadow.com/index.php.
- **Summary of SAMHSA mental health programs by advocacy groups**: http://www.mhlg.org/appropfy2008.pdf.
- **NAMI**: "Grading the States," a report that finds a mental health system in "shambles", www.nami.org/content/navigationmenu/grading_the_states/project_overview/overview.htm.

Biomedical Advanced Research and Development Authority (BARDA)

In a Nutshell

The most recent addition to the U.S. Public Health Service is the Biomedical Advanced Research and Development Authority (BARDA). It was authorized by Congress in the closing days of 2006, to assist the faltering "Project BioShield." BioShield was established in 2004 to stockpile medical countermeasures for potential terrorist attacks using chemical, biological, radiological, or nuclear (CBRN) weapons.

Background

In July 2004, because few medical countermeasures existed to respond to terrorist attacks using CBRN weapons, Congress established Project BioShield. The BioShield Act had two key provisions. First, BioShield sought to encourage private sector development of medical countermeasures by *offering a government-market guarantee for products that would not otherwise have a market.* HHS would be able to obligate funds to purchase countermeasures while they were still in development, but companies would receive payment only when the countermeasure was delivered. Second, the BioShield Act authorized the HHS Secretary to temporarily allow the *emergency use of countermeasures in advance of FDA approval (Emergency Use Authorization).* Congress advance appropriated $5.6 billion to be available for BioShield contracts over a 10-year period.

However, by 2006 it was clear that Project BioShield was failing. HHS, which had the lead responsibility for implementing BioShield, failed to assess the greatest risks to the U.S. population, to develop a rational and comprehensive countermeasure acquisition strategy, and to coordinate detailed response plans with the Departments of Defense and Homeland Security, as well as State and local governments.[179] The Congressional Research Service reported in June 2007 that "the interagency process responsible for deciding which countermeasures to procure (through BioShield) has changed multiple times since this program's inception" in 2004.[180]

With private sector companies becoming increasingly skeptical about the wisdom of working with BioShield, and Members of Congress becoming increasingly restive about the lack of progress on stockpiling medical countermeasures, Congress enacted in late 2006 the Pandemic and All-Hazard Preparedness Act,[181] which established BARDA. BARDA is not designed to replace BioShield funding; rather, the concept of BARDA is to further incentivize private sector development of medical countermeasures by making government grants available during the *development phase.* In addition, the Act placed BARDA and BioShield under the administrative direction of a new Assistant Secretary for Preparedness and Response at HHS, who is responsible for setting priorities and coordinating interagency, and Federal, State, and local emergency responses.[182]

Issue: Katrina Times 100?

It is too early to assess whether this latest bureaucratic reshuffling and addition of new financial incentives from BARDA will advance the nation toward better preparedness for chemical, biological, radiological, and nuclear terrorist threats. However, there is sufficient reason for skepticism. HHS has thus far failed to stockpile countermeasures for the most destructive

CBRN threats. Moreover, HHS lacks the resources, experience, and logistical infrastructure necessary for rapid delivery of hundreds of thousands of medical countermeasures in the aftermath of a terrorist attack using weapons of mass destruction. Our nation faces the possibility of a catastrophe 100 times worse than Katrina, unless the White House and Congress put in place a credible CBRN preparedness strategy without further delay.[183]

"Five years after September 11, 2001, the United States remains dangerously unprepared to deal with the aftermath of a terrorist attack involving nuclear weapons, dirty bombs or explosions at nuclear power plants. . . . We found that the U.S. government lacks a workable plan to respond to the likely medical needs. Thousands of American civilians injured by a nuclear terrorist attack could survive with better preparedness." —Physicians for Social Responsibility[184]

Notes

1. Testimony of Peter R. Orszag, Director, Congressional Budget Office, Senate Budget Committee, June 21, 2007, 1.

2. CRS analysis of data from the March 2006 Current Population Survey. Chris Peterson, "Health Insurance Coverage: Characteristics of the Insured and Uninsured Populations in 2005," 96-891 EPW (Washington, D.C.: Congressional Research Service, August 30, 2006), 2. See also Kaiser Family Foundation, "Medicaid: A Primer," March 2007, 1.

3. A break in coverage is defined as "63 days or more." The intent of HIPAA is to make group health coverage "portable."

4. See chapter 3-1 for details.

5. Because an enormous demand exists for VA health care, services are provided on a priority basis. There are eight priority levels or "groups." Assignment to a particular priority group depends on whether a veteran has a service-connected injury or disability, the veteran's disability rating, and income level. See chapter 3-3 for details.

6. Jacqueline Rae Roche and Sidath Viranga Panangala, "Health Care for Dependents and Survivors of Veterans" RS22483 (Washington, D.C.: Congressional Research Service, August 1, 2006).

7. The two-year waiting period is waived for people with ALS (Lou Gehrig's Disease). People with end-stage renal (kidney) disease are also entitled to immediate Medicare coverage.

8. For a description of the Massachusetts health reform plan, see April Grady, "The Massachusetts Health Reform Plan," RS22447 (Washington, D.C.: Congressional Research Service, May 26, 2006). According the CRS report, the plan "aims to achieve near-universal health insurance coverage by expanding Medicaid and SCHIP eligibility, providing premium subsidies for certain individuals, and mandating the purchase of insurance for those who can afford it." The legislation also "creates a public entity called the Connector to serve as a clearinghouse for the purchase of insurance by small employers and individuals who are not offered subsidized insurance by a large employer."

9. See http://hcr.vermont.gov/.

10. See Marilyn Werber Serafini, "Cover Story—The States Step Up," *National Journal*, March 17, 2007. See also www.statehealthfacts.org, sponsored by the Kaiser Family Foundation, and National Governors Association (NGA) Center for Best Practices at www.NGA.org.

11. See Bernadette Fernandez, "Health Insurance: State High Risk Pools," RL31745 (Washington, D.C.: Congressional Research Service, January 31, 2007). The ability to join these pools is also sometimes

extended to people whose COBRA continuation coverage has recently expired. See the details of the Maryland high risk pool at http://www.marylandhealthinsuranceplan.net/.

12. Chris Peterson, "Health Insurance Coverage: Characteristics of the Insured and Uninsured Populations in 2005," 96-691 EPW (Washington, D.C.: Congressional Research Service, August 30, 2006), 1.

13. In 1986, Congress passed the landmark Consolidated Omnibus Budget Reconciliation Act (COBRA) health benefit provisions. The law amends the Employee Retirement Income Security Act (ERISA), the Internal Revenue Code and the Public Health Service Act to require, in most cases, the option to purchase 18 months of continuation of group health coverage that otherwise might be terminated when leaving a job. For more details, see http://www.dol.gov/ebsa/faqs/faq_consumer_cobra.html.

14. The Health Insurance Portability and Accountability Act of 1996 (HIPAA) amended ERISA to provide new rights and protections for people who have had continuous group health insurance coverage. In particular, if a worker finds a new job that offers health coverage, or is eligible for coverage under a family member's employment-based plan, HIPAA includes protections for coverage under group health plans that limit exclusions for preexisting conditions and prohibit discrimination against employees and dependents based on their health status. For people who lose group coverage and must apply for an individual policy for themselves or their family, HIPAA includes protections for individual policies that guarantee access to individual policies for people who qualify and guarantee renewability of individual policies. For more details, see http://www.dol.gov/ebsa/faqs/faq_consumer _hipaa.html.

15. This reflects *gross outlays* of the Medicare program; source: CBO's March 2007 baseline. Net total outlays, including offsetting premium payments and other collections, are $370 billion.

16. If offsetting premiums and other collections are included, the net total spending for Medicare is about 13% of the budget.

17. Lewis D. Eigen and Jonathan P. Siegel, *The Macmillan Dictionary of Political Quotations* (New York: Macmillan, 1993), 276.

18. Medicare eligibility begins after receiving Social Security disability for at least two years.

19. Almost all elderly are automatically eligible at 65 because they or their spouse paid payroll tax during their career. The two-year disability waiting period is waived for people diagnosed with ALS (Lou Gehrig's disease).

20. Source for Medicare coverage numbers: *The 2007 Annual Report of the Boards of Trustees of the Federal Hospital Insurance and Federal Supplementary Medical Insurance Trust Funds* (Washington, D.C.: Boards of Trustees, Federal Hospital Insurance and Federal Supplementary Medical Insurance Trust Funds, April 23, 2007), 2.

21. Eigen and Siegel, *The Macmillan Dictionary of Political Quotations*, 276.

22. The Commonwealth Fund, "Medicare at 40: Taking Stock," by Karen Davis, June 26, 2005.

23. "Potential Effects of the 'Premium Support" Proposal on the Security of Medicare," *Journal of the American Medical Association*, November 10, 1999, 1761.

24. In FY 2007.

25. The Medicare Part A Trust Fund also receives a portion of the proceeds of taxing Social Security benefits for high-income beneficiaries.

26. Medicare Part B is also called Supplementary Medical Insurance, or "SMI."

27. "Potential Effects of the 'Premium Support" Proposal on the Security of Medicare," *Journal of the American Medical Association*, November 10, 1999.

28. See Jennifer O'Sulllivan, "Medicare: Part B Premiums," RL32582 (Washington, D.C.: Congressional Research Service, February 14, 2007).

29. *Coinsurance* is a percentage owed by the insured. *Copayments* are another type of beneficiary cost sharing that refers to a specific dollar amount paid for a medical service by the insured person.

30. Medicare Advantage replaced the Medicare+Choice managed care program in 2003.

31. CBO, Testimony of Peter Orszag on the Medicare Advantage Program before the House Budget Committee, June 28, 2007. The Commonwealth Fund, *"The Cost of Privatization: Extra Payments to Medicare Advantage Plans"* November 2006.

32. Kaiser Family Foundation, "Medicare: A Primer," March 2007, www.kff.org/medicare/upload /7615.pdf.

33. Transfers from States are a source of income for Medicare Part D, reflecting the transfer of prescription drug coverage for low-income beneficiaries from the Federal-State Medicaid program to the Federal-only Medicare program. *The 2007 Annual Report of the Boards of Trustees of the Federal Hospital Insurance and Federal Supplementary Medicare Insurance Trust Funds* ,table II.B1 (Washington, D.C.: Boards of Trustees, Federal Hospital Insurance and Federal Supplementary Medical Insurance Trust Funds, 2007), 5.

34. The average monthly beneficiary premium in 2006 is $35. CBO, "Overview of the Medicare Prescription Drug, Improvement, and Modernization Act of 2003," December 6, 2004, 8.

35. See appendix Q for an explanation of the FPL.

36. Jennifer O'Sullivan, "Medicare: Enrollment in Medicare Drug Plans" (Washington, D.C.: Congressional Research Service, November 29, 2006).

37. Jennifer O'Sullivan, "Medicare Prescription Drug Benefit: Low-Income Provisions," RL32902 (Washington, D.C.: Congressional Research Service, March 21, 2007).

38. MedPAC, "Data Book: Health Care Spending and the Medicare Program," June 2003.

39. *The 2007 Annual Report of the Boards of Trustees of the Federal Hospital Insurance and Federal Supplementary Medicare Insurance Trust Funds,* 33.

40. Medicare drug plans vary widely, since they are permitted to offer plans that are "actuarially equivalent" (of equal value) to the standard benefit. However, according to the Kaiser Foundation, most Part D plans have a coverage gap. Kaiser Family Foundation, "Medicare: A Primer," 7. www.kff.org/medicare /upload/7615.pdf.

41. Kaiser Family Foundation, "Medicare: A Primer," 7. www.kff.org/medicare/upload/7615.pdf.

42. Families USA Press Release, "Drug Plan Coverage for Seniors in 'Doughnut Hole' Will Be Scarcer and Less Affordable in 2007," November 1, 2006, http://www.familiesusa.org/resources/newsroom/press-releases/2006-press-releases/drug-plan-coverage-for.html.

43. See the Commonwealth Fund, "How Beneficiaries Fare under the New Medicare Drug Bill," Marilyn Moon, June 2004.

44. CBO projects Medicare spending of $851 billion in 2017. Congressional Budget Office, *The Budget and Economic Outlook: Fiscal Years 2008 to 2017* (Washington, D.C.: Author, January 2007), 55.

45. *The 2007 Annual Report of the Boards of Trustees of the Federal Hospital Insurance and Federal Supplementary Medicare Insurance Trust Funds,* 27.

46. *The 2007 Annual Report of the Boards of Trustees of the Federal Hospital Insurance and Federal Supplementary Medicare Insurance Trust Funds,* 17.

47. *The 2007 Annual Report of the Boards of Trustees of the Federal Hospital Insurance and Federal Supplementary Medicare Insurance Trust Funds,* 33.

48. Medicare Prescription Drug, Improvement, and Modernization Act of 2003, P.L. 108-173.

49. Section 804, Medicare Prescription Drug, Improvement, and Modernization Act of 2003, P.L. 108-173.

50. This reflects the Federal portion of this joint Federal-State program.

52. Kaiser Family Foundation, "Medicaid: A Primer."

53. Low-income childless adults are generally *not* covered by Medicaid.

54. The Social Security Amendments of 1965; P.L. 89-87.

55. See Elicia Herz, "Medicaid Cost-Sharing under the Deficit Reduction Act of 2005," RS22578 (Washington, D.C.: Congressional Research Service, January 25, 2007).

56. Kaiser Family Foundation, "Medicaid: A Primer," 1.

57. Source: CBO, *Budget and Economic Outlook,* January 2007, 54–55.

58. The focus of this analysis is the nonelderly poor, because nearly all elderly are covered by Medicare.

59. Elicia Herz, "How Medicaid Works—Program Basics," RL32277 (Washington, D.C.: Congressional Research Service, January 4, 2006), 2.

60. Kaiser Family Foundation, "Medicaid: A Primer."

61. "Under EPSDT, children receive well-child visits, immunizations, laboratory tests, and other screening services at regular intervals. In addition medical care that is necessary to correct or ameliorate identified defects, physical and mental illness, and other conditions must be provided, including optional services that states do not otherwise cover in their Medicaid programs." CRS, "Medicaid: A Primer," December 22, 2005, 4–5.

62. Known as Qualified Medicare Beneficiaries. In addition, Medicare Part B premiums are paid where incomes do not exceed 120% of the FPL (known as Specified Low-Income Medicare Beneficiaries; some Part B premiums are paid where incomes do not exceed 135% of the FPL (known as Qualifying Individuals); and Medicare Part A premiums are paid where incomes of persons previously entitled to Medicare on the basis of disability do not exceed 200% of the FPL (Qualified Disabled and Working Individuals, or QDWIs).

63. April Grady, "Medicaid: The Federal Medical Assistance Percentage (FMAP)," RL32950 (Washington, D.C.: Congressional Research Service, May 15, 2007).

64. For background on eligibility, see Herz, "How Medicaid Works," 2–12.

65. "Budget neutral," meaning that it does not result in increased Federal Medicaid reimbursements to the State.

66. CRS: "Medicaid: A Primer," December 22, 2005, 9; "Medicaid and SCHIP Section 115 Research and Development Waivers," March 5, 2004.

67. Marilyn Werber Serafini, "Balancing Act," *National Journal,* August 13, 2006, 2574.

68. Julie Stone, "Medicaid Coverage for Long-Term Care," RL33593 (Washington, D.C.: Congressional Research Service, January 5, 2007).

69. Kaiser Family Foundation, "Medicaid: A Primer," 7.

70. Kaiser Family Foundation, "Medicaid: A Primer," 6.

71. Kaiser Family Foundation, "Medicaid: A Primer," 8.

72. CRS, "Medicaid Issues for the 109th Congress," by Jean Hearne, April 10, 2006, 4.

73. CBO, *The Budget and Economic Outlook: FYs 2008 to 2017* (Washington, D.C.: Author, January 2007), 55.

74. Jean Hearne, "Medicaid Disproportionate Share Payments," 97-483 (Washington, D.C.: Congressional Research Service, January 10, 2005), 9-10.

75. Kaiser Commission on Medicaid and the Uninsured, "The Continuing Medicaid Budget Challenge: State Medicaid Spending Growth and Cost Containment in FYs 2004 and 2005," October 2004; and "Medicaid Budgets, Spending and Policy Initiatives in State FYs 2005 and 2006," October 2005.

76. See CRS, "Medicaid Issues for the 109th Congress."

78. CRS, "Medicaid Issues for the 109th Congress," 6.

79. Medicaid Commission, "Report to Secretary Leavitt," September 1, 2005, pp. 7-8.

80. Erik Eckholm, "More Americans Are Spending Time below the Poverty Line," *New York Times,* May 9, 2006.

81. CRS, "Medicaid Issues for the 109th Congress," 5.

82. AHRQ press release, April 26, 2006, www.ahrq.gov/news/press/pr2006/meddrugpr.htm.

83. August 1, 2003, letter to Senator Bill Frist from 40 U.S. Senators regarding IME cuts in pending Medicare legislation.

84. See Association of American Medical Colleges (AAMC) at www.aamc.org.

85. In 1982, the Department of Health and Human Services reported to Congress that "the process of graduate medical education results in very intensive treatment regimens . . . there is no question that

hospitals with teaching programs have higher patient care costs than hospitals without." Department of Health and Human Services, "Hospital Prospective Payment for Medicare: A Report to Congress," December 1982, 48–49. In establishing the special Medicare payments to teaching hospitals, the Congress noted "factors such as severity of illness of patients requiring the specialized services and treatment programs provided by teaching institutions and the additional costs associated with the teaching residents." House Ways and Means Committee Rept. No. 98-25, March 4, 1983; and Senate Finance Committee Rept. No. 98-23, March 11, 1983.

86. Source: CMS Office of the Actuary via Association of American Medical Colleges, August 2007.

87. *Budget Options* (Washington, D.C.: Congressional Research Service, February 2007), 171–72.

88. Source: CMS Office of the Actuary via Association of American Medical Colleges, August 2007.

89. *Budget Options,* 173.

90. CBO, "Medicare and Graduate Medical Education" (Washington, D.C.: Congressional Budget Office, September 1995), ix.

91. Source: "A 50-State Survey" (November 2006) prepared by Tim Henderson for the Association of American Medical Colleges.

92. OMB, *Budget of the United States,* FY 2008 (Washington, D.C.: Author, 2007), 68.

93. Health Resources and Services Administration, discussed later in this chapter.

94. Association of American Medical Colleges, "Bush Budget Means Uphill Battle for Academic Medicine," March 2006, www.aamc.org/newsroom/reporter/march06/budget.htm.

95. Conversations the author had with Senator Moynihan during 1999–2000, as his Chief Health Counsel at the Senate Finance Committee.

96. See www.aamc.org/advocacy/library/gme/gme0011.htm.

97. See AAMC, "AAMC calls for 30 Percent Increase in Medical School Enrollment," www.aamc.org/newsroom/pressrel/2006/060619.htm.

98. This reflects the Federal portion of this joint Federal-State program.

99. Centers for Medicare and Medicaid Services at the Department of Health and Human Services.

100. The Balanced Budget Act of 1997, P.L. 105-33.

101. CBO, "The State Children's Health Insurance Program" (Washington, D.C.: Congressional Budget Office, May 2007), vii.

102. As of FY 2006, 25 States and D.C. had established upper income limits at 200% FPL; another 15 States exceeded 200% FPL; and the remaining 9 States set limits below 200% FPL. Elicia Herz and Chris Peterson, "State Children's Health Insurance Program," RL30473 (Washington, D.C.: Congressional Research Service, January 30, 2007), 2.

103. The higher matching rate is sometimes known as the "enhanced FMAP." Under the formula, allocations to states are based on the number of low-income uninsured children in the State, the number of total low-income children, and a geographic health care cost factor. Herz and Peterson, "State Children's Health Insurance Program," 8.

104. However, as discussed later in this chapter, if a State chooses the Medicaid option, the State may not turn away applicants who qualify for eligibility—even after the SCHIP funds run out. The Medicaid option therefore, effectively expands the Medicaid entitlement.

105. Because the program is not an entitlement, it is subject to amounts available under the appropriation. States can therefore exhaust their share of the annually available funds. However, SCHIP contains a mechanism to redistribute unused funds from low spending states to cover shortfalls in the higher spending states. See Chris Peterson, "SCHIP Financing: Funding Projections and State Redistribution Issues," RL32806 (Washington, D.C.: Congressional Research Service, January 30, 2007).

106. Dawn Horner and Beth Morrow, "Outreach Strategies for Medicaid and SCHIP" (Washington, D.C.: Kaiser Commission on Medicaid and the Uninsured, April 2006).

107. For a State-by-State breakdown, see www.cms.hhs.gov/LowCostHealthInsFamChild/downloads/SCHIPStatePlanActivityMap.pdf.

108. As of November 2006, 10 States reported enrolling 639,000 adults in SCHIP. Herz and Peterson, "State Children's Health Insurance Program," 9–10.

109. Institute of Medicine, "The Future of the Public's Health in the 21ˢᵗ Century," November 2002, 2. The report continues: "Several trends are worth noting. . . . [T]he vast majority of Health Care spending, as much as 95 percent by some estimates, is directed toward medical care and biomedical research. However, there is strong evidence that behavior and environment are responsible for over 70 percent of avoidable mortality, and Health Care is just one of several determinants of health."

110. For a history of the PHSCC, go to www.usphs.gov/html/history.html.

111. GAO, "Federal Personnel: Issues on the Need for the Public Health Service's Commissioned Corps," GAO/GGD-96-55 (Washington, D.C.: Author, May 1996).

112. AHRQ is funded through Public Health Service evaluation funds, which are included in other agency budgets. The Federal Budget therefore does not show any net new budget authority for AHRQ. Pamela Smith, "Public Health Service (PHS) Agencies: Background and Funding," RL34098 (Washington, D.C.: Congressional Research Service, July 23, 2007), 5.

113. The CDC's Director also serves as the Administrator of HHS's Agency for Toxic Substances and Disease Registry (ATSDR), which focuses on environmental health–related issues.

114. *Perinatal:* at the time of birth.

115. Centers for Disease Control and Prevention, "Budget Request Summary, FY 2007," February 2006.

117. FDA, "The Food and Drug Administration Celebrates 100 Years of Service to the Nation," January 4, 2006, www.FDA.gov.

118. FDA, "FDA Overview: Protecting Consumers, Promoting Public Health," slides 1–2, www.FDA.gov.

119. Geoffrey Becker and Donna Porter, "The Federal Food Safety System: A Primer," RS22600 (Washington, D.C.: Congressional Research Service, June 18, 2007), 2.

120. Becker and Porter, "The Federal Food Safety System: A Primer," 3.

121. CRS, "Food Safety Issues in the 109th Congress," 5.

122. GovExec.Com, "Food Safety Advocates Recommend Overhauling Inspection System," March 30, 2004.

123. CRS, "Food Safety Issues in the 109th Congress," 6.

124. CRS, "Food Safety Issues in the 109th Congress," 11.

125. See the Prescription Drug User Fee Act of 1992.

126. "Generic Drugs Hit Backlog At FDA: No Plans to Expand Review Capabilities," *Washington Post,* February 4, 2006, A01.

127. GAO, "Drug Safety: Improvement Needed in FDA's Postmarket Decision-making and Oversight Process," March 2006.

128. Duke University, Fuqua School of Business, "Study Examines Pharmaceutical Spending on Post-Approval Drug Safety," March 7, 2006. See also ConsumersUnion.org, "Health, Consumer Groups Urge Congress to Put Prescription Drug, Medical Product Safety on Its Priority Agenda for Year," February 15, 2006.

129. For more background, see http://www.fda.gov/fdac/features/2002/602_squad.html.

130. "New Drug Label Rule is Intended to Reduce Medical Errors," *New York Times,* January 19, 2006.

131. Barnaby Feder, "FDA Imposes Long-Delayed Rule to Require Tracking of Prescription Drugs," *New York Times,* June 10, 2006.

132. The Department of Transportation/National Highway Traffic Safety Administration has jurisdiction over cars, trucks and motorcycles; FDA has jurisdiction over food, drugs, cosmetics, and medical devices; the Bureau of Alcohol, Tobacco and Firearms has jurisdiction over those items; EPA has jurisdiction over pesticides; and the Coast Guard has jurisdiction over boat safety. See http://www.cpsc.gov/Federal.html.

133. CPSC, "2007 Performance Budget Request," February 2006, iii; Statement of the Honorable Thomas H. Moore, Commissioner, on the FY 2006 CPSC appropriations request, http://www.cpsc.gov /pr/app2006stm.pdf.

134. GAO, "High Risk Series: An Update," January 2007; GovExec.com, "Food safety advocates recommend overhauling inspection system," March 30, 2004.

135. National Association of Community Health Centers, "History of Community Health Centers," www.nachc.com/about/aboutcenters.asp.

136. Source: National Association of Community Health Centers, www.nachc.com.

137. GAO, "Medicaid Payment for FQHCs and RHCs," June 2005, 7.

138. National Association of Community Health Centers and the George Washington University, *A Nation's Health at Risk III: Growing Uninsured, Budget Cutbacks Challenge President's Initiative to Put a Health Center in Every Poor County* (Washington, D.C.: Authors, March 2005), 1.

139. National Association of Community Health Centers, "History of Community Health Centers," www.nachc.com/about/aboutcenters.asp. See also "Results from the Patient Experience Evaluation Report System," http://www.nachc.com/press/files/PEERSreport-finaldraft0226.pdf.

140. Speech on January 27, 2005, Cleveland, Ohio, www.whitehouse.gov.

141. National Association of Community Health Centers and the George Washington University, *A Nation's Health at Risk III*, 1.

142. Kaiser Daily Health Policy Report, March 2, 2006, www.kaisernetwork.org.

143. The Rural Health Clinic Services Act of 1977, P.L. 95-210.

144. However, in 2005 the HHS Inspector General found that "279 RHCs are located in areas that HRSA has not designated as shortage areas or that Census has designated as urbanized areas."

145. See www.aapa.org/gandp/rhc.html.

146. AIDS Drug Assistance Program (ADAP). See www.sfaf.org/policy/adap/.

147. CRS, "AIDS: Ryan White CARE Act," October 26, 2005, 1.

148. Centers for Disease Control and Prevention, "HIV/AIDS Surveillance Report," 2003, vol. 15: 12.

149. Judith Johnson, "AIDS Funding for Federal Government Programs," RL30731 (Washington, D.C.: Congressional Research Service, March 8, 2007), 1.

150. Johnson, "AIDS Funding for Federal Government Programs," 17. See also Tiaji Salaam-Blyther, "HIV/AIDS International Programs: Appropriations, FY2003-FY2006," RS21181 (Washington, D.C.: Congressional Research Service, January 3, 2006); Tiaji Salaam-Blyther, "The Global Fund to Fight AIDS, Tuberculosis, and Malaria: Progress Report and Issues for Congress," RL33396 (Washington, D.C.: Congressional Research Service, June 11, 2007). For an analysis of the effectiveness of U.S. international expenditures on HIV/AIDS, see "Botswana's Gains against AIDS Put U.S. Claims to Test," *Washington Post*, July 1, 2005, A01.

151. CRS, "AIDS in Africa," March 9, 2006.

152. CRS, "AIDS Orphans and Vulnerable Children: Problems Responses, and Issues for Congress," October 26, 2005.

153. The Kaiser Family Foundation, "Trends in U.S. Government Funding for HIV/AIDS—FY s 1981 to 2004," p. 1.

154. Smith, "Public Health Service Agencies."

155. Association of Maternal and Child Health Programs, www.amchp.org.

156. See http://nhsc.bhpr.hrsa.gov/about/.

157. The NHSC is headquartered at the Health Resources and Services Administration (HRSA)—the agency within the Department of Health and Human Services that focuses on access to health care for the poor, uninsured, and geographically isolated.

158. See http://nhsc.bhpr.hrsa.gov/publications/factsheets.asp.

159. Urban Institute, "A National Roundtable on the Indian Health System and Medicaid Reform," August 31, 2005, 2.

160. Smith, "Public Health Service Agencies," 24; and Urban Institute, "A National Roundtable," 14–15.

161. Urban Institute, "A National Roundtable," 8.

162. Indian Health Service, "A Quick Look," January 2006.

163. Urban Institute, "A National Roundtable," 7.

164. "Life and Labor in Indian Country," *Congressional Quarterly Weekly,* January 30, 2006, 265.

165. Smith, "Public Health Service Agencies," 28.

166. The coalition is known as the "Ad Hoc Group for Medical Research Funding." See http://www.aamc.org/research/adhocgp/news.htm.

167. Although in inflation-adjusted dollars, it was short of the doubling.

168. In addition to scientific peer review, grant proposals are also subject to a second review by "independent advisory councils." "NIH FY 2007 Performance Budget Overview," February 2, 2006, 2, http://officeofbudget.od.nih.gov/ui/2007Budget.htm..

169. National Institutes of Health, "Summary of the FY 2007 President's Budget," 6, http://officeofbudget.od.nih.gov/pdf/Press%20info%20final.pdf.

170. See http://grants.nih.gov/grants/partners/0106Nexus.htm for general information on NIH extramural grants.

171. Pamela Smith, "NIH: Organization, Funding, and Congressional Issues," RL33695 (Washington, D.C.: Congressional Research Service, December 19, 2006), 18.

172. Smith, "Public Health Service Agencies," 37.

173. Joseph Loscalzo, "The NIH Budget and the Future of Biomedical Research," *New England Journal of Medicine,* April 20, 2006.

174. The President's New Freedom Commission on Mental Health, "Achieving the Promise: Transforming Mental Health Care in America," July 2003, http://www.mentalhealthcommission.gov/reports/FinalReport/downloads/FinalReport.pdf.

175. The Campaign for Mental Health Reform, "Background Materials," Fall 2005 (uncredited author: Charles S. Konigsberg).

176. See NAMI, "Grading the States," 2006, http://www.nami.org/content/navigationmenu/grading_the_states/project_overview/overview.htm.

177. See "Appropriations Recommendations," Mental Health Liaison Group, http://www.mhlg.org/appropfy2008.pdf.

178. The Garrett Lee Smith Memorial Act of 2004 (P.L. 108-355)—named for the son of Senator Gordon Smith (R-Oreg.), who suffered the tragic loss of his son to mental illness.

179. See, for example, Greg Gordon, "U.S. Unprepared for Nuclear Terror Attack, Experts Say," *McClatchy Newspapers,* March 1, 2007; and Eric Lipton, "Bid to Stockpile Bioterror Drugs Stymied by Setbacks," *New York Times,* September 18, 2006.

180. Frank Gottron, "Project BioShield: Appropriations, Acquisitions, and Policy Implementation Issues for Congress," RL33907 (Washington, D.C.: Congressional Research Service, June 11, 2007).

181. P.L. 109-417.

182. §102, Pandemic and All-Hazards Preparedness Act, P.L. 109-417.

183. See the assessment of the Katrina response in chapter 3-2.

184. Ira Helfand, "The U.S. and Nuclear Terrorism: Still Dangerously Unprepared," press conference, Physicians for Social Responsibility, August 31, 2006, Washington, D.C., http://www.psr.org/site/DocServer/Good_PSR_Nuclear_Terrorism_News_Release_Printing.doc?docID=801.

Education and Children's Programs

In FY 2007, Federal spending for education totaled **$71 billion**, or 2.4% of the Federal Budget. Education programs include elementary and secondary education grants, higher education grants and loan assistance, and vocational and adult education. Children's programs for FY 2007 were funded at **$42 billion** and include child nutrition, the Women, Infants, and Children (WIC) food program, foster care and adoption assistance, Head Start, child care, and child support enforcement.

Head Start

FY 2007 Spending for Head Start: $6.9 billion

See www.GovBudget.com for updated numbers.

In a Nutshell

Head Start provides grants to local organizations to operate early childhood development programs for more than 900,000 children from low-income families per year. Services include child development, education, health, nutrition, and social activities. Programs are either full-day or half-day programs. About half of eligible four-year-olds are enrolled, and a third of eligible three-year-olds. Early Head Start covers children from birth to age three, but enrollment is very low due to lack of funds. The Department of Health and Human Services provides funds direct to *local* grantee organizations (rather than through States), and the funds are allocated based on the number of children below the poverty line in each State.[1] Funding has grown rapidly, tripling from 1990 to 1999, and has reached nearly $7 billion.

FIGURE 3-7.1 Children's Programs and Education Programs in FY 2007

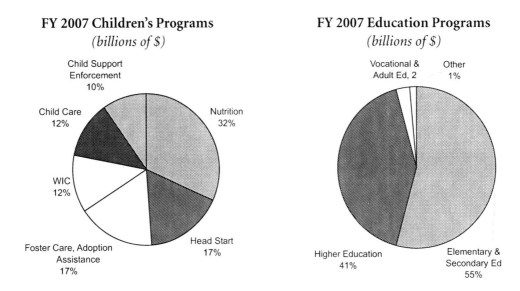

FY 2007 Children's Programs
(billions of $)

Child Support Enforcement 10%
Child Care 12%
Nutrition 32%
WIC 12%
Foster Care, Adoption Assistance 17%
Head Start 17%

FY 2007 Education Programs
(billions of $)

Vocational & Adult Ed, 2
Other 1%
Higher Education 41%
Elementary & Secondary Ed 55%

Background

Head Start is one of the largest Federal early childhood programs, established in 1965 as part of the Johnson Administration's War on Poverty. Many studies have demonstrated the critical role of high-quality, early education in child development and success in kindergarten and beyond. Head Start–funded programs serve nearly one million low-income children every year—more than 23 million since the program's inception.[2]

Head Start is unique in its funding design: it provides grants *directly to local organizations* rather than to States. Local grantees deliver preschool education and other early childhood developmental services to poor children and their families. In addition to preschool educa- tion, Head Start services include health screenings, immunizations, assistance in accessing health services, dental care, psychological services, nutritional services, and social activities intended to promote healthy child development. Head Start grantees generally operate their programs during the school year.[3]

Head Start grantees include over 1,600 local organizations including community agen- cies, school systems, for-profit and nonprofit organizations, other government agencies, and tribal governments or associations. The grantees operate nearly 19,000 Head Start centers in all 50 States and D.C.[4] Head Start grantees must match their Federal grants with 20% of their own resources—which can include in-kind contributions, local or State funds, or donations. The grant program is administered by the Administration for Children and Families (ACF) at the Department of Health and Human Services (HHS).[5]

The program was originally aimed at three- to five-year-olds. In 1994, the program was expanded to serve children from birth to age three (and pregnant women) through **Early Head Start (EHS).** The law requires that a portion of Head Start's funds be set aside for EHS. About half of the EHS slots are in center-based programs; the other half are home-based. In

2002, an HHS study found that two-year-old children with at least one year of EHS performed better on measures of cognitive, language, and emotional development.[6]

In order to target Head Start to children most in need, Federal regulations require that at least 90% of the children enrolled in Head Start come from families with incomes *at or below the Federal Poverty Level (FPL)* or from families receiving public assistance or families caring for a foster child.[7] In addition, at least 10% of the slots must be reserved for children with disabilities. In 2004, about 28% of children enrolled in Head Start were from homes where English was not the primary language.[8]

More than one-third of eligible low-income three-year-olds are served by Head Start, and more than half of eligible 4-year-olds are served. However, despite the views of many experts that the first three years are critical to child development—and profoundly impact later life— less than 1 in 30 eligible low-income children *under age three* are served by Early Head Start, due to limited funding (see table 3-7.1).

This is a reflection of how near-sighted the budget process can be—looking only at the subsequent year's budget, rather than the *long-term impact* of budget investments. An additional $3 billion invested annually in early childhood development to cover all eligible children might avoid tens of billions in expenditures down the road for remedial education, public health and welfare expenditures, foregone income taxes, and—in the worst case—incarcerations. The lesson here is that some Federal expenditures should be treated as investments in the future. To focus only on the next fiscal year is, according to the old adage, penny-wise and pound-foolish.

Evidence of the long-term benefits of early childhood development programs has been reported in the Chicago Longitudinal Study, which found that participants in Chicago's Child-Parent Centers program were more likely to finish high school, less likely to be charged in juvenile court, and less likely to repeat a grade. The study calculated a "return to society" of more than $7 for every dollar invested in the program.[9]

Issues

Controversial issues regarding Head Start include proposals by the Administration to redirect Head Start funds from local grantees to State agencies (to facilitate coordination with preschool, child care, and other State programs); to allow grantees to discriminate in hiring on the basis of religion (to encourage faith-based organizations to become grantees); and to transfer the program to the Department of Education.[10]

TABLE 3-7.1 Head Start Eligibility and Participation

Age	General Population	Eligible Children (i.e., below Poverty Line)	FY 2005 Enrollment	Percent Receiving Services
Under 3	12.3 million	2.9 million	91,000	3 %
Age 3	4.0 million	871,000	308,000	35 %
Age 4	4.1 million	927,000	472,000	51 %

Source: Congressional Research Service.[11]

Child Care

FY 2007 Spending on Child Care: $5.0 billion

See www.GovBudget.com for updated numbers.

In a Nutshell

The Federal Government's principal source of funding dedicated to child care subsidies for low-income families is the $5 billion Child Care and Development Fund (CCDF). The 1996 welfare reform legislation[12] was the catalyst for boosting child care funding because of the expectation that new work requirements would increase the need for child care services. CCDF, which subsidizes child care for children under age 13, consists of two parts: (1) mandatory funding to States (funded at $2.9 billion in FY 2007) and (2) discretionary grants to States (funded at $2.1 billion in FY 2007). (Additionally, States are permitted to use up to 30% of their TANF[13] block grant for child care subsidies.) States are given broad authority to design their respective child care subsidy programs. Recent estimates are that 1.8 million children per year receive child care subsidies funded by CCDF.[14]

Background

This unusual funding arrangement, illustrated in figure 3-7.1 resulted from *combining* a number of predecessor programs that fell within multiple congressional committee jurisdictions.

The *mandatory funding stream* (i.e., funding that flows directly from authorizing legislation without Appropriations Committee action) is the result of combining three predecessor programs under the jurisdiction of the Senate Finance and House Ways and Means Committees: (1) the AFDC Child Care program (Aid to Families with Dependent Children was the old "welfare" program), (2) the Transitional Child Care Program, and (3) the At-Risk Child Care program. A portion of these funds is *guaranteed* to States based on amounts received under the three pre–welfare reform programs; *additional matching Federal funds* from the mandatory stream are tied to States maintaining pre–welfare spending levels on child care (referred to as a State's "maintenance of effort.")[15]

The *discretionary* (annually appropriated) funding stream of CCDF, called the Child Care and Development Block Grant (CCDBG), was first authorized by legislation originating in the Senate Health, Education, Labor, and Pensions (HELP) Committee and the House Education and Workforce Committee in 1990. These funds support child care on a sliding fee scale for children under age 13 whose family income does not exceed 85% of State median income. Funds are allocated to States based on a formula intended to reflect the number of low-income children and the State's per capita income.[16]

Research has shown that child care is a key factor in staying employed.[17] Consequently, in addition to CCDF funds, States are permitted to use Temporary Assistance for Needy Families (TANF) funds and Social Services Block Grant (SSBG) funds to supplement their Federal CCDF dollars.[18]

Issue: Funding for Child Care—How Much Is Needed?

Total child care funding—including TANF funds and State funds—tripled after the enactment of welfare reform increasing from about $3 billion in FY 1996 to over $9 billion by FY 2000. Since

FIGURE 3-7.2 1996, Welfare Reform Combined 4 Child Care Programs into the Child Care and Development Fund (CCDF)

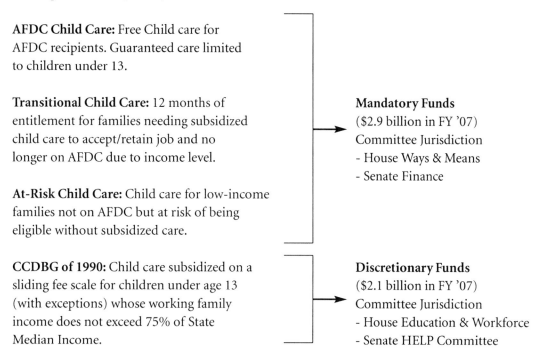

AFDC Child Care: Free Child care for AFDC recipients. Guaranteed care limited to children under 13.

Transitional Child Care: 12 months of entitlement for families needing subsidized child care to accept/retain job and no longer on AFDC due to income level.

At-Risk Child Care: Child care for low-income families not on AFDC but at risk of being eligible without subsidized care.

CCDBG of 1990: Child care subsidized on a sliding fee scale for children under age 13 (with exceptions) whose working family income does not exceed 75% of State Median Income.

Mandatory Funds
($2.9 billion in FY '07)
Committee Jurisdiction
- House Ways & Means
- Senate Finance

Discretionary Funds
($2.1 billion in FY '07)
Committee Jurisdiction
- House Education & Workforce
- Senate HELP Committee

2002, however, Federal child care funding has increased only marginally—not enough to keep pace with inflation.[19] This has triggered an intense debate about whether enough funds are being allocated to realistically enable people to "move from welfare to work." For example, GAO reported to Congress in 2003 that "half of the states do not provide child care assistance to all the families who apply and are eligible for such assistance under the states' eligibility policies."[20]

Child Nutrition and WIC

> **FY 2007 Spending for Child Nutrition and WIC: $18.4 billion**

See www.GovBudget.com for updated numbers.

In the long view, no nation is any healthier than its children or more prosperous than its farmers; and in the National School Lunch Act, the Congress has contributed immeasurably both to the welfare of our farmers and the health of our children.—Harry S. Truman, June 4, 1946[21]

In a Nutshell

Federal Child Nutrition programs and the Women, Infants, and Children (program) provide nutritional support for 39 million low-income children and 2 million low-income women. ***Child nutrition programs*** include School Lunch, School Breakfast, Special Milk, Summer Food Service, and Child Care Food programs—at a cost of $13.2 billion in FY 2007.

The WIC program is spending $5.2 billion in FY 2007 providing low-income, pregnant and postpartum women, infants, and children with vouchers for food packages, nutrition education, and health and immunization referrals. Child nutrition programs are *entitlements:* federal funding and food commodities are guaranteed to schools and other local providers based on the number of subsidized or free meals, snacks, or amount of milk served to poor children, infants, and mothers. By contrast, WIC is a *discretionary* spending program.

Background

The **National School Lunch Program (NSLP)** began in 1946, with the **School Breakfast Program (SBP)** following in 1966. Both programs provide free or low-cost meals to low-income children (although any child at a participating school may purchase an NSLP lunch). In order to participate, school meals must meet the USDA's nutritional standards. The USDA reimburses States based on the number of meals purchased.

The **Child and Adult Care Food Program (CACFP)** subsidizes meals and snacks served by child care centers (typically, 30–50 children) and day care homes (typically, 4–6 children). Each day nearly 3 million children receive meals and snacks through CACFP. (The program also serves 86,000 adults at adult day care centers.)

The **Special Milk** program operates in schools and other locations *without* a lunch program and subsidizes all milk served.

For many low-income children, the only nutritious meal they receive all day is their school lunch from NSLP. Recognizing the need to continue providing children with nutritious meals during the summer, in 1969 Congress established the **Summer Food Service Program** (SFSP). Over 115 million SFSP meals are served each summer by schools, public agencies, and private nonprofit organizations such as recreation centers.

The **Special Supplemental Food Program for Women, Infants, and Children (WIC)** serves about 7.9 million persons per month. WIC provides nutrition services, cash, commodities, food vouchers, and other assistance to low-income pregnant and postpartum women, as well as infants and children considered to be at nutritional risk. Unlike the lunch programs where *school agencies* play a large role on the local level, WIC is administered by local *health agencies*. Similar to NSLP and SBP, the goal of WIC is to prevent developmental problems in infants by providing nutritious meals that meet USDA standards.

The nutrition programs are funded by the Department of Agriculture and are operated—with State oversight—by 300,000 local providers including schools, child care centers, and health clinics. Most subsidies are cash payments, but about 10% is in the form of federally donated food.[22]

WHY AREN'T SCHOOL LUNCHES HEALTHIER?

In 2003, GAO reported to Congress that school lunches were not meeting the required 30% limit for calories from fat. GAO found that "barriers to providing nutritious meals and encouraging healthy eating included budget pressures and competing time demands. . . . [O]fficials said that when they introduce healthier foods, they take the risk that students will buy fewer school lunches resulting in a loss of needed revenue. . . . Also, schools paid for special activities or other items not covered in the school's budget with profits from vending machines and snack bar sales." [23]

The Child Welfare System: Foster Care and Adoption Assistance

> FY 2007 Spending for Foster Care and Adoption Assistance: $6.9 billion

See www.GovBudget.com for updated numbers.

On any given day in the United States, half a million children and youth are in foster care, removed from their homes because of abuse or neglect. . . . While in care, many children do not receive appropriate services, whether they are infants suffering the effects of trauma or older adolescents about to leave foster care to live on their own. —The Pew Commission on Children in Foster Care [24]

In a Nutshell

States have primary responsibility for administering child welfare services; however, the Federal government plays a significant role by providing funds to States for Foster Care and Adoption Assistance programs and conditioning those funds on meeting certain requirements. The Foster Care program provides matching grants to States for the costs of providing foster care for children removed from low-income homes because of neglect or abuse.[25] Adoption Assistance helps parents who adopt low-income children with special needs.

Background

Foster Care and Adoption Assistance, while generally referred to collectively, are actually two separate programs. The **Foster Care program** is an entitlement program that provides matching payments to States for the costs associated with placing low-income children in foster care. Of the $6.9 billion cited earlier, nearly $5 billion was spent in 2007 for foster care entitlement payments to the States. The Department of Health and Human Services (HHS) estimates that in 2008, an average of 211,000 low-income children *per month* will be placed in Foster Care.

Similar to Medicaid, the Foster Care program is an "open-ended entitlement," which means that any qualifying State expenditure will be partially reimbursed, or "matched," without limit.

In order for States to receive Federal Foster Care funds, the removal and foster care placement must be for a *low-income*[26] child based on a voluntary agreement signed by the child's parents, or there must be a judicial determination that remaining in the home would be contrary to the child's welfare (due to neglect or abuse). In addition, there must be reasonable efforts to eliminate the conditions that led to the child's removal to foster care and to facilitate the child returning home. Based on these criteria, States receive Federal payments for roughly half of the children placed in foster homes.[27] The amount of Federal foster care matching payments varies among the States; payments are determined using the Medicaid matching rate, which, as explained in chapter 3-6, can range from 50% to 76%.

The **Federal Adoption Assistance Program**, an entitlement spending $2 billion in FY 2007, supports monthly subsidies for families adopting eligible low-income children[28] with special needs. HHS estimates that in 2008 an average of 427,000 children per month will be supported with Federal subsidies. Similar to the Foster Care program, the Adoption Assistance program is an entitlement program that provides matching payments to States—in this case, for assistance payments for qualified children who are adopted, as well as for administrative expenses and training of adoption professionals. Adopted low-income children with special needs are also eligible for Medicaid (see chapter 3-6 for an explanation of Medicaid).

A related program is the John H. Chafee Foster Care Independence Program (formerly called Independent Living). This $140 million per year program is aimed at assisting youths ages 16–21 in making the transition from foster care to independent living. States are entitled to a portion of the $140 million based on their share of the nation's foster care population.

Elementary and Secondary Education and the No Child Left Behind Act

> FY 2007 Outlays for Elementary and Secondary Education: $23.2 billion

See www.GovBudget.com for updated numbers.

Our progress as a nation can be no swifter than our progress in education. Our requirements for world leadership, our hopes for economic growth, and the demands of citizenship itself in an area such as this all require the maximum development of every young American's capacity. The human mind is our fundamental resource.—President John F. Kennedy, 1961[29]

In a Nutshell

While the vast majority (91%) of public school education in the United States is funded at the State and local levels, the Department of Education funds programs that support America's schools and students in a variety of ways, including funding to improve the achievement of economically disadvantaged students, as well as funding for reading programs, school improvement projects, drug abuse prevention, after-school programs, English language instruction, professional development of teachers, expansion of charter schools, education of Native Americans, education of migrant children, and Impact Aid (see figure 3-7.2).[30] More recently, with the enactment of the No Child Left Behind Act (NCLBA) in 2001, Federal education funding is being used to leverage significant—and controversial—changes in how public elementary and secondary schools educate our children. This degree of Federal involvement in local schools is unprecedented.

Background

Federal elementary and secondary education programs are authorized by the Elementary and Secondary Education Act (ESEA), which was initially signed into law in 1965 and, most recently, was amended by the No Child Left Behind Act (NCLBA) of 2001.

Title I of the ESEA authorizes Federal aid for the education of disadvantaged students. "Title I grants," as they are generally referred to, amounted to $14.5 billion in FY 2007 with services provided to more than half of all public schools and one-third of all students; services are concentrated in prekindergarten through grade 6.[31] The grants are provided for

- Supplemental education funding for students and schools in high poverty areas;
- Assistance to schools in meeting the requirements of the NCLBA;

FIGURE 3-7.3 Elementary and Secondary Education Programs (in billions of dollars)

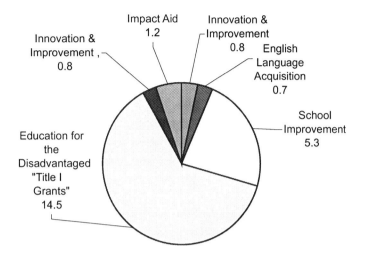

THE NO CHILD LEFT BEHIND ACT (NCLBA)

NCLBA dramatically increased Federal involvement in education by making Federal funding to the States contingent on acceptance of strict Federal regulations. NCLBA set a goal of bringing *all* students to a proficient level of achievement in reading, math, and science by the end of the 2014 school year.

The Act relies heavily on testing in order to measure student proficiency and judge improvement from year to year. Under the NCLBA, States are required to test students in **math and reading in each of grades 3 through 8**, and at **three grade levels in science** by the end of the 2008 school year. In addition, a **National Assessment of Educational Progress** test must be administered to fourth and eighth graders in alternate years.

Much of the intense debate surrounding the efficacy of NCLBA is a result of its Adequate Yearly Progress (AYP) determinations. In order to meet the larger goal of reading, math, and science proficiency by 2014, NCLBA requires States to set AYP testing goals for each school. Failure to meet these AYP goals for consecutive years results in a series of consequences *for schools receiving Title I funds*. After two years of failure, a school is designated as needing improvement, and its students are offered the choice of switching to another local school the following year. After three years, students from low-income families are offered the opportunity to receive private tutoring to supplement their education. After four years of failure to meet AYP testing goals, corrective actions must be taken that can include replacing staff and management as well as developing a new curriculum. Finally, after six years, a school must be restructured; options include "reopening as a charter school, replacing all or most school staff, [or a] state takeover of school operations." [32]

Teacher quality standards are another major requirement of NCLBA. The Act requires that all teachers at schools receiving Title I funds be "highly qualified," meaning that they possess at least a bachelor's degree and have passed a test demonstrating their subject-area proficiency and teaching skills.

WHAT IS A CHARTER SCHOOL?

Charter schools are public schools granted the flexibility to operate outside of typical State and local (and certain Federal) regulations. In return for this special autonomy, they agree to the terms of a multiyear "charter" or contract that holds them accountable for student outcomes. Forty States and the District of Columbia have laws allowing public charter schools, and as of 2004, 3,000 public charter schools nationwide educated more than 600,000 students.[33] The Federal Government provides more than $200 million per year in public charter school grants.[34] However, the efficacy of charter schools is a subject of intense and continuing debate.[35]

- Reading programs including Reading First and Early Reading First (which were funded at $1 billion and $118 million, respectively, in FY 2007);[36]
- School Library Grants;
- the Even Start Family Literacy Program;[37]
- Programs for Children who are Neglected, Delinquent, or At-Risk;[38] and,
- Educational services for children of migratory farmworkers.

The next largest slice of ESEA funds is for **school improvement programs**, which received $5.3 billion in FY 2007. School improvement grants are aimed at supporting NCLBA testing, improving teacher quality, supporting community learning centers in high-poverty areas, enhancing education technology, promoting teaching skills for math and science, supporting rural schools with high concentrations of poor students, providing education for homeless children, and improving education for Native Americans.

The Department of Education's **Office of Innovation and Improvement** (with an FY 2007 budget of $841 million) funds a number of programs authorized by ESEA, including the recruitment and training of high-quality teachers, and the establishment of **public charter schools** and **magnet schools.**

Other elementary and secondary education programs authorized by ESEA and funded by the Education Department include:

- The **Safe and Drug-Free Schools program,** which is the Federal government's primary initiative to prevent drug abuse and violence in and around the nation's public schools ($732 million in FY 2007);
- **Impact Aid,** a $1.2 billion dollar program aimed at replacing lost revenue for school districts due to the presence of students who live on military bases or Indian lands (which are exempt from local property taxes); and
- **English Language** acquisition services for immigrants students.

Issue: Effectiveness of No Child Left Behind

No Child Left Behind has been highly controversial. Many educators, including the National Educators Association (NEA), believe that NCLB "imposes invalid one-size-fits-all measures on students," failing to leave room for creativity and teaching methods that work best for individual students.[39] The NEA and other educators also feel that NCLB takes the "stick" approach too far (i.e., loss of Federal funds) and that a "carrot," or rewards-based system, would better serve students.[40] Others believe that the emphasis on narrow testing goals for reading, math, and science is providing students with a less well-rounded education. The Center on Education Policy reports that "71% of districts reported reducing instructional time in elementary schools for one or more subjects in order to make more time for reading and/or math."[41] The overwhelming concern is that schools are "teaching to the test" rather than focusing on a well-rounded education.

Others argue that NCLB's shortcomings are due, in some degree, to inadequate funding. NCLB funds have been appropriated at several billion dollars below their authorized levels. Some, including Senator Edward Kennedy (D-Mass.), who played a key role in creating NCLB, argue that the original intent was to fund NCLB up to the authorization levels (although, as explained in Part II of this book, it is not at all unusual for Congress to appropriate below a program's authorized levels; it is risky to assume full funding of any program unless the funding is made "mandatory"—i.e., not subject to annual appropriations decisions).[42]

Special Education and the Individuals with Disabilities Education Act (IDEA)

> **FY 2007 Federal Spending on IDEA: $11.8 billion**

This Nation has long embraced a philosophy that the right to a free appropriate public education is basic to equal opportunity and is vital to secure the future and prosperity of our people. It is contradictory to that philosophy when that right is not assured equally to all groups of people with the Nation.—U.S. Senate Report (1975)[43]

In a Nutshell

The Individuals with Disabilities Education Act (IDEA) is both a civil rights law and a funding authorization. As a rights law, the IDEA has required since 1975 that children with disabilities be provided with special education services so they can benefit from a "free appropriate public education" (FAPE).[44] As a funding law, the IDEA authorizes Federal grants to defray part of the costs incurred by States in meeting the FAPE requirement. IDEA's guaranteed services include *early intervention* for infants and toddlers, *preschool services,* and *special education* up to age 21. The IDEA authorizes Federal grants to States to cover up to 40% of State costs incurred in providing special education services, although Congress has never appropriated more than 18% of special education costs incurred by the States. For the 2006–2007 school year, 6.8 million children received IDEA-funded services at an average federal cost of $1,551 per student.[45]

Background

At a time when our society is recognizing an escalating number of children with developmental delays, autism spectrum disorders, learning disabilities, physical disabilities, and other disabilities that pose challenges for children, parents, and their public school educators, the IDEA is increasingly important.

The IDEA requires the provision of a "free appropriate public education" for children with disabilities as a *prerequisite* for States to receive Federal education funds. In order to implement the general principle of a free appropriate public education, the IDEA requires that each child with a disability must be provided an Individualized Education Program (IEP), developed in consultation with the child's parents, aimed at ensuring that each child is educated with their nondisabled peers "to the maximum extent appropriate."

Recognizing the inability of State and local governments to fully fund a free and appropriate public education for all children with disabilities, the IDEA authorized the Federal government to fund 40% of each State's additional costs for educating children with disabilities. The Federal grants are used by States and school districts for early intervention services for infants and toddlers, grants for preschool services, and special education services for children and youth up to age 21.

If public schools are unable to provide appropriate services, school authorities may pay for tuition to place a child in a private school in order to fulfill the FAPE obligation. Alternatively, if parents decide unilaterally to place their child in private school, the IDEA requires that certain services be provided; and, in certain cases, courts may order that school districts cover the services.[46]

Despite the intent of the IDEA that the Federal government cover 40% of States' special education costs, annual grants to States have never come close to the authorized level. For example, recent Federal IDEA funding has covered *less than 18% of States' special education costs*. In FY 2007, this amounted to $10.8 billion.[47] The "underfunding" of the IDEA—as compared with the 40% funding goal—has been a source of continuing concern among State governments, educators, parents, and special education advocates.

Concerns about under-funding led to enactment in 2004 of amendments to the IDEA[48] that set *authorized* funding levels for each year through FY 2011 designed to build up to the IDEA's 40% funding goal. However, as explained in chapter 2-2, the Appropriations Committees of Congress are not required—and often do not—fund programs up to their authorized amounts. As table 3-7.2 illustrates, while IDEA grants to States increased dramatically between 1995 and 2005—growing from 7.8% of State special education costs to 18.5%—Federal IDEA funding is now declining as a percentage of State costs and never went half way to the promised 40 percent level.

From a budgetary perspective, this highlights the lesson that grandiose statements made when *authorization* bills are enacted and signed into law need to be examined with a critical eye; it's the actual appropriation of funds that matter.

Higher Education

FY 2007 Federal Spending on Higher Education: $29.3 billion

See www.GovBudget.com for updated numbers.

This act has many provisions, but it has only one purpose: to nourish human potential today, so that our Nation can realize its rich promise tomorrow.—President Lyndon B. Johnson on signing the Higher Education Act of 1965[49]

TABLE 3-7.2 Underfunding of IDEA Grants to States (in billions of dollars)[50]

Fiscal Year	Federal IDEA Part B State Grant Program[51]	Grants as Percentage of State Special Ed. Costs*
1995	$2.3	7.8 %
1996	$2.3	7.3 %
1997	$3.1	9.2 %
1998	$3.8	10. 5%
1999	$4.3	11.1 %
2000	$5.0	12.0 %
2001	$6.3	14.1 %
2002	$7.5	15.5 %
2003	$8.9	17.1 %
2004	$10.1	18.4 %
2005	$10.6	18.5 %
2006	$10.6	17.7 %
2007	$10.8	17.2 %

*Note that Federal spending for IDEA has never been close to the authorized contribution level of 40%.

In a Nutshell

The Higher Education of Act of 1965 authorizes Federal aid to support postsecondary education. The largest student aid program, *in terms of Federal spending*, is the Pell Grant program, serving more than five million undergraduates at a cost of nearly $14 billion per year. The largest volume of student aid is generated by the Federal government's two major student loan programs: the Federal Family Education Loan (FFEL), formerly known as Guaranteed Student Loans, and the William D. Ford Direct Loan programs. Both programs are entitlement programs; that is, any student or parent of a student who qualifies can obtain specified loans, and both programs offer the same varieties of repayment terms on low-interest loans. The two programs differ only with respect to the source of the loan funds (private lenders and the Federal government, respectively). Together, the two loan programs are projected to leverage student loan financing of $65 billion in FY 2007, with a Federal cost of about $11 billion. Additional student financial aid is provided under three older "campus-based" programs: the Federal Supplemental Educational Opportunity Grant (FSEOG), the Federal Work-Study program, and the Federal Perkins Loan program.[52]

Background and Issues

GRANTS.—**Pell Grants,** the largest Federal college assistance program, are *needs-based grants* for undergraduate students.[53] In FY 2007, more than five million undergraduates received grants of *up to $4,310* to help pay for postsecondary education. (The maximum grant amount is set in the annual Labor-HHS-Education appropriations bill.) In total, the Federal govern-

Graduation at Kenyon College, Gambier, Ohio. Reprinted by Permission

ment spent nearly $14 billion on Pell Grants in FY 2007. The grants are disbursed by colleges and universities from funds provided by the Department of Education. Congress generally makes Pell Grant appropriations available for two years, so the Department can, in effect, borrow from the next year to cover the current year's Pell Grants; this is why these grants are sometimes viewed as a "quasi-entitlement," although the program continues to be subject to annual appropriations decisions.

Major issues under discussion are whether to convert the Pell Grant program to an entitlement program, whether the $4,310 cap on individual Pell Grants should be increased due to rapid increases in higher education costs,[54] and whether academic merit should have a role in consideration of Pell Grant awards.[55] It should be noted that converting Pell Grants to an entitlement would be politically very difficult since the estimated future costs of the program over the next 10 years would have to be offset by entitlement spending cuts or tax increases in order to comply with Congress' PAYGO rules (explained in chapter 2-4).

Federal Supplemental Educational Opportunity Grants (FSEOGs) are generally available to Pell Grant recipients with exceptional financial need. SEOG grants range from $100 to $4000 in amount and were funded at $772 million in FY 2007. SEOG grants are referred to as a "campus-based program" because funds are allocated directly to colleges for award to students.

Academic Competitiveness and SMART[56] Grants are two new types of college assistance. Academic Competitiveness Grants (ACG) offer up to $750 for college freshmen and $1,300 for sophomores who took rigorous courses in high school, are enrolled full-time in college, and have maintained a 3.0 grade point average. Students must be eligible for a Pell Grant in order to receive an ACG.

The SMART Grant provides up to $4,000 and is available to third- and fourth-year college students who are eligible for the Pell Grant. Students must have majored in one of the specified sciences, technology, math, or a language considered critical to national security and in high demand, while maintaining a 3.0 GPA.[57] For FY 2007, the outlays were estimated to total $789 million for both new grant programs.

LOANS.—The **Federal Family Education Loan Program (FFELP),** previously called Guaranteed Student Loans, is projected to leverage $52 billion in FY 2007 student loans by providing Federal guarantees to private lenders. The objective of the program is to promote access to postsecondary education by making low-interest loans available to students from low- and middle-income families. Under FFELP, "private lenders fund the loans, and the government guarantees lenders a minimum yield and repayment if borrowers default. When the interest rate paid by borrowers is lower than the guaranteed minimum yield, the government pays lenders special allowance payments."[58] In addition, the Federal government has boosted the availability of capital by establishing a secondary purchase market for FFEL loans through Sallie Mae, the Student Loan Marketing Association. The budgeted Federal cost of the FFEL program for FY 2007 was $5.7 billion, which reflects fees to guarantee agencies, special allowance payments, interest subsidies, and the cost of projected defaults. (See chapter 2-5 for an explanation of the Federal Credit Reform Act, which requires that certain sums be appropriated up front, when the government guarantees loans.)[59]

The William D. Ford Federal *Direct Loan* Program (FDLP) provides loan funds directly to postsecondary institutions, which originate the loans. The direct loans of $13 billion in FY 2007 are considered to be Federal expenditures in the year the funds are disbursed, but the *net cost* of the program also includes loan repayments from prior year loans. After including repayments, the net cost of the program in FY 2007 was $5.2 billion. The Direct Loan program was originally intended to phase in and gradually replace Guaranteed Student Loans (GSLs) as a more cost-efficient means of providing low-interest fixed rate loans to students. However, both programs—direct and guaranteed loans—have substantial support and consequently they are continuing to function as parallel programs.

While the FFEL Guaranteed Loans and Direct Loan programs rely on different sources of capital (private capital and Federal funds, respectively), they nevertheless offer the same set of low-interest loan options to undergraduate and graduate students and parents of undergraduates: subsidized and unsubsidized "Stafford" loans for undergraduate and graduate students, and PLUS loans for parents of undergraduates. These loan options are summarized in table 3-7.3.

Perkins Loans are low-interest Federal loans for college students with financial need. The FY 2007 cost is about $500 million. The interest rate is fixed at 5%, and no interest accrues before repayment begins. The aggregate amount an undergraduate can borrow is $20,000; for graduate and professional students, it is $40,000. Loans can be canceled, if the borrower works a period of time in public service. An undergraduate can borrow up to $4,000 per year. Graduate students and professionals can borrow up to $6,000 per year.

Other Types of Student Aid.— **Work-Study** is known as a "campus-based" program because funds are awarded to postsecondary institutions, which use the funds to pay 75% of a student's wages for part-time jobs. The $1 billion program assists nearly 900,000 undergraduate and graduate students each year and encourages community service–based job opportunities.

TABLE 3-7.3 Types of Higher Education Low-Interest Loans

Loan Type	Source of Loan Capital	Terms and Conditions	Annual Amount Available
Subsidized Stafford Loans	FFEL (GSLs) and Direct Loans	Department of Education pays interest while borrower is in school and during grace and deferment periods; student must be at least half-time and have financial need.	$3,500–$8,500
Unsubsidized Stafford Loans	FFEL (GSLs) and Direct Loans	Borrower responsible for all interest; student must be at least half time; no showing of financial need required.	$3,500–$20,500 (less any subsidized amounts received)
PLUS Loans (Parent Loans for Undergraduate Students)	FFEL (GSLs) and Direct Loans	For parents of dependent undergraduate students who are enrolled at least half-time and for graduate and professional students. Financial need not required. Borrower is responsible for all interest payments.	Maximum amount is cost of attendance minus any other financial aid student receives.

Source: "Student Aid at a Glance," www.FederalStudentAid.ed.gov/pubs, accessed August 26, 20007.

Notes

1. Funding is also allocated in part, based on historical funding rates. Melinda Gish, "Head Start: Background and Issues," RL30952 (Washington, D.C.: Congressional Research Service, July 26, 2007), 5.

2. Center for Law and Social Policy, "Still Going Strong: Head Start Children, Families, Staff, and Programs in 2004," November 2005, 1.

3. CRS, "Head Start: Background and Issues," July 13, 2006.

4. Ron Haskins and Isabel Sawhill, "The Future of Head Start" (Washington, D.C.: Brookings Institution, July 2003), 1.

5. GAO, "Head Start: Comprehensive Approach to Identifying and Addressing Risks Could Help Prevent Grantee Financial Management Weaknesses," February 2005.

6. Center for Law and Social Policy, "From the Beginning: Early Head Start Children, Families, Staff, and Programs in 2004," March 2006, 1 (citing a study by the Department of Health and Human Services, *Making a Difference in the Lives of Infants and Toddlers and Their Families: The Impacts of Early Head Start* (Washington, D.C.: 2002).

7. In 2004, "three quarters of Head Start children were eligible to participate because family income was below 100 percent of the poverty level at the time of program enrollment. An additional 18 per-

cent were eligible based on enrollment in public assistance. Just 1 percent of children qualified for Head Start because of status as a foster child. Six percent . . . lived in families earning above the Federal poverty line at the time of enrollment." Center for Law and Social Policy, "Still Going Strong: Head Start Children, Families, Staff, and Programs in 2004," November 2005, 1.

8. Center for Law and Social Policy, "Still Going Strong," 1.

9. Chicago Longitudinal Study: http://www.education.umn.edu/ICD/CLS/docs/Newsletter2 .pdf.

10. See Gish, "Head Start."

11. Gish, "Head Start," 11.

12. Personal Responsibility and Work Opportunity Reconciliation Act of 1996. P.L. 104-93.

13. TANF, as noted later, is Temporary Assistance for Needy Families, which replaced Aid to Families with Dependent Children as part of the 1996 welfare overhaul.

14. Melinda Gish, "The Child Care and Development Block Grant: Background and Funding," RL30785 (Washington, D.C.: Congressional Research Service, April 20, 2007), 1–6.

15. Melinda Gish: "Child Care: Funding and Spending under Federal Block Grants," RL31274 (Washington, D.C.: Congressional Research Service, March 19, 2002), 5.

16. Gish, "The Child Care and Development Block Grant," 1–6.

17. GAO, "Child Care: Child Care Subsidies Increase Likelihood That Low-income Mothers Will Work," December 1994.

18. Gish: "Child Care," 9–11.

19. Gish, "The Child Care and Development Block Grant," table 1. Note that the figure for FY 2007 consists of $1.986 billion in mandatory spending plus $956 million in advance appropriated discretionary spending.

20. GAO, "Child Care: Recent State Policy Changes Affecting the Availability of Assistance for Low-Income Families," GAO-03-588 (Washington, D.C.: May 2003), 2.

21.Statement upon signing the National School Lunch Act.

22. Joe Richardson, "Child Nutrition and WIC Programs: Background and Recent Funding," RL33307 (Washington, D.C.: Congressional Research Service, July 12, 2006).

23. GAO, "School Lunch Program: Efforts Needed to Improve Nutrition and Encourage Health Eating," GAO-03-506 (Washington, D.C.: May 2003).

24. The Pew Commission on Children in Foster Care, "Fostering the Future: Safety Permanence and Well-Being for Children in Foster Care," May 2004, 7.

25. See Department of Health and Human Services, "Federal Foster Care Financing: How and Why the Current Funding Structure Fails to Meet the Needs of the Child Welfare Field" (Washington, D.C.: August 2005).

26. The determination of "low-income" for this purpose is based on the family's eligibility for Aid to Families with Dependent Children (AFDC) as it existed prior to 1996 welfare reform. Committee on Ways and Means, U.S. House of Representatives, *2004 Green Book* (Washington, D.C.: Government Printing Office, 2004), 11–18.

27. Committee on Ways and Means, *Green Book,* 11–19.

28. In this context, "low income" refers to SSI- or AFDC-eligible children (based on pre–welfare reform AFDC criteria).

29. Alex Ayres, ed., *The Wit and Wisdom of John F. Kennedy* (New York: Penguin Books, 1996), 57.

30. Impact Aid is compensation for school districts with diminished property tax revenues due to the presence of Federal lands or facilities within the school district.

31. Wayne Riddle, "Education for the Disadvantaged: Reauthorization Issues for ESEA Title I-A under the No Child Left Behind Act," RL33731 (Washington, D.C.: Congressional Research Service, August 6, 2007), 1.

32. W. Riddle et al., "K–12 Education: Highlights of the No Child Left Behind Act of 2001 (P.L. 107-110)" (Washington, D.C.: Congressional Research Service, RL31284, January 2006), 7.

33. Diana Jean Schemo, "Charter Schools Trail in Results, U.S. Data Reveals," *New York Times*, August 17, 2004.

34. David P. Smole, "Funding for Public Charter School Facilities: Federal Policy under the ESEA," RL31128 (Washington, D.C.: Congressional Research Service, February 8, 2006), 10. See also David P. Smole, "Public Charter School Accountability," RL31184 (Washington, D.C.: Congressional Research Service, January 24, 2007);

35. Diana Jean Schemo, "Study of Test Scores Finds Charter Schools Lagging," *New York Times*, August 23, 2006.

36. Both Reading First and Early Reading First were authorized by the NCLBA. Under the Reading First program, schools with high percentages of low-income students receive grants to improve reading programs for students in grades K–3. Early Reading First provides competitive grants to reach children at younger ages. Gail McCallion, "Reading First and Early Reading First: Background and Funding," RL31241 (Washington, D.C., Congressional Research Service, July 31, 2007).

37. The Even Start Family Literacy Program provides education services jointly to disadvantaged parents and their young children, with the objective of integrating early childhood education, adult basic education, and parenting skills. However, future funding is in doubt due to skepticism about the program's efficacy. See Gail McCallion, "Even Start: Funding Controversy," RL33071 (Washington, D.C.: Congressional Research Service, July 31, 2007).

38. Authorizes grants for the education of children and youth in state institutions for the neglected or delinquent. Wayne Riddle and Rebecca Skinner, "The Elementary and Secondary Education Act," 6.

39. National Education Association, "No Child Left Behind Act/ESEA," http://www.nea.org/esea/more.html.

40. National Education Association at http://www.nea.org/esea/more.html.

41. "From the Capital to the Classroom: Year 4 of the No Child Left Behind Act," Center on Education Policy, March 2006,www.cep-dc.org/_data/global/nidocs/CEP-NCLB-Report-4.pdf.

42. Diana Jean Schemo, "Kennedy Demands Full Funding for School Bill," *New York Times*, April 7, 2004.

43. S.Rep. No. 168, 94th Cong., 1st Sess., cited in Nancy Lee Jones, "The Individuals with Disabilities Education Act: Congressional Intent," 95-669 A (Washington, D.C.: Congressional Research Service, May 19, 1995), 3.

44. 20 U.S.C. §1400 et seq. The IDEA was formerly referred to as the "Education for All Handicapped Children Act." Jones, "The Individuals with Disabilities Education Act," 1.

45. Congressional Budget Office, *Budget Options,* February 2007, 130.

46. See Richard Apling and Nancy Lee Jones, "IDEA: Parentally Placed Children in Private Schools," RL33368 (Washington, D.C.: Congressional Research Service, April 24, 2007).

47. Richard Apling and Ann Lordeman, "Individuals with Disabilities Education Act (IDEA): Current Funding Trends," RL32085 (Washington, D.C.: Congressional Research Service, April 4, 2007).

48. P.L. 108-446.

49. Statement by President Lyndon B. Johnson following Passage by the Senate of the Higher Education Bill on September 2, 1965. The Higher Education Act of 1965 was approved by the President on November 8, 1965.

50. Table is based on data in Richard Apling and Ann Lordeman, "Individuals with Disabilities Education Act (IDEA): Current Funding Trends," RL32085 (Washington, D.C.: Congressional Research Service, April 4, 2007).

51. These figures do not include the preschool grants program (funded at $381 million in FY 2006), the infants and families State grants program (funded at $436 million in FY 2006), and national activ-

ities such as information centers, technology and media services (funded at $253 million in FY 2006). Apling and Lordeman, "IDEA," 3.

52. For details on the campus-based programs see David Smole, "Campus-Based Student Financial Aid Programs under the Higher Education Act," RL31618 (Washington, D.C.: Congressional Research Service, May 14, 2007).

53. In 2005–2006, approximately 79% of all Pell Grant recipients had incomes less than or equal to $30,000. However, there is no set income threshold that determines who is eligible for a Pell Grant. Eligibility is determined to a great extent on the "expected family contribution," which can be affected by a number of factors, including family income, family size, number in college, the student's dependency status, and assets. Charmaine Mercer, "Federal Pell Grant Program of the Higher Education Act: Background and Reauthorization," RL31668 (Washington, D.C.: Congressional Research Service, March 19, 2007), 17; Rebecca Skinner, "Memorandum to Senator Tom Coburn" (Washington, D.C.: Congressional Research Service, July 16, 2007), 1.

54. According to the College Board, "the percentage tuition, fees, room, and board at the average public four-year college covered by the maximum Pell Grant declined from 42 percent in 2001–02 to 33 percent in 2005–06." College Board, "Trends in Student Aid," 2006, 5.

55. Mercer, "Federal Pell Grant Program."

56. National Science and Mathematics Access to Retain Talent Grant (National SMART Grant).

57. Department of Education, "$790 Million in New Grants for College Students Available July 1," June 29, 2006. http://www.ed.gov/news/pressreleases/2006/06/06292006a.html.

58. GAO, "Federal Student Loans: Challenges in Estimating Federal Subsidy Costs," GAO-05-874 (Washington, D.C.: September 2005).

59. Adam Stoll, "The Administration of the Federal Family Education Loan and William D. Ford Direct Loan Programs: Background and Provisions," RL33674 (Washington, D.C.: Congressional Research Service, September 29, 2006), 1.

Helping People in Need

This chapter covers the Earned Income Tax Credit, Supplemental Security Income (SSI), the Food Stamp Program, Temporary Assistance for Needy Families (TANF), Housing Assistance, Low Income Home Energy Assistance, and Unemployment Compensation.

Earned Income Tax Credit (EITC)

FY 2007 Spending on the Earned Income Tax Credit: $36.5 billion

Another means of silently lessening the inequality of property is to exempt all from taxation below a certain point.—Thomas Jefferson, 1785 letter to James Madison[1]

In a Nutshell

The Earned Income Tax Credit is the largest antipoverty entitlement program with over 22 million low-income tax filers receiving income tax relief and supplements to their wages. It is designed to "make work pay"—that is, to ensure that a full-time minimum wage worker receiving EITC, along with Food Stamps, and Medicaid, will be lifted above the Federal Poverty Level. EITC is a "refundable" tax credit, which means that if a worker qualifies for a tax credit greater than his or her tax liability, the IRS "refunds" the remaining amount of the credit as a supplement to that person's wages. Working families with incomes below $33,000 to $40,000 (depending on marital status and number of children) and individual workers without children with income below $13,000 are entitled to the EITC. A recent study for Congress reported that families with two or more children received an *average* EITC of $2,669; families with one child received an average of $1,728; and childless adults received much lower assistance of $218.[2]

Background

The EITC has broad bipartisan support. It was established in the 1970s during the Ford administration as a temporary program to offset the regressive payroll (Social Security/ Medicare) tax burden on the working poor.[3] The program was made permanent during the

Carter Administration, expanded by the Reagan Administration, and became a central fixture of the Clinton Administration's antipoverty efforts. As reflected in figure 3-8.1, EITC's benefits are concentrated in families with adjusted gross income between $5,000 and $20,000 per year.

The concept of the EITC is to "make work pay." At very low wage levels, the EITC increases as work increases. It does this by eliminating the income taxes that very low-wage workers pay and by supplementing their wages (with a "refund") in order to lift low-income working families over the poverty line. Most of the EITC is received as a "refund."[4]

The EITC is heavily weighted towards families with children (see figure 3-8.2). In a recent tax year, 98% of the benefits went to families with children.[5]

A study of the EITC expansions between 1984 and 1996 found that half of the large increase in employment of single mothers could be attributed to the EITC.[6] The Committee for Economic Development, an organization of 250 corporate executives and university presidents, concluded in a report released in 2000 that "the EITC has been a powerful force in dramatically raising the employment of low-income women in recent years."[7] Another study reported that "census data show that the EITC lifts more children out of poverty than any other single program or category of programs."[8]

Moreover, in combination with the minimum wage, food stamps, and Medicaid, the EITC has helped to ensure that a family of four with a full-time minimum-wage worker does not have to live in poverty. (In recent years, the EITC/Food Stamps/Minimum Wage combination fell short of this goal due to the eroding purchasing power of the minimum wage; however, in May 2007, Congress enacted the first minimum wage increase in 10 years, boosting it from $5.15 to $7.25 an hour.[9])

Issue: Strengthening the EITC

Low-income workers without children are eligible only for minimal EITC benefits, averaging about $220. This amount simply offsets taxes owed and does not supplement wages. The same rationales that apply to the EITC for families—"making work pay" and lifting minimum wage

FIGURE 3-8.1 EITC Benefits Concentrated at Low Wage Levels

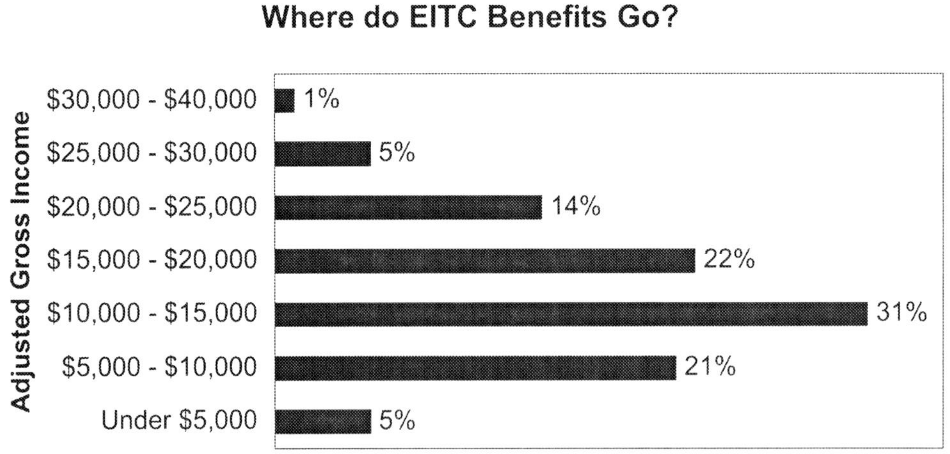

Where do EITC Benefits Go?

FIGURE 3-8.2 At low wage levels, EITC increases as work increases

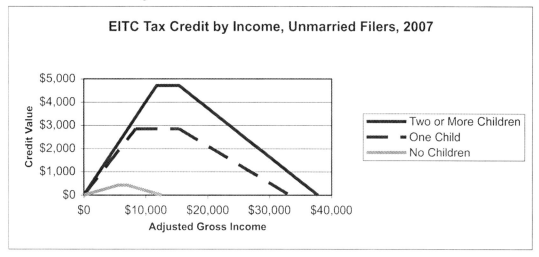

workers above the poverty line—applies equally to workers without children, making this a logical area for expanding the reach of the EITC's benefits.

Supplemental Security Income for the Aged, Blind, and Disabled (SSI)

Estimated FY 2008 Spending on SSI: $41 billion

In a Nutshell

Supplemental Security Income is a Federal assistance program that ensures a minimum cash benefit to aged, blind, or disabled persons with *low incomes* and *minimal assets*. It is a safety net of last resort for those not covered by Social Security Disability Insurance. In order to be considered disabled under SSI an individual must be unable to work, taking into account age, education, and work experience.[10] SSI recipients living alone (or in a household where all residents receive SSI benefits) are also automatically eligible for Food Stamps and, in most States for Medicaid.

Background

The Social Security Act, as originally enacted in 1935, included income support programs for needy aged and blind individuals, and in 1950, disabled individuals were added. At the time, the three categories were administered by state and local governments with partial Federal funding. Due to increasing inconsistencies among the various State and local programs, in 1972 Congress created the SSI program.

SSI provides benefits primarily to adults and children with disabilities who are not eligible for Social Security Disability Insurance (SSDI) benefits. Table 3-8.1 compares the SSI and SSDI programs.

TABLE 3-8.1 Comparing Disability Benefits under SSI and SSDI[11]

Supplemental Security Income	Social Security Disability Insurance
Means-tested entitlement (available only to low-income individuals who have **very limited income and assets**)	*Non*-**means-tested entitlement**—individuals are eligible if they have paid into the Social Security system and satisfy a work requirement.
SSI provides a **flat cash benefit** to individuals meeting the definition of "disabled."	Benefits in **amounts related *to* the disabled worker's former earnings**
Generally, the individual must be **unable to do any kind of work** taking into account age, education, and work experience.	**Same**
Children under age 18 are eligible if they qualify as disabled.	Eligible only as children of a disabled worker
Funded by **general revenues**	Funded by **payroll taxes**
Average monthly benefit at the end of 2006 was **$469 for adults**, $536 for disabled children, and $374 for adults age 65 and over.	**Average monthly SSDI benefit** at the end of 2006 was **$946** (*plus* $249 for spouses and $280 for children).
At the end of 2006, over **7.2 million** individuals were receiving SSI payments (6 million of which were on the basis of disability or blindness).	At the end of 2006, nearly **8.6 million** disabled workers and their dependents were receiving SSDI benefits.

To be eligible for SSI, an individual must *fall below federally mandated income and resource limits.* On the income side, most earned income, is counted, while in-kind assistance from government programs, such as Food Stamps and public housing, are not. On the resources side, the limit for countable resources is $2,000 for an individual and $3,000 for a couple.[12]

SSI provides a number of incentives for individuals with mental or physical disabilities to transition to the workforce. First, under the Plans to Achieve Self-Support (PASS) program, disabled SSI recipients may submit a plan that outlines how he or she will achieve work-related goals, such as receiving specialized training or starting up a business. Once SSA approves the plan, money set aside or spent in the pursuit of one's plan will not be counted as income or assets against federal SSI benefit. The money can be used for a wide variety of activities, including employment services, tuition, transportation to work, or supplies to start a business.[13]

Second, under the Ticket to Work and Self-Sufficiency Program, disabled SSI recipients are given a voucher to purchase vocational rehabilitation services from state agencies. Its goal is to increase opportunities and choices for individuals who are disabled.

Third, for people already receiving SSI payments, earned income is not automatically subtracted from the maximum federal benefits. Instead, the SSA disregards the first $65 of income each month (called the earned income exclusion), after which federal benefits are reduced only $0.50 for each dollar earned as an incentive to transition to work.

SSI also helps low-income parents meet the additional economic burdens associated with their child's disability. It seeks to replace the lost earning of a parent who must stay home to care for the child and to compensate for medical and nonmedical expenses.

The Food Stamp Program

> ***Estimated FY 2008 Spending on Food Stamps: $37 billion***

In a Nutshell

The Food Stamp Program (FSP) is a Federal entitlement that provides monthly food assistance to low-income Americans. To be eligible, a household must have a combined gross income of less than 130% of the Federal Poverty Level. *Monthly benefits vary* with household size, income, and nonfood expenses such as high shelter costs and dependant care expenses.[14] In 2006, the *average* monthly benefit was $94 per person (about $1 per meal), and the program served nearly 27 million participants.[15] About 80% of food stamp recipients are in households with children, and nearly one-third are seniors or people with disabilities. The Food and Nutrition Service of the Department of Agriculture (USDA) sets eligibility standards and allocates Food Stamp funds to the States; State agencies are responsible for day-to-day operations.

Background

Food Stamp benefits are delivered via debit cards and can be used to purchase food in thousands of stores across the country.

FSP is highly responsive to economic conditions. During the 1990s, the number of Food Stamp recipients fell for six straight years, from 27 million to 17 million, due to the strong economy. However, since 2001, the number of recipients has increased due the recession, the failure of the recovery to extend to America's poorest families,[16] and growth in the number of individuals eligible for benefits.[17] By 2006, the number of Food Stamp recipients was back up to 27 million.

FSP also plays a critical role in disaster response. In 2005, the Department of Agriculture provided over $900 million of food stamps to about 4 million individuals in the aftermath of Hurricanes Katrina, Rita, and Wilma.[18]

With poverty in America on the rise, it is surprising that only two-thirds of people eligible for Food Stamps actually participate in the program.[19] Participation rates vary greatly across the country, ranging from a low of 27% in San Diego to a high of 99% in Memphis.[20]

"Welfare"—Temporary Assistance for Needy Families (TANF)

> *FY 2007 Federal Spending on TANF: $17.1 billion*

> *Myth:* A mid-1990s survey by the Kaiser Family Foundation found that 40% of respondents believed "welfare" to be one of the two largest areas of federal spending.
>
> *Fact*: At the time of the survey, the two largest areas of federal spending were Social Security and Defense (as they are today). The Federal government's spending on "welfare," now called Temporary Assistance for Needy Families (TANF), is actually *less than 1%* of the Federal Budget.[21]

In a Nutshell

Temporary Assistance for Needy Families (TANF) was enacted in 1996, as part of sweeping welfare reform legislation[23] that replaced the Depression-era welfare programs: Aid to Families with Dependent Children (AFDC), and Job Opportunities and Basic Skills Training (JOBS). In contrast to AFDC, which was an individual entitlement,[24] TANF is a block grant[25] that provides Federal funds to States for cash assistance, as well as for benefits and services such as transportation, child care, and training aimed at helping recipients move into the workforce. *TANF requires that a family have a dependent child to be eligible for assistance.*

TANF's basic annual grants range from $22 million in Wyoming to $3.7 billion in California.[26] TANF is a joint Federal-State program; in order to receive an allocation from TANF, States must contribute matching funds amounting to 75% of the Federal block grant, ranging from $11 million in Wyoming to $2.7 billion in California.

States are permitted to use TANF funds (and State matching funds) in any manner "reasonably calculated" to achieve TANF's four goals: provide assistance to needy families with children, end dependence on government benefits, reduce out-of-wedlock pregnancies, and promote two-parent families. Although TANF is a block grant to States (which generally provide significant flexibility), Federal law attaches some conditions designed to end dependence on government benefits. Foremost among these conditions is a five-year limit on cash assistance (although 20% may continue to receive assistance for reason of "hardship.")

Background

The transformation of "welfare" from an entitlement to a block grant was aimed at reducing needy families' dependence on welfare, requiring adults with children (mostly single mothers) to move into jobs, increasing the flexibility of States, and capping the cost of Federal welfare spending. Proponents of welfare reform argued that AFDC benefits, "instead of promoting self-reliance . . . were widely believed to promote further dependence, and to be associated with the transmission of dependence to succeeding generations."[27]

The welfare reform law substantially increased the discretion States have in the design and operation of their respective public assistance programs, allowing States to determine forms of assistance, the amount of cash benefits, and specific eligibility requirements. However, the welfare reform law did set forth some specific national standards that each State must meet:

- *Lifetime Limit:* TANF, as a *temporary* assistance program, established a five-year lifetime limit on cash assistance for families (although up to 20% of families can be excluded from the lifetime limit for a variety of reasons such as a parent having a disability, a parent caring for a child with a disability, families dealing with domestic violence, and families with an elderly head of household).[28]
- *Work Participation Requirements:* In general TANF requires 30 hours[29] of work per week in order to receive benefits after two years. In order to enforce this requirement, *States face a loss of block grant funds if less than half of their benefit recipients are engaged in work activities.*[30] "Work activities" include full- or part-time employment in the public or private sector, TANF-subsidized employment, community service, training, caring for a child so another TANF recipient can do community service, and completion of high school.[31]
- *State Funds:* TANF requires States to sustain 75–80% of their historic level of spending under AFDC (known as "maintenance of effort" or MOE funds), but provides flexibility on how those funds can be used by the States.[32]
- **Unmarried teen mothers** must live at home (or in an adult-supervised setting) and stay in school in order to receive public assistance.

The 1996 law that originally established TANF expired in 2002. Due to disputes over the appropriate amount of child care funding as well as work rules for adult participants, reauthorization of the law was delayed for more than three years—with the TANF law extended under a series of 12 temporary measures until it was finally reauthorized as part of the FY 2006 Budget Reconciliation law.[33] The reauthorization law extended the program through FY 2010, at a level of $16.5 billion per year for basic block grants.

Housing Assistance

FY 2007 Spending by HUD for Housing Assistance Programs: $35 billion

In a Nutshell

The Departments of Housing and Urban Development (HUD) and Agriculture (USDA) fund various housing assistance programs for low-income households generally, low-income households in rural areas, and people who are homeless. Following are the principal programs:

- **Section 8 Rental Subsidies** assisting nearly 3.5 million low-income households. Section 8 consists of two programs: the *Housing Choice Voucher program* that gives more than two million low-income households vouchers to help pay for housing in the private market, and a *Project-Based Subsidy program* that attaches Federal subsidies to 1.3 million units creating a supply of subsidized low-income housing. (In FY 2007, the voucher program was funded at $16 billion and the project-based program at $6 billion).
- **Public housing** includes *capital funding* for improvements in public housing projects (FY 2007: $2.4 billion) and *operating subsidies* (FY 2007: $3.8 billion) to cover the gap between rental income and costs. In addition, a small program, HUD's *HOPE VI program,* provides funding to renovate or demolish dilapidated public housing and replace it with mixed income housing (FY 2007: $99 million).
- **HOME Investment Partnership Program** provides block grants to States to fund the development and rehabilitation of low-cost housing and, in so doing, to strengthen communities and reduce homelessness (FY 2007: $1.8 billion).
- **McKinney-Vento Homeless Assistance Grants** (from HUD) fund four programs that provide housing and other services for homeless persons: Emergency Shelter Grants, Supportive Housing, Section 8 Moderate Rehabilitation Assistance for Single-Room Occupancy Dwellings, and Shelter + Care (FY 2007: $1.4 billion). In addition to these HUD-sponsored programs, HHS, the VA, the Department of Labor, the Department of Justice, and FEMA administer a number of smaller programs for the homeless (FY 2007: $577 million).[34]
- **Rural Housing Service programs,** at the Department of Agriculture, provide rental assistance, interest subsidies, grants, and loans to increase the availability of affordable housing in rural areas (FY 2007: $1.4 billion).[35]

Background

Since the U.S. Housing Act of 1937, the Federal government has engaged in efforts to address the housing needs of low-income Americans. Housing assistance has never been provided as an entitlement for all persons in need, however over four million people currently receive Federal housing assistance, primarily through programs administered by HUD.[36]

The primary goal of housing assistance programs is to make suitable housing affordable for low-income households. Studies show that a large percentage of poor families spend more than half of their income on housing costs, limiting their ability to meet other basic needs and increasing the risk of homelessness. In addition, studies show that a lack of low-cost housing options can serve as a barrier to stable employment.[37]

Section 8 Housing Programs.—Established by the Housing and Community Development Act of 1974 (P.L. 93-383), Section 8 programs have become the foundation of Federal housing assistance, accounting for nearly $22 billion in Federal spending in FY 2007. Section 8 consists of the *Housing Choice Voucher program* that provides vouchers to eligible low-income households and the *project-based rental assistance* that attaches subsidies to specified housing units.

The Voucher Program is the nation's largest low-income housing assistance program, providing vouchers to more than two million very low-income families, elderly, and disabled Americans.[38] Vouchers are used by the recipient households to lower their rental costs to a maximum percentage of their income (generally 30% although in certain cases up to 40%), with the HUD vouchers covering the balance up to a limit. Housing choice vouchers are administered by local public housing agencies (PHAs) and funded entirely by the Department of Housing and Urban Development. The program has broad-based political support due to its use of the private market and its efficient delivery of substantial assistance to very low-income households.

Section 8 housing vouchers are not an individual entitlement program; the number of available vouchers is determined by Congress' annual appropriations. The eligibility rules limit vouchers to "very low-income families," with gross income less than 50% of the local area median income, although three-quarters of the vouchers must go to "extremely low-income families" with less than 30% of area median income. Even so, the number of available vouchers is far exceeded by the number of eligible families seeking rental assistance. In 2006, the GAO reported that *only 27%* of all renter households with very low incomes received housing assistance from Section 8 or another federal housing program.[39]

The other Section 8 program—which predates the Voucher Program—is known as *Section 8 "Project-Based"* assistance, where HUD rental subsidies are tied to particular units of privately owned housing (rather than to tenants as in the voucher program). Low-income families that live in Section 8 project-based units generally pay 30% of their incomes toward rent. When a family leaves, the owner of the housing continues to receive payments as long as he or she can move another low-income household into the unit. Total rent on these units is negotiated between HUD representatives and the landlord and are adjusted annually. Most of today's project-based subsidies were initially established during the 1970s and early 1980s.

By the mid-1980s, the Section 8 program's emphasis shifted from Project-Based subsidies to the new Housing Choice Voucher program, because of concern that the existing project-based approach was concentrating low-income families in high poverty areas.

Public Housing.—New public housing developments have not been built in many years, yet over 1.3 million households and over 2 million people currently live in federally funded public housing. Established under the U.S. Housing Act of 1937, the federal public housing program provides housing for eligible lower income families, elderly people, and individuals with disabilities. Public housing ranges from single family homes to high-rise apartment buildings for elderly people and often includes other services. The program is managed by local housing agencies and financed by the Department of Housing and Urban Development.[40] Congress appropriates discretionary funds annually for two accounts: the *Operating Fund*[41] and the *Capital Fund*.

Over 50% of families living in public housing have extremely low incomes—that is, below 30% of the area median income.[42] The waiting lists for public housing are long, and in many large cities, the waiting period may last up to 10 years.[43] A family's rent is based on anticipated gross annual income less certain deductions. A household may stay in public housing as long as it complies with the terms of the lease, and a family cannot be required to move out unless it can afford housing in the private market.

Since 1992, Congress has funded a small public housing revitalization program, known as *HOPE VI* (Housing Opportunities for People Everywhere). The objective of HOPE VI is to avoid concentrations of poverty "by placing public housing in non-poverty neighborhoods and promoting mixed-income communities."[44] In so doing, HOPE VI seeks to address the problems that plague many housing developments including high rates of violence and other crimes.

Programs for the Homeless.—Many theories have been advanced on why homelessness has dramatically increased in America: dramatic changes in state mental health policies in the 1970s leading to discharges of patients from mental hospitals, the failure to follow-up the discharges with establishment of adequate community-based outpatient mental health services, lack of affordable housing, substance abuse and the lack of needed services, domestic violence, lack of prisoner reentry programs, and changing mores on taking in homeless family members. What is no longer debated is that homelessness persists as a major national problem in the United States.[45]

The most recent estimates of HUD are that "754,000 people were homeless in the U.S. on a given night in January 2005 . . . [and] among these . . . 339,000 were unsheltered." About two-thirds of the homeless were "unaccompanied adults and youth," and one-third were "homeless adults and children." The profile also estimated that 25% of the homeless are disabled, 19% of the adult homeless are veterans, and 23% are chronically homeless.[46] Other studies estimate that, over the course of a year, the number of homeless in America is between 2.3 million and 3.5 million.[47]

Most of HUD's funding for homeless assistance grants is awarded through three programs, which are *competitive grant programs*: the Supportive Housing Program (SHP), Shelter Plus Care (S+C), and Single Room Occupancy (SRO). Nonprofit organizations compete for these grants along with State and local governments.

The SHP competitive grants, funded at nearly $900 million, provide funds for *transitional* housing for homeless individuals and families for up to 24 months, as well as permanent housing for disabled homeless individuals, and supportive services such as case management, health and child care, and employment assistance. The S+C program, funded at more than $300 million, provides *permanent* supportive housing through rent subsidies for disabled homeless individuals and their families. The third competitive grant, the SRO program, provides permanent housing to homeless individuals in efficiency units similar to dormitories, although this program is poorly funded at less than $1 million.

In addition to the three competitive grant programs, the Emergency Shelter Grants (ESG) program, funded at nearly $160 million, distributes funds to States, counties, and metropolitan areas for short-term needs of the homeless, such as emergency shelter.[48]

Are these HUD programs, and other programs administered by HHS, the VA, the Dept. of Labor, and FEMA meeting their stated objectives? The 2006 annual survey of Hunger and Homelessness by the U.S. Conference of Mayors casts doubt on the effectiveness of current efforts. The Mayors' report found that

> an average of 23 percent of the requests for emergency shelter by homeless people overall and 29 percent of the requests by homeless families alone are estimated to have gone unmet during the last year. In 86 percent of the cities, emergency shelters may have to turn away homeless families due to lack of resources; in 77 percent they may also have to turn away other homeless people. . . . In 55 percent of the cities, families may have to break up in order to be sheltered. . . . Mental illness and the lack of needed services lead the list of causes of homelessness identified by city officials.[49]

Low-Income Home Energy Assistance (LIHEAP)

> *FY 2007 Spending for LIHEAP: $2.2 Billion*

In a Nutshell

The Low-Income Home Energy Assistance Program (LIHEAP) makes grants to States to assist low-income households with essential energy costs in order to avoid loss of life due to extreme temperatures. Federal LIHEAP funds are allocated to States by the Department of Health and Human Services and are disbursed to eligible households by the States.

Background

Rising energy prices disproportionately impact low-income households. According to the *LIHEAP Home Energy Notebook* released by the Department of Health and Human Services, the "mean individual energy burden" was 6.3% of income. However, the energy burden for low-income households was 13.6% of income, more than twice the energy burden of all households.[50]

LIHEAP is not an entitlement program; it is a discretionary block grant under which the Federal government allocates funds to States to operate home energy assistance programs for their residents. Each year, the Appropriations Committees of the Congress determine how much funding is to be available for allocation. State allocations range from $2 million for Hawaii to $248 million allocated to New York State.[51] As with many block grant programs, the formula for allocation to the States is complex, due to competing regional interests.[52]

Congress appropriates two types of LIHEAP funds: "regular funds," which are allocated to States under a statutory formula, and "contingency funds," which are disbursed at the discretion of the Administration for emergency needs. For FY 2007, Congress appropriated $1.98 billion for regular funds and $181 million for contingency funds.[53]

States can use LIHEAP funds to finance several types of energy assistance:

- Direct assistance to low-income households for heating or cooling bills;
- Low-cost weatherization projects (e.g., window replacement or other home energy–related repairs);
- Services to reduce energy consumption (e.g., needs assessments and counseling on how to reduce energy consumption); and
- Emergency assistance during extreme conditions in the winter or summer.[54]

Although LIHEAP is not an entitlement, Federal law sets basic eligibility guidelines. States are required to limit energy assistance payments to households with incomes no higher than 150% of the Federal Poverty Level or 60% of the State's median income. (States may set lower limits, though no lower than 110% of the FPL.)[55]

Within these guidelines, States have broad discretion in how they operate their respective energy assistance programs. For example, States may choose to make LIHEAP eligibility automatic for households in which one member receives TANF, SSI, Food Stamps, or low-income veterans' benefits. States can impose other eligibility tests, including giving priority to households with the greatest energy cost burdens or households with disabled, elderly, or young children.

Nearly 35 million Americans fall within the Federal eligibility guidelines. However, in FY 2005, the most recent year for which figures are available, only 5 million households actually received assistance, with an average benefit of $304.[56]

This is a clear example of the difference between an entitlement and a discretionary spending program. If LIHEAP were an entitlement, 35 million people would receive a set benefit, determined by law. However, since LIHEAP is a discretionary program, the amount of funds appropriated each year—and the details of the State programs—determine how many low-income Americans receive assistance and how much assistance they receive.

Unemployment Compensation

> ***Estimated FY 2008 Spending on Unemployment Compensation: $36 billion***

In a Nutshell

The Federal-State Unemployment Insurance (UI) program provides temporary, partial wage replacement to unemployed workers and also serves to stabilize the economy during recessions. Regular unemployment benefits—averaging $280 in 2007—generally continue for a maximum 26 weeks, and extended benefits (available during higher levels of unemployment) can add another 13 to 20 weeks. The Federal government collects a 0.8% unemployment tax from employers (FUTA), and State governments collect state unemployment taxes from employers (SUTA), *all of which is deposited in the Federal Unemployment Trust Fund.* Unemployment benefits are paid by the States and are reimbursed from the Trust Fund. State unemployment taxes pay for *regular* UI benefits and half of *extended* UI benefits. Federal taxes pay for administrative costs of the State programs and the other half of extended benefits.

Background

Established by the Social Security Act of 1935, Unemployment Insurance (often referred to as Unemployment Compensation, or UC), is a joint Federal-State program designed as *temporary assistance* for workers who become unemployed through no fault of their own. UI payments replace some of the lost earnings of involuntarily unemployed workers while they seek other employment. From a macroeconomic perspective, the program also serves to stabilize the economy during times of economic downturn by sustaining consumer spending.

As a joint Federal-State program, the U.S. Department of Labor establishes Federal guidelines that the States and territories must follow in administering their respective UI programs, such as categories of workers that must be covered. However, States set most of the specific eligibility rules. In general, States require that in order to receive UI benefits, a worker must:

- have lost a job through no fault of his or her own (i.e., the person was not fired for cause);
- be actively seeking new work;
- have the ability to work (i.e., not prevented from working due to a disability); and
- have worked a minimum number of weeks or quarters and/or earned a minimum amount of wages.[57]

A claimant is usually disqualified if he or she quit voluntarily, was discharged for job-related misconduct, refused suitable work without good reason, or is unemployed as a result of a labor dispute.

Weekly benefits are calculated as a percentage of average weekly income, usually between 50% and 70% up to a state-determined maximum. In addition, some states adjust benefits for the number of dependents and other sources of income. Weekly maximum benefits range from $210 in Mississippi to $862 in Massachusetts.[58] In most states, individuals can receive benefits for up to 26 weeks.

During periods of economic growth, most UI beneficiaries return to work before their 26 weeks of benefits expire. (In FY 2006, the average duration was 15 weeks.[59]) But during economic slow-downs, individuals are more likely to exhaust benefits without finding new employment. In those instances, UI benefits may be extended *at the State level* for an additional 13 to 20 weeks by the Extended Benefits (EB) program. The EB program's most recent activity was in Louisiana during the aftermath of Hurricanes Katrina and Rita.

UI benefits are financed through an unusual combination of Federal and State *employer* taxes.[60] The Federal tax, known as FUTA (Federal Unemployment Tax Act), generally requires employers to pay 0.8% on the first $7,000 paid annually to each employee.[61] States also levy their own payroll taxes on employers, known as SUTA taxes (State Unemployment Tax Act). The SUTA tax rates, and the amount of income subject to the tax, vary greatly among the States.[62]

Both FUTA and SUTA taxes are deposited in the Federal Unemployment Trust Fund and are counted as Federal revenues (and reimbursement of States for benefits paid are counted as Federal outlays). SUTA taxes pay for regular UI benefits and half of extended UI benefits. FUTA taxes pay for administrative costs of the State programs and the other half of extended UI benefits.

For FY 2007, Congress appropriated $2.5 billion from the Trust Fund to pay for Federal and State program administrative costs and the Federal share of *extended* UI benefits. These funds are *discretionary* appropriations. Payments for actual benefit payments were projected at $31.3 billion and are considered to be *mandatory spending* because States are entitled to reimbursement of their benefit payments from the Federal Unemployment Trust Fund. (Each State has an account within the Trust Fund and may borrow from the Federal Treasury if their account is depleted.)

In a recent report to Congress on the UI program, it was reported that "in March 2007, 2.6 million unemployed workers received UI benefits in a given week and the average weekly UC benefit was $281."[63]

During some economic recessions, the Federal government steps in and establishes a *Federal-funded* Temporary Extended Unemployment Compensation (TEUC) program (sometimes called emergency benefits). Congress has acted five times—in 1971, 1974, 1982, 1991, and 2002—to provide up to 13 additional weeks of Federally funded benefits for unemployed workers whose regular UC benefits have been exhausted. Most recently, Congress enacted emergency benefits in FY 2002, as reflected in table 3-8.2.

TABLE 3-8.2 Comparing UI Revenues and Outlays Outlays: Fiscal Years 2002 and 2007 *(billions of $)*

	FY 2002	*FY 2007*
UI Revenue, Total	**27.5**	**44.9**
FUTA Taxes	6.6	7.3
SUTA Taxes	20.9	37.6
UI Outlays, Total	**53.8**	**34.7**
Regular Benefits	42	30.8
Extended Benefits	0.16	0.0
Emergency Benefits	7.9	—
Administrative Costs	3.7	3.9

Source: CRS.[64]

Notes

1. Daniel B. Baker, ed., *Political Quotations* (Detroit: Gale Research, 1990), 218.

2. Christine Scott, "The Earned Income Tax Credit (EITC): An Overview," RL31768 (Washington, D.C.: Congressional Research Service, March 15, 2007), 5. The *maximum* EITC amounts for FY 2007 are $4,716 for families with two or more children, $2,853 for families with one child, and $428 for families with no children.

3. A tax is "regressive" when it impacts disproportionately on lower income taxpayers. Payroll taxes (Social Security and Medicare tax) are regressive because the 7.65% paid by a low-income worker is far more burdensome than the 7.65% tax paid by a worker earning $90,000 per year. Conversely, a tax is viewed as "progressive" when the tax rate on lower-income workers is a lower percentage than the tax rate on middle- and high-income workers.

4. In 2004, 88% of the EITC was received as a refund. Scott, "The Earned Income Tax Credit," 8.

5. Scott, "The Earned Income Tax Credit," 10.

6. Bruce Meyer and Dan Rosenbaum, "Making Single Mothers Work: Recent Tax and Welfare Policy and Its Effects," in *Making Work Pay: The Earned Income Tax Credit and Its Impact on America's Families,* ed. Bruce Meyer and Douglas Holtz Eakin (New York: Russell Sage Foundation, 2001), as cited in Robert Greenstein, *The Earned Income Tax Credit: Boosting Employment, Aiding the Working Poor* (Washington, D.C.: Center on Budget and Policy Priorities, August 17, 2005), fn. 2.

7. CED, "Welfare Reform and Beyond: Making Work *Work*" (New York: Committee for Economic Development, 2000), 7, http://www.ced.org/projects/welfare.shtml. 7

8. Greenstein, *The Earned Income Tax Credit,* 3.

9. HR 2206 (110th Congress, 1st Sess.)

10. For adults, *disability* is defined as the inability to engage in substantial gainful activity due to a medically determinable physical or mental impairment expected to last at least 12 months or result in death. Scott Szymendera, "Supplemental Security Income (SSI): A Fact Sheet," 94-486 (Washington, D.C.: Congressional Research Service, December 26, 2006), 1.

11. Sources: Szymendera, "Supplemental Security Income (SSI)"; and Scott Szymendera, "Primer on Disability Benefits: Social Security Disability Insurance (SSDI) and Supplemental Security Income (SSI)," RL 32279 (Washington, D.C.: Congressional Research Service, December 26, 2006).

12. For a complete list of countable and uncountable resources, see http://www.socialsecurity.gov/notices/supplemental-security-income/text-resources-ussi.htm.

13. See http://www.socialsecurity.gov/disabilityresearch/wi/pass.htm.

14. Joe Richardson, "Food Stamps: Background and Funding," 98-59 EPW (Washington, D.C.: Congressional Research Service, November 7, 2000), summary. See also Dorothy Rosenbaum, "The Food

Stamp Program Is Growing to Meet Need" (Washington, D.C.: Center on Budget and Policy Priorities, July 12, 2006), 4.

15. USDA, "Food Stamp Program Monthly Data," http://www.fns.usda.gov/pd/34fsmonthly.htm (accessed September 2, 2007).

16. According to a recent study, "real median wages for the bottom one-fifth of full-time workers fell in 2003, 2004, and 2005." Rosenbaum, "The Food Stamp Program," 3.

17. The 2002 Farm Bill restored food stamp eligibility for some *legal* immigrants and Food Stamps are now available in many States to people who own a reliable car. Rosenbaum, "The Food Stamp Program," 3.

18. Rosenbaum, "The Food Stamp Program," 5.

19. Kari Wolkwitz, "Trends in Food Stamp Program Participation Rates: 1999–2005" (Washington, D.C.: Mathematica Policy Research, June 2007), xi.

20. "Food Stamp Access in Urban America: A City-by-City Snapshot," *Food Research and Action Center*, October 2006, http://www.frac.org/pdf/cities2006.pdf.

21. Kaiser Family Foundation/Harvard Program on the Public and Health/Social Policy Survey, http://www.kff.org/kaiserpolls/1001-welftbl.cfm. Even if one adds other income security and social services programs aimed at helping low-income Americans—SSI, EITC, Child Care, Housing Assistance, LIHEAP, Food Stamps, Head Start, SCHIP, Community Health Centers, Child Nutrition, and WIC— the funds expended amount to just over 7% of the budget.

23. The Personal Responsibility and Work Opportunity Reconciliation Act of 1996, P.L. 104-193.

24. Under AFDC, poor families with children were entitled to Federal-State public assistance benefits according to an income-based formula.

25. "Block grants" are generally lump sum allocations of Federal funds to States, with significant flexibility on how States may use the funds.

26. Gene Falk, "The Temporary Assistance for Need Families (TANF) Block Grant: A Primer on TANF Financing and Federal Requirements," RL32748 (Washington, D.C.: Congressional Research Service, April 23, 2007), 3–4.

27. House Committee on Ways and Means, "A Decade since Welfare Reform: 1996 Welfare Reforms Reduce Welfare Dependence," February 26, 2006, 2.

28. According to the GAO, States have generally permitted extensions for "families they considered hard to employ, families who were working but not earning enough to move off of TANF, and families that were cooperating with program requirements but had not yet found employment." General Accounting Office, "Welfare Reform: With TANF Flexibility, States Vary in How They Implement Work Requirements and Time Limits" (Washington, D.C.: Author, July 2002), 3.

29. Thirty-five to 55 hours for two-parent families and 20 hours for single parents caring for preschool children. The requirement is waived for single parents if child care is unavailable.

30. Department of Health and Human Services, Administration for Children and Families, "Office of Family Assistance Fact Sheet," www.acf.hhs.gov/opa/fact_sheets/tanf_printable.html. See also General Accounting Office, "Welfare Reform," 1.

31. Falk, "Primer on TANF," table A-1.

32. See General Accounting Office, "Welfare Reform," 6–7.

33. The Deficit Reduction Act of 2005. See appendix N.

34. FEMA/DHS: Emergency Food and Shelter Program; HHS: Health Care for the Homeless, Projects for Assistance in Transition from Homelessness, Consolidated Runaway and Homeless Youth Program, Runaway and Homeless Youth-Street Outreach Program; ED: Education for Homeless Children and Youth; VA: VA Supportive Housing Program; DOL: Homeless Veterans Reintegration Program; DOJ: Transitional Housing Assistance for Child Victims of Domestic Violence, Stalking, or Sexual Assault. For a description of these programs, see Libby Perl, "Homelessness: Targeted Federal Programs

and Recent Legislation," RL 30442 (Washington, D.C.: Congressional Research Service, August 3, 2007).

35. See Bruce Foote, "USDA Housing Program," RL33421 (Washington, D.C.: Congressional Research Service, July 27, 2007).

36. Jeffrey M. Lubell, Mark Shroder, and Barry Steffen, "Work Participation and Length of Stay in HUD-Assisted Housing," *Cityscape* 6, no. 2 (2003).

37. *Section 8 Housing Choice Voucher Program: Funding and Related Issues*, CRS Report for Congress.

38. U.S. Department of Housing and Urban Development, *Housing Choice Voucher Fact Sheet*, http://www.hud.gov/offices/pih/programs/hcv/about/fact_sheet.cfm

39. GAO, *Rental Housing Assistance: Policy Decisions and Market Factors Explain Changes in the Costs of the Section 8 Program* (Washington, D.C.: April 28, 2006).

40. U.S. Department of Housing and Urban Development, "HUD's Public Housing Program," April 25, 2006, http://www.hud.gov/renting/phprog.cfm.

41. See Maggie McCarty, "Public Housing: Fact Sheet on the New Operating Fund Formula," RS22557 (Washington, D.C.: Congressional Research Service, April 13, 2007).

42. U.S. Department of Housing and Urban Development, "Resident Characteristic Report," August 31, 2006. http://pic.hud.gov/pic/RCRPublic/rcrmain.asp

43. National Coalition for the Homeless, *Federal Housing Assistance Programs: NCH Fact Sheet #16*, June 2006, http://www.nationalhomeless.org/publications/facts/Federal.pdf.

44. HUD, "About HOPE VI" (Washington, D.C.: U.S. Department of Housing and Urban Development, August 4, 2006), www.hud.gov/offices/pih/programs/ph/hope6/about/. See also Maggie McCarty, "HOPE VI Public Housing Revitalization Program: Background, Funding, and Issues," RL32236 (Washington, D.C.: Congressional Research Service, March 30, 2007).

45. Libby Perl, "The HUD Homeless Assistance Grants: Distribution of Funds," RL33764 (Washington, D.C.: Congressional Research Service, August 3, 2007), 1; United States Conference of Mayors, "Hunger and Homelessness Survey," December 2006, 4; and conversations the author had with Senator Daniel Patrick Moynihan on the causal relationship between closure of State mental hospitals across the country and the epidemic of homelessness.

46. Department of Housing and Urban Development, "The Homeless in America: A Profile Based on the First Annual Homeless Assessment Report (AHAR)," http://www.hud.gov/offices/cpd/homeless/library/homelessnessfactsheet.pdf.

47. Libby Perl, "Homelessness: Targeted Federal Program and Recent Legislation," RL30442 (Washington, D.C.: Congressional Research Service, August 3, 2007), summary.

48. Funding levels for homeless grants are FY 2006 funding. Source: Perl, "The HUD Homeless Assistance Grants," table 1.

49. U.S. Conference of Mayors, "Hunger and Homelessness Survey: A 23-City Survey," (Sodecho, Inc., December 2006), 3–4.

50. Accessed at http://www.acf.hhs.gov/programs/liheap/data/notebook/notebook.html.

51. Libby Perl, "The Low-Income Home Energy Assistance Program (LIHEAP)," RL31865 (Washington, D.C.: Congressional Research Service, July 3, 2007, 14.

52. See Libby Perl, "Low-Income Home Energy Assistance Program (LIHEAP) Allocation Rates: Legislative History and Current Law, RL33275 (Washington, D.C.: Congressional Research Service, August 21, 2007).

53. Perl, "The Low-Income Home Energy Assistance Program (LIHEAP)," 2.

54. Perl, 6–7.

55. Perl, 6.

56. Perl, 9.

57. CRS, "Unemployment Insurance: Available Unemployment Benefits and Legislative Activity," May 23, 2006, 2–3

58. Julie Whittaker, "Unemployment Compensation: The Cornerstone of Income Support for Unemployed Workers," RS22538 (Washington, D.C.: Congressional Research Service, April 26, 2007), 2.

59. Whittaker, "Unemployment Compensation," 3.

60. Three states require minimal employee contributions. See www.workforcesecurity.doleta.gov/unemploy/uifactsheet.asp.

61. This rate applies provided the State program complies with Federal rules. If a State fails to comply, the State's employers can be required to pay the maximum FUTA tax rate of 6.2%.

62. The SUTA taxes are "experience rated," which means that the more UC benefits paid to its former employees, the higher the tax rate of the employer. Whittaker, "Unemployment Compensation," 4.

63. Whittaker, "Unemployment Compensation," 1, 3.

64. Julie Whittaker, "Unemployment Insurance: Available Unemployment Benefits and Legislative Activity," RL33362 (Washington, D.C.: Congressional Research Service, April 23, 2007).

Transportation Programs

To be immobile is to be in chains. —Abraham ibn Ezra, 12th-century biblical scholar and philosopher famous for his wanderings through Europe and North Africa[1]

The transportation budget for FY 2007 totaled about $65 billion, funding highways and bridges, airports, air traffic control, mass transit, Amtrak, and transportation safety.

FIGURE 3-9.1 FY 2007 Transportation Spending (billions of dollars)

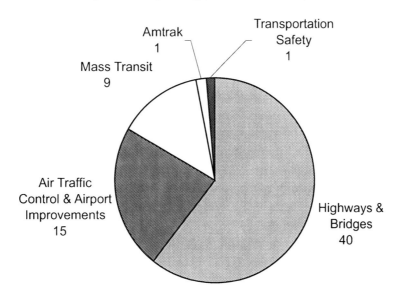

Federal-aid Highway Program (Highways and Bridges)

FY 2007 Spending for Highways and Bridges: $40 billion

See www.GovBudget.com for updated numbers.

In a Nutshell

Federal spending on highways and bridges is funded by gasoline, diesel, and other Federal taxes[2] credited to the "Highway Trust Fund." Every five or six years, Congress enacts a multi-year "highway bill" that sets total highway and bridge spending for each year (based on revenues flowing into the Trust Fund) and establishes *allocation formulas* for dividing available revenues among the States. Establishing these allocation formulas is often a long and politically contentious process. Once established, the formulas are annually adjusted to keep spending authority aligned with projected revenues.[3] Based on the highway bill formulas, the Federal Highway Administration (FHWA) annually apportions to States *authority to enter into contracts* obligating the Federal government to pay a share of project costs. This allocation is known as *contract authority.*

When various phases of contract work are completed, a State notifies FHWA, which authorizes the U.S. Treasury to disburse funds to the State covering the Federal obligation. This disbursement represents Federal outlays. The highway authorization bill enacted in 2005, known by its acronym SAFETEA-LU,[4] provided $199 billion in contract authority for the highway program over fiscal years 2005 to 2009, including $40 billion for FY 2007.[5]   Even though efforts are made to align *contract authority* with projected revenues, CBO projects that the Highway Trust Fund will be insolvent by 2009, due to insufficient tax revenues to cover projected outlays.

Background

Funding of highway and bridge projects is unlike the typical budget process described in Part II of this book. Typically, authorizing committees set the *desired* funding levels for a program, and the Appropriations Committees set *actual* funding levels. In the case of highway funding, however, the authorizers (the Environment and Public Works Committee in the Senate, and the Transportation and Infrastructure Committee in the House) have at least as much impact as the Appropriations Committees. The authorizers craft their multiyear highway bills in a way that permits States to obligate the Federal government as partners on highway and bridge projects without an appropriation.

This authority to enter into contracts that obligate Federal resources, in advance of appropriations, is known as *contract authority.*[6] Contract authority is generally prohibited by the Congressional Budget Act because it allows the annual appropriations process to be circumvented. However, the Budget Act provided a special exception for contract authority derived from trust funds, such as the Highway Trust Fund, that are funded by dedicated taxes.[7] Put another way, because the Federal highway aid program is funded by dedicated taxes, the authorizing committees can determine how those revenues will be used outside the usual appropriations process.

SOLVENCY OF THE HIGHWAY TRUST FUND

In March 2007 testimony, the Congressional Budget Office projected that "the highway account of the Highway Trust Fund will become exhausted at some point during fiscal year 2009 [and] the mass transit account will [only] have sufficient revenues to cover its expenditures until 2012."[8] The reason for the projected insolvency is that the growth in Federal *outlays* for highways, bridges, and mass transit programs are outpacing revenue increases. As explained by CBO, "fuel taxes do not grow as rapidly as the economy . . . . [I]f fuel taxes are extended, revenues from them will grow about 1.5 % per year from 2007 to 2017, less than the nominal growth of the economy, at 4.6%." Moreover, as Americans gradually shift to hybrid and other fuel-efficient vehicles, the current fuel tax based revenue stream for highway spending will erode. Consequently, Congress is approaching a critical decision point on highway spending, and it will have to choose among slowing highway and mass transit projects, raising Federal fuel taxes, taxing other items, and supplementing available funds from general revenues (which would generate higher Federal deficits). These options should be considered in light of GAO's finding that "federal-aid highway grants have influenced state and local governments to substitute federal funds for state and local funds that otherwise would have been spent on highways."[9] In other words, increased Federal resources do not necessarily translate into a greater national investment in highways. Analyzing the various financing options is the task assigned to the National Surface Transportation Infrastructure Financing Commission established by SAFETY-LU.[10]

In some years, however, there has been a tug of war between the authorizing committees and the Appropriations Committees. This occurs when the Appropriations Committees set annual limits on highway spending levels—called *obligation limitations*—lower than the contract authority levels set in the highway bill.[11] In those instances, the obligation ceiling in the appropriations bill "trumps" the spending levels in the multiyear highway authorization bill, under the general legal principle that the *most recently enacted legislation controls*. As explained in the text box, the impending insolvency of the Highway Trust Fund may require the Appropriations Committees to tighten obligation limitations and take additional steps to reduce outlays from the Highway Trust Fund.

Issue: Distribution of Funding among the States

Negotiating the details of the multiyear highway bill consumes more of Congress' time than most other legislation. (Before enactment of SAFETEA-LU in 2005, the previous highway bill had expired in 2003, and the funding pipeline was continued with 11 temporary extensions while Congress and the Administration struggled to reach agreement.) The major reason for difficulty in reaching an agreement on the highway bill is no mystery: disputes about how to slice the budget pie among the 50 States. This is often called the "donor-donee issue," with *donor* States paying more in Federal fuel taxes than they receive in Federal highway aid, and *donee* States receiving more aid than taxes paid. (Southern, midwestern, and western States are often donor States, and northeastern States are generally donee States, with their aging infrastructure.) The drafters of SAFETY-LU eventually reached a compromise that ensured donor States a 92% return on their fuel taxes.[12] With few exceptions, Federal-aid highways must be matched by the States; the State match is usually 20%.

Issue: Are the Nation's Bridges Safe?

In the wake of the sudden collapse of the I-35W bridge in Minneapolis on August 1, 2007, the Congressional Research Service reported to Congress that "of the 600,000 public road bridges listed in the National Bridge Inventory, roughly 12% or 74,000 are classified as structurally deficient." CRS estimates that *at current spending levels* (see table 3-9.1), the number of deficient bridges would only be cut in half by 2024. Reducing the backlog to zero would require about a 20% increase in the bridge program.[13] It should also be noted that while the Federal Highway Bridge Program provides a significant share of the funding for bridge repairs and replacement, the States are responsible for inspecting bridges, signing contracts, and managing the actual work.

Issue: Earmarks

> *A Congressman is never any better than his roads, and sometimes worse.—Will Rogers*[14]

As reflected in Will Rogers' timeless wit, directing Federal highway dollars to one's State or District is a congressional tradition. Yet, this runs counter to the commonsense principle that dollars to maintain the safety of highways and bridges ought to be apportioned on the basis of need. Particularly with bridges, safety should be the paramount factor in distributing Federal aid highway program dollars.

However, increasing amounts of highway dollars are apportioned based on the seniority and committee assignments of Senators and Representatives—not on an objective assessment of safety and need by engineers and transportation planners. The current highway bill, SAFETEA-LU, contains a record number of earmarks: over 5,600 with a value of more than $24 billion (more than 12% of highway spending over five years).[15] Significantly, this is nearly three times the number of earmarks in the prior highway bill (TEA-21). It remains to be seen whether the new earmark disclosure rules (discussed in chapter 2-9) will moderate the number or amount of earmarks in the next highway bill (set to be negotiated in 2009).

TABLE 3-9.1 Overview of the Federal Aid Highways Program[16]

Major Programs/ Projects	Explanation	FY 2007 Spending (bilions of dollars)
Equity Bonus Program	Provides additional funds to States to ensure that all "donor states" receive at least a 92% return on their Federal fuel taxes by 2009	8.3

Major Programs/ Projects	Explanation	FY 2007 Spending (bilions of dollars)
Surface Transportation Program	Flexible funds that may be used by States or cities for highway, bridge, transit, and intracity or intercity bus transportation	6.4
National Highway System	Expenditures to continue building the nation's 161,000-mile National Highway System (of which 47,000 roadways are part of the Interstate Highway System)	6.1
Interstate maintenance program	Finances projects to maintain the Interstate Highway System	5.0
Highway Bridge Replacement and Rehabilitation Program (HBRR)	Replacement, rehab, and preventive maintenance	4.1[17]
"High Priority Projects" and "Projects of National & Regional Significance"	More than 5,000 *earmarked* congressional projects	3.4
Congestion mitigation & air quality improvement (CMAQ)	Directs funds to projects aimed at reducing ozone, carbon monoxide, and particulate matter	1.7
Highway safety improvement	Supports innovative approaches to reducing motor vehicle fatalities (42,642 in 2006)[18]	1.3
Other	Includes highways on Federal lands, Appalachian Highway System, transportation financing programs, "national corridors" to promote economic growth, emergency aid (e.g., the Minneapolis bridge collapse on August 1, 2007), and adjustments due to revenue flows (RABA[19]) and obligation limitations	3.4
TOTAL	**Federal Aid Highways Program (FY 2007)**	**39.7**

Public Transportation

FY 2007 Spending for Public Transportation: $9 billion

See www.GovBudget.com for updated numbers.

In a Nutshell

The Highway Trust Fund, in addition to funding the Federal-Aid Highway program, also funds public transportation programs. SAFETEA-LU authorized $45 billion in funding for public transportation over the five-year authorization, including $9 billion for FY 2007.[20] The Federal Transit Administration (FTA) distributes these Federal fuel tax revenues to State and local governments for a variety of public transportation programs, ranging from new construction to maintenance. CBO projects that the Mass Transit Account in the Highway Trust Fund will be insolvent by 2012, due to the imbalance of slowly increasing fuel taxes and high rates of spending authorized in the highway bill.[21]

Background

When Federal fuel taxes are deposited in the Highway Trust Fund, almost one-fifth of the funds are deposited in the Mass Transit Account. Table 3-9.2 provides a brief overview of the $9 billion authorized by SAFETEA-LU for public transportation grants in FY 2007.

TABLE 3-9.2 Overview of Public Transportation Funding[22]

Major Programs/ Projects	Explanation	FY 2007 Spending (billions of dollars)
Urbanized Area Formula Grants	Funds may be used by urban areas for any transit capital projects; small cities can also use the funds for operating costs.	3.6
Fixed guideway modernization	Funding for heavy and light rail, commuter trains, and ferryboat operations	1.4
Major capital investment	Major capital investment grants of $75 million or more	1.4
Bus and bus facility grants	Grants for bus-related capital projects	0.9
Other formula and capital investment grants	Includes grants for nonurban areas, special needs, commuter needs, and transportation planning	1.7
TOTAL	**Public Transportation (FY 2007)**	**9.0**

Financing Air Traffic Control and Airport Improvements

> **FY 2007 Spending for Airports and Air Traffic Control: $14.5 billion**

See www.GovBudget.com for updated numbers.

The current approach to managing air transportation is becoming increasingly inefficient and operationally obsolete. . . . The Next Generation Air Transportation System . . . will entail precision satellite navigation; digital, networked communications; an integrated weather system [and] layered, adaptive security.—Government Accountability Office, 2006[23]

In a Nutshell

The Federal Aviation Administration (FAA) operates and maintains the nation's air traffic control system, and it provides grants to airports for improvements and expansion. With the nation's air traffic expected to double or triple by 2025,[24] Congress is examining a variety of financing options to pay for a next generation air traffic control system as well as major airport expansions.

Background

The FAA's activities are funded *annually through the appropriations process*. Most of the FAA's funds are appropriated from the Aviation Trust Fund[25] consisting of the 7.5% tax on passenger tickets, a tax on international arrivals and departures, and a tax on aviation fuel. General tax revenues pay for the remaining operations expenses not covered by Trust Fund revenues. Table 3-9.3 provides an overview of the FAA's programs and funding sources.

Issue: Financing the New Air Traffic Control System and Airport Expansion

There is an ongoing debate about whether to modify the current system for financing FAA operations and capital costs. The FAA and others have expressed concerns about the adequacy of the current funding stream, particularly in light of the resources required to launch a "next generation" air traffic control system by 2025 (called Next Generation Air Transportation System, or NGATS). Estimates are that keeping NGATS development on track could cost up to $76 billion by 2025. However, achieving agreement on modifications to FAA funding is a formidable political task. Policymakers must weigh and balance the interests of commercial airlines versus general aviation (corporate and recreational aircraft). The airlines argue they bear a disproportionate share of the current financing system, with the largest source of current revenues derived from passenger ticket taxes. General aviation interests are typically opposed to changing the current financing structure. Other financing options that could be considered include a user fee structure based on aircraft weight and distance flown—a system used by many nations.[26]

TABLE 3-9.3 Overview of Aviation Spending in FY 2007[27]

Major Programs, Projects, Activities (and funding)	Explanation	FY 2007 Spending (billions of dollars)
FAA Operations & Maintenance *(2/3 funded by taxes and fees paid into the aviation trust fund; 1/3 paid by general revenues)*	Supports the air traffic control system, enforcement of airline safety regulations, and administrative costs.	8.3
Airport Improvement Program (AIP) *(funded by taxes and fees paid into the aviation trust fund)*	AIP funds are used to increase airport capacity with additional runways and terminal space, as well as for safety, security, and noise reduction. Airport improvements are also funded by non-Federal sources, including tax-exempt bonds, passenger facility charges, state and local grants, and airport revenue.	3.5
Facilities & Equipment *(funded by taxes and fees paid into the aviation trust fund)*	F&E funds technological improvements to the air traffic control system; FAA and NASA are leading a multiagency effort (known as "Vision 100") to design and implement the Next Generation Air Transportation System (NGATS) aimed at accommodating up to three times the air traffic by making more efficient use of the nation's airspace.[28]	2.5
Research, Engineering, & Development *(funded by taxes and fees paid into the aviation trust fund)*	These FAA projects are aimed at creating greater capacity, improving safety, and addressing environmental concerns.	0.1
TOTAL	**Aviation Programs (FY 2007)**	**14.5**

Amtrak

FY 2007 Spending for Amtrak: $1.3 billion

See www.GovBudget.com for updated numbers.

The current model for providing intercity passenger service continues to produce financial instability and poor service quality. Despite multiple efforts over the years to change Amtrak's structure and funding, we have a system that limps along, is never in a state-of-good-repair, awash in debt, and perpetually on the edge of collapse. —Mark Dayton, Department of Transportation Inspector General[29]

In a Nutshell

Amtrak is the only U.S. intercity passenger rail service. Amtrak is structured as an independent corporation (the National Railroad Passenger Corporation) but has a federally appointed Board, and virtually all of its shares are held by the Department of Transportation. Amtrak's financial condition is described by the GAO as "precarious, requiring a federal subsidy of more than $1 billion annually."[30]

Background

Amtrak was established by Act of Congress in 1970 to provide a minimum level of national intercity passenger rail service—an area the private sector had found to be unprofitable. Amtrak operates 44 routes over 22,000 miles of track, almost all of which is owned by freight rail companies. Amtrak runs an operating loss each year, relying on Federal subsidies to continue current operations. While subsidies have been substantial—over a billion dollars per year since 2003—they have not been sufficient to enable significant maintenance projects.[31]

In recent reports to Congress, the GAO concluded that Amtrak:

- lacks a meaningful strategic plan with clear public goals by which to measure performance (such as mitigating transportation congestion);
- cannot keep pace with its deteriorating infrastructure, despite the billion-dollar-plus Federal subsidy;
- lacks adequate data and financial controls on the purchase of goods and services;
- maintains cross-country routes accounting for 15% of riders but 80% of financial losses; and
- lacks the transparency, accountability, and oversight essential to achieving success because it is neither a publicly traded company nor a public entity.

In a separate report to Congress, CBO concluded that "there are only limited conditions under which passenger rail service in the United States could be economically viable without subsidies."[32]

Transportation Safety

FY 2007 Spending for Transportation Safety: $1.4 billion

See www.GovBudget.com for updated numbers

In a Nutshell

The National Highway Transportation Safety Administration (NHTSA) is an educational, research, and regulatory agency within the Department of Transportation that conduct research and provides highway traffic safety grants. A separate agency at DOT, the Federal Motor Carrier Safety Administration (FMCSA), is tasked with reducing crashes, injuries, and fatalities involving large trucks and buses. The National Transportation Safety Board (NTSB) is an *independent* agency that investigates all civil aviation accidents in the United States, as well as significant accidents in other modes of transportation (highway, marine, railroad, pipeline).

Background

NHTSA, funded at $800 million per year, conducts research on motor vehicle safety, is developing a system to enable States to communicate about dangerous drivers, and administers Highway Traffic Safety Grants to States. FMCSA, funded at $500 million, administers motor carrier safety grants, conducts research, and supports enforcement of truck safety regulations (in particular at the United States–Mexico border).

The NTSB, funded at $78 million in FY 2007, was initially established as part of the Department of Transportation but in 1974 was transformed into an independent commission in order to ensure independent assessments of DOT's regulatory and oversight activities, as well as independent recommendations on avoiding future accidents. NTSB consists of a five-member board and a staff of 400. Recent concerns have been expressed about inadequate staffing at NTSB, particularly with regard to the percentage of small plane crashes it has been able to investigate.[33]

Notes

1. Lewis D. Eigen and Jonathan P. Siegel, *The Macmillan Dictionary of Political Quotations* (New York: Macmillan, 1993), 666.

2. Other taxes include taxation of gasohol as well as a retail sales tax on trucks, heavy-vehicle use taxes, and a tax on truck tires.

3. Known as revenue aligned budget authority (RABA).

4. On August 10, 2005, President Bush signed the Safe, Accountable, Flexible, Efficient Transportation Equity Act-A Legacy for Users.

5. John W. Fischer, "SAFETEA-LU: Selected Major Provisions," RL33119 (Washington, D.C.: Congressional Research Service, October 18, 2005), table 2.

6. In addition, the authorizing committees have attempted to ensure that *all* fuel taxes are expeditiously made available for the highway program by including in SAFETEA-LU a funding mechanism know as "revenue-aligned budget authority (RABA)." As explained by CBO, "under RABA, the Admin-

istration estimates revenues for the highway account and compares those estimates with the revenue amounts anticipated in SAFETEA-LU and with the estimates made the previous years. On the basis of that comparison, the Administration . . . is required to adjust contract authority for programs funded from the highway account." However, CBO explains, "the obligation limitations set in appropriations acts . . . do not necessarily reflect RABA adjustments." Donald B. Marron, Deputy Director, Congressional Budget Office, Testimony before the Subcommittee on Highways and Transit, U.S. House of Representatives, March 27, 2007, 3.

7. P.L. 93-344, §401(c)(1)(B).

8. Marron, "Testimony," 1.

9. GAO, "Federal-Aid Highways: Trends, Effect on State Spending, and Options for Future Program Design," GAO-04-802 (Washington, D.C.: Government Accountability Office, August 2004), 3.

10. See http://financecommission.dot.gov/index.htm.

11. The highway bill itself also includes obligation limitations that reflect spending levels in that bill; however, the appropriators in the annual Transportation-HUD appropriations bill can modify those obligation limitations.

12. Fischer, "SAFETEA-LU," 6–7.

13. See Robert Kirk and William Mallett, "Highway Bridges: Conditions and the Federal/State Role," RL34127 (Washington, D.C.: Congressional Research Service, August 10, 2007), 5.

14. Eigen and Siegel, *The Macmillan Dictionary of Political Quotations*, 667.

15. Fischer, "SAFETEA-LU," 5–6.

16. Source for individual programs: Fischer, "SAFETEA-LU," table 2; source for Federal-Aid Highways total: Marron, "Testimony," table 2.

17. Kirk and Mallett, "Highway Bridges," 7.

18. www.nhtsa.gov: "2006 Traffic Safety Annual Assessment," July 2007.

19. See note 5 for an explanation of the RABA mechanism.

20. Fischer, "SAFETEA-LU," 34–35.

21. Marron, "Testimony," 1.

22. Source for individual programs: Fischer, "SAFETEA-LU," table 2; source for Transit total spending: OMB, FY 2008 Budget, Analytical Perspectives, table 27-1, adjusted to reflect FY 2007 joint funding resolution.

23. GAO, "Next Generation Air Transportation System," GAO-07-25 (Washington, D.C.: Government Accountability Office, November 2006), 1.

24. Bert Elias, "Federal Aviation Administration," RL33789 (Washington, D.C.: Congressional Research Service, January 9, 2007), 7.

25. Also known as the Airport and Airways Trust Fund, established by the Airport and Airway Revenue Act of 1970 (P.L. 91-258).

26. Elias, "Federal Aviation Administration," 1–2, 7.

27. Source: David Peterman and John Frittelli, "Transportation-Treasury-HUD FY 2007 Appropriations," RL33551 (Washington, D.C.: Congressional Research Service, June 4, 2007), table 4; and John Fisher, "Aviation Finance," RL33913 (Washington, D.C.: Congressional Research Service, March 12, 2007).

28. P.L. 108-176, the Vision 100—Century of Aviation Reauthorization Act, enacted in 2003, created the Joint Planning Development Office.

29. Statement of Mark Dayton, DOT Inspector General, before the Senate Committee on Appropriations, March 16, 2006, as cited by John Frittelli, "Amtrak: Budget and Reauthorization," RL33492 (Washington, D.C.: Congressional Research Service, July 20, 2007), 2.

30. GAO, "Amtrak Management: Systemic Problems Require Actions to Improve Efficiency, Effectiveness, and Accountability," GAO-06-145 (Washington, D.C.: Government Accountability Office, October 2005), highlights.

31. Peterman and Frittelli, "Transportation-Treasury-HUD FY 2007 Appropriations," 1.

32. CBO, "The Past and Future of U.S. Passenger Rail Service" (Washington, D.C.: Congressional Budget Office, September 2003), preface.

33. Sara Kehaulani Goo, "NTSB Goes to Fewer Crashes; Backlogged Investigators Pass on Small-Plane Accident Sites," *Washington Post*, February 8, 2006, A17.

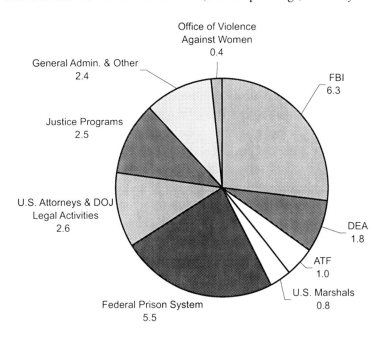

Law Enforcement and Administration of Justice

The Department of Justice (DOJ), created in 1870, has a $23 billion budget that supports the work of the Federal Bureau of Investigation, Drug Enforcement Administration, Bureau of Alcohol Tobacco and Firearms, Federal Prisons, Litigation Divisions and U.S. Attorneys, the Office of Violence against Women, and a range of programs assisting State and local jurisdictions (see figure 3-9.1). This chapter surveys DOJ expenditures.

FIGURE 3-10.1 FY 2007 Law Enforcement and Justice Spending *(billions of dollars)*

The Federal Bureau of Investigation (FBI)

> ### FY 2007 Spending for the FBI: $6.3 Billion
> FY 2007 Personnel: 12,500 Special Agents and 18,000 Support Staff

See www.GovBudget.com for updated numbers.

In a Nutshell

The FBI is the nation's primary Federal law enforcement agency responsible for protecting the United States from terrorist threats, enforcing the criminal laws of the United States, and providing leadership and support to Federal, State, local, and international law enforcement agencies.

Background

President Theodore Roosevelt's Administration established the FBI (originally known as the Bureau of Investigation) in 1908 as a force of Special Agents to fight crime and corruption during what historians came to call America's Progressive Era. Over the ensuing years—during the 48-year directorship of J. Edgar Hoover—the FBI grew rapidly, assuming a broad set of responsibilities: investigating suspects who attempted to evade prosecution by crossing State lines; counterespionage, domestic intelligence, and enforcing the draft during wartime; tracking criminals by means of fingerprint identification records; fighting organized crime; conducting background investigations on present and prospective government employees; using forensic science to assist state and local law enforcement agencies; and conducting civil rights investigations.

During the post-Watergate era, the FBI focused its broad responsibilities on three priorities: foreign counterintelligence, organized crime, and white-collar crime.[1] In 1982, following the increase of terrorist incidents worldwide, FBI Director William H. Webster added counterterrorism as a fourth FBI priority. Webster also beefed up the FBI's efforts to counter political corruption (as reflected in ABSCAM and other operations), as well as investigating financial fraud during the Savings & Loan crisis of the 1980s. In the late 1980s, drug investigations and violent crime became the FBI's fifth and sixth priorities. In the 1990s, FBI Director Louis Freeh forged strong international law enforcement partnerships with European nations and the newly independent Russia to enhance efforts against terrorism, drug trafficking, and organized crime. At the end of the decade, the FBI's National Infrastructure Protection Center was established to investigate cybercrimes.[2]

The September 11 terrorist attacks and subsequent recommendations of the 9/11 Commission led to major changes at the FBI. The foremost was realigning Bureau resources and personnel to *counterterrorism*—the new top priority. In FY 2007, more than one-third of the Bureau's $6 billion budget is dedicated to counterterrorism.[3]

Issue: Has the FBI made Progress on Counterterrorism since 9/11?

The 9/11 Commission reported that "in the summer of 2001, DCI Tenet, the Counterterrorist Center, and the Counterterrorism Security Group did their utmost to sound a loud alarm, its basis being intelligence indicting that al Qaeda planned something big. But . . . FBI field offices apparently saw no abnormal terrorist activity, and headquarters was not shaking them up."[4] Based on this failure, the Commission recommended the following:

> A specialized and integrated national security workforce should be established at the FBI consisting of agents, analysts, linguists, and surveillance specialists who are recruited, trained, rewarded, and retained to ensure the development of an institutional culture imbued with a deep expertise in intelligence and national security.[5]

However, the Commission added a caveat:

> Our recommendation to leave counterterrorism intelligence collection in the United States with the FBI still depends on an assessment that the FBI—if it makes an all-out effort to institutionalize change—can do the job.[6]

The paramount issue currently confronting the FBI is whether the Bureau has made swift and significant progress in realigning its resources and personnel to fulfill its lead responsibility in domestic counterterrorism. It should therefore be a matter of grave concern to all Americans that the 9/11 Commission, in its December 2005 follow-up "report card," found that efforts to create an FBI national security workforce deserved a grade of "C":

> The FBI's shift to a counterterrorism posture is far from institutionalized, and significant deficiencies remain. Reforms are at risk from inertia and complacency; they must be accelerated, or they will fail. Unless there is improvement in a reasonable period of time, Congress will have to look at alternatives.[7]

More recently, the GAO has reported deficiencies in the FBI's efforts to launch "Sentinel," a database designed to "meet the Bureau's pressing need for a modern, automated capability to support its field agents and intelligence analysts' investigative case management and information sharing requirements."[8] Sentinel is intended to replace the FBI's failed Virtual Case File (VCF) program.

DEA, ATF, and U.S. Marshals Service

FY 2007 DOJ Spending for
DEA: $1.8 billion • ATF: $1.0 billion • U.S. Marshals: $825 million

---

See www.GovBudget.com for updated numbers.

In a Nutshell

In addition to the FBI, the DOJ is home to three smaller law enforcement organizations with highly defined missions. The **Drug Enforcement Administration** (DEA) is the lead Federal agency tasked with reducing the supply and abuse of illegal drugs through drug interdiction and seizing of revenues and assets from drug traffickers. In discharging these responsibilities, the

DEA works closely with Federal, State, local, and foreign law enforcement officers. The **Bureau of Alcohol, Tobacco, Firearms, and Explosives** (ATF) is the lead law enforcement agency charged with administering and enforcing Federal laws related to the manufacture, importation, and distribution of firearms and explosives, as well as alcohol and tobacco. ATF also investigates arson cases where there is a Federal interest involved. The **U.S. Marshals Service** (USMS) has broad law enforcement and judicial security responsibilities that include protecting judges, witnesses, and jurors, as well apprehending fugitives and seizing forfeited property.

Background

Drug Enforcement Administration. The mission of the DEA is to enforce U.S. drug laws and to bring to justice organizations and individuals involved in growing, manufacturing, or distributing illegal drugs. In practical terms, this includes investigating and apprehending major drug traffickers and members of drug gangs; managing a national drug intelligence program; seizing illegal drugs and assets connected with drug trafficking; coordinating drug enforcement investigations with Federal, State, and local agencies; and engaging in joint operations— such as crop eradication and substitution—with drug enforcement authorities in foreign countries. (DEA has 57 offices in foreign countries.)

Much of DEA's work is focused on the southwest border with Mexico, where they estimate 85% of illegal drugs are smuggled into the United States. DEA has nearly 11,000 employees, about half of whom are special agents. [9] The DEA's $1.8 billion budget is reviewed as a part of the broader, multiagency National Drug Control Program Budget developed by the Director of the Office of National Drug Control Policy (ONDCP), located in the Executive Office of the President.[10] According to ONDCP, about two-thirds of the $12 billion National Drug Control Budget is expended to disrupt the *supply* of illegal drugs and about one-third on reducing *demand*.

Bureau of Alcohol, Tobacco, Firearms, and Explosives. ATF was transferred in 2003 from the Treasury Department to the Department of Justice. As a law enforcement agency, ATF is tasked with investigating and reducing crime involving firearms and explosives, acts of arson,

---

STATUS: "THE WAR ON DRUGS"

In 2006, an estimated 20.4 million Americans aged 12 or older were current illicit drug users, meaning they had used an illicit drug during the month prior to the survey interview. This estimate represents 8.3% of the population aged 12 years old or older.[11]

"Efforts to significantly reduce the flow of illicit drugs from abroad into the U.S. have so far not succeeded. Moreover, over the past decade, worldwide production of illicit drugs has risen dramatically: opium and marijuana production has roughly doubled and coca production tripled."—Congressional Research Service[12]

The international Monetary Fund estimates that money laundering, the process drug traffickers use to conceal their drug money in legitimate financial markets, amounts to about $600 billion annually.[13]

and illegal trafficking of alcohol and tobacco products. ATF also has regulatory authority covering explosives storage facilities. More than 5.5 billion pounds of explosives are used each year in the United States by private sector and government entities. (ATF's former tax collection responsibilities remain in the Treasury Department.)

The ATF operates numerous programs to fight gun and arson crimes. One program is the National Integrated Ballistic Information Network, which uses ATF's Integrated Ballistic Identification System (IBIS) to identify and compare gun crime evidence in Federal, State, and local criminal investigations. Another ATF program, the Violent Crime Impact Teams (VCIT), operates in 22 cities nationwide to target gun crime "hot spots." In addition to its domestic responsibilities, ATF frequently assists foreign governments investigating crimes involving explosives.

U.S. Marshals Service. USMS is the nation's oldest Federal law enforcement agency, dating back to 1789 when it was established by the first Congress. During its first century, it had expansive and diverse responsibilities, including law enforcement in U.S. territories, taking the census, disseminating presidential proclamations, and protecting the borders.

A major priority for the Service is protecting the nation's Federal judiciary. There are 94 presidentially appointed U.S. Marshals, one for each Federal judicial district, supported by more than 3,000 deputy marshals. Among their current duties, marshals arrest more than half of all Federal fugitives (arresting more than 35,000 in 2005), protect Federal judges, operate the Witness Security Program, transport Federal prisoners, and seize property acquired by criminals through illegal activities. Currently, a high-profile issue for USMS is improving security for Federal judges following the murders of family members of a Chicago Federal judge in 2005.

Federal Prison System

FY 2007 Spending for the Federal Prison System: $5.4 Billion

See www.GovBudget.com for updated numbers.

More people now live in U.S. prisons and jails than in Wyoming, Vermont, and Alaska combined.[14]

In a Nutshell

The Justice Department's Bureau of Prisons maintains Federal penal institutions nationwide.

Background

As of 2007, there were nearly 194,000 *Federal* inmates in 114 penal institutions.[15] However, this is only a fraction of the total prison population in the United States. According to the Bureau of Justice Statistics, as of June 2006, more than *2.2 million prisoners* were held in Federal or State prisons or in local jails.[16] The U.S. prison population far exceeds that of any developed nation, as reflected in table 3-10.1.[17] Moreover, the U.S. prison population is projected to continue its rapid growth, with the number of Federal inmates projected to grow by 10% between 2007 and 2010.

TABLE 3-10.1 U.S. Prison Population Rate Compared with Other OECD Nations

| | *Prison Population Rate: Number per 100,000 Population* | | |
	1992	*1998*	*2004*
United States	505	669	725
Poland	153	148	210
Mexico	98	133	178
UK	90	125	139
Spain	90	114	138
OECD Average	**102**	**122**	**132**
Korea	130	152	121
Canada	123	126	107
Turkey	54	102	100
Italy	81	85	97
Germany	71	96	96
France	84	86	91
Greece	61	68	82
Switzerland	79	85	81
Sweden	63	60	81
Norway	58	57	65
Japan	37	40	58

Source: OECD Factbook 2007.

Issues

Dividing the number of *Federal* inmates (about 200,000) into the $5.4 billion annual budget for the Bureau of Prisons, the current cost per Federal inmate is $27,000 per year. In order to incarcerate a Federal inmate for a 10-year sentence costs well over a quarter million dollars.

The U.S. prison system rarely receives close scrutiny by Members of Congress or the media, yet many Federal prison issues deserve serious, sustained, and thoughtful examination:

1. Why is the U.S. prison population radically higher than that of any other developed nation? (Snapshot of U.S. prison population: According to the Bureau of Justice statistics, in 2003: Fifty-two percent of *State* inmates were incarcerated for violent crimes, 21% for property crimes, 20% for drug crimes, and 7% for public-order crimes.[18] By contrast, more than half of all *Federal* inmates are incarcerated for drug offenses.[19])
2. Considering the staggering public costs of incarcerating 200,000 Federal inmates and more than 2.2 million total inmates, might there have been effective ways to invest public funds early in the lives of these inmates in ways that could have avoided at least some of the criminal activity? Are there better ways to facilitate reentry into society that could reduce the recidivism rate? With regard to drug offenders, compare the $27,000 per year incarceration cost with the $6,800 cost for long-term residential drug treatment.[20]
3. Another ongoing issue deserving the attention of policymakers is prison overcrowding. Bureau of Prisons facilities are estimated to be operating at *36% above capacity* in FY 2007.[21]

United States Attorneys and DOJ Legal Activities

FY 2007 Spending on General Legal Activities and U.S. Attorneys: $2.3 Billion

See www.GovBudget.com for updated numbers.

In a Nutshell

The litigating divisions at the DOJ and the 94 U.S. Attorneys offices located throughout the United States enforce Federal *criminal laws* and represent the U.S. government in *civil litigation* where the Federal government is a party.

Background

DOJ's budget for the 94 U.S. Attorneys offices in each of the Federal judicial districts is $1.7 billion. Each U.S. Attorney is the *chief Federal law enforcement officer* within his or her Federal judicial district. U.S. Attorneys and their staffs of Assistant U.S. Attorneys (AUSAs) handle a broad range of litigation, including white-collar crime, health care and other program fraud, firearms crimes, public corruption, organized crime, drug trafficking, international and domestic terrorism, crimes against children, immigration violations, discrimination cases, bankruptcies, and Habeas Corpus cases in which the U.S. is defending the detention of an individual.

DOJ's $700 million budget for "general legal activities" supports the operations of the litigating divisions at "main Justice," which are the Antitrust Division, Civil Division (which handles commercial, consumer, immigration, tort, and other litigation involving Federal programs), Civil Rights Division, Criminal Division, Environment and Natural Resources Division, and Tax Division.

Justice Programs: Grants for State and Local Law Enforcement

FY 2007 Spending on Justice Grant Programs: $2.5 Billion

See www.GovBudget.com for updated numbers.

There is one transcendent advantage belonging to the province of the State governments, which alone suffices to place the matter in a clear and satisfactory light—I mean the ordinary administration of criminal and civil justice.—Alexander Hamilton, Federalist No. 17

In a Nutshell

As highlighted by Alexander Hamilton more than two centuries ago, States and localities have the *primary* responsibility for crime prevention and law enforcement, while the Federal government's role is limited. The Department of Justice assists State and local law enforcement agencies through a variety of "Justice programs."

Background

The *State and Local law enforcement assistance program*, funded at $1.3 billion, provides grants, training, and technical assistance to State and local governments to assist them in addressing violent crime, criminal gang activity, and illegal drug activity. Included in this funding is the Violent Crime Reduction Partnership Initiative, aimed at reducing violent crime by forming multijurisdictional law enforcement partnerships, and the Byrne Program, which is a flexible grant program.

The *Office of Violence against Women* administers a competitive grants program, funded at nearly $400 million, designed to support State and local efforts aimed at prevention and prosecution of domestic violence, dating violence, sexual assault, and stalking.

The *Community Oriented Policing Services (COPS) program*, established in 1994 and funded at more than $500 million in FY 2007, awards grants to State and local law enforcement agencies for hiring and training additional police officers in order to advance community policing.

Juvenile Justice programs, funded at $338 million, support State and local efforts designed to reduce juvenile delinquency and crime, protect children from sexual exploitation, and provide treatment and rehabilitative services tailored to the needs of juveniles and their families.

The *DNA Initiative*, funded at over $100 million, is aimed at advancing the use of DNA to solve crimes, protect the innocent, and identify missing persons.

The *Weed and Seed program*, funded at $50 million, supports community based cooperative strategies designed to reduce violent crime, drug abuse, and gang activity.

Smaller programs include *Drug Courts* aimed at judicially supervised rehabilitation of nonviolent offenders; the *Prisoner Re-entry Initiative* designed to help nonviolent offenders return to their communities; and the *Paul Coverdell Grant Program* that assists state and local governments with improving the use of forensic sciences in law enforcement.

Notes

1. "White collar crime refers to non-violent fraudulent enterprises committed by persons while engaged in legitimate occupations." Todd Masse and William Krouse, "The FBI: Past, Present, and Future," RL32095 (Washington, D.C.: Congressional Research Service, October 2, 2003), 32.

2. History of the FBI, http://www.fbi.gov/libref/historic/history/historymain.htm.

3. Derived from data in OMB, *FY 2008 Budget of the United States, Analytical Perspectives* (Washington, D.C.: Office of Management and Budget, February 2007), table 3.5.

4. 9/11 Commission, *Final Report of the National Commission on Terrorist Attacks upon the United States* (New York: Norton, 2004), 359.

5. 9/11 Commission, *Final Report*, 425–26.

6. 9/11 Commission, *Final Report*, 424.

7. Final Report on 9/11 Commission Recommendations, December 5, 2005, www.9-11pdp.org.

8. GAO, "FBI Following a Number of Key Acquisition Practices on New Case Management System, but Improvements Still Needed," GO-07-912 (Washington, D.C.: July 2007), highlights. See also GAO, "FBI Needs to Address Weaknesses in Critical Network," GAO-07-368 (Washington, D.C.: April 2007); and GAO, "FBI Has Largely Staffed Key Modernization Program, but Strategic Approach to Managing Program's Human Capital Is Needed," GAO-07-19 (Washington, D.C.: October 2006).

9. http://www.dea.gov/agency/staffing.htm.

10. Mark Eddy, "War on Drugs: Reauthorization of the Office of National Drug Control Policy," RL32352 (Washington, D.C.: Congressional Research Service, January 31, 2007), 12–13.

11. SAMHSA: http://www.oas.samhsa.gov/nsduh/2k6nsduh/2k6Results.pdf.

12. Raphael Perl, "Drug Control: International Policy and Approaches," IB88093 (Washington, D.C.: Congressional Research Service, February 2, 2006), summary page.

13. DEA: http://www.dea.gov/programs/moneyp.htm.

14. Eric Lotke and Peter Wagner, "Prisoners of the Census: Electoral and Financial Consequences of Counting Prisoners Where They Go, Not Where They Come From," *Pace Law Review* 24, no. 587: 588.

15. William Krouse, "Commerce, Justice, Science, and Related Agencies: FY 2008 Appropriations," RL34092 (Washington, D.C.: Congressional Research Service, September 7, 2007), 38.

16. http://www.ojp.usdoj.gov/bjs/prisons.htm.

17. Organisation for Economic Co-Operation and Development, *OECD Factbook 2007* (Paris: 2007).

18. http://www.ojp.usdoj.gov/bjs/prisons.htm.

19. U.S. Department of Justice, "State of the Bureau: 2005" (Washington, D.C.: Federal Bureau of Prisons, 2005), 51.

20. See Larry Schulenberg, "Are We Getting Our Money's Worth?" Federal Prison Policy Project, www.fppp.org, June 2005, 6.

21. Krouse, "Commerce, Justice, Science," 38.

Environment, Energy, and Natural Resources

We are prone to speak of the resources of this country as inexhaustible; this is not so.
—President Theodore Roosevelt, 1907[1]

The budget for environment, energy, and natural resources for FY 2007 was $35 billion, funding the Environmental Protection Agency, energy research, regulation of nuclear power, the Forest Service and National Park Service, the Fish and Wildlife Service, and related programs.

FIGURE 3-11.1 Environmental Protection Agency Spending (billions of dollars)

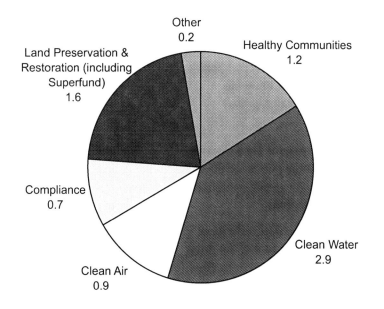

FY 2007 EPA spending allocated among EPA's five major goals: clean water, clean air, healthy communities, land preservation and restoration, and compliance initiatives.

Environmental Protection Agency

FY 2007 Spending for the EPA: $7.7 Billion

See www.GovBudget.com for updated numbers.

In a Nutshell

The core functions of the Environmental Protection Agency (EPA) include regulatory, research, and grant programs to serve as the public's advocate for clean air, clean water, cleanup of hazardous wastes, and control of toxic substances.

EPA's Spending by Budget Item	Purpose of Spending	FY 2007 Budget Authority
Grants to States	Two-thirds of this grants funding is used to capitalize the Clean Water and Safe Drinking Water Revolving Funds, which make low-interest loans to States (and Indian tribes) for construction of wastewater treatment and safe drinking water infrastructure.	$3.2 billion
Environmental programs and management	This appropriation supports programs on each of EPA's five core goals: clean air, clean water, land preservation and restoration, assisting communities at risk, and compliance with environmental laws.	$2.4 billion
Superfund	Congress established the "Superfund" to clean up contamination of sites that pose significant threats to health and the environment. Superfund pays for cleanup of sites where no financially viable responsible party can be identified or located.	$1.2 billion
Science and technology	Science and tech programs fund research and technology to provide a scientific basis for EPA's clean air, clean water, and other environmental regulations.	$764 million
Leaking Underground Storage Tank Trust Fund	Provides funds to remediate leaks from underground petroleum tanks. The Trust Fund is financed by a 0.1 cent per gallon tax on motor fuels.	$100 million

EPA's Spending by Budget Item	Purpose of Spending	FY 2007 Budget Authority
Other spending	Includes Office of Inspector General, and buildings & facilities	$90 million
TOTAL EPA Budget Authority (FY 2007)		**$7.7 billion**[2]

See www.GovBudget.com for updated numbers.

Background

As reflected in figure 3-11.1, EPA's state grants, environmental programs, and other expenditures are aimed at five major environmental goals:

1. *Clean air* activities include research to provide a scientific basis for EPA's national air quality standards and to understand effects of air pollutants on human health, development of technologies for cleaner and more efficient cars, programs aimed at reducing the quantity of toxic air pollutants emitted from industrial and manufacturing processes, efforts to improve indoor air quality, and competitive grants to locales that have not achieved National Air Quality Standards.
2. *Clean and safe water* activities include research to provide a scientific basis for EPA's water quality and safe drinking water standards, strategies to protect the U.S. water supply, programs to promote cost-effective solutions to local and regional water problems, and grants to capitalize the Clean Water State Revolving Funds (SRFs) and Drinking Water SRFs, which provide low-interest loans for construction of wastewater treatment and safe drinking water infrastructure.
3. *Land preservation and restoration* includes research to advance EPA' ability to accurately assess risks posed by contaminated sediments and to study the spread of contaminants through groundwater; programs to reduce waste generation at its source, recycle waste, prevent spills of toxic materials, clean up contaminated properties, and reduce leakage from underground storage tanks; and grants to assist States in implementing hazardous waste programs. Included in this area is EPA's *Superfund Program*, established to clean up contamination at sites that pose significant threats and where no financially viable responsible party can be identified or located.
4. *Healthy Communities* includes efforts to protect or restore the health of communities through research on pesticides, mercury, and other toxic substances; programs to develop safer chemicals; and grants to States to restore bodies of water, reduce exposure to lead, and support "Brownfields" projects (tracts of land developed for industrial purposes, polluted, then abandoned).
5. *Compliance* includes EPA's efforts to improve environmental performance through incentives to governments, businesses, and the public; programs to prevent pollution-at-the-source; collaboration with industry to build pollution prevention into the design of new manufacturing processes; and grants to States to promote compliance with environmental laws.

Energy Programs

FY 2007 Spending on (nondefense) Energy Programs: $8.3 billion

See www.GovBudget.com for updated numbers.

In a Nutshell

Nearly two-thirds ($16 billion) of the Department of Energy's (DOE) $24 billion budget is appropriated for *defense-related* nuclear weapons activities (reviewed in chapter 3-1). The remaining one-third ($8 billion) is dedicated to civilian energy programs, including sophisticated research on a broad range of alternative energy sources (e.g., hydrogen, biofuels, solar, wind, geothermal, hydro/ocean energy), new technologies to improve productivity and reduce emissions and waste from fossil fuels and nuclear power, and incentives to expand the use of nuclear power as one means of addressing global warming.

Background

As reflected in table 3-11.1, the $8.3 billion in *nondefense* expenditures by the Department of Energy consists of $6.5 billion in basic science and energy research, $1.1 billion in associated environmental cleanup costs, and $164 million to maintain the Strategic Petroleum Reserve.

TABLE 3-11.1 Department of Energy Programs (Nondefense)[3]

Energy Budget Item	Purpose of Spending	FY 2007 Budget Authority
Office of Science (Basic Research)	Conducts basic scientific research in six program areas: • Basic energy sciences ($1.3 b); • High-energy physics ($752 m); • Biological and environmental research ($484 m); • Nuclear physics ($423m); • Fusion energy sciences ($319m); and • Advanced scientific computing ($283 m)	$3.797 billion
Energy efficiency and renewable energy (EERE)	The EERE program is aimed at reducing America's dependence on imported energy by developing renewable fuels (e.g., hydrogen, biofuels, solar, wind, geothermal, hydro/ocean energy) and improving energy efficiency of vehicles and buildings.	$1.474 billion
Electricity delivery and energy reliability	Energy storage technologies in support of intermittent wind and solar power production.	$137 million

TABLE 3-11.1 Department of Energy Programs (Nondefense) (Continued)

Energy Budget Item	Purpose of Spending	FY 2007 Budget Authority
Fossil energy R&D	A significant portion of this R&D is related to high-tech coal utilization, including "clean coal" technologies that capture greenhouse gases.	$593 million
Nuclear energy	R&D intended to secure nuclear energy as a long-term viable commercial energy option; also includes assistance with costs of regulatory approval to incentivize new reactors.	$482 million
	SUBTOTAL: Energy Research & Development	**$6.5 billion**
Uranium decontamination and decommissioning	Funds projects to decontaminate and remediate plants at Portsmouth, Ohio; Peducah, Kentucky; and Oak Ridge, Tennessee.	$557 million
Nondefense environmental cleanup	DOE's expenditures for managing the environmental cleanup of fossil energy project sites.	$350 million
Nuclear waste disposal (Office of Civilian Radioactive Waste Management)	Funds to develop a deep geologic nuclear waste repository at Yucca Mountain, Nevada. The long-delayed project is now aiming to be operational in 2017.	$99 million[4]
Other	Includes Legacy Management (long-term monitoring of sites) and other smaller programs.	$61 million
	SUBTOTAL: Environmental Cleanup Subtotal	**$1.1 billion**
Strategic Petroleum Reserve	Created in response to the 1973–1974 Arab oil embargo; about 700 million barrels are stored in hollowed-out salt domes in Louisiana and Texas.	$164 million
Other	Other nondefense expenditures by the Department of Energy, including Power Marketing Administrations.[5]	$583 million
TOTAL Budget Authority: (Nondefense) DOE Programs (FY 2007)		**$8.3 billion**

See www.GovBudget.com for updated numbers.

Federal energy expenditures also include the activities of the Nuclear Regulatory Commission (NRC) and the Federal Energy Regulatory Commission (FERC).

The NRC, with a budget of more than $800 million, is an independent regulatory agency that formulates policies and regulations governing the civilian use of nuclear materials, and licenses and oversees nuclear power plants. A less visible agency for the last 30 years, NRC's activities are now increasing as it reviews the first applications for new nuclear power plants since the 1970s. Nuclear power, which currently generates one-fifth of U.S. electricity, is increasingly being considered as an alternative to burning fossil fuels, given the growing con-

---

FEDERAL EXPENDITURES ON BASIC SCIENCE, RESEARCH AND DEVELOPMENT

The more than $5 billion spent by the Energy Department's Office of Science and the EERE program is a major component of the Federal Government's investment in basic science and research. The other major Federal investments in science and research are conducted by

- The Department of Defense with an RDT&E budget of *$77 billion*;[6]
- The National Institutes of Health (NIH), with a budget of *$28.8 billion*;[7]
- The National Aeronautics and Space Administration (NASA) with a "science, aeronautics, and exploration" budget of *$9.1 billion*;[8]
- The National Science Foundation (NSF), which supports basic science with a research budget of about *$4.6 billion*;[9]
- The National Oceanic and Atmospheric Administration (NOAA), an agency in the Department of Commerce, which invests nearly *$800 million* in research to understand and predict changes in the Earth's environment;[10]
- The U.S. Geological Survey (USGS), an agency in the Department of Interior, which invests more than *$500 million* annually in research on changing terrain, geologic hazards, and water resources;[11] and
- The National Institute of Standards and Technology (NIST), an agency in the Department of Commerce, which invests more than *$600 million* annually developing measurement standards essential to many areas of research, development, and engineering.[12]
- Other research is conducted by the Departments of Agriculture ($2.6 billion), Homeland Security *($1.2 billion)*, Transportation *($800 million)*, and EPA *($600 million)*.[13]

While the combined resources of these agencies and programs amounts to more than $130 billion annually, there is an ongoing and vigorous debate among policymakers and researchers about whether the U.S. is making a sufficient investment in basic science and research. The National Academy of Sciences recently reported to Congress that "in a world where advanced knowledge is widespread and low-cost labor is readily available, U.S. advantages in the marketplace and in science and technology have begun to erode. A comprehensive and coordinated federal effort is urgently needed to bolster U.S. competitiveness and pre-eminence in these areas."[14]

cerns about global warming. In addition, nuclear power is increasingly attractive economically due to improving reactor efficiency, higher prices for natural gas, pollution abatement requirements that could be imposed on coal, and tax incentives and loan guarantees included in the Energy Policy Act of 2005.[15] However, a vexing issue that continues to complicate the nuclear energy debate is whether the proposed Yucca Mountain nuclear waste repository can safely sequester nuclear waste for thousands of years.[16]

FERC, an independent agency within the Department of Energy, regulates key interstate aspects of the electric power, natural gas, oil pipeline, and hydropower industries. FERC's costs are covered by fees paid by regulated businesses.

Natural Resources: Stewardship of Public Lands, Waterways, and Wildlife

In a Nutshell

The Federal Government owns 672 million acres—30% of the land in the United States—most of which is in the West and Alaska. Four agencies administer nearly all of this land: the *Forest Service*, the *National Park Service*, the *Bureau of Land Management*, and the *Fish and Wildlife Service*, with combined budgets totaling more than $10 billion. The responsibility for maintaining and improving U.S. waterways belongs to the *Army Corps of Engineers*. The management of "offshore" Federal lands (the Outer Continental Shelf) belongs to the *Minerals Management Service*. The *Fish and Wildlife Service* protects fish, wildlife, plants, and their habitats.

Background

As reflected in figure 3-11.2, seven Federal agencies share the responsibilities for stewardship of America's vast natural resources:[17]

- *The Forest Service* (FS), located in the Department of Agriculture, manages a network of 155 National Forests covering 192 million acres—more than one-quarter of all public lands. The annual Forest Service budget is $4.8 billion, which funds the administration of FS lands for multiple uses, including recreation, logging, grazing, watershed protection, and fish and wildlife protection. More than $2 billion is dedicated to fighting forest fires.
- *The National Park Service* (NPS), in the Department of the Interior (DOI), administers 79 million acres of parkland. Park visits total 271 million annually. The NPS $2.3 billion budget includes park operations, U.S. Park Police, recreation and preservation, construction, and land acquisition.
- *The Bureau of Land Management* (BLM), in DOI, administers 262 million acres of public lands (13% of total U.S. land) used for energy and mineral development, logging, livestock grazing, fish and wildlife habitat, wilderness preservation, archaeological research, and recreation. BLM's annual budget is $1.9 billion.
- *The Fish and Wildlife Service* (FWS), in DOI, works to ensure the conservation and protection of fish, wildlife, plants, and their habitats through oversight of the 95-million-acre National Wildlife Refuge System and implementation of the Endangered Species Program. The annual FWS budget is $1.3 billion.

FIGURE 3-11.2 FY 2007 Spending on Stewardship of Natural Resources (billions of dollars)

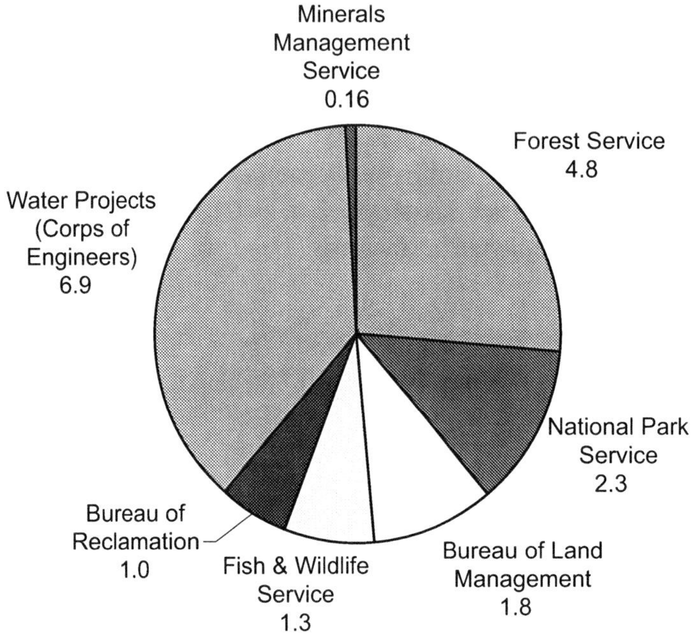

See www.GovBudget.com for updated numbers

- *The Bureau of Reclamation*, in DOI, constructs dams, power plants, and canals. With a budget of nearly $1 billion, the Bureau is the largest wholesaler of water in the country and the second-largest producer of hydroelectric power in the western United States.
- *The Minerals Management Service* (MMS), in DOI, administers leasing of offshore Federal lands (the Outer Continental Shelf) for extraction of oil, gas, and other minerals. The MMS annual budget is $160 million.
- *The Army Corps of Engineers*, in the Department of Defense,[18] is responsible for maintaining and improving the nation's waterways. With a budget of nearly $7 billion in FY 2007,[19] the Corps' original mission of improving and maintaining navigable channels has been expanded to include flood control, emergency and disaster response, environmental restoration, and municipal water infrastructure.[20] Many projects require cost sharing with state and local entities; depending on the type of project, the Federal share can range from 40% to 100% of project costs.[21] (The Corps' budget also has the distinction of being the most heavily earmarked budget of the Federal government; see chapter 2-8 on congressional earmarks).

Notes

1. Lewis Eigen and Jonathan Siegel, *The Macmillan Dictionary of Political Quotations* (New York: Macmillan, 1993), 164.

2. David Bearden and Robert Esworthy, "EPA: FY 2007 Appropriations Highlights," RS22386 (Washington, D.C., Congressional Research Service, June 1, 2007), 2.

3. Source: Carl Behrens, "Energy and Water Development: FY 2008 Appropriations," RL34009 (Washington, D.C.: Congressional Research Service, July 13, 2007).

4. The defense nuclear waste disposal program spent $347 million on the Yucca mountain project, which will serve as a nuclear waste depository for both civilian and defense nuclear waste. Behrens, "Energy and Water Development," 29.

5. Other nondefense expenditures include Power Marketing Administrations (PMAs), Inspector General, General Administration, Energy Information, Northeast Home Heating Oil Reserve, and Naval Petroleum and Oil Shale Reserves. Behrens, "Energy and Water Development," table 7. DOE operates four PMAs that sell wholesale electric power to publicly or cooperatively owned utilities. Nic Lane, "Power Marketing Administrations: Background and Current Issues," RS22564 (Washington, D.C.: Congressional Research Service, January 3, 2007), 1.

6. See table 3-1.1.

7. See table 3-6.7 and figure 3-6.3.

8. The total NASA budget is $16.3 billion. In addition to the science and aeronautics budget, NASA has an "exploration" budget of $6.2 billion that funds space operations, including the space shuttle, the International Space Station, and space and flight support.

9. NSF supports science and engineering and funds basic research, most of which is conducted at U.S. universities. NSF supports the construction of research facilities and equipment, including super-computer centers, earth simulators, and observatories. Source for the $4.6 billion figure: Michael Davey, "Federal Research and Development Funding: FY 2007," RL33345 (Washington, D.C.: Congressional Research Service, March 13, 2007), 21.

10. The mission of NOAA is to understand and predict changes in the Earth's environment and conserve and manage coastal and marine resources to meet our nation's economic, social, and environmental needs. Source for the $800 million figure: Davey, "Federal Research and Development Funding," 26.

11. The USGS provides research and scientific data to support the Interior Department's management of U.S. land and water resources. USGS focuses on changing terrain, geologic hazards, water resources, and management of biological resources.

12. The National Institute of Standards and Technology researches measurement standards and provides standard reference materials for U.S. industry and researchers. Programs include the Center for Neutron Research and the Center for Nanoscale Science and Technology.

13. Davey, "Federal Research and Development Funding," tables 1, 7, 10, and 12.

14. National Academy of Sciences, "Rising above the Gathering Storm: Energizing and Employing America for a Brighter Economic Future," 2007, available online at www.nap.edu/catalog.php?record _id=11463#description.

15. Larry Parker and Mark Holt, "Nuclear Power: Outlook for New U.S. Reactors," RL33442 (Washington, D.C.: Congressional Research Service, March 9, 2007), summary page. See also Mark Holt, "Nuclear Energy Policy," RL33558 (Washington, D.C.: Congressional Research Service, July 12, 2007).

16. See Mark Holt, "Civilian Nuclear Waste Disposal," RL33461 (Washington, D.C.: Congressional Research Service, July 9, 2007).

17. See Carol Hardy Vincent, "Federal Land Management Agencies: Background on Land and Resources Management," RL32393 (Washington, D.C.: Congressional Research Service, August 2, 2004).

18. While operating as part of the Army, the Corps has a largely civilian workforce. Nicole Carter and Betsy Cody, "The Civil Works Program of the Army Corps of Engineers: A Primer," RS20866 (Washington, D.C.: Congressional Research Service, September 20, 2006), 1.

19. Including FY 2007 supplemental appropriations.

20. Carter and Cody, "The Civil Works Program of the Army Corps of Engineers," 1.

21. Carter and Cody, "The Civil Works Program of the Army Corps of Engineers," table 1.

Farm Programs

Were we directed from Washington when to sow, and when to reap, we should soon want bread. —Thomas Jefferson, 1821[1]

FY 2007 Spending on Farm Programs: $29 billion

See www.GovBudget.com for updated numbers.

As reflected in the quote from Thomas Jefferson, the debate over the appropriate amount of Federal involvement in the agricultural sector is as old as the Republic. Currently, the Department of Agriculture (USDA) provides substantial support to farmers in the United States through a variety of farm programs, including three types of commodity payments aimed at stabilizing farm income; conservation programs to protect soil, water, and other natural resources; marketing and export promotion programs; crop insurance to protect against crop failure; direct and guaranteed loans; and disaster relief (see figure 3.12-1).

The commodity programs, crop insurance, and most of the conservation programs are mandatory spending; that is, the spending levels are *determined directly by authorizing legislation, without going through the annual appropriations process.* The relevant authorizing legislation is the multiyear "Farm Bill" drafted about every five years by the *authorizing* committees in the House and Senate (the House Agriculture Committee and the Senate Agriculture Nutrition and Forestry Committee). The remaining programs are discretionary spending, with spending levels set by the *annual* Agriculture-Rural Development-FDA Appropriations bill.[2]

Commodity Programs: Farm Price and Income Supports

In a Nutshell

The Commodity Credit Corporation (CCC), located in the Department of Agriculture (USDA), makes farm commodity payments to stabilize farm income which is vulnerable to the

FIGURE 3-12.1 FY 2007 Spending on Farm Programs (billions of dollars)[2]

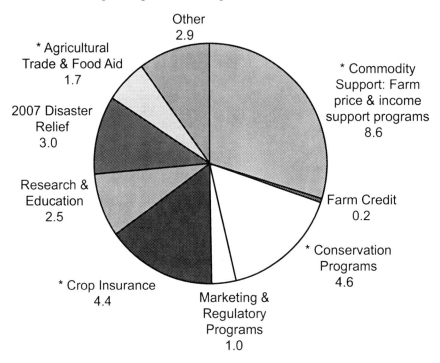

Other
2.9

* Agricultural
Trade & Food Aid
1.7

2007 Disaster
Relief
3.0

Research &
Education
2.5

* Crop Insurance
4.4

Marketing &
Regulatory
Programs
1.0

* Commodity
Support: Farm
price & income
support programs
8.6

Farm Credit
0.2

* Conservation
Programs
4.6

[* includes mandatory spending]

agriculture sector's inherently unstable prices and production. There are three types of commodity payments estimated to cost $8.6 billion[4] in FY 2007: (1) direct payments, (2) countercyclical payments, and (3) marketing assistance loans.

Background

Why does the farm sector receive special assistance? The economic justification for Federal price supports for farm commodities, in contrast to other goods and services, is that farm markets

> do not efficiently balance commodity supply with demand. Imbalances in agricultural markets develop because consumers do not respond to price changes by buying proportionally smaller or larger quantities and, similarly, farmers do not respond to price changes by proportionally reducing or increasing production. The imbalances then often result in inadequate or exaggerated resource adjustments by farmers. The imbalances are further exacerbated by the long time lag between crop planting (or livestock breeding) and harvest, during which economic and yield conditions may dramatically change.[5]

The farm commodity programs were therefore enacted to stabilize and support farm incomes by shifting some of the risks of market fluctuations to the Federal government.

THE COMMODITY CREDIT CORPORATION

The USDA's Commodity Credit Corporation (CCC) is not a program; rather, it is a funding mechanism. USDA's commodity price and income support programs, as well as certain conservation and trade programs, are funded by CCC which has a $30 billion line of credit with the United States Treasury. CCC receives an annual appropriation to replenish its line of credit. CCC's line of credit allows USDA programs to operate smoothly and without delay, despite the fact that commodity program price and income supports—which are tied to rapidly changing market prices—cannot be accurately projected in advance.

Commodity price supports are concentrated in five commodities: corn, cotton, soybeans, wheat, and rice (accounting for over 85% of government commodity payments).[6] In order to receive payments, individuals must share in the risk of producing a crop and comply with land and resource conservation requirements (discussed later).

Commodity program outlays vary dramatically from year to year because the payments are used to compensate for highly variable commodity prices. For example, outlays for corn price supports varied from a recent low of $1.4 billion in FY 2003 to a high of $8.9 billion in FY 2006.[7] However, in FY 2007, corn price supports dropped by almost half because of higher crop prices resulting from strong demand from abroad, increased demand for ethanol, and crop damage due to bad weather.[8]

There are three types of farm commodity payments:

1. *Annual direct payments* based on historical production (unrelated to current production or prices);
2. *Countercyclical payments,* adopted in the 2002 farm bill, are triggered when prices fall below target prices; and
3. *A marketing assistance loan program* that effectively guarantees a minimum price for the crop. (Producers take out marketing loans at harvest using their crops as collateral. The amount of the loan is tied to a minimum price for the crop. If the market price subsequently drops below the minimum, CCC covers the shortfall through partial forgiveness of the loan.)

Each commodity payment has an annual payment limit per farm or farmer, but as a practical matter, the limits are not effective because large farms can be reorganized into separate entities to circumvent the limits.[9]

Farm price supports are controversial for a number of reasons. In some years they can be very expensive (nearly $17 billion in 2006); payments are concentrated among a relatively small number of large agribusinesses (in 2005, about 55,000 farms with sales over $500,000 received $5.7 billion)[10]; price supports for milk[11] and sugar[12] maintain prices *above market* levels; some of the payments may conflict with international agreements prohibiting subsidies (although the 2002 Farm Bill gave the Secretary of Agriculture authority to make adjustments in domestic commodity support payments when needed to comply with Uruguay Round[13] Trade Agreements).[14]

Conservation Programs

In a Nutshell

Conservation programs, with an FY 2007 budget of $4.6 billion, are designed to protect soil, water, wildlife, and other natural resources on the nation's vast agricultural lands. The Natural Resources Conservation Service (NRCS) and the Farm Service Agency (FSA) in the USDA administer 20 distinct conservation programs that provide technical or financial assistance to farmers who wish to practice conservation on their agricultural lands. Unlike commodity payments which tend to be concentrated among large producers, conservation payments tend to go to smaller and midsized producers.[15]

Background

Most of the USDA's conservation programs respond to existing resource problems. Some of the conservation funding is used to pay landowners to retire land from production for a period of time. Other funding is aimed at improving resource conditions through contour farming, nutrient management, controlling soil erosion, groundwater and wetlands conservation, grasslands conservation, wildlife habitat protection, tree planting, pest control, irrigation, and waste management. The largest conservation programs are:

- The *Conservation Reserve Program*, a $2 billion program that pays farmers to replace crops on highly erodible and environmentally sensitive land with long-term resource conservation plantings;
- The *Environmental Quality Incentives Program* (EQIP), a $1.0 billion program that provides Federal cost sharing support to farmers and land owners for implementing conservation practices[16]; and
- The *Conservation Operations and Technical Assistance Program*, with over $760 million,[17] which provides technical assistance for conservation planning through USDA field staff.

Crop Insurance and Emergency Assistance

In a Nutshell

The Federal Crop Insurance program, with a $4.4 billion budget, protects farmers from losses caused by drought, flooding, pest infestation, and other natural disasters. In addition to crop insurance, Congress periodically makes additional emergency assistance available to farmers and ranchers—most recently $3 billion in the FY 2007 supplemental appropriations bill.[18]

Background

USDA's Risk Management Agency (RMA) administers the Federal crop insurance program. Under the program, farmers can choose among insurance policies that provide various levels and types of protection—for example, against yield losses only, or against both yield losses and low prices. The insurance policies are sold and serviced by *private insurance companies* that receive reimbursements for administrative expenses from the Federal government. The insurance companies share the underwriting risk with the Federal government and, in theory, can gain or lose depending on the extent of crop losses and claims.

The reality, however, is that the crop insurance program has been rife with waste and abuse. In June 2007 testimony to Congress, the GAO testified that "from 2002 through 2006, USDA paid the insurance companies underwriting gains of $2.8 billion, which represents an average annual rate of return of 17.8 percent. In contrast, according to insurance industry statistics, the benchmark rate of return for companies selling property and casualty insurance was 6.4 percent." The GAO urged Congress to "give RMA authority to periodically renegotiate the financial terms of its agreement with companies to provide reasonable cost allowances and underwriting gains."[19]

Agricultural Research and Education

In a Nutshell

USDA's extensive research and education activities are conducted by four agencies: the *Agricultural Research Service* conducts long-term research; the *Cooperative State Research, Education, and Extension Service* provides Federal funds to Colleges of Agriculture to support State-level research and education; the *Economic Research Service* provides economic analysis of agriculture issues; and the *National Agricultural Statistics Service* collects data to support ongoing research. The combined appropriations for the four agencies amount to $2.5 billion.

Background

The $1.1 billion budget of the Agricultural Research Service (ARS) funds USDA's in-house scientific research aimed at improving the safety of U.S. agricultural products and providing producers with technologies to compete effectively. Specific areas of research include soil and water conservation, genetics and specialty crops, food safety, renewable energy, plant and animal sciences, nutrition and obesity, and information services. More recently, ARS research resources have been focused on homeland security efforts to protect the nation's food supply. In 2006, ARS submitted 83 new patent applications, licensed 25 new products, and developed 51 new plant varieties.[20]

The $1.2 billion budget of the Cooperative State Research, Education, and Extension Service (CSREES) provides Federal research funds to land grant colleges of agriculture. (The land grant system began in 1862 with the Morrill Act, which gave States public lands provided the lands be sold or used for profit and the proceeds used to establish at least one college that would teach agriculture and the mechanical arts.) Close to 60% of the CSREES budget supports State-level research and teaching programs, and the remainder provides funds primarily for continuing education and outreach activities of the "Extension System."

The Economic Research Service has a $75 million budget, and the National Agricultural Statistics Service has a budget of about $150 million.

Marketing and Regulatory Programs

In a Nutshell

USDA's billion-dollar marketing and regulatory budget includes $851 million for the Animal and Plant Health Inspection Service; $38 million for the Grain Inspection, Packers, and Stockyards Administration; and $113 million for the Agricultural Marketing Service.[21]

Background

The Animal and Plant Health Inspection Service (APHIS) is tasked with protecting U.S. agriculture from pests and diseases. In recent years, the APHIS has received considerable funding to lead USDA efforts to monitor and prepare for a possible outbreak of avian influenza. (The other major inspection activity of the USDA is inspecting all meat and poultry sold in the United States. This is conducted by USDA's Food Safety and Inspection Service, discussed in chapter 3-6.)

The Grain Inspection, Packers, and Stockyards Administration sets standards for grain and seeks to ensure competition in livestock and meat markets.

The Agricultural Marketing Service provides funds to trade associations, commodity groups, and for-profit firms to assist them in building markets overseas for a wide variety of U.S. agricultural products.

Myth: The United States has a substantial agricultural trade surplus that helps to offset the general trade imbalance.

Fact: The United States has an agricultural trade surplus, but *less than is commonly assumed.* USDA is projecting agricultural exports of $83.5 billion for FY 2008 and agricultural imports of $75 billion, with a net trade surplus of less than $9 billion.[22] Major export markets are Canada, Mexico, Japan, the European Union, China, South Korea, and Taiwan. The United States' biggest import suppliers are the European Union, Canada, and Mexico.

Agricultural Trade and Food Aid

In a Nutshell

USDA operates food aid programs funded through annual discretionary appropriations ($1.3 billion) and export promotion programs funded directly by the Commodity Credit Corporation ($262 million[23]). Because the export promotion programs are funded through the multiyear Farm Bill, rather than annual appropriations, they are considered to be mandatory (i.e., nondiscretionary) spending.

Background

The export promotion programs, operated by USDA's *Foreign Agriculture Service* (FAS), include the Market Access Program, Export Enhancement Program, the Foreign Market Development Program, and the Export Credit Guarantee Program.

The *Market Access Program* (MAP) subsidizes efforts by private and nonprofit firms to develop foreign markets for U.S. agriculture through advertising, consumer promotions, market research, and technical assistance.

The *Foreign Market Development Program* (FMDP), jointly funded by government and industry groups, is similar to MAP. The principal difference is that unlike MAP, which is oriented toward consumer goods and brand-name products, FMDP is oriented toward bulk commodities.

The *Export Enhancement Program* (EEP) provides export subsidies. Each year FAS announces target countries for EEP subsidies that allow U.S. agricultural exporters to negotiate the sale of commodities with foreign importers *at reduced prices* and then receive a subsidy payment from the CCC to cover the cost of the price reduction. The program was used in the past most often for wheat exports, although use of the program has declined in recent years (due to ongoing U.S. efforts to end agricultural subsidies in global trade).

The *Export Credit Guarantee program* operates as a government loan guarantee program. Private U.S. banks extend financing to countries desiring to purchase U.S. agricultural exports, and the CCC guarantees the loans (i.e., it will repay the loans in the event of a default by the foreign purchaser). In 2005, the major recipients of export credit guarantees were Turkey, Mexico, South Korea, Russia, and China. USDA estimates that in FY 2006 the amount of credit guaranteed was $3.1 billion, although, as explained in chapter 2-5, the actual cost to the government is the anticipated default rate. For example, as of early 2006, Iraq was in default of more than $3 billion of previously extended guarantees.[24]

The principal food aid program, costing $1.2 billion per year, is known as the *P.L. 480*[25] *Food for Peace program*. USDA administers Title I of the program, which provides for long-term, low-interest loans to developing countries for their purchase of U.S. agricultural commodities. Titles II and III of the program, administered by USAID (see chapter 3-13), provides for donation of U.S. agricultural commodities and grants to governments to support long-term growth.[26]

Another discretionary food aid program operated by USDA is the $100 million McGovern-Dole International Food for Education and Child Nutrition Program, which funds school nutrition programs in developing countries.

Farm Credit

In a Nutshell

The Federal government assists farmers to obtain credit in two ways: (1) credit is available through the Farm Credit System, which is a network of borrower-owned lending institutions operating as a government-sponsored enterprise; and (2) USDA's Farm Service Agency makes or guarantees loans to farmers who cannot qualify at other lenders. The annual Federal cost for FSA direct loans and loan guarantees is $150 million.[27]

Background

The Farm Credit System (FCS) is a Federally-chartered, cooperatively owned commercial lender organized to serve the needs of *creditworthy* farmers.

USDA's Farm Service Agency (FSA) provides direct loans and loan guarantees to farmers who do not otherwise qualify for regular commercial credit. FSA is therefore considered to be a *lender of last resort.*

The Congressional Research Service reports that commercial banks are the largest source of farmers' credit (37%), followed by FCS (30%), individuals and others (21%), and life insurance companies (5%). As a lender of last resort, FSA provides a relatively small amount: 3% through direct loans and 4% through loan guarantees.[28]

Notes

1. Lewis Eigen and Jonathan Siegel, *The Macmillan Dictionary of Political Quotations* (New York: Macmillan, 1993), 6.

2. See chapter 2-9 for more background on mandatory versus discretionary spending.

3. The "other" category includes Farm Service Agency salaries and expenses, the Risk Management Agency salaries and expenses, the Tobacco Trust Fund, and other farm programs.

4. Ralph Chite, "Farm Bill Budget and Costs: 2002 vs. 2007," RS22694 (Washington, D.C.: Congressional Research Service, July 17, 2007), 2.

5. Jasper Womach, "Previewing a 2007 Farm Bill," RL33037 (Washington, D.C.: Congressional Research Service, January 3, 2007), 12.

6. Jim Monke, "Farm Commodity Programs and the 2007 Farm Bill," RS21999 (Washington, D.C.: Congressional Research Service, August 3, 2007), 1.

7. Womach, "Previewing," 14.

8. CBO, *Budget Options* (Washington, D.C.: Congressional Budget Office, February 2007), 81.

9. Jim Monke, "Farm Commodity Programs: Direct Payments, Counter-Cyclical Payments, and Marketing Loans," RL33271 (Washington, D.C.: Congressional Research Service, March 1, 2006), summary page.

10. Put another way, 6.2% of the recipient farms received 36% of the payments. Womach, "Previewing," 16.

11. The 2002 Farm Bill authorized a new countercyclical dairy payment program called the Milk Income Loss Contract (MILC) program, under which dairy farmers nationwide are paid whenever the monthly price for milk in a specified market falls below a certain level. In addition, USDA provides dairy export subsidies and USDA purchases of surplus dairy products. Jasper Womach, "The USDA Farm Bill Proposal," RL33916 (Washington, D.C.: Congressional Research Service, March 12, 2007), 7–8.

12. "Sugar utilizes nonrecourse loans and a system of import tariff rate quotas and domestic marketing allotments to limit supplies and support prices." Womach, "Previewing," 16.

13. Under the auspices of the General Agreement on Tariffs and Trade (GATT), the Uruguay Round of international trade negotiations negotiated an ambitious set of trade liberalization agreements—reducing tariffs on industrial goods by an average of 40%, reducing agricultural subsidies, and creating a new global organization, the World Trade Organization (WTO), to monitor and regulate international trade. For background on the Uruguay Round, see http://www.wto.org/english/thewto_e/whatis_e/tif_e/fact5_e.htm.

14. Womach, "The USDA 2007 Farm Bill," 11.

15. This conclusion was reached by the USDA Economic Research Service, as cited in Jeffrey Zinn, "Conservation and the 2007 Farm Bill," RL34060 (Washington, D.C.: Congressional Research Service, July 16, 2007).

16. Jeffrey Zinn and Tadlock Cowan, "Agriculture Conservation Programs: A Scorecard," RL32940 (Washington, D.C., Congressional Research Service, January 3, 2007), 3.

17. Jim Monke, "Agriculture and Related Agencies: FY 2008 Appropriations," RL34132 (Washington, D.C.: Congressional Research Service, August 27, 2007), 39.

18. P.L. 110-28 (H.R. 2206, 110th Congress); Ralph Chite, "Agricultural Disaster Assistance," RS21212 (Washington, D.C.: Congressional Research Service, June 26, 2007), 1.

19. Robert A. Robinson, Testimony before the House Subcommittee on General Farm Commodities and Risk Management, GAO-07-944T (Washington D.C.: Government Accountability Office, June 7, 2007).

20. OMB, *Budget of the United States, Appendix, FY 2008* (Washington, D.C.: Office of Management and Budget, February 2007), 68; and Monke, "Agriculture and Related Agencies," 13.

21. Monke, "Agriculture and Related Agencies," 39.

22. Charles Hanrahan, "U.S. Agricultural Trade: Trends, Composition, Direction, and Policy," 98-253 (Washington, D.C.: Congressional Research Service, September 5, 2007).

23. Ralph Chite, "Farm Bill Budget and Costs: 2002 vs. 2007" RS22694 (Washington, D.C.: Congressional Research Service, July 17, 2007), 1.

24. Charles Hanrahan, "Agricultural Export and Food Aid Programs," IB98006 (Washington, D.C.: Congressional Research Service, March 9, 2006), 6.

25. P.L. 480 is the Agricultural Trade Development and Assistance Act of 1954.

26. Hanrahan, "Agricultural Export," 7.

27. Monke, "Agriculture and Related Agencies," 39.

28. Jim Monke, "Agricultural Credit: Farm Bill Issues," RS21977 (Washington, D.C.: Congressional Research Service, July 25, 2007), 1.

International Affairs

See www.GovBudget.com for updated numbers,

As reflected in figure 3-13.1, the International Affairs budget covers a broad range of programs: State Department and Foreign Service operations, economic development aid, humanitarian aid, military aid, contributions to the United Nations and other international organizations, and international drug control efforts.

Contrary to the widespread misconception that foreign aid is a substantial portion of the Federal Budget[1], humanitarian and economic assistance amount to about $20 billion per year, which is *less than 1% of the Federal Budget*. Moreover, purely humanitarian aid is only 0.3% of the Federal Budget.

FIGURE 3-13.1 FY 2007 Spending on International Affairs Programs
(billions of dollars)

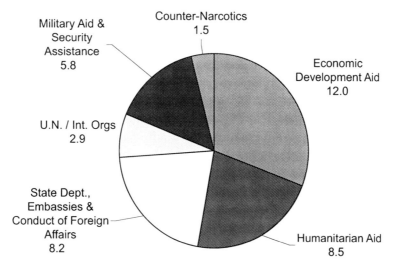

Economic Development Aid

In a Nutshell

Economic Development Aid programs, amounting to about $12 billion, include development assistance, the Economic Support Fund, the Millennium Challenge program, assistance to new democracies in Eastern Europe and states of the Former Soviet Union (FSU), multilateral development banks, the Peace Corps, and USAID operations (see table 3-13.1).

Background and Issues

U.S. Agency for International Development (USAID). United States economic development and humanitarian programs are operated primarily by the U.S. Agency for International Development (USAID), which is an *independent* Federal agency (but closely linked to the State Department, which provides foreign policy guidance). The close coordination of the State Department and USAID was further reinforced in 2006 by the appointment of a "Director of Foreign Assistance" at the State Department, who also serves concurrently as the USAID Administrator. Critics of the new structure are concerned that it will overly politicize aid programs.[2] Supporters of the new structure assert that foreign aid is appropriately viewed as an instrument of foreign policy.

Economic Support Fund (ESF). The ESF, the largest single category of foreign aid, is intended to advance U.S. strategic goals through economic assistance to allies and countries in democratic transition. Principal beneficiaries include Afghanistan, Egypt, Pakistan, Jordan, and Colombia, which together account for two-thirds of all ESF aid.[3]

Millennium Challenge Account. President George W. Bush proposed the creation of the Millennium Challenge Corporation in 2002 to provide assistance, through a competitive selection process, to developing nations pursing political and economic reforms. A key difference from traditional foreign aid is that the grants are intended to be awarded solely based on the performance of the applicant countries and without regard to U.S. foreign policy objectives. The Administration sought about $10 billion for FY 2004–FY 2007; Congress appropriated $6 billion. Recipients have been Madagascar, Honduras, Cape Verde, Nicaragua, Georgia, Benin, Vanuatu, Armenia, Ghana, Mali, El Salvador, Mozambique, Lesotho, Morocco, Mongolia, and Tanzania.[4]

World Bank. The World Bank makes loans and grants to low- and middle-income countries to reduce poverty and promote economic development. It consists of two unique development institutions owned by 185 member countries—the *International Bank for Reconstruction and Development (IBRD)* and the *International Development Association (IDA).* The IBRD focuses on middle-income and creditworthy poor countries, while IDA focuses on the poorest countries in the world. Together they provide low-interest loans, interest-free credit, and grants to developing countries for education, health, infrastructure, and communications. Since the founding of the World Bank, the United States has contributed the largest amount of resources—about $26 billion as of FY 2007.[5] The largest IDA *borrowers* in 2006 were Pakistan, receiving over a billion dollars in new assistance, followed by Vietnam, Tanzania, Ethiopia, India, Bangladesh, Nigeria, Congo, Ghana, and Afghanistan.[6]

TABLE 3-13.1 FY 2007 Funding: Economic Development Aid

Foreign Aid Program	Program Objectives	FY 2007 Funding
Economic Support Fund (ESF)	Provides economic development and stabilization funds to allies, countries making democratic transitions, and countries important in the "Global War on Terror"	$5.1 billion* (includes $2.6 billion supplemental)
Millennium Challenge Account (MCA)	Authorized in 2004, MCA concentrates higher amounts of U.S. aid in a few countries that have demonstrated a strong commitment to political, economic, and social reforms. Aid awarded on a competitive basis.	$1.8 billion
World Bank	U.S. annual contribution to the World Bank	$1.0 billion
Other Multilateral Development Organizations	Includes Asian Development Bank, African Development Bank, African Development Fund, and International Fund for Agricultural Development	$254 million
Development Assistance (DA)	Assist developing countries in several areas: Agriculture, Education, Energy & Technology, Environment, and democratic institutions. Beneficiaries include Afghanistan.	$1.5 billion
Support for East European Democracy (SEED)	Strengthen democratic institutions and market economies in Kosovo, Serbia, Bosnia, Macedonia, and Albania	$488 million*
Independent States of the former Soviet Union (FSA: FREEDOM Support Act[7])	Consolidate the process of political and economic transition to market democracies, and address regional stability issues. Key 2005 beneficiaries: Georgia, Russia, Ukraine, Armenia, and Azerbaijan.	$452 million
Peace Corps	Nearly 200,000 Peace Corps volunteers have been invited by 139 developing countries to provide technical knowledge and training and increase cross-cultural communication.	$320 million

(Continued)

TABLE 3-13.1 FY 2007 Funding: Economic Development Aid (Continued)

Foreign Aid Program	Program Objectives	FY 2007 Funding
Transition Initiatives (TI)	Support for transition to democracy and long-term development of countries in crisis.	$40 million
USAID operating expenses	Operating expenses to maintain USAID resident staff in more than 70 foreign countries[8]	$744 million
TOTAL: U.S. Humanitarian and Economic Development Aid in FY 2007		**$12 billion**

*Includes FY 2007 Supplemental Funds.

Sources: Office of Management and Budget; Congressional Research Service.[9]

U.S. Assistance to the Former Soviet Union. Since 1992, the United States has provided more than $28 billion in assistance to the 12 nations of the former Soviet Union, about $11 billion of which came from the FSA program (FREEDOM Support Act).[10] FSA funds have been focused on projects to support the transition to democracy and market economies, providing humanitarian relief (at critical points in the 1990s when several countries experienced food shortages); promoting security by controlling the proliferation of nuclear, chemical, and biological weapons; and, more recently, fighting terrorism. Since 2002, FSA funding has been trending downward, but a new source of funding is now available with establishment of the Millennium Challenge Corporation. For example, in 2005 an agreement was signed with Georgia providing nearly $300 million over five years to improve infrastructure and stimulate private enterprise.[11]

Peace Corps. Established by President John F. Kennedy in 1961, the Peace Corps is one of the most successful government-sponsored development programs. Volunteers spend two years living in developing countries working on projects related to education (35%), health (21%), business development (16%), environment (14%), youth (6%), and agriculture (5%). (Parenthetical percentages reflect the allocation of Peace Corps resources in FY 2006).[12] The Peace Corps mission is to assist less developed countries that need skilled individuals, as well as promoting cross-cultural communication between the United States and the world's developing countries. Since 1961, more than 182,000 American volunteers have been invited to serve in 138 countries.

U.S. Lags behind Others in Providing Aid. We like to think of America as one of the world's most generous nations. However, as reflected in Figure 3-13.2, an apples-to-apples comparison by the Organisation for Economic Co-operation and Development (OECD)[13] shows the United States lagging behind nearly all other developed nations in the percentage of Gross National Income dedicated to development assistance. A long-standing United Nations goal for foreign aid from developed nations is 0.7% of gross national income. The average development assistance is 0.47 %, while U.S. assistance in 2005 was only 0.22%.[14]

FIGURE 3-13.2 U.S. Lags behind Other Nations in Providing Development Aid

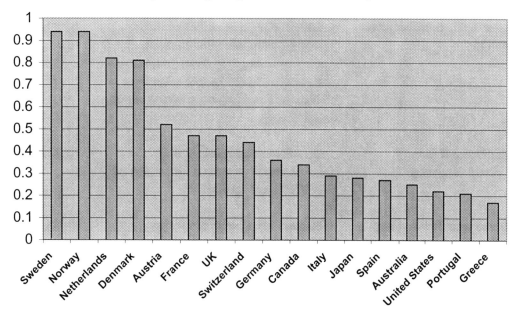

Net Government Development Assistance
as a percentage of gross national income, 2005

Source: *OECD Factbook 2007.*

Humanitarian Aid

In a Nutshell

Humanitarian Assistance programs, amounting to $8.5 billion, include food aid, child survival and health assistance, family planning, the Global HIV/AIDS Initiative, and migration and refugee assistance (see table 3-13.2).

Background

Food Aid. P.L. 480, the authorizing law that governs food assistance, has three titles. Title I, Trade and Development Assistance, is administered by the U.S. Department of Agriculture (USDA) and provides for government to government sales of U.S. agricultural commodities. The food commodities may then be sold in the recipient country and the proceeds used to support agricultural, economic, or infrastructure development. Title II, administered by USAID, provides for the donation of food to meet emergency and nonemergency needs. Title III, also administered by USAID, provides for government-to-government grants to support long-term growth in the least developed countries. Other U.S. food aid programs include Food for Progress, which provides for the donation of U.S. commodities to emerging democracies; the section 416(b) program which provides for overseas donations of surplus commodities; and the McGovern-Dole International Food for Education (FFE) program, which provides for donations of agricultural products for school feeding and maternal and child nutrition projects.

TABLE 3-13.2 FY 2007 Funding: Humanitarian Aid

Foreign Aid Program	Program Objectives	FY 2007 Funding
Global HIV/AIDS Initiative (GHAI)	A multiyear program to combat HIV/AIDS in the 15 hardest-hit countries; also, U.S. contributions to the Global Fund. Recipient nations: Uganda, Kenya, South Africa, Zambia, and Nigeria.	$3.2 billion
P.L. 480 and other Food Aid programs	Includes several food aid and development programs administered by USDA and USAID.[15]	$1.8 billion
International Disaster & Famine Assistance (IDFA)	Humanitarian relief to foreign countries struck by natural or man-made disasters; administered by USAID.	$0.5 billion*
Child Survival and Health Programs (CSH)	Major health issues addressed by CSH include HIV/AIDS, tuberculosis, malaria, infectious diseases, infant mortality, family planning, and reproductive health.	$1.9 billion*
Migration and Refugee Assistance (MRA)	Addresses the protection and humanitarian needs of refugees, migrants, and conflict victims worldwide, and provides assistance to refugees resettling in the United States. Funds are concentrated in Africa and the Middle East.	$1.0 billion*
Emergency Refugee and Migration Assistance (ERMA)	Enables the President to provide emergency assistance for unexpected/ urgent refugee and migration needs worldwide	$110 million*
TOTAL: U.S. Humanitarian Aid in FY 2007		**$8 billion**

*Includes FY 2007 Supplemental Funds.

Sources: Office of Management and Budget; Congressional Research Service.[16]

International Disaster and Famine Assistance Program. Administered by USAID, this program provides temporary shelter, blankets, food, water, medical supplies, and agricultural rehabilitation aid including seeds and hand tools. It is increasingly taking on complex tasks such as Iraq reconstruction and the massive displacement of people from Darfur in the Sudan.

Child Survival and Health Programs. Activities include immunization, nutrition, and sanitation programs, as well as training for health workers. Principal beneficiary nations in 2005 were Nigeria, India, Ethiopia, Bangladesh, and Uganda.

Restrictions on Family Planning Funding. Since 1965 the United States has provided financial support for international family planning efforts (currently funded at $440 million, primarily through the Child Survival and Health Account). In 1984, the Reagan Administration introduced restrictions that denied U.S. funds to any nongovernmental organizations (NGOs) that were involved in voluntary abortion activities, even if such activities were undertaken with non-U.S. funds. President Clinton reversed this policy in 1993, but President George W. Bush resumed the restrictions.[17]

Military Aid and Security Assistance

In a Nutshell

Military aid consists of the foreign military financing program and grants for military education and training. In addition, Congress appropriates funding for "Nonproliferation, Antiterrorism, and Demining," and for peacekeeping operations (non-UN) (see table 3-13.3).

Background

The *Foreign Military Financing (FMF) program* provides funding to allies for the purchase of American military equipment. A majority of the funds go to Israel and Egypt, with significant funds going to Pakistan, Jordan, and Colombia.[18] The program objective is to enhance U.S. security by assisting well-equipped, well-trained allies to maintain regional and global stability. The State Department handles policy decisions for the FMF program, while the program itself is implemented by the DOD's Defense Security Cooperation Agency (DSCA).

The *International Military Education and Training (IMET) program* provides grants for military education and training of personnel from foreign countries. In addition to assisting countries in moving toward self-sufficiency in defending themselves, the program also aims to expose foreign students to democratic values and military respect for civilian control. Beneficiaries have included Turkey, Jordan, Thailand, Pakistan, and Poland.

The *Nonproliferation, Anti-Terrorism, Demining and Related Programs (NADR)* are designed to assist nations in halting the proliferation of nuclear, chemical, and biological weapons; enhance the ability of law enforcement personnel to interdict and deter terrorists; and advance the humanitarian objectives of the demining program. Since 9/11, this account has grown from $170 million to nearly a half billion dollars per year.

Peacekeeping Operations (PKO) support multilateral peacekeeping and regional stability operations that are *not* funded by the United Nations. PKO funding supports the Multinational Force Observers (MFO) in Egypt's Sinai Peninsula, peacekeeping initiatives in Africa,

TABLE 3-13.3 FY 2007 Funding: Military Aid and Security Assistance

Foreign Aid Program	Program Objectives	FY 2007 Funding
Foreign Military Financing	Funding to allies for purchase of U.S. military equipment	$4.8 billion*
Nonproliferation, Anti-Terrorism, Demining	Assist nations in halting the proliferation of nuclear, chemical, and biological weapons	$464 million*
Peacekeeping Operations (non-UN)	Peacekeeping activities not funded through the UN	$453 million*
International Military Education & Training	Grants for military education and training of personnel from foreign countries	$86 million
TOTAL: U.S. Military Aid and Security Assistance in FY 2007		**$5.8 billion**

*Includes FY 2007 Supplemental Funds.

Sources: Office of Management and Budget; Congressional Research Service.[19]

as well as the Global Peace Operations Initiative, which works to increase the peacekeeping abilities of other nations.[20]

Counter-Narcotics and Law Enforcement

In a Nutshell

In FY 2007, Congress appropriated $725 million for international narcotics control (including supplemental funds) and $722 million for the Andean counterdrug initiative.

Background and Issues

The *International Narcotics Control and Law Enforcement program (INCLE)* supports country-specific as well as global efforts to combat the illegal drug trade. The two largest recipient countries in FY 2007 were Afghanistan and Iraq, with $297 million and $255 million, respectively. Afghanistan's opium poppy-based economy, in addition to being the world's largest source of heroin, presents a major security risk to the region because it continues to fund Afghan warlords, the resurgent Taliban, and some Al Qaeda operatives.

In 2007, CRS reported a general lack of progress in fighting opium poppy production, finding that "in spite of ongoing efforts by the Afghan government, the United States and their partners, Afghanistan is now the source of 93% of the world's illicit opium." Afghan President

Hamid Karzai called the opium economy "the single greatest challenge to the long-term security, development, and effective governance of Afghanistan."[21]

The *Andean Counter-drug Initiative (ACI)* is a multiyear counter narcotics initiative aimed at combating the drug trade in Colombia and six neighboring countries (Bolivia, Brazil, Ecuador, Panama, Peru, and Venezuela). Ninety percent of the cocaine in the United States originates in or passes through Colombia. The ACI was developed as part of "Plan Colombia," a six-year plan developed by former Colombian President Pastrana to end Colombia's armed conflict, eliminate drug trafficking, and promote development.[22] From FY 2000 through FY 2007, the United States provided nearly $6 billion in ACI funds.

Despite the enormous commitment of resources, critics have warned that ACI would be of limited value given the continuing intractable U.S. demand for illicit drugs.[23] Despite some measurable progress in Colombia's internal security,[24] CRS reported to Congress in late 2006 that "efforts to significantly reduce the flow of illicit drugs from abroad into the United States have so far not succeeded.... Over the past decade, worldwide production of illicit drugs has risen dramatically: opium and marijuana production has roughly doubled and coca production tripled."[25] Moreover, "street prices of cocaine and heroin have fallen significantly in the past 20 years, reflecting increased availability."[26]

State Department and Conduct of Foreign Affairs

In a Nutshell

For FY 2007, Congress appropriated $8.3 billion to fund State Department operations, U.S. embassies in 180 countries, educational and cultural exchange programs, international broadcasting, and other foreign affairs activities.

Background

State Department Operations. The State Department spends over $5 billion per year on operations in Washington, D.C., operating embassies and diplomatic posts in 180 countries; processing over 9 million visa applications to travel, study, and live in the United States; issuing passports to U.S. citizens; and performing all other activities associated with the conduct of foreign policy. In order to carry out these functions, the State Department employs 9,000 Foreign Service Officers, 6,500 civil service employees, and over 30,000 Foreign Service Nationals (foreigners working at U.S. embassies in their home countries). In budget-speak, this is often called the "diplomatic and consular budget."

Embassy Security, Construction, and Maintenance. Following the two embassy bombings in East Africa in August 1998,[27] Congress substantially increased funding to enhance U.S. embassy security around the world, with the FY 2007 appropriations reaching $1.5 billion.

International Broadcasting. Congress invests over $600 million per year in international broadcasting operations, including Voice of America, Radio Free Europe, Radio Free Asia, broadcasting to Cuba (known as Radio and TV Martí), and the Middle East Broadcasting Network (see table 3-13.4). In order to maintain the independence and credibility of U.S. broadcasting operations, Congress established the Broadcasting Board of Governors as a separate entity from the State Department.

TABLE 3-13.4 U.S. Government-Sponsored International Broadcasts

U.S. Government-Sponsored International Broadcasts		
Station	Languages	Content
Voice of America	44	Radio, TV, and Internet broadcasts of U.S. and world news
Al-Hurra	Arabic	Satellite TV: news and special reports to the Middle East
Radio Sawa	Arabic	U.S. and world news and local music for the Middle East
Radio Farda	Persian	U.S. and world news and local music geared toward Iran
Radio Free Europe/ Radio Liberty	29	U.S. and world news for Central, Southeastern, and Eastern Europe, the Caucasus, and Central and Southwestern Asia
Radio Free Asia	9	U.S. and world news for Asian countries
Radio and TV Martí	Spanish	News and entertainment aimed at Cuba

U.S. International Broadcasting received strong support in its early years when the Voice of America provided information to those living under Nazi occupation during World War II and, later on, to countries under Soviet occupation during the Cold War. However, the most recent ventures—broadcasting to Cuba and now to the Middle East—have been met with skepticism. A 2005 CRS report to Congress noted that "Arabs don't consider Al-Hurra a first choice for news and . . . only 3.8% picked it as a second choice."[28] A 2003 State Department Inspector General's report found that in 2001, only 5% of Cubans regularly listened to Radio Martí.[29]

Contributions to the United Nations (UN) and other international organizations

In a Nutshell

In FY 2007 Congress appropriated $1.2 billion for United States *assessed* contributions to international organizations, including the United Nations; $1.4 billion for UN peacekeeping operations; and $326 million for U.S. *voluntary* contributions to UN System Programs.

Background

Assessed Contributions to International Organizations (CIO) includes the U.S. assessment for the regular UN budget, which in 2007 amounted to $423 million. The UN assessment scale, which is generally based on a country's capacity to pay, requires the United States to pay 22% of the UN regular budget, with the next highest assessments being Japan at 16.6 % and Germany at 8.6 %.[30]

The remainder of the $1.2 billion in assessed contributions is allocated to Specialized Agencies affiliated with the United Nations[31] and to the International Atomic Energy Agency (IAEA).[32] Major budget items in this area include a $101 million assessment for the World Health Organization; $92 million for the Food and Agriculture Organization; $87 million for the IAEA; $72 million for the United Nations Educational, Scientific, and Cultural Organization (UNESCO); $67 million for the International Labor Organization; and $33 million for War Crimes Tribunals.[33]

Contributions to International Peacekeeping Activities (CIPA), like the UN itself, are typically funded through assessments—although the amount of U.S. peacekeeping assessments has been an issue of some controversy, as discussed later.

Voluntary contributions[34] finance special programs created by the UN system, as well as providing additional funding to UN Specialized Agencies.[35] FY 2007 voluntary contributions included among other budget items, $123 million for the UN Children's Fund (UNICEF), $95 million for the UN Development Program (UNDP), $10 million for the UN Democracy Fund (UNDEF), and $5 million for the Intergovernmental Panel on Climate Change and the Framework Convention on Climate Change (IPCC and UNFCC).[36]

Issues

Is the U.S. Assessment Excessive? The United States has been, and continues to be, the single largest contributor to the United Nations due to the size of the U.S. economy. However, the question of which economic factors are most relevant in establishing UN assessments is a source of continuing controversy. For example, the United States has suggested at various times that the formula currently used by the UN results in an excessive U.S. assessment. Members of the Administration and Congress have argued that the formula should take into account a Member Nation's purchasing power and foreign currency rates (in addition to Gross National Income). However, despite a recent UN review of the assessment schedule, the 2007 U.S. assessment for the UN regular budget remained at 22%.[37]

U.S. Arrearages. Another ongoing issue has been U.S. arrearages (dues outstanding). Since 1980, Congress has, at various times, used U.S. payment of assessments as leverage on policy issues and proposed reforms of UN operations. For example, in 1980 Congress began prohibiting dues payments for a number of UN programs and activities such as projects benefiting the Palestine Liberation Organization (PLO) and the South West Africa People's Organization, construction of a conference center in Addis Ababa, and implementation of the "Zionism equals racism" resolution. In 1987, Congress tied payment of dues to reforms by the UN of its budget process and reductions in its staff, and in 1993 payment of dues was linked to establishment of an independent auditing office inside the United Nations. In 1999, negotiations between the Clinton Administration and congressional leaders led to the Helms-Biden plan linking payment of arrearages to various reform benchmarks. According to the UN, despite recent arrears payments, as of December 31, 2006, the United States still owed assessments of more than $1 billion.[38]

Notes

1. "Americans on Foreign Aid and World Hunger—A Study of U.S. Public Attitudes" University of Maryland Program on International Policy Attitudes (PIPA), WorldPublicOpinion.org, February 2, 2001, 6–7.

2. See Connie Veillette, "Restructuring U.S. Foreign Aid: The Role of the Director of Foreign Assistance in Transformational Development," RL33491 (Washington, D.C.: Congressional Research Service, January 23, 2007).

3. House Report 110-197, accompanying H.R. 2764 (110th Congress), State Foreign Operations, and Related Programs Appropriations Bill, 2008, 69–70.

4. Curt Tarnoff, "Millennium Challenge Account," RL32427 (Washington DC: Congressional Research Service, September 24, 2007).

5. Martin Weiss, "The World Bank's International Development Association," RL33969 (Washington D.C.: Congressional Research Service, July 18, 2007), 18.

6. Weiss, "The World Bank's International Development Association," 7.

7. The acronym FSA stems from the FREEDOM Support Act of 1992.

8. Operations spending also includes capital investments for security and information technology, and the Office of the Inspector General.

9. Connie Veillette, "State, Foreign Operations, and Related Programs: FY 2008 Appropriations," RL34023 (Washington, D.C.: Congressional Research Service, September 10, 2007), appendix C.

10. Curt Tarnoff, "U.S. Assistance to the Former Soviet Union," RL32866 (Washington, D.C.: Congressional Research Service, March 1, 2007).

11. Tarnoff, "U.S. Assistance," 4–5.

12. Peace Corps Fact Sheet 2007, http://peacecorps.gov/multimedia/pdf/about/pc_facts.pdf.

13. The OECD, an organization of 30 developed democracies, "brings together the governments of countries committed to democracy and the market economy from around the world to: support sustainable economic growth; boost employment; raise living standards; maintain financial stability; assist other countries' economic development; and contribute to growth in world trade." Source: "About OECD," www.oecd.org.

14. *OECD Factbook 2007: Economic, Environmental and Social Statistics* (Paris: Organisation for Economic Co-operation and Development, 2007), 200–1.

15. See "Fact Sheet: Food Aid," U.S. Department of Agriculture, www.fas.usda.gov/info/factsheets/Food%20Aid.pdf.

16. Veillette, "State, Foreign Operations, and Related Programs," appendix C.

17. See Luisa Blanchfield, "International Population Assistance and Family Planning Programs: Issues for Congress," RL33250 (Washington, D.C.: Congressional Research Service, September 21, 2007).

18. House Report 110-197, 1119–27.

19. Veillette, "State, Foreign Operations, and Related Programs," appendix C.

20. House Report 110-197, 127–30.

21. Christopher Blanchard, "Afghanistan: Narcotics and U.S. Policy," RL32686 (Washington D.C.: Congressional Research Service, September 14, 2007), summary.

22. Connie Veillette, "Plan Colombia: A Progress Report," RL32774 (Washington D.C: Congressional Research Service, January 11, 2006), summary.

23. Raphael Perl, "International Drug Trade and U.S. Foreign Policy," RL33582 (Washington D.C.: Congressional Research Service, November 6, 2006), 13.

24. Veillette, "Plan Colombia," summary.

25. Perl, "International Drug Trade," summary.

26. Raphael Perl, "Drug Control: International Policy and Approaches," IB88093 (Washington D.C.: Congressional Research Service, February 2, 2006), summary.

27. In the 1998 U.S. Embassy bombings (August 7, 1998), over 200 people were killed and over 4,000 injured in simultaneous car bomb explosions at the U.S. embassies in the East African capital cities of Dar es Salaam, Tanzania, and Nairobi, Kenya. The attacks were linked to local members of Al Qaeda. Source: http://www.pbs.org/newshour/bb/africa/embassy_bombing/map.html.

28. Jeremy Sharp, "The Middle East Television Network: An Overview" (Washington, D.C.: Congressional Research Service, August 17, 2005), 4.

29. Office of the Inspector General, "Review of the Effectiveness and Implementation of Office of Cuba Broadcasting's New Program Initiatives" (Washington DC, U.S. Department of State, January 2003), 14.

30. Marjorie Ann Browne and Kennon Nakamura, "United Nations System Funding: Congressional Issues," RL33611 (Washington D.C.: Congressional Budget Office, September 17, 2007), 13.

31. The Specialized Agencies include FAO (Food and Agriculture Organisation), ILO (International Labor Organisation), UNESCO (United Nations Educational, Scientific, and Cultural Organisation), UNIDO (United Nations Industrial Development Organisation) since 1986, WHO (World Health Organisation), ICAO (International Civil Aviation Organization), IMO (International Maritime Organisation), ITU (International Telecommunication Union), UPU (Universal Postal Union), WIPO (World Intellectual Property Organization), WMO (World Meteorologial Organization) and IAEA (International Atomic Energy Agency). The IAEA although not formally a Specialized Agency, is also financed by assessed contributions. Source: www.globalpolicy.org.

32. The IAEA is an autonomous international organization established by representatives of more than 80 countries in 1956.

33. UN Specialized Agencies and the IAEA are autonomous organizations; some use the same assessment scale as the UN, while others adopt their own assessment scale. For example, U.S. assessments for ILO, FAO, and UNESCO are 22%, while the IAEA assessment is 26%. Browne and Nakamura, "United Nations System Funding," 10, 15.

34. From the International Organizations and Programs or "IOP" Account.

35. The Programs and Funds include UNCDF (United Nations Capital Development Fund) since 1973, UNDP (United Nations Development Programme), UNEP (United Nations Environment Program) since 1973, UNFPA (United Nations Population Fund), UNHCR (Office of the United Nations High Commissioner for Refugees), UNICEF (United Nations Children's Fund), UNIDO (United Nations Industrial Development Organization) until 1986, UNITAR (United Nations Institute for Training and Research), UNRWA (UN Relief & Works Agency for Palestinian Refugees in the Near East), UNU (United Nations University) since 1975, and WFP (World Food Programme). Source: www.globalpolicy.org.

36. Browne and Nakamura, "United Nations System Funding," 11.

37. Browne and Nakamura, 12–15.

38. Browne and Nakamura, 15–30.

REVENUES: HOW AMERICA RAISES
$3 TRILLION PER YEAR

Taxes are what we pay for civilized society. —Justice Oliver Wendell Holmes Jr., 1904 [1]

Overview of U.S. Taxes

In FY 2007, revenues flowing into the Treasury amounted to $2.568 trillion. The *individual income tax* is the largest source of Federal revenue, bringing in about $1.2 trillion—45% of Federal revenues.

The next largest source of Federal revenues are *payroll taxes* (including Social Security, Medicare Hospital Insurance, and Unemployment Insurance), amounting to $870 billion in FY 2007, or 34% of Federal revenues.

Corporate income taxes are a distant third as a Federal revenue source, bringing in $370 billion, or 14% of Federal revenues.

The remaining items that complete the revenue pie (see figure 4.1) are *excise taxes* accounting for 3% of revenues; *estate and gift taxes* and *customs duties, each accounting for 1% of revenues;* and *miscellaneous receipts* accounting for the remaining 2% of total revenue.

Individual Income Taxes

The art of taxation consists in so plucking the goose as to obtain the largest possible amount of feathers with the smallest possible amount of hissing.—Jean Baptiste Colbert, 1665[2]

As displayed in figure 4.2 the Federal individual income tax applies increasing levels of taxation—based on income bracket—to various types of income including wages, salaries, tips, interest, investments, and noncorporate business income. After all types of income are

FIGURE 4.1 Overview of FY 2007 Revenues

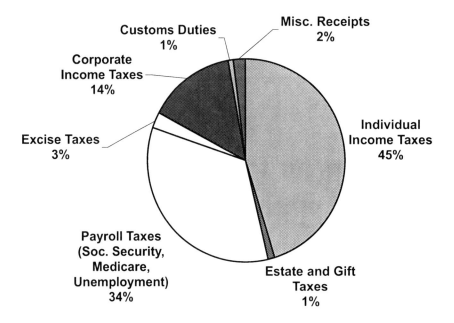

Source: U.S. Treasury Department.[3]

totaled up, certain adjustments are applied that *reduce* total income for tax purposes, such as contributions to certain IRAs, alimony paid, self-employed health insurance premiums, and some interest on student loans; these adjustments generate a number called *adjusted gross income (AGI)*.

AGI is then *reduced* by a "standard deduction"[4] or "itemized deductions" and is further reduced by the number of personal or dependent exemptions. This generates a number called *taxable income*.

Taxable income is then taxed according to rates set by law (see figure 4.2). The resulting tax can then either be *increased* by the Alternative Minimum Tax (explained later) or *decreased* by certain tax credits such as the child tax credit.

Unlike "deductions," which reduce the amount of income that is taxed, tax "credits" reduce the *amount of taxes owed.* Certain tax credits are referred to as "refundable," which means that if the amount of the credit exceeds the tax bill, the Treasury will make a direct payment of the balance to the taxpayer. In other words, a refundable tax credit can, in addition to erasing one's tax liability, result in a check from the Federal government. Examples of refundable credits include the Earned Income Tax Credit[5] and the Child Tax Credit. From a budgetary perspective, the amount of the credits that offset tax liability is scored as a revenue reduction, while the amounts that exceed tax liability and are paid directly to taxpayers are scored as budgetary outlays.

Nonrefundable credits include the Child and Dependent Care Credit (for the costs of care for children and dependents)[6] and the Hope and Lifetime Learning Credits for expenses of postsecondary education.[7]

FIGURE 4.2   The Federal Income Tax in a Nutshell

Individual Income Tax Is Assessed on:
wages, salaries, tips, interest, dividends, capital gains, business income, rent, royalties,
unemployment compensation, pension and annuity income, alimony received, and
Social Security benefits (for higher-income taxpayers)

Reduced by:
IRA and other retirement contributions
SEP, SIMPLE, and other self-employed retirement plans
Alimony paid; Health Savings Accounts
Self-employed health insurance premiums
Certain student loan interest
Moving expenses
One-half of self-employment tax

Adjusted Gross Income

Reduced by:
Standard Deduction[8]
or
Itemized Deductions including:
Home mortgage interest
State/local income taxes
State/local property taxes
Charitable contributions
Medical expenses (over 7.5% AGI)
and
Personal and dependent exemptions

Taxable Income

Taxable Income was taxed at the following incremental rates in 2007
(except for capital gains and dividend income, which are generally taxed at 15%):[9]

Tax Rate	Single Return	Joint Return
10%	Up to $7,825	Up to $15,650
15%	Up to $31,850	Up to $63,700
25%	Up to $77,100	Up to $125,500
28%	Up to $160,850	Up to $195,850
33%	Up to $349,700	Up to $349,700
35%	Over $349,700	Over $349,700

For example, an individual with taxable income of $30,000, pays 10% on the amount *up to* $7,825, and 15% on the amount over $7,825. In this way, the tax rates apply to *increments* of income.

Resulting taxes owed can be *increased* by the Alternative Minimum Tax (AMT) or *reduced* by tax credits such as the earned income tax credit (EITC), child tax credit, education tax credit, credit for elderly or disabled, and credit for child and dependent care expenses.

Alternative Minimum Tax (Amt): Created to Prevent Tax Avoidance by the Few, but Now Poised to Impact Millions

The growing reach of the AMT is "the most serious problem" facing individual taxpayers.
—Office of the National Taxpayer Advocate, 2003 Annual Report to Congress[10]

Congress has often used the Tax Code as a means of promoting various economic and social policies through tax incentives, deductions, and exemptions. While many of these goals are laudable, at the same time it is not surprising that some individuals, particularly in upper income brackets, have been able to structure their activities in ways that take excessive advantage of various tax incentives and preferences. In 1969, after Congress learned that 155 taxpayers with incomes above $200,000 had paid no 1966 Federal tax,[11] lawmakers enacted what later became known as the "Alternative Minimum Tax" (AMT) in order to ensure that everyone pays a minimum amount of tax, regardless of how many tax preferences or deductions they may technically be entitled to.

In general, the AMT operates by requiring people to recalculate their taxes under alternative rules that (1) *include* certain forms of income exempt from regular tax and (2) *disallow* certain exemptions, deductions, and preferences. More specifically:

- First a taxpayer adds back to his or her taxable income certain tax preferences, generating an amount known as the *AMT tax base.* (Personal exemptions, itemized deductions for state and local taxes, and miscellaneous itemized deductions account for 90% of the preference items added back.[12])
- Next, a standard exemption amount[13] is calculated and subtracted from the AMT tax base.
- The resulting amount is then subject to the AMT's two-tiered tax rate of 26% on income up to $175,000 and 28% over that amount.
- Finally, and most importantly, the taxpayer then pays whichever amount is greater—their AMT tax liability or their regular income tax liability (calculated as described at the beginning of this chapter).

Myth: The AMT impacts only high-income taxpayers.

Fact: While the AMT was first enacted to ensure that upper-income individuals pay a "fair share" of the tax burden, in recent years upper-middle and middle-income taxpayers are increasingly finding themselves subject to the AMT, as shown in table 4.1. This has occurred for two reasons. First, while the regular income tax is indexed for inflation, the AMT is not.[14] Second, recent income tax rate reductions have narrowed the differences between regular and AMT tax liabilities. In the table, note the impact on taxpayers at the $50,000–$100,000 and $100,000–$200,000 levels beginning in 2007.

TABLE 4.1 Taxpayers with AMT Liability by Adjusted Gross Income

Adjusted Gross Income (in 2005 dollars)	2005	2007	2008	2009	2010
Less than $50,000	0.0%	0.8%	1.4%	2.2%	3.3%
$50,000 –$100,000	**1.3%**	**42.8%**	**50.5%**	59.0%	65.9%
$100,000–$200,000	**16.7%**	**86.2%**	**90.7%**	93.0%	95.3%
$200,000–$500,000	66.6%	85.2%	86.5%	83.5%	85.7%
$500,000–$1,000,000	27.5%	28.4%	30.7%	28.4%	30.3%
Over $1,000,000	21.2%	23.1%	24.9%	23.8%	25.5%
All taxpayers	2.1%	13.2%	14.7%	16.3%	17.9%

Source: Congressional Budget Office.[15]

According to CBO, until 2000, less than 1% of taxpayers paid AMT in any year.[16] In 2001, 2003, and 2006, Congress enacted *temporary* increases in the *AMT exemption amounts* in order to mitigate the AMT's increasing impact on middle-income taxpayers. However, if AMT relief is not extended beyond 2006, the Congressional Research Service estimates that in 2007, 24 million taxpayers would be subject to the AMT.[17] Moreover, if the 2001 and 2003 tax rate cuts are made permanent (as the Administration and many Members of Congress have been calling for), the reach of AMT would extend to 50 million taxpayers by 2016.[18]

Options to address the growth of the AMT include (1) extending the increased exemption level, (2) indexing the AMT for inflation, or (3) repealing the AMT. However, all of these potential "fixes" for the AMT face the major hurdle of identifying offsetting revenue raisers. As explained in chapter 2-4, Congress is once again operating under PAYGO rules that require revenue raisers to offset the costs of any tax changes that would lose revenue (as all of the AMT "fixes" would). For example, it is estimated that if the 2001 and 2003 tax cuts are extended, repealing the AMT would cost nearly *$1 trillion* in lost revenues over 10 years.[19] Similarly, *even a one-year AMT fix*—usually referred to as a "patch" due to its short-term effect—would cost *$55–$60 billion*.[20] Because of the enormous costs of a permanent AMT fix, Congress appears to be settling into the routine of annually enacting a short-term patch to prevent the AMT from ensnaring upper-middle- and middle-income taxpayers.

Payroll Taxes: Social Security and Medicare Hospital Insurance

As reflected in figure 4.1, payroll taxes will bring in 34% of Federal revenues for FY 2007. Payroll taxes are comprised almost entirely of Social Security taxes and Medicare Hospital Insurance taxes.[21]

Social Security and Medicare payroll tax rates are, respectively, 12.4% and 2.9%, half paid by the employer and half by the employee (i.e., 7.65% each). (Self-employed individuals pay *self-employment tax*, which is roughly equivalent to both halves of the tax.[22]) Revenues from

Social Security payroll taxes pay for retirement and disability benefits, while the Medicare payroll tax pays for Medicare Part A, which is the portion of Medicare that provides elderly and disabled Americans with hospital insurance (HI). (See chapter 3-4 on Social Security and chapter 3-6 on Medicare.)

Social Security payroll taxes are levied on the first $102,000 of wages (as of tax year 2008), with this cap on taxable wages adjusted annually for increases in average wages in the economy.[23] The amount of income subject to Medicare payroll taxes used to be similarly capped; however, that cap was lifted as part of the deficit reduction legislation of 1993, and *all* wage income is now subject to the Medicare (HI) tax.

(For a description of the 0.8% net Federal payroll tax paid by employers to support the unemployment insurance program, see chapter 3-8.)

Myth: The largest tax bill for most American workers is the income tax.

Fact: As of 2005, nearly 80% of American households paid more in payroll taxes than in income taxes. Many argue that this casts a shadow of unfairness on the U.S. tax system because the payroll tax is a highly regressive tax. For example, a middle-class family with four children, earning $97,500 per year, pays the same amount in Social Security payroll taxes as a corporate CEO earning millions, due to the cap on taxable wages.

Myth: A worker's payroll taxes are deposited into a personal account at the Social Security Administration (SSA) from which their benefits will be drawn when they retire.

Fact: This is a common misconception. As displayed in figure 4.3, Social Security is actually a pay-as-you-go system in which the payroll taxes paid by *current* workers are used to pay the benefits of *current* retirees and people on disability. (Any excess payroll taxes—referred to as the "Social Security surplus"—are invested in nonmarketable U.S. Treasury securities. The SSA will begin redeeming those securities when Social Security expenditures exceed incoming payroll taxes—projected to begin around 2017–2019.)

Corporate Income Taxes

Corporate taxable income is subject to a set of graduated tax rates—15%, 25%, 34%, and 35%—with smaller firms often taxed at the lower rates and the bulk of corporate income, earned by larger firms, taxed at the higher rates.

FIGURE 4.3 Current Workers' Payroll Taxes Pay for Current Retirees' Benefits (with Surplus Revenues Invested in Treasury Securities)

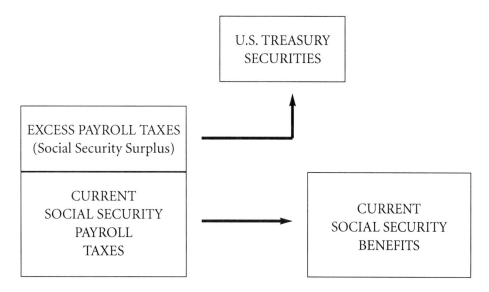

The income base subject to corporate taxes is roughly equal to gross revenue minus expenses. Deductible expenses include wages, materials, and interest paid on debt instruments (sometimes called *debt capital*). In addition, firms can deduct tangible assets—such as machines, equipment, and structures—over time according to a depreciation schedule.

Economists and policymakers have long debated whether it is reasonable to tax corporate profits. Opponents of the corporate tax point out that corporate equity profits are, in reality, taxed twice—once at the corporate level and again when they are received by individual stockholders as dividends or capital gains. Supporters of the corporate tax point out that it discourages the use of corporations as shelters from individual income tax and that it may add to the overall progressivity of the tax system.

In 2003, the Jobs and Growth Tax Relief Reconciliation Act (JGTRRA) reduced the tax rate individuals pay on corporate-source dividends and capital gains to 15%, which some may view as moving in the direction of relieving the "double taxation" of corporate income. On the other hand, this provision has also led some to argue that benefits from recent tax cuts are skewed in the direction of wealthier taxpayers.

Estate and Gift Taxes: Myths and Facts

Of all forms of taxation this seems the wisest. Men who continue hoarding great sums all their lives, the proper use of which for public ends would work good to the community from which it chiefly came, should be made to feel that the community . . . cannot thus be deprived of its proper share. By taxing estates. . .at death the State marks its condemnation of the self-ish millionaire. —Andrew Carnegie, from The Gospel of Wealth *(1901)*

The Federal estate and gift tax is a high-profile public policy issue that, unfortunately, is widely misunderstood due to a lot of ideology muddying the waters. Here are the facts.

As reflected in figure 4.1, the estate and gift tax is a minor slice of the revenue pie, accounting for only 1% of Federal revenues. Furthermore, because of the estate and gift tax "exemption," as well as various deductions, the estate and gift tax impacts only a tiny percentage of Americans. For example, only 2% of all deaths in the United States. in tax year 2001 resulted in estate tax liability; in 2008, an estimated 0.5% of estates are taxed, due to the increasing exemption.[24]

The Federal estate tax is applied when property is transferred at death. *After deductions and exemptions,* the remaining amount is subject to graduated rates of taxation up to 45% as estate size increases. An unlimited marital deduction is allowed for property transferred to a surviving spouse. Other allowable deductions include charitable contributions and estate administration expenses. In addition, the so-called unified credit *exempts* the first $2 million of an estate from tax. This is the primary reason why the estate tax impacts only a very small percentage of the estates in the nation. Under current law, the $2 million exemption will increase to $3.5 million in 2009, and the estate tax will be fully repealed in 2010, before it bounces back in 2011.[25]

As reflected in table 4.2, the major tax cut legislation enacted in 2001 phases out the estate tax over 2002 to 2010. However, due to the Senate's Byrd Rule (explained in chapter 2-2), which was designed to prevent the use of expedited budget procedures for passage of legislation that would increase deficits over the long term, the estate tax reverts to pre-2001 law in 2011. This means that—absent a change in tax law—as of January 1, 2011, the estate tax will be reinstated with a pre-2001 exemption level of $1 million.

The Federal gift tax operates in conjunction with the estate tax to prevent people from shielding their property from estate taxes by making gifts to heirs prior to death. Each year individuals can make gifts of $12,000[26] to as many individual recipients as they wish, without being subject to the gift tax. However, any amount in *excess* of this per-person gift limit is applied to a lifetime gift exclusion amount of $1 million. At time of death, the cumulative amount of gift tax exclusion used by the decedent reduces the estate tax exemption (currently set at $2 million). In this way, the gift tax operates in a unified manner with the estate tax.

TABLE 4.2 Estate Tax Filing Requirement

Year of Death	Threshold for Filing Requirement
2004 and 2005	$1,500,000
2006 through 2008	$2,000,000
2009	$3,500,000
2010	Estate tax repealed
2011	$1,000,000

Myth: The estate tax broadly impacts America's families.

Fact: Actually, *99.5%* of Americans pay no estate tax due to the large exemption amount—currently $2 million. Only the wealthiest 0.5% of Americans pay estate tax. By 2009, when the exemption amount increases to $3.5 million, the coverage of the estate tax will shrink to 0.2%.[27]

Myth: The estate tax poses a serious threat to the survival of small farms and other types of small businesses that lack the liquidity to pay the estate tax.

Fact: According to CRS, "recent estimates suggest that only a tiny fraction of family-owned businesses (less than one-half of 1%) are subject to the estate tax but do not have readily available resources to pay the tax."[28] With regard to farmers, a CBO study in 2005 estimated that when the estate tax exemption level increases to $3.5 million in 2009, only 65 farm estates nationwide would owe any tax, and only 13 might lack sufficient liquidity to pay the estate tax.[29] In 2005, the *New York Times* reported that neither the American Farm Bureau Federation nor the National Cattleman's Beef Association could cite a single case of a farm lost to estate taxes.[30]

Myth: Repeal of the estate tax will not increase the Federal Debt.

Fact: Enacting legislation to permanently repeal the estate tax would cost the Treasury $281 billion over FY 2011 to FY 2015—at a time when the U.S. Treasury will already be burdened with rapidly escalating Medicare, Medicaid, Social Security, defense, and homeland security expenditures.[31]

Opponents of repealing the estate tax also point out that (1) it provides a strong incentive for charitable giving (which is deductible from estates), (2) it taxes capital gains that would otherwise be shielded from tax since heirs receive a "stepped-up" basis,[32] and (3) the estate tax furthers the stability of our democracy by mitigating the increasing concentration of wealth in the United States.[33]

Recommended Sources for More Information on the Estate and Gift Tax

- Michael J. Graetz and Ian Shapiro, *Death by a Thousand Cuts: The Fight over Taxing Inherited Wealth* (Princeton, NJ: Princeton University Press, 2005).
- **CBO:** "Effects of the Federal Estate Tax on Farms and Small Businesses," July 2005.
- **CRS:** "Estate and Gift Taxes: Economic Issues," RL30600, January 26, 2007, www.opencrs.com/document/RL30600/; "Economic Issues Surrounding the Estate and Gift Tax: A Brief Summary" RS20609, April 24, 2007, www.opencrs.com/document/RS20609/; "Asset Distribution of Taxable Estates: An Analysis," RS20593, February 07, 2007, www.opencrs.com/document/RS20593/.
- **American Institute of Certified Public Accountants**, "Study on Reform of the Estate and Gift Tax System," February 2001.

Excise Taxes, Duties, and Miscellaneous Receipts

A tax paid on the day you buy is not as tough as asking you for it the next year when you are broke.—Will Rogers, 1931 [34]

Excise Taxes. In FY 2007, excise taxes raised $65 billion in revenues, less than 3% of total Federal revenues.[35] Excise taxes are a form of "consumption tax"; that is, they are imposed on the consumption of specific goods and services, rather than on income. Unlike sales taxes, which are generally imposed on broad categories, Federal excise taxes apply to specific commodities. Another difference is that excise taxes are imposed per unit of a product (e.g., a pack of cigarettes), rather than as a percentage of the price.

Federal excise taxes are imposed on a variety of products, the largest excise tax being on gasoline, which comprises nearly one-third of excise tax receipts. Other excise taxes include those on diesel fuel, domestic air passengers, distilled spirits, beer, cigarettes, and telephone services.

Most Federal excise taxes are deposited into special "trust funds" dedicated to specific Federal activities. For example, the Federal excise taxes on gasoline, diesel fuel, and heavy tires go into the Highway Trust Fund, which is dedicated to highway construction and maintenance, and mass transit (see chapter 3-9). Economists refer to the gasoline excise tax as a "manufacturer's excise tax" because the government levies it at the production phase for ease of collection, and the producers, refiners, or importers then pass it along to consumers in the form of higher prices. The gasoline excise tax currently amounts to 18.4 cents per gallon, of which 15.44 cents is dedicated to highways, 2.86 cents is dedicated to mass transit, and 0.1 cent goes to the Leaking Underground Storage Tank Trust Fund.[36]

Other excise taxes were imposed purely to raise revenues, such as telephone excise taxes and alcohol taxes.

Finally, some excise taxes—in addition to raising revenue—are also imposed to influence behavior or reflect the societal impact of certain activities, such as the Federal excise taxes on tobacco. It is frequently argued that increasing the Federal tobacco tax would discourage teenage smoking, provide funds for anti-tobacco programs, and charge smokers for increased public health care costs.

Unlike estate taxes and income taxes, which are generally viewed as "progressive" (i.e., imposing higher rates on higher increments of income), excise taxes on consumer products are viewed as "regressive" because they are passed on to consumers as higher prices that consume a higher proportion of income for lower-income people than for those with higher incomes.

Because excise taxes are selectively imposed on certain commodities, they also tend to raise issues of "fairness." For example, the commercial truck transportation industry complains that while heavy tires are taxed, no similar excise taxes are imposed on shipping competitors such as railroads and waterways.[37]

Customs Duties. In FY 2007, customs duties raised $26 billion—about 1% of Federal revenues.[38] There are currently two trends affecting the level of customs duties being collected on imported products. First, because the level of imports into the United States is rising, the overall level of customs duties will tend to rise. However, this effect is partially offset as various bilateral, multilateral, and global trade agreements require the reduction or elimination of tariffs on imported goods.

Miscellaneous Receipts. Miscellaneous Receipts raised $47 billion in FY 2007, almost 2% of Federal revenues.[39] About two-thirds of this amount is attributable to receipts from Federal Reserve System earnings. These earnings arise from (1) interest that the Federal Reserve earns on its portfolio of securities and (2) gains from holdings of foreign currency.[40] Miscellaneous Receipts also includes income from the Universal Service Fund—which taxes interstate and international telecommunications in order to subsidize service in schools, rural areas, and high-costs areas.

The "Tax Gap"

Law is not what the Congress passes. Law is what you are willing to enforce.
Law without enforcement might just as well never be enacted.
—*Former IRS Commissioner and Chief Counsel Sheldon Cohen*

The "tax gap" refers to the difference between the amount of taxes individual and corporate taxpayers owe under the law and the amount actually paid—in short, unpaid taxes. The "gross tax gap" refers to the total amount not paid on time, and the "net tax gap" subtracts out the amount that is eventually collected. For example, as displayed in figure 4.4, the IRS estimates that in tax year 2001 (the most recent year for which data has been collected and analyzed[41]), $345 billion in taxes owed were not paid on time, and after collection efforts, $290 billion remained unpaid.[42] To get a sense of the magnitude of this shortfall, consider that the $290 billion net tax gap for 2001 is nearly double the most recent unified Federal Budget deficit of $163 billion.

The tax gap is important for two fundamental reasons. First, as discussed in Part VI, our nation is facing rapidly growing and unsustainable debt as far as the eye can see due to rapidly rising Medicare and Medicaid spending, retirement of the baby boomers, and escalating defense spending. Closing the tax gap is one important component in making progress to redress the nation's long-term fiscal imbalance.

Second, the U.S. tax system is based on voluntary compliance. Needless to say, it is demoralizing to law-abiding taxpayers, and damaging to overall compliance, to learn that hundreds of billions of dollars in taxes are not being paid. "The vast majority of Americans pay their

FIGURE 4.4 The Tax Gap

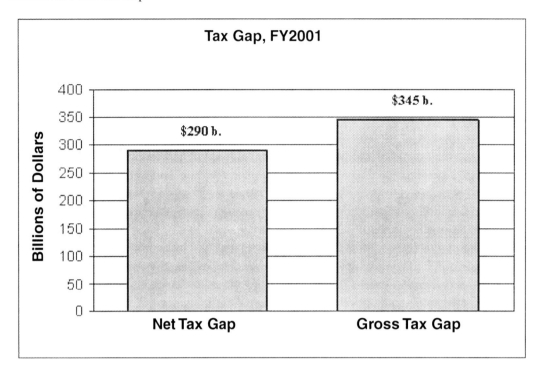

taxes accurately and are shortchanged by those who don't pay their fair share," said IRS Commissioner Mark W. Everson in commenting on recent tax gap data.[43]

As reflected in table 4.3, according to the IRS, the largest component of the tax gap in 2001 was due to *underreporting* tax liability (by underreporting income or overstating deductions or credits). The remainder was due to underpayment of taxes due from filed returns and nonfiling of required returns (altogether or on time).

The IRS also found—not surprisingly—that compliance is greatest where there is both third party reporting and withholding. For example:

- Wages and salaries (which are subject to both third party reporting and withholding) have an underreporting percentage of only 1%;
- Interest and dividend income (which are subject to third party reporting but no withholding) have an underreporting percentage of 4.5%;
- Capital gains (which are subject to only partial reporting and no withholding) have an underreporting percentage of 8.6%; and
- Sole proprietor income and "other income," which are not subject to third party reporting or withholding, have a net underreporting percentage of 54%.[44]

Another contributing factor to the tax gap is the poor record of the Federal government in withholding procurement contracts from companies that are known to have underreported or underpaid their taxes. For example, the GAO reported that in 2002, more than 27,000 Defense contractors owed more than $3 billion in Federal taxes, yet many of these contractors continued to receive Federal contract awards.[45]

TABLE 4.3 Breakdown of the Gross Tax Gap: Tax Year 2001

Description of Taxes Unpaid in 2001 (most recent year for which data are available)	Gross Tax Gap ($ in billions)	Share of Total Gap
Individual Income Tax—Underreporting	197	57%
Underreported Business Income	109	
Underreported Nonbusiness Income	56	
Overstated Adjustments, Deductions, Exemptions, Credits	32	
Employment Tax—Underreporting	54	16%
Self-employment taxes (Social Security and Medicare taxes or the self-employed)	39	
FICA (Social Security and Medicare Payroll Taxes) and Unemployment Taxes	15	
Corporate Income Tax—Underreporting	30	9%
Large Corporations	25	
Small Corporations	5	
Estate, Excise Taxes—Underreporting	4	1%
Underpayment of Reported Income	33	10%
Nonfiling of Timely Tax Returns	27	8%
Gross Tax Gap (Noncompliance Rate: 16%)*	345*	100%

*After collection efforts, $290 billion remained unpaid (referred to as the "net tax gap").
Source: IRS.

There are differing views on how to close the tax gap. Treasury Department officials, in consultation with the IRS Oversight Board,[46] have asked Congress to enact provisions that would (1) require credit and debit card companies to report their customers' gross business receipts to IRS, (2) clarify the circumstances in which employee-leasing companies can be held liable for their clients' employment taxes, (3) expand information reporting on procurements by governmental entities, and (4) expand the signature requirement and penalty provisions applicable to paid tax return preparers.[47]

At the same time, the union that represents IRS employees blames cuts in IRS staffing for the ongoing tax gap. The union asserts that the number of tax returns filed grew from 115 million in 1995 to 130 million in 2003.[48] However, over the same time period, the number of IRS revenue officers and revenue agents shrunk by 40% and 30%, respectively.[49]

In reviewing the tax gap, the GAO suggested a results-oriented strategy: "Long-term, quantitative compliance goals, coupled with updated compliance data, would provide a solid base upon which to develop a more strategic, result-oriented approach to reducing the tax gap."[50] However, politics may get in the way. The Administration and Congress have traditionally been reluctant to beef up IRS enforcement capacity.

Recommended Sources for More Information on the Tax Gap

- **IRS:** Tax Gap Graphic: www.irs.gov/pub/irs-news/tax_gap_figures.pdf; Senate Testimony of Commissioner Mark Everson, September 26, 2006, http://hsgac.senate.gov/_files/Everson926.pdf.

- **Department of the Treasury**, Office of Tax Policy: *A Comprehensive Strategy for Reducing the Tax Gap*, September 26, 2006, http://www.ustreas.gov/press/releases/hp111.htm.
- **GAO:** Tax Compliance—Better Compliance Data and Long-term Goals Would Support a More Strategic IRS Approach to Reducing the Tax Gap, GAO-05-753 (Washington DC: July 18, 2005); Capital Gains Tax Gap, GAO-06-603 (Washington DC: June 2006).
- **2006 Annual Report of IRS Oversight Board:** "Tax Gap a Serious Concern," January 25, 2007, www.treas.gov/irsob/releases/2007/01252007.pdf.
- **National Treasury Employees Union:** "White Paper: Reducing the Tax Gap," September 26, 2006.
- **U.S. Congress, Joint Committee on Taxation:** Options to Improve Tax Compliance and Reform Tax Expenditures, JCS-02-05, January 27, 2005.

How Do U.S. Taxes Compare with Those in Other Countries?

> *Myth:* The tax burden for American taxpayers is higher than in most other Western nations.
>
> *Fact:* Taxes in the United States are, in fact, low compared with those in most other developed countries. This is reflected in data collected by the Organisation for Economic Cooperation and Development (OECD) (see figure 4.5). The OECD is a group of 30 democratic countries with market economies, known for its expertise in collecting statistics.[51]

U.S. total tax revenue in 2003 was equivalent to 25.6% of the nation's Gross Domestic Product.[52] Federal taxes amounted to 16.5% of GDP, and State and local taxes account for the remainder.[53] Japan and Korea had total tax revenue as a percentage of GDP roughly equal to the United States. Mexico is the only OECD member coming in lower, with a total tax rate of 19% of GDP.

Compared with the United States, the following countries had higher total tax revenues, as a percentage of GDP, in 2003: Switzerland, Australia, Turkey, Canada, Poland, Spain, Germany, United Kingdom, Greece, Czech Republic, Hungary, Netherlands, Italy, Austria, France, Norway, Finland, Belgium, Denmark, and Sweden. *Note that the U.S. tax rate of 25.6% of GDP is substantially lower than the average OECD rate of 36% and significantly lower than the European Union average rate of 40.5%.*[54]

Note also the low corporate tax rate in the United States as a percentage of GDP, compared with other market economies.

Tax Fairness, Reform, and Distribution of the Tax Burden

People want just taxes, more than they want lower taxes. They want to know that every man is paying his proportionate share according to his wealth.—Will Rogers, 1924[55]

This quote from the great American humorist Will Rogers is insightful. Most people understand that if we want the nation to be well defended; our laws enforced; Social Security, Medicare, and Medicaid benefits paid to America's elderly, disabled, and needy; our disabled

FIGURE 4.5 Tax Revenue as a Percentage of GDP, 2003

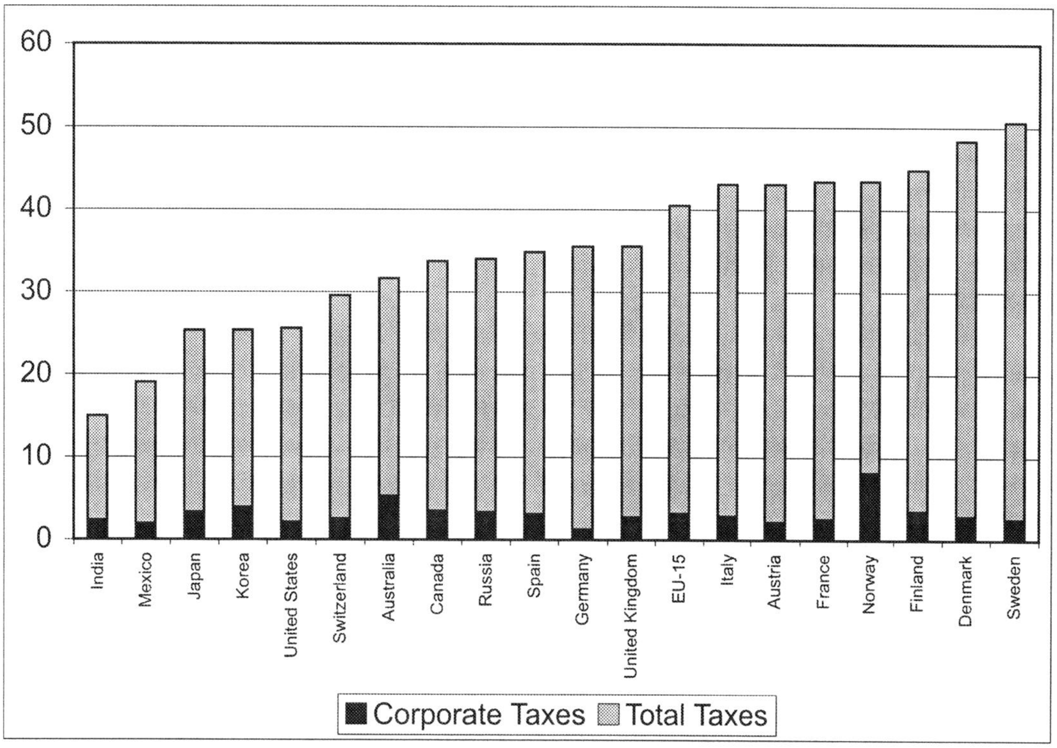

Source: OECD Factbook 2006.

veterans cared for; our highways and bridges maintained; the water we drink, the air we breathe, and the food we eat to be healthy; prescription drugs to be safe; and our children to receive a solid education that gives them equal opportunities to succeed, a sufficient amount of tax revenue must be raised. At the same time, people want to know that everyone is paying their "fair share." Determining the "fair share" is, of course, the complex issue.

Tax Fairness and the Flat Tax. In recent years, some have argued that a flat tax—under which everyone would pay the same percentage of their income—would be "simple" and "fair." Unfortunately, no tax system is "simple," because every tax system must define which "income" is subject to tax. Most everyone would agree that "income" includes wages, salaries and fees, but that is where the agreement ends. Should taxable income include interest? Dividends? Tips? Rental income? Earnings from retirement plans? Social Security benefits? Employer-provided health insurance? Disability benefits? Capital gains? Alimony? Employer-provided retirement benefits? Gifts? Inheritance? This is lesson No. 1 in the "metaphysics of taxation": *The issue of "What is income?" is inherently complex. No tax system can avoid this complexity.*

Addressing the question of "What is fair?" would seem on its face to be less complex than defining income. For example, what if we simply determined what level of taxation would raise the same amount of revenue as the current system if we applied a flat rate percentage across the board to all taxpayers (once we've determined what "income" is)? If, for the sake of argument, a 20% "flat" tax rate would accomplish this, would it not be the fairest way to raise revenues?

Consider the following examples. Under a flat 20% tax rate, a family of four with an income of $30,000 would pay $6,000—money that would come at the expense of the most basic life necessities—food, clothing medicine, and shelter. A family of four with an income of $75,000 would pay $15,000 in tax—a significant burden, though not quite as difficult as the burden on the lower-income family. A family of four with an income of $125,000 would pay $25,000—resulting in important, but less critical, choices. A family of four with an income of $200,000 would pay $40,000 in tax—likely to be less than they are currently paying and not a sum that would impinge on the basics. Jumping up to a family of four with a million-dollar income: they would pay $200,000 in tax. Some would argue this amounts to little or no burden at all.

In sum, under a 20% flat tax, the family earning $30,000 would pay to Uncle Sam money needed for the most basic necessities of life. As incomes go up, the burdensome nature of the flat tax would decrease and eventually be no burden at all to upper income taxpayers. This is lesson No. 2 in the metaphysics of taxation: *A tax system, such as the "flat tax," that may appear "fair" on its face, may not be fair at all when the real-life impact on families is closely examined.*

Tax Fairness and the Progressive Tax. This, in fact, is why the United States has settled on a "progressive" income tax, under which higher "brackets" of income are progressively taxed at higher rates. For example, in 2007, joint return income up to $15,650 is taxed at a 10% rate, while income over $349,700 is taxed at a 35% rate—with four additional tax brackets in between.

The "fairness" of the progressive tax system has for many years been the premise of the Treasury Department's analyses of proposed tax changes. In analyzing proposed changes, the Department typically examines the "distributional effects" of proposed tax legislation. (*Distributional effects* refer to how specific tax proposals would impact taxpayers at various income levels.) In a 1999 white paper discussing distributional analysis, the Department of the Treasury's Office of Tax Analysis suggested that a "fair" tax law is generally considered to be "one under which individuals with equal abilities to pay taxes pay equal amounts, and individuals with greater abilities to pay taxes pay greater amounts."[56] The Treasury analysis concluded that the best way to measure the distributional fairness of tax legislation is by examining the *percentage change in after-tax income* at each of the various income levels. The rationale for focusing on after-tax income is that it reflects the actual income available to families to spend or save.

An important caveat in any discussion of the progressive income tax system is that *nearly 80% of Americans pay more payroll tax than income tax.* While the income tax is progressive, the payroll tax is highly regressive. Each worker pays the same percentage, 7.65%, whether they earn $20,000 per year or $90,000 per year. Adding to the regressive nature of the payroll tax is that the Social Security portion of the tax (6.2%) is capped; that is, the tax is not levied on salaries or wages in excess of $97,500. Consequently, a head of household earning $97,500 per year pays the same Social Security payroll tax as a multibillionaire. This is lesson No. 3 in the metaphysics of taxation: *Any analysis of the progressivity of the U.S. income tax must be tempered by the regressivity of the Federal payroll tax.*

Distributional Effects of Recent Tax Cuts. The tax cuts enacted since 2001 have been the subject of much debate. Table 6.1 (in Part VI) summarizes the six major tax cuts enacted since 2001. Briefly, the two largest tax cuts occurred in 2001 and 2003 and lowered marginal

FIGURE 4.6 Distributional Effects of the 2001–2006 Tax Cuts

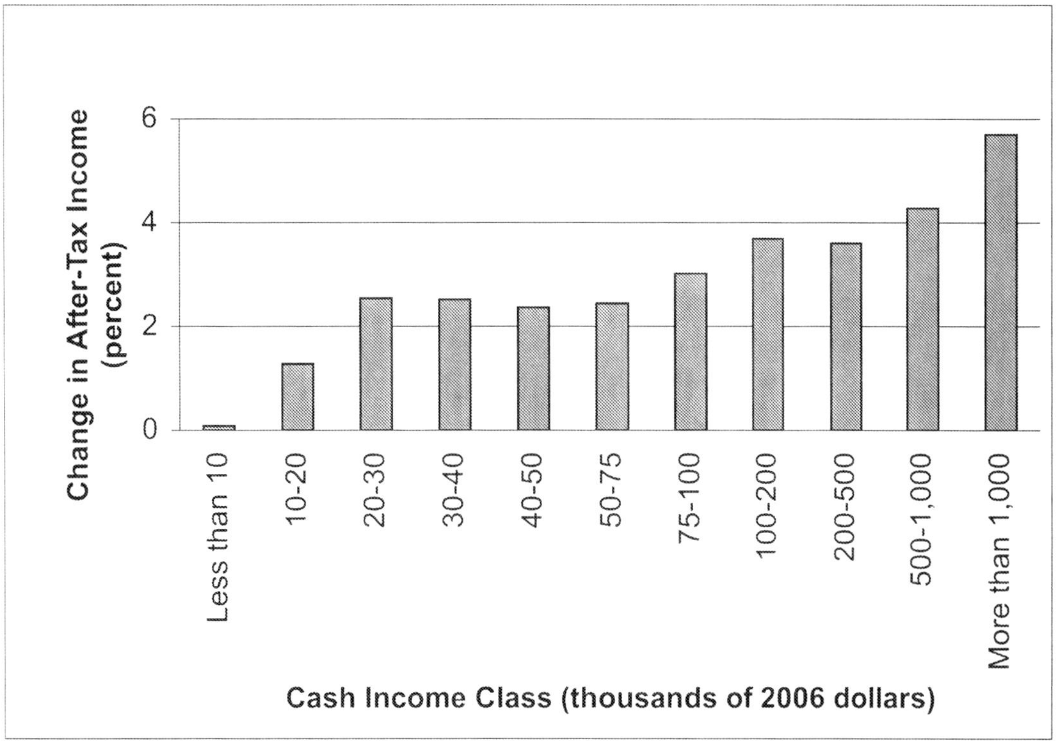

Source: www.taxpolicycenter.org, October 31, 2006.

tax rates, increased the child tax credit, provided marriage penalty relief, temporarily reduced the alternative minimum tax, began a phase-out of the estate tax, and reduced rates on dividend and capital gains income. Figure 4.6 displays the combined effects of the recent cuts on *after-tax income.* Analyzed from the perspective of how much the tax cuts increased after-tax income, taxpayers in the lower- and middle-income brackets saw their after-tax incomes increase between 2% and 4%, with the average increase being 3.2%. Taxpayers at the high end—the top one-fifth of 1% of income earners—benefited the most, with after-tax income increasing close to 6%.

Another way to analyze the 2001–2006 tax cuts is to examine the *share of the combined tax benefits* accruing to each of the income groups (see figure 4.7). From this perspective, what stands out is that the largest share of the tax benefits—nearly one-quarter—accrued to the $100,000–$200,000 income group even though this income group constitutes only 10.4% of taxpayers. The other figure that stands out—and which has caused considerable debate—is that *nearly 17% of the cumulative tax cut benefits accrued to the 0.2% of taxpayers earning over $1 million per year.* The often-debated issue from a budgetary perspective is whether the several hundred billion dollars (over 10 years) in deficit financing required to pay for this high-income portion of the tax cuts was fiscally or economically justified. Some argue that the high-income cuts stimulate significant economic activity; others disagree, emphasizing the long-term economic costs of deficit-financing the cuts.

FIGURE 4.7 The 2001–2006 Tax Cuts: Distribution of Tax Benefits

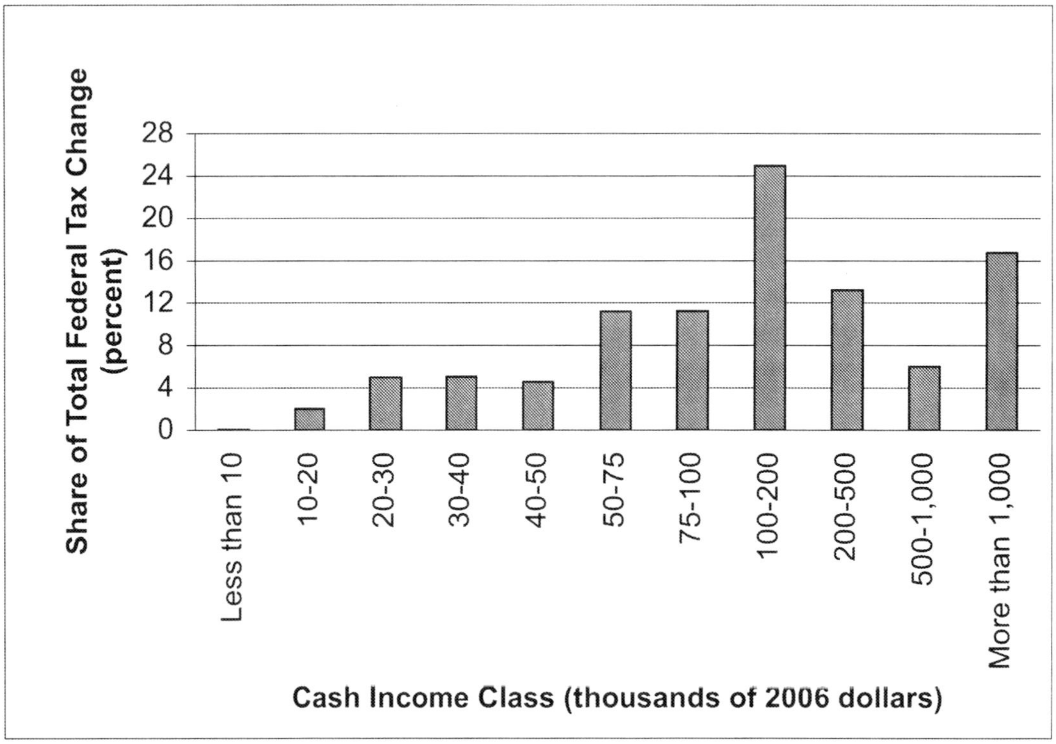

Source: www.taxpolicycenter.org, October 31 2006.

Recommended Sources for More Information on Tax Fairness, Reform, and Distribution of the Tax Burden

- **CBO:** *Historical Effective Tax Rates: 1979 to 2002,* March 2005, www.cbo.gov.
- **CRS:** "Flat Tax Proposals and Fundamental Tax Reform: An Overview," IB95060, www.opencrs .cdt.org/document/IB95060.
- **Final Report of the President's Advisory Panel on Federal Tax Reform:** www.taxreformpanel .gov/final-report/.
- **Joint Committee on Taxation:** "Distributional Effects of the Conference Agreement on H.R. 1836" (JCX-52-01) May 26, 2001.
- **Tax Policy Center:** "Distributional Effects of the 2001and 2003 Tax Cuts and Their Financing," by William Gale, **Peter Orszag (current CBO Director)**, and Isaac Shapiro, www.taxpolicycenter.org/ publications/url.cfm?ID=411018.

Notes

1. Daniel B. Baker, ed., *Political Quotations* (Detroit: Gale Research, 1990), 220.

2. Baker, ed., *Political Quotations,* 218. Colbert was controller general of finance (from 1665) and secretary of state for the navy (from 1668) under King Louis XIV of France. He carried out the program of economic reconstruction that helped make France the dominant power in Europe. "Colbert,

Jean-Baptiste," in *Encyclopædia Britannica* from Encyclopædia Britannica 2006 Ultimate Reference Suite DVD].

3. Data accompanying "Joint Statement on Budget Results for Fiscal Year 2007 (Washington D.C.: Treasury Department and Office of Management and Budget, October 11, 2007), table 2, http://treas.gov/press/releases/reports/ad,ditionaltable2.pdf.

4. The elderly and blind are allowed an additional standard deduction. CRS, "Overview of the Federal Tax System," June 2, 2006, 1.

5. See chapter 3-8.

6. The maximum Child and Dependent Care Credit is 35% of costs up to $3000 for one individual and $6,000 for two or more individuals. The rate is reduced when the taxpayer's AGI exceeds $15,000. CRS, "Overview of the Federal Tax System," June 2, 2006, 5.

7. These education credits, enacted in 1997, provide benefits for postsecondary education. For those who are eligible, a credit of 100% of a portion of tuition and 50% of an additional portion applies for the first two years of undergraduate tuition. CRS, "Overview of the Federal Tax System," 5.

8. Extra standard deductions are allowed for the blind and elderly.

9. 2007 Federal Tax Rate Schedule: www.irs.gov/formspubs/article/0,,id=164272,00.html.

10. "The Taxpayer Advocate Service is an IRS program that provides an independent system to assure that tax problems, which have not been resolved through normal channels, are promptly and fairly handled. . . . Each state and campus has at least one local Taxpayer Advocate, who is *independent of the local IRS office* and reports directly to the National Taxpayer Advocate. The goals of the Taxpayer Advocate Service are to protect individual and business taxpayer rights and to reduce taxpayer burden. The Taxpayer Advocate independently represents (taxpayer) interests and concerns with the IRS." See www.irs.gov/advocate/.

11. National Taxpayer Advocate, "2003 Annual Report to Congress," 5.

12. CRS, "Alternative Minimum Taxpayers by State," March 17, 2005, 1.

13. The AMT exemption amount as of 2006 is $58,000 for joint returns and $40,250 for single and head of household returns, but these amounts may revert to lower levels if AMT relief is not extended in 2007.

14. More specifically, the regular income tax brackets are indexed annually for inflation (a measure adopted in the 1980s in response to so-called bracket creep), while the AMT exemption amount is not indexed for inflation.

15. Gregg Esenwein and Steven Maguire, "The Potential Distributional Effects of the Alternative Minimum Tax," RS22200 (Washington, D.C.: Congressional Research Service, June 15, 2007), 4.

16. CBO, "Revenue and Tax Policy Brief: The Alternative Minimum Tax," April 15, 2004, p1.

17. Esenwein and Maguire, "The Potential Distributional Effects," 2.

18. Gregg Esenwein and Steven Maguire, "The Alternative Minimum Tax for Individuals," RL30149 (Washington D.C.: Congressional Research Service, August 22, 2007), summary.

19. Esenwein and Maguire, "The Alternative Minimum Tax for Individuals," 8.

20. Greg Esenwein and Jane Gravelle, "Modifying the AMT: Revenue Costs and Potential Revenue Offsets," RL33899 (Washington D.C.: Congressional Research Service, March 6, 2007), summary; and Heather Rothman, "Finance May Move One-Year AMT Patch with Two-Year Tax Extenders Provision" (Washington D.C.: BNA Daily Tax Report, October 17, 2007), G-7.

21. Unemployment Insurance tax receipts amount to about 5% of payroll tax receipts.

22. See chapter 3-4, note 1.

23. U.S. Social Security Administration, *Fact Sheet on 2008 Social Security Changes,* October 2007.

24. Jane Gravelle, "Economic Issues Surrounding the Estate and Gift Tax: A Brief Summary," RS20609 (Washington D.C.: Congressional Research Service, January 23, 2006), 2.

25. In 2010, the estate tax will be replaced with a provision to tax appreciation on inherited assets.

26. Married couples can make gifts of $24,000 to each individual.

27. Jane Gravelle, "Economic Issues Surrounding the Estate and Gift Tax: A Brief Summary," 2.

28. Jane Gravelle and Steven Maguire, "Estate Taxes and Family Businesses: Economic Issues," RL33070 (Washington D.C.: Congressional Research Service, September 8, 2006), summary.

29. Congressional Budget Office, "Effects of the Federal Estate Tax on Farms and Small Businesses," July 2005, 13–15.

30. *New York Times*, "Few Wealthy Farmers Owe Estate Taxes, Report Says," July 10, 2005, 21.

31. Joint Committee on Taxation, *Estimated Revenue Effects of H.R. 8, the Death Tax Permanency Act of 2005*, JCX-20-05, 109th Congress, April 13, 2005.

32. Property passing from a decedent's estate generally receives a "stepped-up" basis, which means that the heirs' basis in the inherited property is the fair market value of the asset as of the date of death (or an alternate valuation date up to six months after death). This stepped-up basis allows a beneficiary of an estate who sells the property to avoid tax on any appreciation in the property's value that occurred before the decedent's death.

33. See, for example, www.forbes.com/lists/2006/54/biz_06rich400_The-400-Richest-Americans_land.html.

34. Reba Collins, ed., *Will Rogers Says . . .* (Oklahoma City: Neighbors and Quaid, 1993), 23.

35. Henry Paulson, Secretary of the Treasury, and Jim Nussle, OMB Director, "Joint Statement on Budget Results for Fiscal Year 2007," October 11, 2007, table 2.

36. See Pamela Jackson, "The Federal Excise Tax on Gasoline and the Highway Trust Fund: A Short History," RL30304 (Washington D.C.: Congressional Research Service, April 4, 2006).

37. See Louis Alan Talley and Pamela Jackson, "Federal Excise Tax on Tires: Where the Rubber Meets the Road," RL30302 (Washington D.C.: Congressional Research Service, October 6, 2005).

38. Paulson and Nussle, "Joint Statement," table 2.

39. Paulson and Nussle, "Joint Statement," table 2.

40. Congressional Budget Office, *The Budget and Economic Outlook: Fiscal Years 2007 to 2016*, January 2006.

41. In order to develop estimates of the tax gap for FY 2001, the IRS launched the National Research Program, a three-year study involving the review and examination of 46,000 randomly selected returns. The audits were completed by the end of 2005. Internal Revenue Service, "IRS Updates Tax Gap Estimates" (IR-2006-28), February 14, 2006.

42. Internal Revenue Service, "IRS Updates Tax Gap Estimates."

43. Internal Revenue Service, "IRS Updates Tax Gap Estimates."

44. Internal Revenue Service, Written Testimony of Commissioner Mark Everson before the Senate Homeland Security and Governmental Affairs Committee on Uncollected Taxes and the Issue of Transparency, September 26, 2006, www.hsgac.senate.gov/_files/Everson926.pdf.

45. Internal Revenue Service, National Taxpayer Advocate, *2004 Report to Congress*, executive summary, II-4.

46. The IRS Oversight Board was created by law in 1998. The mission of the nine-member board is to "oversee the IRS in its administration, management, conduct, direction, and supervision of the execution and application of the internal revenue laws and to provide experience, independence, and stability to the IRS so that it may move forward in a cogent, focused manner." See www.trea.gov/irsob/index.html.

47. Internal Revenue Service, Written Testimony of Commissioner Mark Everson.

48. Bureau of National Affairs, "Everson Says Legislative Proposals, Funding Key to Closing Annual $290 Billion Tax Gap," *Daily Tax Report*, February 16, 2006.

49. The number of IRS revenue officers and revenue agents shrunk by 40% (8,139 to 5,004) and 30% (16,078 to 11,513), respectively. National Treasury Employees Union (NTEU) press release, September 26, 2006, http://www.nteu.org/PressKits/PressRelease/PressRelease.aspx?ID=967.

50. U.S. Government Accountability Office, "Tax Compliance: Better Compliance Data and Long-term Goals Would Support a More Strategic IRS Approach to Reducing the Tax Gap," GAO-05-753, July 2005.

51. For more information on the OECD, see www.oecd.org.

52. *OECD Factbook 2006*, Public Finance: Total Tax Revenue as a percentage of GDP (2003).

53. Office of Management and Budget, *Budget of the U.S. Government: FY 2008, Historical Tables* (Washington DC: Government Printing Office, February 2007), 24.

54. *OECD Factbook 2006*, Public Finance: Total Tax Revenue as a percentage of GDP (2003).

55. Collins, ed., *Will Rogers Says . . .* , 25.

56. Department of the Treasury, Office of Tax Analysis, *U.S. Treasury Distributional Analysis Methodology* (OTA Paper 85), September 1999, www.ustreas.gov/ota/ota85.pdf.

PART

V

TAX EXPENDITURES: SPENDING ON THE REVENUE SIDE

The nation's long-term fiscal imbalance provides an . . . impetus for reexamining all major spending and tax provisions. This includes tax incentives and subsidies intended to promote various social and economic objectives.—Government Accountability Office, 2005

Tax expenditures are *reductions in tax liabilities* that result from

- *excluding or exempting* items from gross income ("tax exclusions"),

- *deducting* items from either gross income or adjusted gross income ("tax deductions"),

- granting *preferential tax rates* for certain items of income ("tax preferences"),

- *applying credits* to directly reduce taxes owed ("tax credits"), or

- *deferring* tax liability on certain types of income ("tax deferrals").

In the context of budgeting, these are collectively referred to as "tax expenditures" because the government foregoes revenues it would have otherwise collected.[1] (Colloquially, they are often referred to as "tax preferences" and "tax breaks"—or as "tax loopholes" by those who disagree with particular provisions.)

In effect, tax expenditures are "spending on the revenue side" of the budget because policymakers have written into the Tax Code provisions that reduce Federal taxes in order to achieve specific policy outcomes such as encouraging home ownership, financing postsecondary education, assisting a particular industry, or stimulating research and development.

Tax expenditures may also be viewed as the revenue equivalent of spending entitlements (see chapter 2-9). For example, just as Americans 65 and older are legally entitled to Medicare hospital insurance benefits (on the spending side of the Federal Budget), employees who receive health insurance from their employers are *entitled* to exclude the employer-paid premiums from their gross income. In both examples, eligible individuals are legally entitled to specific benefits—one on the spending side of the Budget, the other on the revenue (tax) side.

Annual tax expenditures are growing both in number and in dollar amount. From 1974 to 2004, the number of tax expenditures reported by the Treasury Department more than doubled, from 67 to 146;[2] some were repealed during that time, but many more were added. As reflected in figure 5.1, *the aggregate dollar amount of tax expenditures is approaching a trillion dollars per year—nearly as much as total discretionary spending.*

As with spending programs, one cannot generalize about tax expenditures. As displayed in table 5.1, tax expenditures are as varied in purpose and operation as programs on the spending side of the budget. Nevertheless, because of the enormous aggregate impact[3] of tax expenditures on Federal revenues, it is important to understand their global impact on the Federal Budget and U.S. economy.

The GAO recently conducted a comprehensive review of tax expenditures and recommended that the "Office of Management and Budget (OMB), consulting with the U.S. Department of the Treasury, take several steps to ensure greater transparency of and accountability for tax expenditures by reporting better information on tax expenditure performance and more fully incorporating tax expenditures into federal performance management and budget review processes."[4]

This is sound advice for two reasons: (1) oversight of Federal programs can only be fully effective if policymakers examine spending programs *and* related tax expenditures, and (2) the unsustainable explosion of Federal debt projected as far as the eye can see (discussed in Part VI) requires that policymakers carefully and regularly review the efficacy of all Federal tax expenditures. Unfortunately, OMB rejected the GAO recommendations[5] and has thus far not applied either the GPRA or PART performance review processes (explained in chapter 2-7) to the nearly $1 trillion of annual tax expenditures.

FIGURE 5.1 Comparison of Spending, Revenues, and Tax Expenditures

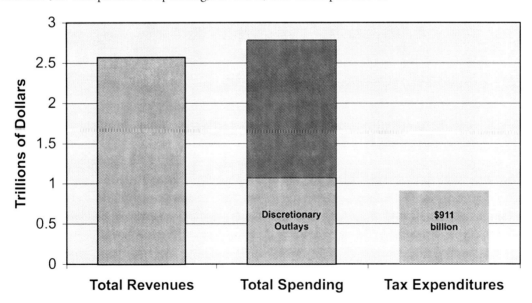

Sources: CBO, CRS, and GAO.[6]

TABLE 5.1 FY 2007 Estimated Tax Expenditures (in billions of dollars)

MAJOR TAX EXPENDITURES—INDIVIDUAL AND CORPORATE
(FY 2007 Estimates in Billions of Dollars)

TAX EXPENDITURE	*DESCRIPTION/ PURPOSE*	*Est. 2007 Cost*	*Ind.*	*Corp.*	*Estimated 2007 Total Cost by Category*
Health	Exclusion: employer-paid health premiums	141	X		**200**
	*Exclusion of Medicare benefits	40	X		
	Deductibility of medical expenses	4	X		
	Deductibility of self-employed health premiums	4	X		
	Deductibility: health-related charitable contributions	5	X	X	
	Medical/Health Savings Accounts	1	X	X	
	Exclusion-interest on hospital construction bonds	4	X	X	
	Payments to employers to maintain Rx drug plans	1			
	Tax credit for orphan drug research	0.3		X	
Home Ownership	Deduction of mortgage interest	80	X		**134**
	Capital gains rollover	37	X		
	Deductibility of property taxes on owner-occupied	16	X		
	Exclusion of interest on mortgage subsidy bonds	1	X	X	
Business-related	Accelerated depreciation-machinery/equip	51	X	X	**117**
	Deferral of income: controlled foreign corps	12		X	
	Deduction—U.S. production activities	11	X	X	
	Expensing R&E costs	6		X	
	Expensing of small investments	5		X	
	Graduated corporate income tax rate	4		X	

(Continued)

TABLE 5.1 FY 2007 Estimated Tax Expenditures (in billions of dollars) (Continued)

TAX EXPENDITURE	DESCRIPTION/ PURPOSE	Est. 2007 Cost	Ind.	Corp.	Estimated 2007 Total Cost by Category
Business-related	Exclusion—income earned abroad by U.S. citizens	3	X		
	*Deferral of gain on like-kind exchanges	3		X	
	Special Employee Stock Option Plan Rules	2	X	X	
	Extraterritorial income exclusion	2		X	
	Tax Deferral for Financial Firms	2		X	
	Expensing of Research and Experimentation	6	X	X	
	Credit for increasing research activities	10	X	X	
Pension/ Retirement	Exclusion of employer pension contributions	50	X		**111**
	Exclusion of 401(k) contributions	42	X		
	Exclusion of "Keogh" contributions	11	X		
	Exclusion of IRA contributions/earnings	6	X		
	Additional deduction for elderly	2	X		
Capital gains	Preferential 15% rate for capital gains income (except agriculture, timber, iron ore, coal)	52	X		**52**
Religious/ charitable	Deductibility of religious and charitable contributions (*other than* education or health)	40	X	X	**41**
	Clergy: "housing allowance"	0.5	X		
Children/ Families	Child Tax Credit	33	X		**35**
	Adoption credit and exclusion	0.6	X		
	Exclusion of foster care payments	0.5	X		
	Assistance—adopted foster children	0.4	X		

TABLE 5.1 FY 2007 Estimated Tax Expenditures (in billions of dollars) (Continued)

TAX EXPENDITURE	DESCRIPTION/ PURPOSE	Est. 2007 Cost	Ind.	Corp.	Estimated 2007 Total Cost by Category
State/local taxes	Deductibility of nonbusiness state and local taxes (other than an owner-occupied home)	34	X		**34**
Community Development	Exclusion: interest on state and local bonds for various public purposes	30	X	X	**33**
	Empowerment zones and renewal communities	1	X	X	
	Exclusion: interest on airport/dock bonds	1	X	X	
	New markets tax credit— $830M	0.8	X	X	
Capital gains on inherited property	At death, heirs receive a "stepped-up" basis on property (i.e. they are not taxed on the appreciation).	33	X		**33**
Social Security benefits	Exclude retiree benefits (except for higher-income beneficiaries who are taxed on a portion of benefits)	18	X		**26**
	Exclude Social Security disability benefits	5	X		
	Exclude dependents' and survivors' benefits	3	X		
Employee benefits	*Exclusion of miscellaneous fringe benefits	7	X		**23**
	Exclusion of workers' comp benefits	6	X		
	*Exclusion—income earned by voluntary employee beneficiary associations	2	X		
	Exclusion—reimbursed employee parking	3	X		

(Continued)

TABLE 5.1 FY 2007 Estimated Tax Expenditures (in billions of dollars) (Continued)

TAX EXPENDITURE	DESCRIPTION/ PURPOSE	Est. 2007 Cost	Ind.	Corp.	Estimated 2007 Total Cost by Category
	Exclusion of premiums: group term life insurance	2	X		
	Exclusion of employee meals and lodging	1	X		
	Exclusion of employer-provided child care	0.9	X		
	Exclusion of employer-provided transit passes	0.6	X		
	Exclusion of accident/ disability insurance	0.3	X		
Insurance	Exclusion of interest on life insurance savings	20	X	X	**22**
	*Special treatment—life insurance company reserves	2		X	
Higher education	Deductibility: charitable contributions for education	5	X	X	**21**
	HOPE tax credit	3	X		
	Lifetime Learning tax credit	2	X		
	Parental personal exemption for students ages 19–23	3	X		
	Exclusion of scholarship and fellowship income	2	X		
	Exclusion of interest on bonds for private education	2	X	X	
	Deduction for higher education expenses	1	X		
	Deductibility of student loan interest	0.8	X		
	Exclusion: earnings of 529 education savings accounts	0.8	X		
	Exclusion of employer-provided assistance	0.6	X		
	Exclusion of interest on student loan bonds	0.6			

TABLE 5.1 FY 2007 Estimated Tax Expenditures (in billions of dollars) (Continued)

TAX EXPENDITURE	DESCRIPTION/ PURPOSE	Est. 2007 Cost	Ind.	Corp.	Estimated 2007 Total Cost by Category
Rental housing	Accelerated depreciation-rental housing	11	X	X	**19**
	Exception from passive loss rules: rental housing	7	X		
	Interest exclusion-rental housing bonds	1	X	X	
Low-income assistance	Earned Income Tax Credit (revenue loss) [7]	5	X		**15**
	Credit for low-income housing investments	5	X	X	
	Credit for child/dependent care expenses	3	X		
	Low-income savers' credit	0.7	X		
	Exclusion of public assistance benefits	0.5	X	X	
	Work Opportunity Tax Credit	0.4	X	X	
	Welfare-to-Work Tax Credit	0.1	X		
Military and Veterans' benefits	Exclusion of vets' death benefits/ disability comp	4	X		**10**
	Exclusion—Armed Forces benefits	3	X		
	*Exclusion—medical care and TRICARE medical insurance for military dependents, retirees	2	X		
	Exclusion of GI bill benefits	0.3	X		
	Exclusion of veterans pensions	0.2	X		
	Exclusion of military disability pensions	0.1	X		
Energy, environment, natural resources[8]	Alternative fuel production credit	2	X	X	**7**
	Expensing of fuel exploration and development	0.9	X	X	
	New technology credit	0.7	X	X	
	Fuels: excess percentage over cost depletion	0.8	X	X	

(Continued)

TABLE 5.1 FY 2007 Estimated Tax Expenditures (in billions of dollars) (Continued)

TAX EXPENDITURE	DESCRIPTION/ PURPOSE	Est. 2007 Cost	Ind.	Corp.	Estimated 2007 Total Cost by Category
	*Special tax rate for nuclear decommissioning	0.6	X		
	Exclusion of interest on bonds for waste facilities	0.6	X	X	
	Expensing—timber growing costs	0.3	X	X	
	Credit for energy efficiency improvements	0.4	X		
	Nonfuel minerals: excess over cost depletion	0.5	X	X	
	Credit/deduction: clean-fuel vehicles	0.3	X		
	Energy-efficient commercial buildings	0.2	X	X	
	Amortize geological expenditures/oil exploration	0.1	X	X	
	Biodiesel producer credits	0.1	X		
Credit unions	Exemption of credit union income	1		X	**1**
Savings bonds	Deferral of interest on savings bonds	1	X		**1**
Agriculture related[9]	Agriculture-related tax preferences	1	X	X	**1**

Note: This table includes all tax expenditures costing more than $2 billion per year and a sampling of tax expenditures costing less than $2 billion per year. Source: Treasury Department estimates as set forth in the President's Budget for FY 2008, except for items marked with an (*) asterisk, which are Joint Committee on Taxation estimates.[10]

Significant Tax Expenditures

Health Care

The largest tax expenditure in the Tax Code is the exclusion of employer-paid health insurance premiums from employee income. The exclusion is designed to encourage employer-provided health insurance. The estimated cost of this tax expenditure in FY 2007 is $141 billion. In order to provide a similar type of tax benefit to self-employed individuals, the Congress amended the Tax Code to make self-employed health insurance premiums fully deductible.

Other health-related tax expenditures include (1) the exclusion from income of Medicare benefits, (2) the deductibility of medical expenses exceeding 7.5% of adjusted gross income (AGI), (3) the exclusion of interest earned on government bonds issued to finance hospital construction, and (4) a tax credit for the clinical testing of "orphan drugs" (i.e., drugs that treat rare physical conditions or rare diseases).

Home Ownership

The second-largest tax expenditure—and probably the best known—is the deduction for mortgage interest paid on owner-occupied homes. Taxpayers who itemize their deductions are permitted to deduct this interest on primary and secondary homes. In addition, home owners may deduct interest on up to $100,000 of home equity loans.

The mortgage interest deduction is one of the best examples of using the Tax Code to encourage particular behaviors and boost certain sectors of the economy. This tax expenditure, projected to cost $80 billion in FY 2007, encourages Americans to own their homes. In addition, from a macroeconomic perspective, it is also a cornerstone of the home-building sector.

Another tax expenditure that boosts home ownership is the capital gains exclusion on home sales. A homeowner can exclude from tax up to $500,000 ($250,000 for singles) of the capital gains from the sale of a principal residence.

A third item that assists homeowners is the deduction for property taxes paid on owner-occupied houses. This provision also assists the localities in which the homes are located by, in effect, reducing the financial impact of property taxes on homeowners—thereby allowing localities to raise higher amounts of revenue.

Families and Children

Another well-known tax credit is the "child tax credit." Under this provision, middle- and low-income taxpayers with children under age 17 are entitled to a $1,000 per child credit against the Federal taxes they owe.[11] In addition, the tax credit is "partially refundable," which means that even if a family does not owe any tax against which to apply the credit, they will nevertheless receive a "refund" check from the Treasury for part of the $1,000 credit. These "refund" checks are treated as Federal outlays (on the spending side of the budget). The estimated FY 2007 cost of the Child Credit is $33 billion in reduced revenues and $15 billion in outlays.

Several smaller tax expenditures assist families in other ways. The adoption credit allows taxpayers a tax credit for various types of adoption expenses (phased out for higher-income taxpayers). Taxpayers may also exclude certain adoption expenses from income.

Foster parents who provide a home and care for children who are wards of the State may exclude compensation received for this service from their calculation of adjusted gross income.[12]

Higher Education

The Tax Code includes more than a dozen tax expenditures for higher education, totaling over $20 billion. The largest of these is the deductibility of charitable contributions for education, estimated at $4 billion for FY 2007.

The largest item specifically created for higher education is the HOPE tax credit, which allows lower- and middle-income families up to a $1,500 credit for a student's tuition and fees during the first two years of higher education. A similar credit, the Lifetime Learning Credit, allows up to a $2,000 credit per year for lower- and middle-income families for both undergraduate and graduate education. Together, the two tax expenditures cost about $5 billion per year.[13]

Other provisions include permission for parents to claim a personal exemption for dependent students between 19 and 23; an exclusion for scholarship and fellowship income; an exclusion for interest earned on government bonds to finance construction of education facilities; a deduction for up to $2,500 of interest paid on an education loan; an exclusion of earnings on Section 529 college savings accounts; an exclusion from income for employer-provided education assistance; an exclusion for interest earned on State and local bonds issued to finance student loans; and income earned on "education IRAs" when used to pay for tuition and fees.

Business-Related Tax Expenditures

The Tax Code includes a number of significant tax provisions to stimulate various economic activities. For example, research and experimentation (R&E) costs can be "expensed"—that is, deducted in the year incurred. In addition, the R&E tax credit reduces a business's corporate income taxes if it *increases* R&E above a specified base amount.

Certain industries have been provided with industry-specific tax preferences. For example, the energy industry has been provided with significant tax incentives to spur domestic production of oil and gas, as well as to develop alternative energy sources.

Other sectors receiving special tax preferences include the nonfuel minerals industry, the timber industry, the agriculture industry, credit unions, and the life insurance industry. The nonfuel minerals industry is permitted to expense (deduct in their entirety in the year incurred) capital outlays associated with exploration and development of nonfuel minerals.[14] Certain timber sales are taxed at the lower capital gains rate rather than as ordinary income, and most of the production costs of growing timber may be expensed in the year incurred rather than deducted when the timber is sold.[15] The largest agricultural tax expenditure permits sales of certain agricultural products, such as unharvested crops, to be taxed at the capital gains rate rather than as ordinary income. Other provisions allow farmers to expense items such as feed and fertilizer in the year of purchase. Farmers are also permitted to lower their tax liability through income-averaging over a three-year period.[16] Credit unions receive favored tax treatment by not being taxed on undistributed earnings.[17] Investment income earned on certain types of life insurance contracts is exempt from income tax, and small life insurance companies are entitled to a special deduction.[18]

Religious and Charitable Contributions

Under the Establishment Clause of the Constitution, the government is clearly prohibited from providing *direct* financial support for *specific* religious institutions or activities. However, the Federal government, through the Tax Code, does provide substantial *indirect support* for religious activities.

First, there is an interesting provision called the "parsonage allowance." It used to be the case that many churches provided a house for their clergy called *parsonages.* As church property, such parsonages were regarded as tax exempt and were therefore not taxed as income to the clergy residing there. Eventually many churches—along with most synagogues—began providing their clergy with "housing or parsonage allowances" in lieu of an actual parsonage. The IRS responded by determining that a member of the clergy living in a parsonage building owned by the Church, or receiving a monetary allowance for private housing, should be equally treated as exempt from taxation. The result is that this half-billion-dollar annual tax expenditure allows religious organizations to declare a portion of their clergy's salary as a "housing allowance," making a significant portion of their salary effectively exempt from Federal income tax.

The Tax Code provides a second type of indirect, but substantial, support of religious activities, by making contributions to religious organizations tax deductible as charitable contributions. In effect, this means that contributions made specifically to support the religious activities of a church, synagogue, or mosque are treated as fully deductible, whether paid as "annual dues," a tithe, or in whatever form collected. Neither the President's Budget for FY 2007 nor the JCT estimates specify how much of charitable contributions are aimed specifically at support of religious activities. However, since deductibility of charitable contributions "other than education and health" is estimated at $40 billion, one may surmise that deductible religious contributions are substantial. Similar to the parsonage allowance, the deductibility of these contributions are, in effect, *indirect* government support of religious activities.

Encouraging Americans to Save for Retirement

Various pension provisions are good examples of using the Tax Code to encourage particular behavior—in this case, setting aside money for retirement. Pension-related tax expenditures are estimated to cost $111 billion in FY 2007.

The largest of these provisions is the exclusion of employer-provided pension contributions from employees' income. In addition, the earnings from the employer's contribution are not taxed until funds are withdrawn by the employee. These provisions together amount to a $50 billion tax expenditure and are an incentive for employers and employees to make pension contributions part of compensation packages.

Employee contributions to 401(k) or similar retirement savings plans are also excluded from income. 401(k) plans are retirement savings plans offered by a company to its employees, allowing them to set aside income for retirement purposes. The income placed in the accounts is excluded from taxation. In some cases, employers match employee contributions dollar-for-dollar. For FY 2007, employees may contribute $15,500 of income to their 401(k)— all of which is exempt from tax. The *investment income* earned by 401(k)-type plans is deferred until withdrawn. This provision is estimated to cost about $42 billion in FY 2007.

Similar types of tax-preferred retirement savings plans are available for self-employed individuals and small businesses. These retirement plans—known as Keogh, SIMPLE, and SEP plans—all permit the self-employed individual or small business to annually exclude from gross income a specified percentage up to a maximum dollar amount. In each case, like the

401(k), *earnings* on funds placed in the account are not taxed until withdrawn. The tax expenditure for Keogh contributions in FY 2007 is estimated at $11 billion.

Individual retirement accounts (IRAs) are another type of tax incentive aimed at encouraging people to save for retirement. A *traditional IRA* allows an eligible individual to place up to $4,000 annually in the account and deduct the entire amount from AGI. *Roth IRAs*, while not providing an up-front deduction, allow *earnings* to grow tax-free. For those whose income level is too high to qualify for the traditional IRA or Roth IRA, *nondeductible IRAs* are available that defers tax on earnings until funds are withdrawn at retirement. For FY 2007, the tax expenditure for all types of IRAs is estimated at $6 billion.

Energy and Environment

Tax provisions related to energy production and environmental protection provide additional examples of how tax policy can be used to influence behavior. For example, several Tax Code provisions are designed to stimulate domestic energy production:

- Costs incurred in drilling oil and gas wells can be expensed (deducted) during the year they are incurred—within certain limitations—rather than amortized (spread out) over the productive life of the well.
- Independent fuel mineral producers (oil, gas, oil shale, coal, uranium) are permitted to deduct a percentage of gross income, rather than deducting costs over the life of the property. Unlike depreciation or amortizing costs, percentage depletion is permitted to exceed the cost of the investment.
- Accelerated depreciation (deduction of capital costs over time) is used to incentivize new gas distribution pipelines.

Other provisions are designed to spur conservation as well as development of alternative, environmentally-friendly energy sources:

- A credit for synthetic fuels produced from coal, as well as gas produced from biomass (energy from wood, garbage, and agricultural waste);
- A new technology credit for equipment that produces energy from solar, wind, geothermal, biomass, poultry waste, small irrigation, municipal waste, and certain types of coal;
- An income tax credit for use of ethanol;
- A tax credit and deduction for clean-fuel vehicles (e.g., gas-electric hybrids);
- A tax credit for investing in clean coal facilities;
- A deduction for energy-efficient commercial buildings and credits for new energy-efficient homes, energy efficiency improvements to existing homes, and installation of solar technology;
- A credit for the manufacture of energy-efficient home appliances;
- A gasoline excise tax credit for use of alternative fuels; and
- A tax credit for farmers using biodiesel fuel.

Subjecting Tax Expenditures to a Reasonable Level of Scrutiny

A significant anomaly of the current budget process is that *spending* programs typically receive close scrutiny by multiple congressional committees, but *tax expenditures* receive comparatively little scrutiny. Part of this is undoubtedly due to ideology. Any proposal to terminate a tax expenditure can easily be criticized by opponents as a "tax increase."

In addition, neither the Congress nor the Executive Branch is structured in ways that submit tax expenditures to performance-based assessments. For example, the higher education tax expenditures are rarely, if ever, analyzed by the congressional committees with expertise in education, nor does the Department of Education review the education tax expenditures. The expenditures are designed, considered, and legislated by the Department of the Treasury, the House Ways and Means Committee, and the Senate Finance Committee.

The Century Foundation Working Group on Tax Expenditures recently proposed that tax expenditures be subjected to the following scrutiny:

- Why is a government tax expenditure program necessary at all?
- What are the objectives of the tax expenditure, and how will success or failure be measured?
- What evidence can be cited that suggests the tax break will accomplish these objectives at an acceptable cost?
- Why is a tax break better than a direct spending program for accomplishing this purpose?

Considering that tax expenditures cost nearly a trillion dollars each year—nearly as much as total discretionary spending—it would seem a matter of common sense to require routine, performance-based reviews that include scrutiny by the agencies of government and congressional committees possessing relevant knowledge and expertise.

Recommended Sources for More Information Tax Expenditures

- **U.S. Congress, Joint Committee on Taxation:** "Estimates of Federal Tax Expenditures for Fiscal Years 2007–2010," (JCS-3-07), September 24, 2007; "Options to Improve Tax Compliance and Reform Tax Expenditures," JCS-02-05, January 27, 2005.
- **GAO:** "Tax Expenditures Represent a Substantial Federal Commitment and Need to Be Reexamined," GAO-05-690, September 2005.
- **OMB:** *Budget of the U.S. Government, FY 2008, Analytical Perspectives,* 285–327, http://www.whitehouse.gov/omb/budget/FY2007/pdf/spec.pdf.
- **U.S. Congress, Senate Budget Committee:** "Tax Expenditures: Compendium of Background Material on Individual Provisions," S. Prt. 108-54.
- **CRS:** "Tax Expenditures: Trends and Critiques," RL33641, September 13, 2006.
- **Harvard University Press:** *Tax Expenditures,* by Stanley Surrey and Paul McDaniel, 1985.
- **The World Bank:** *Tax Expenditures—Shedding Light on Government Spending through the Tax System,* 2004.

Notes

1. The term *tax expenditure* was first used in the mid-1960s by Stanley Surrey, the Assistant Secretary for Tax Policy in the Johnson Administration. See Thomas Hungerford, "Tax Expenditures: Trends and Critiques," RL33641(Washington D.C.: Congressional Research Service, December 7, 2006). The term was later defined in §3(3) of the Congressional Budget and Impoundment Control Act of 1974 (P.L. 93-344) as "those revenue losses attributable to provisions of the Federal tax laws which allow a special exclusion, exemption, or deduction from gross income or which provide a special credit, a preferential rate of tax, or a deferral of tax liability."

2. GAO, "Government Performance and Accountability: Tax Expenditures Represent a Substantial Federal Commitment and Need to Be Reexamined," GAO-05-690 (Washington D.C.: Government Accountability Office, September 2005), 21.

3. The Office of Management and Budget has estimated total tax expenditures for FY 2007 at $911 billion. U.S. Office of Management and Budget, *Budget of the U.S. Government: FY 2008, Analytical Perspectives,* table 19-1, 287. However, note the Government Accountability Office's caveat that "the sum of the individual revenue loss estimates has important limitations in that any interactions between tax expenditures will not be reflected in the sum. . . . [T]ax expenditure revenue loss estimates for specific provisions do not take into account potential behavioral responses to changes in these provisions on the part of taxpayers, and, in turn, no potential behavioral response would be reflected in the sum of the estimates. Thus, the revenue loss from all or several tax expenditures together might be greater or less than the sum of the estimated revenue losses from the individual tax expenditures, and no measure of the size or the magnitude of these potential interactions or behavioral responses to all or several tax expenditures is available." GAO, "Government Performance and Accountability," 3.

4. GAO, "Government Performance and Accountability," highlights.

5. GAO, highlights.

6. Spending, revenue, and deficit figures: Congressional Budget Office, *The Budget and Economic Outlook: An Update,* August 2006; Tax expenditures estimate: Congressional Research Service, *Tax Expenditures: Trends and Critiques,* September 13, 2006; and Tax gap estimate: interview of Senate Finance Committee staff, October 31, 2006.

7. The Earned Income Tax Credit is a "refundable tax credit," which means that it not only erases low-income workers' tax liability (resulting in a revenue loss) but also entitles eligible low-income workers to a Federal payment (resulting in Federal outlays of $36 billion in FY 2007).

8. For a complete list of tax expenditures in this category, see U.S. Office of Management and Budget, *Budget of the U.S. Government: FY 2008, Analytical Perspectives,* Table 19-1, 287.

9. For a complete list of tax expenditures in this category, see U.S. Office of Management and Budget, *Budget of the U.S. Government: FY 2008, Analytical Perspectives,* Table 19-1, 287.

10. U.S. Office of Management and Budget, *Budget of the U.S. Government: FY 2007, Analytical Perspectives,* 287–290. For an alternative set of estimates, see U.S. Congress, Joint Committee on Taxation, *Estimates of Federal Tax Expenditures for Fiscal Years 2007–2011* (JCS-3-07), September 24, 2007.

11. The maximum credit declines to $500 per child after 2010. The credit is phased out for higher-income taxpayers. See U.S. Office of Management and Budget, *Budget of the U.S. Government: FY 2007, Analytical Perspectives,* 313.

12. See U.S. Office of Management and Budget, *Budget of the U.S. Government: FY 2007, Analytical Perspectives,* 313.

13. See U.S. Office of Management and Budget, *Budget of the U.S. Government: FY 2007, Analytical Perspectives,* 311.

14. The Tax Code also permits most nonfuel mineral extractors to use percentage depletion rather than cost depletion. U.S. Office of Management and Budget, *Budget of the U.S. Government: FY 2007, Analytical Perspectives,* 306.

15. See U.S. Office of Management and Budget, *Budget of the U.S. Government: FY 2007, Analytical Perspectives,* 306.

16. See U.S. Office of Management and Budget, *Budget of the U.S. Government: FY 2007, Analytical Perspectives,* 307.

17. See U.S. Office of Management and Budget, *Budget of the U.S. Government: FY 2007, Analytical Perspectives,* 307.

18. See U.S. Office of Management and Budget, *Budget of the U.S. Government: FY 2007, Analytical Perspectives,* 307–8.

PART

VI

IN THE WINK OF AN EYE: FROM DEFICITS TO SURPLUSES AND BACK TO DEFICITS

Those who cannot remember the past are condemned to repeat it.—George Santayana[1]

A Brief History of Deficits and Surpluses

A budget deficit or surplus is calculated very simply by calculating the difference between outlays and revenues for a given fiscal year. For example, in FY 2007, outlays and revenues were $2.731 trillion and $2.568 trillion, respectively, yielding a budget deficit of $163 billion.[2] (Note that for purposes of calculating deficits, "outlays" are used rather than "budget authority" because outlays reflect actual cash disbursements. Budget authority, as explained in chapter 2-9, is the legal authority Congress appropriates to agencies to enter into financial obligations that eventually result in outlays.)

In contrast to an "annual deficit," the "Federal debt" is the *accumulated* debt of the Federal government. Whenever the Federal government runs an annual budget deficit, the additional borrowing to finance the deficit spending adds to the accumulated Federal debt. By contrast, whenever the Federal government runs a budget surplus, the accumulated Federal debt *decreases* because Treasury securities are redeemed using surplus revenues rather than issuing additional debt.

Budget records from the United States' first century are sketchy. Estimates are that from 1789 to 1849, the United States had a cumulative surplus of $70 million; and from 1850 to 1900, the Federal government had a cumulative deficit of nearly a billion dollars. Annual record keeping improved by the turn of the century and we know that in 1901 the Federal Treasury ran a budget surplus of $63 million, with total outlays of $525 million.[3]

As one might expect the first wave of significant budget deficits in the 1900s occurred during World War I. A budget surplus in 1916 gave way to an $853 million deficit in 1917 (not insignificant for a total budget of $1.9 billion). In 1918, the deficit exploded to more than $9 billion because total Federal spending rose to more than $12 billion. And by 1919, the deficit was more than $13 billion, with total Federal spending of more than $18 billion.

363

With the end of the war, Federal spending quickly declined, and the Treasury saw an immediate return to budget surpluses until the Great Depression.

In 1933, with the country in the grip of the Depression, unemployment had skyrocketed to nearly 25%, and the Federal deficit reached 4.5% of the Gross Domestic Product (GDP). However, by 1938, President Roosevelt's New Deal legislation was showing results, with significant decreases in unemployment and a Federal Budget nearly in balance. Then the United States entered World War II.

In 1939, Federal outlays were slightly more than $9 billion. Due to the war, outlays grew to $35 billion by 1942, $78 billion by 1943, and $92 billion by the end of the war. Federal deficits during the last two years of World War II grew to $47 billion about 22% of the nation's GDP. Even more startling is the accumulated Federal Debt Held by the Public, which grew as a percentage of GDP from 52% before the war to 121% after the war. In other words, *the accumulated Federal debt at the end of the war was significantly larger than the entire economy.*

But the post–World War II era saw a rapid decline in Federal deficits. With dramatic reductions in defense spending, Federal deficits dropped from $47 billion in 1945 to $15 billion in 1946 and the budget was already in surplus by 1947. Moreover, with a rapidly expanding postwar economy, the accumulated Federal debt, as a percentage of GDP, saw a relatively steady decline from 121% at the end of the war to 94% in 1950, 56% in 1960, 38% in 1970, and 33% in 1980. Then the fiscal situation changed dramatically with the triple-digit deficits of the 1980s.

The Triple-Digit Deficits of the 1980s

Deficits skyrocketed from $74 billion in 1980, to $128 billion by 1982, and $208 billion by 1983. Similarly, *as a percentage of the GDP*, deficits increased from 2.7% in 1980 to 4% by 1982 and 6% by 1983. The last time deficits had been that large as a percentage of the economy was World War II. Not even at the height of the Vietnam War were deficits, as a percent of GDP, close to those levels.

The reasons for these skyrocketing deficits in the 1980s were several: (1) an economic recession; (2) a massive tax cut in 1981; (3) massive increases in defense spending; and (4) significant growth in entitlement programs, particularly Medicare and Medicaid.

With economic recovery in the mid- to late 1980s, deficits began to moderate. They dropped from $221 billion in 1986 (5% of GDP) to $152 billion in 1989 (2.8% of GDP).

The Budget Agreements of the 1990s Lead to Surpluses

However, by 1990, the deficit picture had again deteriorated. With the nation once again in recession, record outlays required to resolve the savings and loan crisis, and record interest payments required to finance accumulated debt from the 1980s, the deficit rose to $221 billion, nearly 4% of GDP.[5] This set the stage for the first of three historic deficit reduction laws that moved the Federal Treasury from deep deficits into surpluses by the end of the decade.

Budget Summit Agreement of 1990. The first of these deficit reduction laws came to be known as the "Budget Summit Agreement of 1990." The senior officials of the George H. W.

Bush Administration, feeling intense public pressure over soaring deficits, came together with Democratic congressional leaders for two weeks of intense, bipartisan closed door negotiations at Andrews Air Force Base and produced a historic bipartisan budget agreement: the Omnibus Budget Reconciliation Act of 1990.

The Act included a record $500 billion in deficit reduction measures (spending cuts and tax increases over the 1991–1995 budget period) and also enacted the historic Budget Enforcement Act of 1990, which set forth the very successful discretionary spending caps and pay-as-you-go (PAYGO) requirements for tax and entitlement legislation (described in chapter 2-4). President Bush suffered a great deal of criticism for the 1990 Budget Summit Agreement because it included tax increases as well as spending cuts, but the economic facts are that this politically courageous bipartisan agreement laid the foundation for subsequent deficit reduction laws in 1993 and 1997 that moved the Treasury from the huge deficits of the early 1990s into the surpluses and booming economy of the late 1990s.

OBRA 1993. Unlike the 1990 Agreement, the deficit reduction legislation enacted in 1993 was not bipartisan. It was negotiated by President Clinton and congressional Democrats and passed Congress without any Republican votes in August of 1993. The deficit reduction package included roughly equal amounts of tax increases and spending reductions and ended up reducing deficits by far more than the $500 billion over five years projected at the time. In its annual report of January 1994, the nonpartisan Congressional Budget Office noted that "the deficit picture is significantly brighter than it appeared one year ago when CBO projected that the deficit would soar above $350 billion by FY 1998. CBO now projects that the Federal Budget deficit will fall from $223 billion in the current year to below $170 billion in 1996.... The dramatic improvement ... is largely the result of ... the Omnibus Budget Reconciliation Act of 1993 (OBRA-93)."[6]

Balanced Budget Act of 1997. After the enactment of OBRA-93, the political winds changed, and Washington once again entered an era of divided government—a Democratic President and a Republican Congress. The clash of ideologies led to a dramatic political standoff in 1995 that witnessed the most serious Federal government shutdown in history (as discussed in chapter 2-2). The negative political fallout from the shutdown, together with political pressure to reach a balanced budget, eventually brought both sides together in 1997 to enact the third milestone budget agreement of the 1990s. On July 31, 1997, Congress completed action on twin pieces of legislation—the Taxpayer Relief and Balanced Budget Acts of 1997—which the President signed into law on August 5, 1997. Unlike the deficit reduction laws of 1990 and 1993, the 1997 legislation cut taxes, rather than increasing taxes, but nevertheless produced net deficit reduction due to entitlement program cuts and extension of the fiscal restraints of the Budget Enforcement Act through 2002. This led CBO to report in January 1998 that "the Federal Budget deficit is likely to be essentially balanced for the next 10 years if current policies remain unchanged. CBO ... projects single-digit deficits for fiscal years 1998, 1999, and 2000, followed by a small surplus in 2001 and growing surpluses through 2008."[7]

As it turns out, the economy did even better than anticipated and surging Federal revenues brought the Budget into surplus that same year—FY 1998—with a surplus of $69 billion. The surpluses continued, with $126 billion in FY 1999, $236 billion in FY 2000, and $128 billion in FY 2001.

Current Decade: Exploding Deficits Lead to Massive Debt

In 2002, the deficit picture for the first decade of the new millennium shifted dramatically. The $128 billion surplus of 2001 was followed by *deficits* of $158 billion in 2002, $378 billion in 2003, $413 billion in 2004[8], $319 billion in 2005, $248 billion in FY 2006, and $163 billion in FY 2007.[9] *Excluding Social Security surpluses,* the respective deficits were $317 billion in 2002, $538 billion in 2003, $568 billion in 2004, $494 billion in 2005, $435 billion in 2006, and $344 billion in 2007 (figure 6.1) (Excluding Social Security surpluses is a more accurate measure of the nation's fiscal health because the temporary Social Security surpluses will dry up around 2017.)

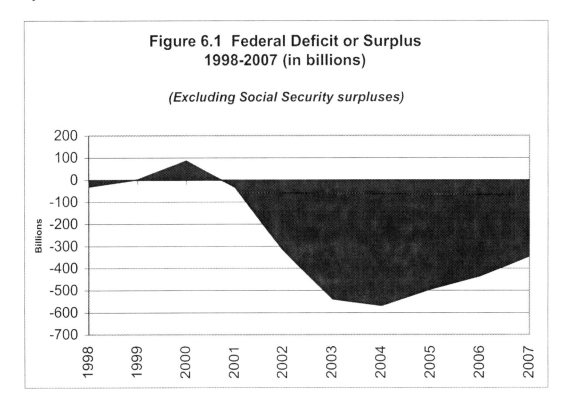

Figure 6.1 Federal Deficit or Surplus 1998-2007 (in billions)

(Excluding Social Security surpluses)

The most troubling results of these annual deficits are the rapid increases in the accumulated Federal debt. In January 2001, CBO projected a 10-year *budget surplus* (2002–2011) of $5.6 trillion, which would have dramatically reduced Federal Debt.

One year later, in January of 2002, CBO revised downward the previous year's 10-year surplus projection of $5.6 trillion to $1.6 trillion—*a precipitous decline of $4 trillion in projected surpluses.* Shortly thereafter, the projected surpluses disappeared and were replaced with projections of long-term deficits.

As shown in figure 6.2, Gross Federal Debt (composed of "Debt Held by the Public" and debt held by government trust funds) has in fact grown from $5.8 trillion in 2001 to nearly $9 trillion at the end of FY 2007. Debt Held by the Public, that is, the cumulative total debt that the Federal Treasury owes to individuals, institutions, and other governments—has grown from $3.3 trillion in 2001 to more than $5 trillion in FY 2007. Using either measure of debt, *our nation's accumulated debt has grown by more than 50% in six years*—a staggering increase.

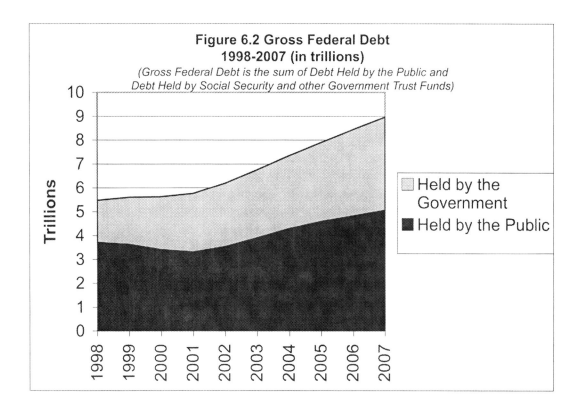

Figure 6.2 Gross Federal Debt
1998-2007 (in trillions)
(Gross Federal Debt is the sum of Debt Held by the Public and Debt Held by Social Security and other Government Trust Funds)

Causes of the Deficit/Debt Explosion

This dramatic reversal in our nation's fiscal outlook, from rapidly accumulating surpluses to rapidly accumulating debt, is due largely to tax cuts, the recession, and increases in defense spending. Quantifying with any precision how much of the massive fiscal shift is attributable to each factor is analytically difficult, to say the least. The task of providing nonpartisan analysis of the fiscal picture belongs to the Congressional Budget Office. In arriving at its estimates, the CBO considers the advice of an outside advisory council composed of economists spanning the political spectrum. By examining the evolving CBO projections, one can piece together a rough snapshot of the factors leading to the debt explosion of the current decade.[10]

Tax cuts. As noted, in January 2001 CBO projected an FY 2002 *surplus* of $313 billion and a 10-year *surplus* (2002–2011) of $5.6 trillion. One year later, CBO revised its projections to reflect a $4 trillion decline in the projected surpluses (soon to be followed by the disappearance of all projected surpluses and the emergence of projected deficits). CBO attributed the largest single factor in this precipitous decline to the tax cuts enacted in 2001. When debt service costs are included, CBO estimated that nearly $1.7 trillion (more than 40%) of the $4 trillion decline in the nation's fiscal health was due to revenue losses associated with the 2001 tax cuts.[11]

While the 2001 tax bill contained the largest cuts in recent years, there have actually been six significant tax cut bills enacted in this decade (as of 2006). Table 6.1 briefly describes the tax cuts and includes the 10-year revenue loss projections associated with each of the measures *at the time the tax cuts were enacted.*[12]

TABLE 6.1 Recent Tax Cuts: Description and Revenue Scoring[13]

Tax Act	Brief Description	10-year Projected Revenue Losses
2001: Economic Growth and Tax Relief Reconciliation Act (EGTRRA, P.L. 107-16)	• Reduced marginal tax rates and created a new 10% bracket for 2001 through 2004[14] • Increased child tax credit from $500 to $1000 and extended refundability to smaller families • "Marriage penalty relief" (standard deduction and 15% tax bracket for joint returns set at twice the level as for single returns) • Temporary reduction in the Alternative Minimum Tax (AMT) • Phased out the estate tax over 2002 to 2010, but reverts to prior law after 2010 (Note: EGTRRA's provisions were phased in over time and expire after 2010 due to the Senate's Byrd Rule—see chapter 3-2.)[15]	$1.349 trillion[16]
2002: Job Creation and Worker Assistance Act (JCWAA, P.L. 107-147)	• Accelerated depreciation for business investment • Temporary extension of the net operating loss carryback period (refers to years in the past, the income from which, a firm can deduct losses over prior years)	$30 billion[17]
2003: Jobs and Growth Tax Relief Reconciliation Act (JGTRRA, P.L. 108-27)	• Accelerated phase-in of the EGTTRA tax cuts (except for estate tax reduction) • Extended and expanded accelerated depreciation under JCWAA • Reduced tax rates on dividend and capital gains income • Increased the Alternative Minimum Tax (AMT) exemption[18]	$320 billion[19]
2004: Working Family Tax Relief Act of 2004 (WFTRA, P.L. 108-311)	• Extended many of the JGTRRA tax provisions scheduled to expire at the end of 2004 (not the capital gains or dividend reductions) • One-year extension of the JGTRRA AMT exemption • Extended four energy tax subsidies	$147 billion[20]

Tax Act	Brief Description	*10-year Projected Revenue Losses*
2005: Energy Policy Act of 2005 (P.L. 109-58)	• Incentives for oil and gas production, refining, distribution • Incentives for coal production • Electricity restructuring provisions • Incentives for efficiency, renewables, and alternative fuels[21]	$11.5 billion[22]
2006: Tax Increase Prevention and Reconciliation Act of 2005 (TIPRA, P.L. 109-222)[23]	• Extended the JGTRRA dividend and capital gains reductions for two years (through 2010) • Extended AMT relief for one year (2006) • Extended increased expensing for two years (through 2009)	$69 billion[24]

Note: All of these tax cuts were deficit financed; that is, they were paid for by Treasury borrowing. However, the revenue loss estimates do not include the additional budgetary impact of higher debt service costs. Therefore, actual costs of the tax cuts are significantly higher.

In considering the role of these tax cuts in the debt explosion of the current decade, it is important to keep in mind that all of the tax cuts have been "deficit financed"—that is, paid for by Treasury borrowing. In that sense, the tax cuts—which may cost more than $2.5 trillion over 10 years when debt service costs are included—are, in the view of some economists, the single-largest factor in our nation's currently rising debt.

On the other hand, other economists assert that the tax cuts have had a stimulative effect on the economy, thereby shortening the length of the 2001–2002 recession. If that has been the case, the total cost of the tax cuts should be offset by the Federal revenue increases directly attributable to the shortening of the recession.

Unfortunately, this type of econometric analysis is far from a perfect science. As CRS has pointed out:

> [I])t is hard to be certain what effects the tax cuts have had on the economy because there is no way to compare actual events to the . . . case where the tax cuts were not enacted. . . . Most estimates predict that . . . tax cuts will increase economic growth in the short term and reduce it in the long run. . . . The period encompassing the tax cuts featured a recession of average duration but below-average depth, an initially sluggish recovery, a deep and unusually long decline in employment, a small decline in hours worked, a sharp and long lasting contraction in investment spending, a significant decline in national saving, and an unusually large trade deficit. Opponents [of the tax cuts] see this as evidence that the tax cuts were ineffective; proponents argue that the economy would have performed worse in their absence. . . . One should also consider that some, perhaps most, of the recovery was due to monetary rather than fiscal stimulus.[25]

There is no obvious answer to the question of whether the tax cuts are *principally* responsible for the current deficit picture. Nevertheless, whatever conclusion one reaches about these past decisions, it is vital that policymakers thoughtfully consider the fiscal costs of permanently extending the tax cuts.

There has been extensive congressional debate about *extending* many of the tax cuts summarized in table 6.1, nearly all of which are due to expire by the end of 2010. *A recent CBO report estimates that extending the 2001 and 2003 tax cuts and other expiring tax provisions (along with indexing the Alternative Minimum Tax exemption so that it doesn't counteract the resulting tax relief*[26]*) would cost more than $3 trillion over a 10-year period.*[27] Regardless of one's conclusions about the principal causes of recent deficits, incurring an additional $3 trillion of deficit-financed tax cuts—at the same time health care costs are skyrocketing, the boomers are retiring, and the nation is at war—ought to raise some very sobering fiscal concerns.

Recession. As noted, in January 2002, CBO attributed more than 40% of the $4 trillion decline in the nation's previously projected surpluses to the 2001 tax cuts. The second-largest factor, according to CBO was the recession, with nearly one-quarter of the fiscal decline attributed to the economic slump.[28] The impact of a recession on the U.S. Treasury is threefold: (1) reduced revenues,[29] (2) increased debt service costs, and (3) increases in entitlement spending (e.g., outlays from unemployment benefits and other low-income programs). Figure 6.3 displays CBO's relative apportionment of the causes of the 2001–2002 fiscal decline.

Defense Spending. Along with tax cuts and the recession, the rapid growth in defense spending has provided significant fuel to the rising debt of the current decade. As discussed

FIGURE 6.3 Causes of the $4 Trillion Decline in the Fiscal Outlook from FY2001 to FY2002

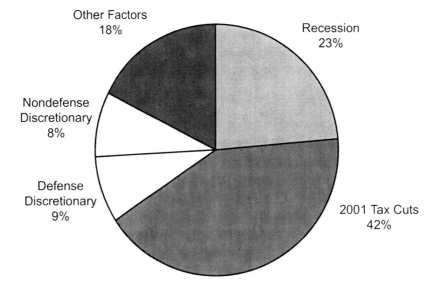

Source: Based on CBO's *Budget and Economic Outlook*, January 2002, summary table 1.

Note: Increased interest payments resulting from changes in the Federal debt are distributed proportionally.

in chapter 3-1, defense spending nearly *doubled* between fiscal years 2001 and 2007. A significant portion of this rapid increase is attributable to the wars in Iraq and Afghanistan, which by 2007, had already cost more than $600 billion.[30]

Entitlements. Entitlement spending growth is sometimes blamed as a factor in the massive shift from trillions of dollars in projected surpluses to trillions in new debt, but the facts suggest otherwise. As figure 6.3 indicates, CBO did not attribute any of the massive $4 trillion shift in the fiscal outlook to entitlement spending. Moreover, if one examines CBO's January 2001 projections for major entitlement spending (when major budget surpluses had been projected) and compare them with actual entitlement spending over 2001–2007, the actual spending for Social Security and Medicaid are very close to the 2001 projections, as displayed in table 6.2. The one exception is Medicare, which began to grow beyond earlier projections in FY 2005, with the phasing in of the new Medicare Prescription Drug benefit (see chapter 3-6).

Nevertheless, it is critical to underscore the following point: Although growing entitlement spending was not a cause of the 2001–2002 decline in the fiscal outlook, the projected growth in entitlements—Medicare and Medicaid in particular—is the central factor in the *perilous fiscal outlook currently facing our nation.*

Top Economic Officials Agree the United States Is on a Dangerous Fiscal Path

There is broad agreement among our nation's top economic officials that the United States is currently on a perilous fiscal path leading to massive and unsustainable Federal Debt that threaten the stability of the U.S. economy.

TABLE 6.2 Entitlement Growth Not a Key Factor in 2001–2002 Shift from Surpluses to Deficits

(billions of dollars)					
Social Security		*Medicare*		*Medicaid*	
Jan. '01 CBO Projections	*Actual Spending*	*Jan. '01 CBO Projections*	*Actual Spending*	*Jan. '01 CBO Projections*	*Actual Spending*
FY 2002 452	452	252	253	141	148
FY 2003 474	471	270	274	153	161
FY 2004 498	492	290	297	166	176
FY 2005 523	519	317	333	180	182
FY 2006 550	549	333	372	194	181
FY 2007 578	586	363	441	211	191
Totals 3,075	3,069	1,825	1,970	1,045	1,039

UNITED STATES ON A DANGEROUS FISCAL PATH

- In January 2007, the CBO's **Budget and Economic Outlook** warned Members of Congress that "the aging of the population and continuing increases in health care costs are expected to put considerable pressure on the budget in coming decades. Economic growth alone is unlikely to be sufficient to alleviate that pressure as Medicare, Medicaid, and (to a lesser extent) Social Security require ever greater resources under current law."[31]

- On January 11, 2007, **Comptroller General of the United States David Walker** told the Senate Budget Committee that "Our current financial condition is worse than advertised. Our long-term fiscal outlook is both imprudent and unsustainable. . . . Long-term fiscal simulations by GAO, CBO and others all show that we face large and growing structural deficits driven primarily by rising health care costs and known demographic trends."[32]

- On January 18, 2007, in an uncharacteristically candid assessment for a **Fed Chairman, Ben Bernanke,** Chairman of the Federal Reserve Board, delivered a similar warning to the Senate Budget Committee, observing that because of rising entitlement costs, a "vicious cycle may develop in which large deficits lead to rapid growth in debt and interest payments, which in turn adds to subsequent deficits. . . . Ultimately, this expansion of debt would spark a fiscal crisis. . . . [T]he effects on the U.S. economy would be severe."[33]

Myth: The decline in (unified) budget deficits from $413 billion in 2004 to $319 billion in 2005, $248 billion in FY 2006, and $163 billion in FY 2007 is an indicator of an improving fiscal outlook.

Fact: Unfortunately, this recent downward "trend" in annual deficits does *not* signal a positive fiscal outlook for our nation. First, these *deficit numbers*—used by the Administration and Congress—are *misleading* because they include Social Security surpluses that will soon disappear. (See chapter 2-9 on the Unified Budget and Social Security.) More important, this brief "downward trend" in unified budget deficits will be short-lived. Several factors—as outlined in table 6.3—will place *increasingly powerful upward pressures on the Federal debt* in the next decade and beyond.

TABLE 6.3 Major Factors Placing LongTerm U.S. Fiscal Stability At Risk

Factors	Explanation
Continuing growth in Health Care costs	Of the three major entitlement programs, Medicare and Medicaid, by far, pose the greatest long-term fiscal challenge. According to CBO, health care costs are likely to continue to grow faster than the economy. CBO notes that between 1960 and 2003, the average annual rate of growth of national health expenditures exceeded the rate of growth of GDP—known as *excess cost growth*—by 2.6%. At that rate, Federal spending for Medicare and Medicaid could rise from 4.5% of GDP today to more than 20% in 2050.[34]
Retirement of the baby boom generation, beginning in 2008[35]	Retirement of the baby boom generation will cause significant increases in Social Security, Medicare, and Medicaid spending— Social Security and Medicare because the elderly are the principal beneficiaries and Medicaid because a significant portion of Medicaid spending covers nursing home expenditures for low-income seniors. The magnitude of these pressures are reflected in the startling statistic that over the next half century, the number of people age 65 or older will double and the number of adults under 65 will increase by just 12%.[36]
Proposed Extension of the 2001 and 2003 tax cuts	The Administration and many in Congress have been pushing for permanent extension of the 2001 and 2003 tax cuts, due to expire in 2010. The estimated costs of such extensions (and an accompanying offsetting fix to the Alternative Minimum Tax) are $3 trillion over 10 years.

Taken together, and unchecked, these factors will seriously worsen an already dangerous accumulation of Federal debt and create a long-term fiscal outlook described by CBO as "unsustainable."[37] Similarly, the nonpartisan GAO concluded recently that "under any reasonable set of expectations about future spending and revenues, the risks posed to the Nation's future financial condition are too high to be acceptable."[38]

Do Deficits Matter?

Debts, public and private, are neither good nor bad, in and of themselves. Borrowing can lead to overextension and collapse, but it can also lead to expansion and strength. There is no single, simple slogan in this field that we can trust.—President John F. Kennedy, 1962 [39]

To be sure, there are times when deficits are necessary and appropriate. During World War II, our nation ran annual deficits as high as 30% of our GDP, and Gross Federal Debt exceeded the size of the entire economy by the end of the war. However, as soon as the war ended, the Federal government began running budget surpluses in order to bring down the accumulated debt. Unfortunately, no efforts are currently under way to adopt policies that will generate surpluses and turn around the current maelstrom of growing debt and interest payments. In fact, as explained earlier, absent quick action by Congress and the Administration to curb the growth of Medicare, Medicaid, and Social Security, the current outlook is for rapidly increasing deficits, debt, and interest payments in the next and subsequent decades.

Ron Suskind, in his fascinating book about former Bush Treasury Secretary Paul O'Neill, reports on a White House meeting where O'Neill was "arguing sharply that the government 'is moving toward a fiscal crisis.'" As O'Neill recalled, Vice President Cheney responded bluntly that "Reagan proved deficits don't matter." [40]

People who take the Cheney position point to the data in table 6.4. The economy did in fact have a healthy economic expansion during fiscal years 1983 through 1989 (**the first shaded area**). However, at the same time, the Federal Debt Held by the Public *nearly doubled*—and net interest payments grew from $90 billion to $169 billion. Therein lies the key point.

The *high interest payments* that accompany high Federal debt should be avoided for three reasons:

- First, our nation gets nothing in return for these enormous annual interest payments— homeland security isn't improved, medical research doesn't advance, our children don't have greater access to early learning or higher education, nor can the funds be used for urgently needed middle-class tax relief.
- Second, every family understands: the dangerous cycle of high debt leading to higher interest payments, leading to even higher debt. Our nation fell into this vicious circle in the 1980s, and it continued into the 1990s, with Debt Held by the Public growing to $3 trillion by 1992. Fortunately, as discussed earlier, our nation was able to climb out of the deficit ditch due to the deficit reduction agreements of 1990, 1993, and 1997—the 1990 and 1997 agreements being the product of strong bipartisan efforts based on the prevailing view that deficits *do matter*. From 1998 through 2001 these laudable deficit reduction efforts yielded budget surpluses—and debt started to decline (the **second shaded area** in table 6.4). Unfortunately, the deficits of 2002 through 2008 have led our nation back into the cycle of growing debt, with Debt Held by the Public exceeding $5 trillion, Gross Federal Debt exceeding $9 trillion, and net interest payments exceeding $250 billion—a shameful waste of taxpayer resources.
- Third, as a matter of values, no parent wants his or her children, grandchildren, and subsequent generations to inherit hundreds of billions of dollars of annual interest payments on debt accumulated by the shortsightedness of our own generation.

In addition to the dangers of high interest payments, there are other compelling reasons to be deeply concerned about ongoing deficits and growing accumulated debt:

Exporting U.S. dollars: Our nation—already the world's largest debtor nation—is increasingly indebted to Japan, China, and other foreign nations, sending hundreds of billions of dollars in interest payments abroad, which, in turn, reduces our own economic growth.

TABLE 6.4 Deficits, Debt, Interest Payments, and Economic Growth

FY	Annual Deficit (billions of $)	Debt Held by the Public	Net Interest Payments (billions of $)	Economic Growth % Change in Real GDP
1981	- 79	789	69	2.5
1982	-128	925	85	-1.9
1983	-208	1,137	90	4.5
1984	-185	1,307	111	7.2
1985	-212	1,507	130	4.1
1986	-221	1,741	136	3.5
1987	-150	1,890	139	3.4
1988	-155	2,052	152	4.1
1989	-153	2,191	169	3.5
1990	-221	2,412	184	1.9
1991	-269	2,689	194	-0.2
1992	-290	3,000	199	3.3
1993	-255	3,248	199	2.7
1994	-203	3,433	203	4.0
1995	-164	3,604	232	2.5
1996	-107	3,734	241	3.7
1997	-22	3,772	244	4.5
1998	69	3,721	241	4.2
1999	126	3,632	230	4.5
2000	236	3,410	223	3.7
2001	128	3,320	206	-0.8
2002	-158	3,540	171	1.6
2003	-378	3,913	153	2.7
2004	413	4,296	160	4.2
2005	-318	4,592	184	3.5
2006	-248	4,829	220	3.3
2007	-163	4,993	235	2.1
2008	-155	5,163	253	2.9
2009	-215	5,392	267	3.0
2010	-255	5,661	281	3.0

Sources: CBO 2007 August Update and *Economic Report of the President* (February 2007).

Crowding out of private investment capital: Continuing rapid increases in U.S. Treasury borrowing can cause a domestic and global shortage of investment capital, "crowding out" funds available at reasonable interest rates for private investors. Particularly with the recent credit crunch in the housing market, Federal fiscal policies that soak up available global credit are increasingly problematic.

Recommended Sources for More Information Deficits, Debt, and the Fiscal Outlook

- **CBO:** "The Budget and Economic Outlook," released each January and updated each August, www.cbo.gov.
- **FED Chairman Bernanke:** "The Coming Demographic Transition: Will We Treat Future Generations Fairly?" October 4, 2006, www.federalreserve.gov/newsevents/speech/bernanke20061004a.htm.
- **GAO:** "The Nation's Long-Term Fiscal Outlook, August 2007 Update: Despite Recent Improvement in the Annual Deficit, Federal Fiscal Policy Remains Unsustainable," GAO-07-1261R, September 28, 2007.
- **Brookings:** *Restoring Fiscal Sanity,* (2005, 2006, and 2007), Alice Rivlin, Isabel Sawhill, Joseph Antos.
- **CBPP:** "The Long-Term Fiscal Outlook Is Bleak," January 29, 2007, www.cbpp.org/1-29-07bud.pdf.
- **Committee for Economic Development (CED):** "The Emerging Budget Crisis: Urgent Fiscal Choices," May 2005, www.ced.org/docs/report/report_budget2005.pdf.
- **Concord Coalition:** "Improving the Long-Term Fiscal Outlook: Does It Take a Commission?" May 15, 2006, National Press Club, http://207.57.22.22/events/060515-commission/transcript.htm.
- **Heritage Foundation:** www.heritage.org/research/Budget/FWUT.cfm.
- **Urban Institute President Bob Reischauer:** Testimony before the Senate Budget Committee, January 30, 2007, www.urban.org/publications/901038.html.

Notes

1. *Notable Quotations from George Santayana: Life of Reason, Reason in Common Sense* (New York: Scribner's, 1905), 284.

2. Henry Paulson, Secretary of the Treasury and Jim Nussle, OMB Director, "Joint Statement on Budget Results for Fiscal Year 2007," October 11, 2007, table 4.

3. These numbers and all subsequent numbers in this section are from Office of Management and Budget, "FY 2007 Historical Tables," U.S. Government Printing Office 2006.

4. Lewis D. Eigen and Jonathan P. Siegel, *The Macmillan Dictionary of Political Quotations* (New York: Macmillan, 1993), 23.

5. See Congressional Budget Office, "The Economic and Budget Outlook: Fiscal Years 1992–1996" (Washington D.C.: Government Printing Office, January 1991).

6. Congressional Budget Office, "The Economic and Budget Outlook: Fiscal Years 1995–1999" (Washington D.C.: Government Printing Office, January 1994).

7. Congressional Budget Office, "The Economic and Budget Outlook: Fiscal Years 1998–2008" (Washington D.C.: Government Printing Office, January 1998), xv.

8. This was a record deficit in dollar terms, but at 3.6% of GDP, it reflected a smaller share of the economy than the deficits of the mid-1980s and early 1990s when deficits frequently exceeded 4% of GDP. CBO, "The Budget and Economic Outlook: An Update" (Washington D.C.: Government Printing Office, September 2004), ix.

9. Office of Management and Budget, *Budget of the United States, FY 2008*, historical tables (Washington D.C.: Government Printing Office, February 2007), 22; and Paulson and Nussle, "Joint Statement on Budget Results for Fiscal Year 2007," table 4.

10. All of the references in the following chronology are drawn from the annual (January) *Economic & Budget Outlook* publications of CBO or the relevant summer update published in August or September.

11. Calculations based on CBO, "Budget and Economic Outlook" (Washington D.C.: Government Printing Office, January 2002), summary table 1, xiv.

12. Projected revenue losses were calculated by Congress' Joint Committee on Taxation (a nonpartisan staff of tax professionals that provides revenue estimates to the Congressional Budget Office).

13. These are revenues losses projected at the time of enactment by Congress' Joint Committee on Taxation. Estimates do not include costs of additional debt service. CRS notes that "actual tax receipts fell significantly more than predicted. . . . This suggests that the tax cuts may have resulted in more revenue loss than predicted." CRS, "What Effects Have the Recent Tax Cuts Had on the Economy?" RL32502 (Washington D.C.: Congressional Research Service, April 14, 2006), footnote 2.

14. Prior to the Act, the tax code's rates were 15%, 28%, 31%, 36% ,and 39.6%; the Act reduced these to 10%, 15%, 25%, 31%, and 35%. In addition, the Act eliminated the overall limit on itemized deductions and phased out the tax code's restriction on personal exemptions. CRS, "Major Tax Issues in the 109th Congress," December 8, 2005.

15. For further information, see CRS, "2001 Tax Cut: Description, Analysis, and Background," December 9, 2002.

16. Marc Labonte, "What Effects Have the Recent Tax Cuts Had on the Economy?" RL 32502 (Washington D.C.: Congressional Research Service, April 14, 2006), 2. The figures for the 2002 and 2003 tax cuts are also derived from the same source.

17. CRS notes that "since accelerated depreciation is a revenue loser in the short term and a revenue raiser in the medium term, the 10-year cost of JCWAA is smaller than the short-term cost." CRS, "What Effects Have the Recent Tax Cuts Had on the Economy?" July 30, 2004, p. 2.

18. For further information see CRS, "Tax Cut Bills in 2003: A Comparison," July 31, 2003.

19. CRS, "What Effects Have the Recent Tax Cuts Had on the Economy?" 2.

20. CRS, "Major Tax Issues in the 109th Congress," 20.

21. For more details, see CRS, "Energy Tax Policy," May 25, 2006.

22. This is a revenue loss projection for 11, rather than 10, years. CRS, "Energy Tax Policy."

23. TIPRA was enacted in response to Reconciliation instructions adopted in 2005, but the conference was not completed until May 2006.

24. U.S. Congress, Joint Committee on Taxation, "Estimated Revenue Effects of the Conference Agreement for the Tax Increase Prevention and Reconciliation Act of 2005," JCX-18-06, May 9, 2006, 3.

25. CRS, "What Effects Have the Recent Tax Cuts Had on the Economy?" summary.

26. According to CRS, "if the reductions in the individual income tax are extended beyond 2010, then the number of taxpayers subject to the AMT will increase from about 1.8 million in 2001 to 23 million in 2007, and then to over 50 million in 2017." Gregg Esenwein, "Extending the 2001, 2003, and 2004 Tax Cuts," RS21992 (Washington D.C.: Congressional Research Service, January 26, 2007), 3.

27. CBO, "Budget and Economic Outlook: Fiscal Year 2008 to 2017" (Washington D.C.: January 2007), 16.

28. CBO, "Budget and Economic Outlook" (Washington D.C.: , January 2002), summary table 1, pg. xiv.

29. According to CBO, the decrease in revenues from 2001 to 2002—nearly 7%—was the largest annual drop in percentage terms since 1946. CBO, "The Budget and Economic Outlook," January 2002, xvii.

30. CBO, "The Budget and Economic Outlook: An Update" (Washington D.C.: , August 2007), 11.

31. CBO, "The Budget and Economic Outlook," January 2007, xi.

32. Testimony delivered to the Senate Budget Committee on January 11, 2007, available at http://budget.senate.gov/democratic/testimony/2007/Walkers%20Long-term%20Testimony.pdf, 1, 5.

33. Testimony delivered to the Senate Budget Committee on January 18, 2007, available at http://budget.senate.gov/democratic/testimony/2007/Bernanke_LongTerm011807.pdf, 4–5.

34. CBO, "The Budget and Economic Outlook," January 2007, 10–11.

35. The "baby-boom generation" generally refers to the large number of people born between 1946 and 1964.

36. CBO, "The Budget and Economic Outlook," January 2006, 22–23

37. CBO, "The Budget and Economic Outlook," January 2005, xiii–xiv.

38. U.S. GAO, "The Nation's Long-Term Fiscal Outlook: September 2006 Update," 1.

39. Alex Ayres, ed., *The Wit and Wisdom of John F. Kennedy* (New York: Penguin Books, 1996), 44.

40. Ron Suskind, *The Price of Loyalty: George W. Bush, the White House, and the Education of Paul O'Neill* (New York: Simon & Schuster, 2004), 291.

PART

VII

NONPARTISAN PRINCIPLES TO SECURE OUR NATION'S FUTURE

Despite some improvement in the annual deficit estimate for this fiscal year, the long-term fiscal outlook . . . is clearly unsustainable—ever larger deficits lead to a Federal debt burden that ultimately spirals out of control.—GAO, August 2007

America's economic future is at risk. As discussed in Part VI, there is broad agreement among our nation's top economic officials, across the political spectrum, that our current fiscal path is unsustainable. At the same time, we should gain confidence from the knowledge that, throughout our history, America has faced and overcome numerous challenges requiring equal or greater resolve.

The key to success in securing our nation's economic future is addressing key fiscal policy issues *now* and in a spirit of *bipartisan cooperation*. There are tough fiscal issues to be decided, essential changes to be made. The following principles are offered as a framework for bipartisan progress.

1. **Leaders of both political parties should endorse the conclusion, reached independently by the leaders of the Federal Reserve Bank, the Government Accountability Office, and the Congressional Budget Office, that the United States is on an unsustainable fiscal course.** Too much public and media attention has been focused on *temporary* reductions in annual deficits and projected "balanced budgets" by 2012—which achieve "balance" only by using Social Security surpluses to mask large structural deficits.

2. **Curtail the rapid growth of Medicare and Medicaid by reducing the overall growth in health care costs.** The rapid growth of Medicare and Medicaid expenditures are the principal contributors to the projected explosion of Federal debt. The main cause of Medicare and Medicaid growth is general health care inflation; health care costs are growing considerably faster than the economy. *Progress lies in reforming the nation's overall health care*

system in a manner that slows the growth in health care costs and improves public health. The following objectives provide a starting point for bipartisan action:

- Reduce the number of emergency room visits, the most expensive type of health care, by ensuring all Americans access to primary care physicians.
- Lower the rate of growth in health insurance premiums by enabling all Americans to participate in group health insurance, spreading costs across larger pools of beneficiaries.
- Foster competition in the health insurance industry by following the example of the Federal Employee Health Benefits Program, which offers participants a broad range of *health insurance choices.*
- Improve the quality of care by promoting *competition* among health care providers on medical outcomes.
- Reduce medical error rates by facilitating the transition to electronic medical records.
- Increase and better target NIH research funds in order to translate scientific advances into new treatments.
- Establish protocols that reduce the high rate of hospital acquired infections in the United States.

Meeting these objectives requires that politicians stop fomenting fears of "socialized medicine." No serious participants in the health care debate are proposing a Federal takeover of medicine; no one is suggesting that doctors become Federal employees. The public debate must remain focused on how to *guarantee that all Americans purchase affordable health insurance enabling them to choose their own doctor—the same opportunity available to every Medicare participant, every Member of Congress, and every Federal employee.*

3. **Secure the long-term solvency of Social Security.** While less urgent than Medicare and Medicaid reform—and less complex—Social Security reforms should be adopted *before the end of this decade,* when the boomers start to retire. Social Security is a pay-as-you-go program with current workers paying for the benefits of current retirees. *Annual benefits are projected to exceed annual payroll tax revenues as early as 2017; this will trigger massive borrowing by the Treasury unless adjustments are made to the program* (see chapter 3-4).

   A balanced package of reforms could include *modest* adjustments to payroll taxes, the rate of growth in benefit payments, and/or the retirement age. *The sooner the adjustments are put in place, the smaller they will need to be.* This opportunity could also be used to make payroll taxes, which exceed income taxes for most Americans, less regressive. Individual accounts are a good idea, provided they are a *supplement*—not a substitute—for the current program.

4. **Enhance national security by merging defense, intelligence, and homeland security spending into a single, unified national security budget that allocates resources based on today's terrorist threats—not yesterday's Cold War scenarios.** Maintaining the current artificial separation between the defense and homeland security budgets interferes

with a sensible, *risk-based* allocation of national security resources. The massive defense budget remains fixed in Cold War thinking, while the relatively meager homeland security budget inadequately addresses today's terrorist threats. A unified national security budget should focus on:

- Securing "loose nukes" in the Former Soviet Union and keeping enriched uranium and other WMD materials out of the hands of Al Qaeda and other terrorists;
- Speeding up development and deployment of technology—with the urgency of the Manhattan Project—to scan all incoming cargo for nuclear and other WMD materials;
- Coordinating and focusing defense, homeland security, and intelligence assets on tracking down and disabling WMDs and terrorist cells throughout the world; and
- Stepping up comprehensive emergency planning for all high-risk urban areas in the United States, including prepositioning medical countermeasures.

At the same time, the United States can reduce anti-Western terrorist recruitment by stepping up foreign aid (which lags behind that of most other developed nations). Robust U.S. relief efforts in response to natural disasters, famine, and pandemics make lasting and profound impressions on people in need throughout the world.

5. **Reenact the Budget Enforcement Act, negotiated in the bipartisan Budget Summit Agreement of 1990.** The triple-digit deficits of the early 1990s turned into the budget surpluses of the late 1990s, in no small measure, due to the budgetary discipline imposed by the Budget Enforcement Act. The fundamental pay-as-you-go principle that new tax cuts and new entitlement spending should be paid for is sound and sensible. If the bipartisan budget discipline of the 1990s had been in place during the current decade, our nation would not be facing a *public debt 50% higher than seven years ago.* (See Part II.)

6. **Tax expenditures, nearing $1 trillion per year, should receive the same level of results-oriented scrutiny as spending programs.** Similar to spending programs, if tax expenditures are achieving their intended public purpose, they should continue. If not, they should be scrapped. Closing an ineffective tax break is a public savings, not a tax increase. Moreover, closer scrutiny of tax breaks will generate the budgetary offsets needed for a renewed commitment to pay-as-you-go (PAYGO) principles. (See Part V.)

7. **Finally, make room in the budget for "public investments" that cost money in the short run,** *but save money over the long run.* One of the serious inadequacies of the current budget process is the fixation on annual budgeting, to the detriment of long-term investments in our people and infrastructure. For example:

- More infrastructure spending in the short run—such as stronger levees in New Orleans, retrofitting buildings in California to survive earthquakes, and accelerating the replacement of dangerous bridges—can save hundreds of billions of dollars in the long run.
- Making college affordable today for *all* young Americans who are motivated to attend will generate substantial innovation and economic growth for tomorrow.

- More robust tax incentives for "green technologies" will generate new and highly productive industries, as well as reduce the ruinous consequences of global warming.
- More funding for community-based mental health can lead to decreases in expensive inpatient care, homelessness, and incarcerations, and generate tax revenues from healthy, productive citizens.
- Fully funding the Individuals with Disabilities Education Act will enable all Americans, no matter what challenges they face, to maximize their full potential and add their unique creativity and drive to our economy.

All of these principles can be a common starting point for policymakers, across the political spectrum, to undertake the serious work of aligning our Federal Budget with America's most urgent national and international priorities.

Budget Process Timetable

DATE	ACTION
Calendar Year Prior to Year in Which Fiscal Year Begins	
Spring	Office of Management and Budget (OMB) issues policy and planning guidance to departments and agencies for the budget beginning October 1 of the following year.
Spring and summer	Departments and agencies begin developing of budget requests.
July	OMB issues annual update to "Circular A-11," providing detailed instructions for departments and agencies on submission of budget data and material for budget requests.
Fall	Departments and agencies submit initial budget requests to OMB.
October–November	OMB conducts "Fall Review" analyzing budget requests; OMB Director makes policy decisions.
Late November	OMB Director briefs the President on the draft budget and receives the President's guidance on key policy issues. OMB informs departments and agencies of decisions, commonly referred to as "OMB Passback."
December	Departments and agencies may appeal to the OMB Director, and ultimately the President, to reverse or modify passback decisions. Departments and agencies submit computer data and materials to OMB for preparation of budget documents.

DATE	ACTION
Calendar Year in Which the Fiscal Year Begins	
Late January (but no later than February 15)	CBO releases *The Budget and Economic Outlook.*
1st Monday in February	President's Budget, *requesting* specific funding levels for all government programs and new initiatives, is submitted to Congress.
Not later than 6 weeks after President submits Budget	House and Senate committees submit "views and estimates" to their respective Budget Committees.
March	House and Senate Budget Committees mark-up their respective budget plans, known as "Budget Resolutions," and report them to the House and Senate.
April 15	Congress completes action on the Budget Resolution (which does not require presidential signature).
	Appropriations Committees begin work on the 12 regular appropriations bills (based on the total amount of discretionary spending allowed by the Budget Resolution).
	If optional Reconciliation instructions are contained in the Budget Resolution, authorizing committees begin work on Reconciliation legislation to change entitlements and/or tax laws; the deadline for committees to report such legislation is included in the Budget Resolution instructions.
May 15	Annual appropriations bills may be considered in the House (in the absence of a Budget Resolution).
June 10	House Appropriations Committee reports last of the 12 regular appropriations bills.
June 30	House completes action on annual appropriations bills.
July 15	President submits "Mid-Session Review" updating the February Budget submission.
July or August	CBO releases *Budget and Economic Outlook: An Update.*
October 1	**New Fiscal Year begins:** if all 12 annual appropriations bills are not yet enacted, Congress passes a *continuing resolution* (CR) to keep unfunded government departments functioning; multiple CRs are often required to keep departments operating as funding negotiations continue.
Beginning of fiscal year	OMB "apportions" appropriated budget authority to agencies by time period, program, project, or activity.

DATE	ACTION
During fiscal year	Departments and agencies obligate available budget authority to operate programs, projects, and activities and, if necessary, ask OMB to request supplemental appropriations from Congress.
	The President may "defer" availability of budget authority to later in the fiscal year, or propose to Congress a "rescission" of specific budget.
	The Congress enforces the Budget Resolution through parliamentary points of order that may be raised against legislation that would breach spending ceilings or revenue floors, or violate other congressional rules such as the PAYGO requirement.

Source: Congressional Budget Act of 1974, as amended, 2 USC 631 et. seq. and OMB Circular A-11.

Budget Points of Order in the Senate and House

A *point of order* is a procedural objection that a Representative or Senator may raise against a bill, resolution, amendment, or conference report on the House or Senate Floor, respectively. In general, if the Presiding Office, advised by the Parliamentarian, sustains the point of order (i.e., finds it to be a valid objection), the offending bill, resolution, amendment, or conference report "falls" (i.e., it is removed from consideration by the House or Senate).[1]

In the following table, "leg." = bills, resolutions, motions, amendments, and conference reports; "BR" = Budget Resolution; "BA" = Budget Authority; "OT" = outlays.

An asterisk (*) in the Senate Waiver Requirement column means that the 60-vote supermajority waiver requirement in the Senate is due to expire in 2017, as provided for in the FY 2008 Budget Resolution.

Section numbers refer to sections of the Congressional Budget and Impoundment Control Act of 1974, as amended, unless otherwise noted.

For updates to this chart, see www.washingtonbudgetreport.com.

Budget Act Section	Description	Applies to: Senate	House	Senate Waiver Requirement[2]
Points of Order against Budget-Busting Spending Legislation				
302(c)	Prohibits consideration of appropriations bills **until the 302(b) suballocations are made**	X	X	60 votes*
302(f)	**Exceeding Committee Allocations:** Prohibits consideration of leg. that would cause a committee to **exceed either its 302(a) committee allocation** (or a 302(b) suballocation in the case of the	X[3]	X[4]	60 votes*

Budget Act Section	Description	Applies to: Senate	House	Senate Waiver Requirementii
	Appropriations Committee) in either the budget year or the total of (5 years) covered by the BR			
	Important note: This point of order against breaching committee allocations applies to BA and Outlay allocations in the Senate, but just BA allocations in the House.			
303(a)	Prohibits consideration of leg. that would make **new spending effective for a fiscal year before a BR** for that fiscal year has been adopted	X	X[5]	60 votes*
303(c)	**Prohibits consideration in the Senate of any appropriations measure until** a BR has been agreed to and a 302(a) allocation has been made to the Appropriations Committee	X		60 votes*
311(a)	**Exceeding Spending Aggregates:** Prohibits consideration of leg. that would **cause the BR's aggregate spending levels for BA or OT to be exceeded** for the first year covered by the BR (except for "emergency requirements")[6]	X	X[7]	60 votes*
Sec. 206 of FY'08 BR	**Limits on Advance Appropriations:** Prohibits the consideration of advance appropriations, except for the FY 2009 and 2010 appropriations specified in the FY 2008 BR conference report	X[8]	X	60 votes
Sec. 204 of FY'08 BR	**Limit On Emergency Designations:** Spending provisions designated as "emergencies"[9] are exempted from the sec. 302 and 311 points of order described above. However, Senators can make a point of order to strike emergency designations from spending legislation unless supporters of the emergency designation can muster 60 votes to waive the point of order.[10]	X		60 votes

(Continued)

Budget Act Section	Description	Applies to: Senate	House	Senate Waiver Requirementii
Sec. 207 of FY'08 BR	**Discretionary Caps:** Prohibits the consideration of leg. that would **exceed any of the discretionary limits for FY 2007 and FY 2008** set forth in the BR. However, the limits can be adjusted upward for certain program integrity or tax enforcement expenditures.	X		60 votes
Sec. 201 of FY'08 BR	**Senate PAYGO Point of Order:** Prohibits consideration of direct spending (entitlement) legislation that would increase or cause a non–Social Security deficit in either of two budget periods: (1) the period of the current fiscal year, the budget year, and the ensuing 4 fiscal years; or (2) the period of the current fiscal year, the budget year, and the ensuing 9 fiscal years	X		60 votes*
Sec. 405 of H.Res. 6, 110th Congress (2007)	**House PAYGO Point of Order:** Prohibits consideration of direct spending (entitlement) legislation that would increase the deficit or reduce the surplus for either of the same two budget periods noted above in the Senate's PAYGO rule.		X	N/A
Sec. 203 of FY'08 BR	**Legislation Increasing Long-Term Deficits:** Prohibits consideration of leg. that would cause a net increase in deficits in excess of $5 billion in any of the four 10-year periods beginning in 2018 and ending in 2057.	X		60 votes*
Points of Order against Budget-Busting Revenue Legislation				
303(a)	Prohibits consideration of legislation that makes changes in revenues for a fiscal year before a budget resolution for that fiscal year has been adopted.	X	X	60 votes*

Budget Act Section	Description	Applies to: Senate	House	Senate Waiver Requirementii
311(a)	Prohibits consideration of leg. that would cause the BR's revenue floors for the budget year, or the total for all years covered by the BR, to be breached.[11]	X	X	60 votes*
Sec. 201 of FY'08 BR	**Senate PAYGO Point Of Order:** Prohibits consideration of tax cuts that would increase or cause a non–Social Security deficit in either of two budget periods: (1) the period of the current fiscal year, the budget year, and the ensuing 4 fiscal years; or (2) the period of the current fiscal year, the budget year, and the ensuing 9 fiscal years	X		60 votes*
Sec. 405 of H.Res. 6, 110th Congress	**House PAYGO Point Of Order:** Prohibits consideration of tax cuts that would increase the deficit or reduce the surplus for either of the same two budget periods noted above in the Senate's PAYGO rule		X	N/A
Restrictions on Earmarks				
H.Res. 6 (110th Congress, 1/4/07)	**House:** Requires disclosure of earmark sponsors, as well as justifications for earmarks, and written certification that earmarks will not benefit their House sponsor		X	N/A
Section 521 of S. 1 (P.L. 110-81, 9/14/07) amended Senate Rule 44	**Senate:** An *earmark* is defined as "a congressionally directed spending item, limited tax benefit, and limited tariff benefit." Rule 44 prohibits consideration of leg. unless the committee chair or majority leader certifies that all earmarks in legislative or report language have been identified by sponsor and are publicly available on the Internet for 48 hours. Senators must provide to the committee the name and location of the earmark beneficiary, and they must certify no financial interest. Prohibits "air-dropping," i.e., inserting *new* earmarks into conference reports.	X		60 votes

(Continued)

Budget Act Section	Description	Applies to: Senate	House	Senate Waiver Requirementii
Limitations on Entitlement and other "Backdoor Spending"				
401(a)	Subject to certain exceptions, prohibits consideration of leg. providing new authority to enter into contracts or to borrow funds or to lend funds unless limited to amounts provided in appropriations acts.	X	X	Majority
401(b)(1)	Prohibits consideration of entitlement leg. that is to becomes effective during the current fiscal year.	X	X	Majority
Sec. 209 of FY'08 BR	No Changes in Mandatory Programs (ChIMPS). Would allow Senators to make a point of order against provisions in appropriations bills that constitute ChIMPs. Provisions meeting the criteria would be stricken from the bill.	X		60 votes*
Federal Credit Reform				
504(b)	Requires that new direct loan obligations and new loan guarantees may be incurred **only to the extent that** new budget authority to cover their costs is provided in advance in an appropriations act. Does not apply to entitlements such as student loans or veterans' home loans, or agriculture loans under the CCC.	X	X	Majority
Protections for Social Security				
301(i)	Prohibits consideration of a BR that would decrease the Social Security surplus in any of the years covered by the Resolution.	X		60 votes*
310(g)	Prohibits consideration of Reconciliation bills, amendments, or conference reports that contain "recommendations with respect to OASDI.[12]	X	X	60 votes*

Senate

Budget Act Section	Description	Applies to: Senate	House	Waiver Requirementii
311(a)(3)	Prohibits consideration of leg. that would cause a decrease in Social Security surpluses or an increase in Social Security deficits (except for tax changes having only an "incidental" Social Security effect).	X		60 votes*
13302(a) of 1990 BEA	Prohibits consideration of legislation in the House that would provide for a net increase in Social Security benefits or decrease in Social Security taxes in excess of 0.02% of the present value of future taxable payroll for a 75-year period.[13]		X	N/A

Protecting the Integrity of the Budget Process

Budget Act Section	Description	Applies to: Senate	House	Waiver Requirementii
301(g)	Prohibits consideration of a BR using more than one set of economic assumptions.	X		Majority
306	Prohibits consideration of leg. within the jurisdiction of the Budget Committee— such as directed scoring provisions—unless reported by the Budget Committee.	X	X	60 votes
309	Prohibits adjourning for the July 4th recess until the House has approved all regular appropriations bills.		X	N/A
310(f)	Prohibits adjourning for the July 4th recess until the House has completed action on the Reconciliation Bill (in years when the BR calls for Reconciliation legislation).		X	N/A

Unfunded Mandates Reform Act

Budget Act Section	Description	Applies to: Senate	House	Waiver Requirementii
425(a)(1)	Prohibits consideration of legislation reported by a committee unless the committee has published a CBO report on direct costs of Federal mandates in the legislation.	X	X	60 votes*

(Continued)

Budget Act Section	Description	Applies to: Senate	Applies to: House	Senate Waiver Requirementii
425(a)(2)	Prohibits consideration of legislation that would increase the cost of federal intergovernmental mandates (i.e., mandates on state or local governments) by more than $50 million (adjusted for inflation) in the first year of the bill's operation or any of the 4 ensuing years *unless* sufficient direct spending authority is provided in the bill or funds are authorized (and identified) to cover the costs. See chapter 2-6 for more information.	X	X	60 votes*
426	Prohibits consideration of a "Rule" in the House that would waive section 425		X	N/A
Procedures Relating to Consideration of the Budget Resolution				
305(c)(4)	Prohibits consideration of nongermane amendments to "amendments in disagreement" between the House and Senate.	X		60 votes
305(b)(2)	Prohibits consideration of nongermane amendments to BR.	X		60 votes
305(d)	Prohibits a vote on a BR unless the figures contained in the resolution are mathematically consistent.	X		Majority
Procedures Relating to Consideration of Reconciliation Legislation				
310(d)(2)	Prohibits amendments to Reconciliation Bills that would decrease spending cuts or reduce tax increases, unless deficit neutral through offsetting provisions.	X		60 votes
310(e)	Prohibits consideration of nongermane amendments to Reconciliation Bills or to "amendments in disagreement" between the House and Senate.	X		60 votes*
313	**Byrd Rule:** Prohibits consideration of "extraneous," i.e. nonbudgetary or deficit-increasing legislation, in a Reconciliation Bill. Offending provisions are stripped out of the Reconciliation	X		60 votes

Budget Act Section	Description	Applies to: Senate	House	Senate Waiver Requirementii
	Bill if the point of order is sustained. See chapter 2-3 and appendix L for more details on the Byrd Rule.			
Sec. 202 of FY'08 BR	**Limiting Reconciliation Leg. to Deficit Reduction:** Prohibits consideration of Reconciliation legislation that would increase deficits or reduce surpluses in either of two budget periods: (1) the period of the current fiscal year, the budget year, and the ensuing 4 fiscal years; or (2) the period of the current fiscal year, the budget year, and the ensuing 9 fiscal years.	X		60 votes

Note: Section numbers refer to sections of the Congressional Budget and Impoundment Control Act of 1974, as amended, unless otherwise noted.

Notes

1. Under section 312(f) of the Congressional Budget Act, if the Presiding Officer in the Senate sustains a point of order against a bill or resolution, it is automatically sent back to the committee of jurisdiction. Under section 312(d), a point of order cannot be raised in the Senate while an amendment that would remedy the problem is pending.

2. There are no supermajority waiver requirements in the House of Representatives. The 3/5 waiver requirement in the Senate was, most recently, extended to September 30, 2017, by the FY 2008 Budget Resolution. For additional history, see James Saturno, "Points of Order in the Congressional Budget Process," 97-865GOV (Washington D.C.: Congressional Research Service, July 2, 2007), note 7.

3. However, in the Senate, "reserve funds" permit allocations to be adjusted upward to reflect new spending that is budget neutral.

4. Point of order does not apply in the House to legislation that is deficit neutral.

5. The point of order does not apply to appropriations bills in the House after May 15.

6. However, "reserve funds" may be included in the Budget Resolution that permit the BA or Outlay ceilings to be adjusted upward to accommodate additional spending that is paid for with revenue increases.

7. However, in the House, (1) the so-called Fazio exception allows appropriations measures to exceed the aggregate ceiling on new budget authority or outlays if they do not exceed the appropriate committee's 302(a) budget allocation, and (2) this limit on total spending does not operate if a Declaration of War is in effect.

8. In the Senate, provisions violating this point of order can be stricken from a conference report.

9. Sec. 204 of the 2008 Budget Resolution sets forth five criteria for determining if an emergency designation is warranted.

10. In recent years, war funding has been designated as emergency spending and thereby exempted from section 302 and section 311 points of order.

11. However, "reserve funds" may be included in the Budget Resolution that permit the revenue floor to be adjusted downward to accommodate tax cuts that are paid for with spending cuts.

12. This point of order would bring down the entire Reconciliation Bill; alternatively, in the Senate, the Byrd Rule could be used to strip out the offending provision.

13. However, section 13302(b) of the Budget Enforcement Act provides that the point of order would not apply to legislation that reduces Social Security taxes in excess of the threshold amounts if the reductions are offset by equivalent increases in Medicare taxes. James Saturno, "Points of Order in the Congressional Budget Process" (Washington, D.C.: Congressional Research Service, Library of Congress, May 19, 2005), 13, footnote a.

14. For more information on the Anti-Deficiency Act, see http://www.gao.gov/ada/antideficiency.htm

Major Laws Governing the Federal Budget Process

Law	Description
Anti-Deficiency Act (enacted in 1870 as part of the legislative appropriations bill), 31 U.S.C. 1341-42; 1511-1519	Provides that no department or government official can make payments, or obligate the U.S. government by contract, in excess of congressional appropriations (with criminal penalties for violations).[14] The Act enforces Congress' constitutional authority over the public purse. The Act also triggers government shutdowns when Congress fails to appropriate funds by the beginning of a new fiscal year.
Budget and Accounting Act of 1921, P.L. No. 67-13, 42 Stat. 20 (June 10, 1921)	Centralized Federal budgeting by creating the Bureau of the Budget (the predecessor to OMB) and codified submission of the President's Budget. Also established the General Accounting Office (now the Government Accountability Office) to provide Congress with an independent audit of executive accounts and to report on violations of fiscal statutes.
Legislative Reorganization Act of 1946, P.L. 79-601, §206, 60 Stat. 812, 837 (Aug. 2, 1946)	Directed the GAO to make expenditure analyses of executive branch agencies with reports to relevant congressional committees.
Accounting and Auditing Act of 1950, P.L. 81-784, §117(a), 31 U.S.C. §3523(a)	Authorized the GAO to audit the financial transactions of most executive, legislative, and judicial agencies and to prescribe, in consultation with the President and the Secretary of the Treasury, accounting standards.

(Continued)

Law	Description
Legislative Reorganization Act of 1970, P.L. 91-150, §204, 84 Stat. 1140, 1168 (Oct. 26, 1970)	Expanded the focus of GAO's audit activities to include program evaluations as well as financial audits.
Congressional Budget and Impoundment Control Act of 1974, P.L. 93-344, 88 Stat. 297 (July 12, 1974)	Established the congressional budget process, including the requirement for an annual Budget Resolution, created the House and Senate Budget Committees and the Congressional Budget Office, and established rescission and deferral procedures to limit presidential impoundment authority.
Balanced Budget and Emergency Deficit Control Act of 1985 (Gramm-Rudman-Holllings), P.L. 99-177, Title II, 99 Stat. 1037, 1038 (Dec. 12, 1985)	Established declining maximum deficit amounts (intended to lead to a balanced budget in FY1991) and a sequestration process (automatic budget cuts) as enforcement; also amended the '74 Budget Act.
Balanced Budget and Emergency Deficit Control Reaffirmation Act of 1987, P.L. 100-119, 101 Stat. 754 (Sept. 29, 1987)	Moved the sequester trigger from GAO to OMB (due to a constitutional challenge) and revised and extended the deficit targets, aiming at a balanced budget in 1993. See *Bowsher v. Synar* (478 U.S. 714, 1986).
Budget Enforcement Act of 1990, P.L. 101-508, Title XIII, 104 Stat. at 1388-573 (Nov. 5, 1990)	Replaced the ineffective G-R-H deficit targets with (1) discretionary spending limits and (2) a pay-as-you-go (PAYGO) requirement to offset entitlement increases and tax cuts—both enforced through automatic sequesters; enacted the Federal Credit Reform Act of 1990; and amended the '74 Budget Act
Government Performance and Results Act (GPRA) P.L. 103-62, 107 Stat. 285 (Aug. 3, 1993)	Requires agencies to submit to Congress multiyear strategic plans, annual performance plans, and annual performance reports. See chapter 2-7 for details.
Omnibus Budget Reconciliation Act of 1993, P.L. 103-66, Title XIV, 107 Stat. 312, 683 (Aug. 10, 1993)	*Extended* the discretionary spending limits and PAYGO process through FY '98.
Unfunded Mandates Reform Act of 1995 (UMRA), P.L. 104-4, 109 Stat. 50 (Mar. 22, 1995)	*Unfunded mandates* are Federal statutes or regulations that require state or local governments or private sector entities to achieve certain goals or fulfill certain functions without being provided any Federal funding. UMRA (1) requires congressional committees

Law	Description
	and CBO to identify and provide information on potential unfunded Federal mandates in legislation and (2) permits Members of Congress to raise certain points of order. (See chapter 2-6 for details.)
Line Item Veto Act, P.L. 104-130, 110 Stat. 1200 (April 9, 1996). (Ruled unconstitutional in 1998)	Granted the President authority to cancel discretionary spending, new direct spending, and limited tax benefits in legislation; later ruled unconstitutional by the Supreme Court.
Budget Enforcement Act of 1997, P.L. 105-33, 111 Stat. 251 (Aug. 5, 1997)	*Extended* the discretionary spending limits and PAYGO process through FY 2002. Amended the '74 Budget Act.
TEA-21, P.L. 105-178, 112 Stat. 107 (June 9, 1998)	The Highway Bill (Transportation Equity Act for the 21st Century or "TEA-21") established additional spending caps on highway and mass transit spending through 2003.
FY 2001 Interior Appropriations Act, P.L. 106-291, 114 Stat. 922 (Oct. 11, 2000)	The FY 2001 Interior Appropriations Act established a set of caps on conservation spending through 2006 (including acquisition, conservation, and maintenance of Federal and nonfederal lands and resources as well as payments in lieu of taxes).
A bill to eliminate preexisting PAYGO balances, P.L. 107-312, 116 Stat. 2456 (Dec. 2, 2002)	Required the Director of the Office of Management and Budget to reduce to zero any PAYGO balances of direct spending and receipts legislation for all fiscal years under the Balanced Budget and Emergency Deficit Control Act of 1985 (Gramm-Rudman-Hollings Act).

Statutory Definition of Entitlement

The term *entitlement* was statutorily defined, for the first time, in section 401 of the Congressional Budget Act. The provision sets forth entitlement authority as one of three types of "back-door spending authority"—a term first introduced by the Joint Study Committee on Budget Control in 1973. By introducing the concept of back-door spending authority, the Joint Committee was seeking to control the proliferation of authorizing legislation that was financially committing the Federal Government *outside the scope of the annual appropriations process.*

Section 401(a) of the Budget Act places restrictions on the ability to create the first two types of back-door spending authority: contract authority and borrowing authority.

Section 401(b) places restrictions on the third type of back-door spending: "legislation providing new entitlement authority." The provision restricts the effective date of new entitlements to the upcoming fiscal year, in order to assure that any new entitlement authority will be created within the context of Budget Resolution limitations.

The three types of back-door spending authority are defined in section 401(c). The third type, entitlement authority, is defined in subparagraph 401(c)(2)(C) as follows:

§401(c) DEFINITIONS.—

(1) For purposes of this section, the term "new spending authority" means spending authority not provided by law on the effective date of this section, including any increase in or addition to spending authority provided by law on such date.

(2) For purposes of paragraph (1), the term "spending authority" means authority (whether temporary or permanent)—

(A) [definition of contract authority];

(B) [definition of borrowing authority];

(C) *to make payments (including loans and grants), the budget authority for which is not provided for in advance by appropriation Acts, to any person or government if, under the provisions of the law containing such authority, the United States is obligated to make such payments to persons or governments who meet the requirements established by such law.* [emphasis added]

The Budget Act's definition may be understood as setting forth a three-part test for defining programs as entitlements:

1. **Specified benefits**: The program's authorizing legislation specifies particular sums of money to be paid.
2. **Specified beneficiaries**: The payments are to be made to a class of persons or governments who meet specified eligibility requirements.
3. **Federal government has a legal obligation to pay that is not subject to appropriations**: The payment is not discretionary; that is, the legislation obligates the United States to make the specified payments to the eligible class, and the legal obligation to make the specified payments to the eligible class of recipients is not contingent on appropriations being enacted. Therefore, if insufficient appropriations are available, the government, in theory, may be sued for payment of the benefits.

Note that although entitlements legally obligate the United States to make specified payments, funds must still be appropriated to cover those payments. Some entitlement programs, such as Social Security, are permanently appropriated. Others are annually appropriated. Both permanently appropriated and annually appropriated entitlements share the common characteristic that the cost of the program has been determined outside of the appropriations process through the establishment of a formula-driven program. Although annually appropriated entitlements might appear to be subject to annual funding decisions of the Appropriations Committees, in reality they are not.

Revenue Bills and the Origination Clause

Article I, section 7 of the U.S. Constitution (otherwise known as the Origination Clause) provides that "All bills for raising revenues shall originate in the House of Representatives; but the Senate may propose or concur with Amendments as on other Bills." The reason for the Origination Clause is that the House—at the time—was the only body directly elected by the people. Even after the 17th Amendment applied direct election to the Senate, the Origination Clause remained in force.

Although the origination clause requires that revenue vehicles must originate in the House, it does not preclude the Senate from beginning its consideration of tax legislation before a House-originated tax vehicle is transmitted to the Senate. For example, the Senate may consider a revenue bill in the form of a Senate or (S.-bill) and then await transmittal of a revenue bill from the House. The Senate can then add or substitute provisions of the S.-bill as an amendment to the H.R.-revenue vehicle and send the H.R.-revenue vehicle back to the House of Representatives requesting a conference, or the House's concurrence on the differing provisions.

When the House believes that the Senate has encroached on its constitutional prerogative to originate revenue bills, it passes a House resolution stating that the Senate provision "in the opinion of the House, contravenes the first clause of the seventh section of the first article of the Constitution of the United States and is an infringement on the privilege of the House and that such bill be respectfully returned to the Senate with a message communicating this resolution." This practice is referred to as "blue slipping" because the resolution returning the offending bill to the Senate is printed on blue paper.

Source: This appendix has been drawn from U.S. Senate, Committee on Finance, *Program Descriptions and General Budget Information for FY 1995*, S. Prt. 103-80, 103d Congress, 2d Session, p. 128. Uncredited author: Charles S. Konigsberg, General Counsel.

Historical Table—Budget Resolutions

FY	First Concurrent Resolution on the Budget Adopted[1]	Second Concurrent Resolution on the Budget Adopted[2]
1976	May 14, 1975 (H.Con.Res. 218)	December 12, 1975 (H.Con.Res. 466)
1977	May 13, 1976 (S.Con.Res. 109)	September 16, 1976 (S.Con.Res. 139)[3]
1978	May 17, 1977 (S.Con.Res. 19)	September 15, 1977 (H.Con.Res. 341)
1979	May 17, 1978 (S.Con.Res. 80)	September 23, 1978 (H.Con.Res. 683)
1980	May 24, 1979 (H.Con.Res. 107)	November 28, 1979 (S.Con.Res. 53)[4]
1981	June 12, 1980 (H.Con.Res. 307)	November 20, 1980 (H.Con.Res. 448)
1982	May 21, 1981 (H.Con.Res. 115)	December 10, 1981 (S.Con.Res. 50)
1983	June 23, 1982 (S.Con.Res. 92)	
1984	June 23, 1983 (H.Con.Res. 91)	
1985	Oct. 1, 1984 (H.Con.Res. 280)	
1986	August 1, 1985 (S.Con.Res. 32)	
1987	May 15, 1986 (H.Con.Res. 337)	
1988	June 25, 1987 (H.Con.Res. 93)	
1989	June 6, 1988 (H.Con.Res. 268)	
1990	May 18, 1989 (H.Con.Res. 106)	
1991	Oct. 9, 1990 (H.Con.Res. 310)	
1992	May 22, 1991 (H.Con.Res. 121)	
1993	May 21, 1992 (H.Con.Res. 287)	
1994	April 1, 1993 (H.Con.Res. 64)	
1995	May 12, 1994 (H.Con.Res. 218)	
1996	June 29, 1995 (H.Con.Res. 67)	
1997	June 13, 1996 (H.Con.Res. 178)	
1998	June 4, 1997 (H.Con.Res. 84)	
1999	*No Budget Resolution Conference Report Adopted*[5] *(House deemed H.Con.Res. 284; Senate deemed S.Res. 209, 312)*	

(Continued)

FY	First Concurrent Resolution on the Budget Adopted[1]	Second Concurrent Resolution on the Budget Adopted[2]
2000	April 15, 1999 (H.Con.Res. 68)	
2001	April 13, 2000 (H.Con.Res. 290)	
2002	May 10, 2001 (H.Con.Res. 83)	
2003	**No Budget Resolution Adopted[6]** (House deemed H.Con.Res.353)	
2004	April 11, 2003 (H.Con.Res. 95)	
2005	**No Budget Resolution Adopted[7]** (House deemed conf. rep. on S.Con.Res.95; Senate deemed Appropriations allocations)	
2006	April 28, 2005 (H.Con.Res. 95)	
2007	**No Budget Resolution Adopted[8]** (House deemed H.Res. 376; Senate deemed 302 allocations)	
2008	May 17, 2007 (S.Con.Res. 21)	

Notes

1. From FY 1976 through FY 1986, the deadline for adopting the spring Budget Resolution was May 15. Gramm-Rudman-Hollings (GRH) changed the deadline to April 15, beginning with FY 1987.

2. As originally enacted, the Budget Act required a first and second Budget Resolution for each fiscal year. The First Budget Resolution spending and revenue totals served only as targets for congressional action on spending and revenue bills. Spending and revenue totals were not binding (i.e., not enforced by parliamentary points of order) until adoption of a Second Budget Resolution. Beginning with FY 1983, the Congress discontinued the formulation of Second Budget Resolutions and made First Budget Resolution totals binding with the start of the fiscal year on October 1. Beginning with FY 1987, Gramm-Rudman-Hollings made the Budget Resolution totals immediately binding upon adoption of the one Budget Resolution each spring. U.S. Senate Comm. on the Budget, "Gramm-Rudman-Hollings and the Congressional Budget Process," 99th Cong., 1st sess., 1985, S.Prt. 99-119, appendix I. (Uncredited author: Charles S. Konigsberg, Staff Attorney.)

3. A third concurrent resolution on the budget for FY 1977 was adopted by the Congress on March 3, 1977 (S.Con.Res. 10).

4. Replaced S.Con.Res. 36.

5. Congress did not complete action on a Budget Resolution for FY 1999. Instead, the House agreed to H.Res. 477 on June 19, 1998, and H.Res. 5 on January 6, 1999 *deeming* the budget levels contained in the House-passed Budget Resolution (H.Con.Res. 284) to have been adopted by the full Congress for budget enforcement purposes; likewise in the Senate with passage of S.Res. 209 on April 2, 1998, and S.Res. 312 on October 21, 1998. Bill Heniff Jr., "Congressional Budget Resolutions: Selected Statistics and Information Guide," RL30297 (Washington D.C.: Congressional Research Service, February 10, 2006), 6.

6. Congress did not complete action on a Budget Resolution for FY 2003. Instead, the House agreed to H.Res. 428 on May 22, 2002 and H.Res. 5 on January 7, 2003, *deeming* the budget levels contained in the House-passed budget (H.Con.Res. 353) to have been adopted by the full Congress for budget enforcement purposes. The Senate did not take similar action. Heniff, "Congressional Budget Resolutions," 6.

7. Congress did not complete action on a Budget Resolution for FY 2005. The House-Senate conference committee reported S.Con.Res. 95; the House adopted the conference report, but the Senate never considered it. In the absence of a Budget Resolution, the House deemed the conference report to have been agreed to for purposes of budget enforcement in the House (by operation of H.Res. 649, the "Rule" governing consideration of the conference report). The Senate included a provision, §14007, in the Defense Appropriations Act (2005) setting forth the FY 2005 spending allocation for the Senate Appropriations Committee. Heniff, "Congressional Budget Resolutions," 6.

8. Congress did not complete action on a Budget Resolution for FY 2007. Instead the House deemed the budget levels in the House-passed Budget Resolution (H.Con.Res. 376) to have been adopted by the full Congress for budget enforcement purposes; the deeming language was included in H.R. 5386, the FY 2007 Interior-Environment Appropriations Bill. The Senate included a provision in the FY 2006 supplemental appropriations bill (HR 4939) to establish a total discretionary appropriations level for the Senate Appropriations Committee.

Example of Budget Resolution Totals

(Excerpted from S.Con.Res. 21, the FY 2008 Budget Resolution)

SEC. 101. RECOMMENDED LEVELS AND AMOUNTS.
The following budgetary levels are appropriate for each of fiscal years 2007 through 2012:

(1) FEDERAL REVENUES- For purposes of the enforcement of this resolution:

 (A) The recommended levels of Federal revenues are as follows:
Fiscal year 2007: $1,900,340,000,000.
Fiscal year 2008: $2,015,858,000,000.
Fiscal year 2009: $2,113,828,000,000.
Fiscal year 2010: $2,169,484,000,000.
Fiscal year 2011: $2,350,254,000,000.
Fiscal year 2012: $2,488,301,000,000.

 (B) The amounts by which the aggregate levels of Federal revenues should be changed are as follows:
Fiscal year 2007: -$4,366,000,000.
Fiscal year 2008: -$34,938,000,000.
Fiscal year 2009: $6,902,000,000.
Fiscal year 2010: $5,763,000,000.
Fiscal year 2011: -$44,296,000,000.
Fiscal year 2012: -$108,795,000,000.

(2) NEW BUDGET AUTHORITY- For purposes of the enforcement of this resolution, the appropriate levels of total new budget authority are as follows:
Fiscal year 2007: $2,380,535,000,000.
Fiscal year 2008: $2,496,028,000,000.
Fiscal year 2009: $2,517,132,000,000.
Fiscal year 2010: $2,569,696,000,000.
Fiscal year 2011: $2,684,889,000,000.
Fiscal year 2012: $2,719,268,000,000.

(3) BUDGET OUTLAYS- For purposes of the enforcement of this resolution, the appropriate levels of total budget outlays are as follows:
Fiscal year 2007: $2,300,572,000,000.
Fiscal year 2008: $2,469,636,000,000.
Fiscal year 2009: $2,566,481,000,000.
Fiscal year 2010: $2,600,036,000,000.
Fiscal year 2011: $2,692,104,000,000.
Fiscal year 2012: $2,703,556,000,000.

(4) DEFICITS- For purposes of the enforcement of this resolution, the amounts of the deficits are as follows:
Fiscal year 2007: $400,232,000,000.
Fiscal year 2008: $453,778,000,000.
Fiscal year 2009: $452,653,000,000.
Fiscal year 2010: $430,552,000,000.
Fiscal year 2011: $341,850,000,000.
Fiscal year 2012: $215,255,000,000.

(5) DEBT SUBJECT TO LIMIT- Pursuant to section 301(a)(5) of the Congressional Budget Act of 1974, the appropriate levels of the public debt are as follows:
Fiscal year 2007: $8,932,264,000,000.
Fiscal year 2008: $9,504,150,000,000.
Fiscal year 2009: $10,073,725,000,000.
Fiscal year 2010: $10,622,023,000,000.
Fiscal year 2011: $11,077,407,000,000.
Fiscal year 2012: $11,419,028,000,000.

(6) DEBT HELD BY THE PUBLIC- The appropriate levels of debt held by the public are as follows:
Fiscal year 2007: $5,047,318,000,000.
Fiscal year 2008: $5,312,560,000,000.
Fiscal year 2009: $5,561,383,000,000.
Fiscal year 2010: $5,774,487,000,000.
Fiscal year 2011: $5,881,776,000,000.
Fiscal year 2012: $5,850,852,000,000.

Note: Spending and revenue levels exclude Social Security spending and revenues, which are technically "off-budget." (See chaper 2-9).

Example of Budget Resolution Reconciliation Instructions

(Excerpted from H.Con.Res. 95, the FY 2006 Budget Resolution)

Note: Reconciliation Instructions require committees to report legislative provisions that achieve specified changes in spending and/or revenue levels within their jurisdiction, but they do not identify specific programmatic or tax changes. Specific changes are "assumed" by the Budget Committee when the dollar targets are drafted, but the authorizing committees need not—and often do not—follow the Budget Committee assumptions.

SEC. 202. RECONCILIATION IN THE SENATE

(a) SPENDING RECONCILIATION INSTRUCTIONS- In the Senate, by September 16, 2005, the committees named in this section shall submit their recommendations to the Committee on the Budget. After receiving those recommendations, the Committee on the Budget shall report to the Senate a Reconciliation bill carrying out all such recommendations without any substantive revision.

(1) COMMITTEE ON AGRICULTURE, NUTRITION, AND FORESTRY- The Senate Committee on Agriculture, Nutrition, and Forestry shall report changes in laws within its jurisdiction sufficient to reduce outlays by $173,000,000 in fiscal year 2006, and $3,000,000,000 for the period of fiscal years 2006 through 2010.

(2) COMMITTEE ON BANKING, HOUSING, AND URBAN AFFAIRS- The Senate Committee on Banking, Housing, and Urban Affairs shall report changes in laws within its jurisdiction sufficient to reduce outlays by $30,000,000 in fiscal year 2006, and $470,000,000 for the period of fiscal years 2006 through 2010.

(3) COMMITTEE ON COMMERCE, SCIENCE, AND TRANSPORTATION- The Senate Committee on Commerce, Science, and Transportation shall report changes in laws within its jurisdiction sufficient to reduce outlays by $10,000,000 in fiscal year 2006, and $4,810,000,000 for the period of fiscal years 2006 through 2010.

(4) COMMITTEE ON ENERGY AND NATURAL RESOURCES- The Senate Committee on Energy and Natural Resources shall report changes in laws within its jurisdiction sufficient to reduce outlays by $2,400,000,000 for the period of fiscal years 2006 through 2010.

(5) COMMITTEE ON ENVIRONMENT AND PUBLIC WORKS- The Senate Committee on Environment and Public Works shall report changes in laws within its jurisdiction sufficient to reduce outlays by $4,000,000 in fiscal year 2006, and $27,000,000 for the period of fiscal years 2006 through 2010.

(6) COMMITTEE ON FINANCE- The Senate Committee on Finance shall report changes in laws within its jurisdiction sufficient to reduce outlays by $10,000,000,000 for the period of fiscal years 2006 through 2010.

(7) COMMITTEE ON HEALTH, EDUCATION, LABOR, AND PENSIONS- The Senate Committee on Health, Education, Labor, and Pensions shall report changes in laws within its jurisdiction sufficient to reduce outlays by $1,242,000,000 in fiscal years 2005 and 2006, and $13,651,000,000 for the period of fiscal years 2005 through 2010.

(8) COMMITTEE ON THE JUDICIARY- The Senate Committee on the Judiciary shall report changes in laws within its jurisdiction sufficient to reduce outlays by $60,000,000 in fiscal year 2006, and $300,000,000 for the period of fiscal years 2006 through 2010.

(b) REVENUE RECONCILIATION INSTRUCTIONS- The Committee on Finance shall report to the Senate a Reconciliation bill not later than September 23, 2005 that consists of changes in laws within its jurisdiction sufficient to reduce the total level of revenues by not more than: $11,000,000,000 for fiscal year 2006, and $70,000,000,000 for the period of fiscal years 2006 through 2010.

(c) INCREASE IN STATUTORY DEBT LIMIT- The Committee on Finance shall report to the Senate a Reconciliation bill not later than September 30, 2005, that consists solely of changes in laws within its jurisdiction to increase the statutory debt limit by $781,000,000,000.

Example of Budget Resolution Reserve Funds (S.Con.Res. 21, FY 2008)

Note: "Reserve Funds" are an *optional* component of a Budget Resolution that allow a Budget Resolution's total spending and committee allocations to be adjusted upward to accommodate additional spending for a specifically defined purpose. Because most reserve funds require that the new legislation be "deficit neutral" (i.e., paid for by new spending cuts or tax increases), the use of the term *reserve fund* is actually a misnomer, since *a Budget Resolution "reserve fund" does not provide any funds.* In fact, the only scenarios in which a "reserve fund" has any purpose at all (other than to make a political statement) is where a mechanism is needed to allow the Budget Committees to adjust committee allocations to accommodate a new program that is to be paid for by tax increases or spending cuts in another committee's jurisdiction. If a new program is paid for by spending cuts within a committee's own jurisdiction, there is no *net* increase in the committee's spending or in total Federal spending, so no adjustments to the Budget Resolution are required, and "reserve fund" authority is unnecessary.

Reserve Funds in Title III of S.Con.Res. 21 (FY 2008 Budget Resolution):

Sec. 301. Deficit-neutral reserve fund for SCHIP legislation.

Sec. 302. Deficit-neutral reserve fund for veterans and wounded service members.

Sec. 303. Deficit-neutral reserve fund for tax relief.

Sec. 304. Deficit-neutral reserve fund for Medicare improvements.

Sec. 305. Deficit-neutral reserve funds for health care quality, effectiveness, efficiency, and transparency.

Sec. 306. Deficit-neutral reserve fund for higher education.

Sec. 307. Deficit-neutral reserve fund for the Farm Bill.

Sec. 308. Deficit-neutral reserve fund for energy legislation.

Sec. 309. Deficit-neutral reserve fund for county payments legislation.

Sec. 310. Deficit-neutral reserve fund for terrorism risk insurance reauthorization.

Sec. 311. Deficit-neutral reserve fund for affordable housing.

Sec. 312. Deficit-neutral reserve fund for receipts from Bonneville Power Administration.

Sec. 313. Deficit-neutral reserve fund for Indian claims settlement.

Sec. 314. Deficit-neutral reserve fund for improvements in health.

Sec. 315. Deficit-neutral reserve fund for child care.

Sec. 316. Deficit-neutral reserve fund for immigration reform in the Senate.

Sec. 317. Deficit-reduction reserve fund.

Sec. 318. Deficit-neutral reserve fund for manufacturing initiatives in the Senate.

Sec. 319. Deficit-neutral reserve fund for the Food and Drug Administration in the Senate.

Sec. 320. Deficit-neutral reserve fund for Medicaid.

Sec. 321. Reserve fund adjustment for revenue measures in the House.

Sec. 322. Deficit-neutral reserve fund for San Joaquin River restoration and Navajo Nation water rights settlements.

Sec. 323. Deficit-neutral reserve fund for selected tax relief policies in the Senate.

Example of Reserve Fund language:

SEC. 301. DEFICIT-NEUTRAL RESERVE FUND FOR SCHIP LEGISLATION.

(a) Senate—

(2) RESERVE FUND—In the Senate, the Chairman of the Senate Committee on the Budget may revise the allocations, aggregates, and other appropriate levels in this resolution for a bill, joint resolution, amendment, motion, or conference report that provides up to $50,000,000,000 in outlays over the period of the total of fiscal years 2007 through 2012 for reauthorization of the State Children's Health Insurance Program (SCHIP), if such legislation maintains coverage for those currently enrolled in SCHIP, continues efforts to enroll uninsured children who are already eligible for SCHIP or Medicaid but are not enrolled, or supports States in their efforts to move forward in covering more children, by the amounts provided in that legislation for those purposes, provided that the outlay adjustment shall not exceed $50,000,000,000 in outlays over the period of the total of fiscal years 2007 through 2012, and provided that such legislation would not increase the deficit over either the period of the total of fiscal years 2007 through 2012 or the period of the total of fiscal years 2007 through 2017.

(b) House Reserve Fund for the State Children's Health Insurance Program—The Chairman of the House Committee on the Budget may revise the allocations of a committee or committees, aggregates, and other appropriate levels for bills, joint resolutions, amendments, or conference reports, which contains matter within the jurisdiction of the Committee on Energy and Commerce that expands coverage and improves children's health through the State Children's Health Insurance Program (SCHIP) under title XXI of the Social Security Act and the program under title XIX of such Act (commonly known as Medicaid) and that increases new budget authority that will result in not more than $50,000,000,000 in outlays in fiscal years 2007 through 2012, and others which contain offsets so designated for the purpose of this section within the jurisdiction of another committee or committees, if the combined changes would not increase the deficit or decrease the surplus for the total over the period of fiscal years 2007 through 2012 or the period of fiscal years 2007 through 2017.

Example of Budget Resolution 302(a) Committee Allocations

(Excerpted from H.Rpt. 110-153, the Conference Report to accompany S.Con.Res. 21, the FY 2008 Budget Resolution)

Note: As explained in chapter 2-2, 302(a) spending allocations to committees reflect only "direct spending" jurisdiction. The allocations do *not* reflect programs that are "authorized" by the various authorizing committees and subsequently funded by the Appropriations Committee. For example, although the HELP Committee has *authorizing jurisdiction* over the National Institutes of Health, NIH's $29 billion budget is not allocated to the HELP Committee; rather, the NIH budget is part of the allocation to the Appropriations Committee since the appropriators make the actual funding decisions each year. Similarly, the Armed Service receives allocations for military retirement, TRICARE, and other mandatory spending, but the bulk of defense spending (which is discretionary) is allocated to the Appropriations Committee.

(millions of dollars)

Senate Committee	Budget Authority FY 2008	Outlays FY 2008	Budget Authority FY 2008–2012	Outlays FY 2008–2012
Agriculture, Nutrition and Forestry	13,464	12,939	67,878	65,557
Appropriations	953,052	1,028,397	*	*
Armed Services	102,125	102,153	546,992	546,679
Banking, Housing and Urban Affairs	13,296	−1,878	64,093	−18,543
Commerce, Science and Transportation	14,457	9,906	75,198	48,684
Energy & Natural Resources	5,071	4,757	25,838	24,730
Environment and Public Works	43,535	1,753	181,487	9,668
Finance	1,078,880	1,079,886	6,018,150	6,022,475
Foreign Relations	14,688	14,690	69,077	65,798

Senate Committee	Budget Authority FY 2008	Outlays FY 2008	Budget Authority FY 2008–2012	Outlays FY 2008–2012
Homeland Security and Governmental Affairs	87,956	85,389	483,868	470,496
Health, Education, Labor and Pensions (HELP)	10,608	10,024	56,565	54,185
Judiciary	8,617	7,504	37,630	37,363
Rules and Administration	70	215	343	532
Veterans' Affairs	1,219	1,300	5,900	6,449
Select Committee on Indian Affairs	452	441	1,748	1,835
Select Committee on Intelligence	263	263	1,415	1,415

*Allocations to the Appropriations Committee are for one year only, since discretionary spending programs are generally funded on an annual basis.

Example of Appropriations Committee 302(b) Sub-Allocations

Fiscal Year 2008
(Budget Authority in billions of dollars)

Appropriations Subcommittee	*House 302(b)*	*Senate 302(b)*
Agriculture—Rural Development—FDA	18.825	18.709
Commerce—Justice—Science	53.551	54.418
Defense	459.332	459.332
Energy—Water	31.603	32.273
Financial Services—General Government	21.434	21.394
Homeland Security	36.254	36.439
Interior—Environment	27.598	27.150
Labor—HHS—Education	151.112	149.236
Legislative Branch	4.024	4.051
Military Construction—Veterans	64.745	64.745
State—Foreign Operations	34.243	34.243
Transportation—HUD	50.738	51.063

Explanation of the Senate's Byrd Rule

The Budget Reconciliation process is particularly significant for the Senate, where legislation is generally subject to (1) unlimited debate and (2) nongermane amendments. In contrast to the normal traditions of open debate and amendment, Reconciliation bills are subject to a very strict—20-hour—time limit and very strict germaneness restrictions on amendments. Because Reconciliation is such a radical departure from the way the Senate normally does its business, Senator Robert C. Byrd in 1985 created the "Byrd Rule" (set forth in 313 of the Budget Act), which limits what can be included in a Reconciliation Bill.

Under the Byrd Rule, all legislation reported pursuant to Reconciliation instructions must be budgetary in nature. Any matter that is not budgetary is considered to be "extraneous." Senators may use a Byrd Rule point of order to *strike specific "extraneous" provisions from a Reconciliation bill or conference report.*

Generally, the Byrd Rule defines as extraneous provisions that (1) have no cost or (2) are significant policy changes with "merely incidental" budgetary effects. Senators may challenge a lengthy provision or very small provisions down to the subsection level. The Byrd Rule, itself, is lengthy, highly technical, and quite arcane. But, in general, the following four-part test may be used in determining if a provision violates the Byrd Rule:

1. Does the provision have a budget effect? Changes in outlays or revenues brought about by changes in the terms and conditions under which outlays are made or revenues are collected are considered to be budget effects (which permitted many provisions in OBRA-93 to survive).

2. If a provision has a budget effect, it does not violate the Byrd Rule (and can remain in the Reconciliation Bill) *unless*

- the budget effect is "*merely incidental*" to the nonbudgetary (policy) components of the provision (for example, if a policy provision doesn't have a budgetary "score" you can't save it from the Byrd Rule by piggybacking it on a minor or "incidental" budgetary provision); *or*
- the provision *decreases revenues* (or increases spending) and the reporting committee has *failed to achieve its Reconciliation instructions* (this is why Senate committees are very careful to fulfill their Reconciliation instructions); *or*

• *in a year beyond the Budget Resolution window* the provision would reduce revenues (or increase spending) and that revenue loss (or spending increase) causes the relevant title of the Reconciliation Bill to become a net deficit increaser in that out-year.

3. If the provision has no budget effect, it violates the Byrd Rule. Examples of "no-costers" that violate the Byrd Rule are reporting requirements, technical corrections, authorizations, and no-cost policy changes.

Exception: Senate-originated provisions which have no budget effect during the budget window do *not* violate the Byrd Rule, if the Chairman *and* Ranking Member of the Budget Committee *and* the authorizing committee certify that one of the following is true:

• the provision mitigates a budgetary provision; *or*
• the provision will result in substantial deficit reduction in an outyear (i.e., a year beyond the budget "window" of the Reconciliation bill); *or*
• budgetary effects are likely to occur in the event of new regulations, court rulings, or statutory triggers; *or*
• budgetary effects are likely but cannot currently be estimated.

4. Also, provisions outside a committee's jurisdiction and provisions affecting Social Security violate the Byrd Rule.

The Byrd Rule and Conference Reports. In general, the Senate's Byrd rule effectively limits Reconciliation legislation to "budgetary" provisions. Although conference reports are normally immune from further amendment, if a Byrd Rule point of order is raised and sustained against a provision in a Reconciliation conference report, the offending provision would be automatically stripped out and the legislative vehicle would cease to be a "conference report." By losing conference report status, the Reconciliation legislation would be sent back to the House, where it would be open to further amendment. (This actually happened in December 2005 when Democrats successfully raised Byrd Rule points of order against the Deficit Reduction Act conference report, with the effect of sending the legislation back to the House of Representatives for another vote on February 1, 2006.)

Historical Table—Reconciliation Bills

Reconciliation Bills	Bill Number	Passed by Congress	Date Signed or Vetoed	Public Law Number
Omnibus Reconciliation Act of 1980	HR 7765	12-03-80	12-05-80	96-499
Omnibus Budget Reconciliation Act of 1981	HR 3982	07-31-81	08-13-81	97-35
Omnibus Budget Reconciliation Act of 1982	HR 6955	08-18-82	09-08-82	97-253
Omnibus Budget Reconciliation Act of 1983	HR 4169	04-05-84	04-18-84	98-270
Consolidated Omnibus Budget Reconciliation Act of 1985 (COBRA)	HR 3128	03-20-86	04-07-86	99-272
Omnibus Budget Reconciliation Act of 1986	HR 5300	10-17-86	10-21-86	99-509
Omnibus Budget Reconciliation Act of 1987	HR 3545	12-22-87	12-22-87	100-203
Omnibus Budget Reconciliation Act of 1989	HR 3299	11-22-89	12-19-89	101-239
Omnibus Budget Reconciliation Act of 1990	HR 5835	10-27-90	11-05-90	101-508
Omnibus Budget Reconciliation Act of 1993	HR 2264	08-06-93	08-19-93	103-66
Balanced Budget Act of 1995	HR 2491	11-20-95	**Vetoed**	
The Personal Responsibility and Work Opportunity Reconciliation Act of 1996	HR 3734	08-01-96	08-22-96	104-93

(Continued)

Reconciliation Bills	Bill Number	Passed by Congress	Date Signed or Vetoed	Public Law Number
Balanced Budget Act of 1997	HR 2015	07-31-97	08-05-97	105-33
Taxpayer Relief Act of 1997	HR 2014	07-31-97	08-05-97	105-34
Taxpayer Refund and Relief Act of 1999	HR 2488	08-05-99	**Vetoed**	—
Marriage Tax Relief Reconciliation Act of 2000	HR 4810	07-21-00	**Vetoed**	—
Economic Growth and Tax Relief Reconciliation Act of 2001	HR 1836[1]	05-26-01	06-07-01	107-16
Jobs and Growth Tax Relief Reconciliation Act of 2003	HR 2	05-23-03	05-28-03	108-27
Deficit Reduction Act of 2005	S 1932	02-01-06	02-08-06	109-171
Tax Increase Prevention and Reconciliation Act of 2006[2]	HR 4297	05-11-06	05-17-06	109-222

Notes

1. H.R. 1836, the Economic Growth and Tax Relief Reconciliation Act, included major provisions from H.R. 3, the Economic Growth and Tax Relief Act; H.R. 6, the Marriage Penalty and Family Tax Relief Act; H.R. 8, the Death Tax Elimination Act; H.R. 10, the Comprehensive Retirement Security and Pension Reform Act; H.R. 622, the Adoption Tax Credits bill; and from S. 896, the Senate Budget Reconciliation bill.

2. S. 1932 and H.R. 4297 are the spending and tax Reconciliation bills, respectively, that emerged from the FY2006 Budget Resolution. The tax bill, HR 4297, was initiated in 2005 but carried over to the 2006 session.

Historical Table—Completion of Appropriations Bills

Only four times since enactment of the Congressional Budget Act has Congress completed all of its regular appropriations bills by the start of the new fiscal year.

FY	Number of Regular Appropriations Bills Enacted by Start of FY	Number of Continuing Resolutions Due to Delay in Completion of Appropriations	Number of Regular Appropriations Bills in Omnibus, CR, or Minibus Measure
1977	**13**	**0**	0
1978	9	3	0
1979	5	1	0
1980	3	2	2
1981	1	2	5
1982	0	4	3
1983	1	2	6
1984	4	2	3
1985	4	5	8
1986	0	5	7
1987	0	5	13
1988	0	5	13
1989	**13**	**0**	0
1990	1	3	0
1991	0	5	0
1992	3	4	0
1993	1	1	0
1994	2	3	0
1995	**13**	**0**	0

(Continued)

FY	Number of Regular Appropriations Bills Enacted by Start of FY	Number of Continuing Resolutions Due to Delay in Completion of Appropriations	Number of Regular Appropriations Bills in Omnibus, CR, or Minibus Measure
1996	0	13	5
1997	**13**[1]	**0**	6
1998	1	6	0
1999	1	6	8
2000	4	7	5
2001	2	21	5
2002	0	8	0
2003	0	8	11
2004	3	5	7
2005	1	3	9
2006	2	3	0
2007	2	4	9
2008	0	3	11

Sources: Sandy Streeter, "Continuing Appropriations Acts: Brief Overview of Recent Practices," RL30343, Washington, D.C.: Congressional Research Service, November 15, 2006); and Sandy Streeter, "The Congressional Appropriations Process: An Introduction," 97-684 (Washington, D.C.: Congressional Research Service, September 8, 2006).

*Unknown at time of publication.

Note

1. The deadline was met by adding five regular appropriations bills to a sixth bill and enacting the other seven bills individually. Sandy Streeter, , "Continuing Appropriations Acts: Brief Overview of Recent Practices," 8.

Appropriations—Rules Governing Floor Consideration and House-Senate Conference

House Rules	Explanation of Provision	Application
Rule XIII, Cl. 5	Provides that appropriations bills are "privileged" and can therefore be brought directly to the House Floor without asking the Rules Committee to report a "Special Rule."	Although "privileged," appropriations bills have increasingly been brought to the House Floor under a "special rule" granted at the request of the Appropriations Chairman. In most cases, these are "open rules" where any Member may offer any amendment consistent with the rules of the House.
"Committee of the Whole"	Appropriations bills are open to amendment with the House sitting as a "Committee of the Whole," after which the Committee of the Whole "rises" and reports the amended bill back to the House for a final vote.	In general, the procedures in the Committee of the Whole, especially relating to offering and debating amendments, are considerably more flexible than House Rules.
Rule XIII, Cl. 3(f)	Reports accompanying appropriations bills must include lists of all unauthorized appropriations, rescissions, transfers of unexpended balances, and provisions changing existing law	Point of order against consideration of the entire bill.

(Continued)

House Rules	Explanation of Provision	Application
Rule XIII, Cl 4(c)	Requires the three-day availability of printed hearings on a general appropriations bill.	Point of order against consideration of the entire bill

Note: The following points of order can be raised against a portion of a paragraph or section, or an entire paragraph or section. If the point of order is sustained, the offending language is stricken. Also, note that the following restrictions are often waived pursuant to a "special rule" adopted for consideration of the appropriations bill since most appropriations measures contain funding for unauthorized agencies or programs as well as legislative provisions changing existing law.

Rule XXI, Cl. 2(a)(1)	Prohibits unauthorized appropriations in a general appropriations bill.	Specific provisions in a reported appropriations bill or consideration of an amendment.
Rule XXI, Cl. 2(a)(2)	Prohibits "reappropriations" in a general appropriations bill.	Specific provisions in a reported appropriations bill or consideration of an amendment.
Rule XXI, Cl. 2(b)	Prohibits legislative provisions in a general appropriations bill (i.e., change in text of existing law; enactment of law where none exists; repeal of existing law; waiver of a provision of existing law).	Specific provisions in a reported appropriations bill or consideration of an amendment.
Rule XXI, Cl. 2(c)	Prohibits legislative amendment from being offered to a general appropriations bill.	Consideration of an amendment to a general appropriations bill.
Rule XXI, Cl. 2(e)	Prohibits nonemergency-designated amendments to be offered to an appropriations bill containing an emergency designation.	Against specific provisions in a reported appropriations bill or consideration of an amendment.
Senate Rules		
Rule XVI (1)	Prohibits amending an appropriations bill by increasing an item of funding in the bill or adding a new item of appropriation unless: it carries out an existing law or treaty; is moved by the Appropriations Committee or relevant authorizing committee; or	However, note that the Appropriations Committee, in reporting a bill to the Senate is *not* limited to the level established by authorizations. This rule limits only the amendments that may be offered on the Senate Floor.

Senate Rules	Explanation of Provision	Application
	is proposed pursuant to a presidential budget estimate required by law.	
Rule XVI (3)	If an amendment is proposed by the relevant authorizing committee to increase an appropriation already in the bill or to add a new item of appropriation, the amendment must be referred to the Appropriations Committee for at least a day.	Purpose is to give the Appropriations Committee an opportunity to review the authorizing committee's amendment before it comes to the Floor.
Rule XVI (2)	Prohibits *reporting an appropriations bill* with new legislative provisions *or* funding limitations that would take effect or cease to be effective based on a contingency (these are generally found in the "General Provisions" section of an appropriations bill).	Paragraph (2) is a point of order against the bill which, if sustained, recommits the bill to Committee. "The theory of funding limitations is that if Congress can decide the objectives for which it wishes to appropriate money, it can also restrict the purposes for which the money should be spent. *Rule XVI mandates that the limitation cannot be contingent.* This means that the limitation may not impose new duties on federal officials or require the officials to make discretionary judgments or determinations." In addition, a funding limitation "cannot reach beyond the pending appropriations bill" (emphasis added).[1] If a point of order is made against an amendment as legislation on an appropriations bill, if the underlying measure is a House-originated bill, the amendment sponsor can raise a "defense of germaneness" to a provision in the House bill. Questions of germaneness are decided by a vote of the full Senate.

(Continued)

Senate Rules	Explanation of Provision	Application
Rule XVI (4)	Prohibits *floor amendments* that propose legislation on an appropriations bill *or* funding limitations that would take effect or cease to be effective based on a contingency. Paragraph (4) also prohibits nongermane amendments whether originating in the Appropriations Committee or from the Senate Floor.	
Rule XVI (5)	Prohibits amending an appropriations bill with a private claim.	
Rule XVI (7)	Committee reports on appropriations bills must identify all unauthorized appropriations.	
Rule XVI (8)	Prohibits "reappropriations" of unexpended balanced in a general appropriations bill.	Point of order against the entire bill and amendments thereto.
House-Senate Conference		
House Rule XXII, Cl. 9.	Generally House rules require that conference agreements must stay within the range of amounts appropriated by the House and Senate bills.	This is not always followed and the House often adopts a special rule waiving this restriction.
Senate Rule XXVIII, paragraphs 2-4.	Under Senate Rule XXVIII, as amended in 2007, a conference committee may not insert in a conference report, provisions that are beyond the scope of the House or Senate bill. Any Senator may make a point of order against "new matter" added by a conference committee, and if the Chair rules the matter to be beyond the scope of the House or Senate bill, those provisions are	This effectively prevents a conference committee from creating omnibus (or minibus) appropriations measures if 40 or more Senators object.

Explanation of Provision	Application
automatically stricken from the conference report. Waiver requires 60 votes.	

Sources: House Committee on Rules, http://www.rules.house.gov/budget_pro.htm; Senate Committee on Appropriations: www.appropriations.senate.gov/budgetprocess/budgetprocess.htm; Martin Gold, *Senate Procedure and Practice* (Lanham, MD: Rowman & Littlefield, 2004), 133–37.

1. Gold, Senate Procedure and Practice, 134–135.

The 2004 PART Questionnaire

Section I: Program Purpose and Design (Yes, No, N/A)
1. Is the program purpose clear?
2. Does the program address a specific and existing problem, interest, or need?
3. Is the program designed so that it is not redundant or duplicative of any other Federal, State, local, or private effort?
4. Is the program design free of major flaws that would limit the program's effectiveness or efficiency?
5. Is the program design effectively targeted, so that resources will reach intended beneficiaries and/or otherwise address the program's purpose directly?

Section II: Strategic Planning (Yes, No, N/A)
1. Does the program have a limited number of specific long-term performance measures that focus on outcomes and meaningfully reflect the purpose of the program?
2. Does the program have ambitious targets and timeframes for its long-term measures?
3. Does the program have a limited number of specific annual performance measures that can demonstrate progress toward achieving the program's long-term goals?
4. Does the program have baselines and ambitious targets for its annual measures?
5. Do all partners (including grantees, subgrantees, contractors, cost-sharing partners, and other government partners) commit to and work toward the annual and/or long-term goals of the program?
6. Are independent evaluations of sufficient scope and quality conducted on a regular basis or as needed to support program improvements and evaluate effectiveness and relevance to the problem, interest, or need?
7. Are Budget requests explicitly tied to accomplishment of the annual and long-term performance goals, and are the resource needs presented in a complete and transparent manner in the program's budget?
8. Has the program taken meaningful steps to correct its strategic planning deficiencies?

Section III: Program Management (Yes, No, N/A)

1. Does the agency regularly collect timely and credible performance information, including information from key program partners, and use it to manage the program and improve performance?
2. Are Federal managers and program partners (including grantees, subgrantees, contractors, cost-sharing partners, and other government partners) held accountable for cost, schedule, and performance results?
3. Are funds (Federal and partners') obligated in a timely manner and spent for the intended purpose?
4. Does the program have procedures (e.g., competitive sourcing/cost comparisons, IT improvements, appropriate incentives) to measure and achieve efficiencies and cost effectiveness in program execution?
5. Does the program collaborate and coordinate effectively with related programs?
6. Does the program use strong financial management practices?
7. Has the program taken meaningful steps to address its management deficiencies?

Section IV: Program Results/Accountability (Yes, Large Extent, Small Extent, No)

1. Has the program demonstrated adequate progress in achieving its long-term performance goals?
2. Does the program (including program partners) achieve its annual performance goals?
3. Does the program demonstrate improved efficiencies or cost effectiveness in achieving program goals each year?
4. Does the performance of this program compare favorably with other programs (including government, private, etc.) with similar purpose and goals?
5. Do independent evaluations of sufficient scope and quality indicate that the program is effective and achieving results?

Note: This list of generic questions excludes additional questions categorized by program type. For the complete list, see Government Accountability Office, GAO-06-28, http://www.gao.gov/new.items/d0628.pdf.

2007 Federal Poverty Level (FPL)

Many low-income entitlement programs—for example, Medicaid and SCHIP—are tied to the Federal Poverty Level (FPL), which is adjusted in January of each year. Following is the FPL for 2007.

2007 Federal Poverty Level (FPL) Guidelines

Persons in Family or Household	48 Contiguous States and D.C.	Alaska	Hawaii
1	$10,210	$12,770	$11,750
2	13,690	17,120	15,750
3	17,170	21,470	19,750
4	20,650	25,820	23,750
5	24,130	30,170	27,750
6	27,610	34,520	31,750
7	31,090	38,870	35,750
8	34,570	43,200	39,750
Additional person, add:	3,480	4,350	4,000

Source: Department of Health and Human Services, http://aspe.hhs.gov/poverty/07poverty.shtml.

Index